More
Super
Trivia

More Super Trivia

Fred L. Worth

GREENWICH HOUSE
DISTRIBUTED BY CROWN PUBLISHERS, INC.
NEW YORK

This book was previously published as *The Complete Unabridged Super Trivia Encyclopedia Volume II*

This 1983 edition is published by Greenwich House, a division of Arlington House, Inc., distributed by Crown Publishers, Inc., by arrangement with Warner Books, Inc.

Manufactured in the United States of America

Library of Congress Cataloging in Publication Data

Worth, Fred L.
  More super trivia.

  Previously published as: The complete unabridged super trivia encyclopedia. v. 2. c1981.
  Summary: Miscellany on a wide variety of topics is presented in a question and answer format.
    1. Questions and answers. [1. Curiosities and wonders. 2. Questions and answers] I. Title.
AG195.W782   1983   031'.02   82-21025

ISBN: 0-517-394111

h g f e d c b a

DEDICATED TO MY BROTHER
James Worth

It is a very sad thing that nowadays there is so little useless information.

—OSCAR WILDE

Nostalgia isn't what it used to be.

—PETER DE VRIES

*I read **War and Peace** in ten minutes; it's about Russia.*

—WOODY ALLEN

Note

One of the worst things that can happen to a trivia buff is to spot or make a mistake. I detest mistakes, but that doesn't stop me from making them. No doubt there are mistakes in *More Super Trivia,* just as there were in *The Super Trivia Encyclopedia,* but with your help they can be eliminated from future editions. One of the advantages of releasing new editions of dictionaries, almanacs, and encyclopedias is that previous mistakes can be corrected.

At present I am working on the updated and corrected version of *The Super Trivia Encyclopedia.* The book will have additional information on most of the existing entries. Also, I am compiling new information for *Super Trivia III,* to be published sometime in the next two years (or so).

If you run across any mistakes, please drop a line to: Fred L. Worth, c/o ILA Ltd., 9601 Wilshire Boulevard, Los Angeles, CA, 90046. And if you wish to add any new facts for future editions, please send them along (that's what the acknowledgments section is all about).

Acknowledgments

I wish to thank all the super-nice people who contributed entries for *More Super Trivia*. As always, special thanks go to Susan Worth. Another special thanks to two very good friends, David Strauss and Steve Tamerius.

Thank you also to the following *More Super Trivia* helpers: Mary Cannedy, James Worth, Ben Fernandez, Jeff Missine, Don McCombs, David Glagovsky, Bob and Judith Seward, Mike Tormey, Hugh Croce, Kathi Swan, Ted Fuery, Bob Donnely, Mark Smeby, Bernie Rolnicki, Darryl L. Rich, Bill Silva, Bud Foster, Doug Ingels, Larry Phillips, Al Hay, Sam Garrison, Bob Wright, Henry McVeigh, Steve Sowers, Frederick H. Ferguson III, Jim Neal, Fred Raymond, Bob Reed, Michael Uslan, Ralph Albi, David C. Crockett, Rev. David Burd, and to all those readers who were so kind as to write me in order to make corrections and to send along new entries.

Introduction

I find it much easier to write 940 pages of manuscript than to sit down to compose an introduction of only a few pages.

Now that I have written an introduction to the introduction, let me go into the subject of this book—trivia. The trivia phenomenon is growing and becoming contagious. Many large magazines now regularly mention trivia facts or offer trivia quizzes, Canadian TV has a trivia program (while we in the United States are still stuck with *The Joker's Wild*), and a number of colleges and universities hold annual trivia contests (the one at the University of Colorado is in its fourteenth year). There is now a fine trivia newsletter, *Trivia Unlimited* (P.O. Box 5213, Lincoln, Nebraska 68505). Radio stations throughout the United States use trivia in their format, many devoting hours to the exchange of inconsequential facts between listeners. Trivia, as you see, is here to stay. The fascinating thing about this game is that everyone can play it. You needn't be six foot six and weigh 250 pounds or be a great athlete. You don't even have to be a great brain (apologies to MENSA). All you need to get in on the game is an interest in what goes on around you and an acquaintance with the American cultural heritage.

Widespread interest in trivia arose during the 1960s, just about the time computers were being introduced into our society. For computers, like the game of trivia, function on detail; they must be programmed with as many facts as possible. In this Computer Age we are attempting to reach a stage of mutuality in which computers are programmed to think like people and people are taught to think like computers.

One last thing: Don't use trivia to boost your own ego. There is no faster way to put others off trivia than to attempt to "stump" them with tough questions. Trivia questions should be asked with the object of getting the other person to answer them successfully. With good clues, any trivia question can be answered. A real trivia buff wants to inform his audience, not embarrass them.

End of lecture.

A1
First automobile license plate issued in Great Britain. It was issued to Lord Russell in 1903.

A4725
Wisconsin automobile license plate of Laverne and Shirley's black $200 Hudson convertible in the TV series *Laverne and Shirley*.

A20284
California State Penitentiary number of Max Dembo (Dustin Hoffman) in the 1978 movie *Straight Time*.

A15042699
M/Sgt. Ernie G. Bilko's Army serial number in the TV series *You'll Never Get Rich* and *The Phil Silvers Show*.

A & A Crop Dusting Service
Company owned and run by Al Bain (Telly Savalas), who flies a dual-wing red airplane, in the 1978 movie *Capricorn One*.

ABCD Powers
Allied nations during World War II: American, British, Chinese, Dutch.

AF
Japanese code for Midway Island during World War II.

AFL franchises
Original eight football teams in the American Football League, founded in 1960: Boston Patriots, Buffalo Bills, Dallas Texans, Denver Broncos, Houston Oilers, Los Angeles Chargers, New York Titans, and Oakland Raiders.

AFL, NFL, AND AAFC
Only two players to have played in all three football conferences: Ben Agajanian and Hardy Brown.

ASCAP

American Society of Composers, Authors, and Publishers, founded in 1914.

ASCAP

California automobile license plate number of George Webber's (Dudley Moore) yellow Rolls-Royce convertible in the 1979 movie *10*.

AUG 865

California license plate number of Fred Rutherford's (Richard Deacon) sedan in the TV series *Leave It to Beaver*.

Aaron

Moses's brother. He was portrayed in the movies by: James Neill in *The Ten Commandments* (1924); John Carradine in *The Ten Commandments* (1956); Anthony Quayle in *Moses the Lawgiver* (1975), and in the TV series *Heroes of the Bible* by Richard Mulligan.

Aaron brothers

Henry and Tommy. They hold the major league home-run record for brothers: Henry hit 755 and Tommy hit 13, for a total of 768.

Aaron, Tommy

Golfer who misscored Roberto De Vincent's first nine holes, giving him a 66 instead of a 65 at the 1968 Masters Tournament. De Vincent unknowingly signed the incorrect scorecard.

Abalone, Arizona

Setting of the 1964 movie *7 Faces of Dr. Lao* as well as the book *The Circus of Dr. Lao* by Charles Finney, on which the movie was based.

Abel and Baker

Chimpanzees that were sent into space from Cape Canaveral on May 28, 1959, becoming the first primates to return to earth.

Abercrombie & Fitch

Famous sporting goods store where many noted celebrities purchased their goods before the store went out of business in 1977. Also the names of the two trash collectors in the *Hi and Lois* comic strip.

Abernathy, Ralph

Head of the Southern Christian Leadership Conference after the death of Rev. Martin Luther King, Jr. He was portrayed in the 1978 TV movie *King* by Ernie Banks.

Able Baker

The chief's (Edward Platt) superior officer in the TV series *Get Smart*. To reach Baker, the code used was Zebra 624.

Abstemiously and Facetiously

Only two words in the English language that have all the vowels in their proper order.

Ace Gasoline

Gasoline station in the town of Wrightsville (1954 movie *The Wild One*).

Ace of Clubs
Nightclub setting on the television soap opera *The Edge of Night*.

Acid Queen
Role played by singer Tina Turner in the 1975 movie *Tommy*.

Acme
Company that supplies Wile E. Coyote with numerous devices in his attempts to capture the Road Runner (cartoons).

Acme
Brand of gasoline sold at Goober Pyle's (George Lindsey) service station (earlier, Wally's Service) in Mayberry, North Carolina, in the TV series *The Andy Griffith* Show.

Acme Book Shop
Los Angeles bookstore in which Dorothy Malone played the proprietress in the 1946 movie *The Big Sleep*.

Acme Cab Co.
Taxi cab (driven by Harry Shannon) that almost collides with a horse carriage being driven by Michael O'Hara (Orson Welles) in the 1948 movie *The Lady from Shanghai*.

Acme Hardware
Store in Rayville where Ed Higgins (Harvey Korman) works in the TV series *The Carol Burnett Show*.

Acme Reversible Shirt Collar
Advertisement from which Mollie Monohan (Barbara Stanwyck) read to the dying Paddy O'Rourke (Regis Toomey), pretending it was a letter from his wife, in the 1939 movie *Union Pacific*.

Acme Rubber Company
Youngstown, Ohio, firm for which Mr. Kaplan (Danny Kaye) worked in the radio series *The Jack Benny Program*.

Acne Statin
Skin cleanser that Pat Boone and his daughters advertised on TV, only to later become embarrassingly disillusioned with the product.

Action Comics No. 1
June 1938 comic book in which Superman debuted. It is one of the most valuable comic books; 100,000 copies of the issue were printed but only 12 are extant. On May 6, 1980, a copy sold at auction for $6,000. Other rare comics are: *Marvel Comics* No. 1 (October 1939), in which The Human Torch debuted (in the fall of 1979 a copy sold for $13,500, making this the most valuable comic); *Whiz Comics* No. 2 (February 1940), in which Captain Marvel debuted; *Motion Picture Funnies Weekly* No. 1 (1939), in which Sub-Mariner debuted (since only four copies are known to exist, this is the rarest—although not the most valuable—comic).

Action Point

Name for the point after touchdown in the defunct World Football League. It had to be scored by a run or a pass, not by a kick.

Adam

First human created by God. He was portrayed in the 1966 movie *The Bible* by Michael Parks.

Adam

How Dr. Victor Frankenstein referred to his monster ("he is my Adam") in the 1816 Mary Wollstonecraft Shelley novel *Frankenstein*. In films the monster generally goes unnamed.

Adam

Son of Samantha and Darrin Stephens in the TV series *Bewitched*. He was born on an episode aired on October 11, 1969, and was played by David Lawrence. Adam was played by David Ankrum in the 1977–1978 TV series *Tabitha*.

Adam

Chimpanzee member of the crew on the Saturday morning TV series *Ark II*.

Adam 47

Officer Ed Wells (Gary Crosby) police unit in the TV series *Adam 12*.

Adams, Franklin P.

Talented writer of the *New York Herald-Tribune* syndicated newspaper column "The Conning Tower." Popularly known as F.P.A., he was a panelist on the radio quiz show *Information Please*. Adams was portrayed in the 1963 movie *Act One* by Drummond Erskine.

Adams, John Quincy

(1767–1848) 6th president of United States and son of the 2nd president. He is the only U.S. president who served as a congressman *after* serving as president. In the 1976 PBS-TV series *The Adams Chronicles*, John Q. Adams was portrayed by David Birney and William Daniels.

Adams, Mary

On August 12, 1965, she became the 50 millionth visitor to enter Disneyland.

Adamson, Cotton

Convicted murderer whom actress Sue Lyon married in 1973 while he was in prison.

Adamson, Joy and George

Married couple who raised Elsa the lioness from birth in February 1956 until they set her free. Their story is told in a series of three books, *Born Free, Living Free* and *Forever Free,* and in the following movies: *Born Free* (1966), with Virginia McKenna and Bill Travers; and *Living Free* (1972), with Susan Hampshire and Nigel Davenport. In the 1974 TV series *Born Free* the Adamsons were portrayed by Diana Muldaur and Gary Collins. On January 4, 1980, Joy Adamson was attacked and murdered in Africa by several men.

Adams, Samuel
(1722–1803) American Revolutionary patriot, signer of the Declaration of Independence, and governor of Massachusetts (1794–1797). He was portrayed by E.G. Marshall in "Paul Revere's Ride," an episode of the TV series *You Are There,* and by Rusty Lane in the 1957 movie *Johnny Tremaine,* and on PBS-TV mini series *The Adams Chronicles* by W. B. Brydon.

Adler, Polly
Famous New York City madam of the 1930s–1940s who owned a penthouse on Park Avenue. She was portrayed in the 1964 movie *A House Is Not a Home* by Shelley Winters. One of Polly's girls in the film was played by Raquel Welch.

Adonis
First dog (English setter) to be registered in the United States (1878).

Aesop
Greek writer of fables. Some historians believe he was a deformed Phrygian slave who lived in the sixth century B.C. On the TV series *The Bullwinkle Show* Charlie Ruggles parodied *Aesop's Fables* in a series of cartoons called "Aesop and Son." In a 1971 CBS-TV special Aesop was played by Bill Cosby.

Affair
The word that appeared in the title of each week's episode of the TV series *The Man from U.N.C.L.E.* and *The Girl from U.N.C.L.E.*

African, The
1967 novel by Harold Courlander. Courlander later charged that three passages from his novel appeared in Alex Haley's book *Roots.* He and Haley settled out of court.

Agent
Allied code name for Prime Minister Winston Churchill during World War II.

Agent 002
Phil Fairbanks of His Majesty's Secret Service, friend of Agent 007 in the James Bond novels.

Agent 99
Agent for CONTROL, played by Barbara Feldon, in the TV series *Get Smart.* Her mother was played by June Dulo. On one episode Agent 99 used the name of Susan Hilton but denied that it was her real name. After her marriage to fellow agent Maxwell Smart, she was known as Mrs. Smart.

Aglets
Name given to the plastic ends of a shoelace.

Agnew
First name called in the Senate role call in the 1939 movie *Mr. Smith Goes to Washington.*

Ah Sin

Play on which Mark Twain and Bret Harte collaborated in 1877. It was not successful.

Ah, Sweet Mystery of Life

Theme song of the radio series *Bachelor's Children*. Also the theme song of Forest Lawn Cemetery. Allan Jones sang it in *The Great Victor Herbert* (1939), and it was the song Nelson Eddy had just finished singing when he suffered a stroke at a nightclub in Miami Beach on March 6, 1967 (he died shortly after). Jeanette MacDonald sang this song at the funeral of Louis B. Mayer in 1957. It was also sung by Madeline Kahn and Terri Garr in Mel Brooks's *Young Frankenstein* (1974). The song's original title was "Dream Melody."

Aïda

Opera composed by Giuseppe Verdi to commemorate the opening of the Suez Canal. It was first performed in Cairo on December 24, 1871. The painter Norman Rockwell was once an extra in a performance in *Aïda* at the Metropolitan Opera House in which Enrico Caruso sang the role of Radames.

Ain't Misbehavin'

Theme song of musician Thomas "Fats" Waller and of comedian George Burns. It was also the name of 1978 Tony Award–winning musicial review of Waller's music.

Aireast 31

Airline flight at 35,000 feet that first reported a UFO to Indianapolis Center in the 1977 movie *Close Encounters of the Third Kind*. TWA 517 was 15 miles in-trail.

Aladdin

Character out of the *Arabian Nights* The son of Mustafa the tailor, Aladdin finds a magic lamp that contains a genie. Movies: *Arabian Nights* (1942), John Qualen; *A Thousand and One Nights* (1945), Cornel Wilde; *Aladdin and His Lamp* (1952), Richard Erdman; *Aladdin and His Magic Lamp* (1968), Boris Bystrov.

Aladdin Hotel

Las Vegas casino/hotel where, on May 1, 1967, Priscilla Beaulieu gave her hand in marriage to Elvis Presley. The ceremony was conducted by Nevada Supreme Court Judge David Zenoff.

Alamo, The

Drive-in restaurant setting of the 1977 movie *Drive-In*.

Alamo Records

Austin, Texas, recording company that released Bobby Ogden's (Peter Fonda) hit song "Outlaw Blues" in the 1977 movie *Outlaw Blues*.

Albertson, Jack

Comedian who co-starred in the TV series *Chico and the Man* as Ed Brown. He also starred in the short lived *Grampa Goes to Washington* and was featured in such other TV series as *The Thin Man, Ensign O'Toole, Room for One More,* and *Dr. Simon Locke.* Jack Albertson was portrayed by Fred Carney, brother of Art Carney, in the 1979 TV movie *Can You Hear the Laughter?*

Al Brown

Pseudonym used by Chicago crime boss Alphonse Capone.

Alcatraz

Federal prison (1933–1963) on an island in the San Francisco Bay. It was the setting of two Clint Eastwood movies: *The Enforcer* (1976) and *Escape from Alcatraz* (1979).

Alden General Hospital

Setting of the daytime TV soap *The Nurses* (aka *The Doctors and the Nurses*).

Alden, John

(1599–1687) One of the Pilgrims who came to the New World on the *Mayflower* and settled at Plymouth, Massachusetts. A signer of the Mayflower Compact, he served as deputy governor from 1664 to 1665 and again in 1677. Alden was portrayed in the 1952 movie *Plymouth Adventure* by Van Johnson and in a 1979 TV movie *The Mayflower: The Pilgrim's Adventure* by Michael Beck.

Aldrin, Edwin "Buzz"

Second man to walk on the moon during the *Apollo 11* landing on July 20, 1969. He was portrayed in the 1976 TV movie *Return to Earth* (from Aldrin's book) by Cliff Robertson.

ALexander 4444

Phone number by which Mervyn Milgrim (Lou Costello) attempts to call a radio station in order to claim the $10,000 jackpot in their Wheel of Fortune contest in the 1942 movie *Who Done It?*

Alexander and His Clarinet

Original title of "Alexander's Ragtime Band," composed by Irving Berlin in 1910.

Alexander the Great

(356–323 B.C.) King of Macedonia and conqueror of the eastern part of the world. Movie portrayals: *Alexander the Great* (1956) Richard Burton; and *Alexander the Great* (1964) William Shatner.

Alexandra

(1872–1918) Empress of Russia, wife of Nicholas II. She was killed by Bolsheviks on July 16, 1918. Movie portrayals: *Rasputin and the Empress* (1932) Ethel Barrymore; and *Nicholas and Alexandra* (1971) Janet Suzman.

Alfie

Sheep dog in the 1973 movie *Serpico*. He was played by Barnaby.

Alfred the Great

(849–899) English king and scholar, portrayed in the 1969 movie *Alfred the Great* by David Hemmings.

Algonquin Hotel

New York City hotel where designer Laura Hunt (Gene Tierney) first met columnist Waldo Lydecker (Clifton Webb) in the 1944 movie *Laura*. The Algonquin was in reality the hangout of an intellectual set of writers including Alexander Woollcott and Dorothy Parker.

Ali Baba

Character out of *Arabian Nights*. Ali Baba, a woodmonger, discovered the hiding place of the Forty Thieves in a cave that opens when one says "Open Sesame" and closes with "Close Sesame." It was Ali's female slave Morgiana who poured the hot oil on the forty thieves, who were hiding in large jars. Ali was played in the movie *Ali Baba and the Forty Thieves* (1944) by Jon Hall (Scotty Beckett as a boy) and in the 1965 movie *The Sword of Ali Baba* by Peter Mann.

Ali, Muhammad

Olympic Gold Medal winner and three-time heavyweight boxing champion of the world, born Cassius Marcellus Clay. He recorded the songs "I Am the Greatest" and "Stand by Me," and has appeared in movies and on TV. Muhammad Ali portrayed himself in the movies *Requiem for a Heavyweight* (1962) and *The Greatest* (1977).

Alice

Woman bartender in the *Andy Capp* comic strip

Alicia Masters

Blind girlfriend of comic book superhero *The Thing*.

All Around Town

Newspaper column written by Hal Towne (Dennis O'Keefe) in the TV series *The Dennis O'Keefe Show*.

Allegretti, Cosmo

Puppeteer on the *Captain Kangaroo* TV series.

Allegro

Nightclub setting in the TV soap opera *The Young and the Restless*, previously named Pierre's. The piano player at Allegro is played by Ben Weisman, who co-wrote 57 songs that were recorded by Elvis Presley.

Allen, Dr. Forrest (Phog)

Member of Basketball's Hall of Fame. He played basketball under James Naismith, the game's inventor. He organized the first NCAA tournament in 1939. Dr. Forrest and Harry S Truman grew up together, living on the same street in Independence, Missouri.

All's Well That Ends Well
Original title of Leo Tolstoi's 1869 novel *War and Peace*.

Along Came Ruth
Song that Irving Berlin composed for George Herman "Babe" Ruth.

Alta Coma, California
Setting (after moving from Fernwood, Ohio) of the TV series *America 2Night*. Alta Coma is the unfinished-furniture capital of the world.

Always
The song that Irving Berlin presented to his wife as a wedding gift in 1926. She received all the publishing rights.

Amalfitano, Joe
Fellow Giant baseball player whose bat Willie Mays borrowed to hit four home runs in a single game on April 30, 1961.

Amazing Grace
Glen Campbell's closing theme song. When the hymn was recorded by the Royal Scots Dragoon Guards in 1972, it became the only million-selling record featuring bagpipes.

Ambassador Hotel
Los Angeles hotel where in the kitchen Robert Kennedy was assassinated by Sirhan Bishara Sirhan on June 5, 1968. Roosevelt Grier and Rafer Johnson were Kennedy's bodyguards that night.

Amboy Dukes
Brooklyn gang featured in the 1949 movie *City Across the River* (based on the novel *The Amboy Dukes* by Irving Shulman); also the name of a late 1960s rock band led by Ted Nugent.

American Eagle Squadron
Roger Ramjet's juvenile assistants: Yank, Doodle, Dan, and Dee (TV cartoons).

American Girl
Magazine of the Girl Scouts of America.

America's Ambassador of Good Will to the World
Nickname conferred upon musician Louis "Satchmo" Armstrong.

America's Sweethearts
Popular nickname of cinema singing duo Nelson Eddy and Jeanette MacDonald.

America's Sweetie
Nickname of Hollywood actress Nancy Carroll.

Ames, Nathan
Inventor of the escalator in 1859.

AMIGO
First California personalized automobile license plate. It was issued on October 26, 1970.

Amin, Idi "Dada"

(Field Marshal Doctor President) Dictator-president of the African country of Uganda from 1971 to 1979. He was portrayed in TV movies by Julius Harris in *Victory at Entebbe* (1976); Yaphet Kotto in *Raid on Entebbe* (1976); and Joseph Olita in *The Rise and Fall of Idi Amin* (1980). Actor Godfrey Cambridge died on November 29, 1976, on the set in which he was portraying Idi Amin in the 1976 movie *Victory at Entebbe* (he was replaced by Julius Harris).

Amman, Jordan

Site of destruction of three skyjacked airliners on September 12, 1970—a TWA 707, a Swissair 707, and a BOAC VC-10—by Arab commandos (PDLP), holding over 600 hostages. A fourth aircraft, a Pan Am 747, was destroyed on the ground at Cairo.

Among My Souvenirs

Song that Al Stephenson (Fredric March) asked Butch (Hoagy Carmichael) to play as his and his wife's favorite in the 1946 movie *The Best Years of Our Lives*.

Amsterdam Queen

Ocean liner on which Duff (Larry Storch) was a first mate in the TV series *The Queen and I*.

Amurao, Corazon

Lone nurse who escaped the massacre of eight young women in a Chicago apartment on July 13, 1966, by Richard F. Speck. Corazon hid under a bed. She later returned to the Philippines, where she was elected to the provincial legislature.

Ana

Elephant displayed at the 1968 Republican National Convention at Anaheim, California.

Anastasia

Youngest daughter of Russian Czar Nicholas II, who was supposedly killed along with her parents, three sisters, and brother on July 16, 1918. Many believed she survived the firing squad. Mrs. Anna Anderson Manahan is the most prominent woman claiming to be the missing Grand Duchess Anastasia Romanov. Anastasia was portrayed in the 1956 movie *Anastasia* by Ingrid Bergman and in the 1971 movie *Nicholas and Alexandra* by Fiona Fullerton. Mrs. Manahan's autobiography is titled *I'm Anastasia*.

Anastasia, Albert

(1903–1957) Lord High Executioner of the Mafia and head man of Murder, Inc., until his assassination in the Park Sheraton Hotel's basement barbershop on October 25, 1957. Arthur Grasso was his barber. Movie portrayals: *The Valachi Papers* (1972) Fausto Tozzi; and *Lepke* (1976) Gianni Russo.

Anchors Aweigh
U.S. Navy hymn. The lyrics were written by Midshipman Alfred Hart Miles especially for the 1906 Army-Navy football game in which Navy first used the forward pass to beat Army 10–0. Lt. Charles A. Zimmerman, the man who invented the autoharp, wrote the music for "Anchors Aweigh."

Andersen, Hans Christian
(1805–1875) Danish writer of children's stories, which were first published in 1835 as *Andersen's Fairy Tales*. He was portrayed in the 1952 movie *Hans Christian Andersen* by Danny Kaye and in the 1966 movie *The Daydreamer* by Paul O'Keefe.

Anderson, George K.
Inventor who patented the first typewriter ribbon on September 13, 1886.

Anderson, Marian
First black to perform at the Met (January 7, 1955). She sang in Giuseppe Verdi's *The Masked Ball*. When the Daughters of the American Revolution, in 1939, would not allow her to perform in Constitution Hall in Washington, D.C., First Lady Eleanor Roosevelt resigned from the DAR in protest. Marian Anderson was born on February 27, 1902, which is also the birthday of author John Steinbeck. Portrayed in the 1977 TV movie *Eleanor and Franklin: The White House Years* by Barbara Conrad.

Anderson, Roland
Most nominated person for an Academy Award. Anderson has been nominated fifteen times for art direction, though the Oscar still eludes him.

And Her Tears Flowed Like Wine
Song performed by Lauren Bacall in *Two Guys from Milwaukee* (1946) and *The Big Sleep* (1946). Andy Williams dubbed the singing.

Andrea Doria
Italian liner that sank on July 26, 1956, after being rammed by the Swedish liner *Stockholm* off Nantucket. The ship's commander was Capt. Piero Calamai, her call letters were ICEH. At the instant of the collision the ship's band was playing "Arrivaderci, Roma" in the ballroom. In the movie theater the 1955 movie *Foxfire* was being shown. On board the *Andrea Doria* were actress Ruth Roman, Cary Grant's third wife, Betsy Drake, and composer Mike Stoller and his wife.

Andy
Spaceship robot (made of spare parts) on the *U.G.S.P.* in the TV series *Quark*. Andy was played by Bobby Porter.

Andy Capp
5-foot 4-inch British bloke Andrew Capp, whose hobby is drinking, he is 46 years old and his wife is named Flo (comic strip *Andy Capp* by Smythe).

Andy Gump
Comic strip character of Sidney Smith's *The Gumps*. Andrew's wife is Min,

his son is Chester. Hope is their pet cat and Buck is their dog. Andy Gump was played in 1923–1928 movie serials by Joe Murphy.

Andy Gump and Pogo

Two comic strip characters who "ran" for president of the United States within their strip—Andy Gump in 1924 and 1952, and Pogo in 1952. In one movie cartoon Betty Boop won.

Andy Panda

Comic book Panda bear created by Walter Lantz: debut in the 1939 cartoon *Life Begins for Andy Panda* (voice of Sara Berner); debut in comic books, *Crackajack Funnies No. 39* (September 1941). Andy Panda's girlfriend is Miranda Panda, his mother is Peremlia Panda, and his father is Papa Panda. They all live in Pandamania.

Angel Falls

Largest waterfall in the world. It was "discovered" by aviator James Angel while he was overflying Venezuela in 1935.

Angels

Cheerleaders for the New Orleans Saints football team since 1978. Prior to that time they were called the Bonnes Amies.

Angola

Louisiana State prison where both singers Huddie Ledbetter (Leadbelly) and Baldemar Huerta (Freddy Fender) spent time—Leadbelly in 1930–1934, Freddy Fender in 1960–1963.

Animal

Nickname of *Los Angeles Tribune* photographer Dennis Price (Daryl Anderson) in the TV series *Lou Grant*. Animal uses a Nikon camera.

Animals, Their Habits, Habitat and Haberdashery

Book written by the world's authority on animal behavior, Professor Ludwig von Complex (Sid Caesar), in the TV series *Your Show of Shows*.

Anna

Actual name of the horse that Rudolph Valentino rode in the 1921 movie *The Sheik*.

Annie

Elephant that broke Sgt. Cutter (Cary Grant) out of the brig in the 1939 movie *Gunga Din*.

Another Evening with Harry Stoones

Off-Broadway play in which Barbra Streisand made her acting debut (October 1961). The show lasted for only one performance.

Ant Hill

German fortification that the French soldiers attacked unsuccessfully in the 1957 movie *Paths of Glory*.

Anthony, Susan B.

(1820–1906) Founder of the women's suffrage movement. Her portrait is depicted on the new $1 coin. She was the first real woman to appear on a U.S. coin. Her portrait on the coin is of her at the age of 48.

Antony, Marc
(83–30 B.C.) Roman soldier and orator who fell in love with Cleopatra. After he was defeated in battle by Octavius, he committed suicide by falling on his own sword. On learning of his suicide, Cleopatra killed herself by allowing a poisonous asp to bite her. Movie portrayals: *Antony and Cleopatra* (1908) Paul Panzer; *Cleopatra* (1917) Thurston Hall; *Cleopatra* (1934) Henry Wilcoxon; *Julius Caesar* (1952) Charlton Heston; *Julius Caesar* (1953) Marlon Brando; *The Serpent of the Nile* (1953) William Lundigan; *Two Nights With Cleopatra* (1954) Ettore Manni; *The Story of Mankind* (1957) Helmut Dantine; *Cleopatra* (1963) Richard Burton; *Caesar the Conqueror* (1963) Bruno Tocci; *Julius Caesar* (1970) Charlton Heston; and *Antony and Cleopatra* (1973) Charlton Heston.

Antoinette, Marie
(1755–1793) Queen of France and wife of Louis XVI who was tried for treason and beheaded during the French Revolution. Movie portrayals: *Madame Du Barry* (1924) Anita Louise; *Marie Antoinette* (1938) Norma Shearer; *Scaramouche* (1952) Nina Foch; *Marie Antoinette* (1955) Michele Morgan; and *The Story of Mankind* (1957) Marie Wilson.

Anyone Can Win
1950 TV game show hosted by cartoonist Al Capp.

Anything Goes
Opening theme song of the 1970 movie *The Boys in the Band*.

Anytime
Theme song of Eddie Fisher's radio/TV series *Coke Time*.

Apache
Horse of cowboy Bob Baker in B westerns.

Ape
George of the Jungle's pet gorilla in the TV cartoon series.

Ape Woman
Character appearing in three Universal films: *Captive Wild Woman* (1943) Acquanetta; *Jungle Woman* (1944) Acquanetta; and *Jungle Captive* (1945) Vicky Lane.

Aphrodite
Theme song of the radio series *The Guiding Light*.

Apollo Airways
California airliner (N5VH) that James Bond (Roger Moore) was pushed out of by Jaws (Richard Kiel) in the 1979 movie *Moonraker*. Don Caltvedt doubled for Moore in the scene, Ron Luginbill doubled for Kiel.

Apollo Theater
Famous Harlem, New York City, theater. On August 16, 1957, Buddy Holly and the Crickets became the first white performers to play there.

April 9, 1978
Date on which Captain Nemo (José Ferrer) and his submarine *Nautilus* were discovered in the TV series *The Return of Captain Nemo*.

April Love
Movie that the Thorn family was watching on television in their home in the 1978 movie *Damien: Omen II*.

Aquaman
Secret identity of superhero Arthur Curry. His sidekick is Aqualad, his wife is Mera. He can stay out of the water for only one hour at a time. Debut: *More Fun Comics* No. 73 (November 1941). Voice of Norman Alden in the TV cartoon series *Super Friends*.

Archaeology for Everyone, or: Don't Lift Heavy Rocks
Basic textbook on archaeology written by the world's expert archaeologist, Professor Ludwig von Fossill, played by Sid Caesar in the TV series *Your Show of Shows*.

Archiekins
Veronica Lodge's nickname for her boyfriend, Archie Andrews (comics).

Ardvark I
CONTROL's computer in the TV series *Get Smart*.

Are there any mechanics here?
Charles Lindbergh's first words upon arriving at Le Bourget Airfield in Paris after his solo nonstop flight across the Atlantic Ocean, May 20–21, 1927. His next question was; "Does anyone here speak English?"

Argo
Wentworth family's pet dog in the 1978 TV movie *The Grass Is Always Greener over the Septic Tank,* based on Erma Bombeck's book of the same name.

Argonaut
Allied code name for the February 4–12, 1945, conference at Yalta between Churchill, Roosevelt, and Stalin.

Ariel Award
Mexico's equivalent of the Academy Awards.

Aries
Space shuttle between Space Station 5 and the Moon in the 1968 movie *2001: A Space Odyssey*.

Aristides
Winner of the first Kentucky Derby, May 17, 1875; ridden by black jockey Oliver Lewis.

Aristotle
(384–322 B.C.) Greek philosopher who is considered to be one of the greatest thinkers in history. He was portrayed in the 1956 movie *Alexander the Great* by Barry Jones.

Ark
Name of the 400-foot-long spaceship launched to the planet Zyra in the 1951 movie *When Worlds Collide* (based on the 1932 Philip Wylie and Edwin Balmer novel of the same name).

Arkansas Traveler, The
Theme song of the radio series *The Bob Burns Show* and title of a 1938 movie starring Bob Burns.

Arlington National Cemetery
Burial place of two U.S. presidents, William Howard Taft (1930) and John F. Kennedy (1963), and where boxer Joe Louis is buried (1981).

Armes, Jay J.
Born Julian Armas, he lost both his hands at age 12 and went on to become one of the most respected private detectives in the United States. He located Marlon Brando's "kidnapped" son Christian in 1972. Armas made an appearance on the TV series *Hawaii Five-O*.

Arnold, Benedict
(1741–1801) American Army officer who during the American Revolutionary War became a traitor when he surrendered West Point to the British in 1780. In 1781 he escaped to Britain, where he lived in disgrace. Arnold was portrayed in the 1945 movie *Where Do We Go from Here?* by John Davidson.

Arnold, Gen. Henry "Hap"
(1886–1950) Commander of the Army Air Corps during World War II. He helped to organize the 8th Air Force's strategic bombing of Germany. Arnold was the first five-star general of the United States Air Force, which he helped to organize in 1947. Movie portrayals: *The Glenn Miller Story* (1954) Barton MacLane; *The Court Martial of Billy Mitchell* (1955) Robert Brubaker; and *The Amazing Mr. Howard Hughes* (1977 TV) Walter O. Miles.

Arnstein, Nicky
Gambler husband of comedian Fanny Brice from 1918 to 1927. Portrayed in the movies *Funny Girl* (1968) and *Funny Lady* (1975) by Omar Sharif and loosely portrayed in the 1939 movie *Rose of Washington Square* by Tyrone Power.

Arrakis
Planet setting of Frank Herbert's science fiction novel *Dune*. (*Dune* was rejected by 13 publishers before it was brought out by the Chilton Book Co.).

Arrow
Oblio's pet dog in the 1971 movie *The Point*. The song "Me and My Arrow" by Harry Nilsson became a hit record and was later used by Chrysler Corp. to advertise its compact car, the Plymouth Arrow.

Arrow Collar Man
Nickname of actor Reed Howes, who advertised Arrow shirt collars in the 1920s.

Arrow–Flite Liner
Bus company featured in the 1956 movie *Bus Stop*.
Arrows
New York City street gang led by Julius Garfinkle (John Garfield) in his youth.
Artful Dodger
Nickname of young thief John Dawkins, a pupil of Fagin, in Charles Dickens' 1838 novel *Oliver Twist*. Played by Anthony Newley in the 1948 movie *Oliver Twist* and by Jack Wild in the 1968 movie musical *Oliver!* In the Broadway musical from which the movie was adapted, the part was played by Davy Jones, who later went on to join the Monkees. Phil Collins, lead singer of Genesis, played the Artful Dodger in a stage presentation of *Oliver Twist*.
Arthur
George Harrison's hair, according to his reply to the question, "What do you call that hairdo?" in the 1964 movie *A Hard Day's Night*. Sybil Burton opened a Manhattan discothèque named Arthur, after the hairdo. Sammy Davis, Jr., was one of her investors.
Arthur, Chester Alan
(1829–1886) 21st president of the United States. He was portrayed in the 1963 movie *Cattle King* by Larry Gates.
Arthur, Jean
American actress who was born Gladys Green in 1905. She was portrayed in the 1980 TV miniseries *Moviola* by Vicki Belmonte.
Art Ross Trophy
Annual award presented to the top scorer in the National Hockey League. It was first awarded to Roy Conacher (1949).
Ashford
Small California hometown of Annette McCleod (Annette Funicello) in the serial "Annette" on the TV series *The Mickey Mouse Club*.
Aspen
Name of the large cabin used by U.S. presidents at Camp David.
Aspercell
Show horse featured in the 1968 movie *The Horse in the Gray Flannel Suit*.
As the World Turns
CBS-TV soap opera that Walter Cronkite interrupted to announce that President Kennedy had just been shot in Dallas, Texas (November 22, 1963).
As Time Goes By
Classic song composed in 1931 by Herman Hupfeld and first recorded by Rudy Vallee. It was Rick Blaine (Humphrey Bogart) and Ilsa Lund Laszlo's (Ingrid Bergman) favorite song in the 1942 movie *Casablanca*. It was the song that Rick instructs Sam (Dooley Wilson) to play. Judy Maxwell (Barbra Streisand) sang the song to Howard Bannister (Ryan O'Neal) in the 1972 movie *What's Up Doc?*

Astor, John Jacob
  (1865–1912) Multimillionaire businessman who lost his life when the liner *Titanic* sank. Movie portrayals: *Titanic* (1953) William Johnstone; and *S.O.S. Titanic* (1979 TV) David Janssen.
Astron Delta
  Planet setting of the 1954 movie *Killers from Space*.
Atlanta
  Navy Cruiser launched by author Margaret Mitchell on September 4, 1941.
Atlantia
  President Adar's (Lew Ayres) battlestar, which was destroyed by Cylon raiders in the 1978 TV movie/series *Battlestar Galactica*.
Atlantic
  Cornelius Vanderbilt's $1 million, 185-foot yacht built in 1903.
Atlantic Casualty and Insurance Company
  Firm that Jim Reardon (Edmond O'Brien) worked for as an investigator in the 1946 movie *The Killers*.
Atlantic Southeastern Airlines
  Fictitious airline whose L1011's were "haunted" by dead flight engineer Dom Cimoli in the 1978 TV movie *Ghost of Flight 401* (based on the factual book *The Ghost of Flight 401* by John G. Fuller). In the film Ernest Borgnine portrayed Cimoli. The airline mentioned in Fuller's book is Eastern.
Atlantis
  Boat used by Honolulu divers in the TV series *The Aquanauts*.
At the Festival of the Sacrosong
  Record album by Pope John Paul II that sold a million copies in 1979.
Attila (The Hun)
  (406–453). Notorious king of the Huns, called the Scourge of God. He was portrayed in the 1954 movie *The Sign of the Pagan* by Jack Palance and in the 1958 movie *Attila* by Anthony Quinn.
Audubon, John James
  (1785–1851) Naturalist painter and bird lover. The Audubon Society, which was organized in 1905 to protect birds, was named in his honor. Audubon was portrayed in the TV series *The Adventures of Jim Bowie* by Robert Cornthwaite.
Auerbach, Red
  Coach of the Boston Celtics basketball team. Whenever he believed that a victory was assured for his team, he would light up a cigar on the bench.
Aura Lee
  Traditional folk song on which Elvis Presley's 1956 hit song "Love Me Tender" was based. In the 1936 movie *Come and Get It* Frances Farmer sang "Aura Lee."
Automatic Jack
  Nickname of NFL player Jack Manders.

Automobile Races

Name	Location
Los Angeles Times Grand Prix	Riverside, California
Yankee 400	Brooklyn, Michigan
Dixie 500	Atlanta, Georgia
Mint 400	Las Vegas, Nevada
Rebel 400	Charlotte, North Carolina
Gator Nationals	Gainesville, Florida
June Sprints	Elkhart Lake, Wisconsin
California 500	Ontario, California
Indianapolis 500	Indianapolis, Indiana
U.S. Grand Prix	Watkin's Glen, New York
British Grand Prix	Silverstone, England

Ava Gardner Award
Annual award (as of 1976) conferred on the year's worst supporting actress by the *Harvard Lampoon*.

Avalon, Frankie, and Annette Funicello
Beach Party (1963); *Bikini Beach* (1964); *Muscle Beach Party* (1964); *Beach Blanket Bingo** (1965); *Ski Party* (1965) (Annette's appearance was uncredited); *How to Stuff a Wild Bikini** (1965); *Fireball 500* (1966) and *Doctor Goldfoot & the Bikini Machine* (1966).

Averill, Earl
Cleveland Indian player who in the 1937 All-Star Game hit pitcher Dizzy Dean with a line drive, breaking Dean's big toe on his left foot. (Averill's son, Earl Jr., played major league ball between 1956 and 1963.)

Away We Go
Original title of *Oklahoma!*, the Oscar Hammerstein–Richard Rodgers adaptation of Lynn Rigg's book *Green Grow the Lilacs*.

Ayatollah Ruhollah Khomeini
Religious leader of Iran who became *Time* magazine's Man of the Year in 1979.

Ayn Rand Award
Annual Award (since 1963) given "to that writer whose bad books make even worse movies" by the *Harvard Lampoon*.

---

*Buster Keaton appeared in this film.

B

B115614
Michigan Department of Corrections number of baseball star Ron LeFlore. Before he began playing baseball in prison, Ron had never played in a hardball game. He was sent to prison in 1970 for robbing Dee's Bar in Detroit with two other men. (See: **Ron LeFlore**)

BC 1234
Bedrock home phone number of Fred and Wilma Flintstone in the TV series *The Flintstones*.

BDR 529
Illinois license plate number of the 1974 Dodge Monaco 440 sedan owned by the Blues Brothers, Elwood (Dan Aykroyd) and Joliet Jake (John Belushi), in the 1980 movie *The Blues Brothers*. The car was formerly a Mount Prospect police car.

BM
Initials in a tattooed heart on the chest of Kovak (John Hodiak) in the 1943 movie *Lifeboat*.

BMW
Bavarian Motor Works.

BR 6
License number of Bill "Bojangles" Robinson's chauffeur-driven Duesenberg.

BSA
Burmingham Small Arms.

Baba
Small Mexican burro given to Clark Gable by actress Grace Kelly in 1953.

Baby Face Nelson
(1908–1934) Nickname of 1930s robber-killer (5 feet ¾ inch tall) Lester

Gillis. Movie portrayals: *Baby Face Nelson* (1957) Mickey Rooney; *The FBI Story* (1959) William Phipps; *Young Dillinger* (1965) John Ashley; and *Dillinger* (1973) Richard Dreyfuss.

Baby It's Cold Outside

Song sung by Rock Hudson and Mae West at the thirtieth Academy Award presentation televised on March 26, 1958. Also sung by Charles Laughton and his wife Elsa Lanchester at the 1960 Academy Awards presentation. The song was composed for the 1949 Esther Williams movie *Neptune's Daughter*, and was introduced in the film by Ricardo Montalban and Esther Williams and later sung comically by Red Skelton and Betty Garrett in the same film. Bob Hope and Dinah Shore sang "Baby It's Cold Outside" on the TV special *The Star-Spangled Review* (April 9, 1950).

Baca, Elfego

Western lawyer who lived in Tombstone, Arizona. He was portrayed in "The Nine Lives of Elfego Baca" on the TV series *Walt Disney Presents* by Robert Loggia.

Bacall, Lauren

American actress (born Betty Joan Perske), who at the age of 19 made her movie debut opposite Humphrey Bogart in the 1945 movie *To Have and Have Not*. Lauren Bacall, nicknamed "The Look," was married to both Humphrey Bogart and Jason Robards, Jr. She was portrayed in the 1979 TV movie *Bogie: The Last Hero* by Kathryn Harrold.

Backlinie, Susan

Actress who played the first victim in the 1975 movie *Jaws,* and again in the 1977 movie *Grizzly*. She swam nude in the 1979 movie *1941*.

Bacon, Francis

(1561–1626) English author and philosopher. He was portrayed in the 1939 movie *The Private Lives of Elizabeth and Essex* by Donald Crisp.

Bad in Every Man, The

Title of Rodgers and Hart's tune "Blue Moon"* when the melody was sung by Shirley Ross in the 1934 movie *Manhattan Melodrama*.

Baden-Powell, Robert

(1857–1941) Founder of the Boy Scouts (1908) who served in the First World War as a British spy against both Russia and Germany.

Badge 3

Badge number of agent Napoleon Solo (Robert Vaughn) in the TV series *The Man from U.N.C.L.E.*

Badge 99

Badge number of the police officer played by Bill "Bojangles" Robinson in the 1937 movie *One Mile from Heaven*.

---

*Originally "Blue Moon" was titled "Prayer" and sung by Jean Harlow in an unproduced movie *Hollywood Revue of 1933*. Lorenz Hart then changed the lyrics and retitled the song "The Bad in Every Man."

Badge 99
> Nashville badge number of police lieutenant Stoney Huff (Claude Akins) in the TV series *Nashville 99*.

Badge 147
> Badge number of police officer Joe Forrester (Lloyd Bridges) in the TV series *Joe Forrester*.

Badge 373
> Badge number of New York police officer Jimmy "Popeye" Doyle (Gene Hackman) in the 1971 movie *The French Connection*.

Badge 416
> Badge number of Capt. Adam Greer (Tige Andrews) in the TV series *Mod Squad*.

Badge 425
> Badge number of Dominic Delvecchio (Judd Hirsch) in the TV series *Delvecchio*.

Badge 436
> Badge number of Los Angeles police lieutenant Columbo (Peter Falk) in the TV series *Columbo*.

Badge 517
> Badge number of San Francisco police lieutenant Tony Carlson (Chevy Chase) in the 1978 movie *Foul Play*.

Badge 627
> Badge number of New York City police lieutenant Theo Kojak (Telly Savalas) in the TV series *Kojak*.

Badge 754
> Badge number of writer Dorothy Uhnak when she worked for the New York City Transit Police. Uhnak's book *Police Woman* was made into the TV series *Get Christy Love*.

Badge 1810
> Officer Dan's (Spencer Tracy) badge number with the 1st Precinct in the 1932 movie *Me and My Gal*.

Badge 1828
> Sgt. Dick Fay's (Spencer Tracy) badge number with the 8th Precinct in the 1932 movie *Disorderly Conduct*.

Badge 4614
> Badge number of Houston police lieutenant Alvin Johnson (John Schuck) in the 1970 movie *Brewster McCloud*.

Badge 5600
> Badge number of CHP officer Francis Poncherello (Erik Estrada) in the TV series CHiPs.

Badge 5712
> Badge number of CHP officer Jon Baker (Larry Wilcox) in the TV series CHiPs.

Badge 7813
Badge number of New York police officer McShane (Lloyd Nolan) in the 1945 movie *A Tree Grows in Brooklyn.*,
Badge 14606
Badge number of New York City cop (21st Precinct) Ed Lacy (Don Murray) in the 1977 movie *Deadly Hero*.
Badge 19818
Badge number of Dick Foran in the 1947 movie *Easy Come, Easy Go*.
Badge 21049
Badge number of Frank Serpico (David Birney) in the TV series *Serpico*.
Badge 26034
Badge number of New York police officer Victor O'Brien (William Bendix) in the 1947 movie *Where There's Life*.
Badge 33131
Officer T. J. McCabe's (James Coleman) badge number in the TV series *S.W.A.T.*
Badge 54362
Badge number of San Francisco officer Falfa, who arrests a young hippie for possession of marijuana, in the 1979 movie *More American Graffiti*.
Badge 84890
Badge number of Mike Danko (Sam Melville) in the TV series *The Rookies*.
Badge 415738
Badge number of Terry Webster (Georg Stanford Brown) in the TV series *The Rookies*.
Bailey, De Ford
4-foot-10-inch-tall harmonica player who in 1927 became the first black artist to perform on WSM radio's *Grand Ole Opry*. He became a regular performer on the program.
Bailey, F. (Francis) Lee
Famous American trial lawyer whose most notable cases were the defense of: the Boston Strangler, Dr. Sam Sheppard, Carl Coppolino, Ernest Medina, and Patty Hearst. He was the author of *The Defense Never Rests* (1971) and *For the Defense* (1975). Bailey was portrayed in the 1975 TV movie *Guilty or Not Guilty: The Sam Sheppard Murder Case* by Walter McGinn. He was also the inspiration for the character Clinton Judd (Carl Betz) in the TV series *Judd, For the Defense*. Bailey hosted the 1967 TV series *Good Company* and appeared on the 1979 TV game show *Who Done It?*
Bakunas, Albert
Stunt man who was killed while filming the 1979 movie *Steel* when a plastic safety bag on which he landed burst after a 323-foot fall from a Kentucky building.

Bal du Paradis
Paris nightclub owned and run by Simone Pistache (Shirley McLaine) in the 1960 movie *Can Can*.

Baldwin
Piano played by Liberace in his 1950s TV series *Liberace*.

Balestrero, Christopher Emmanuel ("Manny")
Man who was falsely arrested for robbery in January 1953. He was portrayed in the 1957 movie *The Wrong Man* by Henry Fonda.

Ball, Ernest
Composer of "When Irish Eyes Are Smiling," who once fought middle-weight champion Stanley Ketchel in order to win enough money for train fare to New York City.

Ball, Lucille
Actress who appeared with her baby son Desiderio Arnaz IV on the cover of the first issue of *TV Guide* (April 3–9, 1953). She was portrayed in 1980 TV miniseries *Moviola* by Gypsi De Young.

Balthasar
Jolyon Forsyte's white and brown dog in *The Forsyte Saga* by John Galsworthy.

Baltimore Clay
Official substance used by umpires to rub down baseballs before every game.

Bambi
Great Prince of the Forest in the 1942 Disney cartoon movie *Bambi*. Who did the voice for Bambi has never been revealed.

Bananas
Capt. Jack Stuart's (John Wayne) pet monkey in the 1942 movie *Reap the Wild Wind*.

Bananas
Monkey on the TV cartoon series *Emergency Plus Four*.

Bandit
Ingalls family pet dog in the TV series *Little House on the Prairie*.

Bandit
Johnny Quest's pet bulldog in the TV cartoon series *Johnny Quest*.

Barabbas
Thief who was released by Pontius Pilate instead of Jesus. Movie portrayals: *King of Kings* (1927) George Seigmann; *King of Kings* (1961) Harry Guardino; *Barabbas* (1962) Anthony Quinn; *The Greatest Story Ever Told* (1965) Richard Conte; *Jesus of Nazareth* (1977 TV) Stacy Keach; and *The Day Christ Died* (1980 TV) Michael Ansara.

Barataria
Land-based home, in the mouth of the Mississippi Delta, of buccaneer Jean Lafitte.

Bar-B-Q

Original title of James M. Cain's 1934 novel *The Postman Always Rings Twice*.

Barfy and Sam

Two pet dogs of the family in Bill Keane's comic strip *The Family Circus*. The family cat is named Kittycat.

Barnes, Ernie

Ex-professional football guard, drafted by the Baltimore Colts in 1960. Barnes is an accomplished artist; the canvas that J. J. Evans (Jimmie Walker) supposedly painted on the TV series *Good Times* was his.

Barnes, Joseph K.

Surgeon general of the U.S. Army who attended to Presidents Lincoln and Garfield after both had been shot.

Barney

Pet Yorkshire terrier of Margaret Pynchon (Nancy Marchand), the publisher of the *Los Angeles Tribune,* in the TV series *Lou Grant* until he was killed by a pit dog in one of the series' episodes.

Barney Bear

MGM cartoon bear, who debuted in the 1952 cartoon *Barney's Hungry Cousin*. His two nephews are Fuzzy and Wuzzy. His sidekick is the little gray donkey Benny Burro.

Baron

White horse ridden by Tom Tyler in B westerns.

Baroudi, Sam

Heavyweight boxer who in 1947 killed his opponent, Glen Newton Smith, in the ring. In 1948, while fighting Ezzard Charles, Sam Baroudi himself died in the ring.

Barracudas

Rival gang of the Faces in the 1977 movie *Saturday Night Fever*.

Barry Chan

Charlie Chan's number-one son in the 1957 TV series *The New Adventures of Charlie Chan*. He was played by James Hong.

Barry, Rick

Only player to have led the NCAA, the NBA, and the ABA in scoring: NCAA (1965) 973 points, University of Miami; NBA (1966–1967) 2,775 points, San Francisco Warriors; ABA (1968–1969) 1,190 points, Oakland Oaks.

Barrymore, Diana

(1921–1960) Daughter of actor John Barrymore and poet Michael Strange. In 1957 she penned her autobiography, *Too Much Too Soon,* which was made into a movie in 1958, with Dorothy Malone portraying Diana Barrymore.

Diana Barrymore was loosely portrayed in the 1952 movie *The Bad and the Beautiful* by Lana Turner (as Georgia Lorrison).

Bartsocchini, Reno
Joe DiMaggio's best man at his wedding to Marilyn Monroe in January 1954. (Reno's San Francisco pub has been the site of many an enjoyable trivia game.)

Bartelt, Gene
Spectator who was injured when he was hit by a golf ball driven by President Gerald Ford at Milwaukee's North Hills Country Club.

Bartley, James
British seaman who, while whale hunting on the *Star of the East* in February 1891 was swallowed by a whale and then lived in the whale's stomach for 2 days. His skin was bleached white from the experience, but he survived until 1926.

Baruch, Bernard
Businessman and statesman who was an adviser to a number of U.S. presidents. His father, Simon Bernard, performed the first operation for appendicitis in the United States in 1888. Movie portrayals: *Wilson* (1944) Francis X. Bushman; and *Funny Lady* (1976) Larry Gates.

Bascomb
Richie Rich's chauffeur (Harvey comics).

Basie, William "Count"
Leader of the first black band to play Carnegie Hall (1939). He appeared in the 1974 movie *Blazing Saddles*.

Basketball
Duration of games:

High school	32 minutes
College	40 minutes
Professional	48 minutes

Bassoon
Musical instrument played by Sherlock Holmes's arch-enemy Professor Moriarty.

Bataan
Gen. Douglas MacArthur's private B17, which he used during World War II and the Korean War. The C54 he used later was also named *Bataan*.

Bates, Charles
FBI agent who was in charge of finding kidnapped heiress Patricia Hearst. He was portrayed in the 1979 movie *The Ordeal of Patty Hearst* by Dennis Weaver.

Bates High School
High school featured in the 1976 movie *Carrie*.

Bathsheba

Biblical wife of Uriah the Hittite. She was the second wife of King David and the mother of King Solomon. Movie portrayals: *David and Bathsheba* (1952) Susan Hayward; and *The Story of David* (1976 TV) Jane Seymour.

Battle

Servant of pulp hero G8.

Battle Hymn of the Republic

Melody written in 1862 by William Steffe, words by Julia Ward Howe. In 1959 the Mormon Tabernacle Choir's version sold a million records. The song was sung at the funerals of Sir Winston Churchill and Robert Kennedy.

Battle of the Bulge Ribbons

Battle ribbons worn by those impersonating White House guards in the 1965 movie *Our Man Flint*. The fact that no such ribbon exists tipped off Derek Flint (James Coburn).

Battle of the Flowers

Original name of the Rose Bowl Parade when it was inaugurated on January 1, 1890.

Baum, Doris Doscher

Movie actress who served as the model for the 1916 U.S. quarter. She was sculpted by Herman Atkins.

Bauman, Charles

Clemson University middle guard whom Ohio State football coach Woody Hayes hit in the neck during the Gator Bowl on December 29, 1978. Hayes was fired the next day. The two ABC-TV announcers, Keith Jackson and Ara Parseghian, did not mention the incident on the air.

Bavetta, Dick

Referee whom coach Gene Shue of the San Diego Clippers hit in a game against Chicago on January 4, 1980. Shue was fined $3,500 and suspended for one week.

Bayes, Nora

(1880–1929) Vaudeville entertainer who, along with her husband Jack Norworth, wrote the song "Shine On, Harvest Moon." She was portrayed in the 1944 movie *Shine On, Harvest Moon* by Ann Sheridan (her husband was portrayed by Dennis Morgan). "Alabamy Bound" was the last song that Nora Bayes sang in public (1928).

Bayonet

Private military parlor railway car in Great Britain of Allied supreme commander Gen. Dwight D. Eisenhower.

Beans

President Calvin Coolidge's Boston bulldog (See: **Peter Pan, Rob Roy, Prudence Prim**).

Bear

Billie Joe McKay's (Greg Evigan) pet chimpanzee in the TV series *B.J. and the Bear,* named after coach Bear Bryant. Bear's real name is Sam. His stand-in was the chimp Jimmy.

Beardsley, Frank

Navy widower with 10 children who married Helen North, a widow with 8 children. They had one child of their own, bringing the total to 19. The couple was portrayed in the 1968 movie *Yours, Mine and Ours* (based on their book *Who Gets the Drumstick?*) by Henry Fonda and Lucille Ball.

Beat the System

Theme song of the TV series *The Kallikaks,* sung by Roy Clark.

Beatle Nut

Special flavor of ice cream created by Baskin-Robbins to celebrate the Beatles' arrival in the United States (February 7, 1964) for their first American tour.

Beatnik

Word coined in 1957 by San Francisco journalist Herb Caen to describe a group of unconventional artists and philosophers.

Beatty, Clyde

World-famous big-game hunter who portrayed himself in the 1951 movie *Perils of the Jungle.*

Beatty, Warren

Actor-brother of actress Shirley MacLaine who is thought to be the subject of Carly Simon's 1972 hit record "You're So Vain"* (Carly Simon was once his girlfriend). Carly Simon is the daughter of Richard Simon, co-founder of the publishing company Simon and Schuster, and the wife of singer-songwriter James Taylor.

Beau

Horse ridden by Rooster J. Cogburn (John Wayne) in the movies *True Grit* (1969) and *Rooster Cogburn* (1975). Beau was played by Dollar.

Beau Geste

There are several movie versions of this 1924 novel by Percival Christopher Wren, an ex-member of the French Foreign Legion.

1926 version:

Role	Actor	As Child
Beau Geste	Ronald Colman	Maurice Murphy
Digby Geste	Neil Hamilton	Philippe DeLacey
John Geste	Ralph Forbes	Mickey McBan

*Mick Jagger sang backup vocal on the recording.

1939 version:

Role	Actor	As Child
Michael "Beau" Geste	Gary Cooper	Donald O'Connor
Digby Geste	Robert Preston	Martin Spellman
John Geste	Ray Milland	Billy Cook

1966 version:

Role	Actor
Beau Geste	Guy Stockwell
John Geste	Doug McClure

1977 spoof (*The Last Remake of Beau Geste*):

Role	Actor
Beau Geste	Michael York
Digby Geste	Marty Feldman

Beaumont, Ginger
Pittsburgh Pirates center fielder who was the first player to bat in the first World Series game (Boston, October 1, 1903). Cy Young, the opposing pitcher, threw a ball that Beaumont hit to Boston center fielder Chick Stahl. Beaumont became the first player to win the batting championship (.357 in 1902) without hitting a single home run.

Beauregard Hotel
English setting of the play and 1958 movie *Separate Tables*.

Beauty
Adam Cartwright's (Pernell Roberts) horse in the TV series *Bonanza*.

Beauty Ranch
Author Jack London's ranch in Glen Ellen, California, where he died on November 22, 1916. Here London built his dream "Wolf House," an expensive home that burned to the ground on August 18, 1913. It was never rebuilt.

Beaver and the Trappers
Rock band that Jerry Mathers toured with after playing the Beaver on the TV series *Leave It to Beaver*.

Beaverbrook, Lord
(1879–1964) Canadian-born British newspaper publisher born William Maxwell Aitken. He was portrayed in the movie *The Magic Box* (1952) by Robert Beatty.

Beaver, Oklahoma
Site of the Annual World Championship Cow Chip Throwing Contest.

Beaver Patrol
Name of the westward-bound wagon train in the TV series *The Travels of Jamie McPheeters*.

Because it is there!
Famous answer by mountain climber George Leigh-Mallory when asked why he (and his partner Andrew Irvine) wanted to climb Mt. Everest in 1924.

Becket, Thomas à
(1118–1170) Archbishop of Canterbury (1162–1170) who was murdered by four knights of the king in Canterbury Cathedral and was later made a saint, only to be expunged from the role of saints of the Church of England in 1538 by Henry VIII. Becket was portrayed in the 1964 movie *Becket* by Richard Burton.

Bedford Falls
New England town setting of the 1946 movie *It's a Wonderful Life*. When George Bailey (James Stewart) wishes never to have been born, the town was renamed Potterville.

Bee Gees
Highly successful Australian rock group of brothers; Maurice, Barry, and Robin Gibb. Their younger brother, Andy Gibb, records as a solo artist.

Beetles
Motorcycle gang led by Chino (Lee Marvin) in the 1954 movie *The Wild One*. It was from this club that the Beatles took their name, altering the spelling. The Beatles also borrowed the movie line "Where are we going, Johnny?" "Straight to the top."

Beheler, Ed
Lookalike of President Jimmy Carter. He portrayed the president in a nonspeaking scene in the 1977 movie *Black Sunday,* and in the 1979 movie *The Cayman Triangle*. He also appeared in several TV commercials.

Behring, Dr. Emil
First recipient of the Nobel Prize (1901). He won it in the field of medicine. Behring was portrayed in the 1940 movie *Dr. Ehrlich's Magic Bullet* by Otto Kruger.

Beiderbecke, Leon Bismarck "Bix"
(1903–1931) Jazz musician of the 1920s who died at the age of 28. The character Rick Martin (Kirk Douglas) in the 1950 movie *Young Man with a Horn* was based on Beiderbecke.

Belafonte, Harry
Singer-actor who became the first black entertainer to win an Emmy. He won it for his special *Tonight with Belafonte*, telecast on December 10, 1959.

Belcher, Sarah Barney
Taunton, Massachusetts, resident who was a common ancestor of Gen. Douglas MacArthur, President Franklin Delano Roosevelt, and Prime Minister Winston Churchill.

Beldingsville
Hometown of Pollyanna, a character in children's books.

Beldone
Futuristic automobile in the 1964 Jerry Lewis movie *The Patsy.**

Belenko, Vikton I.
Soviet pilot who defected from the Soviet Union by landing his MIG-25 in Japan on September 6, 1976.

Belinda, USS
World War II attack transport featured in the 1956 movie *Away All Boats*.

Bell, Alexander Graham
(1847–1922) Inventor of the telephone on March 10, 1876. The very same day that Bell applied for the patent on the telephone, so did Elisha Gray. Movie portrayals: *The Story of Alexander Graham Bell*** (1939) Don Ameche; and *The Story of Mankind* (1957) Jim Ameche (brother of Don Ameche); *The Wings of Kitty Hawk* (1978 TV) John Randolph.

Bellamy, Francis
Creator in 1892 of the Pledge of Allegiance for a Columbus Day celebration.

Belle
Snoopy's sister in the comic strip *Peanuts*. His brother is named Spike.

Bellemere
Hometown of Bunny Brown and Sister Sue in children's books.

Belle Reve
Stella and Blanche's family estate in Tennessee Williams' play *A Streetcar Named Desire*.

Bells of St. Mary's
1945 movie starring Bing Crosby. The movie title appears on marquees within the movies *It's a Wonderful Life* (1946) (at the Bijou Theatre) and *The Godfather* (1972).

Bellvue Hotel
Philadelphia site of the discovery of the deadly legionaire's disease, which took the lives of 29 people in 1976. The source of the bacteria was traced to a cooling tower in Bloomington, Indiana, from where some legionaires came.

Bell Waltz, The
Theme song of the TV series *The Bell Telephone Hour*. It was composed and performed by conductor Donald Voorhees.

---

*Peter Lorre made his last film appearance in this movie.
**Only movie in which the Young sisters—Loretta, Georgiana, Polly, and Ann—appeared together as sisters.

Ben
>Grizzly Adams's 800-pound grizzly bear Ben Franklin. He was captured as a cub in 1854 and died on January 17, 1858.

Bendix, William
>(1906–1964) Actor who, as a boy, served as a batboy for the New York Yankees. According to legend, he was fired when he brought Babe Ruth a dozen hot dogs before a game one day, as Ruth requested. The Babe collapsed after eating the food and was taken to a hospital. Bendix later portrayed Babe Ruth in the 1948 movie *The Babe Ruth Story*.

Ben-Gurion, David
>(Born David Green in 1886) First prime minister of Israel after the country was created in 1948. He was portrayed in the 1979 TV movie *The House on Garibaldi Street* by Leo McKern.

Benjamin Craig Institute
>Los Angeles medical facility featured on the TV series *The Doctors* (as part of *The Bold Ones*).

Benji
>Dog hero of the 1974 movie *Benji*, played by Higgins (of the TV series *Petticoat Junction*). Benji was played by Benji Two in the 1977 movie *For the Love of Benji*, and by Kim in the 1980 movie *Oh Heavenly Dog*.

Bennett, Rheinhart, and Alquist
>Prestigious law firm in Los Angeles for which Martin Kazinsky (Ron Leibman) worked in the TV series *Kaz*.

BEnsonhurst 5520
>New York City home phone number of playwright Moss Hart (George Hamilton) in the 1963 movie *Act One*.

Benton, Al (John Alton)
>Only major league pitcher ever to face both Babe Ruth (1934) and Mickey Mantle (1952).

Berlin, Irving
>(1888–   ) American composer, born Israel Baline in Russia in 1888. His first hit song was "Alexander's Ragtime Band." Berlin composed "White Christmas" and hundreds of other popular songs. He was portrayed by David Levy in the 1978 TV movie *Ziegfeld: The Man and His Women*.

Bern, Paul
>(1889–1932) American director (born Paul Levy) who in 1932 committed suicide shortly after marrying actress Jean Harlow. Paul Bern was portrayed by Peter Lawford in *Harlow* (1965, Paramount) and by Hurd Hatfield in *Harlow* (1965, Magna). Jay Sebring, one of the victims of the Charles Manson cult murders, once lived in the house in which Paul Bern killed himself.

Bernhardt, Sarah

(1844–1923) French stage actress (born Rosalie Bernard). She had one wooden leg and slept in a coffin. She was portrayed by Glenda Jackson in 1976 movie *The Incredible Sarah*.

Bernice

Bert, the *Sesame Street* muppets' favorite pigeon.

Bernice

Whiffle Hen that appeared in Segar's comic strip *Thimble Theater*.

Berrigan, Daniel

Catholic priest who actively opposed the Vietnam War to the point of destroying government records, for which he was sent to jail. He was portrayed in the 1972 TV movie *The Trial of the Catonsville Nine* by Ed Flanders. His brother, Philip Berrigan, was portrayed by Douglas Watson. In 1969 Philip married Elizabeth McAlister, a former nun.

Berry, Capt. Albert

Man who made the first parachute jump from an airplane on March 1, 1912.

Bert's Place

Diner where Rufus Butterworth (Bob Denver) worked in the TV series *The Good Guys*. Bert was played by Herb Edelman.

Bess, Jock, and Jerry

Fictional detective Bulldog Drummond's three pet dogs: a cocker spaniel, a terrier, and a bulldog.

Bessie Mae

Actor Montgomery Clift's affectionate nickname for his close friend Elizabeth Taylor.

Best Friend

Theme song written and sung by Harry Nilsson for the TV series *The Courtship of Eddie's Father*.

Best, Pete

Drummer for the Beatles who was fired in 1963 and replaced by Ringo Starr. He was portrayed by Ryan Michael in the 1979 TV movie *Birth of the Beatles*.

Be sure you're right, then go ahead

Davy Crockett's (Fess Parker) motto in the *Disneyland* TV series.

Betty Crocker

Fictitious symbol of General Mills products, created in 1921. Neysa McMein was the first to show her in a painting. Betty Crocker was once voted the second best known woman (after Eleanor Roosevelt). Betty Crocker is never shown from the waist down. Since 1921 her portraits have been modeled after a real person. (There have been six different portraits so far.)

Betty Ross

Girlfriend of comic book superhero The Hulk.

Beverly Hills Hotel
Famous southern California hotel built in 1912 and nicknamed the Pink Palace. It is the hotel shown on the cover of the Eagles' album *Hotel California*.

Beverly Hills Supper Club
Southgate, Kentucky, nightclub that caught fire and burned on Saturday night, May 28, 1977, claiming 164 lives. John Davidson was the star performer.

Beware! the Blob
1972 sequel movie to *The Blob* (1958). This is the only movie directed by Larry Hagman. The film is also known as *Son of Blob*.

Bezdek, Hugo
Only man to coach a NFL football team and manage a major league baseball team. He managed the Pittsburgh Pirates in 1917–1919, and coached the NFL Cleveland Rams in 1937–1938. Bezdek also coached three teams in the Rose Bowl: Oregon (1916), Great Lakes Navy (1917), and Penn State (1922).

Bib
Gary Gulliver's pet dog in the TV cartoon series *The Adventures of Gulliver*.

Bicentennial Minutes
CBS historical accounts aired each evening at 8:28 P.M. (E.S.T.) from July 4, 1974, until December 31, 1976.

Big Apple
Nickname of New York City, setting of the TV serial *Ryan's Hope*.

Big Beat, The
Short-lived 1957 ABC-TV series featuring Alan Freed and the latest hit songs with the original artists singing them.

Big Bird
Financier Robert Vesco's private Boeing 707, which was repossessed after Vesco fled the country to escape criminal charges.

Big Bopper
Muhammad Ali's CB handle.

Big Bopper, The
(1935–1959) Rock 'n' roll singer Jiles Perry "Jape" Richardson, who was killed in a plane crash with Buddy Holly and Ritchie Valens on February 3, 1959. The Big Bopper was portrayed in the 1978 movie *The Buddy Holly Story* by Gailard Sartain.

Big Daddy
Nickname of NFL player Gene Lipscomb.

Big Deal Records
"The World's Biggest Record Company," headed by B. D. Brockhurst (Donald Pleasance) in the 1978 movie *Sgt. Pepper's Lonely Hearts Club Band*.

Big E Sports Arena

New York City sports facility owned by promoter Eddie Smith (Sheldon Leonard) in the TV series *Big Eddie*.

Bigger they come, the harder they fall, The

Statement made to Jim Jeffries by his manager prior to Jeffries' winning fight with Bob Fitzsimmons on June 9, 1899.

Big Kate

Carter Primus's (Robert Brown) underwater robot in the 1971 TV series *Primus*.

Bigman

John Bigman Jones, the sidekick of David Starr, Space Ranger, in the Lucky Starr novel series by Isaac Asimov under the name Paul French.

Big Mo

Nickname of Cincinnati Royal basketball star Maurice Stokes (Rookie of the Year, All-American, No. 1 draft choice), who was stricken with a fatal illness at the peak of his career. He was portrayed in the 1973 movie *Maurie** by Bernie Casey (as a child, by Ricky Louis). Jack Twyman, his close friend, was portrayed by Bo Svenson.

Big Pictures

Motion picture studio that filmed Mel Funn's (Mel Brooks) movies in the 1976 movie *Silent Movie*.

Big Ragu

Nickname of Carmine Ragusa (Eddie Mekka) in the TV series *LaVerne and Shirley*.

Big Surprise, The

1950s TV quiz show hosted by Jack Barry and Mike Wallace on which actor Errol Flynn appeared as a contestant and won $30,000 answering questions on the subject of sailing

Big Thunder

Fictional Mafia fighter Mack Bolan's .44 Auto Mag pistol, which weighs 3½ pounds unloaded. It was designed by Harry Sanford as the most powerful handgun in the world. (*The Executioner* novel series)

Big Top

1950 TV series on which Ed McMahon was one of the clowns.

Big Town

Hometown of Carter Nash (William Daniels) in the TV series *Captain Nice*.

Bijou

Boston theater that was the first to have its marquee lit by electric lights (December 11, 1882).

---

*Shown on TV under the title *Big Mo*.

Bikila, Abebe
Ethiopian runner who is the only person to have won the Olympic Marathon race twice, in 1960 and 1964. In 1960 he ran it barefoot.

Billboard Chart for April 4, 1964
The top 5 songs were:

1. "Can't Buy Me Love," Beatles (Capitol)
2. "Twist and Shout," Beatles (Tollie)
3. "She Loves You," Beatles (Swan)
4. "I Want to Hold Your Hand," Beatles (Capitol)
5. "Please Please Me," Beatles (Vee Jay)

Billy
Young helper of detective Sherlock Holmes in William Gillette's stage play *Sherlock Holmes*. Billy was played on the London stage by 12-year-old Charles Chaplin in 1903. Terry Kilburn played Billy in the 1939 movie *The Adventures of Sherlock Holmes*.

Billy Beer
Brand of canned beer first manufactured in 1977. It was named after President Jimmy Carter's younger brother Billy, a onetime beer drinker. Advertisement:
"I had this beer brewed up just for me.
I think it's the best I ever tasted and I've tasted a lot.
I think you'll like it, too." Billy Carter.

Bimbo
Betty Boop's pet dog (comic strip/radio/cartoons).

Bimbo
Corky's (Mickey Braddock) pet elephant in the TV series *Circus Boy*.

Bingay, Roberta
First woman ever to enter and finish the Boston Marathon. She finished number 150 in 1964.

Bing Collins
Role played by Bing Crosby in the 1964–1965 TV series *The Bing Crosby Show*.

Bini
West African gray parrot at the Wameru Game Preserve and Research Center in the TV series *Daktari*.

Bip
White-face mute played by French pantomimist Marcel Marceau.

Birchfield
California hometown of the Mulligan family in the 1977 TV series *Mulligan's Stew*.

Birch, John

(1918–1945) U.S. missionary and intelligence officer who was killed in China in 1945. It was John Birch who led Jimmy Doolittle and his crew to safety after they parachuted onto Chinese soil after their famous B25 raid on Tokyo. The John Birch Society was named in his honor, as he is considered to have been the first American killed by the Communists after World War II.

Birdseye

Brand of frozen foods invented by Clarence Birdseye in 1923.

Birmingham Americans

Football team that won the only World Football League championship ever played (December 5, 1974). The score was 22–21 against the Florida Blazers.

Biro, Ladislao

Hungarian journalist who in 1939 invented the ball-point pen.

Birth of the Blues, The

Song performed in the following movies: *Birth of the Blues* (1941); *Painting the Clouds with Sunshine* (1951); *The Jazz Singer* (1953); and *The Best Things in Life Are Free* (1956). Buddy DeSylva and Lew Brown wrote the song lyrics; Ray Henderson was the composer of the music.

Birth of a Nation

1915 movie spectacular directed by D. W. Griffith featuring the "heroics" of the Ku Klux Klan. It was the first movie ever shown at the White House (February 15, 1916).

Bitter Tea of General Yen, The

1933 movie directed by Frank Capra. It was the first movie to play at the Radio City Music Hall.

Black Bart

Notorious California stagecoach robber Charles E. Bolton. He held up 29 stagecoaches with guns that were never loaded. His prisoner number at San Quentin Penitentiary was 11046.

Black Beauty

Western actor Art Acord's horse in movies.

Black, Bill

(1926–1965) Original member of Elvis Presley's backup band. Bill Black played bass on Elvis's Sun recordings, but left Elvis in 1959 to record a successful series of hit records including "Smokie" and "Don't Be Cruel." Today Paul McCartney is the owner of Bill Black's famous bass. Black was portrayed in 1979 TV movie *Elvis* by Elliot Street.

Black Dawn

Maria Vargas's (Ava Gardner) movie debut within the 1954 movie *The Barefoot Contessa*.

Black Jack
    Great Dane that lived with Nancy Blansky (Nancy Walker) on the TV series *Blansky's Beauties*.

Black Maria
    First motion picture studio. It was built by Thomas Edison at a cost of $638. It was named the Black Maria because it resembled a paddy wagon.

Black Pirate
    Secret identity of swashbuckler Jon Valor, who made his debut in *Action Comics* No. 23 in April 1940. The Black Pirate ended with issue No. 42.

Blackstone
    Nickname of prominent American magician Henri Bouton.

Black Swan Records
    First all-black-owned record label. This 1930s company was half owned by W. C. Handy, composer of "St. Louis Blues."

Blake, USS
    Destroyer upon which the action of World War II takes place in the 1952 movie *Okinawa*.

Blair House
    1651 Pennsylvania Avenue. Residence of President Harry Truman and his family in 1950 while the White House was undergoing major repairs.

Blanche
    Wife of Joe Jinks in the comic strip *Joe Jinks*.

Blankers-Koen, Fanny
    Dutch mother of two who in the 1948 Olympic Games in London won four Olympic Gold Medals (for the 100-meter dash, 200-meter dash, 80-meter hurdle, and 400-meter relay). At that time Fanny also held the world's record for the broad jump and high jump, but was not allowed to compete in more than three individual events.

Blarney
    Mr. Callahan's (Forrest Tucker) horse in the TV series *Dusty's Trail*.

Blarney Cock
    Pirate ship commanded by Capt. Ned Lynch (Robert Shaw) in the 1977 movie *Swashbuckler*. The *Golden Hinde* was used for the vessel.

Blatz Beer
    Bottled beer that the Black Rebels Motorcycle Club guzzled by the caseful in Bleeker's Café in the 1954 movie *The Wild One*.

Blaze
    Colonel Elliot Roosevelt's 130-pound bull mastiff who in 1945 was the cause of two servicemen being bumped from a military flight from Newark, New Jersey. One of the servicemen, Seaman 1st Class Leon LeRoy, was on his way to his father's funeral. When the news media picked up the story, the public was outraged. The co-pilot of the aircraft was Gene Autry.

Bleem

2000 Earth years on the planet Ork in the TV series *Mork and Mindy*.

Blessed Virgin Mary

Mother of Jesus and wife of Joseph. Movie portrayals: *Ben Hur* (1925) Betty Bronson; *King of Kings* (1927) Dorothy Cummings; *Song of Bernadette* (1944) Linda Darnell; *King of Kings* (1961) Siobhan McKenna; *The Greatest Story Ever Told* (1965) Dorothy McGuire; *Jesus of Nazareth* (1977) Olivia Hussey; and *The Day Christ Died* (1980 TV) Eleanor Bron. She has appeared on the cover of *Time* magazine 10 times, the most of any woman.

Blip

Space monkey in the TV cartoon series *Space Ghost*.

Bliss, Harry H.

A 68-year-old estate agent who was the first victim of an automobile accident, occurring in New York City on September 13, 1899. After stepping off a streetcar, Bliss was run over by an automobile.

Blob, The

1958 horror movie starring Steve McQueen. Previews of the movie were shown at a drive-in in the 1978 movie *Grease*.

Block, Dora

The 75-year-old Israeli woman who was not rescued at Entebbe Airport on July 4, 1976, because she was in a Uganda hospital. She was never seen again. Dora Block was portrayed by Helen Hayes in the 1976 television movie *Victory at Entebbe*, and by Sylvia Sidney in *Raid on Entebbe* (1977 TV).

Blomberg, Ron

New York Yankee player who became the first designated hitter (April 6, 1973) after the rule became effective in 1973. He was walked by pitcher Luis Tiant.

Blond Blintz

CB handle of Ken "Hutch" Hutchinson (David Soul) in the TV series *Starsky and Hutch*. (See: **Puce Goose**)

Blonde Bombshell

Nickname of actress Jean Harlow.

Blondin, Charles

First person to cross Niagara Falls (1855) on a tightrope (1,000 feet long). He again performed the feat in 1859 and 1860.

Blood

Dog's name in the 1976 sci-fi movie *A Boy and His Dog* (based on a 1969 novella by Harlan Ellison). The voice of the dog was that of Tim McIntire.

Bloomfield

Hometown of Frank Merriwell, his wife, Inza, his son, Frank Jr., and his daughter, Dart (children's books). The family later moved to Elmsport.

Blossom Fell, A
1955 hit song by Nat "King" Cole being played over a car radio to which Kit Carruthers (Martin Sheen) and Holly Sargis (Sissy Spacek) dance in the 1973 movie *Badlands*.

Blount's Landing
Waterfront store in the 1947 movie *The Unconquered*, directed by Cecil Blount DeMille.

Blowhole Beach
Location on the island of Oahu where the famous love scene between Burt Lancaster and Deborah Kerr was filmed in the 1953 movie *From Here to Eternity*.

Blue
Pvt. Will Stockdale's (Sammy Jackson) pet dog in the TV series *No Time for Sergeants*.

Blue Bird Café
Pvt. Gomer Pyle's (Jim Nabors) favorite hangout outside Camp Henderson in the TV series *Gomer Pyle, U.S.M.C.*

Blue Bonnet Café
Laramie restaurant owned by Dru Lemp (Bek Nelson) in the TV series *Laramie*.

Blue Chipp 11
Vessel commanded by Capt. David Scott (Barry Sullivan) in the TV series *Harbourmaster*.

Blue Dragon Café
Phoenix, Arizona, club where Cherie (Marilyn Monroe) sang "That Old Black Magic" in the 1956 movie *Bus Stop*.

Blue Ghost
Name Baretta (Robert Blake) calls his dirty 1966 Chevy in the TV series *Baretta*.

Blue Jays
Alternate name chosen for the Philadelphia Phillies in 1944. The name never caught on and was forgotten.

Blue Jays
Boys who join the Camp Fire Girls (also called Thunderbirds).

Blue Lagoon
Honolulu tavern where Cmdr. Paul Eddington (Kirk Douglas) started a fight in the 1965 movie *In Harm's Way*.

Blue Mist
Nickname of T. E. Lawrence's motorcycle on which he was killed on May 19, 1935, in Dorset, England. The license plate was UL-656. In the 1962 biographical movie *Lawrence of Arabia* in which Peter O'Toole portrayed Lawrence, the license plate was JL 656. Blue Mist was also the name of Lawrence's Rolls-Royce armored car in Arabia.

Blue Moon Boys

Elvis Presley's original backup group with Sun Records. The members were Scotty Moore (guitar) and Bill Black (bass). Elvis and the group were turned down when they auditioned for *Arthur Godfrey's Talent Scouts* in April 1955.

Blue Peter

Flag flown on board a naval vessel as an indicator that the ship is set to sail.

Blue Ridge Chronicle

Small newspaper founded by John-Boy Walton (Richard Thomas) in the TV series *The Waltons*.

Blues Artists

Real first names

Sam	"Lightnin' " Hopkins
Huddie	"Leadbelly" Ledbetter
Alonzo	"Lonnie" Johnson
John	"Sonny Boy" Williamson
Riley	"B.B." King
Peter	"Memphis Slim" Chatman
Aron	"T-Bone" Walker
James	"Slim Harpo" Moore
Elias	"Bo Diddley" McDaniels
McKinley	"Muddy Waters" Morganfield
Chester	"Howlin' Wolf" Burnett

Blue Star

Theme song of the 1954–1956 TV series *Medic*, composed by Edward Heyman and Victor Young.

Blue Train

Famous train that once ran from Paris to Monte Carlo.

Blue Yodel No. 9

Country recording by "The Singing Brakeman," Jimmie Rodgers (in 1930), on which Louis Armstrong played the cornet.

Bodace

Alien planet on which Superman boxed Muhammad Ali in a Special Edition of DC Comics in January 1978. Ali knocked Superman out in the 2nd round, thus saving Earth from destruction.

Boilermaker, The

Nickname of heavyweight boxing champion James Jackson Jeffries.

Bolero

Classic musical piece composed by Maurice Ravel in 1928 for dancer Ida Rubinstein. It is to this song that Bo Derek makes love as it plays on the phonograph in the 1979 movie "10." In the film the song was performed by

Henry Mancini. "Bolero" had previously been the subject of the 1934 George Raft film *Bolero*. The vocal "All My Love," made popular by Patti Page in 1950, is based on Ravel's melody.

Bolero
Code name for the preliminary buildup by the Allied forces for the invasion of Normandy.

Bolo
Nickname of a punch used by welterweight champion Kid Gavilan.

Bolton
Town setting of the TV soap opera *Today Is Ours*.

Bonanza
California ghost town in the Bette Davis–James Cagney 1941 comedy *The Bride Came C.O.D.* The town's cornerstone was laid by William Jennings Bryan on January 14, 1897. The town saloon was the Palace Hotel.

Bonaventure
First starship equipped with warp drive. The U.S.S. *Bonaventure* left Earth to survey other solar systems in 2053 A.D. in the animated TV series *Star Trek*.

Bonavena, Oscar
(1942–1976) Argentine heavyweight champion who in May 1976 was shot to death outside the famed Mustang Ranch brothel in Nevada. 150,000 people went to his funeral in Buenos Aires, the largest crowd ever to attend an athlete's funeral.

Bon Bon
Black singer with Jan Savitt's band. His real name was George Tunnell.

Bond, Julian
Black congressman and civil rights activist. On April 9, 1977, he was the guest host on NBC's *Saturday Night Live*. Bond portrayed himself in the 1978 TV movie *King*.

Bong, Richard
(1920–1945) America's all-time flying ace. In World War II, while flying with the Flying Knights, he shot down 40 Japanese planes in his P38 Lightning. He was killed in a jet aircraft as a test pilot.

BOnneyville 8-1098
Phone number of Roger Thornhill's (Cary Grant) mother Clara (Jessie Royce Landis) in the 1959 movie *North by Northwest*.

Boo
Jonathan "Musty" Muddlemore's (voice of Daws Butler) pet cat in the TV cartoon series *The Funky Phantom*.

Boo-Boo Kitty
Laverne and Shirley's stuffed toy cat. It sits on their sofa in the TV series *Laverne and Shirley*.

Boogie

Mae West's pet monkey that peeled grapes before eating them. This inspired Mae West's famous line, "Beulah, peel me a grape," in the 1933 movie *I'm No Angel*.

Boogie Oogie Oogie

Hit record by Taste of Honey that Boston Red Sox's player Jerry Remy listened to each day of his 19-game hitting streak in 1978.

Book Nook

Bloomington campus hangout near Indiana University Law School where Hoagy Carmichael wrote many of his classic songs, including "Stardust" in 1927. The place today is called the Gables restaurant.

Boone, Daniel

(1734–1820) American frontiersman, pioneer, and founder of the town of Boonesboro in 1775. Movie portrayals: *The Days of Daniel Boone* (1923) Jack Mower; *Daniel Boone Thru the Wilderness* (1926) Roy Stewart; *The Miracle Rider* (1935 serial) Jay Wilsey; *Daniel Boone* (1936) George O'Brien; *The Return of Daniel Boone* (1941) Wild Bill Elliott; *Young Daniel Boone* (1950) David Bruce; and, *Daniel Boone, Trail Blazer* (1956) Bruce Bennett. TV series: *Walt Disney Presents* ("Daniel Boone") Dewey Martinez; *Daniel Boone* Fess Parker; and *Young Dan'l Boone* Rick Moses.

Booth, H. Cecil

English inventor of the vacuum cleaner in 1905.

Booth, John Wilkes

(1838–1865) Shakespearean actor, brother of actor Edwin Thomas Booth. On April 14, 1865, John Wilkes Booth assassinated President Abraham Lincoln at Ford's Theatre in Washington, D.C. Movie portrayals: *The Birth of a Nation* (1915) Raoul Walsh; *Abraham Lincoln* (1930) Ian Keith; *The Prisoner of Shark Island* (1936) Francis McDonald; *Prince of Players* (1955) John Derek (Louis Alexander at age 12); *The Lincoln Conspiracy* (1977) Bradford Dillman; and *The Ordeal of Dr. Mudd* (1980 TV) Bill Gribble.

Boots

Bunny Olsen's (Barbara Stuart) pet cat in the TV series *Gomer Pyle, U.S.M.C.*

Borgia, Caesar

(1476–1507) Italian cardinal, son of Pope Alexander VI, who gave up his church position to become a conqueror of cities and castles in Italy. He had been made a cardinal at the age of 17. His sister was Lucretia Borgia. Movie portrayals: *Don Juan* (1926) Warner Oland (Lucretia by Estelle Taylor); *Bridge of Vengeance* (1949) MacDonald Carey (Lucretia by Paulette Goddard); *Prince of Foxes* (1949) Orson Welles; *Lucretia Borgia* (1952) Pedro Armendariz (Lucretia by Martine Carol); *Nights of Lucretia Borgia* (1959) Franco Fabrizi (Lucretia by Belinda Lee); *The Night of the Great Attack* (1964) Fausto

Tozzi; *The Black Duke* (1964) Cameron Mitchell; and *Conspiracy of the Borgias* (1965) Frank Latimore.

Born in a Trunk
18-minute musical sequence written by Leonard Gershe and sung by Judy Garland in the 1954 movie *A Star Is Born*. The songs sung were: "Born in a Trunk," "Swanee," "I'll Get By," "My Melancholy Baby," and, for the finale, a reprise of "Swanee."

Born Innocent
1974 NBC movie starring Linda Blair that became the subject of a 1978 trial in which it was alleged that the movie had prompted a sexual attack on a young girl.

Born to Be Wild
Song by Steppenwolf that can be heard on the soundtrack of two movies: *Easy Rider* (1969) and *Coming Home* (1978).

Boston
Name that Portland, Oregon, almost became when Asa Lovejoy and Francis Pettygrove flipped a coin. Portland won.

Boston Gob, The
Nickname of heavyweight champion Jack Sharkey (born Joseph Zukauskas). He took his ring name from two fighters he admired, Jack Dempsey (whom he would later fight) and Tom Sharkey.

Boston Memorial Hospital
Setting of the 1978 movie *Coma* (based on the Robin Cook novel of the same name). The comatose patients were transferred to Jefferson Institute after being operated on in OR 8 (Operation Room 8) at Boston.

Boston Symphony
Orchestra in which Robert Dreyfuss (Paul Sand) played bass violin in the TV series *Friends and Lovers.**

Boston Univ
Printing on sweatshirt worn by 4-year-old Barry Builer (Cary Guffey), who is kidnapped by a UFO in the 1977 movie *Close Encounters of the Third Kind*.

Botha, Louis
(1862–1919) Soldier who captured journalist Winston Churchill during the Boer War. (Churchill escaped from the prison camp.) Ironically Winston Churchill would one day become the prime minister of Great Britain, while Louis Botha would become the first prime minister of the Union of South Africa.

BOulder 6170
Boulder, Colorado, phone number of Helen Burger (June Allison) in the 1954 movie *The Glenn Miller Story*.

*Originally titled *Paul Sand in Friends and Lovers*.

Boulder Beach
Resort where Fred Flintstone took his bride Wilma on their honeymoon in the TV cartoon.

Boulder, Colorado
Earth setting of the TV series *Mork and Mindy*.

Bounce
Author Alexander Pope's Great Dane.

Bouncing Belch, The
U.S. Navy PBY aircraft that dropped off several men on a secret mission in the 1958 movie *South Pacific*.

Bowie, Jim
(1790–1836) American soldier and frontiersman who died at the Battle of the Alamo (March 6, 1836). On the TV series *The Adventures of Jim Bowie* Bowie was portrayed by Scott Forbes. Movie portrayals: *Davy Crockett at the Fall of the Alamo* (1926) Bob Fleming; *The Painted Stallion* (1937) Hal Taliaferro; *Man of Conquest* (1939) Robert Armstrong; *Comanche Territory* (1950) MacDonald Carey; *The Iron Mistress* (1952) Alan Ladd; *The Man from the Alamo* (1953) Stuart Randall; *Davy Crockett King of the Wild Frontier* (1955) Kenneth Tobey; *The Last Command* (1955) Sterling Hayden; *The First Texan* (1956) Jeff Morrow; and *The Alamo* (1960) Richard Widmark. Bowie was portrayed by Bernard Kates in "The Siege of the Alamo," an episode in the TV series *You Are There*.

Bowie Knife
Large knife popular on the western frontier that was invented by Jim Bowie's brother, Rezin Bowie. In the TV series *The Adventures of Jim Bowie* Rezin was portrayed by Peter Hanson, and in the 1952 movie *The Iron Mistress* he was portrayed by Richard Carlyle.

Bowling Hall of Fame
ABC American Bowling Congress located in Milwaukee, Wisconsin, since 1941.

Bowzer
Hanks family pet dog in the TV series *Pistols 'n' Petticoats*.

Box
Keeper robot of the frozen food in the 1976 movie *Logan's Run*, played by Roscoe Lee Browne.

Box 7
Box occupied by President Lincoln at Ford's Theatre the night he was assassinated.

Box 191, Radio City Station
New York City mailing address of Ted Mack's *Original Amateur Hour*.

Box K
Ranch saved by William S. Hart in the 1925 silent western *Tumbleweeds*.

Box X10
Detective Bulldog Drummond's London mailbox (novels).

Boxing Hall of Fame
Located in New York City, one block from Madison Square Garden.

Boycott, Charles
Retired captain and land agent against whom farmers conducted a sitdown strike in Erne, Ireland, in 1880. Because of the event his name became part of the English language. Boycott was portrayed by Cecil Parker in the 1947 movie *Captain Boycott*.

Boyd, Jimmy
12-year-old boy whose recording of "I Saw Mommy Kissing Santa Claus" in 1952 sold over 2 million copies.

Boyington, Gregory "Pappy"
World War II Marine pilot and commander. He was the host-narrator of the 1960 TV series *Danger Zone*. Boyington was portrayed in the 1976 TV series *Baa Baa Black Sheep* (a/k/a *Black Sheep Squadron*) by Robert Conrad.

Boys' Club
Group of friends nicknamed the Irish Mafia who met at various Los Angeles restaurants each Thursday evening in the 1930s. The members were: James Cagney, Pat O'Brien, Ralph Bellamy, Frank McHugh, Lynne Overman, Eddie Foy, Jr., Frank Morgan, and George Murphy.

Boy Scouts
Organization founded in 1908 by Lord Baden-Powell. Before he died on January 22, 1959, Cecil B. DeMille was working on a film called *On My Honor*, which was to be a history of the Boy Scouts. Baden-Powell's sister Agnes founded the Girl Guides in 1910.

Bozo
Robot controlled by Hugh Hazard. Debut: *Smash Comics* No. 1 (August 1939).

Bradbury
First landing site (*Viking I*) on Mars, July 20, 1976, which was named for science-fiction writer Ray Bradbury because of his novel *The Martian Chronicles*.

Bradens
Actual family of 8 children that inspired the TV series *Eight Is Enough* about the Bradford family. The series was created by columnist Tom Braden, ex-deputy director of the CIA, and was based on his 1975 book of the same title.

Bradlee, Ben
Managing editor of the *Washington Post* at the time of the Watergate scandal. He was portrayed in the 1976 movie *All the President's Men* by Jason Robards, Jr.

Bradley, Bill

Basketball player for the New York Knicks. In 1965, while attending Princeton University, he won a Rhodes Scholarship. In 1978 Bradley was elected as a U.S. senator from New Jersey.

Bradley, Omar N.

(1893–1981) World War II five-star general who served in Europe. For allowing himself to be portrayed in the movie *Patton,* Bradley received 10 percent of the movie's gross. Omar Bradley was once a contestant on the TV quiz show *You Bet Your Life.* Movie portrayals: *The Longest Day* (1962) Nicholas Stuart; *Is Paris Burning?* (1966) Glenn Ford; *Patton* (1970) Karl Malden; *MacArthur* (1977), Fred Stuthman; and *Ike* (1979 TV miniseries) Richard T. Herd. Omar Bradley and Dwight Eisenhower were classmates at West Point (class of 1915).

Brady, Mathew

(1823–1896) Famous American Civil War photographer. It was the inventor Samuel Morse who taught Brady how to develop photographs in 1843.

Brahms, Johannes

(1833–1897) German composer and pianist who was portrayed by Robert Walker in the 1947 movie *Song of Love.*

Brain Trust

Nickname given to the political advisers of Franklin Roosevelt.

Brands

℞ Barkley Ranch (in the TV series *The Big Valley*).

⌘ Ponderosa Ranch (in the TV series *Bonanza).*

Ⓜ Tom Mix's Melody Ranch.

Brandy

Capt. Tom Custer's dog. The canine was the champion fighter of his regiment in the 7th Calvary.

Brandy

Actual name of the horse ridden by Clint Walker in the TV series *Cheyenne.*

Brannigans, The

Comic strip drawn by Stanley Ford (Jack Lemmon) and syndicated in 463 newspapers in the 1965 movie *How to Murder Your Wife.*

Braun, Wernher von

(1912–1977) German scientist who helped to develop the VI and V2 bombs during World War II. He was portrayed in the 1960 movie *I Aim at the Stars* by Curt Jurgens. Peter Sellers' characterization of Dr. Strangelove was modeled after Braun.

Brazil

Song, a samba, performed in the following motion pictures: *Saludos Amigos*

(1942); *The Gang's All Here* (1943); *Jam Session* (1943); *Brazil* (1944); and *The Eddie Duchin Story* (1956).

Brecher, Irving
Writer who was Groucho Marx's stand-in in many advertisements for the 1940 Marx Brothers film *Go West*.

Breckinridge, John Cabell
(1821–1875) Vice President under James Buchanan. At the age of 36 he became the youngest man to serve as vice president. He was a Confederate general during the Civil War.

Breezin' Along with the Breeze
Song performed in the following movies: *Shine On, Harvest Moon* (1944); *The Jazz Singer* (1953); and *The Helen Morgan Story* (1957). Song lyrics and music by Haven Gillespie, Seymour Simons, and Richard A. Whiting.

Bremen
Ship upon which Marlene Dietrich first came to the United States from Germany in April 1930.

Brenda, Keith, and Brian
British security code names for Queen Elizabeth, Prince Philip, and Prince Charles, respectively.

Brennan, Bud
Spectator who attempted to tackle Tom Harmon at the end of the Michigan Stars' 87-yard touchdown run in a game at Berkeley in November 1940. Brennan missed Harmon on the 4-yard line.

Brenner, David
Comedian who makes numerous appearances on Johnny Carson's *Tonight Show*. In his youth he was a good friend of up-and-coming comic Freddie Prinze. In September 1976 he was supposed to star in a TV series named *Snip,* but the show was canceled just before its debut. Brenner was portrayed in the 1979 TV movie *Can You Hear the Laughter?* by Kenneth Sylk.

Brent, George, and Kay Francis
Films in which the pair appeared: *The Keyhole* (1933); *Living on Velvet* (1935); *Stranded* (1935); *The Goose and the Gander* (1935); *Give Me Your Heart* (1936); and *Secrets of an Actress* (1938).

Br'er Rabbit
Conniving rabbit featured in Joel Chandler Harris's *Tales of Uncle Remus.* Johnny Lee provided the voice of Br'er Rabbit in the 1946 Disney film *Song of the South.* There is a large statue of Br'er Rabbit in Eatonton, Georgia, in front of the courthouse.

Bresnahan, Roger
(1879–1944) New York Giant catcher who in 1908 was the first player to wear shinguards in a baseball game.

Bret Harte High

Alma mater in the TV series *What Really Happened to the Class of '65?*

Brewster

New York hometown of Ann Marie (Marlo Thomas) in the TV series *That Girl.*

Brice, Fanny

(1892–1951) Popular radio comedienne in the 1930s, she also appeared in a number of Ziegfeld Follies. Her most popular radio role was as "Baby Snooks." Movie portrayals: *Rose of Washington Square* (1939) Alice Faye (as Rose Sargent); *Funny Girl* (1968) Barbra Streisand; *Funny Lady* (1975) Barbra Streisand; and *Ziegfeld: The Man and His Women* (1978 TV) Catherine Jacoby.

Brick Bradford

Comic strip hero created by William Ritt and Clarence Giray who debuted in newspapers on August 21, 1933. The character was played by Kane Richmond in the 1947 movie serial *Brick Bradford.*

Bridegrooms

Original (1890) name of the Brooklyn Dodgers baseball team.

Bridger, Jim

(1804–1881) American frontiersman and explorer who was the first white man known to have visited the Great Salt Lake. Movie portrayals: *Kit Carson* (1940) Raymond Hutton; *Tomahawk* (1951) Van Heflin; *Bridger* (1976 TV) James Wainwright; and *The Incredible Rocky Mountain Race* (1977 TV) Jack Kruschen.

Bridger's Wells

Town where the posse is formed in Walter Van Tilburg Clark's novel *The Ox-Bow Incident,* which was made into a movie in 1943.

Bridget

Lucas Tanner's (David Hartman) pet dog in the TV series *Lucas Tanner.* The dog was originally called O'Casey.

Bright Eyes

Name that Dr. Zira (Kim Hunter) gave to the mute George Taylor (Charlton Heston) in the 1968 movie *Planet of the Apes.*

Bringing Up Father

Comic strip created in 1913 by George McManus. When it was discovered in 1948 that the strip was using a code (devised by F.M. Goldsmith Financial Service for its clients) to alert stock market investors to buy or sell certain stocks, it was referred to as "The Wall Street Comic Strip."

Britches

Female member of the Beetles Motorcycle Club, played by Yvonne Doughty in the 1954 movie *The Wild One.*

British Overseas Airways Flight 77
Passenger aircraft that was shot down by a German fighter on June 1, 1943, killing all on board, including actor Leslie Howard. (See: **Chenhalls, Alfred**) The pilot's last recorded words were: "Enemy planes attacking us."

Broadway
Name of the main cell block corridor at Alcatraz prison. The other two corridors were named Michigan Boulevard and Seedy Street.

Broaker, Frank
First person to become a certified public accountant in New York City on December 1, 1896. He was issued Certificate No. 1.

Brodie, Jean
Edinburgh teacher at the Marcia Blaine School for Girls, in the 1962 novel *The Prime of Miss Jean Brodie* by Muriel Spark. She was portrayed in the 1969 movie of the same name by Maggie Smith, who won an Oscar for best actress. Geraldine McEvan played the role in the 1979 Scottish TV miniseries *Prime of Miss Jean Brodie* (the music was composed by Marvin Hamlisch and the show was hosted by Julie Harris).

Broken Heart Saloon
Bar where the action is set in the 1967 movie *El Dorado*.

Broken Wheel Ranch
Ranch outside of Capitol City owned by Jim Newton (Peter Graves) in the TV series *Fury*. Pete (William Fawcett) was the foreman.

Broker's Tip
Horse that won the 1933 Kentucky Derby, ridden by Don Meade. This was the only race that Broker's Tip ever won.

Bromfield, Louis
Pulitzer Prize–winning novelist in whose Mansfield, Ohio, home Humphrey Bogart married Lauren Bacall on May 21, 1945. Bromfield later became the godfather of their son, Steven.

Bromley Technical
The high school in Beckingham, Kent, England, that future rock stars Peter Frampton and David Bowie attended at the same time. Pete's father, Owen Frampton, an art teacher at the school, had Bowie as one of his students. Frampton and Bowie played in rival school bands—David Bowie with George and the Dragons and Peter Frampton with the Little Ravens.

Bronze Peacock
Chicago nightclub in which Caesar Enrico Bandello (Edward G. Robinson) killed Crime Commissioner McClure in the 1930 movie *Little Caesar*.

Brooke, Edward W.
Black former senator (from Massachusetts) elected on November 8, 1966. He was portrayed (as attorney general) by William Marshall in the 1968 movie *The Boston Strangler*.

Brooklyn Heights High School
School attended by both Patty Lane and her cousin Cathy Lane in the TV series *The Patty Duke Show.*

Brooklyn Patriots of Los Angeles
Fraternal organization of which Chester A. Riley (William Bendix) was a member in the TV series *The Life of Riley.*

Brooks, Mel, Neil Simon, and Woody Allen
Former writers for the TV series *Your Show of Shows* starring Sid Caesar. All three have won Academy Awards.

Brother Dominick
5-foot-4 inch 210-pound cherubic monk who makes 500 copies of an assignment by using a Xerox copier in TV commercials. He is played by Jack Eagle (who also played Mr. Cholesterol).

Brother Mathias
6-foot-6 inch Xaverian brother at St. Mary's Industrial School who helped to develop George Herman Ruth into one of the greatest baseball players of all time. Brother Mathias was portrayed in the 1948 movie *The Babe Ruth Story* by Charles Bickford.

Brothers, Dr. Joyce
Only person to win the top prize on both *The $64,000 Question* and *The $64,000 Challenge.* Her subject was boxing.

Brown Bomber
Nickname of heavyweight boxing champion Joe Louis.

Brown Eyes
Cow featured in the 1925 Buster Keaton movie *Go West.*

Brown, Grace
Young woman drowned by Chester Gillette at Big Moose Lake in the Adirondacks in 1906. This murder inspired Theodore Dreiser's 1925 novel *An American Tragedy,* which was made into a play and twice into a movie; in 1931 as *An American Tragedy* and in 1951 as *A Place in the Sun.*

Brown, Helen Gurley
Publisher of *Cosmopolitan* magazine, who is loosely portrayed in the 1964 movie *Sex and the Single Girl* by Natalie Wood. The movie's title was taken from Brown's 1962 book.

Brown, John
(1800–1859) American abolitionist who massacred five slavery adherents on May 24, 1856. He was captured at Harper's Ferry, Virginia, on December 2, 1859, convicted of treason, and hanged. One of the witnesses of his hanging was John Wilkes Booth. Brown was portrayed by Raymond Massey in two movies: *Santa Fe Trail* (1940) and *Seven Angry Men* (1955).

Brown, Lew
(1893–1958) Composer member of the songwriting team of Henderson-De-

Sylva-Brown. He collaborated on such songs as "If You Were the Only Girl" and "Don't Sit Under the Apple Tree." Brown was portrayed in the 1956 movie *The Best Things in Life Are Free* by Ernest Borgnine.

Brown, Louise Joy
World's first test-tube baby (conceived outside her mother's body). She was delivered by cesarean section on July 26, 1978, at 11:47 p.m. at Oldham District General Hospital in London by Drs. Patrick Steptoe and Robert Edwards; she weighed 5 pounds, 2 ounces. Her parents, Lesley and John Brown, were portrayed in the 1980 TV movie *The Miracle Named Louise* by Lynn Redgrave and Ian McShane.

Brown, Myra Gale
Rock musician Jerry Lee Lewis's third cousin, whom he married in 1958 when she was 13 years old, two weeks before his final divorce from his first wife, whom he married when he was 14 years old. The marriage became a scandal in Britain, where Lewis was on tour. It was many years before he was able to make a comeback in rock music.

Brown, Thomas
Onetime governor of Florida who invented the mailbox in 1810.

Brown Wolf
Author Jack London's favorite dog.

Browning, Elizabeth Barrett
(1806–1861) English poet and wife of poet Robert Browning. She was portrayed in the 1934 movie *The Barretts of Wimpole Street* by Norma Shearer.

Browning, Robert
(1812–1889) English poet buried in Westminster Abbey. He was portrayed in the 1934 movie *The Barretts of Wimpole Street* by Fredric March.

Bruce
Honey West's (Anne Francis) pet ocelot in the TV series *Honey West*.

Bruce, Lenny
(1926–1966) Off-color comedian, born Alfred Schweider, who attacked American culture. He died in 1966 after an overdose of narcotics. Bruce was the subject of two documentaries: *Lenny Bruce* (1967) and *Lenny Bruce Without Tears* (1975). Movie portrayals: *Dirty Mouth* (1970) Bernie Travis; and *Lenny* (1974) Dustin Hoffman.

Brummell, Beau
(1778–1840) George Bryan Brummell, English dandy and gambler who died in an insane asylum in France. He was portrayed in the 1954 movie *Beau Brummell* by Stewart Granger.

Brusco, Teresa
Only passenger in the Tenerife, Canary Island, crash of two jumbo Boeing

747's to walk away unscathed. Although others on the Pan Am plane survived, only she was unhurt.

Brutus, Marcus Junius
(85–42 B.C.) Roman politician who headed a conspiracy to assassinate Julius Caesar in 44 B.C. He committed suicide in 42 B.C. Movie portrayals: *Julius Caesar* (1952) David Bradley; *Julius Caesar* (1953) James Mason; and *Julius Caesar* (1970) Jason Robards, Jr.

Bryan, Rebecca
Wife of frontiersman Daniel Boone. TV portrayals: *Walt Disney Presents* ("Daniel Boone") Mala Powers; *Daniel Boone* Patricia Blair; and *Young Dan'l Boone* Devon Ericson.

Bryan, William Jennings
(1860–1925) American lawyer and politician called the Commoner. He was one of the prosecuting attorneys at the famous Scopes Monkey Trial of 1925. He died a few days after the trial ended (July 26, 1925). Movie portrayals: *Wilson* (1944) Edwin Maxwell; and *Inherit the Wind* (1960) Fredric March (as Matthew Harrison Brady).

Buamo
South Pacific island where the survivors of a plane crash were marooned in the TV series *The New People*.

Bubbles in the Wine
Lawrence Welk's theme song.

Buccaneer, The
1938 Cecil B. DeMille movie that debuted at Grauman's Chinese Theatre in the 1975 movie *The Day of the Locust*.

Buck
Matt Dillon's (James Arness) horse in the TV series *Gunsmoke*, played by Marshal.

Buckley's Department Store
New York store where Diana Smythe (Diana Rigg) worked as a fashion illustrator in the TV series *Diana*.

Bucko O'Brien
Detective Brick Bradford's sidekick in the comic strip *Brick Bradford*.

Buck White
Broadway play that starred Muhammad Ali.

Bud
First tropical storm to be named after a male (June 19, 1978).

Buendorf, Larry
Secret Service agent who grabbed the arm of Lynette Alice ("Squeaky") Fromme as she aimed a .45-caliber pistol at President Ford in 1975.

Buffalo Jills
Cheerleaders for the Buffalo Bills football team.

Bugatti
Red automobile in which dancer Isadora Duncan met her death on September 14, 1927, when the long scarf she was wearing got caught in the car's wheel spoke.

Bügerbrau Keller
Munich beer house where on November 19, 1923, Adolf Hitler declared himself chancellor of all Germany.

Bug-Jitter
Two-part password used by the soldiers of the 101st Airborne in the 1949 movie *Battleground*.

Bullseye
Jimmy Dugan's pet dog in the comic strip *Reg'lar Fellers*.

Bunker Hill High
School attended by James Hunter (Lance Kerwin) in the TV series *James at 15*.

Bunny
Ann-Margret's code name when she telephoned Elvis Presley at Graceland.

Bunny and Little Buttercup
Alice and Ralph Kramden's pet names for each other (respectively) when they were first married in the TV series *The Honeymooners*.

Burgess Meredith Award
Annual award (as of 1976) conferred on the year's worst supporting actor by the *Harvard Lampoon*.

Burke, Billie
(1885–1970) American actress (born Mary William Ethelbert Appleton Burk) who was once married to Florenz Ziegfeld. In the 1939 movie *The Wizard of Oz* Billie Burke played Glinda, the Good Witch of the West. Movie portrayals: *The Great Ziegfeld* (1936) Myrna Loy; and *Ziegfeld: The Man and His Women* (1978 TV) Samantha Eggar.

Burnett, Carol
Her comedy characters: Carol Bradford, Eunice Higgins, Nora Desmond (spoof of Gloria Swanson in the movie *Sunset Boulevard*), Zelda the Nudge, Mrs. Wiggins, "Mundane" of Funt and Mundane (with Harvey Korman).

Burnside, Ambrose
(1824–1881) Civil War general and later governor of Rhode Island. His name was lent to the style of facial hair called sideburns. He served as first president of the National Rifle Association.

Burns, Tommy
(1881–1955) (Noah Brusso). Canadian-born boxer who won the world heavyweight crown on February 23, 1906. On March 28, 1906, in San Diego, Burns defended his title twice in the same night when he knocked out Jim O'Brien and Jim Walker, both in the 1st round.

Burnt Cork

Substance worn by singer Al Jolson to blacken his face in vaudeville.

Burr, Aaron

(1756–1836) American Revolutionary officer and U.S. senator who mortally wounded Alexander Hamilton in a duel on July 11, 1804. Burr was vice president of the United States at the time. In 1807 he was arrested, tried, and acquitted of treason. Burr was portrayed in the 1946 movie *The Magnificent Doll* by David Niven.

Burtis, Marilyn

Lovely assistant who provided the Secret Word on a swing when the duck didn't appear on the TV quiz show *You Bet Your Life*.

Burton, Charlie

American inventor of the baby carriage (1848).

Busey, Gary

Actor who played the last person (Harve Daley) to die in the TV series *Gunsmoke*. He died of a brain tumor on the last network telecast episode of the series (September 1, 1975).

Buster

Andy and Florrie Capp's son in the comic strip *Buster*. His debut was May 28, 1960.

Busybody

Byline used by Walter Winchell when he wrote his first column for *Billboard* in 1919.

Butch

Scott Carey's (Grant Williams) pet cat that tried to kill him in the 1957 movie *The Incredible Shrinking Man*.

Butch

Bulldog in Tom and Jerry cartoons.

Butch

Fred and Ethel Mertz's pet dog in the first season (1951) of the TV series *I Love Lucy*.

Butkus

Rocky Balboa's (Sylvester Stallone) pet bull-mastiff dog in the 1976 movie *Rocky*. The dog actually belonged to Stallone.

Butter

On the TV Parkay Margarine commercials Michael Bell's is the voice that says "butter" and "Parkay."

Buttermilk

Horse ridden by Joe Riley (William Smith) in the TV series *Laredo*.

Buttons

Virgil Smith's (Bing Crosby) pet dog in the 1948 movie *The Emperor Waltz*. Buttons resembles Nipper, the RCA Victor dog.

Buttons, Red
Canadian-born (1919) comedian whose real name is Aaron Chwatt. His TV characters on his 1952–1955 *Comedy Variety* series were: Keegelfarver, a German U-boat sailor; Buttons the bellboy; Rocky, a punchy prizefighter; Kupke Kid, a smart-alecky little boy; and Muggsy, the juvenile delinquent. In 1966 he also starred in the TV series *The Double Life of Henry Phyfe*.

Bye-Bye Baby
Phrase used by baseball announcer Russ Hodges to describe a home run for Giants fans.

Bye Bye Blackbird
Song performed in the following films: *Rainbow 'Round My Shoulder* (1952), sung by Frankie Laine; *River of No Return* (1954), sung by Marilyn Monroe; and *The Eddie Cantor Story* (1954), sung by Eddie Cantor. Song lyrics by Mort Dixon, music by Ray Henderson. It was also in the 1975 movie *The Black Bird*.

By Love Possessed
1961 movie starring Lana Turner and Efrem Zimbalist, Jr., that was the first regular-in-flight movie ever shown. It was introduced on TWA's New York–to–Los Angeles route on July 19, 1961.

By Popular Demand
Variety TV show hosted by Robert Alda (father of actor Alan Alda) in 1950. Alda was replaced by Arlene Francis and then went on to host the short-lived TV quiz show *Can Do*.

Byrn, M. L.
American inventor of the corkscrew in 1860.

Byron Lord
(1788–1824) George Gordon Byron, English poet. Movie portrayals: *The Bad Lord Byron* (1948) Dennis Price; *Beau Brummell* (1954) Noel William; *Lady Caroline Lamb* (1972) Richard Chamberlain; and *Frankenstein: The True Story* (1973 TV) David McCallum.

By the River/That's Easy
45 rpm record made in 1960 by Wilt "the Stilt" Chamberlain (END Records).

By the Light of the Silvery Moon
Song performed in the following movies: *Ruggles of Red Gap* (1935); *The Birth of the Blues* (1941); *Sunbonnet Sue* (1945); *The Jolson Story* (1946); and *Always Leave Them Laughing* (1949). Song lyrics by Edward Madden, music by Gus Edwards.

Byzantium
Fuel element used to create a sonic barrier above portions of the United States to protect against a nuclear attack in Clive Cussler's novel *Raise the Titanic* as well as in the 1980 film version.

C

First school letter ever given for collegiate sports. It was issued at the University of Chicago in 1906, the same year Amos Alonzo Stagg organized the first Letterman's Club.

C-3PO

Metallic robot, played by Anthony Daniels in the 1977 movie *Star Wars*.

C854

Ivan's (Tom Courtenay) prisoner number in a Siberian camp in the 1971 movie *One Day in the Life of Ivan Denisovich* (based on the novel by Alexander Solzhenitsyn).

C.A.P.E.R.

Acronym for Civilian Authority for the Protection of Everybody Regardless in the TV series *The Kids from C.A.P.E.R.*

CF-HGO

Canadian call letters of Brian MacLean's (James Cagney) single-engine civilian seaplane in the 1942 movie *Captains of the Clouds*.

C. W. McCall

Truck driver character for Old Home Bread (of Sioux City, Iowa) commercials whose voice is provided by William Fries. Fries, an advertising executive from Omaha, Nebraska, legally changed his name to C. W. McCall. He only voiced the commercials, in a sing-song voice against a musical background. An actor, who never spoke, played C. W. McCall. C. W. McCall's girlfriend was Mavis. William Fries became nationally known via the 1976 hit record "Convoy" and the 1978 movie *Convoy*.

Cabaliers

Cab Calloway's band.

Cactus
Horse ridden by Reese Bennett (Neville Brand) in the TV series *Laredo*.

Cadillac
Consolation prize for contestants who missed the top prize on the TV quiz show *The $64,000 Challenge*. On September 13, 1953, Marilyn Monroe made her TV debut on the *Jack Benny Show*, for which she received a white Cadillac convertible in lieu of a salary.

Caesar
Beauregard Bottomley's (Ronald Colman) pet parrot, whose voice was provided by Mel Blanc, in the 1950 movie *Champagne for Caesar*.

Caesar
Cedric Wehunt's (Chester Lauck) pet hound dog in the radio series *Lum and Abner*.

Caesar, Julius
(100–44 B.C.) Roman general and ruler who was assassinated on March 15. Movie portrayals: *Cleopatra* (1917) Fritz Leiber; *Cleopatra* (1934) Warren Williams; *Caesar and Cleopatra* (1945) Claude Rains; *Julius Caesar* (1952) Harold Tasker; *Julius Caesar* (1953) Louis Calhern; *Spartacus* (1960) John Gavin; *Cleopatra* (1963) Rex Harrison; *Caesar the Conqueror* (1963) Cameron Mitchell; and *Julius Caesar* (1970) John Gielgud.

Café Albert
Berlin pub where Lillian Hellman (Jane Fonda) met Julia (Vanessa Redgrave) in the 1977 movie *Julia*.

Caffrey, James
Contestant from Wakefeld, Rhode Island, who won $24,000 on the radio quiz show *Sing It Again* by guessing correctly the voice of Louis B. Mayer. The $24,000 prize was merchandise, not cash; Caffrey eventually went into debt. James Stewart portrayed Caffrey (as Bill Lawrence) in the 1950 movie *The Jackpot*, in which Lawrence wins $24,000 worth of merchandise on the radio quiz show *Name the Mystery Husband*.

Cain and Abel
Sons of Adam and Eve. They were portrayed in the 1966 movie *The Bible* by Richard Harris and Franco Nero, respectively.

Calcutta
Lawrence Welk's only number-one hit record (1961)—on Dot Records (Dot 16161).

Calhoun, John C.
(1782–1850) American lawyer and statesman who was, successively, a U.S. Representative, secretary of war, vice president, senator, and secretary of state. Calhoun was portrayed in the 1936 movie *The Gorgeous Hussy* by Frank Conroy.

California, Here I Come
Song performed in the following motion pictures: *Lucky Boy* (1929); *Rose of Washington Square* (1939); *The Jolson Story* (1946); and *With a Song in My Heart* (1952). Song lyrics by Al Jolson and Buddy DeSylva, music by Joseph Meyer.

Caligula
(A.D. 12–41) Roman emperor from A.D. 37 to 41 who was assassinated. Movie portrayals: *The Robe* (1953) Jay Robinson; *Demetrius and the Gladiators* (1954) Jay Robinson; *I, Claudius* (1977 PBS-TV) John Hurt; and *Caligula* (1980) Malcolm McDowell.

Callahan, J. T.
On January 23, 1946, he became the first U.S. Navy chaplain to be awarded the Medal of Honor.

Call Me Irresponsible
Song introduced by Jackie Gleason in the 1963 movie *Papa's Delicate Condition*.

Calverley, Ernie
5 foot 10 inch Rhode Island State basketball player who threw a two-handed shot that traveled an estimated 65 feet into the basket in the opening game of the National Invitation Tournament at Madison Square Garden on March 14, 1946. It was a desperation throw with only 2 seconds left to play. The point tied the game with Bowling Green, which won 82–79 in overtime.

Calvin and the Colonel
1961 TV cartoon series featuring the voices of Charles Correll (Calvin) and Freeman Gosden (the Colonel).

Calypso
1956 RCA Victor record album by Harry Belafonte. It was the first LP by a solo artist to sell a million copies.

Calypso II
Philippe Cousteau's PBY-6A amphibian aircraft.

Camels
Detective Philip Marlowe's favorite brand of cigarettes.

Camerons and Stonemans
Two families whose histories are traced in the 1915 silent movie *The Birth of a Nation*.

Campanella, Roy
Brooklyn Dodger catcher (1948–1957) who won the National League MVP three times.* After a January 1958 automobile accident, he became a paraplegic. The first persons "visited" by Edward R. (Roscoe) Murrow on

---

*The only other National League player to win the MVP award three times was Stan Musial.

his TV series *Person to Person* on October 2, 1953, were Roy Campanella, and then Leopold Stokowski and his wife, Gloria Vanderbilt. Campanella was portrayed in the 1975 movie *It's Good to Be Alive* by Paul Winfield.

Campaneris, Bert, and Cesar Tovar

Two major league players who played all nine positions in a single baseball game: Campaneris on September 8, 1965, for the Kansas City Athletics; and Tovar on September 22, 1968, for the Minnesota Twins.

Campbell, Frankie

Young Italian fighter who died after a fight with Max Baer on August 25, 1930.

Camp Crowder

Joplin, Missouri, army post where Rob Petrie (Dick Van Dyke) met his future wife, Laura Meeker* (Mary Tyler Moore), in the TV series *The Dick Van Dyke Show*.

Camp Divine

Outdoor camp for females only in the TV series *Camp Runamuck*.

Camp Greeley

U.S. Army training facility in the 1941 Abbott and Costello movie *Buck Privates*.

Camp Pendleton

California Marine base where Lt. William Rice (Gary Lockwood) was stationed in the TV series *The Lieutenant*.

Canada's Man of the Year (1965)

Title held by Ottawa-born actor Lorne Greene.

Candlestick Park

Baseball and football stadium of the San Francisco Giants and 49er's. On August 29, 1966, it was the site of the last Beatles concert. (In 1961 Candlestick was the home of the Oakland Raiders.)

Can Do

Jinx B17 flown by Col. Greg Brandon (Christopher George) in a daylight raid on a German aircraft factory in the 1969 movie *The 1,000 Plane Raid*.

Candy

Actual name of the horse ridden by Hugh O'Brian in the TV series *The Life and Legend of Wyatt Earp*.

Canoga Falls

Setting of the soap opera takeoff "As the Stomach Turns" in the TV series *The Carol Burnett Show*.

Canonsburg, Pennsylvania

Hometown of singers Perry Como (born 1912) and Bobby Vinton (born 1941). They both grew up on Smith Street.

---

*Richard Meeker was the name of Mary Tyler Moore's first husband. After their divorce the name Meehan was used as her maiden name in the TV series.

Can't Help Lovin' Dat Man
Song sung in the following motion pictures: *Show Boat* (1932) Irene Dunn; *Show Boat* (1951) Ava Gardner; *Till the Clouds Roll By* (1946) Lena Horne; and *The Helen Morgan Story* (1957) Gogi Grant. Song lyrics by Oscar Hammerstein II, music by Jerome Kern.

Capelletti, John
Heisman Trophy winner who had a very close relationship with his younger brother, Joey, who contracted leukemia. John was portrayed in the 1977 TV movie *Something for Joey* by Marc Singer, Joey by Jeff Lynas.

Caper
Word that appeared in the title of every episode of the TV series *77 Sunset Strip*.

Capital Service in the Nation's Capital
Slogan for Stanley Beamish's (aka Mr. Terrific) (Stephen Strimpell) and Hal's (Dick Gautier) Washington garage in the TV series *Mr. Terrific*.

Capitol Cab Co.
Taxi driven by God (George Burns) in the 1977 movie *Oh God!*

Capitol General Hospital
Washington, D.C., hospital headed by Dr. Vincent Campanelli (James Whitmore) in the TV series *Temperatures Rising*.

Caprica
Home planet destroyed by the Cylons, causing the *Galactica* crew to voyage to Earth, in the TV series *Battlestar Galactica*.

Capri Lounge
Fernwood night spot at the Rosemont Bowling Alley where Loretta Billy Jean Susan Antoinette Bowers Parmenter Haggers (Mary Kay Place) sings in the TV series *Mary Hartman, Mary Hartman*. Her biggest hit record was "Baby Boy."

Captain
Role played by Ernie Kovacs in four of his ten movies: *Operation Madball* (1957) Capt. Lock; *Our Man in Havana* (1959) Capt. Segurra; *Wake Me When It's Over* (1960) Capt. Stark; and *Sail a Crooked Ship* (1962) the Captain.

Capt. Amos Burke
Millionaire Los Angeles chief of detectives played on the TV series *Burke's Law* by Gene Barry. Burke graduated from Amherst in 1948. He inherited his fortune from his father, Francis Xavier Burke, who was in the construction business. In an episode on *The Dick Powell Theater* titled "Who Killed Julie Greer?" Dick Powell was the first to play Amos Burke.

Capt. Apollo
Leader of the *Galactica's* fighter squadron and a son of Cmdr. Adama (Lorne

Greene) in the TV series *Battlestar Galactica*. He was played by Richard Hatch.

Capt. Barney Miller
Police captain (played by Hal Linden) at New York City's 12th Precinct in the TV series *Barney Miller* (the pilot was called *The Life and Times of Barney Miller*). His wife, Elizabeth, was played by Barbara Barrie (Abby Dalton in the pilot).

Capt. Bart Friday
San Francisco detective featured in the 1944 radio series *Adventures by Morse* (Carlton E. Morse). Friday was played by Elliot Lewis, David Ellis, and Russell Thorson.

Capt. Benjamin Franklin "Hawkeye" Pierce
Surgeon assigned to the 4077th MASH unit. He was played in the 1970 Robert Altman movie *M*A*S*H* (based on the novel of the same name by Richard Hooker) by Donald Sutherland. In the TV series *M*A*S*H* Alan Alda plays Hawkeye. His hometown is Crabapple Cove, Maine. (In the early episodes Hawkeye stated that he was from Vermont.)

Capt. B. J. Hunnicutt
Surgeon (played by Mike Farrell) who came to the 4077th MASH unit after Capt. John McIntyre left in the TV series *M*A*S*H*. His wife's name is Peggy and his hometown is in Mill Valley, California. His initials were derived from Bea (his mother) and Jay (his father).

Capt. "Cannonball" Bill McCormick
First commanding officer of Fort Courage, played by Willard Waterman, in the TV series *F Troop*.

Capt. Carpenter
Inspector Philip Gerard's supervisor, played by Paul Birch in the TV series *The Fugitive*.

Capt. Chase Reddick
Los Angeles police officer (played by Mitchell Ryan) in charge of a four-man crime fighting team in the TV series *Chase*.

Capt. Gideon Patch
Captain of the ship *Mary Deare*, played by Gary Cooper in the 1959 movie *Wreck of the Mary Deare* (based on the 1956 novel of the same name by Hammond Innes).

Capt. Huxley
Commander of the ocean liner SS *Ocean Queen*, played by Roy Roberts in the TV series *The Gale Storm Show*.

Capt. Jack
Pet alligator of Wally and Beaver Cleaver, named for Capt. Jack (Edgar Buchanan), head of an alligator farm, in the TV series *Leave It to Beaver*.

After the boys gave the alligator away, their parents bought them a pet puppy, which they also named Capt. Jack.

Capt. John F. Xavier McIntyre
Surgeon, nicknamed Trapper John, assigned to the 4077th MASH unit, played in the TV series *M*A*S*H* by Wayne Rogers and in the TV series *Trapper John* by Pernell Roberts as a civilian doctor in contemporary times. Trapper John was played in the 1970 Robert Altman movie *M*A*S*H* (based on the Richard Hooker novel of the same name) by Elliot Gould.

Capt. Judas
Nemesis of Terry Lee in the comic strip *Terry and the Pirates*.

Capt. Patrick Chambers
New York City policeman who is the head of Homicide Division and a friend of private eye Mike Hammer (novels).

Capt. Theocradus Kojakzakilas
Subject of painting hanging on the wall behind Lt. Theo Kojak's (Telly Savalas) desk in the TV series *Kojak*. It's Theo's grandfather.

Capt. Triumph
Secret identity of twin brothers Lance and Michael Gallant. (Michael is dead but still assists his twin.) Debut: *Crack Comics* No. 27. Capt. Triumph was created by Alfred Andriola.

Capt. Windy Scuttlebutt
Old sea captain (marionette) in the TV series *Howdy Doody Time*.

Captured
Title of reruns of the TV series *Gangbusters*.

Cardinal's Mistress, The
Novel written by Benito Mussolini in 1909. It was the only novel the Italian dictator wrote.

Cardway Corporation
California company of which Don Walling (Mitchell Ryan) is president in the TV series *Executive Suite*.

Carefree
Small-town Arizona setting of the TV series *The New Dick Van Dyke Show*. In September 1973 the setting was changed to Tarzana, California.

Carey Walsh's Saloon
Coney Island establishment where Eddie Cantor was employed as a singing waiter and Jimmy Durante as a piano player (circa 1910).

Cargo
Allied code name for President Franklin D. Roosevelt during World War II.

Caribou Ranch
Ranch and recording studio near Boulder, Colorado, of the rock band

Chicago.* The ranch is owned by the group's producer, James William Guerico, and had previously been where the first Arabian horses in America were kept.

Carlson

Manufacturer of the customized superboat used by James Bond (Roger Moore) in the 1979 movie *Moonraker*.

Carlton

Old white bulldog in 1946 movie *The Spiral Staircase*.

Carnac the Magnificent

Swami-type character played in comedy routines on the *Tonight Show* by Johnny Carson, who visions the answers to questions before seeing the questions. Carnac keeps his answers hermetically sealed in envelopes in a mayonnaise jar on the porch of Funk and Wagnall's.

Carnegie Hall

New York City concert hall, former home of the New York Philharmonic. It was built in 1890. Actor Larry Parks was once an usher there.

Carnival

Opera being presented in the 1936 movie *Charlie Chan at the Opera*. Composed by Oscar Levant, it is the only opera ever written expressly for a movie.

Carnival Paints

Brand of paint can that Tony (John Travolta) is carrying in the opening scene of the 1977 movie *Saturday Night Fever*.

Carol Ferris

Girlfriend of comic book superhero the Green Lantern.

Carolina in the Morning

Popular song composed in 1922. It was used by Knute Rockne (Pat O'Brien) to teach his Four Horsemen smooth steps for his famous football shift in the 1940 movie *Knute Rockne—All American*. Song lyrics by Gus Kahn, music by Walter Donaldson.

Caroline

Name of the cow in the first Mickey Mouse cartoon (*Plane Crazy*, 1928).

Carol McKee

Wife of Wash Tubbs in the comic strip *Wash Tubbs*. Their twins sons are Thomas and Jefferson.

Carol's Theme

Theme song of the TV series *The Carol Burnett Show*, composed by Joe Hamilton, the show's producer and Carol's husband.

---

*The band originally called itself the Chicago Transit Authority until it was sued by that city's transit company.

Carolwood–Pacific Railroad
Walt Disney's ⅛th model railroad named for the street—Carolwood Drive—on which the Disneys lived in Holmby Hills. The engine was No. 173. (See: **Lilly Belle**)

Carousel
Name of the ceremony whereby everyone who reaches age 30 is put to death in the city of Domes in the novel/1976 movie TV series *Logan's Run.*

Carr, Charles
Country singer Hank Williams's chauffeur. Carr found the singer dead in the back seat of his Cadillac on January 1, 1953.

Carr, Joe "Fingers"
Pianist (born Louis F. Busch) who has been married to both Janet Blair and Margaret Whiting.

Carry Me Back to Old Virginny
Official song* of the state of Virginia, adopted in 1940. (Words and music by James A. Bland.)

Carson, Kit
(1809–1868). Christopher Carson, American scout, trapper, and Indian agent. Movie portrayals: *The Covered Wagon* (1923) Guy Oliver; *Kit Carson Over the Great Divide* (1925) Jack Mower; *Kit Carson* (1928) Fred Thomson; *Fighting With Kit Carson* (1933) Johnny Mack Brown; *The Painted Stallion* (1937) Sammy McKim; *Overland With Kit Carson* (1939) "Wild" Bill Elliott; *Kit Carson* (1940) Jon Hall; and *Bridger* (1976 TV) Ben Murphy. Bill William portrayed Carson in the 1951 TV series *The Adventures of Kit Carson.*

Carter, Billy
Brother of former President Jimmy Carter. He made his film debut in the 1979 TV movie *Flatbed Annie and Sweetiepie: Lady Truckers.*

Carter, Garnet
American inventor of miniature golf·in 1927 (originally called Tom Thumb Golf).

Carter, Herbert
Member of Capt. Ernest Medina's Charlie Company who testified against Medina at his trial for the murder of civilians in the My Lai 4 incident during the Vietnam War. Carter later became manager of the rock group Sly and the Family Stone.

Carter, Howard
British Egyptologist who in November 1922 discovered the tomb of King Tutankhamun (King Tut). Carter was portrayed in the 1980 TV fiction movie *The Curse of King Tut's Tomb* by Robin Ellis.

---

*"Carry Me Back to Old Virginny" (on the Victor Red Seal label) sung by Alma Gluck in 1915 was the first single recording to sell over a million copies.

Carter, James Earl

39th president of the United States who previously served as governor of Georgia. He is the only president to have reported a UFO sighting (October 1969) and the first to have been born in a hospital.

Carter, June

Daughter of Maybelle Carter, the Mother of Country Music and wife of two country singers, Carl Smith and Johnny Cash. June Carter's great-great-great-grandfather was Henry Addington Sidmouth, prime minister of England (1801–1804).

Cartland, Maj. Ronald

First member of the British Parliament to be killed in World War II. He was the brother of Barbara Cartland, author of popular historical romances.

Caruso, Enrico

Opera (1873–1921) tenor born in Naples, who was the first singer to sell a million records (consisting of various recordings of "Vesti La Giubba," not a single record). Caruso was in San Francisco to sing *Carmen,* staying at the Palace Hotel, on April 18, 1906, the day of the famous earthquake, and he swore he would never return to the city ("San Francisco will never hear my voice again"). He never did. MGM publicity claimed that Mario Lanza was born in 1921, the same year Caruso died, in order to promote the belief that Lanza was Caruso reincarnated. Lanza, who actually was born in 1922, portrayed Caruso in the 1951 movie *The Great Caruso* (Peter Edward Price played the opera singer as a boy).

Carver High School

School setting of the TV series *White Shadow.* An "o" in the word "school" is missing on the name over the front door. Filmed at Notre Dame High School in Los Angeles.

Casanova

(1725–1798) "The World's Greatest Lover," whose full name was Giovanni Jacopo Casanova de Seingalt. Movie portrayals: *Adventures of Casanova* (1947) Turhan Bey; *Casanova's Big Night* (1954) Bob Hope; and *Fellini's Casanova* (1976) Donald Sutherland.

Casey at the Bat

Poem Lauren Bacall read for her TV debut on *The Ed Sullivan Show* in 1954.

Casey, Dan

Phillies baseball player who is believed to have inspired Ernest L. Thayer's poem "Casey at the Bat" when he struck out in the 9th inning in a game played on August 21, 1887. The poem first appeared in the *San Francisco Examiner* on June 3, 1888.

Cassady, Neal

Close friend of Beatnik writer Jack Kerouac. In June 1958 MGM announced that Marlon Brando would portray the Neal Cassady character in the proposed movie *On the Road,* but the film never materialized. (See: **Dean Moriarty**)

Cassius Longinus
Roman general who helped to plot the assassination of Julius Caesar in 42 B.C. He was later killed by his own officers. Movie portrayals: *Julius Caesar* (1953) John Gielgud*; and *Julius Caesar* (1970) Richard Johnson.

Cass Ole
Arabian horse featured in the 1979 movie *The Black Stallion*

Castle, Irene and Vernon
Pseudonym of the dancing team of Irene Foote and Vernon Blythe. They were portrayed in the 1939 movie *The Story of Vernon and Irene Castle* by Fred Astaire and Ginger Rogers. Irene Castle's autobiography is titled *Castles in the Air.*

Castro, Fidel
Communist leader of Cuba. When interviewed by Edward R. Murrow on the TV series *Person to Person* in February 1959, Castro was in his pajamas. In his youth he appeared in several Xavier Cugat movies, such as *Holiday in Mexico* (1946). He was portrayed in the 1969 movie *Che!* by Jack Palance.

Cat
Holly Golightly's (Audrey Hepburn) pet cat in the 1961 movie *Breakfast at Tiffany's,* played by Orangey.

Catch-18
Original title of Joseph's Heller's 1961 novel *Catch-22.*

Caterpillar Club
Collective name of that group of individuals whose lives have been saved by parachuting from a crippled aircraft. On October 20, 1922, Lt. Harold Harris became the first person to parachute out of an uncontrolled airplane.

Cathcart, Dick
Musician who ghosted the cornet playing for Jack Webb in the 1955 movie *Pete Kelly's Blues.*

Catherine the Great
(1729–1796) Catherine II, empress of Russia. Movie portrayals: *The Eagle* (1925) Louise Dresser; *The Scarlet Empress* (1934) Marlene Dietrich; *Catherine the Great* (1934) Elisabeth Bergner; *John Paul Jones* (1959) Bette Davis; and *Great Catherine* (1968) Jeanne Moreau.

Cattle Call
Theme song of Eddy Arnold's 15-minute radio series *Checkerboard Square.*

Cavanaugh, Frank
College football coach, nicknamed the Iron Major. His career record was 145-48-17 coaching for the University of Cincinnati, Holy Cross, Dartmouth,

---

*In the 1970 remake *Julius Caesar* John Gielgud portrayed Julius Caesar, the man he had helped to kill in the 1953 version.

Boston College, and Fordham. He was portrayed in the 1943 movie *The Iron Major* by Pat O'Brien.

Cavell, Edith Louisa

British nurse who during World War I helped 200 soldiers to escape to Holland. She was executed by the Germans on October 12, 1915, along with her accomplice, Philippe Baucq. Cavell was portrayed in the 1939 movie *Nurse Edith Cavell* by Anna Neagle.

Cayce, Edgar

(1877–1945) Famous psychic who from 1901 until his death gave medical diagnoses by clairvoyance. He has been the subject of numerous books and was portrayed in the 1956 movie *The Search for Bridey Murphy* by Noel Leslie.

Cecile Waltz

Theme song of the radio series *Girl Alone*.

Celebrated Criminal Cases of America

Book that sits on detective Sam Spade's night stand in the novel *The Maltese Falcon* by Dashiell Hammett.

Cell 7

Jail cell in the Landsberg Prison, near Munich, where in 1924 Adolf Hitler wrote his autobiography *Mein Kampf* ("My Struggle").

Cell 41

Robert Stroud's (the Birdman of Alcatraz) cell in D Block at Alcatraz Prison.

Cell 2187

Cell in which Princess Leia Organa (Carrie Fisher) was incarcerated while on the *Death Star* in the 1977 movie *Star Wars*.

Cellini, Benvenuto

(1500–1571) Italian goldsmith and sculptor. Movie portrayals: *The Affairs of Cellini* (1934) Fredric March; and *The Burning of Rome* (1960) Brett Halsey.

Centaur Apartments

All-female Los Angeles apartment complex owned by Hogan (Jack Lemmon) in the 1963 movie *Under the Yum Yum Tree*.

Center City

Iowa hometown of Nancy Hudson Smith (Renne Jarrett), daughter of the president of the United States in the TV series *Nancy*.

Center City Examiner

Newspaper for which Walter Burns (John Daly) is editor and Hildy Johnson (Mark Roberts) is a reporter in the TV series *The Front Page*, which is loosely based on the Hecht-MacArthur play of the same name as well as in the 1974 movie of the same name.

Central Airlines

DC-3 airliner that faked an emergency landing at Carswell AFB in the 1955 movie *Strategic Air Command*.

Central America
> Consists of seven countries: Costa Rica, Belize, Guatemala, Honduras, Nicaragua, Panama, and El Salvador.

Central States Appliance Company
> Company for which Elmer Gantry (Burt Lancaster) was employed as a traveling salesman in the 1960 movie *Elmer Gantry* (based on the book of the same name by Sinclair Lewis).

Chadwick, Henry
> Writer of the first baseball rule book in 1858. He laid out the first baseball diamond in July 1846.

Chalkie
> Andy Capp's best friend in the comic strip *Andy Capp*. Chalkie's wife is Rube.

Challenger II
> Space capsule destroyed by a huge piece of rock after a comet hits Orpheus, causing the large rock to spin off in space and collide with *Challenger II*, in the 1979 movie *Meteor*.

Chambers, James
> Inventor of the attachable postage stamp in 1834.

Champagne Bottle Sizes

Magnum	55 ounces
Jeroboam	108 ounces
Rehoboam	163 ounces
Methuselah	216.4 ounces
Salmanazar	324.5 ounces
Balthazar	432.7 ounces
Nebuchadnezzar	541 ounces

Champagne Lady
> Female featured on Lawrence Welk's program. They have been: Lois Best, Jayne Walton, Joan Mowery, Helen Ramsey, Roberta Linn (the first on TV), Alice Lon, and Norma Zimmer.

Champagne Music Makers
> Members of Lawrence Welk's orchestra.

Champagne Tony
> Nickname of golfer Tony Lema.

Championship 10
> Football playoff between the Los Angeles Rams and the Baltimore Colts at the Los Angeles Memorial Coliseum in the 1977 movie *Two Minute Warning*. Howard Cosell and Frank Gifford were the sports announcers, Merv Griffin sang the national anthem.

Champs
> 1950s instrumental group whose biggest hit was "Tequila" (1958). They

recorded on Challenge Records, which was owned by Gene Autry. Autry named the group the Champs after his wonder horse Champion.

Chances Are
1957 hit song by Johnny Mathis (the flip side is "Twelfth of Never"). This is the song that was played on a record player when the UFO landed and kidnapped a small boy (Cary Guffey) in the 1977 movie *Close Encounters of the Third Kind*.

Chanel, Coco
French dress designer, portrayed by Katharine Hepburn in the 1969 Broadway musical *Coco*.

Chanel No. 5
First synthetic scent produced by Gabrielle "Coco" Chanel (1920). Marilyn Monroe claimed to reporters that this perfume was the only thing she wore to bed.

Chani
Robot in the 1955 movie *Devil Girl from Mars*.

Chant
Winner of the 1894 Kentucky Derby. The horse was owned by famed Dodge City deputy sheriff Bill Tilghman.

Chaplain Staneglass
Army officer at Camp Swampy in the *Beetle Bailey* comic strip.

Chaplin, Charles Spencer
(1889–1977) 5-foot 4-inch silent movie comedian nicknamed the Little Tramp who was the first actor to appear on the cover of *Time* magazine (July 6, 1925). He died on December 25, 1977, at age 88. His autobiography is titled *My Autobiography*. Chaplin was portrayed in the 1980 miniseries *Moviola* by Clive Revill.

Charger
Crusader Rabbit's white horse in the TV cartoon series.

Charger
Heath Barkley's (Lee Majors) horse in the TV series *The Big Valley*.

Chargerettes
Cheerleaders for the San Diego Chargers football team, which folded in 1978.

Chariot Horses
Four Arabian stallions driven by Charlton Heston in the 1959 movie *Ben Hur*. The horses were named after stars. Aldebaran, Altair, Rigel, and Antares.

Charlie Clod
Charlie Chan's left-handed cousin—a character played by Ernie Kovacs on TV.

Charles Bogle
Pseudonym used by W. C. Fields as the writer of the 1939 movie *You Can't Cheat an Honest Man.*

Charlestown Chiefs
Federal League hockey team of which Reggie Dunlop (Paul Newman) is player-coach (jersey No. 7) in the 1977 movie *Slap Shot* (filmed in Johnstown, Pennsylvania).

Charlie
Duck that lays golden eggs in the 1971 Disney movie *The Million Dollar Duck.*

Charlie
Charles Townsend, head of Investigative Agency, which employs "Charlie's Angels" in the TV series of that name. He is played by John Forsythe, who voice-records all his parts without going to the set and has never met the three actresses who play the angels.

Charlie Girl
Model Shelley Hack, who advertised Revlon's Charlie perfume on TV commercials.

Charlie's Angels
TV series featuring the beauty of: Sabrina Duncan (Kate Jackson); Jill Munroe (Farrah Fawcett-Majors); Kris Munroe (Cheryl Ladd), Jill's younger sister; Kelly Garrett (Jaclyn Smith); Tiffany Welles (Shelley Hack); and Julie Rogers (Tanya Roberts).

Charlmayne
Pet in the TV cartoon series *Emergency Plus Four.*

Charlotte
Treece's (Robert Shaw) pet dog in the 1977 movie *The Deep.* Played by Saucey.

Charwoman
Cleanup woman with the mop and bucket played by Carol Burnett in skits on her TV series

Chase, Salmon P.
(1808–1873) U.S. senator, governor of Ohio, secretary of the treasury, and chief justice of the U.S. Supreme Court (1864–1873). He was portrayed in the 1942 movie *Tennessee Johnson* by Montagu Love, and in the 1972 movie *1776* by Patrick Hines.

Chateau D'If
Prison in which Edmund Dante, the Count of Monte Cristo, was incarcerated.

Chaucer
Tony's (Chevy Chase) pet schnauzer in the 1978 movie *Foul Play.*

Chauffeurs

Driver	Employer
Tyrone Davis	blues singer Freddie King
Bobby "Blue" Bland	blues singer B. B. King
Larry Williams	singer Lloyd Price
Sebastian Cabot	actor Frank Pettingell
Billy Swan	country singer Webb Pierce
Gerald Peters	Winston Churchill and Elvis Presley
Charles Carr	country singer Hank Williams
Margaux Hemingway	George C. Scott's daughter

Check and Doublecheck
1930 movie featuring Freeman Gosden and Charles J. Correll as Amos 'n' Andy. In the movie a trio in blackface sings "Three Little Words" with Duke Ellington's Orchestra. The trio was actually the Rhythm Boys.

Cheerleaders
Vocal group that sang backup for Gordon MacRae on the 1956 TV series *The Gordon MacRae Show*.

Chelmsford, General Lord
British officer who led 800 British soldiers to their deaths against Zulu warriors in Africa in 1879. He was portrayed in the 1979 TV movie *Zulu Dawn* by Peter O'Toole.

Chelsea
New York hotel where British poet Dylan Thomas drank himself to death on November 9, 1953.

Chemistry
Pet ape of Brig. Gen. Theodore Marley Brook (better known as Ham, a member of Doc Savage's crew).

Chenhalls, Alfred
British movie director who resembled British Prime Minister Winston Churchill. When Alfred Chenhalls boarded a Lisbon-to-Britain flight on June 1, 1943, the Germans believed he was Churchill, returning from Algiers. German fighters shot down the plane, killing all 13 passengers, including actor Leslie Howard.

Chennault, Gen. Claire Lee
(1890–1958) American aviator who served with the rank of general in the Flying Tigers, a volunteer advisory group to Chiang Kai-shek in China before and during World War II. He was portrayed in the 1945 movie *God Is My Co-Pilot* by Raymond Massey.

Cher
Her TV comedy characters: Laverne Lachinsky, the Vamp, Lady Luck,

Donna Jean Bodine, Rosa (waitress in Sonny's Pizza Parlor), Barbara Nauseous, and Holly Farber.

Chesterfield
Brand of cigarettes that Humphrey Bogart smoked in most of his movies.

Chesterfields
Street-corner singing group featured in the 1978 movie *American Hot Wax*.

Chicago
Theme song of comedian Joe E. Lewis.

Chicago (Chicago Transit Authority)
First rock group to play at New York City's Carnegie Hall (April 1971).

Chicago Bulls
Pro basketball team for which coach Ken Reeves (Ken Howard*) played before becoming a high school teacher in the TV series *White Shadow*. He attended Boston College.

Chicago (That Toddling Town)
Song performed in the following motion pictures: *Little Giant* (1933); *The Story of Vernon and Irene Castle* (1939); *Roxie Hart* (1943); *Beyond the Forest* (1949); *Oh You Beautiful Doll* (1949); and *With a Song in My Heart* (1952). Song lyrics and music by Fred Fisher.

Chicken-à la-King
Dish consisting of chicken, peas, and carrots in a white sauce, created by Thomas Jefferson, 3rd president of the United States.

Chicken Little
Crime syndicate code words overheard by Buddy Overstreet (Jack Sheldon) that started the organization's hunt for him in the TV series *Run Buddy Run*.

Chicken sandwich with sliced tomatoes
Food that Robert Erocia Dupea (Jack Nicholson) ordered in a restaurant only to have the waitress (Lorna Thayer) refuse to deliver it to his table in the 1970 movie *Five Easy Pieces*.

Chief
Word painted on the machine gun manned by Al Schmid (John Garfield) in the 1945 movie *Pride of the Marines*.

Chief Canawahchaquaoo
Chief ot the Tuscarora Indians, played by Roosevelt Grier in the TV series *Daniel Boone*. The chief whose name was Gabe Cooper; was a runaway slave.

Chief Nervous Elk
Indian chief played by Paul Lynde in the 1979 movie *The Villain*.

Chief Nok-a-Homa
Full-blooded Ottawa-Chippewa Indian who comes out of his teepee and does a war dance each time one of the Atlanta Braves hits a home run at Atlanta Stadium. His real name is Levi Walker, Jr.

*Son-in-law of columnist Ann Landers.

Chief Red Cloud

Indian chief who raised Cheyenne Bodie (Clint Walker) in the TV series *Cheyenne*. Cheyenne's real father was Lionel Abbot.

Chief Roy Mobey

Redneck police chief of Clinton Corners, Georgia, played the TV series *Carter Country* by Victor French.

Child Is Father to the Man

Award presented by the United States for help given to UNICEF.

Child Psychology

Book by Henrietta Wright, M.A., M.D., that Lina McLaidlaw (Joan Fontaine) was reading on the train in the 1941 movie *Suspicion*.

Children Are People, Only Smaller

Classic book written by the world's best known child psychologist, Dr. Ludwig von Pablum, played by Sid Caesar in the TV series *Your Show of Shows*.

Children's Hour, The

Play written in 1934 by Lillian Hellman, and made into a movie twice (1936 and 1962). The story was based on the case described in William Roughhead's *Bad Companions* (1931). This is the play that Lillian was writing in the 1977 movie *Julia,* in which Jane Fonda portrayed Lillian Hellman and Vanessa Redgrave her friend Julia.

Childs Cup

Trophy awarded for the sport of collegiate rowing.

Chilly Willy

Penguin in Walter Lantz cartoons who made his debut in *Hot and Cold Penguin* (1953). He did not speak; the title theme "I'm Chilly Willy the Penguin" was sung by "Wee" Bonnie Baker.

Chips

K9 dog that became the only animal to win both a Purple Heart and a Silver Star during World War II.

Chita

Head Winkie (motorcycle monkey) in the 1978 movie *The Wiz*. He was played by Carlton Johnson.

Chopin, Frédéric François

(1810–1849) Polish-born composer and pianist and intimate friend of writer George Sand. Chopin was portrayed in the 1945 movie *A Song to Remember* by Cornel Wilde (José Iturbi played the piano), with Maurice Tauzin portraying him as a child; and in *Song Without End* (1960) by Alex Davion.

Chordettes

Female quartet from Sheboygan, Wisconsin, who were the first guests on the national TV series *American Bandstand*.

Chou Chou
Judy Garland's pet poodle that appeared with her in the 1945 movie *The Clock*.

Christabel and Irvin
Monroe family's two dogs in the TV series *My World . . . And Welcome to It*.

Christian
NFL quarterback Sonny Jurgenson's Christian name.

Christian, Dave
Center on the U.S. Olympic hockey team that won the Gold Medal at the 1980 Olympics. Dave Christian is the son of Bill Christian and nephew of Roger Christian, both of whom were on the 1960 U.S. Olympic team that won the Gold Medal. Another uncle of Dave's is Gordon Christian, who played on the Silver Medal–winning U.S. team in 1956.

Christie, Agatha (Dame Agatha Mary Clarissa Miller Christie Mallowan)
(1890–1976) British mystery writer of over 60 detective novels in 55 years. Her play *The Mousetrap* is the longest-running play in history. She created the detectives Hercule Poirot and Miss Marple. On December 4, 1926, Agatha Christie disappeared for 11 days, a period she never talked about. She was portrayed in the 1979 movie *Agatha* by Vanessa Redgrave.

Christman, Allen Bert
Artist who helped to draw Milton Caniff's comic strip *Terry and the Pirates*. As a pilot member of Gen. Chennault's Flying Tiger Squadron in China, he painted the famous faces on the P-40 fighters. Christman was shot and killed by a Japanese pilot while parachuting from his aircraft in January 1942.

Christmas Lullaby
Song recorded on Columbia Records by 62-year-old Cary Grant to celebrate the birth of his and Dyan Cannon's daughter, Jennifer, in 1966. It was his recording debut. Peggy Lee wrote the lyrics.

Christo, Javacheff
Artist who spent $3 million to construct 24½-mile nylon "Running Fence" north of San Francisco in 1975.

Churchill, Lord Randolph
(1848–1895) British statesman and father of Sir Winston Churchill. He was portrayed in the TV miniseries *Edward the King* (1979) by Derek Fowlds, and in the 1972 movie *Young Winston* by Robert Shaw.

Churchill, Sir Winston Leonard Spencer
(1874–1965) British author and statesman. Churchill held more government positions (10) than any other man in British history: under secretary for the colonies (1906); president of the Board of Trade (1908); home secretary (1910); first lord of the admiralty (1911); chancellor of the Duke of Lancaster (1915); minister of munitions (1917); secretary of state for war (1919);

secretary for the colonies (1921); chancellor of the exchequer (1924); and prime minister (1940–1945 and 1951–1955). He was the first honorary citizen of the United States. Portrayals: *Mission to Moscow* (1943) Dudley Field Malone*; *Operation Crossbow* (1965) Patrick Wymark; *Young Winston* (1972) Simon Ward (Russell Lewis at age 7 and Michael Anderson at age 13; *Eleanor and Franklin: The White House Years* (1977 TV) Arthur Gould-Porter; Voice of Peter Sellers in the 1956 movie *The Man Who Never Was;* Voice of Richard Burton in the TV series *The Valiant Years; Ike* (1979 TV miniseries) Wensley Pithey; *A Man Called Intrepid* (1979 TV miniseries) Nigel Stock; *Truman at Potsdam* (1976 TV play) John Houseman; *FDR: The Last Year* (1980 TV play) Wensley Pithey; and *Churchill and the Generals* (1981 TV) Timothy West.

Cigarette me, big boy
Line spoken by Claudette Colbert to Norman Foster (her real-life husband) in the 1930 movie *Young Man of Manhattan*.

Cincinnati Cobra
Nickname of heavyweight champion Ezzard Charles.

Cinderella
Heroine of classic fairy tale based on the popular version by Charles Perrault which was first published in English in 1729. Portrayals: *Cinderella* (1911) Mabel Taliaferro; Walt Disney cartoon movie *Cinderella* (1950), voice of Ilene Woods; *The Wonderful World of the Brothers Grimm* (1962) Pamela Beaird; X-rated *Cinderella* Gemma Craven, *The Slipper and the Rose* (1976) Charyl Smith. Leslie Caron played Ella in the movie musical *The Glass Slipper* (1955), and Lesley Ann Warren played the part in the 1965 Rodgers and Hammerstein TV version. On the 1977 TV presentation of *Cindy* Charlaine Woodard starred in the first black version of the tale. Jerry Lewis played a male version of her in the 1960 movie *Cinderfella*.

Cinderella Girl
Hollywood nickname of actress Linda Darnell.

Cinderella Man
Nickname of heavyweight boxing champion James J. Braddock, coined by Damon Runyon.

Cinque
Leader (general field marshal) of the radical SLA (Symbionese Liberation Army), which kidnapped heiress Patty Hearst. Cinque, whose real name was Donald DeFreeze, was killed in a police shootout in Los Angeles on May 17, 1974. He was portrayed in the 1979 TV movie *The Ordeal of Patty Hearst* by Felton Perry.

---

*Malone had served in real life as assistant secretary of state under President Woodrow Wilson.

Circle G
Elvis Presley's 160-acre ranch in Walls, Mississippi, named for Graceland.

City General Hospital
Medical facility where Dr. Sid Rafferty (Patrick McGoohan) practiced medicine in the TV series *Rafferty*.

City Lights Bookshop
World-famous bookstore located at 261 Columbus Avenue in San Francisco. It was founded in 1953 by Lawrence Ferlinghetti and Peter D. Martin as the first all-paperback bookstore in the United States.

City National Bank
Bank through which John Beresford Tipton dispensed his millions in the 1979 TV movie *The Millionaire*.

Civil War Generals
Those who later became presidents of the United States: Ulysses S. Grant, Rutherford B. Hayes, Chester A. Arthur, James Garfield, and Benjamin Harrison. (William McKinley served as a major.)

Clapton Is God!
Popular graffiti on London walls in 1960s and early 1970s referring to the talents of rock guitarist Eric Clapton. Clapton's wife, Patty, was previously married to former Beatle George Harrison.

Clarabelle Hornblower
Woman who raised John Reid's (the Lone Ranger) nephew Dan Reid. She later took him east to Baltimore, where he was educated.

Clarence Oddbody
293-year-old AS2 (Angel Second Class), played by Henry Travers, who came to earth to help George Bailey (James Stewart) in the 1946 movie *It's a Wonderful Life*.

Claremore Queen
Riverboat captained by Capt. Eli (Irvin S. Cobb) in the 1935 movie *Steamboat 'Round the Bend*.

Claridge, Sharon
Voice of the police radio dispatcher in the TV series *Adam-12*.

Clark, Father Charles Dismas
St. Louis Jesuit priest who devoted his life to rehabilitating criminals by living among them. He was portrayed in the 1961 movie *The Hoodlum Priest* by Don Murray.

Clark, Gen. Mark Wayne
(1896–   ) U.S. Army general who served in both World War I and World War II. In 1943–1944 he was commander of the U.S. 5th Army in North Africa and Italy. Clark was portrayed in the 1968 movie *The Devil's Brigade* by Michael Rennie and in the 1979 TV miniseries *Ike* by Bill Schallert.

Claudia Naughton

The fictional subject of two movies, *Claudia* (1943) and *Claudia and David* (1946), starring Dorothy McGuire as Claudia. In the radio series *Claudia* the character was played by Patricia Ryan and then Katherine Bard. In the 1952 TV series *Claudia, The Story of a Marriage* she was played by Joan McCracken. Claudia was introduced in novels by Rose Franken.

Clavius

Space station set in a crater on the moon in the 1968 movie *2001: A Space Odyssey*.

Clay, Tom

Disc jockey who was once fired for barricading himself in his Buffalo radio station and playing Buddy Holly and the Crickets' "That'll Be the Day" for 17 consecutive hours. The police had to break down the door and drag him out. In the 1978 movie *The Buddy Holly Story* he was portrayed by Fred Travelena as Mad Man Mancusco.

Cleave, Maureen

Reporter for the *London Evening Standard* who conducted the interview with John Lennon on March 4, 1966, in which John made his infamous remark, "We're more popular than Jesus now."

Clemenceau, Georges

(1841–1929) French statesman nicknamed the Tiger. He headed the French delegation at the Versailles Peace Conference after World War I. Clemenceau was portrayed in the 1944 movie *Wilson* by Marcell Dalio and in the 1958 movie *I Accuse!* by Peter Illing.

Clementine

Actor John Barrymore's pet monkey, given to him by actress Gladys Cooper.

Clem Finch

Quiet individual sitting at a restaurant counter to whom Charlie Bratten, the Loud Mouth (Jackie Gleason), gives a bad time. Clem was played by Art Carney in the TV series *The Jackie Gleason Show*.

Cleopatra

(69–30 B.C.) Last queen of Egypt, who married her brother, Ptolemy, and ruled jointly with him. After Caesar's conquest of Egypt she ruled alone as Rome's surrogate. On hearing of the death of her lover Mark Anthony, she committed suicide by having an asp bite her. Movie portrayals: *Cleopatra* (1911) Helen Gardner; *Cleopatra* (1917) Theda Bara; *Cleopatra* (1934) Claudette Colbert; *Ceasar and Cleopatra* (1945) Vivien Leigh; *Serpent of the Nile* (1953) Rhonda Fleming; *The Story of Mankind* (1957) Virginia Mayo; *Cleopatra* (1963) Elizabeth Taylor; *Carry On, Cleo* (1963) Amanda Barrie; and *Anthony and Cleopatra* (1971) Hildegarde Neil.

Cleopatra

Bob and Betty MacDonald's (Fred MacMurray and Claudette Colbert) pig on their small farm in the 1947 movie *The Egg and I*. Their pet dog was called Sport.

Cleveland

Hamburg-American liner on which Rudolph Valentino immigrated to America, arriving on December 23, 1913.

Cleveland, Grover

(1837–1908) 22nd and 24th president of the United States. He once told a 5-year-old boy, "Son, I hope you never become president of the United States." The boy did; his name was Franklin D. Roosevelt. Cleveland was portrayed in the 1940 movie *Lillian Russell* by William B. Davidson, and in the 1976 movie *Buffalo Bill and the Indians* by Pat McCormick.

Cleveland Indians

Baseball team featured in the 1953 movie *The Kid from Left Field*.*

Cliburn, Van

First American musician ever given a ticker tape parade in New York City (May 20, 1958). He was returning from Russia, where he had won the International Tchaikovsky Competition.

Clifton, Nathaniel "Sweetwater"

First black man to play in the NBA in 1950 (for the New York Knickerbockers.)**

Cline, Patsy

(1932–1963) Popular country singer of the 1950s and early 1960s until her death in an airplane accident on March 5, 1963, which also took the lives of singers Harold "Hawkshaw" Hawkins and Lloyd "Cowboy" Copas. She won first place on *Arthur Godfrey's Talent Scouts* on January 28, 1957, singing "Walkin' After Midnight." She also appeared as a contestant on the TV game show *You Bet Your Life*. Patsy Cline was portrayed in the 1980 movie *Coal Miner's Daughter* by Beverly D'Angelo.

Clinkers

Robot couple played by comedy team Robert Shields and Lorene Yarnell.

Clinton Corners

Georgia town setting in the TV series *Carter Country*, just down the road from Jimmy Carter's hometown, Plains.

Clock, The

Comic-book crime fighter whose secret identity is Brian O'Brien.

Clopton, Walter Wingfield

British inventor of lawn tennis in 1874.

Close Encounters

Contacts with a UFO (unidentified flying object): first kind—sighting of a UFO; second kind—physical evidence; third kind—personal contact.

---

*The 1979 TV movie *The Kid from Left Field* featured the San Diego Padres.
**The Boston Celtics had previously drafted the black player Chuck Cooper, but the Knicks opened the 1950 season one night earlier than Boston.

Clothilde
> Tom Jordache's (Nick Nolte) yacht in the TV miniseries *Rich Man, Poor Man*.

Clovell, C. Gary
> Designer of the prizes in Cracker Jack boxes from 1937 until 1965.

Club Durant
> Popular New York nightclub named for comedian Jimmy Durante, who was part owner. The club opened on January 22, 1923. The cost of the sign was $250. The painter left the "e" off the sign and demanded an extra $100 to add it, thus no "e."

Club Safari
> Chicago nightclub where Molly (Kim Novak) worked in the 1955 movie *The Man with the Golden Arm*.

Club Sandwich
> Paul McCartney's fan magazine. Paul is the editor and his wife, Linda, is the photographer.

Club Victoria
> Nightclub setting on the TV soap opera *Love of Life*.

Clyde
> Orangutan (played by Manus) who starred in the 1978 Clint Eastwood movie *Every Which Way But Loose*, as well as in the 1980 sequel *Any Which Way You Can*. Manus's mate, Tiga, appeared in the advertisements for the films.

Clyde Crashcup
> Crazy inventor friend of the Chipmunks on the TV cartoon series *The Alvin Show*. The voice was that of Shepard Menken.

Coal Miner
> Name of country singer Loretta Lynn's custom GMC touring bus. Loretta's CB handle is also Coal Miner.

Cochran, Eddie
> (1938–1960) Rock 'n' roll singer of the 1950s who first recorded with country writer Hank Cochran as the Cochran Brothers, although they were unrelated. His biggest hit was the 1958 recording "Summertime Blues." Cochran was killed on April 17, 1960, in a taxicab accident in London in which Gene Vincent and Sharon Sheeley were injured. Cochran was portrayed in the 1978 movie *The Buddy Holly Story* by Jerry Zaremba.

Cochran, Jacqueline
> (1906 or 1910–1980) Winner of the 1938 Bendix Trophy. In 1953 she became the first woman to exceed the speed of sound (in a F86 Sabrejet). Her autobiography was titled *The Stars at Noon*. Jacqueline Cochran held more aviation trophies than any other female flyer and was the first woman to be elected to the Aviation Hall of Fame.

Code 710

"Do not approach this planet for any reason."—Federation code in the TV series *Star Trek*.

Coffelt, Leslie

Guard who was killed on November 1, 1950, when two men attempted to break into Blair House, where President Truman and his family were living while repairs were being made on the White House.

Cohan, George Michael

(1878–1942) American playwright, actor, and producer. He composed numerous plays and such popular songs as "You're a Grand, Old Flag," Over There," "I'm a Yankee Doodle Dandy," and "Give My Regards to Broadway." He was portrayed by James Cagney in both the 1942 movie *Yankee Doodle Dandy* and the 1955 movie *The Seven Little Foys*. Joel Grey played Cohan in the 1968 Broadway Musical *George M* and Mickey Rooney portrayed him in an episode of the TV series *Bob Hope Presents the Chrysler Theater*.

Coke Girl

Title held by Anita Bryant from 1960 to 1963, when she did advertisements and public relations for the Coca-Cola Company.

College Bowl, The

1950–1951 TV series starring Chico Marx on which 21-year-old Andy Williams was a regular.

Coll, Vincent

(1909–1932) Gangster and murderer nicknamed "Mad Dog." He was himself murdered in a telephone booth. Coll was portrayed in the 1961 movie *Mad Dog Coll* by John Davis Chandler.

Colman, Ronald, and Vilma Banky

Films in which the pair appeared: *The Dark Angel* (1925); *The Winning of Barbara Worth* (1926); *The Night of Love* (1927); *The Magic Flame* (1927); and *Two Lovers* (1928).

Col. Sherman Potter

Commanding officer of the MASH 4077th after the transfer of Col. Henry Blake in the TV series *M*A*S*H*. Potter was played by Harry Morgan.*

Colossus

Computer that attempted to rule the world in the 1970 movie *The Forbin Project* (based on the first book in the D. F. Jones Colossus trilogy). The Soviet computer was named Guardian.

Colson, Charles

Adviser to President Richard Nixon who became involved in the Watergate scandal. Colson was portrayed in the 1979 TV miniseries *Blind Ambition* by Michael Callan and in the 1978 movie *Born Again* by Dean Jones.

---

*Harry Morgan had previously made an appearance on the series as Gen. Bartford Hamilton Steele.

Columbia Electric Victoria

Automobile in which Theodore Roosevelt rode through Hartford, Connecticut, on August 22, 1902, thus becoming the first president to ride in a horseless carriage.

Columbia Records

Only record label for which blues singer Bessie Smith ever recorded.

Columbia, the Gem of the Ocean

Theme song of the radio series *Don Winslow of the Navy*. This was the song the military band played on the USS *Hornet* as the three *Apollo 12* astronauts boarded after their recovery on November 24, 1969.

Columbia University

Dwight Eisenhower once served as president of this university. Lou Gehrig and Jack Kerouac were students there, and Charles Van Doren was an English instructor. Band leader Fletcher Henderson obtained a master's degree in chemistry, actor Nat Pendleton earned a degree in economics, and singer-composer Art Garfunkel earned a degree in mathematics at Columbia.

Columbine

Dwight David Eisenhower's presidential airplane.

Columbo, Russ

(1908–1934) Popular singer of the 1920s and early 1930s. His theme song was "You Call It Madness." Columbo was the 12th child of a 12th child of a 12th child. At the age of 26 he was killed by his friend, Lansing V. Brown, Jr., a photographer, who accidentally discharged a Civil War pistol. His death occurred on September 2, 1934, in the same house in which George Gershwin composed "A Foggy Day in London Town" and his last song "Our Love Is Here to Stay." The house was later the home of José Ferrer and his wife, Rosemary Clooney.

Columbus, Christopher

(1451–1506) Italian explorer who discovered America for the Spanish in 1492. He sailed from Palos on August 3 and arrived in the Bahamas on October 12. Movie portrayals: *Where Do We Go From Here?* (1945) Fortunio Bonanova; *Christopher Columbus* (1949) Fredric March; and *The Story of Mankind* (1957) Anthony Dexter.

Columbus, New Mexico

Border town invaded by Pancho Villa and 400 Mexican horsemen on March 9, 1916.

Comaneci, Nadia

14-year-old Rumanian gymnast at the 1976 Olympics who inspired the name for Barry De Vorzon's instrumental, "Nadia's Theme."

Comeaux, Jerry

Stunt man who jumped a racing boat 110 feet over a road in the 1973 James Bond movie *Live and Let Die*. The jump set a world record.

Comedy of Errors, The
> Only one of his plays in which William Shakespeare mentions America (Act III, Scene 2).

Come Home America
> George McGovern's presidential candidacy theme.

Come On Get Happy
> Theme song of the TV series *The Partridge Family*.

Come Together
> 1969 rock song composed by John Lennon and Paul McCartney for which they were sued for plagiarism. The first two lines are the same as Chuck Berry's 1956 record "You Can't Catch Me."

Command Decision
> 1948 movie in which Clark Gable made his only appearance with an all-male cast.

Cmdr. Adama
> Officer (played by Lorne Greene) in charge of the *Galactica* in the TV series *Battlestar Galactica*.

Cmdr. Adam Quark
> Commander (played by Richard Benjamin) of a patrolling UGSP (United Galaxy Sanitation Patrol) space craft in the TV series *Quark*.

Cmdr. John Koenig
> Commanding officer (played by Martin Landau) of Moonbase Alpha in the TV series *Space: 1999*.

Commando Cody
> Sky Marshal of the Universe Jeff King, played in the 1955 TV series *Commando Cody* by Judd Holdren. Commando Cody was played by George Wallace in the 12-episode serial *Radar Men from the Moon* (1952).

Commissioner Dolan
> Central City police commissioner who is a friend of Denny Colt (the Spirit) in *The Spirit* comic books. His daughter is Ellen.

Comissioner Matthew Gower
> New York City deputy police commissioner in the TV series *The Asphalt Jungle*, played by Jack Warden. In the 1950 movie of the same name John McIntire played the police commissioner, who was called Hardy.

Common Sense Book of Baby and Child Care
> Book written by Navy Lt. Cmdr. Benjamin Spock in 1946 that was the best-selling nonfiction work in the United States next to the Bible.* It became controversial when its "permissive" psychology was held responsible by some for the youth rebellion of the 1960s. Spock was a oarsman member of the Yale crew that won a Gold Medal in the 1924 Olympics in Paris.

---

*Now surpassed by the *Guinness Book of World Records*.

Compact Pussycat

Racing car driven by Penelope Pitstop in the TV cartoon series *The Wacky Races*.

Compass Rose

Royal Navy corvette commanded by Capt. Ericson (Jack Hawkins) in the 1953 movie *The Cruel Sea*.

Compulsion

Novel by Meyer Levin that was made into a play and a movie in 1959. It dealt in fictional form with the kidnapping of Bobby Franks by Nathan Leopold and Richard Loeb in the 1930s. Humphrey Bogart was reading *Compulsion* just before his death on January 14, 1957. Actress Marie McDonald was reading the book before she was kidnapped.

Concerto Macabre

Musical piece composed by Bernard Hermann for the 1945 movie *Hangover Square*.

Concord School

Private school headed by Andy Thompson (Andy Griffith) in the TV series *The Headmaster*.

Cone of Silence

Device employed by the chief in the TV series *Get Smart*. When descended over his desk, the Cone of Silence was used for secret talks.

Conemaugh Dam

Dam that broke, causing the Johnstown, Pennsylvania, flood of May 31, 1889. 2,200 lives were lost.

Congo Bill

Jungle hero was debuted in *Action Comics* No. 37 (May 1940). He was played in the 1948 movie serial *Congo Bill* by Don McGuire.

Connecticut Yankees

Rudy Vallee's orchestra.

Conn Smythe Trophy

Annual award presented to the most valuable player in the Stanley Cup playoffs.

Connolly, Maureen

Youngest woman (nicknamed Little Mo) to win at Forest Hills and Wimbledon, and the first to win the Tennis Grand Slam (1951–1954). She was portrayed in the 1978 TV movie *Little Mo* by Glynnis O'Connor.

Conrad, Robert

Actor who starred in the following TV series: *Hawaiian Eye* (1959–1963); *The Wild Wild West* (1965–1970); *The D.A.* (1971–1972); *Assignment Vienna* (1972–1973); *Baa Baa Black Sheep* (1976–1978); *The Duke* (1979); and *A Man Called Sloan* (1979–1980).

Consolidated Life

New York City insurance company for which Calvin Clinton Baxter (Jack Lemmon) worked at Desk 861 in Section W on the 19th floor, making $94.70 a month, in the 1960 movie *The Apartment*.

Constantine

(A.D. 280–337) Flavius Valerius Aurelius Constantinus, the first Christian emperor of Rome. He converted to Christianity after seeing a cross in the sky with the words *"In hoc signo vinces"* (By this sign thou shalt conquer) on it. He was portrayed in the 1962 movie *Constantine and the Cross* by Cornel Wilde.

Constitution

Ocean liner on which Grace Kelly traveled to Monaco, on April 18, 1956, to be married to Prince Rainier.

Contadora

Panamanian island where the Panama Canal Treaty was signed, where Patty Hearst and her husband, Bernard Shaw, honeymooned, and where the Shah of Iran went to live in December 1979 after leaving the United States.

Continental Flange Company

Firm for which Arnie Nuvo (Herschel Bernardi) worked in the TV series *Arnie*.

Conway

Movie house where James J. (Richard Thomas) watched *East of Eden* four times in the 1977 movie *9/30/55*. At the movie's end the motion picture *The Seven Year Itch* was advertised on the marquee.

Cooke, Sam

(1935–1964) Popular gospel-turned-pop-singer. His biggest hit, "You Send Me," was recorded in 1957. He was shot and killed on December 11, 1964. Cooke was portrayed in the 1978 movie *The Buddy Holly Story* by Paul Mooney.

Cookie

The wife of Smokey Stover in the comic strip *Smokey Stover*.

Coolidge, John Calvin

(1872–1933) 30th president of the United States. He had previously been a state representative, mayor, senator, lieutenant governor, governor, and vice president. Coolidge was sworn into office by his father. He was portrayed in the 1955 movie *The Court Martial of Billy Mitchell* by Ian Wolfe, and in the 1979 TV miniseries *Backstairs at the White House* by Ed Flanders (Lee Grant played his wife, Grace).

Coolie .

Biggest long shot on record. In November 1929 Coolie paid 3401-to-1 at Haydack Park, England.

Cooper, Jackie
> Child actor born in 1921 who appeared in the *Our Gang* shorts and with Wallace Beery in *The Champ* (1931). As an adult he's appeared in numerous movies and in several TV series. Cooper was portrayed in the 1978 TV movie *Rainbow* by Johnny Doran. He swore actor Jay North into the U.S. Navy in 1977.

Cooper, Joseph
> Marshmallow salesman hit by New York Yankees manager Billy Martin in a Bloomington, Minnesota, hotel in October 1979. Because of the incident Martin was fired on October 30.

Cooper, Col. Meriam C.
> (1893–1973) Movie producer and director. He co-wrote and co-directed the classic 1933 movie *King Kong,* as well as the sequel, *Son of Kong* (1933), and *Mighty Joe Young* (1949). During World War II Cooper served as Gen. Claire Chennault's chief of staff in China. He retired from the U.S. Air Force as a brigadier general. He was portrayed in the 1945 movie *God Is My Co-Pilot* by Stanley Ridges.

Cooper, Peter
> American inventor of Jell-O desserts in 1845.

Coors Beer
> 400 cases of this illegal cargo were carried by Bandit (Burt Reynolds) and a truck driver, Cledus (Jerry Reed), in the 1977 movie *Smokey and the Bandit*.

Copper
> Palomino horse ridden in B westerns by singing cowboy Eddie Dean.

Corbett, James J.
> (1866–1933) World Heavyweight Champion boxer (1892–1897). Corbett gained the title when he knocked out John L. Sullivan in the 21st round at a match held on September 7, 1892. The Corbett–Fitzsimmons fight held on March 17, 1897, was the first boxing match recorded on film. Corbett was portrayed in the 1942 movie *Gentlemen Jim* by Errol Flynn.

Cord
> Automobile in which western actor Tom Mix was killed on October 12, 1940. It was also the make of automobile in which George and Marion Kirby were killed in the 1937 movie *Topper*. Cord automobiles were built in Auburn, Indiana.

Cordella, Ohio
> Setting of the TV series *It's a Man's World*.

Corn Beef and Cabbage
> Favorite food of Jiggs in the comic strip *Bringing Up Father*.

Corncracker
> Black colt owned by Dick Handley (Sterling Hayden) as a small boy in the 1950 movie *The Asphalt Jungle*.

Cornwallis, Marquis
(1738–1805) Charles Cornwallis was the British major general in the American War of Independence who surrendered at Yorktown in 1781. He was portrayed in the 1924 movie *Janice Meredith* by Tyrone Power, Sr., and in the 1963 movie *Lafayette* by Jack Hawkins.

Coroebus
First recorded Olympic champion. He was a sprinter who won a 630-foot-long foot race in Olympia in 776 B.C.

Corpses
In the 1931 movie *The Deceiver* John Wayne played a corpse in a single scene, and in the 1935 movie *The Case of the Curious Bride* Errol Flynn played a corpse.

Cosell, Howard
Controversial sports announcer who appeared along with Alex Karras in the 1972 movie *The 500 Pound Jerk*. Cosell was a major in the U.S. Army at the age of 24, the youngest at the time.

Corsair
Treece's (Robert Shaw) boat (No. F641) in the 1977 movie *The Deep*.

Cortez, Hernando
(1485–1547) Spanish conqueror of Mexico in 1519. Movie portrayals: *The Fall of Montezuma* (1912) Francis X. Bushman; and *Captain from Castile* (1947) Cesar Romero.

Costello, Frank
Italian-born racketeer member of the Cosa Nostra under Lucky Luciano. Costello was portrayed loosely in the 1952 movie *Hoodlum Empire* by Luther Adler (as Nickey Mansani).

Cotchford Farm
Estate in Sussex, England, where author A.A. Milne lived. It was Rolling Stones guitarist Brian Jones' home at the time of his death on July 3, 1969.

Count Alucard
Son of Count Dracula, played by Lon Chaney Jr., in the 1943 movie *Son of Dracula*. Alucard is Dracula spelled backward.

Courtney, Clint
Major league player who in 1951 became the first catcher to wear glasses while he played.

Country Club Plaza
First shopping center in the United States. It was opened in Kansas City, Missouri, in 1922 (4629 Wornall Road).

Coward, Charles
World War II British Sergeant-Major who sabotaged Nazi facilities while a POW. He was portrayed in the 1963 movie *The Password Is Courage* by Dirk Bogarde.

Coward, Noel

(1899–1973) British author, composer, playwright, and actor. He was portrayed in the 1968 movie *Star!* by Daniel Massey and in the 1979 TV miniseries *Ike* by Francis Matthes.

Cowardly Lion

Lovable lion who seeks courage from the Wizard of Oz. Portrayals: *The Wizard of Oz* (1903 musical play) Arthur Hill; *The Wizard of Oz* (1939 movie) Bert Lahr; *The Wiz* (Broadway play) Ted Ross; and *The Wiz* (1978 movie) Ted Ross. The Cowardly Lion was played in a New York school (P.S. 41) production by 10-year-old Robert De Niro. In *The Wiz* the Lion's name is Fleetwood Coupe De Ville.

Cowboy and the Indians, The (1949) and The Black Dakotas (1954)

Two movies in which Clayton Moore and Jay Silverheels appeared together, but *not* as the Lone Ranger and Tonto.

Cowboy Hat

Trophy for the winner of the annual Texas University and Oklahoma University football game.

Cowboy Movie Hall of Fame

Located at Owensboro, Kentucky. Western actor Sunset Carson was one of its founders.

Cox, Mark

First amateur tennis player to defeat a professional (Richard "Pancho" Gonzales) in open competition (1968).

Crab Apple Cove

Hometown in Maine of Capt. Benjamin Franklin "Hawkeye" Pierce (Alan Alda) in the TV series *M*A*S*H*. In early episodes Hawkeye said he was from Vermont.

Crapper, Sir Thomas

Inventor of the flush toilet in 1878. He was knighted by Queen Victoria.

Crash Course

Warner Brothers movie that Chris MacNeil (Ellen Burstyn) was filming in the 1973 movie *The Exorcist*.

Crater, Joseph Force

New York Supreme Court justice who mysteriously disappeared on August 6, 1930, never to be heard from again.

Crawford, Joan

(1906–1977) Hollywood actress. Her four husbands were: Douglas Fairbanks, Jr. (1929–1933), Franchot Tone (1935–1939), Phillip Terry (1942–1946), and Alfred N. Steele (1955–1959). She was portrayed in the 1980 TV miniseries *Moviola* by Barrie Youngfellow and in the 1981 movie *Mommy Dearest* with Faye Dunaway.*

---

*Anne Bancroft was originally chosen but bowed out.

Crawfordville, Indiana
Birthplace in 1900 of Mary Worth (comic strip).
Crazy Guggenheim
Character played by Frank Fontaine in the 1950s *The Jackie Gleason Show.*
Crazy Horse
(1848–1877) American Oglala (Sioux) Indian chief whose Indian name was Tashunca-Uitco. He was present at the Battle of the Little Big Horn in 1876 and was killed a year later by Army soldiers for resisting imprisonment. Portrayals: *Custer's Last Stand* (1936) High Eagle; *They Died With Their Boots On* (1942) Anthony Quinn; *Sitting Bull* (1954) Iron Eyes Cody; *Chief Crazy Horse* (1955) Victor Mature; *The Great Sioux Massacre* (1965) Iron Eyes Cody; *The Outlaws Is Coming!* (1965) Murray Alper; *The Incredible Rocky Mountain Race* (1977 TV movie) Mike Mazurki; and *The Legend of Custer* (TV series) Michael Dante.
Cresco
Hometown of the Curlytops (children's books).
Creeper
Horror character played by Rondo Hatton in three Universal films: *The Peril of Death* (1944), *House of Horrors* (1945), and *The Brute Man* (1946).
CRescent 9-9499
Phone number of the Crest Hotel where Little John Starto (Edward G. Robinson) lived in the 1940 movie *Brother Orchid.*
Crescent Star
Ocean liner that hit a mine and sank in the 1957 movie *Abandon Ship!*
Crews, Laura Hope
(1879–1942) Hollywood leading lady and character actress who played Aunt Pittypat in the 1939 movie *Gone With the Wind.* She was portrayed in the 1980 TV miniseries *Moviola* by Audra Lindley.
Crime Does Not Pay
Act that in 1935 toured with the *United Shows of America Carnival,* featuring Bonnie Parker's mother, Emma Parker; Clyde Barrow's mother, Henrietta Barrow; and John Dillinger's father, J.W. Dillinger. They told audiences about their children's life of crime.
Criterion Bar
London pub where Dr. Watson and Sherlock Holmes met for the first time in 1881. They were introduced by Stamford, a student at St. Bartholomew Hospital, where Watson also worked. *(A Study in Scarlet* by Sir Arthur Conan Doyle).
Crocker National Bank
San Francisco institution where Kelly Sherwood (Lee Remick) was employed in the 1962 movie *Experiment in Terror.*

Crockett, Capt. Hanson Gregory
Creator of the hole in doughnuts in 1847. Until then, doughnuts were always solid. There is a memorial to him in Maine.

Cromwell, Thomas
(1485–1540) English statesman and adviser to Cardinal Wolsey who was accused of treason and beheaded. Portrayals: *The Private Life of Henry VIII* (1933) Franklin Dyall; *A Man for All Seasons* (1966) Leo McKern; *Carry On, Henry VIII* (1971) Kenneth Williams; *The Six Wives of Henry VIII* (1971 TV) Wolfe Morris, and *Henry VIII and His Six Wives* (1973) Donald Pleasance.

Cronin, Joe
Player-manager, president of the American League, and member of Baseball's Hall of Fame. Cronin was portrayed in the 1957 movie *Fear Strikes Out* by Bart Burns.

Crook, George
(1829–1890) Civil War general who later fought against Geronimo in the West. Movie portrayals: *Chief Crazy Horse* (1955) James Milican; and *Geronimo* (1962) Lawrence Dobkin.

Crooked Circle, The
1932 motion picture starring Ben Lyon, Zasu Pitts, and James Gleason. On March 10, 1933, it became the first movie to be shown on television (Station WGXOA in Los Angeles).

Crooked Tongue Saloon
Western bar run by Katie (Maureen O'Hara) in the 1950 movie *Comanche Territory*.

Crosby, Bing
(1904–1977) Popular crooner and actor from the 1930s until his death in 1977. He was loosely portrayed by Lee Bowman in the 1947 movie *Smash-Up*.

Crowbar
An Indian, played by Teddy Hart, who appeared in four *Ma and Pa Kettle* movies.

Crown Electric Company
Memphis firm for which Elvis Presley drove a truck in 1953 and 1954 before he became a rock 'n' roll star. Singers Johnny Burnette and his brother, Dorsey, previously had also worked for the company, a year earlier.

Crown Point Cemetery
Chicago cemetery where President Benjamin Harrison, three vice presidents, and gangster John Dillinger are all buried.

Cruella De Ville
Villainess dognapper in the 1961 Disney animated movie *101 Dalmations*.

Actress Mary Wickes modeled for Cruella; the voice is that of Betty Lou Gerason.

Crum, George
Creator of the potato chip. The first person to whom he served potato chips (in 1853) was the man for whom he had made them, Commodore Cornelius Vanderbilt.

Crump, Diane
First female jockey to race in the Kentucky Derby (1970). She finished in 15th place on Fathom.

Crusade in Europe
1949 TV series based on the book by Dwight D. Eisenhower. Another book by a U.S. president that was used as the basis for a TV series was John F. Kennedy's *Profiles in Courage.*

Crystal Ballroom
Los Angeles hall where the USO dances were held in the 1979 movie *1941.*

Cuff and Link
Rocky Balboa's (Sylvester Stallone) pet turtles in the 1976 movie *Rocky.*

Cukor, George
Hollywood director famous for his work with actresses (he was called a "woman's director"). Cukor received an Oscar for best director for the 1964 movie *My Fair Lady.* He was portrayed in the 1980 TV miniseries *Moviola* by George Furth.

Cummings, Robert Orville
Actor whose godfather was aviator Orville Wright

Cundall, Joseph
British creator of the Christmas card in 1846.

Cunningham and Thomas Aircraft
Firm for which Chester A. Riley (William Bendix) worked as a riveter in the TV series *The Life of Riley.*

Curie, Marie and Pierre
Wife-and-husband team that won the Nobel Prize for chemistry in 1911. They were portrayed in the 1944 movie *Madam Curie* by Greer Garson and Walter Pidgeon. Marie Curie was the first person to die of radiation poisoning.

Curragh
Senator Edward Kennedy's 55-foot sloop.

Curtis, Glenn
(1878–1930) American inventor and aviator who set both motorcycle and aviation records. He was portrayed in the 1978 TV movie *The Winds of Kitty Hawk* by Scott Hylands.

Curtis, King
(1934–1971) Saxophone player (born Curtis Ousley) who played sax on most

of the Coaster's hit records, On August 31, 1971, he was stabbed to death outside his New York City apartment building. Curtis was portrayed in the 1978 movie *The Buddy Holly Story* by Craig White.

Curtis, Tony, and Janet Leigh

Films in which the pair (married 1951–1963) appeared; *Houdini* (1953); *The Black Shield of Falworth* (1954); *The Perfect Furlough* (1958); *The Vikings* (1958); and *Who Was That Lady?* (1960).

Custer

Counties that are the geographic centers of both the states of Idaho and Nebraska.

Custer, George Armstrong

(1839–1876) American Civil War general and later Indian fighter who was killed at the Battle of the Little Big Horn on June 25, 1876. Custer graduated at the bottom of a class of 35 at West Point in 1861. His brothers, Tom and Boston Custer, were also killed at Little Big Horn. Tom had twice won the Medal of Honor. Portrayals: *Bob Hampton of Placer* (1921) Dwight Crittenden; *The Flaming Frontier* (1926) Dustin Farnum; *General Custer at the Little Big Horn* (1926) John Beck; *The Last Frontier* (1933) William Desmond; *The World Changes* (1933) Clay Clement; *Custer's Last Stand* (1936) Frank McGlynn, Jr.; *The Plainsman* (1936) John Miljan; *The Oregon Trail* (1939) Roy Barcroft; *Bad Man of Wyoming* (1940) Paul Kelly; *Santa Fe Trail* (1940) Ronald Reagan; *Badlands of Dakota* (1941) Addison Richards; *They Died With Their Boots On* (1941) Errol Flynn; *Warpath* (1951) James Millican; *Bugles in the Afternoon* (1952) Sheb Wooley; *Sitting Bull* (1954) Douglas Kennedy; *Tonka* (1958) Britt Lomond; *The Great Sioux Massacre* (1965) Philip Carey; *The Plainsman* (1966) Leslie Nielsen; *Custer of the West* (1967) Robert Shaw; *Little Big Man* (1971) Richard Mulligan; *Custer* (1967 TV series) by Wayne Mauder; and *The Court Martial of George Armstrong Custer* (1977 TV) James Olson.

Cvetic, Matt

FBI agent who posed as a Communist in order to infiltrate and spy on the party for the U.S. government during the late 1940s. He was portrayed by Frank Lovejoy in the 1951 movie *I Was a Communist for the FBI* and by Dana Andrews in the radio series of the same name.

Cyclops

Coyote Bus Lines' nuclear-powered 106-foot-long bus, using 32 Goodyear tires, in the 1977 movie *The Big Bus*.

Cynara

The poem by Ernest Dowson that suggested both the title of Margaret Mitchell's novel *Gone with the Wind* and the 1948 Cole Porter song "Always True to You in My Fashion."

Czar, The
 Nickname of Will H. Hays, who headed the MPPDA.* He had previously been U.S. postmaster general. Hays was portrayed in the 1979 movie *Hughes and Harlow: Angels in Hell* by Royal Dano.

---

*Motion Picture Producers and Distributors of America, founded in 1922.

D

DD181

U.S. Navy destroyer commanded by Capt. Dan Talbot (John Gavin) in the 1965 TV series *Convoy*.

DLR39019

License plate number of the gold-colored Cadillac in the 1956 movie *The Solid Gold Cadillac*.

Dagat

Carter Primus's (Robert Brown) oceangoing research vessel in the TV series *Primus*.

Daily Worker, The

Official Communist newspaper sold in the United States.

Dairyland School

Chowchilla, California, school whose bus, with its driver, Frank "Edward" Ray, and 26 children, was kidnapped on July 15, 1976. The license number of the bus was 192277.

Daisy

("Bicycle Built for Two") Song that Dr. Langley taught the computer, HAL 9000, to "sing" in the 1968 movie *2001: A Space Odyssey*.

Daisy Hawkins

Original title of the Beatles' hit (Lennon-McCartney composition) "Eleanor Rigby."

Dale, Esther

Pseudonym under which Elaine May wrote the screenplay for the 1971 movie *Such Good Friends*.

Daley, Richard

(1902–1976) Hard-line mayor of Chicago. He was portrayed in the 1978 TV movie *King* by Patrick Hines.

Dalton Brothers

Notorious band of western outlaws who were the cousins of the famed Younger brothers. Bob and Grat were killed on October 5, 1892, at Coffeyville, Kansas, when the gang attempted to rob two banks. Movie portrayals; *When the Daltons Rode* (1940) Bob (Broderick Crawford), Emmett (Frank Albertson), Grat (Brian Donlevy), Ben (Stuart Erwin); *The Daltons Ride Again* (1945) Bob (Kent Taylor), Emmett (Alan Curtis), Grat (Lon Chaney, Jr.), Ben (Noah Berry Jr.); *Badman's Territory* (1946) Bob (Steve Brodie), Grat (Phil Warren), Bill (William Moss); *The Cimarron Kid* (1952) Bob (Noah Beery, Jr.,), Emmett (Rand Brooks), Grat (Palmer Lee), Will (William Reynolds); *Montana Belle* (1952) Bob (Scott Brady), Emmett (Ray Teal); *Jesse James vs. the Daltons* (1954) Bob (James Griffith), Emmett (William Tannen), Grat (John Cliff), Bill (Bill Phipps); and *Belle Starr* (1980 TV) Bob (Jesse Vint), Grat (Alan Vint). In movies Bill, Ben, and Will are the names variously given to the youngest brother, who actually never rode with the gang.

Dalton, Emmett

(1871–1937) Lone survivor of the Dalton brothers' raid on Coffeyville, Kansas, October 5, 1892. After being wounded and spending time in jail, Emmett Dalton starred in several silent films and portrayed himself in the 1918 film *Beyond the Law.* Emmett was portrayed in movies by: *When the Daltons Rode* (1940) Frank Albertson; *The Daltons Ride Again* (1945) Alan Curtis; *The Cimarron Kid* (1952) Rand Brooks; *Montana Belle* (1952) Ray Teal; and *Jesse James vs. the Daltons* (1954) William Tannen.

Damien, Father

François de Veuster (1840–1889) Belgian Catholic missionary who helped the patients at the leper colony on the Hawaiian island of Molokai from 1873 until he died of leprosy in 1889. He was portrayed in the movie *No Greater Love* by Tom Neal and in the 1980 TV movie *Father Damien* by Ken Howard.*

Dana, Richard Henry

(1815–1882) American lawyer and author who in 1840 wrote the autobiographical novel *Two Years Before the Mast.* Dana was portrayed in the 1946 movie by Brian Donlevy.

Dancer

Secret Service code name for First Lady Rosalyn Carter.

Dancer

Sonny Hooper's (Bert Reynolds) beer-drinking horse in the 1979 movie *Hooper.*

Dancing Lollipops

Group of little girls who once danced at the White House for Vice President

---

*Ken Howard replaced David Janssen, who died after 3 days of shooting.

Nixon. One of these girls was Lynette Fromme, who in 1975 attempted to assassinate President Ford.

Danger

Fortune of Brad Runyon (J. Scott Smart) on the radio series *The Fat Man*.

Dangers of Dracula, The

Silent movie starring Esme Gray that Don Lockwood (Gene Kelly) and Cosmo Brown (Donald O'Connor) attended as boys in the 1952 movie *Singin' in the Rain*.

Daniel Webster

Bret Harte's (John Carradine) jumping frog that was filled with buckshot in the 1941 movie *The Adventures of Mark Twain*.

Danny Boy

Pigeon of Joey Doyle, found by Terry Malloy (Marlon Brando) after Doyle "fell" off a building in the 1954 movie *On the Waterfront*.

Danny Danger

Private eye played in comedy skits by Flip Wilson.

Danny's

Quincy's (Jack Klugman) favorite restaurant in the TV series *Quincy*.

Dardanella

Song performed in the following movies: *Baby Face* (1933); *Stella Dallas* (1934); and *Oh You Beautiful Doll* (1949). Song lyrics by Fred Fisher, music by Felix Bernard and Johnny S. Black.

Daredevil

Brom Bones' black stallion in the 1949 cartoon *Legend of Sleepy Hollow*.

Daredevil Jack

1920 movie serial starring boxer Jack Dempsey.

Daring Young Man on the Flying Trapeze, The

Song that the Atlantic Greyhound bus riders sang in the 1934 movie *It Happened One Night*.

Dark Star

Only horse to ever beat Native Dancer. In the 1953 Kentucky Derby Native Dancer lost to Dark Star, his only loss in 22 races.

Dark Tower, The

Play by Alexander Woollcott and George S. Kaufman in which Richard Nixon and Pat Ryan both acted in the 1938 season of the Whittier Community Players. Nixon played Barry Jones and Pat played Daphne Martin. It was while performing in this play that the couple first met.

Dark Victory

1939 movie starring Bette Davis and George Brent with Ronald Reagan. It was the movie being shown in a theater in the 1976 movie *Baby Blue Marine*. *Dark Victory* was remade in 1976 for TV with Elizabeth Montgomery and Anthony Hopkins in the Davis and Brent parts.

Darling Nellie Gray

Opening theme song of the radio series *Just Plain Bill*. The closing theme was "Polly Wolly Doodle."

Darrow, Clarence Seward

(1857–1938) Famous American trial lawyer who never attended law school. His most famous clients were: Eugene V. Debs (1894), Nathan Leopold and Richard Loeb (1924), John Scopes (1925), and the Scottsboro Boys (1932). Darrow was portrayed loosely in two movies: *Compulsion* (1959) Orson Welles (as Jonathan Wilk); and *Inherit the Wind* (1960) Spencer Tracy (as Henry Drummond). Henry Fonda portrayed him in a TV special, *IBM Presents Clarence Darrow* (1974).

Darth Vader

Dark Lord of the Sith and father of Luke Skywalker, played in the movies *Star Wars* (1977) and *The Empire Strikes Back* (1980) by 6-foot 7-inch David Prowse.* Vader's voice was that of James Earl Jones.

Dash, Sam

Senate Watergate Committee's chief counsel. He was portrayed in the 1979 TV miniseries *Blind Ambition* by David Sheiner.

Daughter of the Gods

Movie in which Annette Kellerman performed the first nude scene in films, on October 15, 1916.

Davanna

Home planet of the alien (Paul Birch) in the 1958 movie *Not of This Earth*.

Davenport III, Ormus W.

36-year-old Washington, D.C., patrolman who in 1979 underwent a sex-change operation and became Policewoman Bonnie Davenport.

Davenport, Willie

Black athlete who won a Gold Medal in the 110-meter-high hurdles in the 1968 Olympics. He was the only black American athlete to participate in the United States–boycotted Winter Olympics at Moscow (1980): he entered the four-man bobsled.

David

Italy's equivalent of the Oscar.

David "Lucky" Star

Super-intelligent officer of the Council of Science in sci-fi novels by Paul French (a/k/a Isaac Asimov).

Davies, Joseph Edward

(1876–1958) American lawyer and diplomat. From 1936 to 1938 he served as U.S. ambassador to Russia, and in 1941 he published an account of his time

---

*British weightlifting champion (1962–1964).

in Russia called *Mission to Moscow*. Davies was portrayed in the 1943 movie *Mission to Moscow* by Walter Huston.

Davis, Gary
Stunt man who performed the motorcycle stunts for Evel Knievel in the 1977 movie *Viva Knievel*.

Davis, Jefferson
(1808–1889) President of the Confederate States of America. The First Lady of the Confederacy was Varina Davis. On October 17, 1978, President Carter restored Jefferson Davis's American citizenship. Movie portrayals: *Virginia City* (1940) Charles Middleton; and *Santa Fe Trail* (1940) Erville Alderson.

Dawg
Flagston family dog in the comic strip *Hi and Lois*.

Daybreak
1968 autobiography of folk singer and political activist Joan Baez.

Day, Doris
American actress and singer (born Doris Kappelhoff on April 3, 1924). Her four husbands were Al Jordan (1941–1943); George Weilder (1946–1949); Martin Melcher (1951–1968); and Barry Comden (1976–   ). She was loosely portrayed by Liza Minnelli in the 1977 movie *New York, New York*. Doris Day is mentioned by name in the movies *Grease* (1978) and *The Mirror Crack'd* (1980).

Day the Yankees Lost the Pennant, The
Novel by George Abbott and Douglass Wallop upon which the 1955 Broadway play and 1958 movie *Damn Yankees* were based.

Dayton, Ohio
Hometown of George and Gwen Kellerman (Jack Lemmon and Sandy Dennis) in Neil Simon's 1970 movie *The Out-of-Towners*, which is about the mishaps of a couple who arrive in New York to find that their reservations at the Waldorf-Astoria have been canceled.

Deacon
Secret Service code name for President Jimmy Carter.

Deacon Dan
Nickname of NFL player Dan Towler.

Dean, John W.
White House counsel to President Richard Nixon. Dean was portrayed in the 1979 TV miniseries *Blind Ambition* by Martin Sheen; his wife, Maureen, was played by Theresa Russell.

Dean Moriarty
Central figure in Jack Kerouac's 1955 novel *On the Road*. The character was based on Kerouac's close friend Neal Cassady.

Dear Mr. Gable
Song that the young Judy Garland sang to actor Clark Gable at his 36th

birthday party in the MGM commissary. She sang it to the tune of "You Made Me Love You." Her performance so impressed Louis B. Mayer that he had Judy do the song in the 1937 movie *Broadway Melody of 1938*.

Death to the Fascist insect that preys upon the life of the people
Slogan of the SLA (Symbionese Liberation Army), which kidnapped heiress Patty Hearst.

Deathtrap
Movie being shown in the theater outside of which the bum Navin R. Johnson (Steve Martin) recounts his life story in the 1979 film *The Jerk*.

December 22, 1932
Date on the newspaper held by a newsboy in a photograph that became the key clue in the 1947 movie *Calling Northside 777*.

December 13, 1941
Date of the action in the 1979 movie *1941*.

De Gaulle, Charles
(1890–1979) 6-foot 4-inch general and president of France (1945–1946, 1959–1969). He portrayed by Vernon Dobtcheff in the 1979 TV mini-series *Ike*.

Deep Throat
Washington Post reporter Carl Woodward's name for his secret source during the Watergate investigation. Woodward met with him in the garage of a building.* In the 1976 movie *All the President's Men* Deep Throat was portrayed by Hal Holbrook.

Dejah Thoris
Princess of Mars, wife of Earthman John Carter, in Edgar Rice Burroughs' John Carter series.

Delilah
Philistine woman who deprived Samson of his strength when she had someone cut off his hair. Delilah was portrayed in the 1949 movie *Samson and Delilah* by Hedy Lamarr.

Del Mar Track
Horserace track near San Diego, California, founded in 1937 by Bing Crosby and Pat O'Brien. Each day the song "Where the Surf Meets the Turf," sung by Bing Crosby, was played.

Delomica
First railroad dining car in the United States, put into service in 1868.

Dempsey, Jack Kelly
(1862–1895) Professional prizefighter nicknamed "the Nonpareil." He was both welterweight and middleweight champion from 1883 to 1895. He was

---

*In H. R. Haldeman's book *The Ends of Power* Deep Throat is identified as Fred Fielding.

the only welter/middleweight champ to have the same name as a heavyweight champion.

Denison University
College in Granville, Ohio, attended by Mary Worth (comic strip).

Denton, Cmd. Jeremiah
U.S. Navy fighter pilot who was captured by the North Vietnamese. In 1966, while his "confession" was being filmed, Denton blinked his eyes in Morse Code for the word "torture." He was portrayed in the 1979 TV movie *When Hell Was in Session* by Hal Holbrook. In 1980 he was elected as Alabama's first Republican senator since 1879 (also its first Catholic Senator).

De Paul, St. Vincent
(1581–1660). French priest who helped the needy and sick by founding hospitals in Paris. He was portrayed in the 1947 movie *Monsieur Vincent* by Pierre Fresnay.

Derek, John
Hollywood actor (born Derek Harris) who has been married to three Hollywood beauties: Ursula Andress (1957–1966), Linda Evans (1969–1974), and Bo Derek (born Mary Collins) (1977–   ). The four of them are the best of friends. John Derek photographed all three of his wives for *Playboy* magazine. Derek's first wife was Patricia Behrs (1950–1955).

Derrick Dolls
Cheerleaders of the Houston Oilers football team.

Deserted Mansions
Theme song of the TV soap opera *One Man's Family*.

Desert Hawk
1950 movie in which Jackie Gleason appeared. In an episode of the TV series *The Honeymooners* the Kramdens and the Nortons went to see this film, while in the theater the Nortons won a TV set.

Desert Inn
Las Vegas hotel/casino where Howard Hughes resided from 1966–1976. He rarely left his penthouse apartment.

Desert Palm Motel
Setting in Palm Springs, California, of the TV series *Happy*.

Desilu
Desi Arnaz and Lucille Ball's 34-foot cabin cruiser during their marriage. It was also the name of the couple's production company.

Destiny Waltz
Original theme song (until 1941) of the radio series *One Man's Family*. The later theme song was "Patricia."

DeSylva, Buddy
(1899–1950) Composer who wrote with the song-writing team of Henderson-DeSylva-Brown. He collaborated on such songs as "April Showers" and

"Somebody Loves Me." DeSylva once headed Paramount Pictures. He was portrayed in the 1956 movie *The Best Things in Life Are Free* by Gordon MacRae.

Detective Chano Amenguale

Puerto Rican police officer played by Gregory Sierra in the TV series *Barney Miller.*

Detective Nick Yemana

Oriental police officer played by Jack Soo in the TV series *Barney Miller.*

Detective Phil Fish

Aging police officer played by Abe Vigoda in the TV series *Barney Miller,* and later in his own series *Fish.*

Detective Ron Harris

Wisecracking police officer played by Ron Glass in the TV series *Barney Miller.*

Detective Stanley Taduce "Wojo" Wojohowicz

Polish police officer (Badge No. 549321) played by Maxwell Gail in the TV series *Barney Miller.*

Detective Stuart Bailey

College professor turned private eye played by Efrem Zimbalist, Jr., in the TV series *77 Sunset Strip.* Zimbalist first played the role in an episode of the TV series *Conflict.*

Detective Trace Mayne

Nashville police officer played by Jerry Reed in the short-lived TV series *Nashville 99.*

Detroit

Fitzpatrick family dog in the TV series *The Fitzpatricks.*

Devil

Mr. Hobbs, Lucifer, Satan, Old Nick, Mr. Scratch, Beezlebub (*Lord of the Flies*). Movie portrayals: *The Sorrows of Satin* (1926) Adolphe Menjou; *King of Kings* (1927) Alan Brooks; *All That Money Can Buy* (1941) Walter Huston as Mr. Scratch; *The Devil With Hitler* (1942) Alan Mowbray; *Cabin in the Sky* (1943) Rex Ingram; *Heaven Can Wait* (1943) Laird Cregar; *Angel on My Shoulder* (1946) Claude Rains; *Alias Nick Beal* (1949) Ray Milland; *Meet Mr. Lucifer* (1953) Stanley Holloway; *The Story of Mankind* (1957) Vincent Price; *Damn Yankees* (1958) Ray Walston as Applegate; *The Devil's Eye* (1960) Stig Järrel; *The Greatest Story Ever Told* (1965) Donald Pleasance; *Bedazzled* (1967) Peter Cook; *The Devil in Love* (1968) Vittorio Gassman; *Tales from the Crypt* (1972) Ralph Richardson; *Poor Devil* (1972 TV) Christopher Lee; *The Devil's Daughter* (1972 TV) Joseph Cotten: *Satan's School for Girls* (1973 TV) Roy Thinnes; *A Year at the Top* (1977 TV) Gabriel Dell as Frederick J. Hanover, the son of Satan; *Angel on My Shoulder* (1980 TV) Richard Kiley; *The Devil and Max Devlin* (1980 TV) Bill Cosby; *Wholly*

Moses (1980) John Ritter; TV series *Soap,* voice of Tim McIntire; and TV series *Fantasy Island,* voice of Roddy McDowall.

Devotions upon Emergent Occasions

Series of meditations by John Donne, one of which, Meditation XVII, contains two famous phrases that were used as movie titles: *No Man Is an Island* (1962 movie directed by John Monks) and *For Whom the Bell Tolls* (1943 movie directed by Sam Wood, based on the novel by Ernest Hemingway).

Dewey High School

Modesto high school attended by the teenagers in the 1973 movie *American Graffiti.* Curt's (Richard Dreyfuss) locker number was 2127.

Dewice Cab Co.

Taxicab that crashed through the gates of a Georgetown house after being attacked by locusts in the 1977 movie *Exorcist II: The Heretic.* It was a Checker automobile.

De Witt Clinton

Bronx high school attended by both Neil Simon (Class of '44) and Robert Klein (Class of '58). James Baldwin once served as the editor of the school's newspaper, *The Magpie.*

Dexter Lake Café

All-black club where Otis Day and the Knights were performing when members of the Delta fraternity stopped there to have a drink in the 1978 movie *Animal House.*

DIamond 7-5044

Phone number used to call disc jockey Wolfman Jack to request a song dedication in the 1973 movie *American Graffiti.*

Diamond Horseshoe

Billy Rose's famed New York City nightclub where the young Gene Kelly was dance director and fledgling actress Betsy Blair was a chorus girl. It was featured in the 1945 Betty Grable movie *Diamond Horseshoe.*

Diamond, "Legs"

(1896–1931) American racketeer John Thomas Diamond (born John T. Noland). His last words were: "The bullet hasn't been made that can kill me." He was portrayed in the movies twice by Ray Danton: *The Rise and Fall of Legs Diamond* (1960) and *Portrait of a Mobster* (1961).

Diana Prince

Assumed identity of Wonder Woman (whose real name is also Diana). The real Diana Prince was an Army nurse who became Mrs. Daniel White upon her marriage.

Dice

Pinto horse that Lewt McCanles (Gregory Peck) gave to Pearl Chavez (Jennifer Jones) in the 1946 movie *Duel in the Sun.* Dice was the horse's actual name. Jean Arthur previously rode Dice in the 1940 movie *Arizona.*

Dick
> Spaniel mascot of the naval vessel *USS Constitution* in 1840.

Dick and Dora Charleston
> Husband-and-wife detective team played by David Niven and Maggie Smith in the 1976 movie *Murder by Death*.

Dickerrods
> Yard markers used in the defunct World Football League.

Dickey, Bill
> Catcher for the New York Yankees who served briefly as their manager. He became a member of Baseball's Hall of Fame. He portrayed himself twice in the movies; *The Pride of the Yankees* (1942); and *The Stratton Story* (1949).

Dickinson, Charles
> Man killed by Andrew Jackson in a sword fighting duel on June 5, 1806.

Dick Van Dyke Show, The
> TV series starring Dick Van Dyke and Mary Tyler Moore that Jerry Landers (John Denver) was watching when God (George Burns) came into his apartment (Room 270) in the 1978 movie *Oh God!*

Dietrich, Noah
> Howard Hughes's second-in-command for 32 years. Dietrich was portrayed in the 1977 TV movie *The Amazing Howard Hughes* by Ed Flanders.

Different Worlds
> Theme song of the TV series *Angie*, sung by Maureen McGovern.

Digger
> Butler family's pet dog on the cartoon TV series *Valley of the Dinosaurs*.

Dignity, always, dignity
> Don Lockwood's (Gene Kelly) personal motto, taught to him by his parents, in the 1952 movie *Singin' in the Rain*.

Dike Bridge
> Chappaquiddick Island bridge off which Edward Kennedy drove his Oldsmobile on July 8, 1969. The accident killed his secretary, Mary Jo Kopechne.

Dilly Dilly
> Subtitle of the 1948 song "Lavender Blue."

Dinah
> Audition song sung by Frances Rose Shore on New York radio station WNEW in 1940. She adopted the song title for her stage name, Dinah Shore.

Dinah Shore Show
> TV series on which Loretta Haggar (Mary Kaye Place) made her controversial statement about the Jews "crucifying our Lord" in the TV series *Mary Hartman, Mary Hartman*. It was also the TV series on which Jerry Landers (John Denver) appeared in the 1977 movie *Oh, God!*

Dinucci, Kim
    18-year-old Oroville, California, waitress to whom Richard Burton gave a
    $450 ring while he was filming the movie *The Klansman* (1974).
Dirty Dozen, The
    Indianapolis street gang led by John Dillinger in his youth.
Dirty Shame Saloon
    Bar in the western town of Sawbuck Pass run by Mike (Jane Russell) in the
    1952 movie *Son of Paleface*.
Disco Volante
    SPECTRE's yacht (registered in Panama), commanded by Largo, in the 1965
    movie *Thunderball*. For high-speed chases the yacht could jettison the rear
    half and become a hydrofoil.
Discovery of Buck Hammer, The
    Record album of the boogie-woogie music of a little known dead Mississippi
    artist called Buck Hammer. The album got rave reviews from many critics,
    though it was a hoax—Steve Allen was actually the piano player on the
    album.
Disraeli, Benjamin
    (1804–1881) Prime minister of Great Britain and author of a number of
    novels. Portrayals: *Disraeli* (1929) George Arliss; *Suez* (1938) Miles Mander;
    The Prime Minister (1941) John Gielgud; *The Mudlark* (1950) Alec Guinness;
    Edward the King (1979 TV miniseries) John Gielgud; and *Disraeli: Portrait
    of a Romantic* (1980 TV miniseries) Ian McShane.
District Attorney Frank Scalon
    Only man besides Kato who knows Britt Reid's secret identity as "The Green
    Hornet." He was played in the 1966 TV series by Walter Brooke.
Divine Miss M
    Nickname of singer Bette Midler.
Dixie Bible Company
    Company for which Moses Pray (played by Ryan O'Neal in the 1973 movie
    and by Christopher Connelly in TV series *Paper Moon*) works as a traveling
    salesman.
Dixie Stars
    Pro football team formed by Brick (Paul Newman) in the 1958 movie *Cat on
    a Hot Tin Roof*.
Dr. Anthony "Tony" Menzies
    Chief surgeon (played by Gregory Sierra) at the Adult Emergency Services in
    New York City in the TV series *A.E.S. Hudson Street*.
Dr. Bob
    Surgeon played by Rowlf (Jim Henson's voice) in the TV series *The Muppet
    Show*.

Dr. Demento
Knowledgeable disc jockey of the 1970s who played novelty records of all decades. His real name is Barry Hansen.

Dr. Gilbert Winfield
Dying pediatrician at Blair General Hospital played by Robert Young in an episode of the TV series *Dr. Kildare.*

Dr. Helena Russell
Head medical officer at Moonbase Alpha in the TV series *Space: 1999.* She was played by Barbara Bain.

Dr. Joseph Werner
Chief of staff at Cedars Hospital in the TV soap *The Guiding Light,* played by Anthony Call, who during his collegiate days was quarterback for the University of Pennsylvania.

Dr. Henry Gordon
Physician who amputated the legs of Drake McHugh (Ronald Reagan) in the 1941 movie *King's Row.* He was played by Charles Coburn.

Dr. Lee Wong How
Chinese doctor (played by Keye Luke) who practiced at Blair General Hospital in the *Dr. Kildare* movies.

Dr. Mandrake Kirby
Physician mentioned by Johnny Carson in comedy monologues.

Dr. Mark Piper
Chief medical officer on board the *USS Enterprise* before Dr. Leonard McCoy in the TV series *Star Trek.* Piper was played by Paul Fix.

Dr. Miguelito Loveless
(1848–1880) Enemy agent of the U.S. government, played by Michael Dunn, in the TV series *The Wild, Wild West.* Miguelito Lovelace, Jr., was played by Paul Williams in the 1979 TV movie *Wild Wild West Revisited.*

Dr. Richard Harpo Thorndyke
Director of the Psycho-Neurotic Institute for the Very, *Very* Nervous who won a Nobel Prize at age 42, played by Mel Brooks in the 1978 movie *High Anxiety.*

Dr. Rudy Wells
Surgeon who put Steve Austin and Jamie Sommers back together again, with bionics, in the TV series *The Six Million Dollar Man* and *The Bionic Woman.* Dr. Wells was played by Alan Oppenheimer and, in the last* season, by Martin E. Brooks.

Dr. Steven Hardy
Head of internal medicine at General Hospital in the TV soap *General Hospital.* Hardy is played by John Beradino, who before becoming an actor

---

*By Martin Balsam in the pilot movie.

played baseball (1939–1952) with the St. Louis Browns, Pittsburgh Pirates, and the World Series–winning 1948 Cleveland Indians. His lifetime batting average for 912 games was .249.

Dr. Strange
Master of the Mystic Arts (a/k/a Master of Black Magic)—the secret identity of onetime neurosurgeon, Dr. Stephen Strange, who is Earth's defender against occult menaces. His arch-enemy is Baron Mordo. Dr. Strange was created by Stan Lee and Steve Ditko and made his debut in comics: *Strange Tales* No. 110. The character was played by Peter Hooten in the 1978 TV movie *Dr. Strange*.

Dr. Teeth
Rock 'n' roll band on the TV series *The Muppet Show.* Members: Dr. Teeth—piano (voice: Jim Henson); Animal—drummer (voice: Frank Oz); Zoot—trumpet (voice: Dave Goelz); Janis—Guitar (voice: Frank Oz); and Sgt. Floyd Pepper—Bass (voice: Jerry Nelson).

Dr. Theodore Bassett
Psychiatrist played by Wendell Corey in the TV series *The Eleventh Hour.*

Dr. Theopolis
Round robot brain that Twiki often carries around his neck in the movie/TV series *Buck Rogers in the 25th Century.* The voice is that of Eric Servor.

Dr. Thomas Reynolds
Identity of Ramar—White Witch Doctor, played on the TV series *Ramar of the Jungle* by Jon Hall.

Dr. Who
750-year-old Time Lord of the planet Gallifrey who took the shape of a human. He was played on TV by Tom Baker, Jon Pertwee, William Hartnell, Peter Cushing, and Patrick Throughton. Cushing also played the character twice in the movies: *Dr. Who and the Daleks* (1965) and *Invasion Earth 2150 A.D.* (1966).

Dr. Winston O'Boogie
Pseudonym of singer John Ono Lennon.

Dodger Stadium
Location where the Fleetwood Mac song "Tusk" was recorded live with the U.S.C. Trojan Marching Band in 1979.

Dollar
Horse ridden in western movies by Joel McCrea (1950–1962). Doris Day also rode him in the 1953 movie *Calamity Jane*.

Dolly (Gallagher) Levi
Heroine of Thornton Wilder's play *The Matchmaker* (1938). Movie portrayals: *The Matchmaker* (1958) Shirley Booth; and *Hello Dolly!* (1969) Barbra Streisand. Carol Channing (1964), Pearl Bailey (1967), Ethel Merman (1970), and other actresses played the part of Dolly in the Broadway musical *Hello*

Dolly! The original title of Wilder's play was *The Merchant of Yonkers*. He wrote the role of Dolly for actress Ruth Gordon, who declined the part in 1938 but did play it in 1954.

Dolly: A Damned Exasperating Woman
Original title of the musical play *Hello Dolly!* then *Call On Dolly*, then finally *Hello Dolly!* The play opened with Carol Channing instead, and some years later Ethel Merman took over the role on Broadway.

Do Lord
Single record released in 1954 by the Four Girls. The vocalists were: Connie Haynes, Jane Russell, Beryl Davis, and Della Russell.

Domino
Actual name of the horse Rory Calhoun rode in the TV series *The Texan*.

Domino
Jeff Miller's (Tommy Rettig) pet colt in the TV series *Lassie*.

Dom Pérignon
Champagne preferred by superspy James Bond.

Don Camillo
Catholic priest hero of books by Giovanni Guareschi. He was played in the 1953 movie *Little World of Don Camillo* by Fernandel (English-language version directed and narrated by Orson Welles).

Donerail
Racehorse that on May 10, 1913, won the Kentucky Derby against odds of 91 to 1.

Don Juan
Romantic character created by novelist Gabriel Telleg. He is also the main character of the opera *Don Giovanni* (1787) by Mozart and the subject of the poem *Don Juan* by Lord Byron. Movie portrayals: *Don Juan* (1927) John Barrymore (Yvonne Day at age 5 and Philippe De Lacey at age 10); *The Private Life of Don Juan* (1934) Douglas Fairbanks, Sr.; *Adventures of Don Juan* (1948) Errol Flynn; and *The Devil's Eye* (1960) Jarl Kulle.

Don Juan
Movie Ricky Ricardo (Desi Arnaz) went to Hollywood in 1955 to film, only to have MGM cancel the movie, in the TV series *I Love Lucy*.

Don Juan
Pepe's (Cantinflas) white stallion in the 1960 movie *Pepe*.

Don Pedro O'Sullivan
Swedish man whom the Lone Ranger disguises himself as in order to obtain information in the TV series *The Lone Ranger*.

Donna Diana Overture
Classical piece by Von Reznicek that became the theme song of the radio series *Challenge of the Yukon*.

Donnie
Actress Ann Sothern's Scottie dog that appeared in the 1944 movie *Maisie Goes to Reno* with his mistress.

Donovan, Colleen M.
U.S. Army specialist 4 who posed nude for *Playboy* magazine in November 1979. Her dog tags read 987-65-4320 O-POS.

Donovan, William "Wild Bill"
(1883–1959) Only American to win all four of his country's highest decorations; Congressional Medal of Honor, Distinguished Service Cross, Distinguished Service Medal, and National Security Medal. Donovan was the organizer of the OSS (Office of Strategic Services) in 1942. He was portrayed in the 1940 movie *The Fighting 69th* by George Brent, and in the 1979 TV miniseries *A Man Called Intrepid* by Dick O'Neill.

Don't Do It
Final song of the Band's last concert at Winterland in San Francisco (2:00 a.m., Thanksgiving 1976). It was filmed for the 1978 movie *The Last Waltz*.

Don't Give Up the Ship
Official song of the U.S. Naval Academy, written by Al Dubin and Harry Warren. It was introduced by Dick Powell in the 1935 movie *Shipmates Forever*.

Don't Sit Under the Apple Tree
Song that Gus (William Bendix) sang in a lifeboat accompanied on flute by Joe (Canada Lee) in the 1943 movie *Lifeboat*.

Dooley
Rich boyfriend who wears tan shoes with pink shoelaces in the 1959 song "Pink Shoe Laces" recorded by Dodie Stevens (born Geraldine Ann Pasquale).

Doolittle, James Harold
American Army officer and aviator. He was the first pilot to cross the United States in less than 24 hours; first to perform an outside loop; first man to fly over the Andes solo (he broke both his ankles the day before when he fell out of a window); first person to graduate from MIT with a doctorate in aeronautical engineering. Doolittle flew the first totally instrumental flight (September 24, 1929). In 1931 he won the Bendix trophy. In 1942 he led the famous bombing raid on Tokyo, for which he won the Congressional Medal of Honor. He was portrayed in the 1947 movie *Thirty Seconds Over Tokyo* by Spencer Tracy.

Dorsey Brothers
Tommy and Jimmy, successful orchestra leaders who played themselves in the 1947 movie *The Fabulous Dorseys*. Tommy Dorsey was portrayed by Bobby Troup in the 1960 movie *The Gene Krupa Story*, and by William Tole in the 1977 movie *New York, New York*.

Doss, Desmond T.
World War II soldier and conscientious objector who was awarded the Congressional Medal of Honor for his bravery in the medical corps.

Double Bar M Ranch
Setting of the 1956 TV series *The Gabby Hayes Show*.

Double Eagle II
First balloon (N50DE) to successfully cross the Atlantic Ocean (3,200 miles), manned by Americans Ben Abruzzo, Maxie Anderson, and Larry Newman. They arrived in France at 7:50 p.m. on August 17, 1978. That night Larry Newman and his wife, Sharon, slept in the same bed (single) that Charles Lindbergh slept in after completing his solo flight in 1927.

Douglas, Jennie
First female worker hired by the federal government (1862). She cut and trimmed minted currency.

Douglas, Stephen Arnold
(1813–1861) American politician who in 1858 participated in a series of debates with Abraham Lincoln on slavery. Movie portrayals: *Abraham Lincoln* (1930) E. Alyn Warren; and *Abe Lincoln in Illinois* (1940) Gene Lockhart.

Dous
Only 4 words in the English language end in the 4 letters *dous:* hazardous, horrendous, stupendous, tremendous.

Dove
24-foot sloop in which Robin Lee Graham of California made a solo voyage around the world. He started on July 27, 1965, and completed the voyage on April 30, 1970. He was 16 years old when he began. Graham was portrayed by Joseph Bottoms in the 1974 movie *The Dove*.

Dove, Billie
American actress of the 1920s (born Lilian Bohny in 1900). She was portrayed in the 1977 TV movie *The Amazing Howard Hughes* by Lee Purcell.

Dowding, Sir Hugh Caswall
(1882–1970) British air chief marshal. He headed the RAF fighter command from 1936 to 1940. Dowding was portrayed in the 1969 movie *Battle of Britain* by Laurence Olivier.

Doyle, Jimmy
Only boxer to die during a championship fight. He died in the ring on June 24, 1947, while fighting welterweight champion "Sugar" Ray Robinson.

Doyle, John Joseph
Baseball's first pinch hitter when, on June 7, 1892, he hit a single.

Draconia
Emperor Draco's flagship in the 1979 movie *Buck Rogers in the 25th Century.*

Dragon Prep
Ollie's alma mater in the TV series *Kukla, Fran and Ollie.*

Dragonette, USS
Submarine to which actor Tony Curtis was assigned in the South Pacific during World War II. It was while watching numerous Cary Grant films on board that Curtis learned to imitate Grant's speaking voice (which he used in the 1959 movie *Some Like It Hot*). Ironically, in 1959 Tony Curtis and Cary Grant appeared together in a film about submarines, *Operation Petticoat.*

Dragoon
Ronald Colman's yacht on which Laurence Olivier and Vivien Leigh spent their honeymoon in August 1940.

Drain No 267
Location in the Los Angeles sewer system where the giant ants are finally destroyed in the 1954 movie *Them.*

Drake, Sir Francis
(1540–1596) English explorer who circumnavigated the globe in his vessel the *Golden Hinde* (1577–1580). Movie portrayals: *Marauders of the Sea* (1962) Terence Morgan; *Mission of the Sea Hawk* (1962) Terence Morgan; *Raiders of the Spanish Main* (1962) Terence Morgan; and *Seven Seas to Calais* (1963) Rod Taylor.

Dream Along With Me
Perry Como's theme song for his TV series.

Dreams Are Made for Children
Theme song of the TV series *The Shirley Temple Storybook.*

Dreamy Blues
Original title of the Duke Ellington hit song "Mood Indigo."

Dreiser, Theodore
(1871–1945) American author and editor. Two of his more popular novels were *Sister Carrie* (1900) and *An American Tragedy* (1925). Dreiser was portrayed in the 1942 movie *My Gal Sal* by Barry Downing.

Dresser, Paul
(1857–1906) songwriter brother of author Theodore Dreiser. The 1923 movie *On the Banks of the Wabash* was inspired by his song. Dresser was portrayed in the 1942 movie *My Gal Sal* by Victor Mature.

Dressler, Marie
(1869–1934) American comedy actress (born Leila Von Koeber). She was portrayed in the 1965 movie *Harlow* by Hermione Baddeley.

Driver, William

Yankee clipper captain who first referred to the Stars and Stripes as "Old Glory."

Drop the gun, Louie

Line never said by Humphrey Bogart in the 1942 movie *Casablanca*. What he did say was, "Not so fast, Louie."

Dual Roles

Movies in which an actor or actress played two different parts. A sampling: *The Man Who Lost Himself* (1941) Brian Aherne; *The Phantom President* (1932) George M. Cohan; *The Palm Beach Story* (1942) Claudette Colbert; *Fahrenheit 451* (1967) Julie Christie; *Dead Ringer* (1964) Bette Davis; *The Dark Mirror* (1946) Olivia de Havilland; *The Scapegoat* (1964) Alec Guinness; *The Man in the Iron Mask* (1939) Louis Hayward; *Here Come the Waves* (1944) Betty Hutton; *Cover Girl* (1944) Gene Kelly; *The Parent Trap* (1961) Haley Mills; *Vertigo* (1958) Kim Novak; *Kissin' Cousins* (1964) Elvis Presley; *Keep Em' Flying* (1941) Martha Raye; *The Whole Town's Talking* (1935) Edward G. Robinson; *Kitty Foyle* (1940) Ginger Rogers; and *Honolulu* (1939) Robert Young.

DuBarry, Mme. Marie

(1746–1793) Mistress of King Louis XV and other French nobles. During the French Revolution she was tried, condemned, and then guillotined. She was portrayed in the 1934 movie *Madame DuBarry* by Dolores Del Rio.

Duchess and Rob Roy

Black Beauty's mother and father in Anna Sewell's 1877 novel *Black Beauty*. Duchess was called Pet.

Duchin, Eddy

(1910–1951) Popular piano player and bandleader of the 1930s. His theme songs were "Bettylou" and "My Twilight Dream." He died of leukemia. His son, Peter Duchin, is today a successful piano player. Eddie Duchin was portrayed in the 1956 movie *The Eddy Duchin Story* by Tyrone Power (piano music by Carmen Cavallaro).

Duchin, Peter

Piano-playing son of Eddy Duchin. He played at the White House wedding of Lynda Johnson to Charles Robb on December 9, 1967. He was portrayed in the 1956 movie *The Eddy Duchin Story* by Mickey Maga at age 5 and by Rex Thompson at age 12.

Dudley

Angel played by Cary Grant in the 1947 movie *The Bishop's Wife*.

Duel

1971 TV movie (based on a short story by Richard Matheson) directed by Steven Speilberg and starring Dennis Weaver. The movie is about a chase between a car and tank truck. In a 1978 episode of *The Incredible Hulk* many of the chase scenes, including the wreck, were taken from this movie.

Dueling Banjos

Theme song of the 1972 movie *Deliverance*. It was composed by Arthur "Guitar Boogie" Smith in the late 1940s and originally called "Feuding Banjos."

Dueling Cavalier, The

Silent movie made by Monumental Pictures, remade as a musical titled *The Dancing Cavalier* and then as the 1952 classic *Singin' in the Rain*.

Duffy, Clinton Truman

Warden of California's oldest prison, San Quentin. His father was a guard and he was born and raised on the prison grounds. He married the daughter of a guard. Duffy served as prison warden from 1941 to 1951. He was portrayed by Paul Kelly* in the 1954 movie *Duffy of San Quentin*.

Dula, Tom

Civil War veteran who was hanged in Statesville, North Carolina, in 1868 for the murder of a young Yankee schoolteacher. While waiting to be hanged, he put his confession down in ballad form. He is the subject of the folk song "Tom Dooley."

Dummar, Melvin

Willard, Utah, gas station operator who claimed that Howard Hughes bequested 1/16th of his estate to him because he had once helped Hughes without knowing who he was. The "Mormon Will" was later determined by a jury to be fake. Melvin Dumar's country western band is called the Night Riders. He was portrayed in the 1980 movie *Melvin and Howard* by Paul LeMat.

Duke and Lightning

Horses ridden by Tim Holt in B westerns. Duke's real name was Strike.

Dukes of Dixieland

First artists to put out a commercial stereo record album. It was released in 1957 by Audio Fidelity. On the flip side of the LP were stereo railroad sounds.

Duncan, Donald F.

Founder of Good Humor Ice Cream who in 1929 began producing Duncan Yo-Yos. At one time he owned the Duncan Parking Meter Co., which manufactured 80 percent of all meters in the United States

Duncan, Isadora

(1878–1927) Famous American dancer. She was killed when her scarf became entangled in the wheel of an automobile in which she was riding.

---

*In the 1920s Paul Kelly spent 2 years and 1 month at San Quentin for the manslaughter of fellow actor Ray Raymond.

Movie portrayals: *Isadora Duncan* (1966) Vivian Pickles; and *Isadora (The Loves of Isadora)* (1969) Vanessa Redgrave.

Dundee, Angelo
Onetime fight manager of Muhammad Ali. He was portrayed in the 1977 movie *The Greatest* by Ernest Borgnine.

Dundee, Vince and Joe
Only two brothers to have held boxing crowns. Vince was middleweight champion in 1933, while Joe earlier held the welterweight title (1927–1929). Vince died of Lou Gehrig's Disease.

Dunnis River
Connecticut town setting of the TV series *Soap*.

Dunphy, Don
Popular fight announcer who broadcast his first fight on June 18, 1941. It was the first heavyweight championship fight between Joe Louis and Billy Conn.

Durante, Jimmy
(1893–1980) American comedian, nicknamed "Schnozzola" because of his large nose, which he had insured for $1,000,000 with Lloyd's of London. He was portrayed in the 1954 movie *The Eddie Cantor Story* by Jackie Barnett.

Durocher, Leo
Baseball manager who was the first person to appear twice as a mystery guest on the TV series *What's My Line* (1951 and 1953).

Dusty
"The Boy Detective" Shield's canine sidekick (comic book series *The Shield*). Dusty was the co-leader of the Boy Buddies with Roy. Debut: *Pep Comic* No. 11 (January 1941).

Dusty John
Hippie-type poet played by Bobby Darin in comedy skits in the TV series *The Bobby Darin Show*.

Dutch Boy Paint
Trademark of the Dutch Boy Paint Company. Bill Bohnert, producer of *Dick Clark's Live Wednesday* TV series, posed for the image of the boy when he was a child.

Dutchman, The
Nickname of NFL player Norm Van Brocklin.

Dying Cowboy, The
Theme song of the radio series *Red Ryder*.

Dynamo
Secret Service code name for Amy Carter.

Dynomutt
The Wonder Dog, Blue Falcon's mechanical pet dog (TV cartoon characters).

8

Lois Lane's lucky number.

8:00

Time shown on traditional bars of Dial soap.

8:00

Time of the Grand Opera Opening on a Community Chest Card (Monopoly game). The holder of the card collects $50 from each player.

11

Number of herbs and spices in Kentucky Fried Chicken.

11:15 p.m.

Time when Henry Stevenson (Burt Lancaster) planned to murder his wife, Leona (Barbara Stanwyck), to coincide with the passing of a train in the 1948 movie *Sorry, Wrong Number.*

18LU13

European license plate number of the 4795-pound Lincoln Continental carrying 120 pounds of concealed heroin in the 1971 movie *The French Connection.*

18½ minutes

Erased stretch of the June 20, 1972, tape of a meeting between President Richard M. Nixon and H. R. Haldeman during the Watergate investigations. Although Nixon's secretary, Rose Mary Woods, testified that she accidentally erased the tape, a panel of experts determined on January 15, 1974, that it required five separate manual erasures to create the gap.

81

Miami Dolphins football jersey number of Shake Tiller (Kris Kristofferson) in the 1977 movie *Semi-Tough.*

83

Number of weapons that can be produced from Derek Flint's (James Coburn) cigarette lighter in the 1966 movie *Our Man Flint*.

85

Bing Crosby's golf score at the La Moraleja Club outside Madrid on October 14, 1977. He was playing with pro golfer Juan Tomas Gandarias, whom he beat with his handicap. After playing 18 holes Crosby dropped dead from a heart attack. He was 73. Only three celebrities were allowed to attend his funeral: Bob Hope, Phil Harris, and Rosemary Clooney.

825 DGI

License plate number of Jerry Landers's (John Denver) Pacer automobile in the 1977 movie *Oh God!*

835 Feet

Elevation of the Kings Row Railroad Station in the 1941 movie *Kings Row*.

898

Number of steps to the top of the Washington Monument.

1815

Lifetime major league hits by Stan Musial for both home games and games on the road, for a total of 3,630.

1818

Date on bottles of Smirnoff Vodka.

1874

Year in which the 1974 movie *Blazing Saddles* was set.

1883

Year in which the 1947 movie *Life With Father* was set.

1885

Year in which the 1979 TV movie *Wild Wild West Revisited* was set.

1896

Year in which Sterling Hayden's novel *Voyage* was set. Also the year in which the 1960 movie *Can-Can* was set.

8411½ Sunset Boulevard

Los Angeles office address of detective Lewis Archer (detective stories).

8618

World record–setting number of points accumulated by Bruce Jenner* to win the Decathlon in the 1976 Olympics. Eighty Six Eighteen is the name of a company founded by Jenner.

86-893

Automobile license number of Maxwell Smart's Red Sunbeam Tiger automobile in the TV series *Get Smart*.

---

*Bruce Jenner is a descendant of Edward Jenner, the British physician who developed the vaccine for smallpox.

835-2239

Tom Corbett's (Bill Bixby) office phone number in the TV series *The Courtship of Eddie's Father.*

873-5261

New York City telephone booth phone number from which Elliot Garfield (Richard Dreyfuss) called his own apartment to talk to Paula McFadden (Marsha Mason) in the 1977 movie *The Goodbye Girl.*

11-25-3978

Month, day, and year that the spacecraft showed on its panel when it landed back on the Earth, 2,031 years after taking off (although the crew was in space only 18 months) in the 1968 movie *Planet of the Apes.*

E-124

Call letters of the airplane in which Laurel and Hardy accidentally flew until the plane crashed and Oliver Hardy was killed in the 1939 movie *The Flying Deuces.*

E.E.F.M.S.

Early Eyeball Fraternal Marching Society, a club to which Philadelphia TV viewers of Ernie Kovacs could belong if they made less than $987,648,001.23 per annum and never slept later than 8:03 a.m. The society's password was "It's Been Real."

EGO 22

California license plate number of Burt Reynolds' Cadillac.

EPIC

End Poverty In California—author Upton Sinclair's platform in the 1934 gubernatorial race in California, which he lost.

Eadie, William F.

Navy lieutenant who rescued Eddie Rickenbacker and his men on November 11, 1942, after they had been adrift in the South Pacific for 21 days.

Eagan, Eddie

Only U.S. athlete to win a Gold Medal in both summer and winter Olympics—in 1920, as a light heavyweight boxer, and in 1932, as a bobsledder. From 1945 to 1951 he served as head of the New York State Athletic Commission.

Eagels, Jeanne

(1894–1929) American actress who was nominated for an Oscar for best actress for the 1928 movie *The Letter.* She was portrayed in the 1957 movie *Jeanne Eagels* by Kim Novak.

Eagle

U.S. Coast Guard's last sailing vessel. The 1961-ton three-mast ship was previously the German vessel *Horst Wessel,* launched in 1936.

Eagle City

Alaskan town setting of the TV series *The Alaskans.*

Eagles
> Spaceships belonging to Moon Base Alpha in the TV series *Space 1999*.

East Side Story
> Original title of the musical play *West Side Story*.

East-West Game
> Name of the Rose Bowl Game until 1923, when the Rose Bowl stadium was built.

Eckford, Elizabeth
> 15-year-old black student who attempted to enter Little Rock Central High School on September 25, 1957, in order to desegregate the school system.

Eclipse
> Vessel on which Philippe Charboneau left Britain on July 6, 1772, to sail to the New World in the novel *The Bastard* by John Jakes.

Eclipse Award
> Annual award presented to outstanding horses and jockeys.

Ecuador
> South American country where Panama hats are made.

Eddy-MacDonald
> Movies in which Nelson Eddy and Jeanette MacDonald appeared together: *Naughty Marietta* (1935); *Rose Marie* (1936); *Maytime* (1937); *The Girl of the Golden West* (1938); *Sweethearts* (1938); *New Moon* (1940); *Bitter Sweet* (1940); and *I Married an Angel* (1942).

Eden, Anthony
> British prime minister from April 6, 1955, to January 9, 1957. He succeeded Winston Churchill. Eden had married Churchill's niece, Clarissa Churchill, in 1952. He was portrayed in the 1943 movie *Mission to Moscow* by Clive Morgan.

Edge of Night, The
> TV soap opera actress Tallulah Bankhead was watching when Harry S Truman called her. When informed that the former president was on the phone, Tallulah told her maid to have him call back, as she didn't want to miss her soap opera. She didn't, he called back. On another occasion, in 1956, Tallulah invited Eleanor Roosevelt to tea, only to hush her up until *The Edge of Night* was over.

Edificia Condemanatus Est
> Motto of Cranepool University in the TV series *L.A.T.E.R.*

Ed the Guard
> Jack Benny's watchman who protected Benny's safe in his basement for over 60 years in the radio series *The Jack Benny Show*. A moat ran around the safe. The combination was RT to 44, LT to 60, TR to 15, LT to 110. Jack Benny's secret password was "A fool and his money are soon parted."

Edwards, Gus

Vaudeville impresario. He was portrayed loosely in the 1939 movie *The Star Maker* by Bing Crosby.

Egbert

(755–839) The first king of England.

Ehrlichman, John D.

Chief domestic-affairs adviser to President Nixon. Ehrlichman's novel *The Company* was the basis for the 1977 TV miniseries *Washington: Behind Closed Doors*.

Eichmann, Adolf

(1906–1962) S.S. administrator of the Nazis' Final Solution (the elimination of European Jews). He was portrayed in the 1961 movie *Operation Eichmann* by Werner Klemperer, in the 1978 TV miniseries *Holocaust* by Tom Bell, and in the 1979 TV movie *The House on Garibaldi Street* by Alfred Burke.

Edgar

What Capt. Jeffrey T. Spaulding (Groucho Marx) claimed his middle initial "T" stood for in the 1930 movie *Animal Crackers*.

Einstein, Albert

(1879–1955) German-born physicist who was awarded the Nobel Prize for physics (1921). He was once offered, but turned down, the presidency of Israel. Einstein was portrayed in the 1946 movie *The Beginning of the End* by Ludwig Stossel, and in the 1979 TV miniseries *A Man Called Intrepid* by Joseph Golland.

Eisenhower, Dwight David

(1890–1969) 34th president of the United States. He was the only president to hold a pilot's license and one of only two presidents to shoot a hole in one* (104-yard hole with a 9 iron on February 1968). Portrayals: *The Long Gray Line* (1958) Harry Carey, Jr.; *The Longest Day* (1962) Henry Grace; *The Francis Gray Powers Story* (1976 TV movie) James Flavin; *Tail Gunner Joe* (1977 TV) Andrew Duggan; *Ike* (1979 TV miniseries) Robert Duval; *Backstairs at the White House* (1979 TV miniseries) Andrew Duggan; and *Churchill and the Generals* (1981 TV) Richard Dysart.

Eisenhower, Mamie

Wife of Dwight D. Eisenhower. Movie portrayals of the first lady: *Ike* (1979 TV miniseries) Bonnie Barlett; and *Backstairs at the White House* (1979 TV miniseries) Barbara Barrie.

El Cid

First Navy mascot goat. He made his first appearance at the 4th Army-Navy football game in 1893, which Navy won 6–4. Successor goats were named

---

*Gerald Ford is the other.

Mike, 3–0 Jack Dalton,* Satan, and Bill I through Bill XX. El Cid had previously been the mascot of the cruiser USS *New York*.

Eldridge, USS

Navy destroyer (DE-173) that supposedly vanished from Norfolk, Virginia, only to reappear in Philadelphia on October 28, 1943 in a secret experiment called the Philadelphia Experiment.

Ele 5430 (1655 meters)

Elevation of Boulder, Colorado, as shown on a sign in the opening scene of the TV series *Mork and Mindy*.

Electro

Hero robot invented by Professor Zog who debuted in *Marvel Mystery Comics* No. 4.

Elektro

Westinghouse's 260-pound 7-foot-tall robot, first exhibited at the New York World Fair in 1939. His electric dog was named Sparko.

Elephant, The

Vessel owned by Tom Tom DeWitt (Ted Bessell) in the TV series *It's a Man's World*.

Elephant Man

Name given to a London-born deformed man, John Merrick, whose skin resembled the hide of an elephant. *The Elephant Man* by Bernard Pomerance, a play based on his life, won a Pulitzer Prize. One of the numerous actors to play the part on the stage was rock star David Bowie. Merrick was portrayed in the 1980 movie *The Elephant Man* by John Hurt.

Elinor M

Nickname of the spaceship (MGP-1B) piloted by Cmd. Christopher "Kit" Draper (Paul Mantee) that landed on Mars in the 1964 movie *Robinson Crusoe on Mars*. Elinor M stood for Elinor McReady, wife of Col. Dan McReady (Adam West), Cmd. Draper's fellow astronaut.

Elizabeth of York

(1465–1503) Queen whose face was the model used for the four queens on standard playing cards.

El Jodo

Brentwood home of Douglas Fairbanks, Jr., and his wife, Joan Crawford. They later changed the name to Cielito Lindo.

Elk Mills

Town setting in the midwestern state of Winnemac in Sinclair Lewis's 1925 novel *Arrowsmith*.

---

*Named for Navy kicker Jack Dalton, who defeated West Point 2 years in a row (1910 and 1911) with a single field goal 3–0.

Ellen B
Tammy Tarleton's (Debbie Watson) houseboat in the TV series *Tammy*.
Ellen Dolen
The Spirit's girlfriend in the comic book series *The Spirit*.
Elliot
Invisible dragon in the 1977 Disney movie *Pete's Dragon*. The voice was that
of Charles Callas.
Elmer
Attorney Melvin Belli's skeleton, which he keeps in his San Francisco office
and uses in certain court cases.
Elmo
Pet dog in the TV cartoon series *The Funky Phantom*.
Elmsville
American hometown of the Day family in the TV cartoon series *Those Are
the Days*.
El Sleezo Café
Toughest, meanest, filthiest pesthole on the face of the earth, where Kermit
the Frog stayed in the 1979 movie *The Muppet Movie*. James Coburn was the
owner, Steve Martin a writer, and Paul Williams a piano player.
Elton Thomas
Pseudonym used by Douglas Fairbanks when he wrote movie scripts.
Elwood P. Dowd
Human friend of Harvey, the 6-foot 3½-inch invisible pooka. Elwood was
played in the 1950 movie *Harvey* (based on the Mary Chase play of the same
name) by James Stewart, and in the TV play *Harvey* on the Dupont Show of the
Month (September 22, 1958) by Art Carney.
Elvis
Hole-in-the-Wall Gang's pet dog in the animated TV series *Butch Cassidy
and the Sundance Kids*.
Elvis has left the building
Announcement made by concert hosts to signify to fans that an Elvis concert
was over.
Embraceable You
Song written by George and Ira Gershwin in 1930. It can be heard in the
following films: *Girl Crazy* (1932); *Girl Crazy* (1943); *Rhapsody in Blue*
(1945); *Humoresque* (1947); *Always Leave Them Laughing* (1949); *An
American in Paris* (1951); *With a Song in My Heart* (1952); and *When the
Boys Meet the Girls* (1965).
Emerac
Computer (called Emmy for short) invented by Richard Summer (Spencer
Tracy) in the 1957 movie *Desk Set*. The computer mockup was later used in
the movies *The Invisible Boy* (1957) and *The Fly* (1958). It then became the

shipboard computer on board the *Seaview* in the TV series *Voyage to the Bottom of the Sea*.

Emerald Club

Wild Honolulu club where Sadie Thompson (Rita Hayworth) once sang in the 1953 movie *Miss Sadie Thompson*.

Emil and Emma Glutz

Names that John Agar and his bride Shirley Temple signed on the hotel register while on their 7-day honeymoon in 1946.

Empty Saddles

Song that Rudy Vallee sang at the funeral of Tom Mix in October 1940.

Emma

Cute little lady who talks to the green grapes, purple grapes, apples, and leaves on the TV *Fruit of the Loom* commercial.

Emmaline Quincy, SS

Capt. John Angel's (George Raft) father's vessel, found abandoned in the 1945 movie *Johnny Angel*. The ship was owned by a New Orleans company, Gustafson Lines.

Empire State University

School attended by Peter Parker in *The Spider Man* comic books.

Empress of Japan

Ship on which 14 players of a U.S. baseball team left for Japan from Vancouver, B.C., on October 20, 1934. The players were: Babe Ruth, Lefty Gomez, Jimmie Foxx, Earl Whitehill, Eric McNair, Earl Averill, Clint Brown, Rabbit Warstler, Bing Miller, Joe Cascarella, Lou Gehrig, Charlie Gehringer, Frank Hayes, and Edmund Miller. Manager Connie Mack was also aboard, as well as Princeton-educated Moe Berg, who spoke a dozen languages and was later believed to have been a spy for the United States on this Japan tour.

Emu

Crazy Australian puppet bird of comedian Rod Hull.

Endeavor, The

220-ton vessel commanded by Capt. Chet King (Joe James) in the TV series *Barrier Reef*.

Endicott Building

Building that Maynard G. Krebs (Bob Denver) often asked Dobie (Dwayne Hickman) to go with him to watch being torn down in the TV series *The Many Loves of Dobie Gillis*.

End of the Trail

Very popular sculpture created by James Earl Fraser of an Indian and a horse, both totally exhausted. The Beach Boys used the scene on the cover of their 1971 *Surf's Up* album.

End, William P.
Inventor of the stop sign. He is called the Father of Traffic Safety.

Enemy of the Public
Title of the 1931 James Cagney movie *Public Enemy* when it was released in England. The famous grapefruit scene with Mae Clarke was deleted.

Engine 49
Train engine mentioned in the lyrics of the song "On the Atchison, Topeka and Sante Fe" (from the 1946 movie *The Harvey Girls*).

Enrico Fermi
Nuclear power plant near Monroe, Michigan, that almost went critical on October 5, 1966 ("the day we almost lost Detroit").

Enterprise, Alabama
Site of the first American monument to an insect. The statue of the boll weevil was dedicated on December 11, 1919.

Eephus
High arching lob (up to 25 feet high) that was the trademark of Pirates pitcher Rip Sewell. In the 1946 All-Star Game Ted Williams hit Sewell's famous pitch into the Fenway Park bleachers for a home run. It was Sewell's teammate Maurice Van Robays who coined the term "Eephus" ball.

Erasmus Hall High School
School in Brooklyn, New York, from which Gabriel Kaplan, Beverly Sills, Franchot Tone, Susan Hayward, Barbra Streisand, Barbara Stanwyck, Elia Kazan, Neil Diamond, Dick Powell, Bobby Fischer, Mae West, Robert John, Jeff Chandler, Eli Wallach, and Dorothy Kilgallen all graduated. Barbra Streisand and Neil Diamond sang in the same choir there. In the 1950 movie *All About Eve* Barbara Bates played a young girl named Phoebe who is the president of the Erasmus Hall High School Eve Harrington Fan Club.

Erector Set
Toy comprised of metal beams, girders, screws, and nuts, created by A.C. Gilbert in 1909. Gilbert represented the United States in the pole vault in the 1908 Olympics.

Ergo
Mascot (single-eyed blob of protoplasm) on board the *U.G.S.P.* in the TV series *Quark*.

Eric
Dr. Mirakle's (Bela Lugosi) pet ape, which was trained to kill prostitutes, in the 1932 movie *Murders in the Rue Morgue*.

Erickson, Maj. A. H. "Jimmie"
On January 10, 1911, he became the first person to take a photograph from an airplane. He was overflying San Diego in his Curtis biplane.

Ernie and the Heavyweights
Heavyweight boxer Ernie Terrell's rock group. Ernie's sister, Jean Terrell, became a member of the Supremes when Diana Ross left.

Ernie's Tune
Theme song of Ernie Kovacs. It was an uptempo version of Jack Newton's "Oriental Blues."

Erotica Award
Annual trophy given to the best porno films of the year.

Esmie
Mr. Hennessey's (Burgess Meredith) pet female snake in the 1978 movie *Foul Play*, played by Shirley Python.

Esther
Name of a character played by Judy Garland in two movies: *Meet Me in St. Louis* (1944) and *A Star Is Born* (1954).

Esther Frump
Morticia Frump Addams' (Carolyn Jones) mother, played on the TV series *The Addams Family* by Margaret Hamilton.

Essex
238-ton whaling ship that, on November 20, 1820, was rammed and sunk by a sperm whale.

Etaoin Shrdlu
Most frequently used letters in English in their order of usage.

Ethel
Receptionist at the *Daily Planet* newspaper in the TV series *The Adventures of Superman*. She was played by Yvonne White.

Ethel Carter
Detective Nick Carter's late wife (novel series).

Etting, Ruth
(1907–1978) Torch singer, called the "Sweetheart of Columbia Records." She was portrayed in the 1955 movie *Love Me or Leave Me* by Doris Day.

Eugene
Character played by Ernie Kovacs in his silent TV sketches.

Eureka
Allied code name for the Teheran conference (November 28–December 1, 1943) between Churchill, Roosevelt, and Stalin.

Evans, Bergen
An authority on the English language who wrote the questions for the TV quiz shows *The $64,000 Question* and *The $64,000 Challenge*. He later hosted the TV quiz show *Down You Go*.

Evans, Charles "Chick"
First man to win both the U.S. Open and the U.S. Amateur championships in the same year (1916).

Evanston
Illinois setting of the TV series *The McLean Stevenson Show*.

Eve
First female created by God. She was portrayed in the 1966 movie *The Bible* by Ulla Bergryd.

Everything's Coming Up Roses
Song from the musical play *Gypsy,* which was used as Jack Paar's opening theme song on his nightly TV show, *The Tonight Show*. Ethel Merman sang part of the song in the 1980 movie *Airplane!*

Ewry, Ray
Purdue graduate who won 8 Olympic Gold Medals in track and field. He won 3 medals in 1900, 3 in 1904, and 2 more in 1908.

Exalted Order of Sidekicks
Clubs founded by Pat Buttram and Andy Devine. Some of the members were Jay Silverheels, William Frawley, and Nigel Bruce.

Evillene
Evil witch of the South, killed by Dorothy, in the 1978 movie *The Wiz*. Evillene was played by Mabel King.

Excedrin Headache No. 1040
The Tax Audit—on TV commercials for Excedrin pain reliever.

Ex-Lady
1933 movie in which Bette Davis had her first starring role. This is the old movie Jane Hudson (Bette Davis) was watching on TV in the 1962 movie *What Ever Happened to Baby Jane?* (See: **Sadie McKee**)

Eyes of Texas, The
Song played in the Astrodome whenever a Texas Astro hits a home run. "The Eyes of Texas" uses the same melody as "I've Been Working on the Railroad."

IIII
Roman numeral used for the number 4 on classic Roman numeral clocks (IV is rarely used). Supposedly, the IIII balances out the VIII. Another theory is that King Louis XIV habitually confused IV and VI and hence began the custom of using IIII.

4F
Superman's military status during World War II. While taking an eye test, he accidentally used his X-ray vision and read the eye chart in the next room.

Four Freedoms, The
Painting by Norman Rockwell that is the most reproduced painting in history.

4 Girls 4
Nightclub quartet that began singing together in the late 1970s. The members are: Rosemary Clooney, Rose Marie, Helen O'Connell, and Margaret Whiting.

Four Horsemen of Calumny
Fear, Ignorance, Bigotry, and Smear—from the Declaration of Conscience Speech made by Senator Margaret Chase Smith of Maine in an anti–Joseph McCarthy appeal to the U.S. Senate on June 1, 1950.*

4 Letters
Three U.S. presidents had last names consisting of only four letters: Polk, Taft, and Ford.

4 Sutton Place
New York City address of Roger Smythe's apartment (11B) where his sister, Diana Smythe (Diana Rigg), is living in the TV series *Diana*.

---

*The next day Smith was removed from the Senate Permanent Investigating Committee and replaced by a new senator from California—Richard M. Nixon.

5L5042

Wolf J. Flywheel's (Groucho Marx) automobile license number in the 1941 movie *The Big Store*.

Five Skaters, Three Bikers, Two Catchers

Members of a 21st-century roller ball team in the 1975 movie *Rollerball*.

14AAAAAA

Shoe size worn by Popeye's girlfriend Olive Oyl (comic strip).

14 letters

Largest number of letters allowed in a thoroughbred horse's name.

$14.27

Amount of money mentioned in Roger Miller's 1964 Grammy hit record "Dang Me." It was the money left after he bought five rounds out of six.

15

Members on a hurling team.

15 Men on a Dead Man's Chest

(Yo-Ho-Ho, and a Bottle of Rum) Favorite song of pirate Long John Silver in Robert Louis Stevenson's novel *Treasure Island*.

40 Points

Record number of points scored by a single player in a pro football game. On November 28, 1929, while playing for the Chicago Cardinals against the Chicago Bears, Ernie Nevers scored 6 touchdowns and made 4 extra-point conversions.

41 hours, 17 minutes

Length of time the jury took to deliberate in Lt. William Calley's trial for the My Lai massacre of Vietnamese civilians. He was found guilty on March 29, 1971.

42 hours, 40 minutes

Length of time the jury took to deliberate in the Charles Manson trial for the ritual murders in California. He was found guilty on January 26, 1971.

42nd Division

Los Angeles Police Department division setting of the TV series *Dog and Cat*.

43

Number of Marv Throneberry baseball cards in trade for one Carl Furillo in TV Schlitz Light Beer commercials.

44

Football jersey number worn by Steve Novak (John Derek) in the 1951 movie *Saturday's Hero*.

44 Wins (31 KO's), 20 Losses

Rocky Balboa's (Sylvester Stallone)—the Italian Stallion—fight record before his title bout against Apollo Creed (Carl Weathers), "The Master of Disaster" who won 46 fights without a loss in the 1976 movie *Rocky*.

46 Perry Street

New York City home address (Apartment C) of John and Barbara Gay (played by themselves) on the 1949 TV series *Mr. and Mrs. Mystery* (also titled *Apartment 3-C*).

47

Record number of consecutive games in which Johnny Unitas threw at least one touchdown pass.

48

Jersey number of University of Michigan center Gerald Ford.

50th Anniversary

In 1978 the Academy Awards celebrated its 50th year of presenting Oscars. That year was also Mickey Mouse's 50th birthday.

51 West 57th Street

Address of C. C. Baxter's (Jack Lemmon) apartment (2A) in the 1960 movie *The Apartment*.

52

Number of "fundamental errors" that Parker Brothers found in Charles Darrow's new game *Monopoly* when he first submitted it to them in 1933.

55

Bombing missions flown by Capt. Yossarian (Alan Arkin) during World War II before he went over the hill in the 1970 movie *Catch-22* (based on the novel of the same name by Joseph Heller).

403

Number of steps from the base to the top (in the torch) of the Statue of Liberty.

404 East Court

Madison County, Iowa, address where, on May 26, 1907, Marion Michael Morrison* (John Wayne) was born.

.406

Batting average of Ted Williams in 1941. He was the last player in the major leagues to hit over .400 for a season.

415 Monroe Street

Hoboken, New Jersey, address where 13½-pound Francis Albert Sinatra was born on December 12, 1915.

420 Madison Avenue

New York City address of the Day family in the 1947 movie *Life With Father*.

430 Vallejo Street

San Francisco address of Gloria Mundy (Goldie Hawn) in the 1978 movie *Foul Play*.

433 Prospect Place

New York City address of Dorothy (Diana Ross) in the 1979 movie *The Wiz*.

---

*His birth certificate read: Marion Robert Morrison.

403 APARTMENT NUMBER - ONE DAY AT A TIME.

437 River Street

Address that Charley Malloy (Rod Steiger) gave to the cab driver (Nehemiah Persoff) in the 1954 movie *On the Waterfront*.

441½ O'Farrell Street

San Francisco birthplace of Jerry Helper (Jerry Paris) in the TV series *The Dick Van Dyke Show*.

463 7th Avenue

Manhattan address of Lorelei Fashions where Wendy Nelson (Deirdre Lenihan) worked as a fashion designer in the TV series *Needles and Pins*.

500 Club

Atlantic City, New Jersey, nightclub where singer Dean Martin and comedian Jerry Lewis teamed up for the first time on July 25, 1946.

505 East 50th Street

New York City address of the Williams family (Apartment 781) in the TV series *The Danny Thomas Show* and *Make Room for Granddaddy*.

$516.32 and $712.05

Two different prize checks given to the winners of the TV game show *The Gong Show*.

535 Hudson Street

New York Greenwich Village home address of Mary Worth (comic strip).

550 North Shore Road

Home address of Sheriff Sam Adams (Andy Griffith) in the TV series *Adams of Eagle Lake*.

599 PCE

California automobile license plate of private detective Moses S. Wine's (Richard Dreyfuss) yellow 1969 Volkswagen convertible in the 1978 *The Big Fix*, based on the Roger L. Simon novel of the same name.

4433½ Alma Avenue

Lycurgus, New York, address of Alice Tripp's (Shelley Winters) apartment in the 1951 movie *A Place in the Sun* (based on the novel *An American Tragedy* by Theodore Dreiser).

4482 Bayview Drive

San Francisco home address of Phyllis Lindstrom (Cloris Leachman) in the TV series *Phyllis*.

40,000 A.D.

Time setting of the 1968 movie *Barbarella* (based on the French comic strip of the same name).

44444

Zip code of Newton Falls, Ohio (only single-repeating-digit zip).

45723

Phone number whose last four digits open the safe in which the Odessa file is kept in the 1974 movie *The Odessa File* (based on the 1972 Fredrick Forsyth novel of the same name).

45998

Zip code of Fernwood, Ohio, in the TV series *Mary Hartman, Mary Hartman*.

48642

Robert Montgomery's prison number in the 1930 movie *The Big House*.

50574

Prison number of Vincent Canelli (Edward G. Robinson) in the 1954 movie *Black Tuesday*.

54018

Dallas Police Department number of Lee Harvey Oswald when he was booked for the murder of President Kennedy and Officer J. D. Tippit on November 22, 1963.

583547

U.S. Navy serial number of Lt. Bradville (Gene Kelly) in the 1954 movie *Crest of the Wave*.

421-7596

Lt. Frank Bullitt's (Steve McQueen) San Francisco home phone number in the 1968 movie *Bullitt*.

$5,000,000

Ransom demanded for the San Francisco mayor (played by John Crawford) by the People's Revolutionary Strike Force in the 1977 movie *The Enforcer*.

5432126

Service serial number (shown on his dog tags) of British officer Capt. Jason C. Halliday (Richard Nugent) in the 1943 movie *Sahara*.

555-1271

Private phone number of the Harts on the TV series *Hart to Hart*.

555-2321

Minneapolis home phone number of Mary Richards (Mary Tyler Moore) in the TV series *The Mary Tyler Moore Show* (given as 555-7862 in some episodes).

555-2368

Home phone number of Tony Baretta (Robert Blake) in the TV series *Baretta*.

555-2657

Home phone number in Mill Valley, California, of Capt. B. J. Hunnicutt (Mike Farrell) in the TV series *M*A*S*H.**

555-5624

Phone number of the UBS television studio on the TV series *America 2-Night*.

---

*Actually digital prefixes were not in use during the Korean War.

555-6161
Home phone of the Stevens family in the TV series *Bewitched*.
555-8737
Ted Baxter's (Ted Knight) home phone number in the TV series *The Mary Tyler Moore Show*.
555-9532
Philip K. Fish's (Abe Vigoda) home phone number in the TV series *Fish*.
555-9861
Home phone number of Kate Columbo (Kate Mulgrew) in the TV series *Mrs. Columbo*.
42050227
Serial number of Pvt. Gomer Pyle (Jim Nabors) in the TV series *Gomer Pyle U.S.M.C.* (given as 13029300 in some episodes).
42259077
George William Jorgensen. Jr.'s, U.S. Army serial number. He later became Christine Jorgensen after a sex-change operation.
530-80-4623
Social Security number of Waterhole Ike, a real live pig, born on May 1, 1974.
F Sharp Major
Only key in which composer Irving Berlin could play the piano.
F.I.S.T.
(Federation of Interstate Truckers) Title of a 1978 movie starring Sylvester Stallone as Johnny Novak (a character loosely based on Jimmy Hoffa, head of the Teamsters union).
F.T.D.
Florist Telegraph Delivery, later changed to Florist Transworld Delivery.
Faber College
Pennsylvania college founded by pencil magnate Emil Faber in 1904 and the setting for the 1978 movie *Animal House* as well as the TV series *Delta House*. The college football team is the Mongols, Delta House is the featured fraternity. (Actually the movie was filmed at the University of Oregon.)
Face, The
Nickname of actress/model Anita Colby.
Faces
Bay Ridge, Brooklyn, gang headed by Tony Mareno (John Travolta) in the 1977 movie *Saturday Night Fever*.
Fahning, Emma
Buffalo, New York, woman who on March 4, 1930, became the first female to bowl a 300 game during a sanctioned competition.
Fair Carol
Yacht on which the rock band Wings recorded part of the album *London Town* in the Virgin Islands (May 1–31, 1977).

Fairy Soap Girl
 Fairy Soap's advertising symbol—posed for by actress Madge Evans.
Falcon
 Horse ridden by Buster Crabbe in his B westerns.
Falcon Lair
 Hollywood home of Rudolph Valentino, later owned by mobster moll
 Virginia Hill. Actor Harry Carey also once lived there.
Falcons
 Fonzie's (Henry Winkler) old gang, of which he was the leader, in the TV
 series *Happy Days*.
Falgout, USS
 First U.S warship (a destroyer) commanded by a black (Lt. Cmd. Samuel L.
 Gravely) in 1962.
Fall, Albert Bacon
 (1861–1944) Secretary of the interior under President Harding who was a
 central figure in the Teapot Dome scandal. He was the first Cabinet member
 in U.S. history to be convicted of a crime. Fall was sent to prison for one
 year and fined $100,000 for accepting bribes in an oil deal on November 1,
 1929.
Fame Is the Name of the Game
 1966 pilot movie for *The Name of the Game* TV series.
Fardale
 Prep school attended by Frank Merriwell before he went on to Yale (Frank
 Merriwell stories).
Farfel
 Danny O'Day's dog dummy who sang the commercial on TV ("N-E-S-T-L-E-S,
 Nestles makes the very best C-h-o-c-o-l-a-t-e").
Farmer Al Falfa
 Bald, white-bearded farmer in Paul Terry cartoons. He debuted in 1916 and
 last appeared in the 1950s. He was also known as Farmer Gray.
Farmer, Karen
 First black member of the DAR (Daughters of the American Revolution).
Farmer's Almanac, The
 Annual book of information, begun in 1792 by Robert B. Thomas.
Faro
 Big Eli's (Burt Lancaster) pet dog in the 1955 movie *The Kentuckian*,
 directed by Lancaster.
Farragut, Enterprise, and Republic
 Three United Federation vessels on which James T. Kirk served (*Star Trek*).
Farrell, Charles, and Janet Gaynor
 Movie appearances together: *Seventh Heaven* (1927); *Street Angel* (1928);
 Lucky Stars (1929); *Sunny Side Up* (1929); *Happy Days* (1930); *High Society*

Blues (1930); *The Man Who Came Back* (1931); *Merely Mary Ann* (1931); *Delicious* (1931); *The First Year* (1932); *Tess of the Storm Country (1932);* and *Change of Heart* (1934).

Farringdon

Hometown of Judy Bolton (children's books).

Fashion Hall of Fame

Any person who appears on the Best Dressed List three times enters the Fashion Hall of Fame.

Fat Annie, The

Old ferryboat run by Capt. Cecil Hart (Orson Welles) in the 1959 movie *Ferry to Hong Kong*.

Fat City

Nickname of Stockton, California, especially in the early 1900s when boxing was very popular there.

Father Dave Benson

Young priest played by Robby Benson in the 1978 movie *The End*.

Father Divine

(1877–1965) Black religious leader (born George Baker) who founded the Peace Mission Movement. He was involved in several questionable practices and scandals. Father Divine was portrayed in the 1980 TV movie *Guyana Tragedy: The Story of Jim Jones* by James Earl Jones.

Father Duffy

Horse that Steve Cauthen rode to victory on February 2, 1979, after riding in 110 consecutive races without a win.

Father Fitzgibbon

Older priest of St. Dominic's parish in the 1944 movie *Going My Way*, played by Barry Fitzgerald, who won the Academy Award for best supporting actor. The character was played in the TV series by Leo G. Carroll. On TV his hometown is Ballymora, Ireland.

Father of the American Turf

Title conferred on Leonard Jerome, the maternal grandfather of Winston Churchill.

Father of the Atomic Submarine

Title conferred on Adm. Hyman G. Rickover.

Father of the Soviet H-Bomb

Title conferred on Andrei D. Sakharov.

Father of the Year—1942

Title conferred on General Douglas MacArthur.

Father's Day

Third Sunday in June. The special day was created on June 19, 1910, through the efforts of Mrs. John B. Dodd of Spokane, Washington.

Fats

Dummy in the 1978 movie *Magic* (based on the 1976 William Goldman novel of the same name). $250,000—the most expensive dummy ever made.

Fats Stuff

Mexican friend of Smilin' Jack. In each comic strip a button would pop off his shirt, only to be caught and eaten by a chicken.

Fauvel

Richard Plantagenet's (King Richard the Lion Heart) noble steed, which he rode during the Crusades.

Fawkes, Guy

(1570–1606) British conspirator who, with others, attempted to blow up the Houses of Parliament on the night of November 4–5, 1605, in what became known as the Gunpowder Plot. He was caught and executed.

Fawzia

Fictitious Arabian kingdom setting of 1964 movie *John Goldfarb, Please Come Home*.

Fayetteville Female Academy

School that Katie Scarlett O'Hara attended for two years in the novel *Gone with the Wind*.

Fearsome Foursome

Los Angeles Rams' defensive line of the 1960s: Merlin Olsen, Lamar Lundy, Deacon Jones, and Roosevelt Grier.

February 29

Leap year date and birthday of Superman. Also claimed as birthday by Froggy (Billy Laughlin) in *Our Gang* films. In 1904 band leader Jimmy Dorsey was born on February 29.

Feigner, Eddie

Softball pitcher who played with a three-man team billed as the King and His Court. In an exhibition game on February 18, 1967, he struck out in order: Willie Mays, Willie McCovey, Brooks Robinson, Roberto Clemente, Maury Wills, and Harmon Killebrew.

Felicity Ann

23-foot sloop in which Britisher Ann Davidson became the first woman to solo-voyage the Atlantic Ocean from Plymouth, England, to the West Indies. The journey began on May 18, 1952, and took 17 months.

Fellingham, Virginia

Driver of the stagecoach on Wells Fargo TV commercials. The horses are owned and trained by Virginia.

Fellows, Alvin

Inventor who patented the first tape measure on July 14, 1868.

Felton, Rebecca Latimer

First woman to serve in the U.S. Senate. She was appointed to that position on October 3, 1922, and attended only two Senate sessions (November 21 and 22). Rebecca Felton was a Democrat from Georgia.

Ferdy and Morty

Nephews of Mickey Mouse who attend Public School 12.

Ferguson, Lowell G.

Pilot of the Western Airlines Boeing 737 who on July 31, 1979, landed at Buffalo, Wyoming, mistaking it for his destination, Sheridan, 35 miles away.

Fermi, Enrico

(1901–1954) Italian physicist who was awarded the 1938 Nobel Prize for physics. He was portrayed in the 1946 movie *The Beginning of the End* by Ludwig Stossel.

Fernwood Assembly Plant

Factory where Tom Hartman (Greg Mullavey) worked in the TV series *Mary Hartman, Mary Hartman*. Tom's job was to screw in the dome light inside the cars. He later became general manager for Donally's R. V. City.

Fernwood Courier Press

Fernwood (Ohio) newspaper in the TV series *Mary Hartman, Mary Hartman*. Its motto was: "You Do It, We'll Print It." It cost 17 cents (86 cents beyond 2 miles).

Fernwood Flasher

83-year-old Grandpa Raymond Larkin (Victor Kilian) in the TV series *Mary Hartman, Mary Hartman*.

Fiat

(Fabrica Italiana Automobile Torino). Italian automobile.

Fiddle-dee-dee!

Scarlett O'Hara's favorite expression in the novel *Gone with the Wind*.

Fidler, Jimmy

Popular Hollywood gossip columnist and broadcaster since the 1930s. He was portrayed by Russell Arms in the 1978 TV movie *Bud and Lou*.

Fidelity, Bravery, Integrity

Motto of the Federal Bureau of Investigation (FBI).

Fields, Lew

(1867–1941) Partner in the famous vaudeville comedy team of (Joe) Weber and Fields. The pair portrayed themselves in the 1940 movie *Lillian Russell* and Lew Fields appeared as himself in the 1939 movie *The Story of Vernon and Irene Castle*. He was portrayed in the 1952 movie *Somebody Loves Me* by Ralph Meeker. His daughter, Dorothy Fields, became a famous lyricist: "On the Sunny Side of the Street" and "The Way You Look Tonight" are two of her songs. She was the first woman elected to the Songwriters' Hall of Fame.

Fifteenth Pelican

Book by Tere Ross on which the TV series *The Flying Nun* was based.

Fifth of Beethoven
 Instrumental by Walter Murphy heard in the movies *Saturday Night Fever*
 (1977) and *Ice Castles* (1979). It is a disco adaptation of Beethoven's Fifth
 Symphony.

Fighting Marine
 Nickname of heavyweight boxing champion Gene Tunney. Tunney starred in
 the 1926 movie serial *The Fighting Marines*.

Fillet of Soul
 Harlem nightclub from which James Bond (Roger Moore) was kidnapped in
 the 1973 movie *Live and Let Die*.

Final Scores
 2 to 1: Pirates over Yankees for Pennant in the 1951 movie *Angels in the
 Outfield*. 6 to 2: Brooklyn over New York in the World Series in the 1951
 movie *Rhubarb*. 18 to 16: 4077th M*A*S*H over the 325th EVAC in football
 game in the 1970 movie *M*A*S*H*. 9 to 7: Ridgeville University over Wilton
 College in the 1951 movie *That's My Boy*. 32 to 30: Carlton over Bixby in
 collegiate basketball game in the 1945 Abbott and Costello movie *Here Come
 the Co-Eds*. 49 to 24: San Francisco 49ers over the Los Angeles Rams in
 football game in which private eye Moses Wine (Richard Dreyfuss) lost $100
 in the 1978 *The Big Fix*. 36 to 35: Mean Machine over the Guards in the 1974
 movie *The Longest Yard*.

Findlay's Friendly Appliances
 Store in Tuckahoe, New York, operated by Walter Findlay (Bill Macy) in the
 TV series *Maude*.

Finkelstein, Mel
 New York *Daily News* photographer whom Jackie Kennedy Onassis flipped
 over her knee to the ground as she was leaving a New York theater that was
 showing the Swedish movie *I Am Curious (Yellow)*.

Fink, Mike
 American frontiersman known as the King of the Keelboatmen. He was
 portrayed in the 1955 TV series *Davy Crockett* by Jeff York and in the 1977
 TV movie *The Incredible Rocky Mountain Race* by Forrest Tucker.

Finley
 Name on the mailbox of the mansion at 518 Crestview Drive into which the
 Clampetts moved in the TV series *The Beverly Hillbillies*.

Fireman of the Year
 Annual award (since 1960) given by *The Sporting News* to the outstanding
 relief pitcher in each major league.

Fire Opal
 Ring always worn by The Shadow. It was given to him by the Xinca Indians
 of Guatemala (pulp magazines).

Fire Shovel

Very first item ever sold by F. (Frank) W. (Winfield) Woolworth in his first store in Utica, New York, on February 22, 1879. It was sold at 9:00 a.m. to a woman for 5 cents.

Fireside Inn

Nightclub setting on the TV soap opera *Another World*.

Firpo. Luis Angel

(1876–1960) Heavyweight boxer, nicknamed the "Wild Bull of the Pampas." He was the only man to knock Jack Dempsey out of the ring. This occurred in a bout on September 14, 1923. Dempsey landed on *New York Tribune* reporter Jack Lawrence's portable typewriter, wrecking it.

First Family, The

Comedy album by Vaughn Meader released in 1962 on Cadence Records. It became the best-selling comedy album of all time (4½ million copies). Sales of the album suddenly stopped when President Kennedy was assassinated.

First Lady of Baseball

Nickname conferred upon actress Laraine Day who during her marriage to baseball manager Leo Durocher (1947–1960) took an active interest in the game.

First Lady of Jazz

Title conferred on singer Ella Fitzgerald.

First Mama

CB handle of former First Lady Betty Ford.

First Names

Actors who used their real first names as their stage last names:

Stage Name	Real Name
Paul Muni	Muni Weisenfreund
John Shepperd	Shepperd Strudwick
John Derek	Derek Harris

Actors who used their real last names as their stage first names:

Barry Sullivan	Patrick Barry
Stockard Channing	Susan Stockard
Broderick Crawford	William Broderick

First National Bank

Danfield, Connecticut, institution of which Theodore J. Mooney (Gale Gordon) was president in the TV series *The Lucy Show*. The phone number was 878-5652. (See: **Westland Bank**)

First Queen of the Movies

Title conferred on actress Joan Crawford by *Life* magazine in 1937.

First Years, The

Theme song of the TV series *Paper Chase*, performed by Seals and Croft.

Fisher, Alva J.

American inventor of the electric washing machine.

Fisher, Fred
(1875–1942) American songwriter who composed "Peg o' My Heart," "Dardanella," and "Chicago." He was the father of songwriter Doris Fisher. Together they composed "Whispering Grass" in 1940. Fred Fisher was portrayed in the 1949 movie *Oh, You Beautiful Doll* by S. Z. Sakall.

Fisher, N.A.
Inventor of Lawrence Welk's bubble machine.

Fisk, Jim
(1834–1872) American stock market speculator who, with Jay Gould, helped to wreck the Erie Railroad on Black Friday, September 24, 1869, but failed in his attempt to corner the gold market. Fisk was portrayed in the 1937 movie *The Toast of New York* by Edward Arnold.

Fitzgerald, A. Ernest
Cost analyst who was fired from his government job in 1970 when he revealed a $2 billion cost overrun in the building of the Lockheed C5A transport.

Fitzgerald, F. Scott
(1896–1940) Francis Scott Key Fitzgerald. American novelist and short story writer of the 1920s and 1930s; he coined the phrase "the Jazz Age." He was one of the many writers for the movie *Gone With the Wind* in 1939. He was portrayed in the 1959 movie *Beloved Infidel* by Gregory Peck. Scott and his wife, Zelda, were portrayed in *F. Scott Fitzgerald and the Last of the Belles* (1974 TV) by Richard Chamberlain and Blythe Danner, and in *F. Scott Fitzgerald in Hollywood* (1976 TV) by Jason Miller and Tuesday Weld.

Fiver and Hazel
Main two rabbit characters in Richard Adam's novel *Watership Down*.

Flagship
Freighter commanded by Capt. Ben Foster (John Larch) in the 1965 TV series *Convoy*.

Flakey Wakeys
Diet breakfast cereal whose contest Ralph Kramden (Jackie Gleason) entered by creating the slogan, "Flakey Wakeys add to the taste/But take away from your fat little waist," in "Honeymooners" episodes of *The Jackie Gleason Show* (1966–1967). Ralph won first prize (a $40,000 home), but was disqualified when it became known that he used Ed Norton to fake before-and-after dieting photos. Flakey Wakey wanted to use Ralph's slogan, so they awarded him second prize—a trip to Europe for four.

Flaming Lips
5½-hour movie starring Jerry Benson (Gene Kelly) in 1964 movie *What a Way to Go*.

Flanagan, Betsy
Barmaid of Elmsford, New York, who in 1776 introduced the cocktail drink at the Halls Corners Tavern.

Flash

Dog in TV cartoon series *Emergency Plus Four*.

Flash

Eddie Dean's horse in B westerns. He also rode White Cloud.

Flash

White horse that Gary Cooper rode in the 1927 movies *Arizona Bound* and *The Last Outlaw*.

Flashing Spikes

Title of an episode of the TV series *Alcoa Premieres* that featured James Stewart and Don Drysdale. Directed by John Ford, it was broadcast on October 4, 1962.

Fleet Driver

Horse that Johnny Longden rode to victory at Hollywood Park on May 15, 1952, to become the first jockey to win 4,000 races.

Fleet Frederick

Lookout in the crow's next of the White Star liner *Titanic* who on the night of April 14, 1912, spotted the iceberg just before it collided with the ship.

Flight 19

U.S. Navy flight of five Avenger torpedo bomber aircraft that departed Ft. Lauderdale on December 5, 1945, only to disappear in the Bermuda Triangle without a trace. A Martin Marine PBY sent to find Flight 19 also disappeared. A total of 27 men were lost. In the 1977 movie *Close Encounters of the Third Kind* the aircraft were found intact in the Mexican village of Sonoyita.

Flight 711

Buck Rogers' NASA flight that was in suspended animation for 504 years in the 1979 movie *Buck Rogers*.

Flint

Superspy Derek Flint, played by James Coburn in the movies *Our Man Flint* (1966) and *In Like Flint* (1967) and by Ray Danton in the 1976 TV movie *Our Man Flint: Dead on Target*.

Flint, Michigan

City in which the 1977–1978 TV series *The Fitzpatricks* is set.

Floccinaunihilipilification

Oxford English Dictionary's longest word, defined as estimating something as worthless.

FLoogle 8-900

Jeff's telephone number in the comic strip *Mutt and Jeff*.

Flores, Pedro

Filipino busboy who in 1927 introduced the Yo-Yo to America. He became the first manufacturer of the toy.

Flotsam

Dog featured in the TV series *On Our Own*.

Flowers and Trees
1932 Walt Disney Silly Symphony release that was the first color cartoon. It is this cartoon that the family of Dalmatians watch on TV in the 1961 cartoon movie *One Hundred and One Dalmatians*.

Flower of the Musical World
How Jackie Gleason introduced his band leader, Ray Block, on TV.

Flowers of the Manhattan
Shop owned by Gillian Holroyd (Kim Novak) in the closing scenes of the 1958 movie *Bell, Book and Candle*.

Floyd
Astro chimpanzee found by Lt. Robin Crusoe (Dick Van Dyke) in the 1966 movie *Lt. Robin Crusoe, U.S.N.*

Floyd Bennett
Name of the Ford trimotor airplane (NX4542) in which Richard E. Byrd and pilot Brent Balchen flew over the South Pole on November 28, 1929.

Flub-a-dub
Howdy Doody's pet (originally called Flub-dub) in the TV series *Howdy Doody Time*. He came from South America and was made up of eight animals: he had the feathered body of a dachshund, the neck of a giraffe, the ears of a cocker spaniel, a raccoon's tail, the flippers of a seal, a duck's head, a cat's whiskers, and a memory like an elephant. When he was hungry, he would say, "Meatballs, meatballs" (voice of Dayton Allen).

Flubber
Magic substance that causes an antigravity effect. Recipe: 1 pound of saltwater taffy, 1 heaping tablespoon of polyurethane foam, 1 cake of crumbled yeast. Mix till smooth, allow to rise, pour into saucepan over 1 cup of cracked rice mixed with 1 cup of water. Add topping of molasses, boil until contents lift lid off pan with the sound "Qurlp!" Flubber was used in *The Absent-Minded Professor* (1961) and *Son of Flubber* (1963)—both Walt Disney productions.

Fluffy
Eunice's (Carol Burnett) pet rabbit when she was a child in the TV series *The Carol Burnett Show*.

Fluffy
Ted Baxter's (Ted Knight) toy teddy bear as a child in the TV series *The Mary Tyler Moore Show*.

Flying Dutchman Overture, The
Musical piece by Richard Wagner that was used as the theme song of the TV series *Captain Video and His Video Rangers*.

Flying Fish
Airborne minisub belonging to the atomic submarine *Seaview* in the TV series *Voyage to the Bottom of the Sea*.

Flying Irishman, The
   1939 movie in which Douglas "Wrongway" Corrigan portrayed himself. The movie re-creates Corrigan's famous "wrongway" flight.
Flying Newsroom
   Helicopter used by the reporters of the *Daily Planet (Superman* comics).
Flying Parson, The
   Nickname of mile runner Gil Dodds.
Flying Scot
   Famous train that once ran from London to Edinburgh.
Fly Me to the Moon
   Song played on Jennifer Marlowe's (Loni Anderson) door bell in the TV series *WKRP in Cincinnati.*
Flynn, Joseph
   Air Force lieutenant general who was the highest-ranking American captured during the Vietnam War. He spent 5½ years as a POW.
Foggy Mountain Breakdown
   Theme song of the 1967 movie *Bonnie and Clyde,* performed by Earl Scruggs and Lester Flatt. The song was first recorded by the pair back in 1948.
Foghorn J. Leghorn
   Giant rooster that talks with a southern accent in Warner Brothers cartoons: "I say, I say, howdy, son" (Voice of Mel Blanc). He made his debut in the cartoon *Walky Talky Hawk* (1946).
Foley, Red
   (1910–1968) Country singer, member of the Country Music Hall of Fame and father-in-law of singer Pat Boone. He appeared on the TV scrics *Mr. Smith Goes to Washington* as Cooter Smith. Foley was portrayed loosely in the 1975 movie *Nashville* by Henry Gibson as Haven Hamilton.
Folsom Prison
   California penal institution setting of the 1954 movie *Riot in Cell Block 11.*
Folsom Prison Blues
   Opening theme song for the TV series *The Johnny Cash Show.* "I Walk the Line" was the closing theme.
Fontana, D. J.
   First drummer to perform in Elvis Presley's band. He played behind Elvis from 1955 until 1959. He was portrayed in 1979 TV movie *Elvis* by Ed Begley, Jr.
Foo!
   Favorite expression of comic strip character Smokey Stover.
Food Can Be Habit Forming
   Book written by the world's expert on nutrition, Professor Kurt von Stuffer Sid Caesar in the TV series *Your Show of Shows.*

Food World
   Burbank grocery store where Jerry Landis (John Denver) worked as assistant
   manager in the 1977 movie *Oh God!*

Fooling Around with Love
   Original title of the 1940 hit song "Taking a Chance on Love" (words by
   John Latouche and Ted Fetter, music by Vernon Duke).

Foolish Carriage
   Frank B. Gilbreth, Jr.'s, 1917 Pierce Arrow (novel/movie *Cheaper by the
   Dozen*).

Foozebane
   Planet visited by Kermit to interview its inhabitants in the TV series *The
   Muppet Show*.

Ford, Gerald Rudolph
   38th president of the United States and only president to have been an Eagle
   Scout. He received offers to play football from both the Detroit Lions and the
   Green Bay Packers. Gerald Ford and Nelson Rockefeller were the only
   nonelected president and vice president to serve in office together. Both were
   confirmed as vice president by the House and the Senate.

Ford Model N
   First successful mass-produced automobile.

Forest Street
   Street in Hartford, Florida, where, from 1873 until 1893, Harriet Beecher
   Stowe and Samuel L. Clemens lived in houses situated next to each other.

For He's a Jolly Good Fellow
   Tune played on the Prince of Wales' (Peter Ustinov) snuff box when opened
   in the 1954 movie *Beau Brummell*. Beau Brummell (Stewart Granger) had
   given him the box.

Fort Crown Point
   Headquarters of Maj. Robert Rogers (Keith Larsen) in the TV series *Northwest Passage*.

Fort Hooker
   Western calvary fort setting where misfits in the Union Army were assigned
   in the 1964 movie *Advance to the Rear*.

Fort Knox
   U.S. Army camp near Louisville, Kentucky, where the nation's gold supply
   has been stored since 1936. The nation's silver supply is stored at West Point.

Fortmann, Danny
   Youngest person to have played football in the NFL. He played for the
   Chicago Bears in 1936 at the age of 19.

Fortress, The
   Madam Sally Stanford's house of pleasure, located at 1144 Pine Street in San
   Francisco (1941-1949). The house was built by Harry K. Thaw for actress

Anna Held. Two of Sally's more prominent guests were Errol Flynn and Humphrey Bogart.

Fort Ridiculous

U.S. Calvary post commanded by Col. Fluster in the comic strip *Tumbleweeds*.

Fort Shona

German fort on the Ulanga River passed by the *African Queen* in the 1951 *The African Queen*.

Fortunella

1958 Italian movie, portions of whose musical score were used for the 1972 movie *The Godfather*. This made the film score by Nino Rosta ineligible for an Academy Award nomination.

Fort William Henry Harrison

Training base of the first Special Service Force in Helena, Montana, in the 1968 movie *The Devil's Brigade*.

Foster, Stephen Collins

(1826–1864) Popular American songwriter whose best known compositions are "My Old Kentucky Home," "O Susanna," and "I Dream of Jeannie." Movie portrayals: *Swanee River* (1940) Don Ameche; and *I Dream of Jeannie* (1952) Ray Middleton.

Foster, Vernon

Los Angeles Superior Court judge who "unmasked" Clayton Moore (the Lone Ranger) in court in September 1979.

Fountain Pen

Communication device that agent Napoleon Solo (Robert Vaughn) used to contact U.N.C.L.E. on Channel D in the TV series *The Man from U.N.C.L.E.*

Four Boys and a Guitar

Credit on record labels for many years underneath the Mills Brothers' name.

Fowler, Gene

(1880–1960) American journalist and playwright. He was portrayed in the 1976 movie *W.C. Fields and Me* by Louis Zorich.

Foxfire

1955 movie starring Jane Russell and Jeff Chandler. The movie was being shown on board the *Andrea Doria* at the moment the liner collided with the *Stockholm* on the night of July 26, 1956.

Foxe, Fanne

Stripper (Annabella Battistella) who was found with Arkansas Democratic Representative Wilbur Mills in the Washington Tidal Basin in 1974. The incident led to Mills' resignation as chairman of the House Ways and Means Committee.

Foy, Eddie

(1854–1928) Popular vaudeville entertainer (born Edward Fitzgerald) who fathered seven talented children. Movie portrayals: *Lillian Russell* (1940) Eddie Foy, Jr.; *Yankee Doodle Dandy* (1942) Eddie Foy, Jr.; *Wilson* (1944) Eddie Foy, Jr.; and *The Seven Little Foys* (1955) Bob Hope. Eddie Foy, Jr., and the Osmond Brothers played the "7 Little Foys" in an episode on the TV series *Bob Hope Presents the Chrysler Theatre* broadcast on January 24, 1964. Mickey Rooney played George M. Cohan in the same episode.

Francis
Stagehand in the TV series *Texaco Star Theatre*, played by Arnold Stang.

Francis
Terrier that hid in the wine cellar of the St. Francis Hotel during the fire that swept San Francisco after the earthquake of April 18, 1906. He became such a celebrity that his picture was used on postcards.

Frank Dugan
Employee of the Stenrud Corporation, played by Bob Mathias in the 1959–1960 TV series *Troubleshooters*.

Frank E. Campbell
New York City mortuary (located at 1076 Madison Avenue) where services were held for such noted personalities as Rudolph Valentino in 1928, Judy Holliday in 1965, and Judy Garland in 1969. John Lennon's body was taken there after his death in 1980.

Frank, Gerald
Author of numerous biographical books, including: *Judy, The Boston Strangler,* and *Too Much Too Soon* (with Diana Barrymore). He was portrayed in the 1959 movie *Too Much, Too Soon* by Robert Ellenstein.

Frankie and Johnny
Traditional American folk song originally known in 1888 as "Frankie and Albert."

Franklin
Previous name (1784–1788) of the state of Tennessee.

Franklin, Benjamin
(1706–1790) American statesman, philosopher, scientist, inventor, and writer who published *Poor Richard's Almanac* from 1732 to 1757 under the pseudonym of Richard Saunders. He invented the Franklin stove and used kites to conduct electricity experiments in 1752. Movie portrayals: *Lloyd's of London* (1936) Thomas Pogue; *Marie Antoinette* (1938) Walter Walker; *Lafayette* (1963) Orson Welles; and *1776* (1972) Howard da Silva.

Frank Merriwell
Clean-cut all-American hero of novels by Burt L. Standish. He was captain of the Yale football team. (The character was supposedly based on Louis Sockalexis, the first Indian to play baseball in the major leagues.)

Franz Josef
Emperor of Austria from 1848 until his death in 1916. His nephew and heir,

Archduke Franz Ferdinand, was assassinated at Sarajevo (June 28, 1914), which precipitated World War I. Movie portrayals: *The King Steps Out* (1936) Franchot Tone; *Florian* (1940) Reginald Owen; *The Emperor Waltz* (1948) Richard Haydn; *Forever My Love* (1962) Karl Boehm; and *The Great Waltz* (1960) Prince Johannes Schonburg-Hartenstein; *Oh, What a Lovely War* (1969) Jack Hawkins.

Freckles
Robert Kennedy's pet dog.

Freckles
Dusty's (Bob Denver) horse in the TV series *Dusty's Trail*.

Fred
Scotty's teddy bear in the 1971 song "Watching Scotty Grow," composed by Mac Davis and recorded by Bobby Goldsboro.

Fred
Little Ricky's (Richard Keith) pet puppy in the TV series *I Love Lucy*.

Freddie Johnson
Jive-talking playboy played by Flip Wilson in comedy routines.

Freddie's Dead
Theme song of the 1972 movie *Superfly*, performed by Curtis Mayfield.

Freddy
Hubert's sheepdog in the comic strip *Hubert*.

Freddy and Adam
Dega's (Dustin Hoffman) two pigs in the 1973 movie *Papillon*.

Fred Johnson
One-armed man (played by Bill Raisch) who killed Dr. Richard Kimble's (David Janssen) wife, Helen Regan Kimble, in the TV series *The Fugitive*. He was finally killed on August 29, 1967.

Freeman, Jr., Joseph
First black elder of the Mormon church (June 9, 1978).

Freedman, Mike
ABC TV cameraman punched by Ohio State football coach Woody Hayes, in the closing minutes of the Buckeyes' game at Michigan on November 19, 1977. (See: **Bauman, Charles**).

Freedom
Name of 19½-foot-tall statue situated on the top of the U.S. Capitol building.

Freeway
Pet dog of Jonathan (Robert Wagner) and Jennifer (Stefanie Powers) in the TV series *Hart to Hart*. He is played by Charlie, who was discovered in a dog pound.

French, John Denton
(1852–1925) British field marshal who in 1915 became the commander-in-chief in the United Kingdom. He was portrayed in the 1969 movie *Oh! What a Lovely War* by Laurence Olivier.

Fresca

President Lyndon Johnson's favorite drink. He had special taps installed in the White House to distribute the liquid.

Freud, Sigmund

(1856–1939), Austrian founder of psychoanalysis and author of numerous books on the subject. He was portrayed in the 1962 movie *Freud* by Montgomery Clift and in the 1976 movie *The Seven Per Cent Solution* by Alan Arkin.

Friar Dominic

Role played by Lee Marvin in the San Francisco Opera presentation of *Joan of Arc at the Stake* in October 1954.

Friday

Robinson Crusoe's native companion. Movie portrayals: *Adventures of Robinson Crusoe* (1954) James Fernandez; and *Man Friday* (1976) Richard Roundtree.

Friday 13th

Debut (in September 1974) of the TV series *Kolchak: The Night Stalker*.

Friendship

Fokker trimotor in which Amelia Earhart (as passenger) became the first woman to fly the Atlantic. The crew departed from Newfoundland on June 17, 1928, and arrived in Wales 20 hours and 38 minutes later, Wilmer Stutz was the pilot. The plane was once owned by Cmd. Richard Byrd.

Frisbie Baking Co.

Bridgeport, Connecticut, firm that lent its name to the Frisbie sport. "Frisbie" was inscribed on the company's pie tins, which were the first Frisbies (1950–1957).

Froman, Jane

(1908–1980) Torch singer of the 1940s. She was one of 15 survivors of a Pan Am plane crash in 1943 and later married the pilot who rescued her. Froman was portrayed in the 1952 movie *With a Song in My Heart* by Susan Hayward. On her TV series in 1953 Jane Froman first introduced the song "I Believe."

Fromme, Lynette Alice "Squeaky"

Former member of Charles Manson's "family" who on September 5, 1975, attempted to assassinate President Gerald Ford in Sacramento, California. (A few weeks later, on September 22, Sara Jane Moore attempted to shoot Ford in San Francisco.) Fromme is incarcerated in the federal prison at Pleasanton, California, the same prison in which Patty Hearst served time.

Frosty Palace

Soda fountain hangout of Rydell High students in the 1978 movie *Grease*.

Fug

Profanity adjective coined by Norman Mailer in his 1947 *The Naked and the Dead*. It was created by him to replace a four-letter Anglo-Saxon word that was then taboo.

Fugate, Caril Ann

14-year-old companion of Charles Starkweather. The pair went on a murderous spree in Nebraska in 1958. They were portrayed in the 1973 movie *Badlands* by Sissy Spacek (Holly Sargis) and Martin Sheen (Kit Carruthers).

Full House

B-29 weather-reporting aircraft that overflew Nagasaki before the A-bomb was dropped on the Japanese on August 9, 1945. The craft was piloted by Maj. Ralph R. Taylor.

Fuller, Ida May

First person to receive Social Security benefits, beginning on January 31, 1940. She paid $22 into the fund that gave her $20,000 over the 35 years that she collected from it.

Fulton, Robert

(1765–1815) American inventor of the steamboat. He built the successful *Clermont* in 1807, and spent the remainder of his life building steamboats for the government. Fulton was portrayed in the 1940 movie *Little Old New York* by Richard Greene.

Fumbles

Ed Huddle's pet dog in the TV cartoon series *Where's Huddles*.

FUN

Giveaway word in the very first crossword puzzle (called a word-cross), published in the *New York World* on December 21, 1913. It was created by Arthur Wynne.

Funny Face

Nickname of the woman the singer is to meet at his hometown train station in the classic song "Chattanooga Choo Choo."

Furniture

Word describing women in the 1973 movie *Soylent Green*.

Futureworld

1976 movie (sequel to *Westworld* [1973]) starring Peter Fonda and Blythe Danner. It was the first U.S. movie purchased by mainland China (January 1978).

Fuwalda

British ship from which Lord and Lady Greystoke were put ashore in Africa in 1888 after a mutiny (Tarzan novel series).

Fuzz

German shepherd in the TV series *Chase*.

Fuzzy Q. Jones

Lash LaRue's sidekick in B westerns, played by Al St. John, a nephew of Roscoe "Fatty" Arbuckle.

G. A. Johnson and Mary Ann Evans
Pseudonyms under which Howard Hughes and actress Jean Peters were married in Tonopah, Nevada, on March 13, 1957.
G. C. Luther
Pseudonym used by ball player Ted Williams when he traveled on his fishing trips.
GEC
Three notes played in the NBC tone. GEC stood for General Electric Company, which was once NBC's parent company.
GGG
Glorious Guardians of Good, the fraternal organization in Fernwood, Ohio, of which Tom Hartman was a member in the T.V. series *Mary Hartman, Mary Hartman*. The head man (or Keeper of the Keys) was called the Massah.
G. Dickson
Name on mailbox 201, next to Roy Neary's (Richard Dreyfuss) truck when a UFO appeared in the 1977 movie *Close Encounters of the Third Kind*.
GLD 204
California license plate number of the 1955 Chevy that crashed in a race against Big John's 1932 Ford coupe in the 1973 movie *American Graffiti*. Bob Falfa (Harrison Ford) was the driver of the Chevy. The cars raced on Paradise Road to the tune of Booker T. and the M.G.'s song "Green Onions."
Gable, Clark, and Lana Turner
Films in which the pair appeared: *Honky Tonk* (1941); *Somewhere I'll Find You* (1942); and *Betrayed* (1954).

Galileo

(1564–1642) Italian astronomer and physicist who made numerous astronomical discoveries with the aid of the telescope. He was nearly burned at the stake for maintaining that the earth revolved around the sun, a theory that was held to contradict biblical truth. His life was spared by the Pope when he recanted his theory at the stake. He was portrayed in the 1974 movie *Galileo* (based on the Bertolt Brecht play) by Topol.

Gallant Man

Horse ridden by Willie Shoemaker in the 1957 Kentucky Derby. As he came down the stretch, Shoemaker misjudged the finish line and raised up in the saddle. This error allowed Iron Liege to pass him and win. Iron Liege was the horse that *Sports Illustrated* had chosen to follow from birth in a series of articles.

Gallico, Paul

(1897–1976) Newspaperman, author, and organizer of the first Golden Gloves boxing tournament. His father, Paola Gallico, was Beverly Sills's piano instructor. Two of Paul Gallico's works are *The Snow Goose* and *The Poseidon Adventure*. Gallico was portrayed in the 1978 TV movie *Ring of Passion* by Joseph Campanella.

Galveston Giant, The

Nickname of heavyweight boxing champion Jack Johnson. (Another of his nicknames was Little Artha.)

Game of Death, The

Ironic title of Gig Young's last movie (1979), before his suicide.

Gandhi (Mahatma Coatma Collar Gandhi)

Actress Marion Davies' pet dachshund, given to her by William Randolph Hearst. Gandhi is present in most photographs of Miss Davies.

Gandhi, "Mahatma" Mohandas Karamchand

(1869–1948) Hindu nationalist who led the movement for Indian independence from Britain in a campaign of nonviolent civil disobedience. He was assassinated in 1948. Gandhi was portrayed in the 1963 movie *Nine Hours to Rama* by J. S. Casshyap.

Gangster Story

1960 movie directed by Walter Matthau, his only effort as a director.

Garagiola, Joe

Major league catcher who later became a TV sports announcer and host of the following TV games shows; *Memory Game, Sale of the Century, He Said, She Said,* and *To Tell the Truth.*

Garbo, Greta

Swedish actress (real name is Greta Gustaffson) who was nicknamed "the Dumb Swede" in her early Hollywood days. Garbo was Adolf Hitler's favorite actress. In the 1926 movie *The Torrent* Joel McCrea doubled for Garbo in riding scenes. In ads for the movie *Woman of Mystery* she was depicted as a Sphinx. Garbo was portrayed loosely by Kim Novak in the 1968 movie *The Legend of Lylah Clare*. In 1980 it was revealed that during World War II Garbo spied for the Allies against the Axis powers.

Garcia y Vega Elegantes

Brand of cigars smoked by Lt. Columbo in the TV series *Columbo*.

Gardenia

Flower that singer Billie Holliday always wore in the right side of her hair. The tradition began when singer Sylvia Simms first put the flower on Billie's head. Actress Joan Crawford always carried a gardenia in her hand when she attended a social event, and habitually dined with a gardenia nearby.

Gardner, Erle Stanley

(1889–1969) American lawyer and detective story writer. He authored a large number of Perry Mason novels from 1933 until his death. Gardner wrote under the following pseudonyms: A. A. Fair, Kyle Corning, Charles M. Green, Less Tillray, Carleton Kendrake, Robert Parr, and Charles J. Kenny. He was portrayed in the 1959–1960 TV series *The Court of Last Resort* by Paul Birch. On the last new episode of the TV series *Perry Mason,* titled "The Case of the Final Fade-Out" (May 22, 1966), Erle Stanley Gardner played the judge.

Garfield, James Abram

(1831–1881) 20th president of the United States. He was the first president to use a telephone (1878) while in office. He was also the first left-handed president. Portrayals: *Night Riders* (1939) Lawrence Wolf, and *No More Excuses* (1968) Van Johnson.

Garrick, David

(1717–1779) Very popular English actor and close friend of Samuel Johnson while both attended Lichfield Grammar School. Movie portrayals: *Peg of Old Drury* (1935) Cedric Hardwicke; and *The Great Garrick* (1937) Brian Aherne.

Garson, Greer, and Walter Pidgeon

Movies in which the two appeared together: *Blossoms in the Dust* (1941); *Mrs. Miniver* (1942); *The Young Profession* (1943); *Madame Curie* (1943); *Mrs. Parkington* (1944); *Julia Misbehaves* (1948); *That Forsythe Woman* (1949); *The Miniver Story* (1950); and *Scandal at Scourie* (1953).

Gatling, Richard J.

Inventor of the machine gun in 1862.

Gauguin, Eugène Henri Paul

(1848–1903) French painter who helped to establish the school of Pont-Avien. Movie portrayals: *The Moon and Sixpence* (1942) George Sanders (as Charles Strickland); *Lust for Life* (1956) Anthony Quinn; and *Gauguin the Savage* (1980 TV) David Carradine.

Gaumont
> Theater in Manchester, England, where the Gibb brothers (Barry, Robin, and Maurice) first gave a live performance in 1957. They then called themselves the Rattlesnakes and sang "Lollipop." The three had planned to mime the record, but the record was dropped by accident, so they had to sing live. Today the group is called the Bee Gees.

Gay Abandon
> Wife of Rick O'Shay since 1973 (comic strip *Rick O'Shay*).

Gay Bob
> First homosexual doll (1978). His parents are Fat Pat and Heavy Harry. The 13-inch doll comes in a cardboard closet.

Gayetty, Joseph C.
> Inventor of toilet paper in 1857.

Gedunk Sunday
> Favorite food of Harold Teen (comic strip *Harold Teen*).

Gemstone
> Gordon Liddy's code name for the break-in at the Watergate complex in Washington, D.C., on June 17, 1972.

Gene Gene The Dancing Machine
> Black dancer on Chuck Barris's TV series *The Gong Show*. He is actually a stagehand named Gene Patton.

General Lee
> Good ol' boys' Bo (John Schneider) and Luke (Jon Wopat) red Dodge Charger (with Confederate flag on the roof and 01 on the door) in the TV series *The Dukes of Hazard*. The Georgia automobile license plate is CNH320 and the car's horn plays "Dixie."

General Randall, USS
> Troop ship upon which Pvt. Elvis Presley sailed to Germany on September 19, 1958, from Brooklyn. The army band played "Hound Dog," "All Shook Up," "Don't Be Cruel," "Tutti Frutti," "Dixie," and "Sentimental Journey."

General Services of the U.S. Army
> Branches:

G1	Administration		G4	Quartermaster
G2	Intelligence		G5	Civil Affairs
G3	Operations		G6	Psychological Warfare and Public Relations

General Sterling Price
> Beer-drinking cat in the 1969 movie *True Grit* and in the 1975 sequel *Rooster Cogburn*. He was named for a Yankee Civil War general.

Geneva Convention
> Code by which prisoners of war are treated. Japanese Col. Saito (Sessue

Hayakawa) slapped British Col. Nicholson (Alec Guinness) across the face with a copy of the code in the 1957 movie *The Bridge on the River Kwai*.

Geneviere
Jill Young's (Terry Moore) doll when she was a girl in Africa in the 1949 movie *Mighty Joe Young*.

Genghis Khan
(1162–1227) Mongol conqueror named khan of all the Mongols in 1206. Movie portrayals: *The Conqueror* (1956) John Wayne; and *Genghis Khan* (1965) Omar Sharif.

Genovese, Catherine "Kitty"
28-year-old woman who was stabbed to death on New York City's Austin Street at 3:00 p.m. on Friday, March 13, 1964, three doors from her home. Though there were 38 witnesses to the murder, no one helped the victim as the murderer returned again and again to stab her. Her killer was 29-year-old Winston Moseley.

Genovese, Vito
(1897–1969) Mafia leader known as Don Vitone. He was a hit man in his youth before he became head of the Mafia, after which he ordered a number of murders. He died in Leavenworth in 1969. Lino Ventura portrayed him in the 1972 movie *The Valachi Papers*.

Gent from Frisco, The
Title considered originally for the 1941 Humphrey Bogart film *The Maltese Falcon*.

Gentile, Jim
Baseball player nicknamed Diamond Jim who was the first major league player to hit back-to-back (consecutive innings) grand slams, on May 9, 1961. On June 24, 1968, Jim Northrup became the second player to hit back-to-back grand slams.

George
Janitor on the TV series *The Muppet Show*. His voice is that of Frank Oz.

George
Time traveler played by Rod Taylor in the 1960 movie *The Time Machine* (based on the H.G. Wells novel of the same name).

George
Aunt Elizabeth's (May Robson) pet dog, played by Skippy in the 1938 movie *Bringing Up Baby*.

George Burns Story, The
Billing on marquees for the 1977 movie *Oh God!* when it was shown in Salt Lake City.

George Washington Slept Here
1942 Jack Benny movie given by the submarine USS *Thunderfish* to the

submarine USS *Corbina* in exchange for the 1944 Cary Grant movie *Destination Tokyo* in the 1951 movie *Operation Pacific*.

Georgia on My Mind
State song (as of 1979) of Georgia. (Words by Stuart Gorrell, music by Hoagy Carmichael.)

Georgies
Wrestler Gorgeous George's gold-plated bobby pins.

Georgetown, Colorado
Setting for the 1959 TV series *Hotel De Paree*.

Geraldine
Abner Peabody's pet cat in the radio series *Lum 'n' Abner*.

Geraldine and Josephine
Names that composer Cole Porter gave to his two crushed legs (right and left, respectively) when he was recovering from an injury after a horse fell on him in October 1937.

German, Jacob
New York City cab driver who on May 20, 1899, became the first person to be arrested for speeding. He was traveling at 12 mph.

Geronimo
Traditional yell used by U.S. Army paratroopers when jumping out of an airplane. It was originated by Sgt. Aubrey Eberhart during World War II.

Geronomo, Cesar
Cincinnati Reds outfielder who on July 17, 1974, became Bob Gibson's 3000th strike-out victim. Then on July 4, 1980, Geronomo became Nolan Ryan's 3000th strike-out victim.

Gershwin, George
(1898–1937) American composer. He and his lyricist brother, Ira, composed a number of popular songs such as "Swanee," "I Got Rhythm," and "Love Walked In." George Gershwin also scored the music for dozens of musical plays. He was portrayed in the 1945 movie *Rhapsody in Blue* by Robert Alda (Mickey Ross as a boy) and Ira was portrayed by Herbert Rudley (Darryl Hickman as a boy). Ira Gershwin is the godfather of actress Liza Minnelli.

Gertrude
6-foot-tall doll prop used by Ernie Kovacs in many of his skits on Philadelphia TV.

Gertrude
McCoy family's Model T Ford in the TV series *The Real McCoys*.

Gertrude and Heathcliffe
Two sea gulls who talk to each other in Red Skelton's comedy skit. They were the subject of a children's book written by Skelton.

Gertrude Gearshift and Mabel Flapsaddle
Two telephone operators on the radio series *The Jack Benny Program*, played by Bea Benaderet (Gertrude) and Sara Berner and Sandra Gould (Mabel).

Gestring, Marjorie
U.S. contestant in the springboard competition who became the youngest Gold Medal winner in the Olympics when she won in Berlin in 1936. She was 13 years, 4 months old.

Getacean
Submarine-type vehicle in which Mark Harris (Patrick Duffy) traveled in the TV series *The Man from Atlantis*.

Get a Job
1957 hit record by the Silhouettes. It was from the lyrics of this song that the group Sha Na Na got their name. Joe Namath made his singing debut on Sha Na Na's TV series, singing "Get a Job." The first record made by Smokey Robinson and the Miracles was the 1958 answer song "Got a Job."

Get Dancing
Song that made the top 10 in 1975 by Disco Tex and the Sex-O-Lettes. Disco Tex in actuality was comedian Monti Rock III.

Getting to Know You
Song sung by Anna (Deborah Kerr*) in the 1951 movie *The King and I*, and by Andy Schmidt (Henry Winkler) to Mary Crawford (Kim Darby) in a restaurant in the 1977 movie *The One and Only*. The song was written by Richard Rodgers and Oscar Hammerstein II for the musical play *South Pacific*, but was used instead in *The King and I* with new lyrics.

Getty, John Paul
Wealthiest man in the world. In 1923 he was Jack Dempsey's sparring partner for an upcoming fight with Tom Gibbons. Getty was supposedly the only man ever to knock out Jack Dempsey.

Ghostly Trio
Mischievous ghosts who give Casper the Friendly Ghost a bad time in cartoons/comic books. Their names are Fatso, Fusso, and Lazo.

Gibbons, Cedric
Art director who designed the statuette used for the Academy Awards. Gibbons, who has won the statue 11 times, was once married to actress Dolores Del Rio.

Gibbons, Floyd
(1887–1937) War correspondent and author who was with Pancho Villa during the Mexican Revolution (1915), and later with Gen. Pershing (1916) on the American expedition to Mexico. Gibbons was rescued from the

*Dubbed by Marni Nixon.

torpedoed liner *Laconic* on February 25, 1917. During World War I he served as a correspondent in France. He was portrayed by Stuart Erwin in the 1934 movie *Viva Villa!*

Gibbsville Courier
Newspaper for which Ray Whitehead (Gig Young) was a reporter in the TV series *Gibbsville*.

Gibson, Josh
Black player for the Homestead Grays of the Negro League. Gibson hit 84 home runs in one season and over 800 home runs in his career. In 1934 he missed by only 5 feet of hitting a ball out of Yankee Stadium.

Gibson Man, The
Nickname conferred on handsome silent screen actor J. Warren Kerrigan.

Gideon, Clarence Earl
(1909–1972) Florida handyman who was convicted and sent to prison for 5 years for petty larceny in 1961 after defending himself. He later petitioned the Supreme Court to overturn his conviction on the grounds that his constitutional rights to a proper defense had been violated. The court ruled in his favor in the landmark decision *Gideon* v. *Wainwright*. Gideon was portrayed in the 1980 TV movie *Gideon's Trumpet* by Henry Fonda.

Giddyap Gourmet
TV series hosted by Randy Robinson (Charles Nelson Reilly) within the TV series *Arnie*.

Giesler, Jerry
Famous Hollywood lawyer who has handled cases for a great number of movie industry celebrities. He was once an office boy for famed attorney Earl Rogers*.

Gilbert, John, and Greta Garbo
Films in which the couple appeared: *Flesh and the Devil* (1927); *Love* (1927); *A Woman of Affairs* (1929); *A Man's Man* (1929); and *Queen Christina* (1933). Gilbert and Garbo were portrayed in the 1980 TV miniseries *Moviola* by Barry Bostwick and Kristina Wayborn.

Gilbert, William S.
Half of the songwriting team of Gilbert and Sullivan. As a child in 1839, Gilbert was the victim of a $125,000 kidnapping. He was portrayed in the movie *The Story of Gilbert and Sullivan* by Robert Morley (Sullivan by Maurice Evans).

Gilley's
Pasadena, Texas, nightclub, the largest in the world with 48,000 square feet of floor space. It was the setting of the 1980 movie *Urban Cowboy.* The club

---

*Father of writer Adela Rogers St. Johns.

is co-owned by musician Mickey Gilley, cousin of Jerry Lee Lewis, and Jimmy Swaggart.

Gilliam & Norris Theatrical Agency
Agency that handles Ann Marie (Marlo Thomas) on the series *That Girl*.

Gilmore, Gary
Convicted murderer who was put to death on January 17, 1977, in front of a firing squad in Utah. He was the first person to be executed in the United States in ten years. Gilmore was the illegitimate grandson of magician Harry Houdini. He is the subject of Norman Mailer's 1979 Pulitzer Prize–winning book *The Executioner's Song*.

Gimcrack
Schooner on which the New York Yacht Club was founded on July 30, 1844.

Ginger
Mrs. Gibson's pet dog (Mrs. Gibson was Ralph Kramden's mother-in-law) in the TV series *The Honeymooners*.

Girl in a Black Dress
Other name of the "Portrait of Jennie," painted by Eben Adams in the novel *Portrait of Jennie* by Robert Nathan (not mentioned in the 1948 movie of the same title).

Girl of the North
Projected movie for which Consolidated Pictures conducted a search to find the right actress for the role of a southern belle à la *Gone With the Wind* in the 1939 movie *Second Fiddle*.

Gisele McKenzie Show, The
1957–1958 TV series on which Tom Kennedy replaced his brother, Jack Narz, as announcer.

Gish, Lillian
(1896–   ) "The First Lady of the Silent Screen," sister of actress Dorothy Gish. She was nominated for an Oscar for best supporting actress for the 1946 movie *Duel in the Sun*. Lillian Gish was portrayed in the 1980 TV miniseries *Moviola* by Mackenzie Phillips.

Give My Regards to Broadway
Song written by George M. Cohan in 1904. It can be heard in the following movies: *Yankee Doodle Dandy* (1942); *Give My Regards to Broadway* (1948); *Jolson Sings Again* (1949); *With a Song in My Heart* (1952).

Gladiator
Philip Wylie's 1930 science fiction novel that inspired 17-year-old writer Jerry Siegel and artist Joe Shuster to create *Superman,* which debuted in comic books in June 1938.

Gladstone, William Ewart
(1809–1898) British statesman who served several times as Liberal prime minister. The character of the Mad Hatter in Lewis Carroll's *Alice in*

Wonderland was patterned after him. Gladstone was portrayed in the 1966 movie *Khartoum* by Ralph Richardson.

Glassboro, New Jersey

Site of the 1967 summit meeting between President Johnson and Premier Kosygin.

Glea Girls

Beautiful young models who introduced skits on the TV series *The Jackie Gleason Show.*

Glenn, John

Astronaut (first American in space, May 5, 1961) and senator. In 1962 he was given the biggest ticker-tape parade in history when New York showered 3,474 tons of paper on him.

GLenview 7537

Office phone number of private eye Philip Marlowe (detective stories).

Glidden, J. F.

Inventor of barbed wire in 1874.

Global 33

Boeing 707 flight that accidentally breaks the time barrier and becomes lost in time in "Odyssey of Flight 33," an episode of the TV series *The Twilight Zone.*

Global 802

Boeing 707 flight that had a near miss with a VFR* aircraft and later had to make an emergency landing with an engine on fire in the 1979 TV movie *Crisis in the Skies.* The pilot was Capt. Adam Travis (Don Murray).

Glomar Explorer

36,000-ton ship built at a cost of $550 million. Howard Hughes used the vessel to raise the remains of a Soviet nuclear submarine.

Goal Posts

They stand 10 feet high in football. In collegiate play the goal posts are 23 feet 4 inches across. In pro play they are 18 feet 6 inches across.

Gobelues

Theme song composed and played by John Scott Trotter on the TV series *The George Gobel Show.*

Goddard, Paulette

American actress (born Marion Levy). She was married to Charlie Chaplin, Burgess Meredith, and writer Erich Maria Remarque. Goddard was portrayed in the 1980 TV miniseries *Moviola* by Gwen Humble.

Goebbels, Joseph Paul

(1897–1945) Nazi Germany's minister of propaganda who committed suicide in Hitler's bunker in Berlin along with his wife and children in 1945.

---

*Visual Flight Rules.

Movie portrayals: *Confessions of a Nazi Spy* (1939) Martin Kosleck; *The Nasty Nuisance* (1943) Charles Rogers; *The Hitler Gang* (1944) Martin Kosleck; *Hitler* (1962) Martin Kosleck; and *The Bunker* (1981 TV) Cliff Gorman.

Gobel, William
Governor-elect of Kentucky who was assassinated on his inauguration day in January 1900.

Gogo
Greer Garson's pet dog that appeared with his mistress in the 1945 movie *Valley of Decision*.

Golden Arrow
Famous train that once ran from Paris to Monte Carlo.

Golden Bear
Annual award given by the Berlin Film Festival for the year's best movie.

Golden Boy
1939 Columbia movie that launched the careers of both William Holden and Lee J. Cobb. John Garfield played Holden's role on Broadway in 1951. *Golden Boy* was Garfield's last stage appearance; he died that year.

Golden Dragon
Nightclub setting in the TV series *Hong Kong*. The Golden Dragon was also the restaurant in San Francisco that was attacked by Chinese youths on the night of September 4, 1977; several people were killed.

Golden Driller
76-foot-tall statue symbolizing the petroleum industry that stands in Expo Square in Tulsa, Oklahoma. The figure's shoe size is 394DDD, its hat size is 112.

Goldeneye
Ian Fleming's Jamaican retreat where he wrote his James Bond novels. It was named after Operation Goldeneye (the defense of Gibraltar) during World War II.

Golden Fleece Awards
Monthly awards created by Senator William Proxmire for wasteful spending in the federal government. The first award, in 1975, went to the National Science Foundation for its $84,000 study of why people fall in love.

Golden Globe Awards
Annual awards (begun in 1942) given by the Hollywood Foreign Press Association, honoring TV and motion pictures.

Golden Glove
Amateur boxing competition in the United States (begun in 1923).

Golden Goose Café
Club off Times Square that was the setting of the 1949 TV series *The Morey*

Amsterdam Show, on which future author Jacqueline Susann* played Lola, the cigarette girl.

Golden Lion of St. Mark
Annual award given by the Venice Film Festival for the year's best movie.

Golden Palm
Annual award given by the Cannes Film Festival for the year's best movie.

Golden Rule
Names of J. C. Penney's (James Cash Penney) first store, established in Kemmerer, Wyoming, in 1902.

Golden Safari
New York City nightclub at 4336 West Washington where Jill Young (Terry Moore) appeared with her pet gorilla Joseph Young in the 1949 movie *Mighty Joe Young.*

Golden Sounds
Housing project in John D. MacDonald's novel *Condominium.*

Goldmark, Peter
Inventor of the long-playing record album in 1948. Goldmark was killed on December 7, 1977, in an automobile accident on the centennial of the invention of the phonograph by Thomas Edison.

Gold Medal Award
Annual award (begun in 1920) by *Photoplay* magazine for the year's best picture.

Goldstein, Ruby
Referee who handled numerous championship fights. During the World light heavyweight Championship match at Yankee Stadium, on June 24, 1952, between Joey Maxim and Sugar Ray Robinson, Goldstein had to quit refereeing at the end of the 10th round because of heat exhaustion.

Goldwyn, Samuel
(1882–1974) Warsaw-born movie producer (born Samuel Goldfish). He was involved in the formation of the Jesse L. Lasky Feature Play Company (1913), Adolph Zukor's Famous Players (1916), Metro-Goldwyn-Mayer (1922), and Samuel Goldwyn Productions (1923). He was popular for such Goldwynisms as: "A verbal agreement isn't worth the paper it's written on," and "Anyone seeing a psychiatrist should have his head examined." Goldwyn was portrayed in the 1980 TV miniseries *Moviola* by Lee Wallace.

Goliath
Merchant ship that after being sunk in a 1943 hurricane with a cache of drugs was located in the 1977 movie *The Deep* (based on the 1976 Peter Benchley novel of the same name). The wreck used for the movie was actually the RMS *Rhone,* which sunk on her maiden voyage in 1865. (See: **Grifon**)

---

*Her husband, Irving Mansfield, was the show's producer.

Goliath
Biblical Philistine giant killed by David with a sling and a stone. Goliath was portrayed in the 1951 movie *David and Bathsheba* by Walter Talvn and in the 1961 movie *David and Goliath* by Kronos.

Go Man Van Gogh
Beatnik artist in Beany and Cecil cartoons (voice provided by "Scatman" Crothers).

Gonzo the Great
Resident artist and chicken trainer on the TV series *The Muppet Show* (voice provided by Dave Goelz).

Goodale, William
Inventor of the first paper bag, patented on July 12, 1859.

GOOD BYE
Two words on the bottom of a Ouija Board. Parker Brothers are the owners of the game.

Goodman, Benny
Very popular jazz clarinetist whose career began in the 1920s. Goodman recorded dozens of hit songs. His opening theme song was "Let's Dance," and his closing theme is "Goodbye." In 1939 he wrote his autobiography, titled *Kingdom of Swing*. Benny Goodman's was the first American band to tour the Soviet Union (1962). He was portrayed in the 1955 movie *The Benny Goodman Story** by Steve Allen (Harry James, Lionel Hampton, Teddy Wilson, Gene Krupa, and Ben Pollock portrayed themselves).

Good Morning
Catchy song by Nacio Herb Brown and Arthur Freed. It was sung in the 1941 movie *Babes in Arms* and again in the 1952 movie *Singin' in the Rain*.

Good Night and Good News
Sign-off of WJM-TV anchorman Ted Baxter (Ted Knight) in the TV series *The Mary Tyler Moore Show*.

Good Old Days
Theme song of the Little Rascals (Our Gang) comedies.

Goodrich, Bert
Mr. America of 1938. He was the first to hold the title.

Goon and Jeep
Words coined by Elzie Crisler in his comic strip *Thimble Theater*.

Goose
Nickname of basketball player Reese Tatum of the Harlem Globetrotters.

Gopher Gus
Alaskan prospector sidekick of Barney Baxter in the comic strip *Barney Baxter*.

---

*This film saw the movie debut of Sammy Davis, Jr.

Gopher Prairie

Setting of Sinclair Lewis's 1920 novel *Main Street*. It closely resembled Lewis's hometown of Sauk Centre, Minnesota.

Gordon, Charles "Chinese"

(1833–1885) British general who abolished slavery in China and the Sudan. He was portrayed by Charlton Heston in the 1966 movie *Khartoum,* in which Laurence Olivier portrayed his Arab nemesis, the Mahdi.

Gordon, Ruth

(1896–   ) American stage and screen actress married to writer Garson Kanin. The pair collaborated on a number of successful screenplays. Gordon was portrayed in the 1953 movie *The Actress* by Jean Simmons (as Ruth Gordon Jones). Ruth Gordon and her husband are one of several married couples who have both won an Academy Award. She won hers for her supporting role in *Rosemary's Baby* (1968). Others are: Laurence Olivier and Vivien Leigh; and Mel Brooks and Anne Bancroft.

Gorgon

Barnaby Baxter's talking dog in the comic strip *Barnaby*.

Göring, Hermann

(1893–1946) German politician who during World War I commanded the Richthofen squadron, and years later held high positions in Adolf Hitler's government. While in jail in 1946 he committed suicide. Movie portrayals: *The Nasty Nuisance* (1943) Rex Evans; *The Magic Face* (1951) Herman Ehrhardt; *Hitler* (1962) John Mitchum; *The Battle of Britain* (1969) Hein Reiss; and *Von Richthofen and Brown* (1971) Barry Primus.

Gossamer Albatross

Aircraft that Bryan Allen peddled across the English Channel (22 miles) on June 12, 1979, to a $200,000 prize. It took him 2 hours and 50 minutes.

Gossamer Condor

First human-powered aircraft. On August 23, 1977, the craft, designed by Dr. Paul MacCready, Jr., and piloted by Bryan Allen, completed a mile-long figure-8 course in 6 minutes, 22.05 seconds, to win the $87,000 (£50,000) prize established by British industrialist Henry Kremer.

Goulet, Robert

Ex-Canadian disc jockey and singer who for some reason was hated by Elvis Presley. In 1974 Presley once shot at a television set because Goulet was on the screen. When Goulet sang the "Star-Spangled Banner" at the Muhammad Ali–Sonny Liston fight in February 25, 1964, he forgot some of the words.

Governor Philip Grey

Governor of Hawaii in the TV series *Hawaii Five-O,* played by Richard Denning.

Gowdy, Curt
Radio and television announcer after whom a state park in Wyoming is named.

"Go west, young man, go west"
Saying widely credited to newspaper publisher Horace Greeley but actually coined by newsman John B. Soule in 1851.

Goya y Lucientes, Francisco José de
(1746–1828) Spanish painter famous for his bullfighting and battle scenes. He was portrayed in the 1959 movie *The Naked Maja* by Anthony Franciosa.

Gracie Mansion
Official residence in Carl Schurz Park of New York City's mayors.

Graf Zeppelin II
Sister ship of the *Hindenburg*.

Graham, Bette Claire
Inventor of the fluid used for correcting typewriter mistakes, Liquid Paper. She founded a multimillion-dollar company to manufacture the substance in 1956. Bette Graham is the mother of Michael Nesmith, a former member of the Monkees.

Graham, Calvin
12-year-old U.S. sailor who was awarded the Bronze Star and a Purple Heart. He was stationed aboard the USS *South Dakota* during the Battle of Guadalcanal in 1942. When the Navy discovered his age, it took back its medals, put him in jail, and then discharged him. In May 1978 Graham was finally granted an honorable discharge.

Graham, Sheila
Hollywood columnist who was romantically involved with author F. Scott Fitzgerald. Movie portrayals: *Beloved Infidel* (1959) Deborah Kerr; and *F. Scott Fitzgerald in Hollywood* (1976) Julia Foster.

Graham, Sylvester
Inventor of the Graham cracker.

Grand Central Station
First commercial establishment lighted by electric lights, on September 4, 1882.

Grand Moff Tarkin
Commander of the *Death Star*, played by Peter Cushing in the 1978 movie *Star Wars*.

Grandview
Small-town setting of the 1947 James Stewart movie *Magic Town*. The town newspaper was the *Dispatch*.

Grange, The
Farmers' organization to which Amos McCoy (Walter Brennan) belonged in the TV series *The Real McCoys*.

Grant, George F.
Boston inventor of the golf tee, on December 12, 1899.

Grass Sandwich, A
1915 film considered to be the first American pornographic movie.

Gravitt, Hugh D.
Off-duty taxicab driver who on August 11, 1949, struck author Margaret Mitchell as she and her husband, John, were crossing Peachtree Street in Atlanta, Georgia. Margaret died on August 16, and Hugh Gravitt was sentenced to jail for involuntary manslaughter.

Gray Ghost
Trained horse that Chief Sitting Bull rode as a member of Bill Cody's Wild West Show.

Gray, L. Patrick
Acting director of the FBI after the death of J. Edgar Hoover. Gray was appointed by President Nixon. On April 27, 1973, he resigned, a casualty of the Watergate scandal. He was portrayed in the 1979 TV miniseries *Blind Ambition* by Lonny Chapman.

Graziano, "Rocky"
Rocco Barbella, world middleweight boxing champion. He appeared on the following TV series: *Pantomime Quiz* (regular); *Miami Undercover* (co-star); *The Martha Raye Show; The Keefe Brasselle Show* (regular); and *Henny and Rocky* (co-host). Graziano was portrayed in the 1956 movie *Somebody Up There Likes Me* by Paul Newman.

Grease
Longest-running Broadway play (1972–1980). The movie, starring John Travolta, was released in Mexico as *Vaselina* and in Italy as *Brilliantino*.

Greased Lightnin'
Danny Zucco's (John Travolta) super-customized car in the 1978 movie *Grease*.

Great Artiste and No. 91
Two photoreconnaissance B29's that flew with the *Enola Gay* on her mission to drop the first atomic bomb on Hiroshima, August 6, 1945. Major Charles Sweeney, the pilot of *Great Artiste*, was also the pilot of *Bock's Car*, the B29 that dropped the A-bomb on Nagasaki 3 days later.

Great Krypton!
Favorite expression of Superman (comic books).

Great One, The
Nickname of actor Jackie Gleason.

Great Ormond Street Hospital
London medical facility to which James Barrie bequeathed the copyright of his book *Peter Pan*.

Great Pacific Casualty Company
New Orleans firm for which Michael Longstreet (James Franciscus) worked as an investigator in the TV series *Longstreet*.

Great Western
Hampshire boar bought for $10,200 in 1953 in Byron, Illinois. It was the highest price ever paid for a hog.

Greb, Harry
Only man to defeat Gene Tunney in the boxing ring. The match took place in 1922 for the light-heavyweight title.

Grecian Urn
Award presented to *Sports Illustrated* magazine's Sportsman of the Year. The first recipient was runner Roger Bannister, in 1954.

Greco, El
(1548–1614) Real name: Kyriakos Theotokopoulos. Famous Spanish (Cretan-born) painter who studied under Titian. He was portrayed in the 1966 movie *El Greco* by Mel Ferrer.

Greece
Country whose team always leads the Olympic procession at the opening ceremonies. The last team in the parade is that of the host country.

Greek-French-British
Three national passports carried by Joel Cairo (Peter Lorre) in the 1941 movie *The Maltese Falcon*. His birthdate was given as May 5, 1903.

Greenacres
Name of comic Harold Lloyd's 16-acre estate in Beverly Hills. It had an Olympic-sized swimming pool and a 9-hole golf course.

Green Archer
Secret identity of crime fighter Michael Bellamy, played in the 1940 movie series *The Green Archer* by Kenneth Duncan.

Greenbluff, Illinois
Hometown of Capt. Arthur Black (Nicholas Hammond) in the 1980 TV movie *The Martian Chronicles* (based on the Ray Bradbury collection of short stories of the same name). The town and its inhabitants were duplicated on Mars by the Martians.

Green-Gold-White
Colors of the Oakland A's baseball team uniforms, introduced by Charles O. Finley. The colors' official terms: Kelly Green, Fort Knox Gold, and Wedding Gown White.

Green Grow the Lilacs
Working title of the Rodgers and Hammerstein musical *Away We Go!*, which finally was changed to *Oklahoma!*

Greenland and New Guinea
Two largest islands in the world. (Australia is a continent.)

Green, Robert M.
American inventor of the ice cream soda in Philadelphia in 1874.

Greensleeves
Traditional English ballad whose authorship is attributed by some to Henry VIII.

Greenwood
North Carolina town of which Andy Sawyer (Andy Griffith) was mayor in the TV series *The New Andy Griffith Show*.

Greyhound Hall of Fame
Honors racing dogs and is located in Abilene, Kansas. It was opened in 1973.

Griffin, John Howard
White southern newspaperman who darkened his skin, lived as a black in the South in 1959, and wrote a book about his experiences called *Black Like Me* (1961). Griffin was portrayed by James Whitmore (as John Finley Horton) in the 1964 movie *Black Like Me*.

Griffin, Peck
Brother of TV talk show host Merv Griffin who won the U.S. doubles championship three times. Another brother, Elmer, was featured in several Ripley's *Believe It or Not* segments for his achievements in tennis. Merv himself won three Oregon State titles, all in a single day.

Grifon
French tobacco ship filled with treasure that lies in the same ruins as the military vessel *Goliath* in the 1977 movie *The Deep*. The vessel, one of an 11-ship armada, actually sank on July 31, 1715.

Grilled Soul
Meal eaten by Jame Bond (Sean Connery) on board a train in the 1964 movie *From Russia With Love*.

Grizzly Adams
James Capen Adams, a character of the western frontier who had a pet bear named Ben. Adams was portrayed in the 1974 movie and TV series *The Life and Times of Grizzly Adams* by Dan Haggerty and in the 1972 movie *The Life and Times of Judge Roy Bean* by John Huston.

Groat, Dick
Major league baseball player who was college basketball player of the year for 1951.

Grogan, Perry
Telegrapher who, with the help of sportswriter Jack Lawrence, pushed Jack Dempsey back into the ring at New York's Polo Grounds on September 14, 1923, when Luis Firpo knocked Dempsey out of the ring in the 1st round of the title fight. In the 1976 movie *Rocky* Mickey Goldmill (Burgess Meredith) claimed to have knocked Ginny Russo out of the ring the same night.

Grow Old with Me
Original title of science fiction writer Isaac Asimov's first book, *Pebble in the Sky*, which first appeared in *Galaxy* in 1933.

Gucci
Brand of saddle used by Bart (Cleavon Little) in the 1974 movie *Blazing Saddles*.

Guess Who?
First words spoken by Woody Woodpecker in his debut cartoon *Knock, Knock*. "Guess Who?" later became Woody's trademark.

Guevara, Ernesto "Che"
Cuban guerrilla who infiltrated Bolivia in 1965 to fight against the government troops. Che Guevara was captured and executed on October 8, 1967. Movie portrayals: *El Che Guevara* (1967 Italian) Francisco Rabal; and *Che!* (1969) Omar Sharif.

Guinan, Texas
Mary Louise Cecilia Guinan. Popular nightclub owner of the 1920s who greeted her customers with "Hello, suckers!" Her only talkie movie was *Queen of the Night Clubs** (1929). She had once been a Sunday school teacher, and one of her students was Lowell Thomas. Movie portrayals: *Incendiary Blonde* (1945) Betty Hutton; *The George Raft Story* (1961) Barbara Nichols; and *Splendor in the Grass* (1961) Phyllis Diller. Ruby Stevens (Barbara Stanwyck) and Ruby Keeler were once chorus girls at Texas Guinan's club on West 56th Street in New York.

Gulick, Mrs. Luther Halsey
Founder of the Camp Fire Girls organization on March 17, 1912, at Lake Sebago, Casco, Maine.

Gulliver
Diana Smythe's (Diana Rigg) pet Great Dane in the TV series *Diana*. The dog belonged to Diana's brother, Roger.

Gumm Sisters
Judy, Virginia, and Suzanne, a singing-sister trio. Judy later became Judy Garland. The three sisters were portrayed in the 1978 TV movie *Rainbow* by Andrea McArdle (Judy), Donna Pescow (Virginia), and Erin Donovan (Suzanne).

Gunther, Johnny
(1929–1947) Author John Gunther's teenage son who died of a brain tumor. John Gunther told of his son's bravery in his 1949 book *Death Be Not Proud*. Johnny Gunther was portrayed in the 1975 movie *Death Be Not Proud* by Robby Benson; John Gunther was portrayed by Arthur Hill.

Guppy
Capt'n Crunch's sailing vessel (breakfast cereal).

---

*Movie debut of George Raft.

Gus

Harry Rule's (Robert Vaughn) pet dog in the TV series *The Protectors*.

Guthrie, Gary

Disc jockey for radio station WAKY who first spliced (as a present for his wife) the versions of "You Don't Bring Me Flowers" by Barbra Streisand and Neil Diamond. The popularity of his tape eventually led to the two recording the song as a duet.

Guthrie, "Woody" Woodrow Wilson

(1912–1967) American folk singer and composer of numerous songs including "This Land Is Your Land." His autobiography, *Bound for Glory,* was made into a movie in 1977 with David Carradine portraying Woody. In the 1969 movie *Alice's Restaurant* Woody was portrayed by Joseph Boley, and his son, Arlo, played himself.

Gwyn eich byd a dymunaf i chwi laweydd bob amser

Welsh saying meaning: "May you always be well and be happy." Said by Tom Jones at the conclusion of his weekly TV show.

H Albums
> Albums recorded by the group America: *America,* called their "Horse with No Name" album (1972); *History–America's Great Hits* (1972); *Hat Trick* (1973); *Holiday* (1974); *Hearts* (1975); *Hideaway* (1976); and *Harbour* (1977).

H Bandleaders
> Dizzy Gillespie played in eight bands whose leaders' last name began with *H:* Edgar Hayes, Earl Hines, Fletcher Henderson, Horace Henderson, Les Hite, Claude Hopkins, Woody Herman, and Teddy Hill.

H Bomb
> Whiskey-drinking horse in the 1973 movie *Flap,* played by Old Fooler.

H. J. Bellows and Co.
> Ad agency for which Ozzie Nelson worked in the 1952 movie *Here Come the Nelsons.* On TV he never appeared to have an occupation.

H Presidents
> U.S. presidents whose last names begin with *H:* William Henry Harrison, Rutherford Birchard Hayes, Benjamin Harrison, Warren Gamaliel Harding, and Herbert Clark Hoover.

HMT 598B
> British license number of the white Jaguar XKE on the cover of the Dave Clark Five's *Try Too Hard* album.

HVJ
> Vatican's radio station, which began broadcasting in 1931.

H. W. Bolt & Co., TV Service
> Cover advertisement on the side of Honey West's (Anne Francis) van in the TV series *Honey West.*

Hackard Building
> New York City location of Mike Hammer's detective agency, Hammer Investigative Agency (Suite 808).

Hackensack, New Jersey

Destination of one or two missiles (XK 101 "Army Bird") in the 1978 movie *Superman*. Because Eva Teschmacher's (Valerie Perrine) mother lives there, she freed Superman so he could divert the missile.

Haeberle, Ronald L.

Army combat photographer with C Company who took 40 military black and white photographs and 18 personal color photos of the aftermath of the My Lai 4 massacre on March 16, 1968.

Hale, Nathan

(1755–1776) American Revolutionary hero who was hanged as a spy by the British on September 21, 1776. His last words were: "I only regret that I have but one life to lose for my country." Brandon de Wilde portrayed the young Nathan Hale in the TV series *The Young Rebels*.

Haldeman, H. R. "Bob"

White House chief of staff under President Nixon. He was portrayed in the 1979 TV miniseries *Blind Ambition* by Lawrence Pressman, and in 1978 movie *Born Again* by Richard Caine.

Haley, Alex

Author of the highly popular book *Roots* and the 1977 TV miniseries derived from it. Haley was portrayed in another TV miniseries, *Roots: The Next Generation*, by James Earl Jones (Kristoff St. John as a small boy and Damon Evans as a young man). Haley's family tree:

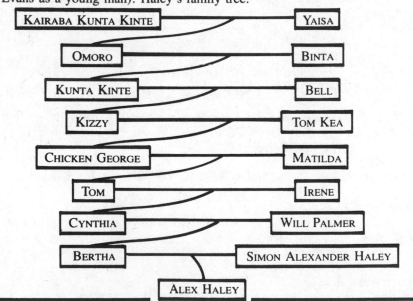

Hall, Donald A.
Ryan Airlines engineer who, in 60 days in 1927, designed and built Charles Lindbergh's *Spirit of St. Louis,* the single-engine aircraft that was the first plane to fly the Atlantic.

Hall, Jon, and Maria Montez
Films in which the pair appeared: *Arabian Nights* (1942); *White Savage* (1943); *Ali Baba and the Forty Thieves* (1944); *Cobra Woman* (1944); *Gypsy Wildcat* (1944); and *Sudan* (1945).

Halsey, William Frederick "Bull"
(1882–1959) American naval officer who commanded the U.S. 3rd fleet in the Pacific during World War II. Bull Halsey was the starting fullback in the 1902 Army-Navy game. The midshipmen lost to the Army, whose team was managed by Douglas MacArthur. Movie portrayals: *The Gallant Hours* (1960) James Cagney; *Tora! Tora! Tora!* (1970) James Whitmore; *Midway* (1976) Robert Mitchum; and *MacArthur* (1977) Kenneth Tobey.

Halverson, Carl S.
American lieutenant who first dropped little parachute bags of candy for the children of Berlin during the Berlin Airlift. The idea soon spread to other crews.

Hamblen, Stuart
Country-western and gospel singer and composer who ran for U.S. president on the Prohibition ticket in 1952. Some of his compositions are: "This Ole House," "It Is No Secret," and "Beyond the Sunset." Elvis Presley recorded several of his gospel compositions.

Hamburger U
McDonald Hamburger's training school at Elk Grove Village, Illinois.

Ham Gravy
Olive Oyl's boyfriend before she met Popeye. She went with Ham for 10 years. Played by Bill Irwin in the 1980 movie *Popeye*.

Hamilton, Alexander
(1755–1804) First U.S. secretary of the treasury (1789–1795). He was wounded in the duel with Aaron Burr on July 11, 1804, and died the next day. Movie portrayals: *Alexander Hamilton* (1931) George Arliss; and *Magnificent Doll* (1946) Arthur Spree.

Hammer, Frank
Texas Ranger captured by Bonnie and Clyde, who forced him to pose for photographs Bonnie then sent to the newspapers. It was Hammer who led the ambush that took the pair's lives. In the 1967 movie *Bonnie and Clyde* Hammer was portrayed by Denver Pyle.

Hammerstein II, Oscar
(1895–1960) Highly successful composer of Broadway musical songs. He

collaborated with George Gershwin, Sigmund Romberg, and Richard Rodgers, among others. A few of his compositions are: "Indian Love Call," "Ol' Man River," and "Some Enchanted Evening." Hammerstein was portrayed in the 1946 movie *Till the Clouds Roll By* by Paul Langton, and in the 1976 TV special *America Salutes Richard Rodgers—The Sounds of His Music* by Gene Kelly.

Hammett, Dashiell

Pinkerton detective (for 8 years) who became a writer of classic detective novels: *Red Harvest, The Maltese Falcon, The Dain Curse, The Glass Key, The Thin Man,* and *The Continental Op.* Hammett created the radio series *The Fat Man.* James Coburn played Hamilton Nash in the TV miniseries *Dain Curse.* Dashiell Hammett was portrayed by Jason Robards, Jr., in the 1977 movie *Julia.*

Hamm, William Jr.

Wealthy brewer kidnapped by Alvin "Old Creepy" Karpis and Fred Hunter for $100,000 ransom. Karpis was personally arrested by the head of the FBI, J. Edgar Hoover, on April 30, 1936. (It was Hoover's first arrest.)

Hammond, John

This great-grandson* of Commodore Vanderbilt was a record company executive and helped develop the careers of Benny Goodman, Count Basie, Duke Ellington, Billie Holiday, Pete Seeger, Bessie Smith, and Bob Dylan. He was portrayed in the 1956 movie *The Benny Goodman Story* by Herbert Anderson. Benny Goodman married Hammond's sister, Alice, in 1942.

Hampstead Apartments

Where George Jefferson (Sherman Hemsley) once worked as a janitor in the TV series *The Jeffersons.*

Hancock, USS

Aircraft carrier from which Milton Berle broadcast his television show on April 3, 1956. Elvis Presley was the featured performer.

Handel, George Frederick

(1685–1759) German-born composer and naturalized British subject who composed a number of oratorios (23), including *The Messiah* (1742) and *Samson* (1743). He was portrayed in the 1942 movie *The Great Mr. Handel* by Wilfred Lawson.

Hamner, Earl Jr.

Creator and narrator of the TV series *The Waltons.*

Handy Housewife Helpers

Kitchen utensils that Ralph Kramden and Ed Norton attempt to sell for 10

---

*John Hammond is also the grandson of William Douglas Sloane, founder of W & J Sloane Furniture Co.

cents each during the commercial break of a telecast of a Charlie Chan movie in the TV series *The Honeymooners*.

Hannibal
(247–183 B.C.) Carthaginian general who fought against Rome. He crossed the Alps in 218 and defeated a Roman army. Hannibal committed suicide in 183 B.C. Movie portrayals: *Jupiter's Daughter* (1955) Howard Keel; and *Hannibal* (1960) Victor Mature.

Hannibal
Ben Calhoun's (Dale Robertson) horse in the 1966 TV western *Iron Horse*.

Hansel and Gretel
Lost boy and girl, subjects of a Grimm fairy tale. The pair were played by Stanley Fafara and Diana Driscoll in the 1962 movie *The Wonderful World of the Brothers Grimm*.

Hansen, Elisa and Lisa
Siamese twins born head to head in 1977 who were separated on May 30, 1979, in a 16½-hour operation. The first operation separating Siamese twins was done in 1956, on Virginia and Teresa Hansen, also 19 months old.

Hap
Labrador retriever that was kept in a lifeboat by his master, Capt. Cyril Lebrecque, after his yacht capsized and sank in 1976. The captain sacrificed the lives of two of his crew members to save the dog's life. At his trial Labrecque was found innocent.

Happy Birthday to You
Probably the most frequently sung song in America. It was composed by sisters Mildred and Patty Hill in 1893 under the original title of "Good Morning to You."

Happy Days
Theme song of the TV series *The Donna Reed Show*. Also the title of the theme song of the TV series, *Happy Days*.

Happy Days Are Here Again
Theme song of Franklin D. Roosevelt's 1932 presidential campaign. (Words by Jack Yellen, music by Milton Ager.)

Happy Endings
Name of Francine Evan's (Liza Minnelli) musical movie in the 1977 movie *New York, New York*.

Happy Kyne and the Mirth Makers
Studio orchestra on the *American 2night* TV series. Happy was played by Frank De Vol.

Happy Through Marriage
Book written by the world's leading marriage expert, Dr. Heinrich von Heartburn (Sid Caesar), in the TV series *Your Show of Shows*.

Harder, USS
World War II submarine that sank 5 Japanese destroyers in 5 days. Cmd. Sam Dealey was posthumously awarded the Medal of Honor after the vessel was lost at sea.

Hardin, John Wesley
(1853–1895) Texas outlaw and murderer who, after being pardoned from prison, was shot in the back and killed by John Selman in the Acme Saloon in El Paso in 1895. He is credited with inventing the shoulder holster. Movie portrayals: *The Texas Rangers* (1950) John Dehner; *The Lawless Breed* (1952) Rock Hudson; and *Dirty Dingus Magee* (1970) Jack Elam. In 1968 Bob Dylan recorded an album titled *John Wesley Harding* in honor of Hardin (his name was deliberately misspelled).

Harding, Warren Gamaliel
(1865–1923) 29th president of the United States. In 1922 he became the first president to broadcast on the radio. He died in San Francisco on August 2, 1923. Harding was portrayed in the 1979 TV miniseries *Backstairs at the White House* by George Kennedy; his wife, Florence, was played by Celeste Holm.

Hard to Get
1955 hit record by Gisele McKenzie on the "X" record label. She introduced the song on an episode of the TV series *Justice*.

Hardwicke, Sir Cedric
(1893–1964) British actor of both stage and motion pictures and narrator of the 1953 movie *War of the Worlds*.

Hardy, Oliver
(1892–1957) American-born comedian who, with British-born Stan Laurel, formed motion pictures' greatest comedy team. Hardy was portrayed in the 1965 movie *Harlow* by John "Red" Foxx. John MacGeorge provided his voice in the 1966 TV cartoon series *The Laurel and Hardy Cartoon Show*.

Harlettes
Bette Midler's female vocal trio. Melissa Manchester was once a member.

Harley Davidson 74
Jim Bronson's (Michael Parks) red motorcycle in the TV series *Then Came Bronson*.

Harmon, Merle, and Alex Hawkins
Broadcasting team for the WFL football games seen on national television.

Harold Teen
Teenage hero of Carl Ed's comic strip *Harold Teen*. The character was played by Arthur Lake in the 1928 movie *Harold Teen*.

Harriet D. Vane
Wife of Peter Wimsey in the detective novels of Dorothy Sayers. She was the

author of the mystery novels *The Fountain Pen* and *Murder by Degrees*. Their three children were Bredon, Paul, and Roger.

Harrigan's Hooligans
TV series in which Richard Richardson (Richard Dawson) appeared within the TV series *The New Dick Van Dyke Show*.

Harrison, George
Lead guitarist of the Beatles. Born February 25, 1943, Harrison was the youngest of the four and became known as the Quiet Beatle. His ex-wife, Patti Boyd, is now married to rock guitarist Eric Clapton. Harrison was the executive producer of the Monty Python film *The Life of Brian* (1979). He was portrayed in the 1979 TV movie *Birth of the Beatles* by John Altman.

Harrison, William
Gangster who was a member of both Al Capone's mob and then Ma Barker's gang until he was killed by the Barkers.

Harris, Townsend
(1804–1878) First diplomat to represent the United States in Japan (1856). He opened Japan's ports to foreign trade. Harris was portrayed by John Wayne in the 1958 movie *The Barbarian and the Geisha*.

Harry, Ray
Actor who has played more corpses in movies than any other person.

Harry the Cat
Cat that advertises Square Meals for 9-Lives cat food.

Harry the Horse
Name of a character played in the 1943 Abbott and Costello movie *It Ain't Hay* by Eddie Quillan and in the 1955 movie *Guys and Dolls* by Sheldon Leonard. Character mentioned in the 1961 movie *Pocketful of Miracles*.

Harry Van and His Six Blondes
Billing for Harry Richmond (Clark Gable) and his six ladies (Virginia Grey, Paula Stone, Joan Marsh, Virginia Dale, Bernadine Hayes, and Lorraine Krueger), who sang "Puttin' on the Ritz" in the 1938 movie *Idiot's Delight*.

Hart, Lorenz
(1895–1943) American lyricist who teamed many times with Richard Rodgers to produce such evergreens as "Blue Moon," "My Heart Stood Still," and "My Funny Valentine," as well as the scores of numerous musical plays. He was portrayed in the 1948 movie *Words and Music* by Mickey Rooney and in the 1976 TV special *America Salutes Richard Rodgers: The Sound of His Music* by Henry Winkler.

Hart, Moss
(1904–1961) American playwright who collaborated with both Irving Berlin and George S. Kaufman. He was portrayed in the 1963 movie *Act One* by George Hamilton.

Hart Trophy
Annual award given for the most valuable player in the National Hockey League. It was first awarded to Frank Nighbor of Ottawa, in 1924.

Harte, Brett
(1836–1902) Francis Brett Harte, American short story writer who went to California during the Gold Rush days. He was portrayed in the 1944 movie *Adventures of Mark Twain* by John Carradine.

Hartford, Connecticut
Site of the installation of the first pay telephone (1899).

Hartford House
Nightclub setting on the TV soap opera *Search for Tomorrow.*

Hartley, Mariette
Actress who co-starred with James Garner in numerous Polaroid camera commercials on TV. Because of the roles they played in the commercials, audiences assumed they were married. In real life Mariette took to wearing a T-shirt with "I am not Mrs. James Garner" printed on it and to dressing her infant daughter, Justine, in a T-shirt that said, "No I'm Not James Garner's Baby." Hartley and Garner played opposite each other in a 1980 episode of the TV series *The Rockford Files*.

Harvey, Raymond Lee
Man arrested in May 1979 for conspiring to kill President Carter. Harvey's friend, who was arrested with him on a different charge, was Osualdo Esponioza (the names Lee, Harvey, Osualdo, and Ray were all strangely coincidental).

Harvey S. Kelsey
President of Kelsey's Nuts and Bolts Factory, a character played by Jim Backus in his radio series. Backus used the Mr. Magoo voice for Kelsey before the Mr. Magoo voice cartoon series.

Hasty Pudding Club
Harvard University's drama society, established in 1848. It is the third oldest theatrical organization in the world. In 1889 the club had its greatest financial failure, under the management of J. P. Morgan. In 1945 Jack Lemmon was its president. Joseph Kennedy, Sr., was a member.

Hat Trick
Term used in hockey when a player scores 3 or more goals in one game.

Haugen, Anders
Recipient of a Bronze Medal in skiing 50 years after the Olympic event took place in France in 1924 because of an error in scoring that wasn't discovered until 1974.

Haunted House Café
Restaurant run by Bing Crosby where Louis Armstrong appeared in the 1936 movie *Pennies from Heaven*.

Hawks, Howard

American movie director who was responsible for such classic films as *To Have and Have Not* (1944) and *Red River* (1948). He was portrayed by Adam Roarke in the 1979 movie *Hughes and Harlow: Angels in Hell.*

Hawky Tawley

Long-necked talking bird in the *Barney Google* comic strip.

Hayes, Billy

American escapee from a Turkish prison who wrote a book describing his ordeal entitled *Midnight Express.* He was portrayed in the 1978 movie *Midnight Express* by Brad Davis.

Head of the Family

Comedy episode starring Carl Reiner that appeared on the July 19, 1960, presentation of the summer replacement TV series *The Comedy Spot.* This was the pilot for the TV series *The Dick Van Dyke Show.*

Heads

Outlaw motorcycle club at odds with C. C. Ryder (Joe Namath) in the 1970 movie *C. C. and Company.* The Heads' leader is named Moon.

Hearst, Patty

Daughter of William Randolph Hearst, Jr., who was kidnapped by the SLA on February 4, 1974. Patty Hearst's photograph adorned the first issue of the revised *Look* magazine* (February 19, 1979). She was portrayed in the 1979 TV movie *The Ordeal of Patty Hearst* (originally titled *Get Patty Hearst*) by Lisa Eilbacher.

Hearst, William Randolph, Jr.

Son of American newspaper publisher William Randolph Hearst, Sr., who once served as a member of the U.S. House of Representatives. Hearst, Jr. is the father of Patricia "Patty" Hearst. He was portrayed in the 1979 TV movie *The Ordeal of Patty Hearst* by Stephen Elliott.

Heartbreak of Psoriasis, The

Soap opera spoof set in ancient Egypt on Sonny and Cher's TV series. Cher played Psoriasis and Sonny played Emperor Bursitis.

Heart Punch, The

First movie starring a heavyweight boxing champion. Champion Jess Willard appeared in this 1919 Universal silent.

Heartland, U.S.A.

Hometown of Sgt. Phineas Patrick Paul Pepper and his parents, Harry and Elinor, in the 1978 movie *Sgt. Pepper's Lonely Hearts Club Band.* Mr. Kite (George Burns) was the town's mayor for 43 years. The town paper was *The Heartland Gazette.*

---

*In the West; the cover in the East was of Nelson Rockefeller.

Heathcliffe
Horse of puppet Snarky Parker in the 1950 TV show *Life With Snarkey Parker.*

Heavy Metal
Rock music term coined by William Burroughs in his book *The Soft Machine.*

He can run, but he can't hide
Comment made by heavyweight champion Joe Louis about his June 18, 1941, opponent Billy Conn.

Hecate, HMS
Destroyer commanded by Capt. Murrell (Robert Mitchum) in pursuit of the German submarine U-121, which was commanded by Kapitan Von Stolberg (Curt Jurgens), in the 1957 movie *The Enemy Below* (produced and directed by Dick Powell).

Hector
8-foot killer robot (first of the Demi-God series) in the 1980 movie *Saturn 3.*

Heffernan, Gladys
American League President Joe Cronin's 60-year-old housekeeper whom Ted Williams hit on the head when his baseball bat slipped out of his hands during a game in September 1956.

Held, Anna
Wife of Flo Ziegfeld. She had several of her ribs surgically removed to obtain a waist of 18 inches. She became famous for taking milk baths. Held was portrayed in the 1936 movie *The Great Ziegfeld* by Luise Rainer, and in the 1978 TV movie *Ziegfeld: The Man and His Women* by Barbara Parkins.

Helen
Late wife of Tom Corbett (Bill Bixby) and the mother of Eddie (Brandon Cruz) in the TV series *The Courtship of Eddie's Father* and in the 1963 movie starring Glenn Ford and Ronny Howard.

Helen Crump
Mayberry schoolteacher whom Sheriff Andy Taylor (Andy Griffith) married on the first episode of *Mayberry R.F.D.* (September 23, 1968). Helen was played by Aneta Corsaut.

Hellman, Lillian
Hollywood screenwriter, playwright, and long-time campanion of detective writer Dashiell Hammett. She was portrayed in the 1977 movie *Julia* by Jane Fonda; Hammett was portrayed by Jason Robards, Jr.

Helot
Word used by the colonel (Walter Brennan) to describe the average person, the heels of the world, in the 1940 movie *Meet John Doe.* The original helots were serfs in ancient Sparta.

Help Me Make It Through the Night
Kris Kristofferson–composed hit record by Sammi Smith. It was the theme song of the 1972 movie *Fat City*.

Helper
Rob and Laura Petrie's next-door neighbors in the TV series *The Dick Van Dyke Show*. Jerry (Jerry Paris) was a dentist and Millie (Ann Morgan Guilbert) was his wife. Their three children were Patty, Freddie, and Ellen.

Helter Skelter
Title of a song composed by John Lennon and Paul McCartney. It was the favorite expression of killer Charles Manson, representing the coming revolution between the whites and blacks. It also became the title of a book on the Manson Cult murders written by Vincent Bugliosi and Curt Gentry. The expression also appears in the lyrics of Don McLean's song "American Pie." Helter Skelter in actuality is a playground slide in Britain.

Hemings, Sally
Black slave with whom Thomas Jefferson was rumored to have carried on a 38-year affair.

Hempel's Department Store
Minneapolis store where Rhoda Morgenstern (Valerie Harper) was employed in the TV series *The Mary Tyler Moore Show*.

Henderson, Fletcher
(1898–1952) American bandleader popular in the 1930s through the late 1940s. His theme song was "Christopher Columbus." He was portrayed in the 1956 movie *The Benny Goodman Story* by Sammy Davis, Jr.

Henderson, Ray
(1896–1970) Composer who was a part of the songwriting trio of Henderson-DeSylva-Brown. He also collaborated with other writers. Two of his most famous songs are "Bye Bye Blackbird" and "The Thrill Is Gone." Henderson was portrayed in the 1956 movie *The Best Things in Life Are Free* by Dan Dailey.

Henning, Tennessee
Hometown of author Alex Haley. The TV series *Palmerstown* was patterned after Henning. (Alex Haley's middle name is Palmer.)

Henny and Rocky Show, The
Short-lived 1955 TV series starring comedian Henny Youngman and boxer Rocky Graziano.

Henrietta
Statuette given by the Foreign Press Association to the year's most popular actor and actress.

Henry
Soul singer Screamin' Jay Hawkins's prop skull.

Henry

Voiceless lad in the comic strip *Henry* by Carl Anderson. Henry was the first comic strip character to appear on a postage stamp (Turkey, issued in 1952).

Henry Bond

Older brother of secret agent James Bond.

Henry, Patrick

(1736–1799) American Revolutionary leader who served twice as governor of Virginia. His speeches helped to incite the colonists to rebellion; his most famous words were: "Give me liberty, or give me death." He was portrayed in the 1959 movie *John Paul Jones* by MacDonald Carey.

Hepburn, Katharine

(1909–   ) Popular Hollywood actress, winner of three Academy Awards. She debuted in the 1932 movie *A Bill of Divorcement*. For many years she was in love with actor Spencer Tracy, who was married. They appeared in nine movies together. Hepburn was portrayed in the 1977 TV movie *The Amazing Howard Hughes* by Tovah Feldshuh and in the 1980 TV miniseries *Moviola* by Merleanne Taylor.

Herald, The

Newspaper originally sold by Billy Batson (Captain Marvel).

Herbert, Victor

(1859–1924) Irish-born American conductor and composer of several light operas, including *Babes in Toyland* (1903) and *The Red Mill* (1906). He was portrayed in the 1939 movie *The Great Victor* by Walter Connolly and in the 1946 movie *Till the Clouds Roll By* by Paul Maxey.

Herbie and the Heartbeats

Rock group that performed at the Dewey High Freshman Hop in the 1973 movie *American Graffiti*. The band was played by Flash Cadillac and the Continental Kids.

Hercules and Peter the Great

U.S. and the Soviet Union space platforms for launching nuclear rockets used to destroy Orpheus in the 1979 movie *Meteor*.

Herd, The

Woody Herman's band.

Here Come the Girls

1953 Bob Hope movie watched by the astronauts in the 1955 movie *Conquest of Space*. They were viewing a scene with Rosemary Clooney.

Here's looking at you, kid

Line used four times by Rick Blaine (Humphrey Bogart) in the 1942 movie *Casablanca*.

Herman Trophy

Annual award given (since 1967) to the outstanding college soccer player. In the first 10 years the award was given to five players from St. Louis University.

Hernandez, Jaime Ramon Mercader del Rio
Assassin of Leon Trotsky (born Lev Davidovich Bronstein in 1879) in Mexico City on August 20, 1939. The killer used an ice ax.

Herndon, William Henry
(1818–1891) Abraham Lincoln's law partner. He was portrayed in the 1930 movie *Abraham Lincoln* by Jason Robards.

Her Nibs
Nickname of singer Georgia Gibbs (real name Fredda Lipson), given to her by comedian Gary Moore. She recorded "Love Me" before Elvis Presley made his million-selling version of the song.

Herod Antipas
Ruler of Judea at the time of the death of Jesus. He beheaded John the Baptist at the behest of his stepdaughter, Salome. Movie portrayals: *Salome* (1953) Charles Laughton; *The Greatest Story Every Told* (1965) José Ferrer; and *The Day Christ Died* (1980 TV) Jonathan Pryce.

Herriot, James
English veterinarian and author of several books on animals. He was portrayed in the 1974 movie *All Creatures Great and Small* by Simon Ward and in the PBS-TV series by Christopher Timothy.

Herwig, Robert
All-American football center for the University of California who during World War II won the Navy Cross and Silver Star. He married a sportswriter named Kathleen Windsor who authored the best-seller *Forever Amber* (Kathleen Windsor also married bandleader Artie Shaw).

Heuer
Brand of stopwatch used on the TV series *60 Minutes*.

Hey Dog
Jason Nichols' (Wright King) pet mutt in the TV series *Wanted: Dead or Alive*.

Heydrick, Gen. Reinhard
(1904–1942) Deputy chief of the Gestapo, called the Hangman. In retaliation for his assassination in Czechoslovakia in 1942, the Nazis murdered the entire male population of the village of Lidice. Heydrich was portrayed in the 1943 movie *Hitler's Madman* by John Carradine.

Hibernia Bank
San Francisco bank robbed by Patty Hearst and three members of the SLA on April 15, 1974.

Hickok Belt
$10,000 prize awarded to the Professional Athlete of the Year.

Hickok, James Butler "Wild Bill"

(1837–1876) Western gunfighter and lawman killed by Jack McCall on August 2, 1876, while holding the famous dead man's hand (aces and eights). Movie portrayals: *Wild Bill Hickok* (1923) William S. Hart; *The Iron Horse* (1924) John Padjan; *The Last Frontier* (1926) J. Farrell MacDonald; *The Last Frontier* (1932) Yakima Canutt; *The Plainsman* (1937) Gary Cooper; *The Great Adventures of Wild Bill Hickok* (1938) Gordon Elliott; *Frontier Scout* (1938) George Houston; *Young Bill Hickok* (1940) Roy Rogers; *Deadwood Dick* (1940) Lane Chandler; *Badlands of Dakota* (1941) Richard Dix; *Wild Bill Hickok Rides* (1942) Bruce Cabot; *Dallas* (1950) Reed Hadley; *The Lawless Breed* (1953) Robert Anderson; *Son of the Renegade* (1953) Ewing Brown; *Jack McCall Desperado* (1953) Douglas Kennedy; *Pony Express* (1953) Forrest Tucker; *Calamity Jane* (1953) Howard Keel; *I Killed Wild Bill Hickok* (1956) Tom Brown; *The Raiders* (1963) Robert Culp; *Seven Hours of Gunfire* (1964) Adrian Hover; *The Outlaws Is Coming* (1965) Paul Shannon; *The Plainsman* (1966) Don Murray; *Deadwood '76* (1971) Robert Dix; and *Little Big Man* (1971) Jeff Corey. TV portrayals: Guy Madison in the series *Wild Bill Hickok* and Lloyd Bridges in the "Wild Bill Hickok—The Legend and the Man" episode of *The Great Adventure* series.

Hi-De-Ho Man

Nickname of orchestra leader Cab Calloway.

High Hopes

Name of the "haunted" colonial house at 112 Ocean Avenue on Long Island where, on November 13, 1974, 24-year-old Ronald De Feo shot and killed his six-member family with a rifle. It is the subject of a 1977 book by Jay Anson, *The Amityville Horror,* and the 1979 movie derived from it.

High Hopes

Official John F. Kennedy campaign song of 1960. It was composed by Jimmy Van Heusen and won an Oscar for best song in the 1959 movie *A Hole in the Head*.

High Sky

Horse ridden during the Civil War by Confederate general Jeb Stuart.

Hilda

Hurricane that hit the Gulf Coast on August 17 in the 1974 TV movie *Hurricane*.

Hilda

Girl whom Dagwood Bumstead stood up at his senior prom (comic strip *Blondie*).

Hildegard

Monastery cow from which little John Sarto (Edward G. Robinson) got 492 quarts of milk in one month in the 1940 movie *Brother Orchid*.

Hi-Life

Country singer Hank Williams's favorite horse.

Hill, Barney and Betty
Married couple who claimed to have been taken aboard a UFO on September 19, 1961. The event is the subject of a 1966 book, *The Interrupted Journey,* by John Grant Fuller. The mixed black-white couple were portrayed in the 1975 TV movie *The UFO Incident* by James Earl Jones and Estelle Parsons.

Hill, Clinton J.
Secret Service agent who pushed Jackie Kennedy back into the presidential limousine the day John F. Kennedy was assassinated (November 22, 1963).

Hill, Howard
Archer who actually did the shooting for Errol Flynn in the 1938 movie *The Adventures of Robin Hood.*

Himmler, Heinrich
(1900–1945) High-ranking member of the Third Reich and head of the S.S. He was captured by the British, and then committed suicide on May 23, 1945. Movie portrayals: *Hitler's Madmen* (1943) Howard Freeman; *The Nasty Nuisance* (1943) Wedgewood Nowell; *The Hitler Gang* (1944) Luis Van Rooten*; *The Magic Face* (1951) Sukman; *Operation Eichmann* (1961) Luis Van Rooten†; *Hitler* (1962) Rick Traeger; *The Eagle Has Landed* (1977) Donald Pleasance; *Holocaust* (1978 TV) Tom Bell; and *The Bunker* (1981 TV) Michael Sheard.

Hindenburg, Paul von
(1847–1934) German general and president (1925–1934) who appointed Adolf Hitler as chancellor in 1933, yielding his power. The giant zeppelin *Hindenburg* was named in his honor. He was portrayed in the 1944 movie *The Hitler Gang* by Sig Ruman and in the 1969 movie *Fraulein Doktor* by Walter Williams.

Hippocrates
(460–377 B.C.) Greek physician called the Father of Medicine. He established a code of medicine embodied in the Hippocratic Oath. He was portrayed in the 1957 movie *The Story of Mankind* by Charles Coburn.

Hires, Charles Elmer
American inventor of root beer in 1869.

Hirohito
(1901–   ) Emperor of Japan since 1926 (he is No. 124 in direct lineage). Movie portrayals: *The Emperor and the General* (1968) Koshiro Matsumoto; and *MacArthur* (1977) John Fujioka.

Hirsch, Elroy
Professional football player, nicknamed Crazylegs. He made All-America at

*Luis Van Rooten's movie debut.
†Final movie appearance of Luis Van Rooten.

the University of Wisconsin. He appeared in three movies: *Crazylegs* (1953), *Unchained** (1955), and *Zero Hour!* (1957).

His Eye Is on the Sparrow
Spiritual sung by Ethel Waters in the play/movie *The Member of the Wedding* (1952). It was also the title of her 1953 autobiography.

Hitchcock
Pet dog (Sealyham terrier) that director Alfred Hitchcock gave to actress Tallulah Bankhead while he was directing her in the 1944 movie *Lifeboat*.

Hit 'em where they ain't
Wee Willie Keeler's explanation for his hitting success in baseball. The complete sentence said by him in 1894 was: "Keep your eye clear and hit 'em where they ain't; that's all."

Hoar, Leonard, and Nathan B. Pusey
Only past presidents of Harvard University who did not have an undergraduate house named after them.

Hodges, Ann
Only person known to have been hit by an object entering the earth's atmosphere. On November 30, 1954, an 8½-pound meteorite struck Mrs. Hodges on the hip after crashing through the roof of her house.

Hogan, Ben
American golfer, winner of four U.S. Open tournaments. Hogan was involved in a serious auto accident in 1949 and it was feared that he would never walk again. He was portrayed in the 1951 movie *Follow the Sun* by Glenn Ford (Harold Blake as a boy).

Hokey Wolf
Friendly wolf who along with his companion, Ding-a-ling, manages to find trouble (Hanna-Barbera cartoons; voice of Daws Butler).

Hole-in-One
Babe Ruth shot a hole-in-one on the 185-yard 3rd hole at Pasadena Golf Club near St. Petersburg, Florida, in 1933. Glenn Miller shot a hole-in-one on the 143-yard 9th hole at Pinehurst, North Carolina, in 1942. Presidents Eisenhower (February 6, 1968, Lake County Club, Palm Springs, Calif.) and Ford also shot holes-in-one. Bob Hope shot four through 1979.

Holiday for Strings
Theme song played by David Rose for the TV series *The Red Skelton Show*.

Holland, USS
First submarine (53 feet long, 74 tons) in the U.S. Navy. It was designed by John P. Holland and bought in 1900 by the Navy.

Hollingshead, Richard, Jr.
Chemical manufacturer who, in 1932 in Camden, New Jersey, built the first drive-in movie.

*"Unchained Melody" was the movie's theme song.

Holloman, Alva Lee "Bobo"
St. Louis Browns pitcher who on May 7, 1953 pitched a no-hitter in his first major league game. It was Holloman's only complete game in the majors. The score was Browns 6, Athletics 0. He ended the year at 3–7 and did not pitch in the majors again.

Holly, Buddy
(1936–1959) Innovative rock 'n' roll artist (born Charles Hardin Holley) whose band was called the Crickets. He died in a plane crash with Ritchie Valens and J. P. Richardson (the Big Bopper) on February 3, 1959. Holly was portrayed in the 1978 movie *The Buddy Holly Story* by Gary Busey.

Holly Goodhead
CIA agent, scientist, and astronaut, played by Lois Chiles in the 1979 movie *Moonraker.*

HOllywood 9-3488
Telephone number used to call in to the radio series *People Are Funny,* hosted by Art Linkletter.

Hollywood Squares
Popular TV game show hosted by Peter Marshall. On the debut show, October 17, 1966, the nine celebrities were: Nick Adams, Charley Weaver, Wally Cox, Rose Marie, Abby Dalton, Sally Field, Morey Amsterdam, Agnes Moorehead, and—in the middle square—Ernest Borgnine. (Bert Parks was the emcee for the pilot show.) The celebrities on the last show (summer of 1980) were: Charlie Callas, Rose Marie, Tom Poston, Marty Allen, Wayland and Madame, Michelle Lee, George Gobel, Leslie Uggams, and Vincent Price. (Note that Rose Marie was on both the first and last shows.)

Hollywood State
Los Angeles movie theater showing the Walt Disney movie *Dumbo,* which Gen. Joseph Stilwell (Robert Stack) attended in the 1979 movie *1941.*

Hollywood Victory Committee
Previous name of the USO (United Services Organization), formed in 1941.

Holm, Celeste
Narrator of the 1949 movie *A Letter to Three Wives.*

Holm, Eleanor
1932 Olympic Gold Medal winner for 100-meter backstroke swimming. She was married to both band leader Arthur Jarnette (she sang with his band) and Billy Rose. Holm was portrayed in the 1975 movie *Funny Lady* by Heidi O'Rourke.

Holme Insurance Company
10-story Chicago building built in 1885—the world's first skyscraper.

Holmes, Oliver Wendell

(1841–1935) Associate justice of the U.S. Supreme Court from 1902 to 1932. His father, also Oliver Wendell Holmes, was a noted author and member of the American Hall of Fame. The judge was portrayed in the 1951 movie *The Magnificent Yankee* by Louis Calhern.

Holverg Suite

Opening theme of the TV series *Mama*. The closing theme was *The Last Spring*.

Holy cow! Holy cow! Holy cow!

Excited exclamation of Yankee announcer Phil Rizzuto upon watching Bucky Dent hit the game-winning home run in the 1978 division playoff between the Yankees and the Red Sox.

Home Is the Sailor

Song that Dennis Morgan sang at the funeral of actor/adventurer Errol Flynn, on October 20, 1959.

Home on the Range

Official song of the state of Kansas, adopted in 1935. President Richard Nixon often played the song on the piano.

Home Pride

Brand name of the stove in the Kramdens' Bensonhurst apartment in the TV series *The Honeymooners*.

Homer Smith

Name of character played by Robert Young in the 1942 movie *Cairo* and by Sidney Poitier in the 1963 *Lilies of the Field*.

Home Sweet Home

Song written by John Howard Payne* (portrayed in the 1914 silent film *Home Sweet Home* by Henry B. Walthall). It was the first song that Louis Armstrong learned to play on the trumpet.

Hondo

1953 movie starring John Wayne and also a 1967 TV series starring Ralph Taeger—the first movie and TV production taken from a book by Louis L'Amour. *Hondo* was the only John Wayne movie filmed in 3D (though it was never shown in 3D).

Honest Hakkum

Arab who sold camels during the commercial break in the 1977 movie *The Last Remake of Beau Geste*. He was played by Avery Schreiber and his pitch was ''Ten Kilos of Free Hash with each Camel—Call toll free (985)47 2189375206751839020977643983056724095798720394709813840284160923855031602748039410283947516037051483059032127374803947582151439827304749274936403150366829403148273058392159030421394738721.''

---

*For writing this song, John Howard Payne became the first musician to be knighted (1842).

Honey Babe
   Million-selling record by Art Mooney, from the 1955 movie *Battle Cry*.
Honey Bears
   Cheerleaders for the Chicago Bears football team.
Honorificabilitudinitatibus
   Longest word in the works of William Shakespeare.
Hooker
   Word derived from Civil War general Joseph Hooker,* who saw that his
   Union troops were supplied with prostitutes. A Hookers Ball is held anually
   in San Francisco.
Hootenanny Saturday Night
   Theme song of the TV series *Hootenanny*.
Hoover, Herbert
   (1874–1964) 31st president of the United States and the first president born
   west of the Mississippi River. Hoover was one of only two Quaker presidents
   (Nixon was the other). He was awarded more honorary degrees (89) than any
   other American. He was portrayed in the 1931 movie *Fires of Youth* by Tom
   Jensen and in the 1979 TV miniseries *Backstairs at the White House* by Larry
   Gates. (His wife, Lou, was played by Jan Sterling in *Backstairs*.)
Hoover, Irwin H. "Ike"
   First chief usher at the White House (1891–1933) and author of the book *42
   Years in the White House*. Movie portrayals: *Wilson* (1944) Roy Roberts;
   Eleanor and Franklin: The White House Years (1977 TV) Colin Hamilton;
   and *Backstairs at the White House* (1979 TV miniseries) Leslie Nielsen.
Hoover, John Edgar
   (1895–1972) Director of the Federal Bureau of Investigation from 1917 until
   his death. He was a lifelong bachelor. Movie portrayals: *Lepke* (1975) Edwin
   Fuller; *The Private Files of J. Edgar Hoover* (1978) Broderick Crawford
   (James Wainwright as a boy); *The Brinks Job* (1978) Sheldon Leonard; *King*
   (1978) Dolph Sweet; and *Blind Ambition* (1979 TV) Logan Ramsey.
Hopkins, Miriam
   (1902–1973) American actress who appeared in both movie versions of
   Lillian Hellman's play *The Children's Hour: These Three* (1936) and *The
   Children's Hour* (1962). She was portrayed in the 1980 TV miniseries
   Moviola by Sheilah Wells.
Hopper, Hedda
   (1890–1966). Hollywood gossip columnist (born Elda Furry) who began her
   career as an actress in silent films. Her many and varied hats became her
   trademark. She was portrayed in the 1976 movie *Gable and Lombard* by
   Alice Backes.

---

*Gen. Hooker is the great-great-grandfather of this author's wife, Susan.

Hornsby, Rogers
Hall of Fame baseball player with the highest season batting average: .424 hit in 1924. He was the only player to own stock in one major league team (Cardinals) while playing for another (Giants). Hornsby was portrayed by Frank Lovejoy in the 1952 movie *The Winning Team*.

Horrible
Mutt found and taken in by the Petries in one episode of the TV series *The Dick Van Dyke Show*.

Horrible Hall
Setting of the TV cartoon series *The Groovie Goolies*.

Horse, The
Nickname of NFL player Alan Ameche.

Horst Wessel Song
Official Nazi anthem, composed by Horst Wessel and adopted by Joseph Goebbels.

Hoskins, John
World War II admiral who lost his leg during a Japanese attack on the U.S. carrier *Princeton* in the Battle of Leyte Gulf in October 1944. He pressed the Navy to allow him to stay in the service, arguing with Adm. Halsey that the Navy did not train a man to think with his leg. He received command of the new *Princeton* at the end of the war. Hoskins was an advocate of putting jet aircraft on carriers. He was portrayed in the 1955 movie *The Eternal Sea* by Sterling Hayden.

Hot Box Niteclub
Nightclub where Adelaide (Vivian Blaine) sang in the 1955 movie *Guys and Dolls*.

Hotel Daniels
San Francisco hotel at 226 Embarcadero Street where Chicago hood Johnny Ross (Pat Renella) was guarded (in Room 634) in the 1968 movie *Bullitt*.

Hotel Flanders
New York City hotel where Felix Ungar (Jack Lemmon) got himself a room (No. 914) for $5 so he could jump out the window in the 1968 movie *The Odd Couple*. His suicide attempt failed when he couldn't get the window open.

Hotel Metropole
Chicago hotel where Al Capone lived while he was the mob's boss.

Hotel Motel
Chicago setting (in the Terrace Casino) of the TV series *Don McNeill's TV Club*.

Hot Foot Teddy
Smokey the Bear's original name when he was found in 1950.

Hot Time in the Old Town, A
Theme song of President Theodore Roosevelt. Bands played the song whenever he appeared. This is the only song that the Hooterville Band could play in the TV series *Petticoat Junction*.

House Party
Novel by Patrick Dennis upon which the TV series *The Pruitts of Southampton* was based.

Houston, Sam
(1793–1863) American soldier and politician. He served as governor of both Tennessee (1827–1838) and Texas (1859–1861). Movie portrayals: *Man of Conquest* (1939) Richard Dix; *Men of Texas* (1942) William Farnum; *Lone Star* (1952) Moroni Olsen; and *The Alamo* (1960) Richard Boone. Philip Bosco played Houston in "The Siege of the Alamo," an episode of the TV series *You Are There*.

Hovatar, Alice, and Juanita Johnson
Two fans who were killed when struck by a drunk driver as they waited with a third girl, Tammy Baiter (who was seriously injured), to view Elvis Presley's body outside of Graceland, where it lay in state (August 18, 1977).

Howard
World's strongest ant in a skit on Ernie Kovacs' TV series.

Howard the Duck
Comic book duck "Trapped in a World he never made!" Howard was hatched in January 1976.

Howard Johnson
Motel chain that paid Connie Francis $2.65 million as a settlement because the singer was raped in their Westbury, New York motel in 1974.

Howard, Joseph E.
(1878–1961) American musical composer. He was portrayed in the 1947 movie *I Wonder Who's Kissing Her Now* by Mark Stevens.

Howard, Leslie
(1890–1943) British actor who helped get Humphrey Bogart his starring role in the 1936 classic film *The Petrified Forest*. He is most famous for his role in the 1939 movie *Gone With the Wind*. Howard died under mysterious conditions when the aircraft he was flying in was shot down during World War II. (See: **British Overseas Airways Flight 777**.) He was portrayed in the 1980 TV movie *Bogie* by Stephen Keep.

Howard, Leslie, and Bette Davis
Films in which the pair appeared: *Of Human Bondage* (1934); *The Petrified Forest* (1936); and *It's Love I'm After* (1937).

Howe, Louie
Friend and adviser to President Franklin D. Roosevelt. Portrayals: *Sunrise at Campobello* (1960) Hume Cronyn; *Eleanor and Franklin* (1976 TV) Ed

Flanders; *Eleanor and Franklin: The White House Years* (1977 TV) Walter McGinn; and (in the 1979 TV miniseries) *Backstairs at the White House* by Woodrow Parfrey.

Howitzer
Yearbook at West Point Academy.

How I Won the War
Song sung by Errol Flynn in the 1943 movie *Thank Your Lucky Stars*.

How to Keep Young Mentally
First article in the first issue of *Reader's Digest* (February 1922).

How to Marry a Millionaire
1953 movie starring Marilyn Monroe, Betty Grable, and Lauren Bacall. It was the first movie shown on NBC's *Saturday Night at the Movies* (September 23, 1961).

How Would You Like to Tussell with Russell?
Part of an $800,000 ad campaign for Howard Hughes' 1943 movie *The Outlaw* starring Jane Russell in her movie debut.

Hoyle, Edmond
First person to publish a set of rules for the card game of whist (1742). As he expounded on more games through the years, Hoyle became *the* authority on card game rules.

Hubbard, Cal
Only member of both the Baseball Hall of Fame (1976) (as an umpire) and the National Football League Hall of Fame (1963).

Hubbard, De Bart
First black to win an Olympic Gold Medal for the United States. He won in the long-jump contest in Paris in 1924.

Hubbard, Gardiner Greene
First president of the National Geographic Society, founded in 1888. He was the father-in-law of Alexander Graham Bell.

Huberie, Montana
Western town setting of the 1953–1954 TV series *Action in the Afternoon*.

Hubert Updyke III
The richest man in the world and a man of distinction—a character played by Jim Backus on his radio series

Hud
Actual name of the horse that Paul Newman rode in the 1969 movie *Butch Cassidy and the Sundance Kid*.

Hudson, Rock, and Doris Day
Films in which the pair appeared: *Pillow Talk* (1959); *Lover Come Back* (1961); and *Send Me No Flowers* (1964).

Hugemobile
Finkerton detective Inch High's automobile in the TV cartoon series *Inch High Private Detective*.

Huggins, Miller
New York Yankee manager who stood 5 feet 4 inches and weighed 146 pounds. Despite his stature, he disciplined and suspended the burly Babe Ruth on numerous occasions. Movie portrayals: *The Pride of the Yankees* (1942) Ernie Adams; and *The Stratton Story* (1949) Cliff Clark.

Huggy Bear Brown
Friend and informant of Dave Starsky (Paul Michael Glaser) and Ken "Hutch" Hutchinson (David Soul) in the TV series *Starsky and Hutch*. He was played by Antonio Fargas.

Hughes, Howard
(1905–1976) Billionaire businessman, aviator, inventor, movie producer, and, later in life, eccentric recluse. He once owned Trans World Airlines* and discovered movie stars Jean Harlow and Jane Russell. Hughes was the winner of the Harmon and Collyer aviation trophies. He broke a world record in 1938 by flying around the world with a crew of four in 91 days. Movie portrayals: *The Amazing Howard Hughes* (1977 TV movie) David Schulman (as a boy), Tommy Lee Jones (in middle age), and Ben Pollock (as as an old man); *Hughes and Harlow: Angels in Hell* (1977) Victor Holchak; and *Melvin and Howard* (1980) Jason Robards, Jr. Hughes was loosely portrayed by Robert Ryan in the 1949 movie *Caught*.

Hugo, Victor
(1802–1885) French author of the classic novels *The Hunchback of Notre Dame* (1831) and *Les Misérables* (1862). He was portrayed in the 1938 movie *Suez* by Victor Varconi.

Hull, Cordell
(1871–1955) American politician who served as secretary of state (1933–1944) during World War II. He was awarded the Nobel Peace Prize in 1945. Movie portrayals: *Sergeant York* (1941) Charles Trowbridge; *Mission to Moscow* (1943) Charles Trowbridge; and *Tora! Tora! Tora!* (1970) George Macready.

Hull, George
Cigar maker who engineered the 1869 hoax, in which the "Cardiff Giant" was supposedly found a mile north of Cooperstown, New York. The giant, which weighs 2990 pounds and stands 10 feet 4½ inches, is now kept at the Farmers' Museum in Coopertown, New York.

Human Body and How to Avoid It, The
Noted book written by Professor Hugo von Gezuntheit, the world's leading

---

*Then called Transcontinental and Western Airlines.

medical authority, who was played by Sid Caesar in the TV series *Your Show of Shows*.

Human Eel, The

Billing of 4-year-old circus performer Harry James when as a child he worked for the Mighty Haag Circus with his performing parents. James later became a popular trumpet player and bandleader.

Hummingbird Hill

Subdivision housing setting of the 1948 movie *Sitting Pretty*.

Hunter College

Institute of higher learning from which Marjorie Morningstar (Natalie Wood) graduated in the 1958 movie *Marjorie Morningstar*.

Hunter, Oscar

California highway patrol officer who gave James Dean a ticket for going 65 mph in a 45-mph zone at 3:30 p.m. on September 30, 1955, just a few hours before Dean's fatal crash (5:45 p.m.).

Huntley, Chet

(1912–1974) American news commentator. He narrated the 1943 Randolph Scott movie *Gung Ho!* and hosted the 1952 TV game show *Who Knows?* He also appeared in the 1949 movie *Arctic Manhunt*.

Hunt, Walter

American inventor of the safety pin in 1849.

Hurd, Peter

Artist who painted the official portrait of Lyndon Johnson. When it was unveiled in January 1967, the president remarked that it was "the ugliest thing I ever saw."

Hurkos, Peter

World-famous psychic who has assisted numerous police departments throughout the world in solving difficult cases. He was portrayed in the 1968 movie *The Boston Strangler* by George Voskovec.

Hurricane Mills

Town north of Nashville owned by Loretta Lynn and her husband, Mooney.

Hurry back

Humphrey Bogart's last words before he died on January 14, 1957. They were said to his wife, Lauren Bacall.

Huskisson, William

Man who on September 15, 1830, became the first person to be run over by a train (Manchester-Liverpool Railroad).

Hussey, Tim, and Ed Finneran

Two DC Comics contest winners. The pair made cameo appearances as members of the Smallville High School football team in the 1978 movie *Superman*.

Huston, John

(1906–   ) Director son of actor Walter Huston. Both Hustons won Academy Awards for the 1948 movie *The Treasure of Sierra Madre*, John for direction, Walter for best supporting actor. In his youth John Huston was the amateur lightweight boxing champion of California. He won 23 of his 25 bouts. He was portrayed in the 1980 TV miniseries *Moviola* by William Frankfather and in the 1980 TV movie *Marilyn: The Untold Story* by John Ireland.

Hutchins, Levi

Inventor of the alarm clock in 1787.

Huygens, Christian

Inventor of the pendulum clock in 1656.

Hyak

Fishing boat that Randal Patrick McMurphy (Jack Nicholson) and other inmates stole in the 1975 movie *One Flew Over the Cuckoo's Nest*.

Hyborian Age

Time setting (approximately 12,000 years ago) of Robert E. Howard's *Conan* series.

Hydrogen Terror, The

Novel written by Congressman Leo Ryan, who was killed in Guyana during the Jonestown massacre.

I

I-19
Japanese submarine commanded by Capt. Akiro Mitamura (Toshiro Mifune) that surfaced off the coast of Santa Monica on December 13, 1941, in the 1979 movie *1941*.

IBC
International Broadcasting Company—the TV network that employed Mickey Mulligan (Mickey Rooney) as a page in the TV series *The Mickey Rooney Show.*

IW59-17
New York State automobile license plate number of the car in which Jesse Owens traveled for the ticker tape parade that welcomed him home from the 1936 Olympics in Berlin. During the parade an unknown person threw a brown paper bag into the car. The bag was later discovered to contain $10,000.

IY-64910
California automobile license number of the 1954 yellow Mercury convertible used to pull the house trailer in the 1954 movie *The Long Long Trailer*.

Iceman, The
Nickname of jockey George Woolf and of singer Jerry Butler.

Ice Station Zebra
1968 Rock Hudson–Ernest Borgnine movie (loosely based on the Alistair Maclean novel of the same name). It was Howard Hughes' favorite movie. He ran it so often (over 150 times) that he had memorized the dialogue. Singer Dobie Gray made his film debut in the movie.

I Cried for You

Song that Judy Garland sang to a photo of Mickey Rooney in the 1939 movie *Babes in Arms*.

Ida (Sweet as Apple Cider)

Theme song of comedian Eddie Cantor, written about his childhood sweetheart and wife, Ida Tobias. In the 1953 movie *The Eddie Cantor Story* Ida was portrayed by Marilyn Erskine.

I'd Like to Teach the World to Sing

1972 hit record by the New Seekers. It was originally heard as a Coca-Cola television jingle sung by the Hillside Singers.

Idol of the Airlanes

Nickname of bandleader Jan Garber.

I Don't Want to Walk Without You, Baby

Song originally written by Jules Styne and Frank Loesser for evangelist Aimee Semple McPherson as "I Don't Want to Walk Without You, Jesus."

Idyll of Miss Sarah Brown, The

Short story by Damon Runyon that is the basis for the musical play *Guys and Dolls*.

I Feel Love

Theme song of the 1974 movie *Benji,* sung by Charlie Rich.

If I Had the Wings of an Angel

Song that the tough gang of kids sang at the close of the 1937 movie *Dead End*.

I Get a Kick Out of You

Song sung by the black railroad gang in the 1974 movie *Blazing Saddles*. Lyle (Burton Gilliam), the white assistant foreman, sang "Camptown Races," a song the black workers were not familiar with.

Iggy

Count Screwloose's cross-eyed dog that wears a Napoleonic hat in the comic strip *Count Screwloose of Tooloose*.

Igor

Grampa's (Al Lewis) pet bat in the TV series *The Munsters*.

Igor

Dr. Bruce Banner's assistant (a spy) who fired the bomb that turned Banner into The Hulk (comic books).

I Got Stung/One Night

Last RCA Victor 78 rpm Elvis Presley recorded, issued in October 1958.

I guess I just forgot to duck

Famous line said by Jack Dempsey after Gene Tunney beat him in the World Heavyweight Championship fight in Philadelphia on September 23, 1926. It was a reply in response to Louella Parsons's question: "But how did it happen?"

Ila
> Adama's (Lorne Greene) dead wife, who was killed by the Cylons, in the TV series *Battlestar Galactica*.

I Like Ike
> Presidential campaign song composed in 1952 by Irving Berlin for Dwight Eisenhower. It was originally titled "They Like Ike."

I'll Get By
> Song composed by Roy Turk and Fred E. Ahlert in 1928. It can be heard in the following movies: *A Guy Named Joe* (1943); *Follow the Boys* (1944); *You Were Meant for Me* (1948); *I'll Get By* (1950); *A Star Is Born* (1954); and *Marciano* (1979 TV).

I'll Love You Till the Rope on the Old Well Bucket Disentwines Its Sacred Knot, Leavin' the Old Bucket Skip and Sink Beneath the Still Cool Waters of the Old Well in the Month of June
> Classic song composed by the world's foremost collector of folk music, Professor Lemuel Cornball (Sid Caesar), in the TV series *Your Show Of Shows*.

I'll Never Smile Again
> Song composed by Ruth Lowe upon the death of her husband, Harold Cohen, in 1939.

I'll Take You Home Again, Kathleen
> Theme song of the radio soap opera *Orphans of Divorce*. It was one of Thomas A. Edison's favorite songs and it was played at his funeral. It was also sung by Ensign Kevin Reilly (Bruce Hyde) on "The Naked Time" episode of the TV series *Star Trek*. Elvis Presley even recorded the song.

I Love Mickey
> Record made by Teresa Brewer and Mickey Mantle (Coral 61700) in 1956.

I Love Ringo
> 1964 Phil Spector–produced novelty record sung by Bonnie Joe Mason (a pseudonym of Cher).

I love you
> The first three words Suzanne Somers spoke in her movie debut in *American Graffiti* (1973). She said them to Curt (Richard Dreyfuss) from her white 1955 T Bird. She received $136.72 for playing the role.

I Love You California
> Official song of the state of California, adopted in 1951.

I'm a Ding Dong Daddy from Dumas/Side by Side
> Two songs sung by a very young barbershop quartet called the Osmond Brothers on their television debut on *The Andy Williams Show,* on December 20, 1962.

I May Be Wrong but I Think You're Wonderful
> Song composed in 1929 by Harry Ruskin and Henry Sullivan. It can be heard

in the following movies: *Swingtime Johnny* (1944); *Wallflower* (1947); *You're My Everything* (1949), sung by Dan Dailey; *Young Man With a Horn* (1950), sung by Doris Day; *On the Sunny Side of the Street* (1951); and *Starlift* (1951), sung by Jane Wyman.

I'm coming home, Mabel, the case is closed
Closing lines spoken by Rocky King (Roscoe Karns) in each episode of the TV series *Rocky King, Detective*.

I'm Forever Blowing Bubbles
Theme song of the 1931 movie *Public Enemy*. Also heard in the following films: *Stella Dallas* (1937); *Men With Wings* (1938); and *On Moonlight Bay* (1951). (The lyrics are by Jean Kembrovin*; John William Kellette wrote the music.)

I'm in the Mood for Love
Song composed by Dorothy Fields and Jimmy McHugh in 1935. It can be heard in the following movies: *Every Night at Eight* (1935), sung by Alice Faye; *Between Two Women* (1944), sung by Gloria De Haven; *The Big Clock* (1948); *That's My Boy* (1951); *Ask Any Girl* (1959); and *The Misfits* (1961).

Imitation of Christ, The
Book by Thomas à Kempis that Pope John Paul I was reading when he died in bed on September 28, 1978.

I'm Just Wild about Harry
Song composed in 1921 by Noble Sissle and Eubie Blake. It can be heard in the following movies: *Rose of Washington Square* (1939), sung by Alice Faye; *Broadway* (1942); *Is Everybody Happy?* (1943), sung by Al Jolson; *Jolson Sings Again* (1949), sung by Al Jolson; and *I'll See You in My Dreams* (1951). "I'm Just Wild about Harry" was Harry S Truman's presidential campaign song in 1948.

I'm mad as hell and I'm not going to take it anymore!
Battle cry of frustrated TV viewers in the 1976 movie *Network*.

Imogene
Dorothy Gale's pet cow in the 1903 musical play *The Wizard of Oz*.

Imperial Hotel
Tokyo hotel built between 1915 and 1922. It was designed by Frank Lloyd Wright† as the first earthquake-proof building.

Imperius Rex
Battle cry of Prince Namor, the submariner (Marvel comics).

Imp Girl
Publicity name of actress Florence Lawrence bestowed on her by the Independent Motion Pictures Company.

---

*Pen name of James Kendis, James Brockman, and Nat Vincent.
†Frank Lloyd Wright, the grandfather of actress Anne Baxter, coined the word "carport."

In a North-Westerly Direction
Working title of the 1959 Alfred Hitchcock movie *North by Northwest*.
Incendiary Blonde
Nickname of actress Betty Hutton.
Inchcliffe Castle
Freighter commanded by Capt. Colin Glencannon (Thomas Mitchell) in the
TV series *Glencannon*.
Independence
28-minute movie made in 1975 that was shown 32 times a day, 7 days a
week, at Independence Hall in Philadelphia. It was directed by John Huston.
Independence, Colorado
Setting of the TV western series *Sam*.
Indescribably delicious
Slogan of Peter Paul candy bars.
India
Country described by Mark Twain as "mother of history, grandmother of
legend, and greatgrandmother of tradition."
Indio, California
Small town where the monster lands in the 1955 movie *The Beast With a
Million Eyes*.
Infanta
John Barrymore's $250,000 yacht.
Infant Island
Home of Mothra (Japanese movie monster).
Inn of the Three Golden Apples
Pub in Heidelberg where Kathie worked in the 1924 musical play *The Student
Prince in Heidelberg*.
Innisfree
Irish hometown of Sean Thornton (John Wayne) in the 1952 movie *The Quiet
Man*.
Innsbruck
German submarine (U202) that dropped four saboteurs off Amagansett, Long
Island, on June 12, 1942. After Seaman 2nd Class John Cullen of the U.S.
Coast Guard confronted the men, they thought they had bought him off for
$260, but they were later captured. The names of the four saboteurs were
George Dasch (leader), Ernest Burger, Henrich Heinck, and Richard Quirin.
Four saboteurs (Edward Kerling, Herbert Haupt, Hermann Neubauer, and
Werner Thiel) were landed off the coast of Florida by another sub. They too
were captured, and six of the eight saboteurs were executed; Dasch and
Burger were merely imprisoned.
In Other Words
Title of the song "Fly Me to the Moon" when first sung in 1954.

Inside the Walls of Folsom Prison
   1951 movie starring Steve Cochran that inspired Johnny Cash's song "Folsom Prison Blues" in 1955.

Inspector Lewis Erskine
   FBI agent played by Efrem Zimbalist, Jr., on the TV series *The F.B.I.* His daughter, Barbara Erskine, was played by Lynn Loring. Director Hoover considered Zimbalist the perfect example of an FBI agent.

Inspector Luger
   Capt. Barney Miller's (Hal Linden) superior officer, played by James Gregory, in the TV series *Barney Miller*.

Inter-Ocean News Syndicate
   News service for which Connie Chesley (Susan Hayward) was a reporter in the 1944 movie *The Fighting Seabees*.

International Transport Trucking Company
   Company for which Mike "Cannonball" Malone (Paul Birch) worked in the TV series *Cannonball*.

International World Films
   Hollywood movie studio headed by Monroe Stahr (Robert DeNiro) in the 1976 movie *The Last Tycoon*.

INTERSECT
   Secret government agency for which Sam Casey (Ben Murphy) was an agent in the TV series *The Gemini Man*.

Interview
   Word that God (George Burns) misspelled in his note to Jerry Landers (John Denver) in the 1977 movie *Oh God!* He spelled it inter*veiw*.

Intrepid
   Code name for the Canadian World War II spy William Stephenson. He was portrayed in the 1979 TV miniseries *A Man Called Intrepid* by David Niven. Stephenson, who was Ian Fleming's superior when Fleming worked for the British secret service, read the manuscript of the first James Bond novel (*Casino Royale*) and told Fleming that it would never sell.

Invictus
   Poem written by William Ernest Henley as a tuberculosis patient in the Edinburgh Infirmary in 1888. It was read by Parris (Robert Cummings) to Drake (Ronald Reagan) in the 1941 movie *King's Row,* and by Louis Howe (Hume Cronyn) to Franklin D. Roosevelt (Edward Bellamy) in the 1960 movie *Sunrise at Campobello*.

Iola Morton and Callie Shaw
   Girlfriends of the Hardy Boys, Joe and Frank, respectively, in novels. In the 1977 TV series *The Hardy Boys Mysteries* Callie was played by Lisa Eilbacher and Iola was noticeably absent.

Iolani Palace
Honolulu headquarters of the Five-O team (5-0 meaning the 50th state) in the
TV series *Hawaii Five-O*.

Iraq
First country to use an adhesive postage stamp.

I Remember Mama—But I Forget Papa
Book written by Professor Lapse von Memory, the world's foremost memory
expert, played by Sid Caesar on the TV series *Your Show of Shows*.

Iron Butt, The
College nickname of Richard Milhous Nixon. In law school, at Duke
University, he was called Gloomy Gus.

Iron Mike
Nickname of the automatic pilot aboard the U.S.O.S. *Seaview* in the TV
series *Voyage to the Bottom of the Sea*.

Iroquois
Indian tribe to which John Hawk (Burt Reynolds) belonged in the TV series
Hawk.

Irregardless
Double negative humorously used by Al Capp in his *Li'l Abner* comic strip.
Although the word is used quite often in common speech, it is actually a
nonstandard adjective for the word *regardless*. (To clarify the grammatical
problem, I have coined the word *unirregardless,* which is a triple negative,
which should bring us back to the original meaning of *regardless*.)

Irving and Christabel
Monroe family dogs in the TV series *My World . . . And Welcome to It*.

Irving Wong
Chinese song composer, a character played by Ernic Kovacs on TV.

Iscariot, Judas
One of Jesus Christ's twelve apostles. He betrayed Jesus and then committed
suicide. Movie portrayals: *The Robe* (1953) Michael Ansara; *The Greatest
Story Ever Told* (1965) David McCallum; *Jesus Christ, Superstar* (1973) Carl
Anderson; *Jesus of Nazareth* (1977) Ian McShane; and *The Day Christ Died*
(1980 TV) Barrie Houghton.

Is everybody happy?
Catch line of bandleader Ted Lewis.

Island Princess
Boat skippered by Sam Bailey (Paul Ford) in the TV series *The Baileys of
Balboa*.

Isotta Faschini
Norma Desmond's (Gloria Swanson) $28,000 leopard-skin-upholstered lim-
ousine in the 1950 movie *Sunset Boulevard*.

I Surrender Dear

Song composed in 1931 by Harry Barris (father of Chuck Barris). It was Bing Crosby's first hit as a solo artist and Red Norvo's theme song "I Surrender Dear" was the song dedicated to the men of the 101st Airborne (Screaming Eagles) by a German radio station in the 1949 movie *Battleground*.

It

The only word that the Knights of Nee can't pronounce in the 1978 movie *Monty Python and the Holy Grail*.

Italia Bella

Benito Mussolini's pet lion that traveled with him.

It happened that way moving west

Closing line said by Walter Coy on the 1955–1956 TV series *Frontier*.

I, the Jury

1947 detective novel by Mickey Spillane that introduced the character Mike Hammer. A paperback copy of the book (Signet) appears in the 1955 movie *Marty* and in the 1971 movie *The Last Picture Show*. The book was also read by the guys at Arnold's on the TV series *Happy Days*.

It Is Very Beautiful Over There

Last words of Thomas A. Edison before he died on October 18, 1931.

It's a Long Way to Tipperary

Song sung by the cast on the last new episode of the TV series *The Mary Tyler Moore Show*.

It's a Most Unusual Day

Song played by a group of violinists in the Palm Court as Roger O. Thornhill (Cary Grant) enters the Plaza Hotel just before being kidnapped in the 1959 movie *North by Northwest*.

It's clobberin' time

Battle cry of the superhero The Thing (Ben Grimm), a member of the Fantastic Four (Marvel comics).

It's Finger Lickin' Good

Slogan for Kentucky Fried Chicken.

It's going, going, gone

How baseball announcer Mel Allen described a home run for his Yankee fans.

It's Only Money

Proposed 1948 movie vehicle for Frank Sinatra, Groucho Marx, and Jane Russell. The film was never made.

Ivan

German shepherd on the TV series *The Inspector*.

Ivanhoe

Knight hero of Sir Walter Scott's 1820 novel *Ivanhoe* and the 1850 sequel

Rebecca and Rowena by William Makepeace Thackeray. He was portrayed in the 1953 movie *Ivanhoe* by Robert Taylor.

I've Got a Lovely Bunch of Coconuts

Merv Griffin's theme song. He received a flat $50 for this 3-million seller, which he recorded in 1948 with Freddy Martin's band.

I've Got You Under My Skin

Song composed in 1936 by Cole Porter. It can be heard in the following movies: *Born to Dance* (1936); *Night and Day* (1946); and *The Mating Game* (1959).

Ivory Soap Baby

Numerous babies have posed for Ivory Soap commercials and ads. One of these babies was Malcolm John Rebennack, a/k/a rock musician Dr. John; another was Brooke Shields (at age 11 months).

I Wanna Be Loved by You

Song written in 1928 by Bert Kalmar, Herbert Strothart, and Harry Ruby and introduced by Helen Kane in the 1928 musical *Good Boy*. It can be heard in the following films: *Three Little Words* (1950), sung by Debbie Reynolds (dubbed by Helen Kane); *Gentlemen Marry Brunettes* (1955), sung by Rudy Vallee, Jane Russell, and Jeanne Crain (dubbed by Anita Ellis); and *Some Like It Hot* (1959), sung by Marilyn Monroe.

I Will Come Back

Judy Garland's closing song on her 1963–1964 TV series.

J. G. Reeder
British detective created by prolific writer Edgar Wallace. Reeder was played in British movies by Gibb McLaughlin in *Mr. Reeder in Room 13* (1938) and by Will Fyffe in *Mind of Mr. Reeder and Missing People* (1935). Hugh Burden played the character on the 1972 TV series *The Mind of Mr. Reed.*

JRH 421
California license plate of the 1955 Chevy in which actor Montgomery Clift crashed on the night of May 13, 1956. He had been following the car of actor Kevin McCarthy. Clift's face was later repaired by plastic surgery. The film he was making at the time was *Raintree County.*

J Trump
First American-bred and trained horse to win the Grand National Steeplechase in England.

JW 1-6223
Number of the phone in Robert T. Ironside's van in the TV series *Ironside.*

Jack
Pet collie of the Ingall family in the TV series *Little House on the Prairie,* played by Bandit.

Jackie Gleason Classic
Annual golf tournament held at the Inverrary Golf Course.

Jackolope
Fictitious animal created in that it is a cross between a jackrabbit and an antelope. It is found in Douglas, Wyoming. The males have antlers. Jackolopes mate only during lightning flashes. They can imitate the human voice. To hunt them, a hunter's IQ must be between 50 and 72.

Jackson, Andrew

(1767–1845) 7th president of the United States, nicknamed Old Hickory. He was the first president on whom an assassination attempt was made—on January 30, 1835, Richard Lawrence fired two shots at Jackson, but both guns misfired. Jackson was the first president to ride in a railroad train (June 1833) and the only president to have been a prisoner of war (in April 1781, when he was 14, he and his brother, Robert, were captured by the British). Movie portrayals: *Eagle of the Sea* (1926) George Irving; *The Frontiersman* (1927) Russell Simpson; *The Goregous Hussy* (1939) John Barrymore; *The Buccaneer* (1938) Hugh Sothern; *Man of Conquest* (1939) Edward Ellis; *The Remarkable Andrew* (1942) Brian Donlevy; *Lone Star* (1952) Lionel Barrymore; *The President's Lady* (1953) Charlton Heston; *Davy Crockett* (1955) Basil Ruysdael; *The First Texan* (1956) Carl Brenton Reid; *The Buccaneer* (1958) Charlton Heston; and *Bridger* (1976 TV) John Anderson.

Jackson City

Montana hometown of Jefferson Smith (James Stewart) in the 1939 movie *Mr. Smith Goes to Washington*. The town newspaper was the *Jackson City Star*.

Jackson, Graham

Black musician who played "Going Home" on his accordion at Franklin D. Roosevelt's funeral in April 1945.

Jadaan

Arabian stallion ridden by Rudolph Valentino in the 1926 movie *The Son of the Sheik*.

Jake

(Zunar J5/90 Doric 4-7) Alien feline in the 1978 movie *The Cat from Outer Space*, played by Rumple (voice of Ronnie Schell).

Jake's Bar & Grill

Inn in Vienna, Austria, run by Jake Webster (Robert Conrad) in the TV series *Assignment Vienna*.

James, Jesse and Frank

Brothers who were notorious western outlaws: Jesse Woodson James (1847–1882) and Alexander Franklin James (1843–1915). Jesse was shot in the back by Robert Ford, but Frank died peacefully at the age of 72, never having been convicted of a crime. Portrayals: *Jesse James Under the Black Flag* (1921) Jesse James, Jr. (Jesse); *Jesse James as the Outlaw* (1921) Jesse James, Jr. (Jesse); *Jesse James* (1927) Fred Thompson (Jesse) and James Pierce (Frank); *Jesse James* (1939) Tyrone Power (Jesse) and Henry Fonda (Frank); *Days of Jesse James* (1939) Donald Barry (Jesse) and Michael Worth (Frank); *The Return of Frank James* (1940) Henry Fonda (Frank); *Jesse James at Bay* (1941) Roy Rogers (Jesse); *Bad Men of Missouri* (1941) Alan Baxter (Jesse); *The Remarkable Andrew* (1942) Rod Cameron (Jesse); *Badman's*

Territory (1946) Lawrence Tierney (Jesse); *Jesse James Rides Again* (1947) Clayton Moore (Jesse); *Adventures of Frank and Jesse James* (1948) Clayton Moore (Jesse) and Steve Darrell (Frank); *I Shot Jesse James* (1949) Reed Hadley (Jesse), and Tom Tyler (Frank); *Fighting Man of the Plains* (1949) Dale Robertson (Jesse); *The James Brothers of Missouri* (1950) Keith Richards (Jesse) and Robert Bice (Frank); Frank James Rides Again, (1950) Don Barry (Frank); *The Return of Jesse James* (1950) Reed Hadley (Frank); *The Great Missouri Raid* (1951) MacDonald Carey (Jesse) and Wendell Corey (Frank); *Kansas Raiders* (1950) Audie Murphy (Jesse) and Richard Long (Frank); *Best of the Badmen* (1951) Lawrence Tierney (Jesse) and Tom Tyler (Frank); *Woman They Almost Lynched* (1953) Ben Cooper (Jesse) and James Brown (Frank); *The Great Jesse James Raid* (1953) William Parker (Jesse); *Jesse James' Women** (1954) Don Barry (Jesse) and Jack Buetel (Frank); *The True Story of Jesse James* (1957) Robert Wagner (Jesse) and Jeffrey Hunter (Frank); *Hell's Crossroads* (1957) Henry Brandon (Jesse) and Douglas Kennedy (Frank); *Alias Jesse James* (1959) Wendell Corey (Jesse) and Jim Davis (Frank); *Young Jesse James* (1960) Ray Stricklyn (Jesse) and Robert Dix (Frank); *The Outlaws Is Coming* (1965) Wayne Mack (Jesse); *Jesse James Meets Frankenstein's Daughter* (1966) John Lupton (Jesse); *A Time for Dying* (1969) Audie Murphy (Jesse); *The Great Northfield Minnesota Raid* (1972) Robert Duvall (Jesse) and John Pearce (Frank); *Belle Starr* (1980 TV) Michael Cavanaugh (Jesse) and Gary Combs (Frank); *The Long Riders* (1980) James Keach (Jesse) and Stacy Keach; (Frank); *The Legend of Jesse James* (TV series) Chris Jones (Jesse) and Allen Case (Frank). Wendell Corey and Don Barry are the only actors to have played both Jesse and Frank James in films.

James, M. E. Clifford
British actor who became Gen. Montgomery's double during World War II. He was portrayed in the 1958 movie *I Was Monty's Double* by John Mills.

Jan and Dean
Jan Berry and Dean Torrence, popular rock 'n' roll duet of the 1960s. In 1965 Jan Berry was involved in a serious automobile accident when his Corvette crashed near Deadman's Curve in Los Angeles (ironically, this occurred a year after the pair recorded the song "Dead Man's Curve"). Jan and Dean were portrayed in the 1978 TV movie *Deadman's Curve* by Richard Hatch and Bruce Davison.

Jane Foster
Girlfriend of comic book superhero Thor.

Jane Hudson
Name of character appearing in two films, *Summertime* (1955) and *What*

---

*Directed by Don "Red" Barry.

Ever Happened to Baby Jane? (1962), played by Katharine Hepburn and Bette Davis, respectively. Both actresses were nominated for best actress for these roles.

Janowicz, Vic
Only Heisman Trophy winner (Ohio State, 1950) to play major league baseball (Pittsburgh Pirates 1953–1954).

January 1st
Traditional day for the Rose Bowl, Sugar Bowl, Cotton Bowl, and Orange Bowl. January 2, 1978, was the first time these games weren't played on the 1st (the 1st was a Sunday, when the pro teams played).

Jarvis, Al
The first disc jockey, he originated his *Make Believe Ballroom* from KFWB in Los Angeles in the 1930s.

Jarvis, Anna
Woman who created Mother's Day, although she was never a mother herself (she was never even married). She began campaigning for the holiday in 1907, and it was finally adopted on May 12, 1914. There is a Mother's Day Shrine in Miss Jarvis's hometown of Grafton, West Virginia.

Jasper
Maxim de Winter's (Laurence Olivier) pet cocker spaniel in the 1940 movie *Rebecca*.

Jawas
Small people who find and sell abandoned robots in the 1977 movie *Star Wars*.

Jaws
James Bond's (Roger Moore) metal-toothed villain in the 1977 movie *The Spy Who Loved Me* and in the 1979 movie *Moonraker*. Jaws was played by 7-foot 2-inch actor Richard Keil (he wears a size 16EEE shoe).

Jay Gatsby
Hero of F. Scott Fitzgerald's novel *The Great Gatsby*. Warner Baxter (1926), Alan Ladd (1949), and Robert Redford (1974) played the part in the three movies made from the novel. Jay Gatsby was born in 1896 and died in 1928.

Jazz Artists' Real First Names
Julian—Cannonball Adderley
Harold—Shorty Baker
William—Count Basie
Leon—Bix Beiderbecke
Roland—Bunny Berigan
Leon—Chuck Berry
Leon—Barney Bigard
Reuben—Ruby Braff
Alexander—Sandy Brown

Charles—Billy Butterfield
Carlos—Don Byas
Cabell—Cab Calloway
Bennett—Benny Carter
Adolphus—Doc Cheatham
Wilbur—Buck Clayton
William—Cozy Cole
Albert—Eddie Condon
Harry—Bing Crosby
George—Bob Crosby
William—Wild Bill Davidson
Warren—Baby Dodds
David—Roy Eldridge
Edmund—Duke Ellington
Lawrence—Bud Freeman
John—Dizzy Gillespie
Benjamin—Benny Goodman
William—Sonny Greer
Lloyd—Tini Grimes
Woodrow—Woody Herman
Albert—Budd Johnson
William—Bunk Johnson
Robert—Jonah Jones
Bill—Yusef Lateef
John—Yank Lawson
Norma—Peggy Lee
Joseph—Windy Manone
James—Bubber Miley
Ernest—Kid Punch Miller
Irving—Miff Mole
Ferdinand—Jelly Roll Morton
Theodor—Fats Navarro
Albert—Wooden Joe Nichols
Ernest—Red Nichols
Kenneth—Red Norvo
Joseph—King Oliver
Edward—Kid Ory
Oran—Hot Lips Page
Joseph—Flip Phillips
Gertrude—Ma Rainey
Robert—Red Rodney
Milton—Shorty Rogers

Charles—Pee Wee Russell
Hezekiah—Stuff Smith
Francis—Muggsy Spanier
Saunders—Sonny Terry
Thomas—Fats Waller
William—Dicky Wells
Charles—Cootie Williams

Jean C. Tarzan
Name under which Tarzan traveled. He also used the name John Caldwell of London, as well as his title, Lord Greystroke (novels).

Jeanie
Cartoonist Bill Mauldin's jeep, which he drove in Europe during World War II.

Jed Clayton, U.S. Marshal
Title of a TV western starring Sam Garrett (Richard Mulligan) as Jed Clayton in the TV series *The Hero*.

Jeff
Sidekick of Augustus Mutt in the comic strip *Mutt and Jeff*. Jeff is short for Jeffries. Within the comic strip, fighter Jim Jeffries convinced the little guy to change his name to Jeff.

Jefferson, "Blind" Lemmon
(1897–1929) Blind blues singer whose style influenced country yodeler Jimmie Rodgers. Jefferson was portrayed in the 1976 movie *Leadbelly* by Art Evans.

Jefferson City
State penitentiary in Missouri where Charles "Sonny" Liston was sentenced to serve three concurrent 5-year sentences for armed robbery. (He served only 2½ years—1950–1952.) It was there that Liston learned to box.

Jefferson County Bridge
Bridge spanning the Ohio River in Louisville, Kentucky, from which Cassius Clay (a/k/a Muhammad Ali) threw his Olympic Gold Medal (from the 1960 Olympics) into the river.

Jefferson, Thomas
(1743–1826) 3rd president of the United States. Along with all his political accomplishments, he was the inventor of the folding bed and the swivel chair. Movie portrayals: *America* (1924) Frank Walsh; *Janice Meredith* (1924) Lionel Adams; *The Man Without a Country* (1925) Albert Hart; *Alexander Hamilton* (1931) Montagu Love; *The Remarkable Andrew* (1942) Gilbert Emery; *Magnificent Doll* (1946) Grandon Rhodes; *The Far Horizons* (1955) Herbert Heyes; *1776* (1972) Ken Howard; and *Independence* (1976 short) Ken Howard.

Jell-O
Gelatine dessert introduced in the 1930s. The original six flavors were

strawberry, raspberry, cherry, orange, lemon, and line. The top of a raspberry Jell-O box was used by Julius Rosenberg's brother-in-law, David Greenglass, as identification when he met Soviet agent Harry Gold to sell him U.S. secrets. Jell-O powder was used to color the horse-of-a-different-color in the making of the 1939 movie *The Wizard of Oz*.

Jenkins Hill
Hill in Washington, D.C., upon which the Capitol was built.

Jennings, Al
(1863–1948) Western outlaw and train robber who was pardoned by President Theodore Roosevelt in 1907 after serving 5 years of a life sentence for robbery. Author O. Henry, who was in prison with Jennings, wrote about a number of his exploits. After being pardoned, Jennings returned to law practice and later became a silent western star, forming his own movie company (Al Jennings Feature Film Company). He served as technical adviser for the 1939 movie *The Oklahoma Kid*. Jennings was portrayed by Dan Duryea in the 1951 movie *Al Jennings of Oklahoma*.

Jensen, Andrew
Only Navy chaplain ever court-martialed for adultery. He was portrayed in the 1975 TV movie *The Trial of Chaplain Jensen* by James Franciscus.

Jerez, Rodrigo de
Spanish explorer who is believed to have been the first European who smoked, being taught by the Indians.

Jerome and Geraldene
Pet baby goats of the Everett family in the TV series *Nanny and the Professor*.

Jerry
Little man who throws confetti in the TV series *The Gong Show*.

Jessel, George
(1898–1981) American vaudeville entertainer who both acted in and produced motion pictures. In his youth he was a bat boy for the New York Giants. He holds the rank of toastmaster general of the United States. Jessel was portrayed in the 1978 TV movie *Rainbow* by Jack Carter.

Jessica
Name of the U.S. Army jeep in the 1944 movie *Four Jills in a Jeep*. The film was based on a novel written by actress Carole Landis.

Jesus
Jesus of Nazareth, who was born approximately 4 B.C. and crucified A.D. 29. Son of Joseph, a carpenter, and the Virgin Mary. Christians believe he is the Son of God. Movie portrayals: *The Holy City* (1913) Robert Frazer; *The Life of Christ* (1914) Monsieur Normand; *From the Manger to the Cross* (1914) Robert Henderson Bland; *Intolerance* (1916) Howard Gaye; *King of Kings*

(1927) H. B. Warner;* *The Robe* (1953) Cameron Mitchell; *Ben Hur* (1959) Claude Heater: *King of Kings* (1961) Jeffrey Hunter; *Barrabas* (1962) Roy Mangano; *The Greatest Story Ever Told* (1965) Max Von Sydow; *Pontius Pilate* (1966) John Drew Barrymore (he also played Judas); *Gospel Road* (1966) Robert Elfstrom; *Johnny Got His Gun* (1971) Donald Sutherland; *Godspell* (1973) Victor Garber; *Jesus Christ, Superstar* (1973) Ted Neeley; *The Passover Plot* (1976) Zalman King; *Jesus of Nazareth* (1977) Robert Powell (Immad Cohen as a boy); *Jesus* (1979) Brian Beacon; *The Day Christ Died* (1980 TV) Chris Sarandon; and *In Search of the Historical Jesus* (1980) John Rubinstein, and *History of the World, Part 1* (1981) John Hurt.

Jethrene Bodine
Sister of Jethro Bodine (both played by Max Baer, with Jethrene's voice supplied by Linda Kaye Henning) in the TV series *The Beverly Hillbillies*.

Jeweler's Shop, The
Play written by Pope John Paul II in 1960 when he was a bishop in his native Poland. The play premiered on Italian radio on March 1, 1979.

Jidge
Nickname that the New York Yankee team had for Babe Ruth. Ruth once gave Lou Gehrig's mother a pet Chihuahua, which she named Jidge.

Jiggs
White bulldog that was the mascot of the U.S. Marine Corps. When Jiggs died in 1927, Jiggs II, presented by boxer Gene Tunney (himself an ex-Marine), took his place.

Jim
Dr. Richard Kimble's (David Janssen) favorite first-name alias in the TV series *The Fugitive*. Among the last names he used were Owen, McGuire, Lincoln, and Russell.

Jimmy Chan
Charlie Chan's (Sidney Tolen) number-two son, played in movies by Victor Sen Young. Young also played number-one son Lee in *Charlie Chan in Honolulu* (1938). In the 1937 movie *Charlie Chan at the Olympics* Charlie, Jr., was number-two son.

Jimmy Doyle
Name of a character in the following films: *Sahara* (1943) Dan Duryea; *The French Connection* (1971) Gene Hackman; and *New York, New York* (1977) Robert De Niro.

Jimmy Walker
Hero of the 1972 Jim Croce hit song "You Don't Mess Around with Jim."

Jim's Bar
Bar where publisher Henry Connell (James Gleason) and John Willoughby

---

*H. B. Warner, Dorothy Cummings (as Mary), and Joseph Schildkraut (as Judas) were uncredited in the film.

(Gary Cooper) have a drink and talk about the Stars and Stripes in the 1940 movie *Meet John Doe*.

Jingle Bells
Song that Frances Gumm (Judy Garland) sang at her stage debut at the age of 3 (1925). Her debut was unplanned—she ran onto the stage, sang a few choruses, and was carried off by her father.

Jip
Dora Copperfield's (David's wife) pet spaniel in Dickens' novel *David Copperfield*.

Jitterbug
$80,000 dance routine omitted from the final version of the 1939 movie *The Wizard of Oz*.

Joanie Phoney
Antiestablishment character who appeared in Al Capp's comic strip *Li'l Abner*, purported to be a takeoff on folk singer Joan Baez. Joan Baez successfully sued Al Capp over the satirization.

Jodie
Imaginary pig in the novel/movie *The Amityville Horror*.

Joe
Gen. Chennault's pet dachshund that served with him in China during World War II.

Joe Patroni
Only continuing character (played by George Kennedy) in the *Airport* movie series: *Airport* (1970); *Airport 1975* (1974); *Airport '77* (1977); and *Concorde: Airport '79* (1979). He died in the last movie.

John Birch Society Talking Blues
Song CBS would not allow Bob Dylan to sing on *The Ed Sullivan Show* in 1963. Dylan then refused to appear on the show.

John Burrows
Code name used by Elvis Presley in answering telephone calls. A second alias was Dr. John Carpenter. Tom Parker used the code name of Col. Snow.

John Doe
Name that Leon F. Czolgosz used to sign the hotel register at the Riggs House on Friday, September 6, 1901, the day he assassinated President McKinley.

John Hamilton
Name used by actor Sterling Hayden when he served as an officer in the OSS during World War II.

John J. Fadozle
America's number-one private eye, in the TV series *Howdy Doody Time*.

John Luckless
Pseudonym of writer Clifford Irving.

Johnny Blood
  Nickname of NFL player John McNally.
Johnny Casino and the Gamblers
  Rock 'n' roll group (played by Sha-Na-Na) that played at the Rydell High
  gym where *National Bandstand* was being broadcast in the 1978 movie
  Grease.
Johnny One-Note
  Song composed by Rodgers and Hart in 1937 for the 1939 movie *Babes in
  Arms*, but used instead in the 1948 movie *Words and Music*. The scene in
  which Judy Garland sang the song in the 1939 movie was cut from the film.
John Paul Jones II, USS
  New Navy destroyer featured in the 1943 movie *Destroyer*.
John Shaft
  New York City black detective played in movies and the TV series by
  Richard Roundtree. Shaft was created by Ernest Tidyman.* Movies: *Shaft*
  (1971); *Shaft's Big Score* (1972); and *Shaft in Africa* (1973).
Johnson, Albert
  Murderer who in 1932 became the subject of the biggest manhunt in
  Canadian Mounted Police history. He was portrayed in the 1980 movie *Death
  Hunt* by Charles Bronson.
Johnson, Amy
  (1903–1941) British aviatrix who was the first woman to make a solo flight
  from London to Australia (1930). She set other aviation records as well. Amy
  Johnson drowned in the Thames estuary after bailing out of an airplane. She
  was portrayed in the 1942 movie *Wings and the Woman* by Dame Anna
  Neagle.
Johnson, Davey
  Only baseball player who has played on the same team with the two greatest
  home run hitters: Hank Aaron (in Atlanta) and Sadaharu Oh (in Japan).
Johnson, Jeremiah
  (1822–1900) Rocky Mountain adventurer, scout, trapper, and Indian fighter.
  In 1974 his body was exhumed, flown to Wyoming, and reburied there.
  (Johnson had once expressed the wish to be buried in the mountains). Robert
  Redford, who portrayed Jeremiah in the 1972 movie *Jeremiah Johnson*,†
  served as one of the pallbearers.
Johnson, Van, and June Allyson
  Movies in which the pair appeared: *Two Girls and a Sailor* (1944); *Till the
  Clouds Roll By* (1946); *High Barbaree* (1947); *The Bride Goes Wild* (1948);
  Too Young to Kiss (1951); and *Remains to be Seen* (1953).

---

*Tidyman wrote the screenplay for the 1971 movie *The French Connection*.
†Country singer Tanya Tucker made her movie debut in a bit role.

John the Baptist
   Prophet who baptized Jesus. He was executed by Herod Antipas. Movie portrayals: *Salome* (1953) Alan Badel; *King of Kings* (1961) Robert Ryan; *The Greatest Story Ever Told* (1965) Charlton Heston; and *Jesus of Nazareth* (1977 TV) Michael York.

Joint, Alf
   Stunt man who jumped from one cable car to another in the 1968 movie *Where Eagles Dare.*

Jolson, Al
   (1886–1950) Jewish-American entertainer (born Asa Yoelson). He appeared in the first talkie picture, *The Jazz Singer,* in 1927. In 1945 he married Erle Chennault, 40 years his junior and the niece of Gen. Chennault. In 1950 he was the first actor to entertain U.N. troops in Korea. Movie portrayals: *The Jolson Story* (1946) Larry Parks; *Jolson Sings Again* (1949) Larry Parks; *The Best Things in Life Are Free* (1956) Norman Brooks; and *Harlow* (1965) Buddy Lewis.

Jonah, HMS
   Experimental submarine disguised as the Loch Ness monster in the 1969 movie *The Private Life of Sherlock Holmes.*

Jonas Grumby
   Skipper of the SS *Minnow,* which ran aground, stranding Grumby and six other people on a South Pacific Island. He was played by Alan Hale, Jr., in the TV series *Gilligan's Island.*

Jonathan Garvey
   Role played by former Los Angeles Rams football player Merlin Olsen in the TV series *Little House on the Prairie.*

Jones
   Yellow tomcat on board the interstellar tug *Nostromo* in the 1979 movie *Alien.*

Jones, James
   American author of a famous World War II triology: *From Here to Eternity* (1951); *The Thin Red Line* (1962); and *Whistle* (1978).
   Character name changes:

From Here to Eternity	*The Thin Red Line*	*Whistle*
1/Sgt. Warden	Sgt. Welsh	Mart Winch
Pvt. Prewitt	Pvt. Witt	Bobby Press
Mess/Sgt. Stark	Mess/St. Storm	John Strange

While in the U.S. Army, Jones twice made noncom and twice was busted back to private. He was in Schofield Barracks when the Japanese attacked Pearl Harbor on December 7, 1941, and was awarded both the Purple Heart and the Bronze Star during the war. He was once a Golden Gloves contender.

Jones died on May 9, 1977, while writing the novel *Whistle;* it was finished from his notes.

Jones, Jim

(1931–1978) Cult leader of the People's Temple who convinced his 900 followers to commit suicide by poison in Jonestown, Guyana, on November 18, 1978. Jones was portrayed in the 1979 movie *Guyana: Cult of the Damned* by Stuart Whitman, and in the 1980 TV movie *Guyana Tragedy: The Story of Jim Jones* by Powers Boothe.*

Jones, Raymond

Lad who walked into Brian Epstein's NEMS Record Store in Liverpool on October 28, 1961 to request a record titled "My Bonnie" by an unknown group called the Beatles. This stirred Epstein's interest and led him to become the Beatles' manager and publicity architect. Raymond Jones became the bass player for Billy J. Kramer and the Dakotas, a group that recorded a number of Lennon-McCartney compositions and was also managed by Brian Epstein.

Jonesy

Ranch cook, played by Hoagy Carmichael, in the TV series *Laramie.*

Jonson, Ben

(1573–1637) English poet, actor, and playwright who is buried in Westminster Abbey in a sitting position (dictated by lack of space).

Joplin, Scott

(1868–1917) Ragtime piano player called the King of Ragtime. He composed numerous rags, including "Maple Leaf Rag" and "The Entertainer," which was used in the 1973 movie *The Sting.* Joplin was portrayed in the 1978 TV movie *Scott Joplin* by Billy Dee Williams (Richard Hyman performed the selections) and by David Hubbard as a boy.

Josef Conrad

Polish freighter sunk by U.S. aircraft during the December 19, 1971, raid on Hanoi harbor.

Joseph, Chief

(1840–1904) American Indian chief of the Nez Percé tribe whose Indian name was Hinmaton-Yalaktit. On October 5, 1877, he was captured by Gen. Nelson A. Miles. Chief Joseph was portrayed in the 1975 TV movie *I Will Fight No More, Forever* by Ned Romero.

Joyce, Joan

Underhand softball pitcher who in exhibition games struck out both Ted Williams and Hank Aaron. She has won 638 games, lost 38, and had 139 no-hitters, including 41 perfect games (as of 1979). She once pitched 229 consecutive scoreless innings.

---

*At the 1980 Emmy presentations Boothe was the only actor present to accept his award (best actor for his Jim Jones role). The other winners all boycotted the ceremonies because of the actors' strike.

Juárez, Benito Pablo
(1806–1872) Mexican politician who served as president of Mexico for many years. He died in office on July 18, 1872. He was portrayed in the 1956 movie *Juarez* by Paul Muni.

Judson, Whitcomb L.
American inventor of the zipper in 1891.

Juice, The
Nickname of football great Orenthal James (O.J.) Simpson.

July 4, 1976
America's Bicentennial. On that date Israeli commandos freed over 100 hostages at Entebbe Airport in Uganda.

Jumper
Coates family mule in the 1957 movie *Old Yeller.*

June Gale
Dr. Rex Morgan's girlfriend (comic strip *Rex Morgan, M.D.*).

Juno Award
Canadian equivalent of the U.S. Grammy Award.

Justice Society of America
Society of crime-fighting superheroes that debuted in *All Star Comics* No. 3 (Winter 1940). The original eight members, clockwise around the society table, were: The Atom, Sandman, The Spectre, The Flash, Hawkman, Dr. Fate, Green Lantern, and The Hour-Man.

Just One of Those Things
Cole Porter song, composed in 1935, that can be heard in the following movies: *Night and Day* (1946), sung by Ginny Simms; *Lullaby of Broadway* (1951), sung by Doris Day; *The Jazz Singer* (1953), sung by Peggy Lee; *Young at Heart* (1955), sung by Frank Sinatra; and *Can Can* (1960), sung by Maurice Chevalier.

Just when you thought it was safe to go back in the water . . .
Promotional line used to advertise the 1978 movie *Jaws 2*.

KAR 120C
British license plate number of the prisoner's (Patrick McGoohan) sports car, which he built by hand, in the TV series *The Prisoner.*

KB 7608163
Dr. Richard Kimble's (David Janssen) police identification number in the TV series *The Fugitive.*

KDAV
Lubbock, Texas, station that in 1953 became the first radio station to broadcast solely country music. In 1958 Waylon Jennings went to work there as a disc jockey. Buddy Holly and Bob Montgomery hosted a radio show on KDAV.

KDKA
Pittsburgh, Pennsylvania, radio station that became the first commercial radio station on November 2, 1920, when it broadcast the presidential election returns in the race between Warren G. Harding and James M. Cox. Dr. Frank Conrad was the broadcaster.*

KFSG
(Four Square Gospel) Sister Aimee Semple McPherson's radio station at her Los Angeles church, Angelus Temple. She was the first woman in the United States to be granted an FCC license.

KGEB
Radio station that broadcast from the landing site in Corona, California, of the Martians in the 1953 movie *The War of the Worlds.*

---

*Conrad coined the word *broadcasting*.

KL5-1251
Telephone number engraved on a Speidel bracelet (Speidel TV commercial).
KLUE
Longview, Texas, radio station that announced a public bonfire of Beatle records and pictures for Friday night August 13, 1966, in retaliation for John Lennon's remark, "We're more popular than Jesus now." The day after the bonfire a lightning bolt struck the transmission tower, knocking station manager Lowell Wolfe unconscious and causing extensive damage to the radio equipment.
KLXA
California television station where Tabitha Stephens (Lisa Hartman) was employed as an assistant producer of "The Paul Thurston Show" in the TV series *Tabitha*.
KRDA
DeQueen, New Mexico, station—"World's smallest television station"—setting of the 1978 TV series *Please Stand By*.
KSF
San Francisco TV station for which Linda Lee Danvers (Supergirl) works.
KVGS
Las Vegas television station for which Larry Parnell (Larry Breeding) worked in the TV series *Who's Watching the Kids?*
KXIV
Phoenix, Arizona, TV station for which Dick Preston (Dick Van Dyke) worked as a host of a talk show in the TV series *The Dick Van Dyke Show*.
KXLA
Los Angeles television station (Channel 3) for which Kimberly Wells (Jane Fonda) and Richard Adams (Michael Douglas) worked in the 1979 movie *The China Syndrome*.
KZAZ
Los Angeles TV station (Channel 5) that broadcast the National Bandstand dance contest from Rydell High gym in the 1978 movie *Grease*.
Kahn, Gus
(1886–1941) American lyricist who composed the evergreens "I'll See You in My Dreams" and "Love Me or Leave Me." He was portrayed in the 1952 movie *I'll See You in My Dreams* by Danny Thomas. His wife, Grace LeBoy Kahn, was portrayed by Doris Day.
Kala Nag
Elephant (played by Irawatha) ridden by Sabu in the 1937 movie *Elephant Boy*.
Kalmar, Bert
(1884–1947) Successful lyricist who, with Harry Ruby, composed many

songs, such as "Who's Sorry Now?" and "Three Little Words." Kalmar was portrayed in the 1950 movie *Three Little Words* by Fred Astaire.

Kalmbach, Herbert W.

President Nixon's personal lawyer. He was portrayed in the 1979 TV miniseries *Blind Ambition* by William Schallert.

Kane, Helen

(1904–1966) American singer (born Helen Schroder) who became known as the Boop-a-Doop girl. Her theme song was "I Wanna Be Loved by You." She was portrayed by Debbie Reynolds in the 1950 movie *Three Little Words* (Helen Kane dubbed the singing).

Kankakee, Illinois

Hometown of the captains of both the West Point (Harry Stella) and the Annapolis (Allen Bergner) football teams in 1939. When the two teams met on a grid-iron, Army was the victor.

Kansas Cyclone

Nickname of football back Dwight Eisenhower at West Point Academy.

Kappa Alpha Theta

First sorority, formed on January 27, 1870, at Indiana Asbury University (now De Pauw University).

Karpis, Alvin "Creepy"

(1908–   ) Former member of Ma Barker's gang. He was once designated Public Enemy Number One. Karpis was Prisoner No 325 at Alcatraz Prison. Later, at McNeil Island Prison (1964–1967), he taught Charles Manson to play the guitar. Karpis spent more time (25 years) in Alcatraz than any other prisoner. In his youth he won the Marbles Championship of Topeka, Kansas. Movie portrayals; *Bloody Mama* (1970) Bruce Dern (as Kevin Dirkman); *F.B.I. Story: The F.B.I. Versus Alvin Karpis, Public Enemy Number One* (1974 TV) Robert Foxworth; *The Kansas City Massacre* (1975) Morgan Paul. and *The Private Files of J. Edgar Hoover* (1978) Brad Dexter.

Kashimo

Charlie Chan's Japanese assistant (novels).

Kate Columbo

Wife of Lt. Columbo, played in the TV series *Mrs. Columbo* by Kate Mulgrew.

Katzenjammers, The

Orchestra formed by singer/actor Dick Haymes.

Kaufman, George S.

(1889–1961) American playwright. He was awarded the Pulitzer Prize for his 1932 play *Of Thee I Sing*. Kaufman was portrayed in the 1963 movie *Act One* by Jason Robards, Jr.

Kayo

Harpo Marx's white dog with black spots that appeared in the 1932 movie *Horse Feathers* along with his master.

Kean, Edmund

(1787–1833) Popular British Shakespearean actor. He was portrayed in the 1922 movie *A Stage Romance* by William Farnum.

Keaton, Joseph "Buster"

(1895–1966) American movie comic whose career began in 1917. He received his nickname "Buster" from his godfather, magician Harry Houdini. In the 1950 movie *Sunset Boulevard* he portrayed himself, and in the 1957 movie *The Buster Keaton Story* he was portrayed by Donald O'Connor.

Keeler, Christine

Englishwoman who became the center of a political scandal (1963) when it was revealed that she was conducting simultaneous affairs with the British minister of war, John Profumo, and the Soviet naval attaché, Yevgeni Ivanov. She was portrayed by Yvonne Buckingham in the 1964 movie *The Christine Keeler Affair,* in which she had a bit part as another character.

Keeler, Ruby

American singer and dancer and one-time wife of Al Jolson who made her film debut in *42nd Street* (1933). She played an extra in the 1969 movie *They Shoot Horses, Don't They?* Keeler was portrayed loosely in the 1946 movie *The Jolson Story* by Evelyn Keyes (as Julie Benson).

Kefauver, Estes

(1903–1963) U.S. senator and vice presidential candidate. He headed a number of congressional committees investigating organized crime. He was portrayed in the 1974 TV movie *The Virginia Hill Story* by Herbert Anderson.

Keller, Helen

(1880–1968) American author and lecturer who at the age of 19 months lost both her hearing and her sight. She was taught to communicate by Anne Sullivan. Keller was portrayed in the 1962 movie *The Miracle Worker* by Patty Duke (Mindy Sherwood at age 5). In a 1979 TV presentation of *The Miracle Worker* Melissa Gilbert portrayed Helen Keller and Patty Duke (Astin) portrayed Anne Sullivan.

Kellerman, Annette

Crippled daughter of an Australian music teacher who regained the use of her limbs through swimming and then went on to become a famous swimmer. She was portrayed in the 1952 movie *Million Dollar Mermaid* by Esther Williams (Donna Corcoran at age 10).

Kelley, Tom

Photographer who took the famous nude calendar picture of Marilyn Monroe, posed for on May 27, 1949. For the now classic photograph Miss Monroe was paid $50.

Kelly, Beverly G.
Lieutenant (jg) who became the first female commanding officer of a U.S. Navy (or Coast Guard) vessel when she took command of the Coast Guard cutter *Cape Newagen* on April 12, 1979.

Kelly, George "Machine Gun"
(1897–1954) Kidnapper and bootlegger who died in Alcatraz in 1954. He was portrayed in the 1958 movie *Machine Gun Kelly* by Charles Bronson.

Kelly, Ned (Edward)
(1855–1880) Famous Australian desperado and murderer who was hanged in 1880. He was portrayed by Mick Jagger in the 1970 movie *Ned Kelly*.

Kemp, Jack
Former pro football player who was elected to the U.S. House of Representatives in 1970. In 1960 he led the AFL in passing (211 completions) as quarterback for the Los Angeles Chargers, becoming the All-AFL quarterback that year.

Kennedy, Harvey
Inventor of the shoelace.

Kennedy, Joseph Patrick, Jr.
(1915–1944) Eldest son of Joseph and Rose Fitzgerald Kennedy. He was killed in action during World War II while flying a drone aircraft (PB4Y-1) full of explosives on a mission to bomb a V1 launching site. He was portrayed in the 1977 TV movie *Young Joe: The Forgotten Kennedy* by Peter Strauss (Lance Kerwin at age 14). Stephen Elliott portrayed Joseph Kennedy, Sr.; Gloria Stroock portrayed Rose Kennedy; and Sam Chew, Jr., portrayed Jack Kennedy.

Kennedy, Patricia
Sister of President John F. Kennedy and one-time wife of actor Peter Lawford. She made a cameo appearance on every episode of the TV series *Dear Phoebe,* in which Lawford starred.

Kennedy, Robert Francis
(1925–1968) Brother of President John F. Kennedy, who appointed him attorney general (1961–1964). Robert Kennedy served in the U.S. Senate from 1965 until his assassination on June 5, 1968. Portrayals: *The Missiles of October* (1974 TV play) Martin Sheen; *The Private Files of J. Edgar Hoover* (1977 movie) Michael Parks; *Young Joe: The Forgotten Kennedy* (1977 TV movie) Lance Kerwin (Shane Kerwin as a boy); and *King* (1978 TV movie) Clift De Young.

Kent State
Site where four college students were shot and killed by the Ohio National Guard on May 4, 1970. The four were portrayed by Jeff Miller (Keith Gordon), Bill Schroeder (Jeff McCracken), Sandra Scheuer (Talia Balsam), and Allison Krause (Jane Fleiss) in the 1981 TV movie *Kent State*. Several

members of the rock group the James Gang attended Kent State, as did New York Yankees catcher Thurman Munson.

Kentucky Derby Winners (fiction)

Winner	*Movie*
Tommy	*Sporting Blood* (1931)
Glory	*Glory* (1956)

Kentucky Derby
Trick of performing the Yo-Yo feat "Around-the-World" with both hands at once.

Kern, Jerome
(1885–1945) American composer of the music for a number of hit songs such as "Ol' Man River," "Smoke Gets in Your Eyes," and "The Way You Look Tonight." He was portrayed in the 1946 movie *Till the Clouds Roll By* by Robert Walker. (Amazingly, though he played the title role, Walker was billed 11th in the credits.)

Kerouac, Jack
Popular Beatnik writer of the 1950s whose most famous novel, *On the Road*, was published in 1957. Kerouac narrated the underground film *Pull My Daisy*. He was portrayed by Jack Heard in the 1978 movie *Heart Beat*.

Kettle Hill
Actual hill in Cuba that Teddy Roosevelt and the Rough Riders charged on July 1, 1898. (In history books San Juan Hill is usually, but mistakenly, named instead.)

Keyes, Evelyn
American actress who debuted in the Cecil B. DeMille movie *The Buccaneer* (1938). She married several famous men: Charles "King" Vidor (1944–1945). John Huston (1946–1950), and Artie Shaw (1957–   ). She authored the novel *I Am a Billboard*.

Keyes, Paul
Head writer for the TV series *Laugh In*. He was also one of Richard Nixon's speech writers.

Kezar Stadium
Previous home of the San Francisco 49er's football team. Also, home of the Scorpio killer (Andy Robinson) in the 1971 movie *Dirty Harry*.

Khariozas
Actor Rock Hudson's 40-foot boat.

Khrushchev, Nikita
(1894–1971) Premier of the Soviet Union from 1958 to 1964. He was portrayed on the 1974 TV play *The Missiles of October* by Howard Da Silva, and by Thayer David in the 1976 TV movie *Francis Gary Powers: The True Story of the U-2 Spy Incident*.

Kidd, Capt. William
(1645–1701) Pirate captain of the ship *Adventure Galley*, who was hanged for piracy and murder. Movie portrayals; *Captain Kidd* (1945) Charles Laughton; *Double Crossbones* (1950) Alan Napier; and *Captain Kidd and the Slave Girl* (1954) Anthony Dexter.

Kids and Company
1951 TV variety series hosted by Johnny Olsen with cartoonist Ham Fisher as his assistant.

Kiko
Kangaroo character in Paul Terry cartoons during the 1930s.

Killer
Lucas Adams's (Tierre Turner) pet dog in the TV series *The Cop and the Kid*.

Killers, The
1964 version of an Ernest Hemingway story (the first version was filmed in 1946). *The Killers* was the first movie ever made for TV (NBC).* In it director Don Siegel made a cameo appearance as a cook in a diner and actor Ronald Reagan made his last movie appearance. (See: **See How They Run**)

Kilmer (Alfred), Joyce
(1886–1918) American poet who authored many popular poems (collected as *Trees and Other Poems* (1914). His father, Fred, invented baby powder for the Johnson & Johnson Company in 1885. Joyce Kilmer was killed in action on July 30, 1918, during World War I. He was portrayed in the 1940 movie *The Fighting 69th* by Jeffrey Lynn.

Kinetics of the Reaction Inactivation of Tyrosinase During the Catalysis of the Aerobic Oxidation of Gatechol
Title of scientist/writer Isaac Asimov's doctoral thesis, written in 1948.

King Ahasuerus
Biblical Persian king, portrayed in the 1960 movie *Esther and the King* by Richard Egan.

King Arthur
Legendary king of the Britons (6th century) who instituted the famous Knights of the Round Table. Movie portrayals: *The Crusades* (1935) Henry Wilcoxon; *King Arthur Was a Gentleman* (1942) Arthur Askey; *A Connecticut Yankee in King Arthur's Court* (1949) Sir Cedric Hardwicke; *Knights of the Round Table* (1953) Mel Ferrer; *The Black Knight* (1954) Anthony Bushell; *Prince Valiant* (1954) Brian Aherne; *Sword of Lancelot* (1963) Brian Aherne; *The Sword in the Stone* (1963 animated cartoon) voice of Rick Sorenson (as a boy); *Siege of the Saxons* (1964) Mark Dignam; *Camelot* (1967) Richard Harris (Nicholas Beaury as a boy); and *Monty Python and the Holy Grail* (1975) Graham Chapman.

---

*Although made for TV, because of the violence in the film, it was released in movie theaters instead.

King Charles I
(1600–1649) English king who succeeded James I in 1625 and ruled until 1649, when he was beheaded. Movie portrayals: *The Crimson Blade* (1964) Robert Rietty; and *Cromwell* (1970) Alec Guinness.

King Charles II
(1630–1685) English king called the Merry Monarch. Movie portrayals; *Hudson's Bay* (1940) Vincent Price; *Forever Amber* (1947) George Sanders; and *The King's Thief* (1955) George Sanders.

King Charles VII
(1403–1461) King of France (1422–1461) who, with the aid of Joan of Arc, regained French territory previously captured by the English. He was portrayed in *Joan the Woman* (1917) by Raymond Hatton and in *Joan of Arc* (1948) by José Ferrer.

King David
King of Judea and Israel who died in 973 B.C. He married Bathsheba, with whom he had a son, King Solomon. Movie portrayals: *David and Bathsheba* (1951) Gregory Peck (Gwyneth Verdon as a boy); *The Story of David* (1960) Jeff Chandler; *David and Goliath* (1961) Ivo Payer; and *The Story of David* (1976 TV) Keith Mitchell.

King Edward I
(1239–1307) King of England (1272–1307), portrayed in the 1950 movie *The Black Rose* by Michael Rennie.

King Edward III
(1312–1377) King of England from 1327 until 1377. He was portrayed in the 1955 movie *The Warriors* by Michael Hordern. One of his descendents is Richard Milhous Nixon.

King Edward IV
(1442–1483) King of England from 1461 until his death. In 1477 he outlawed the game of cricket.* Movie portrayals: *Towers of London* (1939) Ian Hunter; *Richard III* (1956) Cedric Hardwicke; and *Tower of London* (1962) Justice Watson.

King Edward V
(1470–1483) King of England from April to June 1483, when he was murdered in the Tower of London. He was portrayed in the 1962 movie *The Tower of London* by Eugene Martin.

King Edward VII
(1841–1910) King of England, called the Peacemaker. He was portrayed in the 1978 TV series *Edward the King* by Timothy West and in the TV miniseries *Upstairs, Downstairs* by Lockwood West (Timothy West's father).

---

*It wasn't made legal again until 1748.

King Edwards Apartments
Pittsburgh home (Apartment 316) of Pirates manager Aloysius X "Guffy" McGovern (Paul Douglas) in the 1951 movie *Angels in the Outfield*.

King Faisal
(1885–1933) King of Syria (1920) and Iraq (1921–1933). With the help of Col. T. S. Lawrence and Gen. Allenby, he captured Jerusalem on December 9, 1917, and Damascus on October 2, 1918. King Faisal was portrayed by Alec Guinness in the 1962 movie *Lawrence of Arabia*.

King Ferdinand
(1452–1516) King of Sicily, Aragon, and Naples. He married Isabella of Castile and the royal pair financed Columbus's voyage to the New World. Ferdinand was portrayed in the 1949 movie *Christopher Columbus* by Francis Lister.

Kingfisher
Charter fishing boat skippered by Ross Carpenter (Elvis Presley) in the 1962 movie *Girls! Girls! Girls!* Ross later bought the sailboat *The West Wind*.

King Guzzle
Ruler of the land of Moo (comic strip *Alley Oop*).

King George I
(1660–1727) King of Great Britain and Ireland from 1714 to 1727. He was portrayed in the 1954 movie *Rob Roy* by Eric Pohlmann.

King George III
(1738–1820) George William Frederick, king of Great Britain and Ireland from 1760 to 1820. He was portrayed in the 1954 movie *Beau Brummell* by Robert Morley.

King George IV
(1762–1830) King of Great Britain and Ireland (1820–1830) who was portrayed by Ralph Richardson in the 1972 movie *Lady Caroline Lamb*.

King George VI
(1895–1952) Alfred Frederick Arthur George, king of Great Britain and Northern Ireland from 1936 until his death. He succeeded to the throne after his brother, Edward VIII, abdicated on December 11, 1936. He was portrayed in the 1979 TV miniseries *Ike* by Martin Jarvis and in the 1981 TV movie *Churchill and the Generals* by Lyndon Brook.

King Henry II
(1133–1189) King of England from 1154 until 1189. He was twice portrayed in movies by Peter O'Toole: in *Becket* (1964) and in *The Lion in Winter* (1968).

King Henry III
(1207–1272) King of England from 1216 until 1272, portrayed in the 1946 movie *The Bandit of Sherwood Forest* by Maurice R. Tauzin.

King Henry IV
(1367–1413) King of England from 1399 until 1413, portrayed in the 1954 movie *The Black Shield of Falworth* by Ian Keith.

King Henry VI
(1421–1471) King in England who in 1431 was crowned King of France. After being expelled from France, his struggle for power helped to begin the War of the Roses. Henry died a prisoner in the Tower of London. He was portrayed in the 1939 movie *Tower of London* by Miles Mander.

King Henry VIII
(1491–1547) King of England (1509–1547) who broke with the Roman Catholic Church. Movie portrayals: *Deception* (1920) Emil Jannings; *The Private Life of Henry VIII* (1933) Charles Laughton; *The Prince and the Pauper* (1937) Montagu Love; *The Sword and the Rose* (1953) James Robertson Justice; *Young Bess* (1953) Charles Laughton; *A Man for All Seasons* (1966) Robert Shaw; *Anne of the Thousand Days* (1969) Richard Burton; *Royal Flesh* (1970) Lawrence Adams; *The Six Wives of Henry VIII* (1971 TV) Keith Michell; *Crossed Swords* (1977) Charlton Heston.

King Louis XI
(1423–1483) King of France from 1461 until 1483. Movie portrayals: *If I Were King* (1920) Fritz Leiber; *Hunchback of Notre Dame* (1923) Tully Marshall; *Quentin Durward* (1955) Robert Morley; and *The Vagabond King* (1956) Walter Hampden.

King Louis XII
(1462–1515) King of France from 1498 until 1515. He was portrayed by Jean Mercure in the 1953 movie *The Sword and the Rose*.

King Louis XIII
(1601–1643) King of France from 1610 until 1643. Movie portrayals: *The Three Musketeers* (1921) Adolphe Menjou; *The Three Musketeers* (1935) Miles Mander; *The Man in the Iron Mask* (1939) Albert Dekker; *The Three Musketeers* (1939) Joseph Schildkraut; *The Three Musketeers* (1948) Frank Morgan; *The Three Musketeers* (1973) Jean-Pierre Cassel; and *The Four Musketeers* (1974) Jean-Pierre Cassel.

King Louis XIV
(1638–1715) King of France from 1643 until 1715. Movie portrayals: *The Man in the Iron Mask* (1939) Louis Hayward; *Royal Affairs in Versailles* (1954) Sacha Guitry; *Star of India* (1956) Basil Sydney; *The Rise of Louis XIV* (1965) Jean-Marie Patte; and *The Man in the Iron Mark* (1977 TV) Richard Chamberlain.

King Louis XV
(1710–1774) King of France, called "Well Beloved." Movie portrayals: *When a Man Loves* (1927) Stuart Holmes; *Du Barry, Woman of Passion* (1930) William Farnum; *Voltaire* (1933) Reginald Owen; *Madame Du Barry*

(1934) Reginald Owen; *The Loves of Madame Du Barry* (1938) Nares Owen; *Marie Antoinette* (1938) John Barrymore; and *Monsieur Beaucaire* (1946) Reginald Owen.

King Louis XVI
(1754–1793) King of France from 1774 to 1792. He married Marie Antoinette in 1770. In 1793, in the aftermath of the French Revolution, he was tried for treason, found guilty, and guillotined. Movie portrayals: *Captain of the Guards* (1930) Stuart Holmes; *Marie Antoinette* (1938) Robert Morley; and *Lafayette* (1963) Albert Rémy.

King Louis XVIII
1755–1824 King of France from 1814 until his death. He was portrayed in the 1970 movie *Waterloo* by Orson Welles.

King, Martin Luther Jr.
(1929–1968) Nonviolent leader of the American civil rights movement. King was arrested on 120 occasions and was the youngest man to win the Nobel Peace Prize, which was awarded to him in 1964 when he was 35. He was portrayed in 1978 TV movie *King* by Paul Winfield (Coretta Scott King was portrayed by Cicely Tyson). Billy Dee Williams played King on Broadway and Raymond St. Jacques portrayed him in the 1978 movie *The Private Files of J. Edgar Hoover.*

King of Swat
136-to-1 long shot, the first professional mount ridden by jockey Steve Cauthen. The horse finished last.

King of the Twelve-String Guitar
Nickname of folk singer Leadbelly (Hubbie Leadbetter).

King of Thule
Father of Prince Valiant (comic strip).

King of Torts
Title conferred on prominent San Francisco attorney Melvin Belli by *Life* magazine in 1954.

King Philip II
(1527–1598) King of Spain (1556–1598) who married four times. The armada he sent to defeat the English in 1588 was destroyed, mostly by bad weather. Movie portrayals: *In the Palace of Kings* (1923) Sam De Grasse; *The Sea Hawk* (1940) Montagu Love; and *That Lady* (1954) Paul Scofield.

King Philip III
(1578–1621) King of Spain (1598–1621), son of Philip II. He was portrayed in the 1949 movie *Adventures of Don Juan* by Romney Brent.

King Richard I
(1157–1199) King of England called Richard the Lion-Hearted. He fought in the Crusades. Movie portrayals: *The Crusades* (1935) Henry Wilcoxon; *The Adventures of Robin Hood* (1938) Ian Hunter; *King Richard and the Crusaders*

(1954) George Sanders; *Men of Sherwood Forest* (1956) Patrick Holt; *The Lion in Winter* (1968) Anthony Hopkins; and *Robin and Marian* (1976) Richard Harris.

King Richard III

(1452–1485) King of England, member of the house of York. Movie portrayals: *Tower of London* (1939) Basil Rathbone; *Richard III* (1956) Laurence Olivier; and *Tower of London* (1962) Vincent Price. William Windom played the part in the 1950 TV adaptation of *Richard III* on *Masterpiece Playhouse*.

King Saul

First king of Israel. He was succeeded by David. Movie portrayals: *David and Bathsheba* (1951) Francis X. Bushman; and *David and Goliath* (1961) Orson Welles.

Kings and Queens

Face cards in a deck, traditionally named (kings) David, Alexander, Caesar, and Charles; and (queens) Argine, Esther, Judith, and Pallas.

Kings Choppers

Los Angeles motorcycle club in which Edd Byrnes and Micky Dolenz were gang members in an episode of the TV series *Adam 12*.

Kings of Queens

Lodge in Queens, New York, to which Archie Bunker belonged in the TV series *All in the Family*.

Kingston, Cohen, and Vanderpool, Inc.

New York City advertising agency where Don Robinson (Don Rickles) was employed in the TV series *The Don Rickles Show*

King Tut

Prized stud bull bought by Bick Benedict (Rock Hudson) in the 1956 movie *Giant*.

King William III

(1650–1702) King of England, Scotland, and Ireland (1689–1702) who ruled jointly with his wife, Queen Mary. He was portrayed in the 1945 movie *Captain Kidd* by Henry Daniell.

Kinmont, Jill

Skier who in 1955 was injured just before the Olympic tryouts. In 1954 she had been the first U.S. skier to win both junior and senior slalom championships within the same year. Jill Kinmont was portrayed by Marilyn Hassett in the movies *The Other Side of the Mountain* (1975) and *The Other Side of the Mountain Part 2* (1978).

Kipling, Rudyard

(1865–1936) English author born in Bombay, India. He wrote such famous tales as *Soldiers Three, Captains Courageous,* and *The Jungle Book*. He was portrayed in the 1975 movie *The Man Who Would Be King* by Christopher Plummer.

Kipps

1905 novel by H. G. Wells on which the 1963 musical play *Half a Sixpence* is based.

KISS

Flashy rock 'n' roll band of the late 1970s and early 1980s. Its members: Gene Simons (born Gene Klein on August 25, 1949)—bass; Peter Criss (born Peter Crisscoula on December 20, 1947)—drums (he was replaced in 1980 by Eric Carr); Ace Frehley (born Paul Frehley on April 27, 1955)—lead guitar; and Paul Stanley (born Stanley Eisen on January 20, 1950)—rhythm guitar. KISS stands for Knights in the Service of Satan.

Kiss, The

1896 Edison film starring May Irwin and John C. Rice, in which the first screen kiss occurred (it lasted over 30 seconds). This is the film that is being shown in a hotel in the opening scene of the 1946 movie *The Spiral Staircase*.

Kiss, Max

Inventor of the laxative Ex-Lax.

Kit Carson

Colorado town near which Adolf Hitler inherited 9,000 acres of land.

Kitchen Cabinet

Nickname given to the political advisers of President Andrew Jackson because they usually met in the kitchen of the White House.

Kit Kat

Addams family pet lion in the TV series *The Addams Family*.

Kitty

Nickname Anne Frank gave to her diary, which began on Sunday June 14, 1942, and ended on August 4, 1944. "Dear Kitty . . ."

Klein, Mannie

Musician who provided the bugle blowing for Montgomery Clift in the 1953 movie *From Here to Eternity*.

Kleindienst, Richard G.

Successor to John Mitchell as Nixon's attorney general. He resigned in April 1973, at the height of the Watergate scandal. In the 1979 TV miniseries *Blind Ambition* William Windom portrayed Kleindienst.

Klopstockia

Bankrupted country over which the president (W. C. Fields) rules in the 1932 movie *Million Dollar Legs*.

Knockouts, The

Heavyweight champion Joe Frazier's rock 'n' roll band.

Knothead and Splinter
>   Woody Woodpecker's niece and nephew; they debuted in the 1956 cartoon *Get Lost*.

Knowledge Is Good
>   Motto of Faber College* in the 1978 movie *Animal House* and the TV series *Delta House*.

Knox, Frank
>   (1874–1944) U.S. secretary of the navy from 1940 until 1944. He was portrayed in the 1970 movie *Tora! Tora! Tora!* by Leon Ames. His daughter, actress Elyse Knox, married Michigan football great Tom Harmon.

Knox, John
>   (1505–1572) Scottish theologian and statesman who opposed the Catholic Church in Scotland and helped to establish the Presbyterian Church in that country. Knox was portrayed in the 1936 movie *Mary of Scotland* by Moroni Olsen and in the 1971 movie *Mary, Queen of Scots* by Robert James.

Knutson, Gunilla
>   Beautiful former Miss Sweden† who would taunt her audience to "Take it off, take it all off," as the song "The Stripper" was played on TV Noxzema commercials. On the TV series *Petticoat Junction* Miss Knutson played Billie Joe Bradley. In 1966 she was replaced in the role by Meredith MacRae.

Koch, Howard
>   Radio (and later movie) director and producer. He was portrayed in the 1975 TV movie *The Night That Panicked America* by Paul Shenar.

Kodiak
>   Name of a character in two different TV series: played by Keenan Wynn in the 1959 TV series *The Troubleshooters* and by Clint Walker in the 1974 TV series *Kodiak*.

Kohoutek
>   Comet that approached within 75 million miles of the earth in mid-January 1974.

Kopechne, Mary Jo
>   Passenger who was killed when Senator Edward Kennedy's automobile ran off Dike Bridge at Chappaquiddick on July 18, 1969. She was portrayed by Shari Kurgis in the 1981 TV movie (Kennedy was played by Jack Knight).

Korova Milkbar
>   Hangout of Alex and his gang (the Droogs) in the 1971 movie *A Clockwork Orange* (based on the novel by Anthony Burgess).

Kotch
>   Only movie directed by Jack Lemmon (1971).

---

*Founded by Emil Faber in 1904.
†Miss Universe finalist in 1961.

Kovacs, Ernie
> His comedy characters on TV: J. Walter Puppybreath, Percy Dovetonsils, Miklos Molnar, Aunt Gruesome, Matzoh Hepplewhite, and Eugene.

Krause, Kenneth L.
> U.S. Marine sergeant who was wounded and held prisoner by Iranian revolutionaries in February 1979. For his stand at the U.S. Embassy in Tehran he was awarded the Purple Heart and Navy Commendation Medal.

Krents, Hal
> Blind Harvard student who took up skiing and football. He was portrayed in the 1980 TV movie *To Race the Wind* by Steve Guttenberg.

Kristofer Kamel
> Camel in *Krazy Kat* comic strip.

Kristofferson, Kris, and Billy Swan
> Popular recording artists who both once worked as janitors at the Columbia Record Studios in Nashville.

Krockmeyer's Department Store
> Where Walter Burnley (John McGiver) worked as manager of the complaint department in the TV series *Many Happy Returns*.

Kroc, Ray
> Owner of the McDonald hamburger chain and the San Diego Padres baseball team. It was Kroc who hired Freeman Gosden and Charles Correll to play the roles of "Sam and Henry" at Chicago radio station WGN in 1926. "Sam and Henry" later became "Amos 'n' Andy."

Krueger Finest Beer
> Company that, on January 24, 1935, produced the first can of beer.

Krupa, Gene
> (1909–1973) Popular and talented drummer during the swing era. He played for Benny Goodman, Red Nichols, Russ Columbo, Buddy Rogers, and others. He was once arrested for possession of marijuana. He portrayed himself in the 1955 movie *The Benny Goodman Story* and was portrayed by Sal Mineo in the 1959 movie *The Gene Krupa Story.**

Kublai Khan
> (1216–1294) Founder of the Mongol dynasty in China and descendant of Genghis Khan. Kublai Khan ruled China at the time of Marco Polo's visit there in 1271. Movie portrayals: *The Adventures of Marco Polo* (1938) George Barbier; *Marco Polo* (1962) Camillo Pilotto; and *Marco the Magnificent* (1966) Anthony Quinn.

Kudirka, Simas
> Lithuanian seaman who on November 23, 1970, jumped from his Soviet trawler to the U.S. Coast Guard cutter *Vigilant*. The crew of the *Vigilant*

---

*The drum playing during the opening credits of the movie was done by Krupa.

stood by while his shipmates forced him back to their vessel. Kudirka was later allowed to emigrate to this country. He was portrayed by Alan Arkin in the 1978 TV movie *The Defection of Simas Kudirka*.

Kunta Kinte
Slave hero of Alex Haley's book *Roots*. He was portrayed on the 1977 TV miniseries *Roots* by LeVar Burton (in youth) and John Amos (in maturity).

Kurwood Derby
Hat that makes Bullwinkle a genius when he wears it in the cartoon series *Rocky and Bullwinkle*.

Kuusela, Armi
First winner of the Miss Universe contest (1952). Armi represented Finland.

Kwajalein
Island where Capt. Phillip Francis Queeg (Humphrey Bogart) turned his vessel around, leaving a yellow dye marking his retreat, in the 1954 movie *The Caine Mutiny*. This provoked his crew to compose the song "Yellowstain Blues."

Kyser, Kay
Bandleader of the 1930s and 1940s. He hosted the radio program *Kay Kyser's Kollege of Musical Knowledge*, and appeared in a number of films. As a football coach at Rocky Mount High School, Kyser persuaded one of his football players to stay with the game. That player became Coach Bill Murray, today a member of the National Football Foundation Hall of Fame.

LJH 681
   California license plate number of April Dancer's (Stefanie Powers) sports
   car in the series *The Girl from U.N.C.L.E.*
LU2-3100
   Phone number for viewers to call in on the TV series *Ted Mack's Original
   Amateur Hour.*
LUH3417
   Beautiful roommate of THX1138 (Robert Duvall) in the 1971 movie *THX1138.**
   LUH3417 was played by Maggie McOmie.
Laddie
   Pet dog of the Williams Family on the TV series *Make Room for Daddy.*
Ladies of the Chorus
   1948 movie being shown to the troops in the 1952 movie *Okinawa.* The scene
   was of Marilyn Monroe singing "Every Baby Needs a Da-Da-Daddy."
Lady
   Brown trotting horse, which won't be passed by other horses, owned by Jess
   Birdwell (Gary Cooper) in the 1956 movie *Friendly Persuasion.* Jess traded
   his slower horse, Red Rover, for Lady.
Lady and the Tramp
   Canine heroes of the 1955 Walt Disney animated movie *Lady and the Tramp.*
   Barbara Luddy provided the voice of Lady and Larry Roberts provided the
   voice of Tramp.

---

*Some scenes from the movie were filmed in the computer room of the *Oakland Air Route Traffic Con-
trol Center,* where this author works.

Lady Day
   Nickname of blues singer Billie Holiday.
Lady in Red
   Anna Sage (a/k/a Anna Cumpanas) who, on July 27, 1934, fingered John Dillinger for the FBI. Movie portrayals; *The F.B.I. Story* (1959) Jean Willes; and *Dillinger* (1973) Cloris Leachman.
Lady in the Lake, The
   1946 MGM movie directed by and starring Robert Montgomery. The camera records the action from Montgomery's point of view, so he is unseen in the film except as a reflection in mirrors and windows.
Lafayette, Marquis De
   (1757–1834) French military officer who came to America in 1777 to fight on the side of the Colonists in the Revolutionary War. He was the first foreigner awarded honorary citizenship of the United States (1784). Lafayette was portrayed by Philippe Forquet in the TV series *The Young Rebels* and by Michel Le Royer in the 1963 movie *Lafayette*.
Lafitte, Jean
   (1780–1826) French pirate whose home base was New Orleans. He sided with the Americans at the Battle of New Orleans in 1814. Movie portrayals: *The Buccaneer* (1938) Fredric March; *Last of the Buccaneers* (1950) Paul Henreid; and *The Buccaneer* (1958) Yul Brynner.
Lago
   Western town setting of the 1973 Clint Eastwood movie *High Plains Drifter*.
LaGuardia, Fiorello
   (1882–1947) American lawyer who served as the mayor of New York City from 1934 to 1945. Movie portrayals: *The Pride of the Yankees* (1942) David Manley; and *The Court Martial of Billy Mitchell* (1955) Phil Arnold.
Laine, Frankie
   Popular singer who sang the theme song for the 1974 movie *Blazing Saddles*, the theme songs for the TV series *Rango*, *Rawhide*, and *The Misadventures of Sheriff Lobo*, and for the Manhandler soup commercials. From May 26 to October 18, 1932, he and Ruth Smith broke the world's record for marathon dancing (3,501 hours).
Lake Highlands High School
   Setting for the 1978 Ron Howard–directed TV movie *Cotton Candy*.
Lake Tahoe High School
   California school where Shirley Miller (Shirley Jones) taught English in the TV series *Shirley*.
Lamb, Lady Caroline
   (1785–1828) English aristocrat and novelist who had a celebrated affair with Lord Byron. She went insane upon meeting the poet's funeral procession.

Movie portrayals: *The Bad Lord Byron* (1951) Joan Greenwood; and *Lady Caroline Lamb* (1972) Sarah Miles.

LaMotta, Jake

Middleweight boxing champion of the world (1949–1951), nicknamed "the Bronx Bull." He is the only boxer who won a title without ever having had a manager. La Motta was portrayed in the 1980 movie *The Raging Bull* by Robert De Niro.

Lamphier, Thomas Jr.,

P38 pilot who on April 18, 1943, shot down the bomber carrying Japanese Adm. Yamamoto. Lamphier was portrayed in the 1960 movie *The Gallant Hours* by William Schallert.

Lancerfish, USS

Nuclear submarine trapped 1,235 feet under the sea in the 1978 movie *Gray Lady Down*.

Land, Edwin H.

Inventor, in 1947, of the Polaroid camera.

Landis, Carole

(1919–1949) American actress (born Frances Ridste), portrayed loosely by Sharon Tate (as Jennifer North) in the 1967 movie *Valley of the Dolls*.

Landmark Motor Hotel

Hollywood, California, motel where the body of Janis Joplin was found by John Cooke at 7:30 p.m. on October 4, 1970. Her hand clutched $4.50.

Langdon, Harry

(1884–1944) American actor whose plaque, as part of the Walk of the Stars, is directly in front of Grauman's Chinese Theatre (now Mann's) on Hollywood Boulevard.

Lang, Jennings

Agent of actress Joan Bennett who was shot and wounded by Joan's husband, Walter Wanger, on December 13, 1951, in a parking lot across the street from the Beverly Hills Police Station. Wanger believed the pair to be lovers. Jerry Geisler defended Wanger at his trial. Wanger spent 4 months at the Wayside Honor Farm in Castaic, California, and after his release produced two antiprison movies: *Riot in Cell Block 11* (1954) and *I Want to Live!* (1958).

Langley, Samuel Pierpont

(1834–1906) American aviator pioneer. His experiments on the Potomac River resulted in the first flights of mechanically propelled heavier-than-air aircraft (1896). This predated the Wright brothers' plane, but Langley's aircraft were models, not full size. He was portrayed in the 1978 TV movie *The Winds of Kitty Hawk* by John Hoyt.

Langtry, Lillie

(1853–1929) British actress nicknamed the Jersey Lily. Portrayals: *The*

Westerner (1940) Lillian Bond; *The Trials of Oscar Wilde* (1960) Naomi Chance; *The Life and Times of Judge Roy Bean* (1972) Ava Gardner; and *Lillie* (1979 TV miniseries) Francesca Annis.

La Paloma
President Warren G. Harding's favorite song.

La Paloma Courts
Apartment home of Queenie Dugan (Mitzi Green) in the TV series *So This Is Hollywood*.

Lara's Theme
Theme song of the 1965 Carlo Ponti movie *Doctor Zhivago*. With lyrics, the song is titled "Somewhere My Love."

Larches, The
Detective Hercule Poirot's house in the village of King's Abbot in England.

Larry
Laurie Robinson's (Didi Conn) dummy in the 1977 movie *You Light Up My Life*

Larry
Maurice "Buddy" Sorrell's (Morey Amsterdam) pet German shepherd in the TV series *The Dick Van Dyke Show*.

Lasky, Jesse L.
(1880–1958) American motion picture producer. Movie portrayals: *The Legend of Valentino* (1975 TV movie) Milton Berle; and *Valentino* (1977) Huntz Hall.

Last Angry Man, The
1959 movie in which Paul Muni made his last film appearance and Billy Dee Williams made his film debut.

Last Chance Club
Las Vegas nightclub where Linda Rollins (Jane Russell) worked in the 1952 movie *The Las Vegas Story*.

Last Chance Gulch
1860s mining camp that later changed its name to Helena (now the capital of Montana).

Last Chance Saloon
Town saloon in Bottleneck owned and run by Frenchy (Marlene Dietrich) in the 1939 movie *Destry Rides Again*.

Last Kiss, The
Song that Conrad Birdie (Jesse Pearson) sang on *The Ed Sullivan Show* in the 1963 movie *Bye Bye Birdie*.

Last Movie, The
Kris Kristofferson's first movie (1971). It was directed by Dennis Hopper.

Last one up's a sissy
Line said by Max Baer to heavyweight champion Primo Carnera when they

both fell to the canvas in the first round of a championship fight. It was won by Baer (June 1934).

Laughlin, Michael
24-year-old private pilot who took the snapshots of the American Airlines DC10 flight 191 as it crashed at Chicago on May 25, 1979.

Laura Foster
Murder victim of Tom Dula, who was arrested by Sheriff Jim Grayson in the folk song "Tom Dooley."

Laurel Shopping Center
Wheaton, Maryland, shopping mall where ex-Alabama Governor George Wallace was shot and paralyzed by 21-year-old Arthur Bremmer on May 15, 1972. Wallace was then running for the presidency.

Laurel, Stan
(1890–1965) British-born comedian (Arthur Stanley Jefferson) who teamed up with Oliver Hardy to become motion picture's most successful comedy duo. Laurel was portrayed in the 1965 movie *Harlow* by Jim Plunkett. Larry Harmon provided Laurel's voice on the 1966 TV cartoon series *The Laurel and Hardy Cartoon Show*.

Laverne Esposito
Girl in Toledo, Ohio, who married and divorced Corp. Max Klinger (Jamie Farr) via radio (hamstation BS2 XYZ) in the TV series *M*A*S*H*. Laverne was never seen on the show.

La Verne Lashinski
Perfectly tasteless lady of the Laundromat, played by Cher on her TV series. La Verne's husband was named Harry.

Lawrence, Gertrude
(1901–1952) British-born actress whose real name was Gertrude Alexandra Dagmar Lawrence-Klasen. Movie portrayals: *The Man Who Came to Dinner* (1941) Anne Sheridan (loosely); *Star!* (1968) Julie Andrews; and *Ike* (1979 TV miniseries) Patricia Michael.

Lawrence, James
Alias used by criminal John Dillinger.

Lawrence, Marjorie
Australian opera soprano born in 1908. She was portrayed in the 1955 movie *Interrupted Melody* by Eleanor Parker.

Lawrence, Richard
First man who attempted to assassinate a U.S. president. He fired two pistols at President Andrew Jackson at point-blank range on January 30, 1835, but both guns misfired. At his trial on April 11, 1835, the prosecuting attorney was Francis Scott Key.

Lawrenceville

New Hampshire home of Anne Welles (Barbara Parkins) in the 1967 movie *Valley of the Dolls*. The movie was actually filmed in Bedford, New York

Lawson, James

The minister who married James Earl Ray and Anna Sandhu on Friday, October 13, 1978, at Brushy Mountain State Prison. It was Rev. Lawson who had invited Martin Luther King to Memphis, where he was slain by Ray.

Lazy

Song composed in 1924 by Irving Berlin. It can be heard in the following movies: *Alexander's Ragtime Band* (1938); *Holiday Inn* (1942), sung by Bing Crosby; *Belles on Their Toes* (1952); and *There's No Business Like Show Business* (1954) sung by Marilyn Monroe.

Leadbelly

(1888–1949) Nickname of country-blues folk singer Hubbie Leadbetter (a/k/a Walter Boyd). He was imprisoned for murder and pardoned by Texas Governor Pat Neff (it was the governor's last official act). Leadbelly later spent additional time in prison. Perhaps his most famous song is "Goodnight Irene." Leadbelly was portrayed by Paul Benjamin in the 1977 movie *Leadbelly*.

League for Spiritual Discovery

Religion based on LSD founded by Dr. Timothy Leary in 1966. Its motto: "Turn on, tune in, and drop out."

Lee, Gypsy Rose

(1914–1970) Famous striptease dancer and sister of actress June Havoc. She was the assistant for the TV quiz show *Think Fast*. Natalie Wood portrayed her in the 1962 movie *Gypsy*. (Suzanne Cupito* portrayed her as a child.)

Lee, Robert E.

(1807–1870) Son of Henry "Light-Horse Harry" Lee, of Revolutionary War fame. Robert E. Lee commanded the Confederate armies during the Civil War. He was a third cousin, twice removed, of George Washington. Movie portrayals: *The Birth of a Nation* (1915) Howard Gaye; *Abraham Lincoln* (1930) Hobart Bosworth; and *Santa Fe Trail* (1940) Moroni Olsen.

LeFlore, Ron

Detroit Tiger center fielder who spent time in prison for theft. He set a record in 1978 with 27 consecutive stolen bases. LeFlore was portrayed in the 1979 TV movie *One in a Million* by LeVar Burton. (See: **B115614**).

Left Ear

Ear that painter Vincent Van Gogh cut off a part of on Christmas Eve 1888. It is also the ear that Carole Burnett tugged on her TV show as a personal sign to her mother that everything is all right.

---

*Today Suzanne uses the stage name of Morgan Brittany, which was borrowed from a romantic novel.

Legion of Super-Heroes
Futuristic organization in DC Comics. Begun in *Adventure Comics* No. 247 in 1958, the Legion of Super Heroes was set in the 30th century.

Leica
German shepherd that often appeared with his master, Jack Paar, on the TV series *The Tonight Show.*

Leigh, Vivien
(1913–1967) British actress (born Vivien Hartley in Darjeeling, India) best known for her performance as Scarlett O'Hara in *Gone With the Wind* (1939). She was married for a time to Laurence Olivier. Portrayals: *Day of the Locust* (1975) Morgan Brittany; *Gable and Lombard* (1976) Morgan Brittany; *Night Train* (1977 TV movie) Phyllis Davis; and *Moviola* (1980 TV miniseries) Morgan Brittany.

LeMay, Curtis
(1906–) USAF General who advocated strategic bombing in World War II. As head of the 8th Air Force in England, LeMay created a tight formation for U.S. bombers. While in the Pacific, in command of 20th Air Force, he devised the massive firebombing raids of Tokyo. He was portrayed in the 1952 movie *Above and Beyond* by Jim Backus. Curtis LeMay was the vice presidential running mate of George Wallace in 1968 on the American Independent Party ticket.

Lemonade Lucy
Nickname of the wife of President Rutherford Hayes. Lucy Ware Hayes was called Lemonade Lucy because she served that beverage in the White House instead of alcoholic drinks. She was the first First Lady to have graduated from college.

Lemon, Meadow "Meadowlark"
Famed clown member of the Harlem Globetrotters basketball team. He joined in 1956. Scatman Crothers provided the voice of Meadowlark in the TV cartoon series *The Harlem Globetrotters.*

Lennon, John Winston (later Ono)
(1940–1980) Member of the world's most successful rock group, the Beatles. His picture was on the first issue of *Rolling Stone* magazine (November 1967) and he was the recipient of the first Rolling Stone Man of the Year Award in 1969. Lennon was portrayed by Stephen MacKenna in the 1979 TV movie *Birth of the Beatles.* On the evening of December 8, 1980, he was shot and killed in front of the Dakota, his New York residence.

Lenore
Boston Brahmin's (William Powell) mermaid (Ann Blythe) in the 1948 movie *Mr. Peabody and the Mermaid.* The tail for Blythe's mermaid costume cost $18,000.

Leo
William "Bumper" Morgan's (George Kennedy) canine friend in the TV series *The Blue Knight*.

Leo Jr.
Actual name of the quarter horse ridden by Dale Robertson in the TV series *Tales of Wells Fargo*.

La Parisienne
Brewster, New York, restaurant owned by Ann Marie's (Marlo Thomas) parents, Lou (Lew Parker) and Helen (Rosemary De Camp) Marie in the TV series *That Girl*.

Lepke
Nickname of the boss of Murder Inc., Louis Buchalter. He was portrayed in the 1975 movie *Lepke* by Tony Curtis. Lepke was the only gangland leader to be executed by the U.S. government (March 4, 1944).

Lerner, Alan Jay
Composer (with Frederick Loewe) of many modern classics, including "Almost Like Being in Love." His father, Joseph Lerner, founded the woman's clothing store Lerner's. Alan Jay Lerner was born on August 31, 1918, which was also Ted Williams' birth date.

Let Me Go, Devil
Original title of the song "Let Me Go, Lover," composed by Jenny Lou Carson in 1953. "Let Me Go, Lover" was popularized by Joan Webber in a November 15, 1974, episode of the TV series *Studio One*. Webber's version reached No 1 on the charts.

Let's Not Be Sensible Song
Sung by Bing Crosby in the 1962 movie *Road to Hong Kong*. The last word of the song, "Love," was later dubbed in by Mike Sammes after the film was shot because the word hadn't turned out clearly on the soundtrack and Crosby was no longer available.

Lewis, Mrs. Nathan
Woman who was accidentally run down by President Franklin Pierce on horseback. Pierce was arrested and later released.

Liar's Song
Song sung by Fred Astaire and Jane Powell in the 1951 movie *Royal Wedding*. The full title is "How Could You Believe Me When I Said I Loved You When You Know I've Been a Liar All My Life."

Liberty Belles
Cheerleaders for the Philadelphia Eagles football team.

Liberty Coffee Shop
Philadelphia restaurant where Angie Falco (Donna Pescow) has worked as a waitress for 6 years in the TV series *Angie*. The name *Liberty Coffee Shop* reads backward on the glass door as it faces the street. In the second half of the first season Angie became its proprietor.

Liberty Enlightening the World
Official name of the Statue of Liberty.

Liberty—In God We Trust
Words found on the face of all U.S. coins. On the back is: *United States of America* and *E Pluribus Unum*, along with the value of the coin.

Lichtenburg
Fictitious country featured in the 1950 Broadway play *Call Me Madam*.

Licorice
What Charlie Chaplin's shoe, which he ate in the 1925 silent movie *The Gold Rush*, was made from. The shoe cost $200 to create.

Liddy, G. Gordon
Counsel to CRP, The Committee to Re-Elect the President, during the 1972 Nixon–McGovern campaign. He was portrayed in the 1979 TV miniseries *Blind Ambition* by William Daniels.

Lie
Record album (his only one) recorded by Charles Manson on the Awareness label. The cover bore a close resemblance to the cover of an issue of *Life* magazine.

Lt. Ben Logan
Police officer played by Stacy Keach in the 1975 TV series *Caribe*.

Lt. Boomer
Fighter pilot (played by Herb Jefferson, Jr.,) who is the friend of Starbuck in the TV series *Battlestar Galactica*. In the sequel to the series, entitled *Galactica 1980*, he was promoted to the rank of colonel

Lt. Christine Chapel
Head nurse (played by Majel Barrett) on board the USS *Enterprise* in the TV series *Star Trek*. Majel Barrett is married to *Star Trek*'s creator, Gene Roddenberry, and supplied the voice for the *Enterprises*'s computer. In the 1979 movie *Star Trek; The Motion Picture* she was promoted to chief medical officer of the *Enterprise*.

Lt. Col. Donald Penobscot
Army officer whom Maj. Margaret "Hot Lips" Houlihan married in an episode of the TV series *M*A*S*H*. Penobscot was played by Beeson Carroll and, in a later episode, Mike Henry.

Lt. Ilia
Bald female navigator aboard the starship USS *Enterprise*. She was played by Persis Khambatta, a former Miss India, in the 1979 movie *Star Trek: The Motion Picture*.

Lt. Starbuck
Ace fighter pilot, played by Dirk Benedict, in the TV series *Battlestar Galactica*.

Life Among the Lowly
Subtitle of Harriet Beecher Stowe's novel *Uncle Tom's Cabin*.

Life and Loves of Linda Lovely, The
Ongoing soap opera on the *Bob and Ray* TV series.

Life Could Not Better Be
Danny Kaye's TV theme song

Life on the Mississippi
Mark Twain's autobiography of his early years as a riverboat cub pilot. It was first published in 1883. *Life on the Mississippi* was the first paperback published by Bantam Books (January 3, 1946); it cost 25 cents.

Life With Snarky Parker
Children's TV puppet show, broadcast in 1950. It was produced and directed by Yul Brynner.

Lift Every Voice and Sing
Song referred to as the black national anthem.

Light Brigade
Enoch Light's orchestra.

Lightning
Racehorse in the 1969 movie *The Reivers,* (based on the novel of the same name by William Faulkner). He was played by Marauder.

Ligowski, George
Inventor of the first clay pigeon, on September 7, 1880.

Lillums Lovewell
Girlfriend of Harold Teen in the comic strip *Harold Teen.*

Lilly Belle
Locomotive (No. 173) on Walt Disney's scaled-down Carolwood Pacific Railroad, which ran for half a mile on his property in southern California.

Lincoln, Abraham
(1809–1865) 16th president of the United States who served during the American Civil War. He was assassinated on April 15, 1865, by John Wilkes Booth, just 5 days after Lee's surrender. Movie portrayals: *Lincoln's Gettysburg Address* (1912) Ralph Ince; *Lincoln the Lover* (1914) Ralph Ince; *The Birth of a Nation* (1915) Joseph Henaberry; *The Highest Law* (1921) Ralph Ince; *Abraham Lincoln* (1930) Walter Huston; *The Littlest Rebel* (1935) Frank McGlynn, Sr.; *Of Human Hearts* (1938) John Carradine; *Young Mr. Lincoln* (1939) Henry Fonda; *Abe Lincoln in Illinois* (1940) Raymond Massey; *Virginia City* (1940) Victor Kilian; *Prince of Players* (1955) Stanley Hall; *The Story of Mankind* (1957) Austin Green; *How the West Was Won* (1963) Raymond Massey; *The Great Man's Whiskers* (1971 TV) Dennis Weaver; *Sandburg's Lincoln* (1974 TV miniseries) Hal Holbrook; and *The Lincoln Conspiracy* (1977) John Anderson.

Lincoln, Levi and Enoch
Brothers who served as governors of two different states at the same time (1827–1829); Levi of Massachusetts, and Enoch of Maine.

Lincoln Logs
Set of building toy logs that was invented by John Lloyd, son of architect Frank Lloyd Wright.

Lincoln, Mary Todd
(1818–1882) Wife of Abraham Lincoln from November 4, 1842, until his death. In 1875 she was judged to be insane. She was once accused by a congressional committee of being a Confederate spy. The president testified twice before the committee to exonerate her. Movie portrayals: *Abraham Lincoln* (1924) Nell Craig; *Abraham Lincoln* (1930) Kay Hammond; *Abe Lincoln in Illinois* (1940) Ruth Gordon; *Prince of Players* (1955) Sarah Padden; and *Sandburg's Lincoln* (1974 TV miniseries) Sada Thompson.

Lincoln Zephyr
Automobile in which ex-heavyweight champ Jack Johnson was killed outside of Franklinton, North Carolina, on June 10, 1946.

Linda
Song that Jack Lawrence composed in 1944 for his attorney's little girl, Linda Eastman. Today Linda Eastman is the wife of Paul McCartney. The song's first line is: "I count all the charms about Linda." It was introduced in the 1945 movie *The Story of G.I. Joe.*

Linda Loring
Wife of detective Philip Marlowe (novels). He married her when he was 42 years old.

Linda Lovely
Housewife of Bob and Ray's TV satirical soap skit "One Feller's Family." She was played by Audrey Meadows and Cloris Leachman on *The Bob and Ray Show.*

Lindbergh, Anne Morrow
Author wife of Charles Lindbergh. She was the first woman to be issued a glider pilot license.

Lindy's
New York City restaurant alluded to in a majority of Damon Runyon's stories. In "Guys and Dolls" he called it Mindy's.

Lingle, Alfred "Jake"
Chicago Tribune reporter who was gunned down in a Chicago subway station by Al Capone's mob on June 9, 1930. He was portrayed in the 1975 movie *Capone* by Peter Maloney.

Linkletter, Art
Radio/TV host best known for his TV series *Art Linkletter's House Party* (1950–1969) and *People Are Funny* (1951–1961). His portrait is on the $100 bill in the board game Life (his is the only real person's image used in the game).

Lion's Head
London pub where Jack Griffin (Claude Rains) first became invisible in the 1933 movie *The Invisible Man*.

Lipman, Hyman L.
Inventor, in 1858, of the first pencil with an eraser on it.

Liston, Charles "Sonny"
(1932–1970) Heavyweight boxing champion who came from a family of 25 children. He was the only boxer on the cover of the Beatles' *Sgt. Pepper's Lonely Hearts Club Band* album. Liston was portrayed in the 1977 movie *The Greatest* by Roger E. Mosley. He appeared as an extra in the 1968 Monkees' movie *Head*.

Liszt, Franz
(1811–1886) Hungarian-born pianist and composer. He was the father-in-law of composer Richard Wagner.* Movie portrayals: *Suez* (1938) Brandon Hurst; *The Phantom of the Opera* (1943) Fritz Leiber; *A Song to Remember* (1945) Stephen Bekassy; *Song of Love* (1947) Henry Daniell†; *Song Without End* (1960) Dirk Bogarde; and *Lisztomania* (1975) Roger Daltrey.

Little Big Man
121-year-old man named Jack Crabb. Movie portrayals: *Chief Crazy Horse* (1955) Ray Danton; and *Little Big Man* (based on the Thomas Berger novel of the same name) (1970) Dustin Hoffman.

Little Blackie
14-year-old Mattie Ross's (Kim Darby) horse in the 1969 movie *True Grit* (based on Charles Portis's novel of the same name).

Little Bohemia Lodge
Retreat on Lake Michigan in Wisconsin where, on April 22, 1934, Melvin Purvis and his agents shot it out with John Dillinger, Homer Van Meter, John Hamilton, Tommy Carroll, and Baby Face Nelson.

Little Bo-Peep
Little girl who lost her sheep in the nursery rhyme. She was played in the 1934 movie *Babes in Toyland* by Charlotte Henry, and in the 1961 movie *Babes in Toyland* by Ann Jilliann.

Little Buck
Actual name of the horse ridden by Robert Horton in the TV series *Wagon Train* and later by Doug McClure in the TV series *The Virginian*.

Little Caesar
Nickname of United Farm Workers Union President Cesar Chavez.

Little Coyote
Nickname given to Lucy Mallony's baby girl, who was born in Apache

---

*Katharine Delaney O'Hara, the mother of American author John O'Hara, was one of Liszt's students.
†Ervin Nyiregyhazi's hands are seen on the keyboard.

Wells, in the 1939 movie *Stagecoach*. She was played by Mary Kathleen Walker.

Little Dipper School
Elementary school attended by Elroy Jetson in the TV cartoon series *The Jetsons*.

Little Flower, The
Affectionate nickname given to New York City Mayor Fiorello LaGuardia.

Little General
Nickname of NFL player Eddie Le Baron.

Little House on the Prairie
Series of stories by Laura Ingalls Wilder that was made into the TV series starring Michael Landon and Karen Grassle as Charles and Caroline Ingalls. Laura Ingalls was portrayed by Melissa Gilbert. Garth Williams was the illustrator for the books.

Little Luke Leadbetter
Good friend of Bobby Benson, played by Bert Parks, in the radio series *Bobby Benson*.

Little Miss Poker Face
Nickname of tennis champion Helen Wills Moody.

Little Miss Muffett
Subject of a Mother Goose nursery rhyme: Little Miss Muffett who sat on her tuffet. She was played in the 1934 movie *Babes in Toyland* by Alice Dahl.

Little Mo
Nickname of tennis champion Maureen Connally. (See: **Connally, Maureen**).

Little Nell
Mike Conovan's (Spencer Tracy) racehorse in the 1952 movie *Pat and Mike*.

Little Old New York
Ed Sullivan's newspaper column (starting in 1932) in the New York *Daily News*.

Little Professor
Nickname of baseball player Dominic DiMaggio, brother of Joe.

Little Queen of Soap Opera
Title conferred on actress Anne Francis.

Little Red Riding Hood
Popular Grimm fairy tale character. She was played in the 1962 movie *The Wonderful World of the Brothers Grimm* by Ruthie Robinson.

Little Salem
Small Colorado town where Charles Foster Kane was born in 1864 in the 1941 movie *Citizen Kane*.

Lively Lady
Charter fishing boat owned by Bill Greer (Bill Williams) in the TV series *Assignment Underwater*.

Livermore Larruper
Nickname of heavyweight boxing champion Max Baer.

Liza
Song composed in 1929 by Ira Gershwin, Gus Kahn, and George Gershwin. It can be heard in the following movies: *Rhapsody in Blue* (1945); *The Jolson Story* (1946); *The Man I Love* (1946); and *Starlift* (1951). Liza Minnelli was named for the song as Ira Gershwin was her godfather.

Lloyd George, David
(1863–1945) British statesman and prime minister (1916–1922), portrayed in the 1972 movie *Young Winston* by Anthony Hopkins.

Loan, Brig. Gen. Nguyen Ngoc
South Vietnamese police chief who was photographed, executing by pistol, a Vietcong Officer. The photo, taken by AP photographer Eddie Adams, won the Pulitzer Prize.

Lobsinger, Lydia
Recipient of the first payment by the FDIC (Federal Deposit Insurance Corporation) when an East Peoria bank, the Fond Du Lac State Bank, went bankrupt on July 3, 1934.

Lockspur High School
School where Andrea Thomas (secret identity of Isis) teaches in the TV series *Isis*, starring Jo Anna Cameron.

Lodge, Henry Cabot
(1850–1924) U.S. representative and later senator who led the opposition to American membership in the League of Nations. He was portrayed in the 1944 movie *Wilson* by Sir Cedric Hardwicke. Lodge's grandson, John Lodge, began a career as an actor and later became governor of Connecticut (1950–1954) and ambassador to Spain and Argentina.

Logie
Australia's equivalent of the Emmy Awards.

Lollipop Kids
Three tough Munchkin boys who sang to Dorothy in Munchkinland in the 1939 movie *The Wizard of Oz*. Jerry Maren played the boy who gave Dorothy a giant lollipop. The group was also called the Lollipop Guild. The King's Men Quartet (leader Ken Darby) provided their singing voices.

Lolly Willowes; Or The Loving Huntsman
Novel by Sylvia Townsend that became the first selection of the Book-of-the-Month Club when it was established in New York City in April 1926.

Lomax, John Avery
(1872–1948) American folk music historian who with his son, Alan, recorded numerous blues and folk singers throughout the United States for an oral musical history for the Library of Congress. He was portrayed in the 1976 movie *Leadbelly* by James E. Brodhead.

Lombardi, Vince
(1913–1970) College football player for Fordham. He served as head coach at St. Cecilia's High School in 1939–1945, and later was named head coach of the Green Bay Packers. During his time with the Packers (1959–1968) he won eight championships. The Super Bowl trophy is named in his honor. Lombardi's NFL record over 10 years was 141-39-4. He was portrayed by Ernest Borgnine in the 1978 TV movie *Portrait: Legend in Granite*.

Lombard Street
London's equivalent of Wall Street.

Lompoc Daily Picayune Intelligencer
Lompoc daily newspaper in the 1940 W. C. Fields movie *The Bank Dick*.

London, Jack (John Griffith)
(1876–1916) American journalist and novelist. Among his works are *The Sea Wolf* (1900), *The Call of the Wild* (1904), and *White Fang* (1907). While in Hawaii, London became one of the first Americans to learn how to surf. He was portrayed in the 1943 movie *Jack London* by Michael O'Shea.

London Times and Daily Newsgiver
Two newspapers read each day by sleuth Miss Jane Marple (novels).

Long, Huey Pierce
(1893–1935) American lawyer and politician nicknamed 'The Kingfish.'' He served as governor of Louisiana (1928–1931) and as a U.S. senator (1931–1935).He was assassinated on September 8, 1935, by Dr. Carl Weiss. Huey Long was portrayed by Broderick Crawford (as Governor Willie Stark) in the 1949 Academy Award–winning movie *All The King's Men* (based on the Robert Penn Warren novel of the same name), and by Edward Asner in the 1977 TV movie *The Life and Assassination of the Kingfish*.

Long, Luz
German athlete against whom Jesse Owens competed in the 1936 Olympics. Long befriended Owens, helping him to qualify, and the two remained good friends until Long was killed in North Africa during World War II.

Long, Richard Dale
First baseman (left-handed) who caught two games for Chicago Cubs pitcher Bob Scheffing in 1958. In May 1956, while with the Pittsburgh Pirates, Long hit eight home runs in eight consecutive games.

Longstreet, James
(1821–1904) U.S. Army soldier who joined the Confederate Army during the Civil War. He was U.S. minister to Turkey in 1880–1881. Longstreet was portrayed in the 1940 movie *Santa Fe Trail* by Frank Wilcox.

Look
Allied code name for Gen. Dwight D. Eisenhower during World War II.

Look
> Magazine for which Gerald R. Ford modeled winter sports clothing in 1939.

Look for the Union Label
> Theme song of the ILGWA (International Ladies' Garment Workers of America).

Look How Far We've Come
> Theme song of the short-lived TV series *The Family Holvak,* sung by Denny Brooks.

Looking for Love
> 1964 film in which Johnny Carson made his only movie appearance.

Look, The
> Nickname of actress Anita Colby. Lauren Bacall was called "The Looks."

Looper, Selda
> 18-year-old who became the first female page in the U.S. House of Representatives.

Lopez, Al
> Manager of the only two teams to win the American League pennant from 1949 through 1964, other than the New York Yankees. He managed Cleveland (1954) and Chicago (1959).

Lord's Prayer, The
> Hit record sung by Australian nun, Sister Janet Mead, on A & M Records (1974).

Lorraine Motel
> Memphis, Tennessee, motel where on April 4, 1969, Martin Luther King, Jr., was assassinated by James Earl Ray as he stood on the balcony. King was staying in Room 306. Loree Bailey, the wife of the hotel owner, died of a stroke after hearing about the assassination.

Lorre, Peter
> (1904–1964) Hungarian-born actor (Laszlo Löwenstein) who made his movie debut in the classic film *M* (1931). He was portrayed in the 1980 TV movie *Bogie* by Herb Braha.

Lorz, Fred
> U.S. marathon runner who in the 1904 Olympics, in St. Louis rode part of the 26-mile, 385-yard marathon in an automobile, waving to the other runners. He got out of the car 5 miles from the stadium and finished first, only to be disqualified.

Los Angeles Daily Blade
> Newspaper for which Bill Hastings (Peter Lawford) wrote an advice-to-the-lovelorn column under the name of Phoebe Goodheart in the TV series *Dear Phoebe.*

Los Angeles Philharmonic Orchestra
Musical assembly that provided the music for the TV series *Battlestar Galactica*.
Los Angeles Rams
Football team on which Jerry Standish (Dick Gautier) once played in the TV series *Here We Go Again*.
Los Angeles Sun
Newspaper for which Jim Thompson (Don Chastain) was a sports writer in the TV series *The Debbie Reynolds Show*.
Los Angeles Tribune
Newspaper for which Lou Grant (Ed Asner) works in the TV series *Lou Grant*. It is also the newspaper for which Brenda Starr is a reporter (TV series).
Los Rodeos Airport
Canary Island site of the worst accident in aviation history. A KLM Boeing 747, Flight 4805 (*Rhine River*), smashed into a Pan American Boeing 747, Flight 1736 (*Clipper Victor*), on a foggy runway on March 27, 1977, resulting in 582 deaths.
Loughery, Jackie
First winner of Miss U.S.A. contest (1952). She represented New York State.
Louis, Joe
Born Joseph Lewis Barrow: heavyweight boxing champion from 1937 to 1946. As champ, Louis defended his title 25 times. He holds the distinction of having knocked out six men who at one time were heavyweight champions: Schmeling, Baer, Walcott, Sharkey, Carnera, and Braddock. When dressing, Louis always put on his left glove first. He was portrayed by Coley Wallace in the 1953 movie *The Joe Louis Story*, in the 1979 TV movie *Marciano*, and in the 1980 movie *Raging Bull*. He was also played by Bernie Casey, in the 1978 TV movie *Ring of Passion*.
Lousy Awards, The
Humorous awards presented on *The Steve Allen Show* on TV.
Lovable Clown
Theme music played by David Rose for the "Freddie the Freeloader" skits on the TV series *The Red Skelton Show*.
Love Comes But Once
Record made in college by Jimmy Stewart with José Ferrer's college band, the Pied Pipers. The flip side of the record was José Ferrer singing "Sweet Georgia Brown."
Love Is All Around
Theme song of the TV series *The Mary Tyler Moore Show*, sung by Sonny Curtis (ex-member of Buddy Holly's Crickets).

Love Is a Many-Splendored Thing
> 1955 movie based on the autobiography of Han Suyin. The title song from the movie was recorded by the Four Aces and became very popular. This song was played in the opening scene of the 1978 movie *Grease* (before the credits).

Love: It's Cure and Prevention
> Book written by the world's leading psychologist, Professor Ludwig von Hartflopper (Sid Caesar), in the TV series *Your Show of Shows*.

Lovelady, Billy Nolan
> Co-worker of Lee Harvey Oswald at the Texas School Book Depository in Dallas who bore a striking resemblance to Oswald.

Lovely to Look At
> Number-one song performed on the first broadcast of the radio series *Hit Parade* (April 20, 1935). It was introduced by Fred Astaire in the 1935 movie *Roberta*.

Lowell Memorial Hospital
> Los Angeles medical facility where Dr. Jake Goodwin (George Peppard) practiced in the TV series *Doctor's Hospital*.

Luciani, Albino
> Pope John Paul, 263rd pontiff. His reign lasted only 34 days before he died of a heart attack on September 28, 1978.

Luciano, Charles "Lucky"
> (1897–1962) Organized crime syndicate chief who was deported from the United States on the ship *Laura Keene* on February 10, 1946. Movie portrayals: *A House Is Not a Home* (1964) Cesar Romero; *The Valachi Papers* (1972) Angelo Infanti; *Lepke* (1975) Vic Tayback; *Brass Target* (1978) Lee Montague; and *Gangster Chronicles* (TV series) by Michael Nouri.

Lucifer
> Count Baltar's robot assistant, played by 4-foot 11-inch Bobby Porter on the TV series *Battlestar Galactica*. The voice of Lucifer is that of Jonathan Harris.

Luck, Wisconsin
> Onetime yo-yo capital of the world. Duncan yo-yos were produced there between 1946 and 1966.

Lucky
> Packy Lambert's (Roger Mobley) horse in the TV series *Fury*.

Lucky Bag, The
> Name of Annapolis Academy's 7-pound yearbook.

Lucky Dragon No. 5
> Japanese fishing trawler that received fallout from the H-bomb explosion at Bikini atoll on March 1, 1954. The trawler was 120 miles away from the target site.

Lucky Stiff, The
 1949 United Artists movie produced by comedian Jack Benny (his only effort as a producer).

Lucy Hamilton
 Private eye Michael Shayne's secretary, played on the TV series *Michael Shayne, Private Detective* by Patricia Donahue and then Margie Regan.

Ludwig and Wolfgang
 Dr. Henry Frankenstein's two sons. Sir Cedric Hardwicke played Ludwig in *The Ghost of Frankenstein* (1942), and Basil Rathbone played Wolfgang in *The Son of Frankenstein* (1939).

Lugash
 Country to which the Pink Panther Diamond is taken in the 1974 movie *The Return of the Pink Panther.*

Luisetti, Angelo Enrico "Hank"
 Stanford 6-foot 3-inch forward who invented the one-handed shot in basketball. In 1935 he scored 305 points in 18 games.

Luke Short's General Store
 Only establishment in Bug Tussell that has a telephone in the TV series *The Beverly Hillbillies.*

Lulu
 Ed Norton's pet dog, which he lost at Coney Island, in the TV series *The Honeymooners.*

Lulu
 Call sign of the rescue party headed by Lt. Alexander Austin (Alan Ladd) in the 1958 movie *The Deep Six.* "Little Daddy" were the men watching the life rafts.

Lulubelle (L3)
 U.S. Army tank (USAW304512) commanded by Sgt. Frank Tree (Dan Aykroyd) in the 1979 movie *1941.*

Lum, Mike
 Only player to pinch hit for Hank Aaron.

Lumpy
 Chewbacca's son (played by Patty Maloney), as revealed in the 1978 *Star Wars Holiday Special* on TV.

Luna
 Moon-bound spaceship launched from Earth in the 1950 movie *Destination Moon.* The ship landed in the crater Harpalus.

Lustine
 French frigate that sank in 1793. The ship's bell is rung at Lloyd's of London every time a disaster occurs. (The bell is called the Bad News Bell.)

Luther and Nobody Loves An Albatross
 Two plays that up-and-coming actor Guy Woodhouse (John Cassavetes)

appeared in in the 1968 movie *Rosemary's Baby* (based on the Ira Levin novel of the same name).

Luther, Martin

(1483–1546) German leader of the Protestant Reformation who founded the Lutheran denomination after being excommunicated by Pope Leo X. Movie portrayals: *Luther* (1973) Stacy Keach. Albert Finney portrayed Luther in the John Osborne play *Luther,* which premiered at the Theatre Royal in Nottingham on June 26, 1961.

Lux Soap

Product for which Grace Kelly gave a testimonial advertised in magazines during the 1950s. When later interviewed as Princess Grace of Monaco, she denied using the product.

Lynnhaven College

Where Professor Ray McNutley (Ray Milland) taught English in the TV series *The Ray Milland Show.* After the first season, he taught at Comstock University.

Lytheon

Planet setting of the 1968 movie *Barbarella*.

M & M
   Candy manufacturers: Mars and Murray.

Mable
   Fable lady, played by Cher in her TV series.

MacArthur, Douglas
   (1880–1964) Son of Medal of Honor winner General Arthur MacArthur.
   Douglas MacArthur became the Allied supreme commander in the Southwest
   Pacific during World War II and supreme commander of the U.N. forces in
   the Korean War. MacArthur, like his father, was awarded the Medal of Honor.
   As a cadet, he scored the winning run in the very first varsity baseball game
   between Annapolis and West Point, played at Annapolis. The final score was
   West Point 4, Annapolis 3. Movie portrayals: *They Were Expendable* (1945)
   Robert Barrat; *An American Guerilla in the Philippines* (1950) Robert
   Barrat; *The Court Martial of Billy Mitchell* (1955) Dayton Lummis; *Collision
   Course* (1975 TV) Henry Fonda; *MacArthur* (1977) Gregory Peck; and
   Inchon (1981) Laurence Olivier.

Mach 1
   First mascot falcon of the U.S. Air Force Academy (October 5, 1955).

Machus Red Fox
   Detroit restaurant where, on July 30, 1975, Jimmy Hoffa was last seen.

MacKall, John Thomas
   First U.S. paratrooper to be killed in action, on November 8, 1942 (during
   World War II). Camp MacKall in North Carolina is named in his honor.

Mackenzie

Nickname of the canned laughter machine used for TV programs.

Macheath

Name of the central character in the Bertolt Brecht–Kurt Weill play *Threepenny Opera* and subject of the song "Mack the Knife."

MacMillan, Kirkpatrick

Scottish inventor of the bicycle in 1839.

MacMurray, Fred, and Claudette Colbert

Films in which the pair appeared together: *The Gilded Lady* (1935); *The Bride Comes Home* (1935); *Maid of Salem* (1937); *No Time for Love* (1943); *Practically Yours* (1945); *The Egg and I* (1947); and *Family Honeymoon* (1948).

Madame

Wayland Flowers's senior citizen, quick-witted dummy.

Madam Natasha

Girlfriend of comic book superhero *Daredevil*

Madison

New England town setting of the TV series *Margie*.

Madison, Dolley

(1768–1849) Wife of U.S. President James Madison. She became well-known as a gracious Washington hostess. Movie portrayals: *The Buccaneer* (1938) Spring Byington; and *Magnificent Doll* (1946) Ginger Rogers.

Madison High School

Brooklyn school attended by authors Arthur Miller, Irwin Shaw, and Sylvia Porter.

Madison, James

(1751–1836) 4th president of the United States. He was the shortest president (5 feet 4 inches) and the lightest (100 pounds). Burgess Meredith portrayed Madison in the 1946 movie *Magnificent Doll*.

Madison Junior High School

School where John Martin (Herb Edelman) was a science teacher in the TV series *Big John, Little John*.

Madison Square Garden (Old)

New York City auditorium located on Madison Avenue and 23rd Street that was the site of the murder of renowned architect Stanford White by Harry K. Thaw on July 25, 1906. The musical being performed was *Mam'zelle Champagne*.* Thaw was jealous of White's relationship with actress Evelyn Nesbitt, Thaw's estranged wife. The story is told in the 1955 movie *The Girl in the Red Velvet Swing*. Ray Milland portrayed Stanford White, Farley

---

*Sitting at White's table when he was shot was Clinch Smith, who later perished on the *Titanic*.

Granger was Harry Thaw, and Joan Collins was Evelyn Nesbitt. As a brick-layer's helper, author John Steinbeck helped to construct the old Madison Square Garden.

Mad Man Mooney's Hubcap Heaven
Used car lot run by Mooney (Milton Berle) in the 1979 movie *The Muppet Movie*.

MAD Magazine
Zany monthly magazine founded in 1953 by William M. Gaines. The title was taken from the first initials of the names Melvin, Alfred, and David. In July 1955 (issue No. 24) *MAD* changed from a comic book to a magazine. Harvey Kurtzman was *MAD's* art director. The magazine's original full title was *Tales Calculated to Drive you Mad*.

Madrid, New Mexico
Setting of the TV series *Cade's County,* starring Glenn Ford as Sheriff Sam Cade.

Magazine Covers
Mia Farrow adorned the first cover of *People* magazine, March 4, 1974. John Travolta became the first male to appear on the cover of *McCall's* magazine in over 100 years of publication in July 1978. Jean Harlow was the first female movie star to adorn the cover of *Life* magazine (May 3, 1937). John Lennon was on the cover of the first issue of *Rolling Stone* magazine (November 1967). Lucille Ball and her baby, Desi Arnaz IV, graced the very first cover of *TV Guide* (April 3–9, 1953).

Magee, Carl C.
Inventor of the parking meter in 1935.

Maggie
Mrs. Eleanor Roosevelt's pet dog.

Maggie
Award given to the year's best magazine.

Magic in Manhattan
Book that Nicky Henderson (Jack Lemmon) helped Sidney Redlitch (Ernie Kovacs) to write in the 1958 movie *Bell, Book, and Candle*.

Magician, The
Television program that Patty Hearst and Steven Weed were watching in their apartment (No. 4) at 2603 Benvenue Avenue in San Francisco on February 4, 1974, the day Patty was kidnapped. In the 1979 TV movie *The Ordeal of Patty Hearst* the TV series heard (not seen) was *The Guinness Book of World Records,* hosted by David Frost.

Magic Mirror
Mirror of which the evil witch asks, "Mirror mirror on the wall, who's the fairest one of all?" in the Disney cartoon movie *Snow White and the Seven Dwarfs*. The voice of the mirror was that of Moroni Olsen.

Magnificent Wildcat, The
Nickname of actress Pola Negri.

Magruder, Jeb Stuart
Director of White House communications and President Nixon's deputy campaign director in 1972. He was portrayed in the 1979 TV miniseries *Blind Ambition* by Christopher Guest.

Mahout Cigarettes
Cigarette advertisement in the scene in which Gene Kelly dances on a wet street in the 1952 movie *Singin' in the Rain*.

Major Chord
Jimmy Doyle's (Robert De Niro) nightclub in the 1977 movie *New York, New York*.

Maj. Frank Marion Burns
Surgeon assigned to the 4077th MASH unit who had an affair with Maj. Margaret Houlihan (Loretta Swit) in the TV series *M*A*S*H*. Maj. Burns was played by Larry Linville, who left the series before the 1978 season. In the 1970 Robert Altman film *M*A*S*H* Maj. Burns was played by Robert Duvall.

Major Major Major
Character who resembled actor Henry Fonda in Joseph Heller's novel *Catch 22*. He was played by Bob Newhart in the 1970 movie version of the book. When an IBM computer mistakenly promoted him to the rank of major, he became Maj. Major Major Major.

Majuba Diamond
Gem stolen by Noonan (Raymond Burr) in the 1955 Louis and Martin comedy *You're Never Too Young*.

Making Whoopee
Phrase coined by Walter Winchell in his newspaper column for the *Daily Mirror*. It later became the title of a popular song.

Maloney
Actor John Barrymore's favorite pet vulture.

Mama Barks
1950 song recorded by Frank Sinatra and Dagmar. Because Mitch Miller insisted that Sinatra make this recording with the nonsinging sex symbol Dagmar, Sinatra angrily left Columbia Records for the Capitol label.

Mama's Bank Account
Novel by Kathryn Forbes on which the play, 1948 movie and TV series *I Remember Mama* were based.

Ma'm'selle Hepzibah
Skunk that lives in the Okefenokee Swamp in Walt Kelly's comic strip *Pogo*.

Mammoth Pictures
> Movie studio owned by Jed Clampett (Buddy Ebsen) in the TV series *The Beverly Hillbillies*.

Man about the House
> British TV series of which the ABC comedy *Three's Company* is an offspring.

Manatee, The
> Title of the first (No. 1) Harlequin Romance novel. It was written by Nancy Bruff and published in 1949.

Mandarley
> Maxim de Winter's (Laurence Olivier) huge estate in the 1940 movie *Rebecca* (based on the Daphne DuMaurier novel of the same name).

Mandolin
> Musical instrument played by Fibber McGee in the radio series *Fibber McGee and Molly*. He kept it in his hall closet.

Man from Atlantis, The
> First American television series to be broadcast in mainland China (1980).

Manhattan
> New York magazine for which Christine Massey (Loretta Young) became a staff writer in the TV series *The Loretta Young Show*.

Manhattanite Magazine
> Magazine for which John Monroe (William Windom) is a cartoonist in the TV series *My World . . . And Welcome to It*.

Manhattan Magazine
> Magazine for which Ruth Sherwood (Elaine Stritch) worked as a writer in the TV series *My Sister Eileen*.

Manhattan, SS
> Ship upon which 7-year-old Elizabeth Taylor first came to the United States in 1939.

Mannekin-Pis
> Fountain statue of urinating little boy in the Grand Place in Brussels, Belgium. He is continually being clothed for special occasions. Since the statue is often stolen, the original by Jerome Duquesnoy (1619) is kept in the Municipal Museum.

Manson, Charles
> 5-foot 6-inch tall cult leader of a California band of killers. In 1969 his group killed actress Sharon Tate, coffee heiress Abigail Folger, and three others in the home of director Roman Polanski. The next night they killed Leno and Rosemary La Bianca in their home. Charles Manson and his band—Susan Atkins, Patricia Krenwinkel, and Leslie Van Houten—were all found guilty

and sentenced to life imprisonment. A 1976 TV movie called *Helter Skelter* depicted the cult.

Character	Actor
Charles Manson	Steve Railsback
Susan Atkins	Nancy Wolfe
Linda Kasabian	Marilyn Burns
Patricia Krenwinkel	Christina Hart
Leslie Van Houten	Cathey Paine

Vincent Bugliosi, the Los Angeles prosecutor, was portrayed by George Di Cenzo.

Manson, Jean
August 1974 *Playboy* Playmate of the Month. Her recording of "Avant de Nous Dire Adieu" (Before We Say Goodbye) sold one million copies in France, topping that country's hit parade.

Manuel, Dean
Piano player who was killed, along with singer/pilot Jim Reeves, when their plane crashed outside of Nashville on July 31, 1964.

Man Who Plays the Sweetest Trumpet in the World, The
Tag line for band leader Charlie Spivak.

Man with the Perfect Profile
Nickname of actor Robert Taylor.

Mapleton
Hometown of Cicero P. Sweeny (Charles Ruggles) in the TV series *The World of Mister Sweeny*.

Mapleton, Massachusetts
Small town setting of the 1942 movie *The Mummy's Tomb*.

Marathon Hotel
Latigo, New Mexico, setting of the TV series *Black Saddle*.

Maravich, Peter
Basketball player for the New Orleans Jazz. During his 4 years in college he wore the same pair of socks for luck

Marcella
Ballerina-elephant star of the Ringling Brothers, Barnum & Bailey Circus from 1922 until her retirement in 1977.

Marcellino, Muzzy
Musician who provided the whistling for the song "The High and the Mighty"* in the 1954 movie and for the theme song of the 1968 movie *The Good, the Bad, and the Ugly*. Muzzy Marcellino was the band leader for *Art Linkletter's House Party* on TV.

---

*Some sources credit Fred Lowry with providing the whistling.

Marchal Jewelers
   Suppliers of the gold bracelets given to unsuspecting contestants on the TV series *This Is Your Life,* hosted by Ralph Edwards.
Marcheta
   Recurring theme song in the 1945 movie *They Were Expendable.*
March of the Clowns
   Theme song of the TV series *The Greatest Show on Earth.* It was composed by Richard Rodgers.
March of Time
   Newsreel series begun in 1934; narrated by Westbrook Van Voorhees.
March On, March On
   National anthem of China, adapted in 1978.
March 19, 1938
   Birth date (4:31 a.m., to be exact) of the prisoner (Patrick McGoohan) in the TV series *The Prisoner.*
Marcus, David "Mickey"
   (1902–1948) American lawyer who commanded the Israeli Army in 1947. He was mistaken for an enemy and killed by one of his own sentries because he couldn't speak Hebrew. Marcus is the only soldier buried at West Point under a foreign flag. He was the 6th Allied soldier to set foot in France on D-Day. Marcus was portrayed by Kirk Douglas in the 1966 movie *Cast a Giant Shadow.*
Marcus-Nelson Murders, The
   1973 pilot movie for the *Kojak* TV series.
Margaret
   Lucas McCain's (Chuck Connors) deceased wife (her maiden name was Gibbs) in the TV series *The Rifleman.*
Maria Elena
   Popular tune made famous by Jimmy Dorsey in 1946. It was originally composed in 1933 and dedicated to Marie Elena, wife of Mexico's president Pontes Gil. In 1963 Los Indios Tabajaras had a million-seller version of "Maria Elena."
Marie Antoinette
   Wednesday Thursday Addams's (Lisa Loring) headless doll in the TV series *The Addams Family.*
Marilyn Munster
   "Plain" member of the Munster family, played by Beverly Owen and Pat Priest (daughter of Ivy Baker Priest*), in the TV series *The Munsters,* and by Debbie Watson in the 1966 movie *Munster, Go Home.*

---

*One-time Secretary of the Treasury.

Mariposa and Monterey

Sister ships of the Pacific Far East Lines, and the last two luxury liners to fly the American flag. The *Mariposa* made its final docking at Pier 35 in San Francisco on April 7, 1978. It was piloted by Capt. John Caldwell. The bar pilot was Capt. William W. Meyer, whose father had been the *Mariposa*'s first captain.

Mark Savage

Hero of mystery novels read by Lionel "Brownshoe" Whitney (Jeff Goldblum) in each episode of the TV series *Tenspeed and Brownshoe*. The novels' author was Steven J. Cannell (the actual name of the show's producer).

Mark Twain

Associated Press's annual award for Best News Writing.

Marlboro

Pack of cigarettes in which a role of film was hidden in the 1978 movie *Foul Play*.

Marquis of Queensberry

(1844–1900) Sir John Sholto Douglas, patron of boxing, who in 1867 established a code of fair play known as the Marquis of Queensberry Rules. He was portrayed in the 1960 movie *The Trials of Oscar Wilde* by Lionel Jeffries.

Marse, Robert

Name of the horse that pulled the buckboard driven by Rhett Butler (Clark Gable) to safety as Atlanta burned in the 1939 movie *Gone With the Wind* Marse Robert was Negro slang for Gen. Robert E. Lee.

Marshal, Bob

1973 World Champion Steer Wrestler. His 14-year-old son, Mike, was one of the schoolchildren kidnapped in the Chowchilla school bus hijack on July 15, 1976.

Marshall, Jim

Minnesota Vikings defensive end who, after picking up a ball fumbled by 49er halfback Billy Kilmer, ran 66 yards into the wrong end zone in a game played on October 28, 1964. (George Mira threw the pass to Kilmer.) Minnesota won the game, 27–22.

Marshall, George Catlett

(1880–1959) U.S. secretary of state, president of the Red Cross (1950), and the only general to be awarded the Nobel Peace Prize. During World War II Marshall served as chief of staff and general of the Army. Portrayals: *Tora! Tora! Tora!* (1970) Keith Andes; *MacArthur* (1977) Ward Costello; *Ike* (1979 TV miniseries) Dana Andrews; and *Churchill and the Generals* (1980 TV) Joseph Cotten.

Marshall, Peter

(1920–1949) Chaplain of the U.S. Senate 1947–1949. He was portrayed by

Richard Todd in the 1955 movie *A Man Called Peter* (adapted from a book by his wife, Catherine).

Marshall University
College in West Virginia that lost its entire football team in the plane crash of a Southern Airways DC-9 on November 14, 1970.

Martha Washington Hotel
First hotel exclusively for women; opened in New York City in 1903.

Martian
Three-eyed alien in the 1953 movie *The War of the Worlds*. He was played by Charles Gemora*—on his knees.

Martin, George
Producer of the Beatles when they recorded for EMI's Parlophone label until they formed their own company, Apple Records. He was portrayed in the 1979 TV movie *Birth of the Beatles* by Nigel Havers.

Martin, George W. T.
London cab driver who crashed his taxi on April 17, 1960, killing his passenger, rock singer Eddie Cochran. Also injured were passengers Gene Vincent and Cochran's fiancee, Sharon Sheeley.† Martin was later barred from driving a cab for 15 years.

Marwine
51-foot yacht once owned by actor Warner Baxter and later by lawyer Melvin Belli.

Mar-Wyck
140-acre ranch where racehorses were bred during the 1930s. It was owned in partnership by Zeppo Marx and Barbara Stanwyck

Mary Ann
Nickname of the right hand of heavyweight boxer "Fireman" Jim Flynn, the only man who ever knocked out Jack Dempsey (February 13, 1917).

Mary, I'm In Love with You
Theme song of the TV series *The Adventures of Ozzie and Harriet*.

Mary Magdalene
Woman whom Jesus cured of evil spirits. She anointed his feet and dried them with her hair, and Jesus forgave her sins because "she was much loved." Movie portrayals: *King of Kings* (1927) Jacqueline Logan; *Mary Magdalene* (1958) Yvonne De Carlo; *King of Kings* (1961) Carmen Sevilla; *Jesus Christ, Superstar* (1973) Yvonne Elliman; *Jesus of Nazareth* (1977 TV) Anne Bancroft; and *The Day Christ Died* (1980 TV movie) Delia Boccardo.

Mary Queen of Scots
(1542–1587) Mary Stuart, queen of Scotland from the age of 6 days. In 1568

---

*Charles Gemora also played an ape in the movies *The Monster and the Girl* (1940) and *Phantom of Rue Morgue* (1954).
†Composer of Ricky Nelson's 1958 hit "Poor Little Fool."

she fled to England, where she was held prisoner until she was beheaded at the order of Queen Elizabeth in 1587. Movie portrayals: *Dorothy Vernon of Haddon Hall* (1924) Estelle Taylor; *Mary of Scotland* (1936) Katharine Hepburn; and *Mary, Queen of Scots* (1971) Vanessa Redgrave.

Mary's a Grand Old Name
Song sung by James Cagney and Bob Hope for the 1942 movie *Yankee Doodle Dandy*. However, the song was cut from the final print released.

Mary Worth
Comic strip created in 1932 by Mary Orr as "Apple Mary." Mary Worth was born in 1900 in Crawfordsville, Indiana, to Silas and Ella Jackson. She later married John David Worth.

Masquerade for Money
Radio quiz show on which Beauregard Bottomley (Ronald Colman) was a contestant, in the 1950 movie *Champagne for Caesar*. The show was sponsored by Milady Soap Company.

Master Mystery, The
1919 movie serial starring Harry Houdini.

Masters, Edgar Lee
Author of *Spoon River Anthology* (1915), a collection of poems. His autobiography was titled *Across Spoon River*. Masters was once a law partner of Clarence Darrow.

M/Sgt. Maxwell Slaughter
Army soldier played by Jackie Gleason in the 1963 movie *Soldier in the Rain*.

Matlack, Thomas
Man who actually "penned" the Declaration of Independence—it is in his handwriting.

Matlovich, Leonard
31-year-old Air Force sergeant who in March 1975 admitted to being a homosexual. He was portrayed in the 1978 TV movie *Sergeant Matlovich vs. The U.S. Air Force* by Brad Dourif.

Maugham, (William) Somerset
(1874–1965) British novelist and playwright who during World War I spied for the British. His best works are *Of Human Bondage* (1915) and *The Razor's Edge* (1944). Maugham was twice portrayed by Herbert Marshall in the movies: in *The Moon and Sixpence* (1942) and in *The Razor's Edge* (1946).

Maverick, Samuel A.
Texas legislator whose name was given to unbranded cattle.

Max
Pet cat of *Daily Planet* editor Perry White in *Superman* comic books.

Maxie the Taxie
Character created by comedian Eddie Cantor.

Maxim, Hiram Stevens
(1840–1916) American inventor who later became a naturalized British subject and was knighted. He invented a recoil-operated machine gun. His brother, Hudson, invented smokeless powders. His son, Hiram Percy Maxim, invented the silencer for guns. Hiram Maxim was portrayed in the 1946 movie *So Goes My Love* by Don Ameche.

Maximilian (Ferdinand Maximilian Joseph)
(1832–1867) Austrian archduke who became emperor of Mexico in 1864, after French troops drove Juárez from the country. In 1867 Juárez returned to his country, defeated Maximilian's troops, and had the emperor executed. Maximilian was portrayed in the 1939 movie *Juarez* by Brian Aherne.

Maxim, Joey
Only fighter to knock out Sugar Ray Robinson. He did it in the 14th round of the light heavyweight championship fight on June 25, 1952. Robinson announced his retirement after this fight, but went on to box for 13 more years.

Maxim's
Parisian restaurant featured in the 1958 musical *Gigi*.

Maxwell Edison
Role played by comic Steve Martin in the 1978 movie *Sgt. Pepper's Lonely Hearts Club Band*. It was based in part on a character in the John Lennon/Paul McCartney song "Maxwell's Silver Hammer."

May
James Bond's maid in his Chelsea flat on King's Road in London (novels).

Maybelle
Large ship kept by Superman as a trophy in his Fortress of Solitude (comic books).

Mayer, Louis Burt
(1885–1957) Russian-born American motion picture producer. He merged his company with Metro Pictures to form Metro-Goldwyn-Mayer Corp. (MGM). Movie portrayals: *Harlow* (1965) Jack Kruschen; *Gable and Lombard* (1976) Allen Garfield; *Rainbow* (1978 TV) Martin Balsam; and *Moviola* (1980 TV miniseries) Harold Gould.

Mayfield High School
School attended by Wally Cleaver (Tony Dow) in the TV series *Leave It to Beaver*. Wally was a member of the basketball team, the Mayfield Crusaders, and once scored 32 points in a game against Taft. As a freshman, he ran the 440 in 58 seconds flat.

FIRST EPISODE "CAPTAIN JACK"   WARD FROM SHAKER
                                                  HIEGHTS
MINERVA - MAID IN EARLY EPISODES
                                      JUNE FROM EAST ST. LOUIS

May I Sing to You
>Opening theme song sung by Eddie Fisher on the 1953–1957 TV series *Coke Time with Eddie Fisher*.

Maynard, Ken
>Motion picture's original singing cowboy. He first sang in the 1930 movie *Songs of the Saddle*. In 1920 he had held the title Champion Cowboy of the World, and in 1921 he was the top rider with the Ringling Brothers Circus. His brother, Kermit, was billed as Tex Maynard in western films.

Maynardsville
>Tennessee town in which both country superstars Roy Acuff (1903) and Carl Smith (1927) were born.

Mayor Finny
>Mayor of Big Town, U.S.A.; played by Liam Dunn in the TV series *Captain Nice*.

Mayor John Peoples
>Mayor of New City, California; played by Paul Maxey in the TV series *The People's Choice*.

Mayor Merle Jeeter
>Mayor of Fernwood, Ohio; played by Dabney Coleman in the TV series *Mary Hartman, Mary Hartman*.

Mayor Plumpfront
>Character (voice of Jon Arthur) in the radio series *Big Jon and Sparkie*.

Mayor Prometheus J. Gurgle
>Mayor of Dogpatch in the comic strip *L'il Abner*. It was he who first proclaimed Sadie Hawkins Day.

Mayor Thomas Jefferson Alcala
>Mayor of Albuquerque, New Mexico, in the TV series *The Man and the City*. He was played by Anthony Quinn.

Mayor Thomas Russell
>Mayor of the town of Springdale; played by Thomas Mitchell in the TV series *Mayor of the Town*.

Maytag Repairman
>The Maytag appliance repairman who awaits the repair call that never comes, played in TV commercials by Jesse White.

MCA
>Music Corporation of America, founded by Jules Stein in the early 1920s. Joan Crawford's adopted daughter, Christina, was once a receptionist at MCA in New York.

McAdoo, William G.
>(1863–1941) U.S. secretary of the treasury (1913–1918) and Democratic candidate for the presidency in 1920 and 1924. He married President

Wilson's daughter, Eleanor. McAdoo was portrayed in the 1944 movie *Wilson* by Vincent Price.

McCartney, Paul
Born James Paul McCartney on June 18, 1942. He was the rhythm guitarist for the Beatles who, together with John Lennon, composed the majority of the group's hit records. After the breakup of the Beatles in 1970, he formed the successful group Wings. He was portrayed in the 1979 TV movie *Birth of the Beatles* by Rod Culbertson.

McCarthy, Luther
Heavyweight boxer who died in the ring in a bout with Arthur Pelky on May 24, 1913, held in a barn in Canada. As McCarthy lay on the canvas after being knocked down by Pelky, a strange beam of sunlight shone through the roof onto his face. After a few moments, the beam disappeared and the referee found McCarthy dead.

McCormick, Cyrus Hall
(1809–1884) Inventor of the reaper in 1834.

McDonald's and Shell Oil
First two businesses that went dark during a power failure in the 1977 movie *Close Encounters of the Third Kind*.

McGuire, Patti
Playboy magazine's Playmate of the Month for November 1976 who married tennis star Jimmy Connors in 1979.

McKeever, Mike and Marlin
The only twin brothers ever selected for the college All-American football team.

McKinley, William
(1843–1901) 25th president of the United States who always wore a red carnation. As a private during the Civil War, he served under Gen. Rutherford B. Hayes. McKinley was assassinated on September 6, 1901, by Leon Czolgosz. He was portrayed in the 1937 movie *This Is My Affair* by Frank Conroy; in the 1936 movie *Message to Garcia,* his voice was provided by John Carradine.

McLaughlin, Rita
Double for Patty Duke in the TV series *The Patty Duke Show.*

McNulty, Frank
Oakland, California, machinist who spent 49 months in jail for refusing to pay taxes on his $128,000 Irish Sweepstakes winnings. He was released on March 16, 1979.

Meadows, The
Boys' school attended by Timmie Harkinson (Tim Hovey) in the 1956 movie *Toy Tiger.*

Mean Machine

Racing car driven by Dick Dastardly in the TV cartoon series *The Wacky Races*.

Medicine Ball Cabinet

Nickname given to the political advisers of President Herbert Hoover.

Medusa

Planet in the solar system Proxima Centauri and the setting of the 1977 TV series *Star Maidens*.

Meet the Press

Longest-running TV series. It began on November 20, 1947, and is still on the air.

Mellinger, Frederick N.

He established the women's apparel chain *Frederick's of Hollywood* in 1946.

Mellisa

Name of Red Anderson's (Robert Mitchum) pet cow and Boeing 707 aircraft in the 1964 movie *What a Way to Go*. Anderson was killed when he attempted to milk Melrose the bull.

Mellow, Thomas

St. Louis policeman whom boxer Charles "Sonny" Liston was arrested for beating up on August 13, 1960. Liston was given a 9-month sentence.

Melody

Member of the cartoon rock group The Pussycats (voice provided by Cheryl Ladd) in the TV series *Josie and the Pussycats*. Ladd later went on to become one of "Charlie's Angels" in the ABC series of the same name.

Melrose, California

Setting of the TV series *Archer*.

Mel's Sporting Goods Store

Los Angeles store (11425 South Crenshaw Boulevard, Inglewood) robbed by Bill and Emily Harris, with Patty Hearst as lookout, on May 16, 1974. That same day the three kidnapped, and then released, Tom Dean Matthews.

Melvin

Name of the slithering blob on the cover of the first *MAD* comic book (October–November 1952).

Memoirs (Autobiography of the Hon. Galahad Threepwood)

Fictitious book mentioned in numerous novels of P. G. Wodehouse.

Memoirs of a Woman of Pleasure, The

Subtitle of the novel *Fanny Hill* written by John Cleland in Newgate Prison, London, in 1750.

Memorial Hospital

Medical facility in southern California where Jill Danko (Kate Jackson) worked as a nurse in the TV series *The Rookies*.

Memphis Mafia
   Elvis Presley's loyal following of close friends, bodyguards and musicians.
   Members: Bobby "Red" West, Charlie Hodge, George Klein, Nick Adams,
   Jerry Schilling, Marty Lacker, Sonny West, Alan Fortas,* and Joe Esposito.
   Red West appeared as Sgt. Andy Micklin in the TV series *Black Sheep
   Squadron*. Members of the Mafia who were portrayed in the 1979 TV movie
   Elvis: Red West (Robert Gray), Sonny West (Les Lannom) Joe Esposito (Joe
   Mantegna), and Charlie Hodge (Charlie Hodge).
Merchant's Coffee House
   New York City establishment where the New York Stock Exchange was
   formed on May 17, 1792.
Mercury Aviation Company
   Airline company founded in 1919 by director Cecil B. DeMille. It folded in
   1921.
Meredith, James
   First black to attend the University of Mississippi. He enrolled on November
   1, 1961—with the aid of the local police, state troopers, National Guard,
   federal marshals, and FBI.
Merimac
   Town setting of the 1954–1955 TV soap *Road of Love*.
Merlin
   Magician at the court of King Arthur. Movie portrayals; *Knights of the Round
   Table* (1954) Felix Aylmer; *The Sword in the Stone* (1963) voice of Karl
   Swenson; *Sword of Lancelot* (1963) Mark Dignam; *Camelot* (1967) Lawrence
   Naismith; and *Son of Dracula* (1974) Ringo Starr.
Merrill, Carol
   Model who appears on the TV quiz show *Let's Make a Deal*.
Merrill, Frank D.
   (1903–1956) U.S. brigadier general, under Stilwell, who envisioned guerrilla
   warfare tactics against the Japanese on Burma. He was responsible for
   organizing and training Merrill's Marauders, who operated behind enemy
   lines, greatly hindering the Japanese war effort through hit-and-run tactics.
   Merrill was portrayed in the 1962 movie *Merrill's Marauders* by Jeff
   Chandler.
Merrily We Roll Along
   Theme song of Warner Bros.' Merrie Melodies cartoons as well as for the
   radio series *Truth or Consequences*. It was co-written by Eddie Cantor. The
   previous theme song for the cartoons was "Get Happy."
Mertyl and Mike
   Everett family guinea pigs in the TV series *Nanny and the Professor*.

---

*Nephew of former Supreme Court Justice Abe Fortas.

Mesa Grande

Town near Fort Apache in the TV series *The Adventures of Rin-Tin-Tin*.

Meserve, Cyndi

First woman to play in an NCAA-sanctioned varsity basketball game (Pratt Institute, on November 29, 1974).

Messing, Shep

Soccer player for the Oakland Stompers. He became the first American soccer player to make $100,000 a year (1978). Messing once posed nude for a centerfold of *Viva* magazine.

Metaluna

Mutant's home planet in the 1955 movie *This Island Earth*.

Metcalf, Klein, and Associates

Law firm for which John Burton (John Davidson) worked in the TV series *The Girl with Something Extra*.

Methot, Mayo

Third wife of actor Humphrey Bogart (1938–1945). It was Mayo Methot who introduced the song "More Than You Know" in the 1929 musical play *Great Day*. She was portrayed in the 1980 TV movie *Bogie* by Ann Wedgeworth.

Metro Café

Restaurant setting in the TV soap opera *The Guiding Light*.

Metropole

Hotel in Moscow where Ivan (Lou Jacobi) worked as headwaiter in the TV series *Ivan the Terrible*.

Mexican Hat Dance

Record to which Sgt. John M. Stryker (John Wayne) taught a marine to use a bayonet in the 1949 movie *Sands of Iwo Jima*.

Meyers, Ann

First woman to sign a contract in the NBA—she signed with the Indiana Pacers in September 1979, but was cut in the tryouts. Meyers was also the first woman to attend UCLA on a full athletic scholarship.

Michael

Archangel who spoke to Joan of Arc.

Michael's Pub

Manhattan nightclub where Woody Allen plays clarinet with the New Orleans Funeral and Ragtime Orchestra every Monday night. Allen was playing there the night he won the Academy Award for best director and for best screenwriter for *Annie Hall,* which won a total of four Oscars. That very same day—April 3, 1978—John Wayne went into the hospital for open-heart surgery.

Michener, James A.

Highly respected American novelist whose first book about his experiences in

World War II—*Tales of the South Pacific* (1947)—won the Pulitzer Prize and became the basis for the musical *South Pacific*. Michener was portrayed in the 1954 movie *Men of the Fighting Lady* by Louis Calhern.

Mickey Malph
Ralph Malph's (Donny Most) father's name in the TV series *Happy Days*. He was an optometrist and was played by Jack Dodson in several episodes.

Mickey Mouse Park
Name originally considered for Disneyland when it was being planned in 1948.

Mickey Mouse Watch
Watch created in 1933 by Ingersol, originally priced at $3.75. Astronaut Gene Cernan wore one on the Apollo 10 flight.

Midge
Barbie's best friend (Mattel dolls).

Midge Gibson
Eunice's friend (played by Joanne Woodward) in the TV series *The Carol Burnett Show*.

Midnight Man, The
1919 movie serial starring ex-heavyweight boxing champ James J. Corbett.

Midway
Naval battle of June 4–6, 1942. The three American carriers involved were *Enterprise, Hornet,* and *Yorktown.** The four Japanese carriers sunk were: *Kaga, Akagi* (flagship), *Hiryu,* and *Soryu.* It was the first defeat of the Japanese Navy since the 16th century.

Midway Drugs
Boone City store where Fred Derry (Dana Andrews) found a job as clerk after returning from World War II in the 1946 movie *The Best Years of Our Lives*. His weekly pay was $32.50. The store had previously been known as Bullard's Drug Store.

Mig Mad Marine
Name on Maj. John Glenn's F86 fighter during the Korean War.

Mikado, The
Light opera by Gilbert and Sullivan attended by the Pope at the San Francisco Opera House in the 1978 movie *Foul Play*. Cyril Magnin, the man who portrayed the Pope in the film, was not an actor, but the owner of Joseph Magnin's department store in San Francisco.

Mike
Nickname of the first (65-ton) H-bomb. It was exploded near Alamogordo, New Mexico, on October 31, 1952.

---

*Torpedoed on June 6 by the Japanese submarine I-168 and sunk on the 7th.

Mike and Ike

Comic characters created by Rube Goldberg: "Mike and Ike, They Look Alike."

Mildred

Wife of Col. Sherman Potter (Harry Morgan) in the TV series *M*A*S*H*. Her picture always sat on the right side of his desk. (It was actually a photo of actress Spring Byington.)

Miles, General Nelson

U.S. Army general to whom the Apache chief Geronimo surrendered on September 4, 1886. Portrayed by John Litel in the 1956 movie *Comanche*.

Milestone, Lewis

(1895–) American director of such classic films as *All Quiet on the Western Front* (1930) and *Of Mice and Men* (1940). He was portrayed in the 1979 TV movie *The Amazing Mr. Howard Hughes* by Marty Brill.

Miller, Alton Glenn

(1904–1944) Popular dance band leader of the 1930s and early 1940s who joined the U.S. Army to entertain the troops during World War II. In the Army Air Corps his service number was 0-505273. His plane disappeared in the North Sea on December 15, 1944 and he was presumed dead. He appeared with his orchestra in two movies: *Sun Valley Serenade* (1941) and *Orchestra Wives* (1942). He was portrayed by James Stewart in the 1954 movie *The Glenn Miller Story*.

Miller, Herb

Younger brother of Glenn Miller who organized his own orchestra during the early 1940s.

Miller, Marilyn

(1898–1936) Singer and dancer in Broadway musicals and movies. Movie portrayals: *Till the Clouds Roll By* (1946) Judy Garland; *Look for the Silver Lining* (1949) June Haver; and *Ziegfeld: The Man and His Women* (1978 TV) Pamela Peadon. Norma Jean Baker took her screen name, Marilyn Monroe, from Marilyn Miller and President James Monroe.

Miller, Mozelle

Woman whose hands were used for those of Scarlett O'Hara in the close-up of Scarlett pulling a radish from the ground in the 1939 movie *Gone With the Wind*.

Miller, Raymond, and Alma Brown

Couple married by evangelist Marjoe Gortner on January 4, 1949. Marjoe was 4-years old when he performed the ceremony.

Millie and Chilly

Daughter and son of Frosty the Snowman and his wife, Crystal (TV cartoon movie).

Millsburg
Hometown of novelist Cameron Garrett Brooks (Robert Young) on the TV series *Window on Main Street*.

Millville
Home town of Don Sturdy (children's books).

Milo Perrier
Belgian detective played by James Coco in the 1976 movie *Murder by Death*.

Milwaukee Kid
CB handle of Billie Joe McKay (Greg Evigan) in the TV series *B.J. and the Bear*.

Minute Mouse
Sidekick of cartoon hero Courageous Cat.

Miracle Braves
Only baseball team to go from last place on July 4 to a pennant victory. The Boston Braves accomplished this feat in 1914 when they made up a deficit of 15 games.

Miracle Man—Solomon and Sheba
On December 20, 1931, Tyrone Power, Sr., died just after leaving the set of the movie *Miracle Man*. On November 15, 1958, Tyrone Power, Jr., died on the set of the movie *Solomon and Sheba*.

Misha
Russian Olympic mascot bear (1980).

Miss America 1973
Terry Anne Meeuwsen, a member of the New Christy Minstrels since 1969. She entered as Miss Wisconsin.

Miss American Television 1950
Title held by Edie Adams.

Miss Bachrach
Receptionist at the *Daily Planet*, she is seen but infrequently in the TV series *The Adventures of Superman*.

Miss Beth Randall
Jarrod Barkley's wife (played by Sandra Smith) in a single-episode, "Days of Wrath," of the TV series *The Big Valley*. She was killed by Cass Hyatt, an ex-convict.

Miss Bronze 1962
Title held by singer Marilyn McCoo.

Miss California 1969
Title held by 5-foot 11-inch actress Susan Anton. She was second runner-up for Miss America.

Miss Fort Worth 1966
Title held by actress Abby Bradford.

Miss Gwedoline
F-Troop's goat mascot in the TV series *F-Troop*.

Miss Hepburn runs the gamut of emotions from A to B
From a review of Katharine Hepburn's acting by Dorothy Parker.

Miss Idaho 1955
Title won by country singer Judy Lynn.

Mississippi Queen and Delta Queen
Two sternwheelers that presently cruise the Mississippi and Ohio rivers.

Miss Jenny Wren
Cock Robin's sweetheart in *Who Killed Cock Robin?*.

Miss Lea Simmons
Mother of Heath Barkley (Lee Majors) in the TV series *The Big Valley*. She is from the town of Strawberry. Heath's father is Tom Barkley.

Miss Lemon
Detective Mr. Parker Pyne's private secretary (Agatha Christie detective series).

Miss MacTavish
Detective Philo Vance's pet Scottish terrier (novels).

Miss Massachusetts 1924
Title held by actress-comedienne Thelma Todd.

Miss Miami
Title held by actress Veronica Lake. She was disqualified when it was learned that she was underage.

Miss Ohio State
Title held by actress Jean Peters.

Missouri State
College for whose basketball team Darrin Stevens played forward in the TV series *Bewitched*.

Missouri Waltz
Harry S. Truman's favorite song. He played it on the piano—on which Lauren Bacall sat—at the Washington National Press Club in February 1945. The photograph of the scene became very popular with the media.

Miss Piggy
Liberated pig muppet (27-20-32) who is in love with Kermit the Frog in the TV series *The Muppet Show*. She was born in Hog Springs, Iowa, and her voice is provided by Frank Oz. In the 1979 movie *The Muppet Movie* Miss Piggy's singing voice was dubbed by Johnny Mathis. Miss Piggy was educated at Miss Worthington's Conservatory for Piglets. She is a crew member of the spaceship *Swinetrek* in episodes of "Pigs in Space" on *The Muppet Show*. Frank Oz modeled Miss Piggy after Loretta "Hot Lips" Swit of TV's *M*A*S*H* fame.

Miss Pro Tennis 1968
Title held by Farrah Fawcett.

Miss Teasedale
Snooks Higgins's schoolteacher in the radio series *Baby Snooks*.

Miss Teenage America 1961
TV soap (*The Young and the Restless*) actress Janice Lynde.

Miss U.S.A. 1952
Title held by actress Jackie Loughery, the second wife of Jack Webb.

Miss Utah
Title held by actress Marie Windsor.

Miss Viareggio, Italy—1959
Beauty contest title held by actress Elke Sommer (then named Elke Schletz).

Miss Worthington's Conservatory for Piglets
Oxford school where Miss Piggy was educated in the TV series *The Muppet Show*.

Missy
Name of Robert Taylor's $75,000 Beechcraft, named for his wife, Barbara Stanwyck.

Mr. and Mrs. Blandings
Radio series about Jim and Muriel Blandings starring Cary Grant and his wife Betsy Drake. The characters originally came from the 1948 movie *Mr. Blandings Builds His Dream House*, in which Grant co-starred with Myrna Loy.

Mr. America
Secret identity of cowboy Tex Thomson. Debut: *Action Comics* No. 33* (February 1941).

Mr. Bailey
Augustus Smith's boss (comic strip *Smitty*).

Mr. Barnaby Bibbs
Winnie Winkle's boss (comic strip *Winnie Winkle*).

Mr. Binkie
Scottie dog in the 1939 movie *The Light That Failed* (based on Rudyard Kipling's first novel).

Mr. Butler
Name given to the Shetland pony belonging to 4-year-old Bonnie Blue Butler, daughter of Scarlett and Rhett Butler, in the movie *Gone With the Wind*. Bonnie Blue died from a broken neck when she fell off the pony while attempting to jump a hurdle.

Mr. Chairman
Gilbreth family dog, bought for $5, in the 1950 movie *Cheaper by the Dozen*.

*Actually introduced in *Action Comics* No. 1 (June 1938), but as a slightly different character.

Mr. Cholesterol
Overweight man, played by Jack Eagle, in the Fleischmann Margarine TV commercials.

Mr. Henderson
Sally Rogers's (Rose Marie) pet cat in the TV series *The Dick Van Dyke Show.*

Mr. Mefooski
Fictitious Jewish character whom Walter Winchell often wrote about in his newspaper column.

Mr. Mind
Evil caterpillar nemesis of Captain Marvel (comic books). He was convicted for the murder of 186,744 people. Debut: *Captain Marvel* No. 22 (April 1942).

Mr. Muggs
Chimpanzee mascot of Jim Jones's People's Temple in Guyana.

Mister Roberts and Raintree County
Successful novels that were made into movies: *Mister Roberts* in 1955 and *Raintree County* in 1957. Ross Lockridge, Jr., the author of *Raintree County,* and Tom Heggen, the author of *Mister Roberts,* both committed suicide.

Mr. T. Bolt
Man who manages detective Nick Carter's office on Liberty Street in New York (detective novels).

Mr. Television
Nickname of comedian Milton Berle. He debuted on TV in 1929 on a Chicago closed-circuit show.

Mr. Tudball
Mrs. Wanda Wiggin's (Carol Burnett) Swedish boss, played by Tim Conway, in the TV series *The Carol Burnett Show.*

Mr. Withers
Tillie Jones's boss (comic strip *Tillie the Toiler*).

Mr. Yuk
Symbol of the National Poison Center: stick-on faces that indicate to children they shouldn't drink the liquid inside certain bottles.

Mrs. Eskale
Detective Bulldog Drummond's nanny when he was a child (novels).

Mrs. Emmie Webster
Granny character in Warner Bros. cartoons.

Mrs. Housing Development of the United States
Beauty contest conducted for a time on the TV series *You Bet Your Life*.

Mrs. Kissel
Stooped and shortsighted little old lady who was the servant of the Catholic priest in the 1979 movie *10*. She was played by Nedra Volz.

Mrs. Malaprop
Character in Richard Sheridan's 1775 comedy *The Rivals*. She was noted for her misapplication of words (origin of the word *malapropism*).

Mizell, Wilmer (Vinegar Bend)
St. Louis Cardinal pitcher who became a U.S. representative from North Carolina (1963–1974).

Mitchell, Jackie
Female softball pitcher who in an exhibition game in Chattanooga, Tennessee, on April 2, 1931, struck out Babe Ruth and Lou Gehrig. She became the first woman pitcher in organized baseball when she joined the Chattanooga baseball team of the Southern Association. However, she was never allowed to play in a league game.

Mitchell, John
President Nixon's attorney general who was sent to prison (Watergate scandal). Mitchell was portrayed in the 1979 TV miniseries *Blind Ambition* by John Randolph.

Mjolnor
Thor's magic hammer that gives him his super powers (comic books).

Moanin' Low
Song that Gaye Dawn (Claire Trevor) was forced to sing by Johnny Rocco (Edward G. Robinson) in the 1948 movie *Key Largo*.

Moby Dick and Captain Bligh
Nicknames of Phyllis Diller's fictional in-laws in her comedy routines. Her actual in-laws sued her for $100,000 for making them the butt of her jokes. They settled out of court.

Modesto, California
Setting of the 1973 movie *American Graffiti*, actually filmed in Petaluma, California.

Modigliani, Amedeo
(1884–1920) Italian painter and sculptor who was portrayed in the 1957 movie *Montparnasse 19* by Gérard Philippe.

Mohican
American ship that rescued the five survivors of Transoceanic Airways Clipper flight 4, which was shot down by the German destroyer, *Bon Sheen* 300 miles off the English coast in the 1940 movie *Foreign Correspondent*.

Mojo
85-foot cabin cruiser hit by a 25-foot wave on the journey from Morro Bay to Monterey on January 17, 1978. The vessel was chartered by actor George C. Scott, who was on his way to the Bing Crosby Pro-Am Golf Tournament. The Coast Guard cutter *Cape Hedge* came to the rescue.

Molotov, Vyacheslav Mikhailovich
Russian statesman who became prominent during the Russian Revolution of

October 1917. He presided over the Anglo-Soviet conference in Moscow in September 1941. The homemade bomb the Molotov cocktail is named in his honor. He was portrayed by Gene Lockhart in the 1943 movie *Mission to Moscow*.

Mona
Chimpanzee that is Cmdr. Christopher "Kit" Draper's (Paul Mantee) traveling companion in the 1964 movie *Robinson Crusoe on Mars*.

Monck, Charles
Inventor of the monkey wrench.

Money Talks, So Listen!
Book written by the world's foremost economist, Professor Filthy von Lucre, played by Sid Caesar in the TV series *Your Show of Shows*.

Monkey Face
Pet name that Johnnie (Cary Grant) calls his wife Lina (Joan Fontaine) in the 1941 Hitchcock movie *Suspicion*.

Monster That Devoured Cleveland, The
Maynard G. Krebs's (Bob Denver) all-time favorite movie in the TV series *The Many Loves of Dobie Gillis*.

Monstro
Whale in which Pinocchio and Gepetto were trapped in the 1940 Walt Disney movie *Pinocchio*.

Montana State (Golden Bobcats)
Only American college to have lost its entire 11-man football team (1940–1941) in World War II.

Monte Cristo No. One
Brand of expensive Havana cigars that FBI agent Melvin Purvis smoked over the bodies of the following criminals whom he tracked down: "Machine Gun" George Kelly (captured); Wilbur Underhill (killed); "Handsome Jack" Klutas (killed); "Baby Face" (Charles Arthur Floyd) Nelson (killed); and John Dillinger (killed). The cigars had been given to Purvis by agent Ray Caffrey, who was killed in the Kansas City Massacre.

Monte's Pink Flamingo Lounge
Tavern where Mary Jo Rose Foster (Bette Midler) made her debut as a singer in the 1979 movie *The Rose*.

Monterey
Light aircraft carrier on which Gerald Ford served during World War II.

Montez, Lola
(1818–1861) Irish dancer (born Eliza Gilbert) who was portrayed by Yvonne De Carlo in the 1948 movie *Black Bart*.

Montgomery, Sir Bernard Law
(1887–1976) British field marshal during World War II who defeated German Gen. Rommel (the Desert Fox) at El Alamein in 1943. Movie portrayals: *The*

Longest Day (1962) Trevor Reid; *Patton* (1970) Michael Bates; *Ike* (1979) TV miniseries) Ian Richardson and *Churchill and the Generals* (1981 TV) Ian Richardson.

Monti, Carlotta
W. C. Fields' mistress from 1932 until his death in 1946. She was portrayed by Valerie Perrine in the 1976 movie *W. C. Fields and Me*.

Monumental Pictures
Hollywood movie company headed by R. F. Simpson (Millard Mitchell) in the 1952 movie *Singin' in the Rain*.

Moody Blues
First rock band to perform in the People's Republic of China.

Moon Lake House
Saratoga Springs, New York, hotel where potato chips were first served in 1853. The inventor of the product was George Crum, an Indian cook.

Moonlight on the Meadows
Original title of the song "A Kiss to Build a Dream On" (words by Bert Kalmar and Oscar Hammerstein II, music by Harry Ruby).

Moon River
Academy Award winning song of 1961, composed by Henry Mancini for the movie *Breakfast at Tiffany's*. It was Andy Williams' theme song on TV. Johnny Mercer wrote the lyrics.

Moonshine Sonata
Frog that lives in the Okefenokee Swamp in Walt Kelly's comic strip *Pogo*.

Moore, Grace
Noted opera singer. She was portrayed by Kathryn Grayson in her early years (1917–1928) in the 1953 movie *So This Is Love*.

Moore, Scotty
Lead guitarist for Elvis Presley from Presley's recording debut in 1954 until 1968. Scotty Moore also served for a short time as Elvis's (first) manager. He was portrayed in the 1979 TV movie *Elvis* by James Canning.

Moran, George "Bugs"
(1893–1957) American bootlegger, robber, and murderer who belonged to the notorious North Side gang in Chicago. Moran died of cancer in Leavenworth prison. He was portrayed in the 1967 movie *The St. Valentine's Day Massacre* by Ralph Meeker.

More, Sir Thomas
(1478–1535) British statesman who sided with the Catholic Church in its opposition to King Henry VIII's divorce from Catherine of Aragon. More was decapitated and his head put on public display on London Bridge. Movie portrayals: *A Man for All Seasons* (1966) Paul Scofield; and *Anne of the Thousand Days* (1969) William Squire.

More than a Woman

Song by the Bee Gees to which Tony Mareno (John Travolta) and Stephanie Magano (Karen Lynn Gorney) danced for the contest at the 2001 Disco in the 1977 movie *Saturday Night Fever*. In the same film the song was sung another time, by a different group, the Tavarres.

Morgan, Helen

(1900–1941) American singer and actress who once held the title of Miss Illinois. She was portrayed in the 1957 movie *The Helen Morgan Story* by Ann Blyth, and on the May 16, 1957, *Playhouse 90* TV production "The Helen Morgan Story" by Polly Bergen.

Morgan, Sir Henry

(1635–1688) British buccaneer who was appointed acting governor of Jamaica in 1680. Movie portrayals: *The Black Swan* (1942) Laird Cregar; and *Blackbeard, The Pirate* (1952) Torin Thatcher.

Moroni

Angel that first visited Morman leader Joseph Smith on September 22, 1827.

Morris, Frank Lee

Leader of the trio of convicts who became the only men to successfully escape from Alcatraz on January 11, 1960. The other two men were brothers, John and Clarence Anglin. Frank Morris was portrayed by Clint Eastwood in the 1979 movie *Escape from Alcatraz,* and by Ed Lauter in the 1980 TV movie *Alcatraz: The Whole Shocking Story.*

Morris, Kathy

22-year-old singer who, while undergoing brain surgery in 1976, experienced complications and brain damage. She was portrayed in the 1979 TV movie *Seizure: The Story of Kathy Morris* by Penelope Milford (Leonard Nimoy portrayed Dr. Connought).

Morticia Frump

Morticia's (Carolyn Jones) maiden name in the TV series *The Addams Family.*

Morton, William Thomas Green

(1819–1868) American dentist who was the first to use ether as an anesthetic (1846). He was portrayed by Joel McCrea in the 1944 movie *The Great Moment*.

Moses

Old Testament figure who led the Jewish people out of Egypt to the Promised Land of Palestine. Portrayals: *The Ten Commandments* (1923) Theodore Roberts: *The Ten Commandments* (1956) Charlton Heston (Fraser Heston as an infant); *The Story of Mankind* (1957) Francis X. Bushman; *Moses, the Lawgiver* (1975 TV miniseries) Burt Lancaster; and TV series *Heroes of the Bible* John Marley.

Moses, Anna Mary Robertson
Popular American painter, called Grandma Moses, who began painting at the age of 78 in 1938. She died after raising 10 children at the age of 101.

Moshulu
Tramp steamer that transported Vito Andolini (a/k/a Don Vito Corleone), the Godfather, to the United States in Mario Puzo's novel *The Godfather.*

Motel Inn
Very first motel to open (December 12, 1925), in San Luis Obispo, California).

Mother
(MU/TH/UR 6000) Shipboard computer aboard the spacecraft *Nostromo* in the 1979 movie *Alien.*

Mother Goose
Walter Eckland's (Cary Grant) radio code name in the 1964 movie *Father Goose.*

Mother Jones
(1830–1930) Name of Mary Harris Jones, who was a labor leader into her 80s. She was, in fact, arrested for union activities at the age of 82. *Mother Jones* magazine is named in her honor.

Mt. Calvary
Hill in Jerusalem where Jesus was crucified.

Mountain Climbing: What Do You Need It For?
Leading book on mountain climbing written by the world's expert, Professor Sigmund von Fraidy Katz (Sid Caesar), in the TV series *Your Show of Shows.*

Mount Pilot
Town 12 miles down the road from Mayberry in the TV series *The Andy Griffith Show.*

Mouse, The
Dance routine and song made popular by Soupy Sales.

Movin' On
Theme of the TV series *Movin' On,* sung by Merle Haggard.

Movin' On Up
Theme song and title of the autobiography of gospel singer Mahalia Jackson.

Mozart Café
Harry Lime's favorite nightclub in the 1950 movie *The Third Man.*

Mudd, Samuel
Doctor who treated John Wilkes Booth's broken leg, which the actor received tripping over an American flag after shooting Abraham Lincoln. Dr. Mudd was sentenced to life imprisonment and later pardoned (after serving 3 years, 7 months, 12 days): Thus the expression, "his name is mud." CBS Newscaster Roger Mudd is a distant relative of Dr. Mudd. In 1980 President

MUDD, HARCOURT FENTON
HARRY MUDDS REAL NAME - STAR TREK

Carter exonerated Dr. Mudd of all guilt. Mudd was portrayed by Warner Baxter in the 1936 movie *The Prisoner of Shark Island,* and by Dennis Weaver in the 1980 TV movie *The Ordeal of Dr. Mudd.*

Muffitt II

Boxey's (Noah Hathaway) pet daggitt drone in the TV series *Battlestar Galactica,* played by a 4-year-old chimpanzee named Evolution (nicknamed Eve).

Muffy

Laura Manion's (Lee Remick) pet dog, which she taught to carry a flashlight, in the 1959 movie *Anatomy of a Murder.*

Muller, Heinrich

(1896–   ) Head of the Gestapo who was largely responsible for that organization's high degree of efficiency and ruthlessness, although Muller himself was a mild-mannered man. At the end of the war he escaped and is believed to still be alive and working for the Russians. Muller was portrayed in the 1978 TV movie *Holocaust* by Anthony Haygarth. ·

Mummy, The

Muhammad Ali's appellation for George Foreman.

Munchkin Coroner

Official who declares of the Wicked Witch of the East, "She's not only merely dead, she's really most sincerely dead." The character was played by Meinhardt Raabe, who in the 1930s played Oscar the Wiener Man for Oscar Hot Dogs.

Muncie, Indiana

Setting of the 1977 movie *Close Encounters of the Third Kind.*

Municipal Flat Block 18A Linear North

Alex and his family's home in the 1971 movie *A Clockwork Orange.*

Murphy

Singer John Denver's pet dog, who appears on the back cover of the *John Denver's Greatest Hits* album.

Murphy, Audie

(1924–1971) Most decorated soldier in World War II. His 1949 autobiography was titled *To Hell and Back.* Murphy portrayed himself (Gordon Gebert portrayed him as a boy) in the 1954 movie made from his book. Before he joined the Army, Murphy was turned down by both the Marines and the Navy because of his size and age. His 12 medals, all won by the age of 20, were: Medal of Honor; Distinguished Service Cross; Médaille Militaire (France); European, African, and Middle East Campaign; Purple Heart (2 oak-leaf clusters); Legion of Merit; Silver Star (oak-leaf cluster); Bronze Star; Good Conduct Medal; Victory Medal; Croix de Guerre with palm (Belgium); and American Campaign Medal. After the war Murphy starred in a number of movies, including *The Red Badge of Courage* (1951). He also played Tom

"Whispering" Smith in the 1961 TV series *Whispering Smith*. Audie Murphy was the co-writer (with Scott Turner) of the song "Shutters and Boards."

Murphy, Calvin
Shortest basketball player in the NBA (1978) at 5-feet 9-inches. In 1964 he came in second in the National Baton Twirling contest held at the World's Fair in New York.

Murrieta, Joaquin
(1832–1853) California desperado and stagecoach robber supposedly killed by Texas Ranger Harry Love, who cut off and displayed his head. Movie portrayals: *The Robin Hood of El Dorado* (1936) Warner Baxter; *The Last Rebel* (1960 Mexican) Carlos Thompson; and *Firebrand* (1962) Valentin De Vargas.

Musial, Stan
First major league player to hit 5 homers in a double header (May 2, 1954). (Nate Colbert of the Padres became the second on August 1, 1972.) Musial was the only National League player to lead the league in singles, doubles, and triples. Ty Cobb did so for the American League.

Music to Watch Girls By
Former theme song of Pepsi Cola TV commercials. It became a hit song by the Bob Crewe Generation in 1967.

Mussolini, Benito
(1883–1945) Fascist dictator who led Italy into war on the German side in 1940. He was killed by Italian partisans on April 28, 1945. Movie portrayals: *The Great Dictator* (1940) Jack Oakie (as Napaloni); *Star-Spangled Rhythm* (1942) Paul Porcasi; *The Devil With Hitler* (1942) Joe Devlin; *The Nasty Nuisance* (1943) Joe Devlin; *The Miracle of Morgan's Creek* (1944) Joe Devlin; and *Mussolini: Last Days* (1974) Rod Steiger and *Lion of the Desert* (1981) Rod Steiger. Romano Mussolini, son of Benito, is the brother-in-law of actress Sophia Loren.

Mustang Ranch
Brothel outside of Reno, Nevada, that is probably the best-known legal house of prostitution in the United States. It was at the Mustang Ranch that South American heavyweight boxer Oscar Bonavena was shot to death in May 1976. He was killed by security guard Willard Rose Brymer.

Mutual Broadcasting System
Radio network, originally called Quality Group Network, that linked the radio stations WOR (New York), WXYZ (Detroit), WLW (Cincinnati), and WGN (Chicago). It was formed in 1933 to broadcast *The Lone Ranger,* which originated on WXYZ.

My Answer
Rev. Billy Graham's syndicated daily newspaper column.

Mycroft
Computer in Robert A. Heinlein's novel *The Moon Is a Harsh Mistress*.

My Dream
Theme song of Merv Griffin's TV show, composed by Merv.

My First Days in the White House
Book that Senator (ex-Louisiana Governor) Huey Pierce Long was writing at the time of his assassination in 1935.

My Funny Valentine
Song written in 1937 by Lorenz Hart and Richard Rodgers. It can be heard in the following movies: *Babes in Arms* (1939); *Gentlemen Marry Brunettes* (1955); and *Pal Joey* (1957). This was the favorite song of Ted Baxter (Ted Knight) and Georgette Franklin (Georgia Engel) when they were dating (TV series *The Mary Tyler Moore Show*). It was also the song that George Webber (Dudley Moore) played at Truman Capote's party in the 1979 movie *10*.

My Heart Stood Still
Song composed in 1927 by Lorenz Hart and Richard Rodgers. It can be heard in the following films; *A Connecticut Yankee* (1931); *Never Say Goodbye* (1946); *Humoresque* (1947); *Words and Music* (1948); and *Parrish* (1961).

My Kingdom for Love
Argentinian radio soap opera starring Eva Duarte (Eva Peron), beginning in 1943.

My Life as a Director, or: How to Live on $22.50 a week
Autobiography of the world's foremost movie director, Professor Kurt von Closeup (Sid Caesar), in the TV series *Your Show of Shows*.

My Melancholy Baby
Song composed by George A. Norton and Ernie Burnett in 1912. It can be heard in the following movies: *The Birth of the Blues* (1941); *Minstrel Man* (1944); *Scarlet Street* (1945); and *A Star Is Born* (1954).

Myron
White mouse belonging to Greg Brady as part of his science project in the TV series *The Brady Bunch*.

Myron
Dick and Dora Charleston's (David Niven and Maggie Smith) pet white dog in the 1976 movie *Murder by Death*.

My Sheba
Winning horse in the 1953 Dean Martin-Jerry Lewis movie *Money From Home*.

Mystery Machine
Automobile belonging to the teenagers in the TV cartoon series *Scooby-Doo, Where Are You?*

My Sweet Lord
1970 hit composed by former Beatle George Harrison, first recorded on Apple records by Billy Preston. Harrison was successfully sued for plagiarism because "My Sweet Lord" was a copy of the 1968 Chiffon's hit "He's So Fine."

N

9 Days Old
Age of "The Naughty Lady of Shady Lane," 1954 hit record by the Ames Brothers.

9 Lupine Road
Lowell, New Hampshire, house in which author Jack Kerouac was born on March 12, 1922.

19-Gun Salute
British tribute accorded Winston Churchill at his funeral in January 1965. Previously, the most given to a commoner was 17 guns.

19-19-19
Measurements of Popeye's 29-year-old girlfriend, Olive Oyl.

93
Number worn by author Eric Segal as a competitor in the 1967 Boston Marathon.

93 Deathrow
Address of Ajax Mortuary in (Bob) Hudson and (Ron) Landry comedy routine.

94
Number of living clones of Adolf Hitler created by Dr. Josef Mengele (Gregory Peck) in the 1978 movie *The Boys from Brazil* (based on the Ira Levin movie of the same name). Jeremy Black played four of them.

94 Baker Street
London address of the Beatles' Apple Boutique (open from December 5, 1967, to July 30, 1968).

97 St. George's Square
  London address of Peter Wimsey's detective agency (novels). His secretary was Miss Alexandra Katherine Climpson.

921
  Number on the Erie and Lackawanna Railroad train engine in the 1903 silent movie *The Great Train Robbery*.

932 A.D.
  Opening date of the 1979 movie *Monty Python and the Holy Grail*.

965 North Parkway
  San Francisco address of Pallucci's Italian Restaurant, over which Doris Martin (Doris Day) lived in Apartment 207 in the TV series *The Doris Day Show*.

999
  Emergency telephone number in Britain used to call the local police.

1901
  Time setting of Johnny Horton's 1960 hit song "North to Alaska."

1904
  Setting of the 1944 musical movie *Meet Me in St. Louis*.

1905
  Year in which the 1971 movie *Fiddler on the Roof* was set.

1910
  Year the train engine was built that plunged into the Kwai River when the bridge blew up in the 1957 movie *The Bridge on the River Kwai*.

1911
  Time setting of Cher's 1973 hit record "Half Breed" and the 1938 movie *Alexander's Ragtime Band*.

1911 6th Street
  Lubbock, Texas, address of the house where Charles Hardin Holley (Buddy Holly) was born on September 7, 1936.

1912
  Year in which the musical movies *The Music Man* (1962), *My Fair Lady* (1964), and *Porgy and Bess* (1959) were set.

1914
  Time setting of the TV series *Nichols*.

1917
  Time setting of the 1978 movie *Pretty Baby*.

1922
  Time setting of the 1935 movie *The Informer*.

1927
  Time setting of the 1969 Elvis Presley movie *The Trouble with Girls*.

1942
  Time setting of the TV series *Wonder Woman* during its 1st year. During the 2nd season it was updated to contemporary times.

1945

Year at the opening of the 1972 movie *The Godfather*. The location was Long Island. 1945 was also the time setting of the 1977 movie *New York, New York*.

1951

Year in which Tommy Walker became deaf, dumb, and blind in the rock opera and 1975 movie *Tommy*.

1960

Setting of the 1924 movie *The Last Man on Earth*.

1960 Olympic American Basketball Team

U.S. Gold Medal team: Jerry Lucas, Darrall Imhoff, Walt Bellamy, Oscar Robertson, Adrian Smith, Jerry West, Terry Dischinger, and Bob Boozer. John Havlicek was an alternate. All went on to play in the NBA; Robertson, Lucas, Bellamy, and Dischinger became Rookies of the Year.

1970

Setting of the 1933 movie *Men Must Fight*.

1981

Time setting (November 16) of the 1977 movie *Twilight's Last Gleaming*.

1983

Time setting of two TV series: *Land of the Giants* and *Voyage to the Bottom of the Sea*.

1984

Futuristic novel written by George Orwell in 1948 (he just changed the 4 and 8 around).

1987

Year in which Capt. Buck Rogers departed Cape Canaveral in the 1979 movie *Buck Rogers in the 25th Century*. He slept for 504 years.

1998

Setting of the 1979 movie *Americathon*.

9047 and 89691

Prisoner numbers of Duffy and Sandohval, the two inmates who were paged during the recording of Johnny Cash's 1968 album *Johnny Cash at Folsom Prison*.

$99,000 Answer, The

Quiz show on which Ralph Kramden (Jackie Gleason) appeared, only to lose when he failed to recognize the tune "Swanee River," in the TV series *The Honeymooners*.

N23S

Call sign of the Stevens Corporation Boeing 747 that became submerged (27° N-65° W) in the 1977 movie *Airport '77*.

N144PA

Call sign of the Hawker aircraft owned by entertainer Paul Anka. The aircraft can be seen landing in the 1979 movie *The Electric Horseman*.

N803LJ
Derek Flint's (James Coburn) private Lear jet in the 1966 movie *Our Man Flint*.

N882Y
Red Waco airplane won (actually flown by Frank Tallman) by Jonas Cord, Jr. (George Peppard), in a poker game in the 1964 movie *The Carpetbaggers*.

N3149Y
Piper aircraft in which Rocky Marciano died when it crashed on August 31, 1969.

N3220Y
Call numbers of the aircraft on the TV series *Ripcord*.

N9860E
Call letters of Thomas Crown's (Steve McQueen) yellow glider in the 1968 movie *The Thomas Crown Affair*.

N46091
Registration number of the biplane crop duster that attacked Roger Thornhill (Cary Grant) at Prairie Stop in the 1959 movie *North by Northwest*. The plane crashed into a Magnum Oil Co. gas truck.

N51071
Registration number of the DC-3 that crashed on December 13, 1977, killing 29 people, including the University of Evansville basketball team (the Aces). The pilot was a Vietnamese, Ty Van Pham; the co-pilot a Cuban, Gaston Ruiz.

N59492
Registration of the helicopter from which Sonny Hooper (Burt Reynolds) jumped to the ground in the 1978 movie *Hooper*. The stunt man in the 232-foot fall was A. J. Bakunas.

NBC's Best Sellers
1976 TV miniseries that featured four best-selling novels: *Captains and the Kings* (by Taylor Caldwell); *Once an Eagle* (by Anton Myrer); *Seventh Avenue* (by Norman Bogner); and *The Rhineman Exchange* (by Robert Ludlam).

NBC Nightly News
The theme song for the news show was composed by Henry Mancini.

NC500
Call sign of the ill-fated DC-7 in which Roberto Clemente met his death on December 31, 1972.

NC14700
Call letters of Steve Collins's (James Cagney) single-engine airplane in the 1941 movie *The Bride Came C.O.D.*

NR7952
Amelia Earhart's red Lockheed Vega, now hanging in the National Air and Space Museum.

NARA
National Association of Recording Artists, an organization formed in 1936 whose first president was Fred Waring.

N.A.S.C.A.R.
National Association for Stock Car Auto Racing, founded in 1947 by Bill France, Jr.

Nadsat
Slang word coined by author Anthony Burgess for his novel (also a 1971 movie) *A Clockwork Orange*.

Naitamba
3,000-acre South Pacific island, 165 miles northeast of Suva, purchased by actor Raymond Burr, where he now lives.

Naked at Dawn
Lauralee "Lauri" Brooks's (Jaime Lyn Bauer) first published novel in the TV serial *The Young and the Restless*.

Naked Came the Stranger
Best-selling novel by Penelope Ashe (pseudonym of 25 reporters at *Newsday*, including two-time Pulitzer Prize–winning reporter Gene Goltz).

Naked Edge, The
1961 movie for which audiences were barred from entering theaters during the last 13 minutes. It was Gary Cooper's last movie appearance.

Naked Jungle, The
1954 George Pal movie based on the classic Carl Stephenson short story and radio drama *Leiningen vs. the Ants*.

Nancy Blues
Theme song of the TV series *The Nancy Walker Show*.

Nanette
One of the two German shepherd puppies that Corp. Lee Duncan found in a fox hole in Europe on September 15, 1918, and adopted. One, Nanette, died on the voyage to the United States. The pup that survived was renamed Rin-Tin-Tin.

Nanu, Nanu
Greetings of Mork (Robin Williams) in the TV series *Mork and Mindy*.

Napoleon
Orangutan at the London zoo that relieved himself on Prince Philip in May 1968.

Napoleon III
(1808–1873) (Charles) Louis Napoleon Bonaparte, emperor of the French. Movie portrayals: *The Story of Louis Pasteur* (1936) Walter Kingsford; *Juarez* (1939) Claude Rains; and *A Dispatch from Reuters* (1940) Walter Kingsford.

Napoleon and Josephine
Flo Addams's (Ann Sothern) two dogs in the 1940 movie *Brother Orchid*.

Nash

First automobile to offer seat belts (1950).

Nat

New York City, Third Avenue, bar frequented by Don Birnam (Ray Milland) in the 1945 movie *The Lost Weekend*. The owner, Nat, was played by Howard da Silva. Scenes were actually filmed at P.J. Clark's on Third Avenue.

Natasha

Name written on the side of the Buckeye bulldozer that Lt. Cmdr. Wedge Donovan (John Wayne) rode to his death in the 1944 movie *The Fighting Seabees*.

Nathaniel Crosby, SS

Liberty ship launched in 1944. It was christened after Bing Crosby's grandfather, a pioneer sailor of the China–West Coast route and one of the founders of Portland, Oregon, and Olympia, Washington.

National Bowling Hall of Fame

Located in Greendale, Wisconsin.

National Cowgirl Hall of Fame

Located in Hereford, Texas.

National Motors Corporation (NMC)

Detroit automobile manufacturing firm in Arthur Hailey's *Wheels* (made into a TV miniseries in 1978). The firm's phone number was 313-961-9999.

National Soaring Museum

Located at Harris Hill, Elmira, New York.

National Track and Field Hall of Fame

Located in Charleston, West Virginia.

National Trivia Hall of Fame

Located in Lincoln, Nebraska. The first inductee (1980) was Robert L. Ripley.

National Wrestling Hall of Fame

Located in Stillwater, Oklahoma.

Nature Boy

242-pound wrestler Buddy Rogers, who was popular on TV in the 1950s.

Nature Boy

Song written in 1946 by Eden Ahbez and first recorded by Nat King Cole. It was the first song ever to enter radio's *The Hit Parade* at the No. 1 position (1948).

Navy Blue and Gold

Official song of the U.S. Naval Academy at Annapolis.

Nebraska, USS

Battleship setting of the 1927 musical play *Hit the Deck*. When the play was performed in London, the ship became the HMS *Inscrutable*.

Nebula M–78
Home of Ultraman (secret identity of Iota), located in the 40th Galaxy, in TV series *Ultraman*.

Nellie
Quick Draw McGraw's horse (TV cartoons).

Nelly Kelly
Female fan mentioned in the 1908 song "Take Me Out to the Ball Game."

Nelson, Horatio
(1758–1805) British war hero who in 1801 was named Viscount of the British Navy. He died at the Battle of Trafalgar. Movie portrayals: *Nelson* (1926) Cedric Hardwicke; *Lloyds of London* (1936) John Burton; *That Hamilton Woman* (1942) Laurence Olivier; *Lady Hamilton* (1968) Richard Johnson; and *The Nelson Affair* (1973) Peter Finch.

Nero
(A.D. 37–68) Nero Claudius Caesar Drusus Germanicus, Roman emperor from 54 to 68. After years of persecuting Christians, he committed suicide. Movie portrayals: *Quo Vadis?* (1925) Emil Jannings; *The Sign of the Cross* (1932) Charles Laughton; *Quo Vadis?* (1951) Peter Ustinov; and *The Story of Mankind* (1957) Peter Lorre.

Ness, Elliot
U.S. Treasury agent who fought against Al Capone and other organized crime bosses during the Prohibition era. Ness was portrayed in the TV series *The Untouchables* by Robert Stack.

Nevada, USS
Battleship berthed at Pearl Harbor on December 7, 1941, when the Japanese attacked. The ship's band was playing "The Star Spangled Banner" as the attack began. Future actor Leif Erickson was blown off the ship when a bomb exploded nearby. The *Nevada* was later used as the target ship during the Bikini A-bomb tests. It was the only battleship that was present at both Pearl Harbor and at the Normandy landings on D Day (June 6, 1944).

New Bulletin
Newspaper for which Ann Mitchell (Barbara Stanwyck) worked as a columnist in the 1940 movie *Meet John Doe*. The original *Bulletin* was established in 1862.

New Caledonia
South Pacific setting of the TV series *Broadside*.

New Canaan
Connecticut hometown setting of the 1975 TV series *The Montefuscos*.

Newcombe, Don
Only baseball player to have been named: Rookie of the Year (1949); Most Valuable Player (1956); and Cy Young Award Winner (1956).

New Congress Club
Hawaiian nightclub where prostitute Alma (alias Lorraine) (played by Donna Reed) worked in the 1953 movie *From Here to Eternity*. In the novel it was called the New Congress Hotel.

New Era Pictures
Movie studio in the 1976 movie *Won Ton Ton, The Dog Who Saved Hollywood*.

New Haven, Connecticut
First city to utilize a telephone directory (1878). It listed 50 names.

New Moon Café
Restaurant setting on the TV soap opera *The Edge of Night*.

New Orleans
Setting of the following movies: *Panic in the Streets* (1950); *A Streetcar Named Desire* (1951); *Walk on the Wild Side* (1962); *Hotel* (1967); *WUSA* (1970); *The Drowning Pool* (1977); *Pretty Baby* (1978).

Newsboy's Sexlet
Vaudeville singing trio comprised of George Jessel, Eddie Cantor, and Walter Winchell. When Chicago Mayor Anton Cermak was assassinated in 1933, years after the group split, George Jessel and Eddie Cantor were performing at the theater a few blocks away, and Walter Winchell was the first reporter to reach Giuseppe Zangara, the assassin.

Newsom, Bob
Major league baseball player who holds the record for being traded. He was traded 16 times.

Newton, Issac
(1642–1727) English mathematician. According to Voltaire, Newton devised his theory of universal gravitation after watching an apple fall in his garden. Newton was portrayed in the 1957 movie *The Story of Mankind* by Harpo Marx.

New York Banner
Newspaper owned by Gail Wynand (Raymond Massey) in the 1948 movie *The Fountainhead*.

New York Bulletin
Newspaper for which Nick Alexander (Nick Adams) worked as a reporter in the TV series *Saints and Sinners*.

New York Daily News
Newspaper that employed the unnamed reporter who snapped the picture of Ruth Snyder being executed in the electric chair in January 1928. He had a camera strapped to his ankle. James Cagney used the same method to take a picture in Sing Sing Prison in the 1933 movie *Picture Snatcher*.

New York Globe
Newspaper for which Danny Taylor (Harry Guardino) was a reporter in the TV series *The Reporter.*

New York in a Blizzard
Movie being shown in the first movie theater, opened in Los Angeles on April 2, 1902.

Nicholas II
(1868–1918) Czar of Russia who with his family was executed by the Bolsheviks at Ekaterinburg in July 1918. Movie portrayals: *Rasputin and the Empress* (1932) Ralph Morgan; and *Nicholas and Alexandra* (1971) Michael Jayston.

Nichols' Department Store
Store where a man is hanging out of a window in the record album *Inside Shelly Berman*

Nick Stone
Name of the undercover agent played by Mike Connors in the TV series *Tightrope.*

Nicklaus, Jack
Professional golfer who in 1978 landed a 1,358-pound marlin, the biggest fish caught off Australia that year.

Nick's
San Francisco saloon on Pacific Street where Nick (William Bendix) was the bartender in the 1948 movie *The Time of Your Life.*

Nightingale, Florence
(1820–1910) English nurse in the Crimean War who became the first woman to receive the Order of Merit (1907). She was portrayed in the 1936 movie *The White Angel* by Kay Francis, and in the 1951 movie *The Lady with a Lamp* by Anna Neagle.

Night Train
Nickname of NFL player Dick Lane (7th husband of singer Dinah Washington).

Night Train
Tune to which Sonny Liston liked to jump rope while in training.

Nijinsky, Waslau
(1890–1950) Russian dancer who was a member of the Imperial Ballet. In later years he was confined in an asylum for the insane. Nijinsky was portrayed by George De la Peña in the 1980 movie *Nijinsky.*

Nikki
Theme song of the TV series *The ABC Movies of the Week.* It was composed by Burt Bachrach.

Nikko
Head winged monkey in the 1939 movie *The Wizard of Oz,* played by Pat Walsh.

Nikkon

Camera mentioned in the lyrics of the 1973 Paul Simon hit song "Kodachrome."

Nimitz, Chester William

U.S. Naval Academy graduate (1905) who was the commander-in-chief of the U.S. Pacific fleet during World War II (December 1941–November 1945). Movie portrayals: *Hellcats of the Navy* (1957) Selmer Jackson; *The Gallant Hours* (1960) Selmer Jackson; *Midway* (1976) Henry Fonda; and *MacArthur* (1977) Addison Powell.

Nina

Daughter of caricaturist Al Hirschfield and his actress wife, Dolly Haas. Nina's name is hidden somewhere in virtually all of Hirschfield's drawings.

Ninety Days and Nights in Prison

Best-selling book written by Ann Vickers (Irene Dunne) in the 1933 movie *Ann Vickers*.

Ninety Six

Hometown in South Carolina of major league pitcher William S. Voiselle who wore the number 96, thus becoming the first player to wear the name of his hometown on his uniform.

Nini Clock

Wife of Skeezix since 1944 (comic strip *Gasoline Alley*).

Nips

Robinson family's pet monkey in the 1960 movie *Swiss Family Robinson*.

Nirvano gas

Substance breathed in by Anthony "Buck" Rogers that enabled him to sleep for 504 years.

Nissen, George

American inventor of the trampoline in 1926.

Niven, David, and Deborah Kerr

Films in which the pair appeared together: *Bonjour Tristesse* (1958); *Separate Tables* (1958); *Casino Royale* (1967); *Eye of the Devil* (1967); and *Prudence and the Pill* (1968).

Nixon, Pat

Wife of President Richard Nixon. Patricia Nixon was born Thelma Ryan on March 16, 1912 (she took the name Pat in memory of her father). She attended Whittier College and married Richard Nixon on June 21, 1940. Pat Nixon was portrayed in the 1979 TV miniseries *Blind Ambition* by Cathleen Cordell.

Nizer, Louis

Famed criminal trial lawyer who wrote a Broadway play in the late 1960s titled *A Case of Libel*. He was portrayed in the 1975 TV movie *Fear on Trial* by George C. Scott. Nizer is also the author of several books, including *The Implosion Conspiracy.*

No
Only word spoken in the Mel Brooks 1976 movie *Silent Movie*. It was said by Marcel Marceau.

No. 37
First pilot license issued to a female—Harriet Quimby in 1911.

Noa
U.S. destroyer that rescued John Glenn from the water after his reentry into the earth's atmosphere in *Friendship 7* (February 20, 1962).

Nolan, Kathleen
First woman president of the Screen Actors Guild (1975).

No Left Turn
Fictitious movie starring James Coburn and Diana Berry (Maggie Smith) in the 1978 movie *California Suite*. Miss Berry was nominated for an Academy Award for her role.

No More Rivers to Cross
Traditional song sung by midshipmen when they pass their final exam at the U.S. Naval Academy. By the mid-1960s the song was no longer sung.

Nomura, Kichisaburo, and Saburo Kurusu
Japanese admiral and ambassador who were in Washington conferring with Secretary of State Cordell Hull when Japan attacked Pearl Harbor on December 7, 1941.

No Name
Detective John Shaft's favorite bar on Hudson Street in New York City. It is owned by Shaft's 6-foot 9-inch friend, Rollie Nickerson (novels).

None but the Lonely Heart
Theme song (from Tchaikovsky) of the radio series *Kitty Keene*.

Non Silba Sed Anthar
Not for self but for others—motto of the Ku Klux Klan.

Norman Bean
Pen name used by Edgar Rice Burroughs to sign his first novel, *Under the Moon of Mars*, in 1911. He used Norman Bean for his first Tarzan novel, *Tarzan of the Apes*, in 1914. From then on, Burroughs signed only his real name to his fiction.

Norseman
Plane (C-64) in which band leader Glenn Miller (0-505273) disappeared on December 15, 1944, on a flight from Bedford, England, to Paris, France. The pilot was Flight Officer Johnny Morgan. Arranger Jerry Gray missed the flight because he had a cold.

North American Soccer League (1967)

Eastern Conference	*Western Conference*
Atlanta Chiefs	Dallas Tornado
Baltimore Bays	Houston Stars
Boston Beacons	Kansas City Spurs
Chicago Mustangs	Los Angeles Wolves
Cleveland Stokers	Oakland Clippers
Detroit Cougars	California Surf
New York Generals	San Diego Toros
Toronto Falcons	Vancouver Royals
Washington Whips	

North, O. A.
Inventor of the coat hanger in 1869.

Northwest Airlines
Airlines on which Roger Thornhill (Cary Grant) flew from New York to Rapid City in the 1959 movie *North by Northwest*.

Norwegian Doll
Nickname of figure skater Sonja Henie.

Nostromo
800-foot-long interstellar tug (registration No. 180246) commanded by Capt. Dallas (Tom Skerritt) in the 1979 movie *Alien*.

Not Ready for Prime Time Players, The
Billing of the regular comedians who appeared in the NBC series *Saturday Night-Live*.

Now and Forever
1934 movie starring Gary Cooper, Carole Lombard, and Shirley Temple. In the 1951 movie *A Place in the Sun* George Stevens (Montgomery Clift) accidentally sat next to Alice Tripp (Shelley Winters) in a movie theater where *Now and Forever* was being shown.

No Way to Treat a Lady
1968 movie in which Christopher Gill (Rod Steiger) disguised himself as a priest, plumber, hairdresser, cop, prostitute, and caterer, in order to enter women's apartments to strangle them.

Now I Lay Me Down to Sleep
Song composed by Glenn Miller with lyrics by Eddy Heyman. New lyrics were later added and the title was changed to "Moonlight Serenade."

Number 7
Mad Jack's (Denver Pyle) loyal mule in the TV series *Grizzly Adams*.

Number Nine
Laurie Tuttle's (Doris Day) pet dog, the runt of the litter, in the 1955 movie *Young at Heart*.

Nurmi, Paavo Johannes

Finnish track and field athlete who won more Olympic medals than anyone: 9 Gold and 3 Silver (1920, 1924, 1928, in individual and team competition). He received 5 of the Gold Medals in 1924.

Nurse Charlotte Diesel

Head nurse at the Psycho-Neurotic Institute for the Very *Very* Nervous, played by Cloris Leachman in the 1978 movie *High Anxiety*. She was born in North Platte, Nebraska, on October 16, 1939.

Nurse Mildred Ratched

Head nurse of the mental institution in the 1975 movie *One Flew Over the Cuckoo's Nest* (based on Ken Kesey's 1962 novel of the same name). She was played by Louise Fletcher, who won an Oscar as best actress for the role.

Nuttycrest

Institution that Count Screwloose and his cross-eyed dog, Iggy, call home (comic strip *Count Screwloose of Tooloose*).

Nuxhall, Joe

Youngest player, at age 15 years, 10 months, 11 days, to start in the major leagues. In June 1944 he pitched for Cincinnati, giving up five runs. He did not pitch again until he was 23 years old.

1:15 p.m.
Exact time each day that detective Nero Wolf begins his lunch.
1 Snoopy Place
Santa Rosa, California, home address of cartoonist Charles Schulz.
1,2,3,4,5,6,7,8, Schlemiel, Schlemasel, Hassenpfeffer Incorporated!
Chant sung by Laverne and Shirley in the opening sequence of the TV series *Laverne and Shirley.*
100 Center Street
New York City address of the 21st Precinct police station in the 1951 movie *Detective Story.*
100% All Talking, 100% All Singing, 100% All Dancing
Billing for the 1929 movie *Broadway Melody.*
100 St. Germain Street
San Francisco home address of Kelly Sherwood (Lee Remick) in the 1962 movie *Experiment in Terror.*
101 Maple Drive
New York City home address of Cosmo Topper in the TV series *Topper.* He paid $16,000 for the house.
116 years
Length of the Hundred Years War (1337–1453).
117 Schlossergasse
Address of the house in Freiberg, Moravia, Austria, where Sigmund Freud was born on May 6, 1856.
121 Hilldown Avenue
London, England, home of the Glover family in the TV series *Father, Dear Father.*

123½
Street number of Big Bird's nest in the TV series *Sesame Street*.

130 North Weatherly Street
Address of the Royal Weatherly Hotel, home of UCLA student Sandy Stockton (Sandy Duncan) (Apartment 2A) in the TV series *The Sandy Duncan Show*.

132
Number of times that the word *duke* is sung in the 1962 Gene Chandler hit song "Duke of Earl."

132 Post Road
Danfield, Connecticut, home address of Lucy Carmichael (Lucille Ball) in the TV series *The Lucy Show*.

134 West Avenue
Boulder, Colorado, home address of Fred McConnell (Conrad Janis) and Cora Hudson (Elizabeth Kerr) in the TV series *Mork and Mindy*. Their phone number is (303) 555-0694.

136
Record number of opponents knocked out by light-heavyweight Archie Moore.

149 PCE
California automobile license plate number of the red Plymouth Valiant driven by Dennis Weaver in the 1971 TV movie *Duel* (based on a short story by Richard Matheson, who also authored the screenplay).

152 Hadley Drive
Medfield home address of the Daniels family in the 1976 movie *The Shaggy D.A.*

$155
Amount of money paid for the slave Kunta Kinte by his first master, John Reynolds (Lorne Greene), in the TV miniseries *Roots*. In Alex Haley's book the amount was $850.

158
First draft number drawn in November 1940. It was selected at random by Secretary of War Henry Lewis Stimson. The bandage used to cover his eyes was made from a cover of a chair in Independence Hall.

189—Doctor Perry! Come! It's I, Helen
Only words spoken by Helen (Dorothy McGuire) in the 1946 movie *The Spiral Staircase*. They are also the last words of the film.

1001 Franklin Street
Los Angeles home address of thief Arthur Adamson (William Devane) (whose real identity was that of the missing heir Edward Shoebridge) and his wife Fran (Karen Black) in the 1976 movie *Family Plot*.

1049 Park Avenue
New York City address of Oscar Madison's (Jack Klugman) apartment in the TV series *The Odd Couple*.

1112 North Jay Street
Address of the Tacoma, Washington, house where Harry Lillis "Bing" Crosby was born on May 2, 1903.

1163 Rexford Drive
Home address in Beverly Hills, California, of Bentley Gregg (John Forsythe) in the TV series *Bachelor Father*.

1206
Suite at the Plaza Hotel in New York where the Beatles stayed during their first visit to the United States in February 1964.

1313
Number on all the cell doors in the "Jailhouse Rock" song-and-dance routine in the 1957 Elvis Presley movie *Jailhouse Rock*.

1313 Pelican Way
Address of Herman Douglas's (Ned Beatty) coastal house in Santa Monica, California, in the 1979 movie *1941*. The house slides down the cliff in the closing scene of the movie.

1358 Pleasant Vista Lane Place
Raytown home address of Eunice Harper Higgins (Carol Burnett) in the TV series *The Carol Burnett Show*. Her home phone number was 555-3329.

1405 Beechwood
Los Angeles house address of detective Ira Wells (Art Carney) in the 1977 movie *The Late Show*. Marge's (Lily Tomlin) address was 3626 Franklin (near Vermont), apartment 409 (La Paloma Apartments).

1436 Oak Street
Sacramento, California, home address of the Bradford family in the TV series *Eight Is Enough*.

1460 Cambridge Street
Jamestown, Washington, D.C., home address of Karen Angelo (Karen Valentine) in the TV series *Karen*.

1466 East 54th
Address of house stormed by the Los Angeles police in a raid that killed six members of the SLA on May 17, 1974. They were: Nancy Perry, Angela Atwood, William Wolf, Donald De Freeze, Pat Soltysik, and Camilla Hall.

1506 Nix Nix (and) Notary Sojac
Words that appear in every strip of Bill Holman's comic strip *Smokey Stover*. 1506 is supposed to be the apartment number of his friend Al Posen (who created the strip *Sweeney and Son*). Holman once said Notary Sojac means horse manure in Gaelic.

1575

Number of steps from the ground floor to the top of the Empire State Building.

1600 North Hope Street

Address where Jerry Landers (John Denver) was to meet God (George Burns), in Room 2700, in the 1977 movie *Oh, God!* The building actually had only 17 floors.

1619 Pine Street

Boulder, Colorado, house address of Mork of Ork (Robin Williams) and Mindy McConnell (Pam Dawber) in the TV series *Mork and Mindy*. Their phone number is 555-1575. The address is real and the house actually belongs to Samuel Oltman.

1714

Date on the Spanish medallion found by David Sanders (Nick Nolte) in the ruins of a sunken vessel in the 1977 movie *The Deep*.

1730 Ocean Drive

Cyprus Beach, California, home address of Johnny and Scott Stuart in the TV series *Sigmund and the Sea Monster*.

10050 Cielo Drive

Los Angeles address of the house where actress Sharon Tate was killed by Charles Manson's clan. The house had previously belonged to record producer Terry Melcher, son of Doris Day. (It has been speculated that Manson wanted to have Melcher killed because he had refused to record an album for Manson.) Henry Fonda also lived there once. It was in this house that Cary Grant and Dyan Cannon spent their honeymoon in 1965.

12305 Fifth Helena Drive

Brentwood house where housekeeper Eunice Murray found Marilyn Monroe dead on August 5, 1962.

1-30-33

Combination of the safe in the German embassy in Istanbul, Turkey that was opened by the spy Cicero (James Mason) in the 1952 movie *Five Fingers*. The combination was the date Hitler came to power—January 30, 1933. Cicero suggested using 6-18-15, the date of the Battle of Waterloo.

$100,000

The first athletes to be paid $100,000 a season in their sport:

Joe Di Maggio—baseball
Johnny Unitas—football
Wilt Chamberlain—basketball
Bobby Orr—hockey
Earl Anthony—bowling

Shep Messing—American soccer
Tom Ferguson—rodeo

In 1971 Billie Jean King became the first woman athlete to win $100,000 in a single year.

$104,000
Amount that Judge Arthur K. Marshall awarded to Michelle Triola Marvin in her lawsuit against actor Lee Marvin in her lovimony (or palimony) case.

116191
Berlin phone number of Adolf Hitler at Wilhelmstrasse 77, Berlin W 8.

01650295
Lt. Felix Unger's (Tony Randall) U.S. Army serial number in the TV series *The Odd Couple*

10610918
Capt. Tony Nelson's (Larry Hagman) Air Force service number in the TV series *I Dream of Jeannie*.

106-43-2185
Social security number of Hollis P. Wood (Slim Pickens) in the 1979 movie *1941*

0 78375
Serial number of private detective Frank Cannon (William Conrad) when he was a captain in the U.S. Army in the TV series *Cannon*.

OHD 706
California license plate number of the blue Corvette on the cover of the Beach Boys' album *Shut Down Volume 2*.

OSI
Office of Scientific Intelligence, the government agency headed by Oscar Goldman (Richard Anderson) in the TV series *The Six Million Dollar Man* and *The Bionic Woman*.

Oakland, California
Home of the Hell's Angels Motorcycle Club and the Black Panthers. Also the location of the Black Filmmakers Hall of Fame. Gertrude Stein once said of Oakland, "There's no there there." In 1901 Jack London unsuccessfully ran for mayor of Oakland.

Oakley, Annie
(1860–1926) Famed sharpshooting champion (born Phoebe Annie Moses). She adopted the name Oakley from a section of Cincinnati. Annie was nicknamed "Little Sure Shot." In 1876 she married sharpshooter Frank Butler. The Annie Oakley Museum is located in Greenville, Ohio. Movie portrayals: *Annie Oakley* (1935) Barbara Stanwyck; *Annie Get Your Gun* (1950)

Betty Hutton; and *Buffalo Bill and the Indians* (1976) Geraldine Chaplin. Gail Davis played Annie in the 1953–1958 TV series *Annie Oakley.*

Oasis Hotel
Las Vegas casino hotel where Nancy Blansky (Nancy Walker) worked in the TV series *Blansky's Beauties.*

Oberlin College
Ohio learning institute that became the first college to introduce co-education (September 6, 1837).

Object 6633
Skylab satellite tracked by the Space Defense Center.

O'Brien, Marty
Professional boxing ring name of Frank Sinatra in his youth.

O'Callahan, Father Joseph T.
U.S. Navy chaplain who became the first clergyman to win the Congressional Medal of Honor during World War II.

O'Casey
Lucas Tanner's (David Hartman) pet dog in the TV series *Lucas Tanner.* The dog's name was also given on the show as Bridget.

O'Casey, Sean
(1880–1964) Irish playwright. His 1924 play *Juno and the Paycock* won the British Hawthorne Prize in 1926. O'Casey helped to organize the Irish Citizen Army in 1916. He was portrayed in the 1965 movie *Young Cassidy* by Rod Taylor.

Ode to Autumn
Poem by Verlaine. The second line, "Pierce my heart with a dull languor," was the key phrase broadcast by the BBC during World War II to inform the French underground that the D-Day invasion of Normandy was on.

Officer Dibble
New York City 13th Precinct police officer in the TV cartoon show *Top Cat.* The voice was that of Allen Jenkins.

Officer Frank "Ponch" Poncherello
Motorcycle officer for the California Highway Patrol, played by Erik Estrada in the TV series *CHIPS.*

Officer Jon Baker
Motorcycle officer for the California Highway Patrol, played by Larry Wilcox in the TV series *CHIPS.*

Officers Don Burdick and Gil Foley
Pilots of the W.C.P.D. police helicopter in the 1974 TV series *Chopper One.* They were played by Jim McMulland and Dirk Benedict.

Officer Terry Beauregard Webster
Police officer of the SCPD (Southern California Police Department), played

by Georg Stanford Brown, in the TV series *The Rookies*. His serial number
was 84934.

O'Hara, Virginia
Woman who in 1979 settled for $200,000 in a New York City malpractice
case in which she claimed her belly button had been moved 2½ inches off
center by plastic surgeon Dr. Howard Bellin.

Oh, How I Hate to Get Up in the Morning
Song introduced by composer Irving Berlin—he sang it in the 1918 musical
play *Yip, Yip Yaphank* (1918). He sang it again in the 1942 musical/1945
movie *This Is the Army*.

Ohio River
Iced-over river that Eliza crossed in the novel *Uncle Tom's Cabin*.

Oh, You Beautiful Doll, and Ain't We Got Fun
Two songs played on a calliope in the 1951 Hitchcock movie *Strangers on a
Train*. "Strawberry Blonde" was played on a carousel.

O'Keefe, Joseph "Specs"
One of the 9 men who robbed Brink's in Boston for $2.7 million on January
17, 1950. He later served as actor Cary Grant's chauffeur, without Grant's
knowing of his past. O'Keefe was portrayed in the 1979 movie *The Brink's
Job* by Warren Oates.

Oklahoma
Title song of Rodgers and Hammerstein's musical *Oklahoma!*, the first
musical whose sound track was released on a record album. The song
"Oklahoma" has been the official state song of Oklahoma since 1953.
"Oklahoma" was the song sung by the cast in the last network broadcast
episode of the TV series *The Bob Newhart Show*.

Olcott, Chauncey
(1860–1932) American singer and actor who composed and first sang the
song, "My Wild Irish Rose." He was portrayed by Dennis Morgan in the
1947 movie *My Wild Irish Rose*.

Old Blood and Guts
Nickname of Hockey Hall of Famer Eddie Shore.

Old Dollar
John Bernard Books's (John Wayne) horse in the 1976 movie *The Shootist*.

Old Fooler
Stubborn old horse in the TV series *The Rounders*.

Old Moongoose
Nickname of light-heavyweight champion Archie Moore

Old Speed
Henry Lloyd Moon's (Jack Nicholson) horse in the 1978 movie *Goin' South*.

Oleandar Arms
Apartment building at 211 Orchid in Hollywood that is the home of Esther Hoffman (Barbra Streisand) in the 1976 movie *A Star Is Born*.

Olive
Popeye's sailing vessel, named for his girlfriend, Olive Oyl (comic strip).

Oliver Air Force Base
Setting of the 1964–1965 TV series *No Time for Sergeants*.

Oliver, Thelma
Actress who was naked from the waist up in the 1964 movie *The Pawnbroker*.

Ollie
Friendly dragon on the TV puppet show *Kukla, Fran and Ollie*. Ollie's full name was Oliver J. Dragon III. He was born at Dragon Retreat, Vermont, and was educated at Dragon Prep.

Olson, Carl "Bobo"
Middleweight Champion of the World (1953–1955). As a boy of 11, he witnessed the Japanese attack on Pearl Harbor.

Olympia
Original name of the ship *Exodus* in the Leon Uris novel and the 1960 movie *Exodus* before the Jewish imigrants changed it.

Olympic Airlines
Greek national airline once owned by Aristotle Onassis.

O'Malley, Walter
Lawyer-owner of the Brooklyn (now Los Angeles) Dodgers baseball team. He was portrayed in the 1975 TV movie *It's Good to be Alive* by Ramon Bieri.

Omar Khayyám
(1050–1123) Persian mathematician, astronomer, and poet, author of the classic poem *The Rubáiyát*. Movie portrayals: *Son of Sinbad* (1955) Vincent Price; and *Omar Khayyam* (1957) Cornel Wilde.

Omega Base
Home station of Rod Brown (Cliff Robertson) in the TV series *Rod Brown of the Rocket Rangers*.

Omega Theta Pi
Faber College's oldest fraternity and rival of Delta fraternity in the 1978 movie *Animal House*.

Omphale's Spinning Wheel
Theme song of the radio series *The Shadow*.

Onassis, Aristotle
(1906–1975) Greek business tycoon who made his fortune in shipping. He married the widow of President John F. Kennedy, Jacqueline Kennedy, in 1968. Onassis was portrayed loosely in the 1978 movie *The Greek Tycoon* by Anthony Quinn (as Theo Tomasis).

Onassis, Jacqueline Bouvier Kennedy
Widow of President John F. Kennedy (1963) and of Greek millionaire Ari
Onassis (1975). She was portrayed loosely in the 1978 movie *The Greek
Tycoon* by Jackie Bisset (as Liz Cassidy Tomasis).

On a Summer Evening
Theme song for the 1957 TV series *The Andy Williams and June Valli Show.*

On Broadway
Walter Winchell's newspaper column in the 1930s.

Once Upon a Deadman
1971 pilot movie for the *McMillan and Wife* TV series.

One for My Baby and One More for the Road
Theme song of the TV series *Meet McGraw,* starring Frank Lovejoy. The
song is also heard in the following movies: *Roadhouse* (1948); *The Sky's the
Limit* (1949); and *Young at Heart* (1955).

Oneida
Private yacht on which President Grover Cleveland underwent a secret
operation for the removal of a growth in the upper part of his mouth.
The operation took place in July 1893, but wasn't revealed publically until
1917.

O'Neil, Kitty
Hollywood stunt woman and racing car driver who was born deaf. She said,
"A handicap is not a defeat, but a challenge to conquer." She set 22 records,
including: December 6, 1976: Women's land speed record of 618 mph (only
4 miles short of overall world record).
July 7, 1977: Overall world acceleration record in quarter mile from a
standing start—392 mph.
July 7, 1977: World acceleration record in 500 meters from a standing
start—412 mph.
July 11, 1977: Women's world water speed record—275 mph.
August 24, 1977: Overall world record high fall on fire—112 feet.
August 15, 1978: Women's world high-fall record—120 feet.
O'Neil was portrayed in the 1979 TV movie *Silent Victory: The Kitty O'Neal
Story* by Stockard Channing.

O'Neill, Eugene Gladstone
(1888–1953) American playwright who won the Pulitzer and the Nobel Prize.
He attended both Princeton and Harvard Universities. His daughter, Oona,
married comedian Charles Chaplin.

One Long Pan
Oriental detective played by Fred Allen on his radio series *The Fred Allen
Show.*

One on all, all on one
Motto of the Hell's Angels motorcycle gang.

One Tin Soldier
   Hit song by Coven that was used as the theme song of the 1972 movie *Billy Jack*.

Only the Valiant
   1941 Argentinian movie in which Eva Duarte (Eva Peron) made her film debut.

On My Way to a Star
   Theme song of the TV series *The Perry Como Show*.

Ono
   Middle name of John Lennon, which he adopted officially on April 22, 1969. He was named at birth John Winston Lennon.

On the Banks of the Wabash
   Song composed in 1897 by Paul Dresser. It is the official state song of Indiana. The song can be heard in the following movies: *My Gal Sal* (1942); *The Jolson Story* (1946); and *Wait Till the Sun Shines, Nellie* (1952).

On the Road
   Novel written by Jack Kerouac in 1955. It is often referred to as the Beats' Bible (it was originally titled *Beat Generation*.)

On Your Way
   TV game show hosted by Kathy Godfrey, sister of Arthur Godfrey.

Operation Barbarossa
   Code name for the German invasion of Russia during World War II, beginning on June 22, 1941. In the early planning, it was called Operation Otto.

Operation Case Green
   Code name for the German invasion of Czechoslovakia (September 1938).

Operation Dynamo
   British operation to evacuate 45,000 soldiers from Dunkirk in May 1940. A total of 338,000 men were evacuated by 900 vessels from English ports.

Operation Eagle
   German Luftwaffe assault on Britain that began on August 13, 1941. It was intended to precede Operation Sea Lion—invasion—but because of German losses inflicted by British fighter planes in what became known as the Battle of Britain, Operation Sea Lion was postponed, and finally canceled.

Operation Fortitude
   Code name for the diversionary plan designed to convince the Germans that the Allies would not invade at Normandy but at other designated locations.

Operation Greif
   Code name for the German plot on the life of Gen. Eisenhower, attempted on December 13, 1944

Operation Husky
   Code name of the Allied invasion of Sicily on July 10, 1943.

Operation Iceberg
Code name for the invasion of Okinawa by American forces on April 1 (Easter Sunday), 1945.

Operation Market-Garden
Code name for the Allied airborne invasion of Holland to cut off the German Army. It began on September 17, 1944, and ended 10 days later. The 1977 movie *A Bridge Too Far* is a film about this operation.

Operation Olympic and Coronet
Code names for the planned U.S. invasion of Japan. Olympic was to commence on November 1, 1945, at Kyushu; Coronet was to take place 5 months later at Honshu.

Operation Otto
Code name for the German invasion of Austria (March 1938).

Operation Punishment
German code name for the Luftwaffe bombing of Belgrade, Yugoslavia, on April 6, 1941

Operation Skyhook
Offensive operation against the Japanese in the South Pacific in the 1965 movie *In Harm's Way*.

Operation Sunshine
Voyage of the atomic submarine USN *Nautilus* under the North Pole in 1957.

O. P. Henley Textile Mill
Cotton mill in Henleyville unionized by the Textile Workers Union of America (TWUA) by a vote of 425 to 373 in the 1979 movie *Norma Rae*.

Oppenheimer, Jr. Robert
(1904–1967) Head of the atomic laboratory at Los Alamos who was largely responsible for the development of the atomic bomb. He was portrayed in the 1946 movie *The Beginning of the End* by Hume Cronyn, and in the 1980 TV movie *Enola Gay* by Robert Walden.

Orace
Manservant of Simon Templar in novel series *The Saint*.

Orbison, Roy
Popular recording artist since 1955. He is the only person to have toured with Elvis Presley, the Beatles, and the Eagles.

Orca
Carter Primus's (Robert Brown) patrol boat in the TV series *Primus*.

Order of Lenin
Soviet Union's highest military honor.

Oreos
Name of two black female singers who sang with Esther Leona Hoffman (Barbra Streisand) in the 1977 movie *A Star Is Born*.

Orizaba, USS
   Tanker from which American author Hart Crane jumped to his death on April 27, 1932. In his youth Montgomery Clift had sailed on the same vessel.

Ork
   Mork's (Robin Williams) home planet in the TV series *Mork and Mindy*. The capital city is Kork. Ork is 60 bleems* from Earth.

Orson
   Mork's superior, "His Immenseness" on his home planet of Ork, in the TV series *Mork and Mindy*. The character's voice is provided by Ralph James.

Oscar (The Wonder Rodent)
   White mouse used to win prizes on the TV game show *The Cheap Show*.

Osborne Industries
   Firm for which Harry Grafton (Phil Silvers) worked as a maintenance superintendent in the TV series *The New Phil Silvers Show*.

Oscar
   Wilma Flintstone's animal clothes washer in the TV cartoon series *The Flintstones*.

Oski the Bear
   Cheerleader mascot of the University of California.

Oswald, Lee Harvey
   Assassin of President John F. Kennedy on November 22, 1963, in Dallas, Texas. He was killed 2 days later by Jack Ruby. Portrayals: *Ruby and Oswald* (1977 TV) Frederick Forrest; and *The Trial of Lee Harvey Oswald* (1977 TV) John Pleshette.†

Otis Day and the Knights
   House band at J. J.'s Paradise Lounge in Camden, New Jersey, in the 1978 movie *Animal House*. They played a 47-minute version of "Shout" at midnight at the Delta House.

Otis, William
   Inventor of the steam shovel in 1839.

Ott, Fred
   Man whose sneeze was filmed on January 7, 1894, by Thomas Edison. It was the first copyrighted film.

Ottumwa, Iowa
   Hometown of Walter "Radar" O'Reilly (Gary Burghoff) in the TV series *M*A*S*H*.

Our Hearts Were Young and Gay
   Autobiography of actress Cornelia Otis Skinner and title of the 1944 movie in which Gail Russell portrayed Skinner. Russell also portrayed Skinner in the

* Billion light-years.

†Cousin of actress Suzanne Pleshette.

1946 sequel movie, *Our Hearts Were Growing Up*. It was this autobiography that Marine Pvt. Mike McHugh (Martin Milner) had on him when killed by a Japanese sniper in the 1949 movie *Sands of Iwo Jima*.

Our Boat

Houseboat on which a group of men resided in the TV series *The San Pedro Beach Bums*.

Our Lady, Help of Christians

Title of Mary, the Mother of Jesus, under which she is the patron of Australia.

Outland Trophy

Award given annually (since 1946) to the outstanding collegiate lineman.

Outlaw Trail, The

Historical book written by actor Robert Redford.

Over the Rainbow

Academy Award–winning ballad sung by Judy Garland in the 1939 movie *The Wizard of Oz*. The song was taken out of the film by its producers after the sneak preview because it was felt that it slowed the movie down. Judy Garland sang the song over 12,000 times, the last time on March 25, 1969, in Copenhagen. Elizabeth Hartman hummed the song in the 1965 movie *A Patch of Blue*.

Owasso

Turkey mascot of the U.S. Navy LSD *St. Clair County* in the 1961 movie *All Hands on Deck*.

Over Hill, Over Dale, Our Love Will Never Fail

Inscription of Maj. Margaret Houlihan's (Loretta Swit) wedding ring in the TV series *M*A*S*H*.

Owen Cantrell

Husband of Juliet Jones as of 1976 (comic strip *The Heart of Juliet Jones*).

O. W. Jeeves

Pseudonym used by Orson Welles as co-writer of the 1972 movie *Treasure Island*.

Owls

Lodge to which Maj. Hoople belonged (comic strip *Our Boarding House*).

Oxford

University where Carl Hyatt (Sebastian Cabot) had taught as a professor of criminology in the TV series *Checkmate*.

Ozzie Rabbit

Lee Harvey Oswald's nickname in the U.S. Marine Corps (Serial No. 1653230).

P

P-40 (Curtis Warhawk)
Stolen fighter plane flown by 28-year-old Capt. Wild Bill Kelso (John Belushi) in the 1979 movie *1941*.

PPW306R
License plate number of James Bond's special sports car that converts into a submarine in the 1977 movie *The Spy Who Loved Me*.

PT 41
Patrol boat, commanded by John D. Bulkeley, on which Gen. Douglas MacArthur was evacuated from the Philippines on March 11, 1942. MacArthur and his family were taken to Mindanao. Bulkeley was portrayed loosely by John Wayne (as Lt. John Brickley) in the 1945 movie *They Were Expendable*, and by William Wellman, Jr., in the 1977 movie *MacArthur*.

PT 44
Motor torpedo boat on which Ens. Jeremiah Torrey (Brandon de Wilde) was killed while fighting the Japanese in the 1965 movie *In Harm's Way*.

PT 112
Torpedo boat of Squadron 19 commanded by Lt. Elroy Carpenter (Bob Hastings) in the TV series *McHale's Navy*.

PXL 1236
NASA spacecraft on which Junior (Bob Denver) and Barney (Chuck McCann) were accidentally launched into space in the TV series *Far Out Space Nuts*.

Pa and Ma
Nicknames Clark Gable and Carole Lombard used for each other.

Pabst Blue Ribbon
Detective Mike Hammer's favorite brand of beer (novels).

Pacific Edible Seaweed

Business at 2790 Penrose Boulevard in Fresno, California, operated by J. Russell Finch (Milton Berle) in the 1963 movie *It's a Mad Mad Mad Mad World*.

Pacific Princess

Ocean liner of the British P & O lines (registered in London) captained by Merrill Studing (Gavin MacLeod) on the TV series *Love Boat*.

Pacific Technical College

California learning institute where Pat Pemberton (Katharine Hepburn) was a phys. ed. teacher in the 1952 movie *Pat and Mike*.

Packard (1939)

Automobile in Anton Myrer's novel/1979 TV movie *The Last Convertible*.

Packer, Alferd

Only man in the United States ever convicted of cannibalism (1874). There are several Alferd Packer Organizations in the United States.

Paderewski, Ignace Jan

(1860–1941) All-time highest paid concert pianist—his fortune was estimated to exceed $5 million. Paderewski served as prime minister of Poland from 1919 to 1921. He starred in the 1938 movie *Moonlight Sonata* (his only film).

Paganini, Nicolò

(1782–1840) Great Italian violinist and composer. Paganini was portrayed in the 1946 movie *The Magic Bow* by Stewart Granger and in the 1945 movie *A Song to Remember* by Roxy Roth.

Paige, Satchel

Born Leroy Robert Paige on July 7, 1906. Member of Baseball's Hall of Fame who in 1948, when he was 42 years old, made his debut in the American League (6-1). On September 25, 1965, he pitched 3 innings for the Kansas City A's; he was 59 years old (the oldest man to appear in a major league lineup). He struck out one batter and allowed only one hit. Paige was portrayed by Lou Gossett, Jr., in the 1981 TV movie *Don't Look Back* (Milton Stafford in his youth).

Paisley

Cocker spaniel on the TV series *Marge and Jeff*.

Palace

Ballroom in which the singer of the 1930 Rodgers and Hart song "Ten Cents a Dance" works as a dancer.

Palisades Park

New Jersey amusement park once owned by movie producer Joe Schenck. In 1962 Freddie Cannon recorded the hit song "Palisades Park," which was written by Chuck Barris.

Pall Mall

London street that, in 1807, became the first to be lighted by gas. Pall Mall cigarettes are Mack Bolan's (The Executioner) favorite brand (novels).

Palm Beach, USS
Sister ship of the USS *Pueblo*.

Palm Springs Racquet Club
California resort managed by Charlie Farrell in the TV series *The Charlie Farrell Show*. (Charlie Farrell and actor Ralph Bellamy founded the Palm Springs Racquet Club in real life.)

Palo Alto
One of President Warren G. Hardings 12 pet dogs.

Palo Alto Transfer
The moving van (27 feet long, 8 feet high) buried in a rock quarry in Livermore, California, in which the schoolchildren kidnapped from Chowchilla were incarcerated on July 15, 1976.*

Palomino Blonde
Publicity nickname of actress Anne Francis.

Pan American Flight No. 155
Aircraft on which the Ricardos and Mertzes departed from London for New York City on an episode (May 14, 1956) of the TV series *I Love Lucy*.

Pappy's Lambs
Four nurses who appeared in the TV Series *Black Sheep Squadron*. Nurse Nancy was played by Nancy Conrad, who is the daughter of Robert Conrad.

Paradise Bar and Grill
Sgt. Bilko's hangout, referred to as the Snake Pit, in Roseville, Kansas, in the TV series *The Phil Silvers Show*. Mr. Adamapplelis was the proprietor.

Paradise Ranch
Setting for the TV series *Big Hawaii*. It was based on an actual ranch, the Parker Ranch.

Paradise Valley
Former name of the city of Hollywood.

Paragon Records
Record company owned by Frederick J. Hanover (Gabriel Dell) in the TV series *A Year at the Top*. Hanover was the son of the devil whose recording contracts included the selling of one's soul.

Paramount Girl
Studio publicity nickname of actress Anita King.

Paramount on Parade
Theme song of *Paramount News*.

Pardner
Silent film western hero Al Hoxie's horse. (Al was the brother of Jack Hoxie.) (See: **White Fury**)

---

*The rock quarry was located only three blocks from this author's house in Livermore.

Pardon Me
Inscription on the T-shirt Patty Hearst was wearing the day she was pardoned by President Jimmy Carter in February 1979. "Being Kidnapped Is Always Having to Say You're Sorry" was on the back.

Paris
Capital of France where, at the age of 16, James Bond lost his virginity (novels).

Paris Sketchbook
Book that Ernest Hemingway was working on when he killed himself, July 2, 1961.

Paris Underground
Constance Bennett–Gracie Fields 1945 movie being advertised on the marquee of a movie theater in the 1977 movie *New York, New York*.

Parker, Dorothy
(1893–1967) American journalist and short story writer whose pieces were published in *The New Yorker*. It was Dorothy Parker who coined the phrase "Men seldom make passes at girls who wear glasses." She was portrayed in the 1977 movie *Julia* by Rosemary Murphy.

Park Plaza Hotel
New York City hotel where Ramon Raquello and his orchestra were playing (in the Meridian Room) in the Orson Welles radio broadcast of *War of the Worlds* on October 30, 1938.

Parks, Lillian Rogers
Maid at the White House and author of the book *My Thirty Years Backstairs at the White House*. Lillian Parks was portrayed in the 1979 TV miniseries *Backstairs at the White House* by Leslie Uggams. Her mother, Maggie, was portrayed by Olivia Cole.

Parks, Rosa
42-year-old black woman who on Thursday, December 1, 1955, was arrested because she wouldn't give up her seat on a Montgomery, Alabama, bus to a white man. She was fined $14. The incident inspired a black boycott of Montgomery buses that lasted 382 days, until they were integrated. Rosa Parks was portrayed in the 1978 TV movie *King* by Yolanda King (daughter of Martin Luther King, Jr.).

Parnell, Charles Stewart
(1846–1891) Irish nationalist hero until he was involved in an adultery scandal. He was portrayed by Clark Gable in the 1937 movie *Parnell*.

Parole
Winner of a three-horse race held in 1877 that both houses of Congress voted to attend. The other two horses were Ten Broeck and Tom Ochiltree.

Parrish, Mitchell
Songwriter who composed the lyrics to "Stardust" (Hoagy Carmichael wrote

the music). He also composed the lyrics to Glenn Miller's "Moonlight Serenade."

Parrott, The

Television presentation on March 24, 1953, on the *Armstrong Circle Theater.* It was the first operetta composed for commercial TV.

Parsons, Louella

(1880–1972) Hollywood gossip columnist, Hedda Hopper's rival. She hosted the radio series *Hollywood Hotel* and appeared in the 1937 movie of the same name. Parsons was portrayed by Anne Bellamy in the 1980 TV movie *Bogie*, by Priscilla Morrill in the 1980 TV movie *Marilyn: The Untold Story,* and by Jane Kean in the 1980 TV miniseries *Moviola.*

Partner

Monte Hale's horse in B westerns.

Party at Kitty and Stud's

Original title of the 1970 X-rated movie in which Sylvester Stallone appeared. It was rereleased in 1978 under the title *The Italian Stallion,* to capitalize on Stallone's success.

Passing of the Oklahoma Outlaw, The

Pulp novel written by Sheriff William Tilghman. It was the first western read by Louis L'Amour (1922).

Pasteur, Louis

(1822–1895) French chemist who discovered a cure for diseases affecting silkworms, a successful treatment for rabies, and the process of pasteurization (sterilization) of milk. Pasteur was portrayed in the 1936 movie *The Story of Louis Pasteur* by Paul Muni, who won an Oscar for best actor for his performance.

Pastor, Tony

(1837–1908) American actor and theatrical manager. He was portrayed in the 1940 movie *Lillian Russell* by Leo Carrillo.

Pat

President Herbert Hoover's German shepherd.

Patek Philippe

$2,250 watch worn by Thomas Crown (Steve McQueen) in the 1968 movie *The Thomas Crown Affair.*

Paterson, New Jersey

Birthplace of Gilligan (Bob Denver) in the TV series *Gilligan's Island.*

Patterson, William

Air Force pilot who spotted a number of UFO's over Washington, D.C., on the night of July 19, 1952. The objects were also followed on radar. In the 1956 movie *U.F.O.* the voice of Patterson, the pilot of Red Dog 1, is that of Harry Morgan.

Pavlova, Anna
> (1885–1931) Russian classical ballerina best known for her "Death of the Swan." She was portrayed in the 1952 movie *Million Dollar Mermaid* by Maria Tallchief.

Pauley, Jane
> *Today* host who asked the wrong question of Margaret Trudeau, who, in protest, walked off the set of the TV show on April 23, 1979.

Paul Revere
> Radio name of former Hearst newsman Douglas Chandler, who broadcast propaganda for Germany during World War II.

Pazuzu
> King of the evil spirits of the air, the evil Locust who possesses Regan MacNeil (Linda Blair) in the 1973 movie *The Exorcist* and the 1977 sequel *Exorcist II: The Heretic*.

Peabody Award
> George Foster Peabody Broadcasting Award. An annual award (established in 1940) given by the University of Georgia for outstanding achievements in broadcasting, radio, and television.

Peace and Freedom Party
> Party that ran Dr. Benjamin Spock for president of the United States in 1968.

Peach Blossom
> Setting of the short-lived TV series *McDuff, The Talking Dog*.

Peaches
> Vocal group that backed Bobby Vinton in his 1975 TV series *The Bobby Vinton Show*.

Peale, Norman Vincent
> Minister who wrote the best-selling book *The Power of Positive Thinking* in 1952. He was portrayed in the 1964 movie *One Man's Way* by Don Murray. Norman Vincent Peale performed the marriage of Lucille Ball to her second husband, Gary Morton, on November 19, 1961.

Pearl River First National Bank
> Bank in Pearl River, New York, of which Pearson Norby (David Wayne) was vice president in the 1955 TV series *Norby*.

Pearson, Billy
> Jockey who won $64,000 on the TV quiz show *The $64,000 Question*. His subject was art.

Pearson, Drew
> (1897–1969) Columnist who wrote the syndicated column "Washington Merry-Go Round," and the novel *The Senator* (1968). He also narrated the 1949 movie *City Across the River*.* Pearson was portrayed by Robert F. Simon in the 1977 TV movie *Tail Gunner Joe*.

---

*From Irving Shulman's novel *The Amboy Dukes*.

Pebbles
Daughter of Fred and Wilma Flintstone (TV cartoons). Jean Vanderpyl, Sally Struthers, and Mickey Stevens all did her voice (for several different TV series).

Pecos
Wrangler Jane's (Melody Patterson) horse in the TV series *F Troop*.

Pedro
Turkey that got cooked for Thanksgiving dinner in the 1956 movie *Giant*.

Pee Wee
White dog belonging to a young baseball fan whom Babe Ruth (William Bendix) accidentally hit with a baseball in the 1948 movie *The Babe Ruth Story*.

Pegasus
Carter Primus's (Robert Brown) vehicle for underwater exploration in the TV series *Primus*.

Pegasus
Maj. Charles Emerson Winchester III's (David Ogden Stiers) polo pony in the TV series *M*A*S*H*.

Pelosi, James
West Point cadet who was accused of violating the honor code and given the silent treatment by all the cadets for 2 years. Pelosi was portrayed by Richard Thomas in the 1975 TV movie *The Silence*.

Penn, William
(1644–1718) Quaker founder of the colony of Pennsylvania (1681), which he named for his father. William Penn lived in the first brick house in America. He was portrayed in the 1944 movie *Courageous Mr. Penn* by Clifford Evans.

Pennants in Both Leagues
The following managers won a pennant in both major leagues:

Manager	American	National
Joe McCarthy	1932, 1936–1943—New York Yankees	1929—Chicago Cubs
Alvin Dark	1974—Oakland A's	1962—San Francisco Giants
Yogi Berra	1964—New York Yankees	1973—New York Mets

Penguin
Logo of the rock band Fleetwood Mac.

Penistone Crags
Large boulder where Cathy and Heathcliff went to be quietly together in the novel and film *Wuthering Heights*.

Pennies from Heaven

Song written in 1936 by Johnny Burke and Arthur Johnson. It can be heard in the following movies: *Pennies from Heaven* (1936); *Cruisin' Down the River* (1953); *From Here to Eternity* (1954); and *Picnic* (1956).

Pepper

Horse of Hopalong Cassidy's sidekick Johnny Nelson (novel series).

Pepper, Buddy

Accompanist of singer Judy Garland who helped her on her feet when she accidentally fell during her opening night performance at the London Palladium on April 14, 1951.

Pepsi and Milk

Laverne De Fazio's (Penny Marshall) favorite drink in the TV series *Laverne and Shirley.*

Peralta

Vessel upon which Frank Medlin (Errol Flynn) was sailing when he heard about the San Francisco earthquake in the 1938 movie *The Sisters.*

Percival Popp

Sidekick of *The Spectre* (comic books).

Percy

12-foot mechanical moray eel used in the filming of the 1977 movie *The Deep.* Actually, 3 Percys were built.

Perry Brothers

Capt. Oliver H. Perry (1785–1819) was the hero of the Battle of Lake Erie in 1813. His brother, Commodore Matthew C. Perry (1794–1858), opened Japan to western trade in 1853.

Perry, Gaylord and Jim

The winningest pitcher-brothers in the major leagues, with over 400 wins between them.

Pershing, Gen. John Joseph

(1860–1948) Called "Black Jack" Pershing. In 1916 he commanded the U.S. expeditionary force that went into Mexico in pursuit of Pancho Villa, and in World War I he was the commander-in-chief of the American Expeditionary force. He also won a Pulitzer Prize for history (1932). Movie portrayals: *Sergeant York* (1941) Joseph Gerard; *The Court Martial of Billy Mitchell* (1955) Herbert Heyes; *The Long Gray Line* (1955) Milburn Stone; and *Cannon for Cordoba* (1970) John Russell.

Peruggia, Vicenzo

Employee of the Louvre Museum in Paris who on August 21, 1911, stole the Mona Lisa. He kept the painting for 2 years, and then was arrested when he attempted to sell it.

Petacci, Clara
Benito Mussolini's mistress who was shot and hanged with him in Milan on April 29, 1945. The next day Hitler and Eva Braun took their lives.

Pete
Horse ridden by Gary Cooper in the 1940 movie *The Westerner.*

Pete Fletcher
Husband of Mary Perkins in the comic strip *On Stage.* The couple were married in 1959.

Pete Ross
Boy who lived in Smallville and learned that his friend Clark Kent was actually Superboy (*Superboy No. 90*). Superboy didn't realize that Peter knew his identity.

Peter Pan
President Calvin Coolidge's wire-haired terrier. (See: **Rob Roy, Beans, Prudence Prim**)

Peters, Gerald
Elvis Presley's chauffeur. He previously served in that capacity for Sir Winston Churchill.

Peters, Lana
Name that Joseph Stalin's daughter, Svetlana Alliluyeva, adopted upon becoming a U.S. citizen after defecting to the United States in 1967.

Peterson, James B.
Barber who shaved off Pvt. Elvis Presley's hair in the Army book camp at Fort Chaffee, Arkansas, on March 24, 1958. The scalping cost Elvis 65 cents.

Petrox Explorer
Oil company research vessel (P0710) commanded by Capt. Ross (John Randolph) in the 1976 movie *King Kong.* The actual ship used in the movie was leased from the University of California.

Petit, Philippe
Frenchman who on August 7, 1974, walked across a wire between the World Trade Center towers in New York City. The towers are 1,350 feet high.

Petrified Forest, The
Play by Robert Sherwood that was presented on the NBC TV series *Producer's Showcase* on May 30, 1955. This was Bogart's only dramatic appearance on television. Henry Fonda and Lauren Bacall also appeared in the production.

Petty, Lee and Richard
Father-and-son professional automobile race drivers. They were portrayed in the 1972 movie *Smash-Up Alley* by Darren McGavin and Richard Petty.

Peyton Place Clarion
Town newspaper in the New England town of Peyton Place (TV series).

Phantasmo

"The Master of the World," secret identity of Phil Anson. Debut: *The Funnies* comics No. 45 (July 1940). His sidekick is a bellhop named Whizzer McGee.

Pharoahs

Tough gang of youths who "befriended" Curt (Richard Dreyfuss) in the 1973 movie *American Graffiti*. The gang cruised around in a 1951 Mercury (license DLW796).

Phédre

Play by Racine that is the basis of the libretto used in the opera staged in the 1941 movie *Citizen Kane*. Bernard Herrman conducted the orchestra.

Philbin, Regis

Joey Bishop's announcer on his ABC TV series *The Joey Bishop Show*.

Philadelphia 23, Cubs 22

Final score in a 10-innning ball game played on May 17, 1979. There were 50 hits in the game.

Philip of Macedonia

(382–336 B.C.) Military genius who conquered Greece. He was the father of Alexander the Great. Philip was portrayed in the 1958 movie *Alexander the Great* by Fredric March.

Phippsboro Bulletin

Newspaper owned and edited by Robert Major (Robert Sterling) in the TV series *Ichabod and Me*.

Phoebe Figalilly

Everett family nanny (played by Juliet Mills) in the TV series *Nanny and the Professor*.

Pickett, Bill

Black cowboy who invented bulldogging.

Pickett, George Edward

(1825–1875) Confederate Army general who led the famous charges at Gettysburg (July 3, 1863) that were repulsed by the Union Army. He was portrayed in the 1940 movie *Santa Fe Trail* by William Marshall.

Pickles

Buddy Sorrell's (Morey Amsterdam) wife, whose maiden name as a showgirl was Fiona Conway, in the TV series *The Dick Van Dyke Show*. Pickles was first played by Barbara Perry and then by Joan Shawlee, wife of George "Papa Bear" Halis, owner of the Chicago Bears football team.

Pidge

Tramp's pet name for his love, Lady, in the 1955 movie *Lady and the Tramp*.

Pie

James Stewart's favorite horse in his western movies. He rode him for the first time in the 1950 movie *Winchester '73,* and for the last time in *Bandolero* (1968).

Piedmont, New Mexico

Small town (population 68) whose inhabitants were killed by foreign micro-organisms in the 1971 movie *The Andromeda Strain* (based on the 1969 novel by Michael Crichton).

Pie Eye

Pianist played by Duke Ellington in the 1959 movie *Anatomy of a Murder.*

Pierce, Franklin

(1804–1869) 14th president of the United States. He attended Bowdoin College at the same time as Henry Wadsworth Longfellow and Nathaniel Hawthorne. On the way to his inauguration Pierce witnessed his son's death in a train mishap. He was portrayed in the 1944 movie *The Great Moment* by Porter Hall.

Pierre's

Nightclub setting on the TV soap opera *The Young and the Restless.* In later episodes Pierre's became the Allegro.

Piersall, Jimmy

Major league baseball outfielder who, on hitting his 100th home run, ran the bases backward. In 1977 Piersall underwent open-heart surgery. The physician was Dr. Robert Brown, one-time third baseman for the New York Yankees. Piersall was portrayed by Anthony Perkins in the 1957 movie *Fear Strikes Out* (based on his autobiography of the same name).

Pieta, The

Only sculpture signed by Michelangelo.

Pilar

Ernest Hemingway's 40-foot vessel, now on display at the Hemingway Museum in Cuba. It was named after a character in his novel *For Whom the Bell Tolls* (she was played by Katina Paxinou* in the 1943 movie).

Pilate, Pontius

Procurator of Judea under Emperor Tiberius. He tried and sentenced Jesus to be executed. Portrayals: *King of Kings* (1927) Victor Varconi; *Last Days of Pompeii* (1935) Basil Rathbone; *The Robe* (1953) Richard Boone; *Salome* (1953) Basid Sydney; *Ben Hur* (1959) Frank Thring; *King of Kings* (1961) Hurd Hatfield; *Barabbas* (1962) Arthur Kennedy; *The Greatest Story Ever Told* (1965) Telly Savalas; *Jesus Christ, Superstar* (1973) Barry Dennen; *Jesus of Nazareth* (1979 TV miniseries) Rod Steiger; and *The Day Christ Died* (1980 TV movie) Keith Mitchell.

Pin Blasters

Dagwood Bumstead's bowling team *(Blondie* comic strip).

---

*Paxinou won an Oscar for her performance, her first film role.

Pinafore

Secret Service code name for First Lady Betty Ford.

Pincus in the Pines

Favorite vacation resort of Molly Goldberg and her family in the TV series *The Goldbergs*.

Ping Girl, The

Short-lived studio publicity nickname for actress Carole Landis.

Pink Cadillac

Automobile driven by Hud Bannon (Paul Newman) in the 1963 movie *Hud*.

Pinkettes

Pinky Tuscadero's (Roz Kelly) female gang in the TV series *Happy Days*.

Pink Ladies

Gang of tough girls at Rydell High School in the 1978 movie *Grease*. They rode around in a pink Studebaker (California license FLM336).

Pinkville

U.S. Army's code name for the Vietnam hamlet of My Lai.

Pinky Tuscadero

Hard, sexy woman with whom Fonzy fell in love in the TV series *Happy Days*. Pinky, the leader of the Pinkettes, was played by Roz Kelly; her sister, Leather Tuscadero, was played by singer Suzi Quatro.

Pipp, Wally

(1893–1965) Walter Clement Pipp. He played first base for the New York Yankees for 10 years, then was replaced by rookie Lou Gehrig on June 2, 1925. Earlier, when he played for Detroit, Pipp was sent down to Columbia University to try to sign Gehrig to the team. Pipp was portrayed in the 1942 movie *The Pride of the Yankees* by George McDonald.

Pirate Girl

Assistant to host Jan Murray on the TV game show *Treasure Hunt*. She was played by Marian Stafford.

Pistol Packin' Mama

Song composed and recorded in 1937 by Al Dexter. It became the first country song to be sung on the radio series *Your Hit Parade*.

Pitt, William ("the Younger")

(1759–1806) He became prime minister of England at the age of 24 (December 1783). He was portrayed in the 1942 movie *The Young Mr. Pitt* by Robert Donat and in the 1954 movie *Beau Brummell* by Paul Rogers.

Pittsburgh Crawfords

Baseball team of the Negro league for which both Satchel Paige (pitcher) and Josh Gibson (catcher) played at the same time.

Pittsburgh Pirates

Baseball team featured in the 1951 movie *Angels in the Outfield*.

Pittsburgh Pitts
> Women's roller derby team on the TV series *Rollergirls*.

Pixilated
> Word coined in the 1936 movie *Mr. Deeds Goes to Town*. It was used by Jane and Amy Faulkner (Margaret Seldon and Margaret McWade) to describe Longfellow Deeds (Gary Cooper).

Pizza Bowl
> Restaurant owned by Frank De Fazio (Phil Foster), father of Laverne, in the TV series *Laverne and Shirley*.

Plains, Georgia
> Hometown of President Jimmy Carter. The town newspaper, *The Plains Georgia Monitor*, was bought by *Hustler* magazine publisher Larry Flynt.

Plank, Doug
> Defensive back with the Chicago Bears who intercepted the last pass of Joe Namath's career on October 10, 1977. The Bears won 24–23.

Platinum Bombshell
> Nickname of actress Jean Harlow.

Platinum Turkey Awards
> Annual award for the year's best fiascos in rock music presented by *Rolling Stone* magazine.

Play Misty for Me
> 1971 movie billed on a San Francisco movie theater marquee in the 1971 Clint Eastwood movie *Dirty Harry*. *Play Misty for Me* was directed by Eastwood, who also starred in it.

Plaza Hotel
> New York City hotel where the Beatles stayed during their first visit to the United States in February 1964, when they appeared twice on *The Ed Sullivan Show*. The incident is partly told in the 1978 movie *I Want To Hold Your Hand*. The Plaza was also the hotel from which Roger Thornhill (Cary Grant) was kidnapped (from the Oak Room bar) in the 1959 movie *North by Northwest*. It is also the New York home of comic strip character Eloise (created by Kay Thompson). Her pet dog is Weenie, who looks like a cat. *Eloise* was supposedly based on the mischievous childhood of Liza Minnelli. She was played by Evelyn Rudie in a production of *Playhouse 90*. (1956 TV). And finally, the Plaza is the setting of the 1971 movie *Plaza Suite* (based on the Neil Simon play of the same name).

PLaza 3–9098
> Sally Rogers' (Rose Marie Curly) phone number in the TV series *The Dick Van Dyke Show*.

Plea for Mercy, A
> Song composed by Huddie Ledbetter, later known as Leadbelly, the composer

of "Goodnight Irene." While in a Texas prison, Leadbelly sang "A Plea for Mercy" to Governor Pat Neff in 1934. The governor pardoned him.

Pleasantville, New York
Hometown of *Reader's Digest* magazine, first published February 1922 (cost: 25 cents).

Plimpton Cup
Award given to the World Amateur backgammon champion.

Plimpton, J. L.
American inventor of the four-wheeled roller skate in 1863.

Plink, Plank, Plunk
Theme song of the TV series *I've Got a Secret,* composed by Leroy Anderson, who in May 1952 had the No. 1 song in the United States—"Blue Tango."

Plowshare
Code name of the United States program to find peaceful uses for atomic energy.

Plunderers of Painted Flat
Last movie made by Republic Pictures; it was released in 1959.

Plunger, The
$150,000 painting stolen in the 1944 Abbott and Costello comedy movie *In Society.*

Plutonium
Planet setting of the 1962 movie *The Road to Hong Kong.*

Plymouth Club
Reserved Boston club, founded in 1797, into which Mayor Frank Skeffington (Spencer Tracy) entered uninvited in the 1958 movie *The Last Hurrah.* He discovered his opponents in the Cotton Mather Room.

Plymouth Hotel
Chicago flophouse at 16 South Van Buren where Jake and Elwood lived in the 1980 movie *The Blues Brothers.* It was blown up by Carrie Fisher.

Pocahontas
(1595–1617) American Indian princess, daughter of Chief Powhatan. In 1608 she saved the life of Capt. John Smith when her father was about to kill him. Her real Indian name was Matoaka, and her Christian name was Rebecca. In April 1614 she married colonist John Rolfe. Pocahontas was portrayed in the 1953 movie *Captain Smith and Pocahontas* by Jody Lawrence.

Podhajsky, Col. Alois
Director of the Spanish Riding School in Vienna who, with Allied help, led the prized Lipizzan horses to safety during World War II. He was portrayed in the 1963 movie *The Miracle of the White Stallions* by Robert Taylor.

Poe, Edgar Allan
(1809–1849) American poet and author of numerous bizarre stories. Some of

his works are classics: e.g., "The Raven" and "The Fall of the House of Usher." Poe was thrown out of West Point in 1831 when he showed up for inspection stark naked. He was portrayed in the 1915 movie *The Raven* by Henry B. Walthall, and in the 1942 movie *The Loves of Edgar Allen Poe* by John Shepperd (a/k/a Shepperd Strudwick). Roy Wanders and Freddie Mercer played Poe as a child.

Poe, USS
Navy destroyer on which Lt. Alexander Austin (Alan Ladd) served in the 1958 movie *The Deep Six*. The ship was commanded by Cmdr. Meredith (James Whitmore). The movie was filmed aboard the USS *Stephen Potter.*

Poinsett, Joel
(1779–1851) U.S. minister to Mexico who discovered the poinsettia flower (named for him) and brought it to the United States.

Point Clare
Chicago suburban setting of the 1977 TV series *Friends and Lovers.*

Poker Cabinet
Nickname given to the political advisers of President Harding.

Polidor
Sister atomic submarine of the *Seaview* in the TV series *Voyage to the Bottom of the Sea.*

Polish Prince, The
Nickname of popular singer Bobby Vinton. It is also the title of his 1978 autobiography.

Polk, James Knox
(1795–1849) 11th president of the United States and the first president to be photographed. The photographer was John Plumbe, who was also the first man to photograph the White House. Portrayed in the 1959 movie *The Oregon Trail* by Addison Richards.

Polly Benedict
Girlfriend of Andy Hardy (Mickey Rooney) in a dozen Andy Hardy films. She was played by Ann Rutherford.

Pollywog
One who has not yet crossed the equator by ship.

Polo, Marco
(1254–1324) Italian explorer who traveled to China, where he became a diplomat for Kublai Khan. Movie portrayals: *Adventures of Marco Polo* (1938) Gary Cooper; *Marco Polo* (1962) Rory Calhoun; and *Marco the Magnificent* (1966) Horst Buchholz.

Polydor
German record label for which the Beatles, and later the Bee Gees, recorded.

Polynesia Paradise Cafe

Encino, California, restaurant owned by Jerry Standish (Dick Gautier) in the TV series *Here We Go Again*.

Pond House

Lillian Carter's house in Plains, Georgia.

Pontiac Greeting Card Company

Fictitious company for which CONTROL agents Maxwell Smart and Agent 99 claimed to work as salesmen in the TV series *Get Smart*.

Pony Express

Cheerleaders for the Denver Broncos football team.

Poor, Poor Ophelia

Novel by Carolyn Weston that is the basis of the TV series *The Streets of San Francisco*.

Pope Alexander III

Orlando Bandinelli, Pontiff of the Catholic Church from 1159 until his death in 1181. He cannonized Thomas à Becket over the protests of King Henry II of England. He was portrayed in the 1964 movie *Becket* by Paolo Stoppa.

Pope Gregory X

(1210–1276) Teobaldo Visconti. Head of the Catholic Church from 1271 until his death. Pope Gregory X sent explorer Marco Polo to China in 1271. He was portrayed in the 1966 movie *Marco the Magnificent* by Guido Alberti.

Pope John XXIII

(1881–1963) Angelo Guiseppe Roncalli. Head of the Catholic Church from 1958 until his death. He was portrayed by Rod Steiger in the 1968 movie *A Man Named John*, and by Raymond Burr in the 1973 TV special *Portrait: A Man Whose Name Was John*.

Pope John Paul II

Karol Wojtyla, a Pole, the first non-Italian Pope in 455 years. He was elected in 1979.

Pope Julius II

(1443–1513) Giuliano del'la Rouere. Head of the Catholic Church from 1503 until his death. He was Michelangelo's patron and was portrayed in the 1965 movie *The Agony and the Ecstasy* by Rex Harrison.

Pope Kiril I

Fictitious Russian pope played by Anthony Quinn in the 1968 movie *The Shoes of the Fisherman* (based on the Morris L. West bestseller of the same name).

Pope Paul VI

He became the first pope to fly when he visited the Holy Land in 1964.

Pope Pius VII

(1742–1823) Luigi Barnaba Chiaramont. Pope Pius VII crowned Napoleon emperor (1804) and was later held prisoner by him. He was portrayed by Leonard George in the 1954 movie *Desirée*.

Population 2013
Population of Salem's Lot in the 1979 TV movie *Salem's Lot* (based on the 1975 Stephen King novel of the same name). The elevation was 289 feet.

PORSCHE
Most requested 7-digit personalized automobile license plate in California. It is owned by Mark Schumacher of Long Beach, who put it on a Toyota.

Port Charles
Town setting of the TV soap *General Hospital*.

Port Charleston
Boat on which the picnickers travel to Kittiwah Island in the 1959 movie *Porgy and Bess*.

Porter, Cole
(1893–1964) American composer and lyricist and member of the French Foreign Legion. He wrote such classic songs as "Begin the Beguine," "What Is This Thing Called Love?" and "I've Got You Under My Skin." He also composed the songs for a number of musicals, such as *Can Can* and *Kiss Me Kate*. Cole Porter was portrayed in the 1946 movie *Night and Day* by Cary Grant and in the 1953 movie *Kiss Me Kate* by Ron Randell.

Porto Bello
British island setting of the 1956 TV series *Long John Silver*.

Portrait of Geraldine J.
Painting by Mary B. Titcimb of a young girl named Geraldine Jacobi. The painting was exhibited in San Francisco in 1915 at the Panama-Pacific Exposition. It later hung in the White House and in the home of Woodrow Wilson's widowed wife. The painting's subject is the young girl who grew up to become the mother of actress Jane Russell.

Portsmouth, New Hampshire
Site where the treaty ending the Russo-Japanese War was signed on September 5, 1905.

Poseidon
Charter fishing boat owned by Crunch Adams (Forrest Tucker) and Des (Sandy Kenyon) in the TV series *Crunch and Des*.

Possessed
Title of two different movies in which actress Joan Crawford appeared; a 1931 MGM film starring Clark Gable and a 1947 Warner Bros. film with Van Heflin.

Post Toasties Girl
Picture of a healthy girl adorning cereal boxes of Post Toasties. The girl is actress Anita Louise when she was young.

Post, Wiley

(1900–1935) Famous American aviator who twice flew his aircraft, *Winnie Mae,* around the world. He and Will Rogers were killed in an aircraft accident near Point Barrow, Alaska, on August 15, 1935. Post was portrayed in the 1952 movie *The Story of Will Rogers* by Noah Beery, Jr.

Poteet

Steve Canyon's adopted cousin who was raised in the Little Dogie Orphanage in Poteet, Texas, but left on his doorstep (comic strip *Steve Canyon*). The real-life model, in 1956, for Poteet was Nancy O'Neal. In the town of Poteet, Texas, stands a life-size tile mural of Poteet.

Potomac

Presidential yacht bought by Elvis Presley in 1964 and then given by him to Danny Thomas for St. Jude's Hospital in Memphis, Tennessee.

Pottawatomie Giant

Nickname of heavyweight boxing champion Jess Willard.

Powell, Boog

First baseball player to play in both the Little League World Series (Lakeland, Florida) and in the Major League World series (for Baltimore).

Powell, Dick

(1904–1963) American actor who made his acting debut in 1932. He was the husband of actresses Joan Blondell (1936–1944) and June Allyson (1945–1963). It was Dick Powell who sold the yacht *Santana* to Humphrey Bogart. He was portrayed in the 1975 movie *The Day of the Locust* by Dick Powell, Jr.

Powell, Dick, and Ruby Keeler

Films in which the pair appeared: *42nd Street* (1933); *Gold Diggers of 1933* (1933); *Footlight Parade* (1933); *Dames* (1934); *Flirtation Walk* (1934); *Shipmates Forever* (1935); and *Colleen* (1936).

Powell, William, and Myrna Loy

Films in which the pair appeared: *Manhattan Melodrama* (1934); *The Thin Man* (1934); *Evelyn Prentice* (1934); *The Great Ziegfeld* (1936); *Libeled Lady* (1936); *After the Thin Man* (1936); *Double Wedding* (1937); *Another Thin Man* (1939); *I Love You Again* (1940); *Love Crazy* (1941); *Shadow of the Thin Man* (1941); *The Thin Man Goes Home* (1944); *Song of The Thin Man* (1947); and *The Senator Was Indiscreet* (1947).

Power, Myrtle

70-year-old grandmother who won $32,000 in the TV series *The $64,000 Question* in 1955. Her subject was baseball.

Power to the People

Motto of the Black Panthers.

Powers, John A. (Shorty)

Voice of Mission Control who provided the countdowns at Cape Canaveral (a/k/a Cape Kennedy).

Power, Tyrone, and Loretta Young
Films in which the pair appeared: *Ladies in Love* (1936); *Love Is News* (1937); *Café Metropole* (1937); *Second Honeymoon* (1937); and *Suez* (1938).

Precious Memories
Song sung by Susan Raye as the theme of the 1979 movie *Hardcore*.

Prentiss Hat Company
Hackensack, New Jersey, company that was robbed of $254,912 on July 20, 1940, in the 1946 movie *The Killers*.

Prescription: Murder
1968 pilot movie for the *Columbo* TV series. It was not bought as a series until a second pilot was made, *Ransom for a Dead Man*, in 1971.

Presidential Football Coaches and Players
Coaches
Calvin Coolidge—Amherst College
Woodrow Wilson—Wesleyan/Princeton
Herbert Hoover—Stanford (as a student)

Players
Dwight Eisenhower—West Point
Gerald Ford—University of Michigan
Ronald Reagan—Eureka College
(At one time Teddy Roosevelt tried to outlaw football because too many young men were getting killed.)

Presley, Elvis
(1935–1977) World's most successful rock 'n' roll artist who was born in Tupelo, Mississippi, on January 8, 1935. His first record, "That's All Right (Mama)" (flip: "Blue Moon of Kentucky"), was recorded for Sun Records. Presley was portrayed in the 1979 TV movie *Elvis* by Kurt Russell (Randy Gray as a boy); Gladys Presley was played by Shelley Winters. Portrayed in the 1981 TV movie *Elvis and the Beauty Queen* by Don Johnson. Presley's film roles: *Love Me Tender* (1956), as Clint Reno; *Loving You* (1957), as Deke Rivers (Jimmy Tompkins); *Jailhouse Rock* (1957), as Vince Everett; *King Creole* (1958), as Danny Fisher; *G.I. Blues* (1960), as Tulsa McCauley; *Flaming Star* (1960), as Pacer Burton; *Wild in the Country* (1961), as Glenn Tyler; *Blue Hawaii* (1961), as Chad Gates; *Follow that Dream* (1962), as Toby Kwimper; *Girls! Girls! Girls!* (1962), as Ross Carpenter; *It Happened at the World's Fair* (1963), as Mike Edwards; *Fun in Acapulco* (1963), as Mike Windgren; *Kissin' Cousins* (1964), as Josh Morgan; *Viva Las Vegas* (1964), as Lucky Jordon; *Roustabout* (1964), as Charlie Rogers; *Girl Happy* (1965), as Rusty Wells; *Tickle Me* (1965), as Lonnie Beale; *Harum Scarum* (1965), as Johnny Tyronne; *Frankie and Johnny* (1966), as Johnny; *Paradise— Hawaiian Style* (1966), as Rick Richards; *Spinout* (1966), as Mike McCoy;

Easy Come, Easy Go (1967), as Ted Jackson; *Double Trouble* (1967), as Guy Lambert; *Clambake* (1967), as Scott Heywood; *Stay Away, Joe* (1968), as Joe Lightcloud; *Speedway* (1968), as Steve Grayson; *Live a Little, Love a Little* (1968), as Greg; *Charro!* (1969), as Jesse Wade; *The Trouble With Girls* (1969), as Walter Hale; *Change of Habit* (1970), as Dr. John Carpenter*; *Elvis That's The Way It Is* (1970), as himself; and *Elvis on Tour* (1973), as himself.

Presley, Priscilla Beaulieu
Wife of singer Elvis Presley from 1967 until their divorce in 1972. She was portrayed in the 1979 TV movie *Elvis* by Season Hubley, who married Kurt Russell (who portrayed Elvis) after the completion of the movie. She went on to become one of the hosts of the ABC TV series *Those Amazing Aminals* (1980).

Pretty Boy Floyd
(1901–1934) Nickname of the 1930s thief and killer Charles Floyd. Movie portrayals: *Pretty Boy Floyd* (1960) John Ericson; *Young Dillinger* (1965) Robert Conrad; *A Bullet for Pretty Boy* (1970) Fabian Forte; *Dillinger* (1973) Steve Kanaly; *A Story of Pretty Boy Floyd* (1974 TV movie) Martin Sheen; and *The Kansas City Massacre* (1975 TV movie) Bo Hopkins. Woody Guthrie composed a song about the outlaw called "The Ballad of Pretty Boy Floyd."

Pretty Penny
Estate of actress Helen Hayes.

Price and Pride
Two store clerks in A & P TV commercials. They were played by Ted Pugh (Price) and Ralph Strait (Pride).

Price, Victoria, and Ruby Bates
Teenage girls who claimed they were raped by 12 black men in 1931. The celebrated case became known as the *Scottsboro Boys Case* They were portrayed in the 1976 TV movie *Judge Horton and the Scottsboro Boys* by Ellen Barber and Susan Lederer.

Pride, Charlie
Highly successful country singer who was the first baseball player cut in the Angel's first spring training camp (1961).

Pride of New Bedford
Vessel commanded by Capt. Bering Joy (Lionel Barrymore) in the 1949 movie *Down to the Sea in Ships*.

Prince
Sigmund Ooz's (Billy Barty) pet lobster in the TV series *Sigmund and the Sea Monster*.

Prince
German shepherd that lived at the Wameru Game Reserve and Research Center in the TV series *Daktari*.

---

*By one of the strange ironies of life, the director of the 1979 TV movie *Elvis* was also named John Carpenter.

Prince
    Great Dane in the 1939 movie *Wuthering Heights*.
Prince Albert
    (1819–1861) Albert Francis Charles Augustus Emmanuel of Saxe-Coburg-Gotha. In 1840 he married Queen Victoria of England, his first cousin. Movie portrayals: *Victoria the Great* (1937) Anton Walbrook; *Sixty Glorious Years* (1938) Anton Walbrook; *The Dark Avenger** (1955) Errol Flynn; and *The Swan* (1956) Alec Guinness.
Princess
    Stray dog belonging to the youngest Day family son, Harlan (Derek Scott), in the 1947 movie *Life With Father*.
Princess Anne
    Only person who competed in the 1976 Montreal Olympics (in Equestrian Riding) who was not given a sex test.
Princess Misha'al
    Saudi Arabian princess who was publicly shot to death for adultery (her lover, a student, was beheaded at the same time). She was portrayed in the controversial 1980 PBS-TV movie *Death of a Princess* by Suzanne Abou Taleb.
Princess Narda
    Nemesis of Mandrake the Magician (comic strip).
Princess Theatre in Pocatello, Idaho
    Where Esther Blodgett (Judy Garland) claimed she was born in the 18-minute musical sequence "Born in a Trunk" in the 1954 movie *A Star Is Born*.
Princeton
    College from which James Stewart and Presidents James Madison and Woodrow Wilson graduated. John Kennedy attended the university for a short time. Edgar Allan Poe and his five brothers played football there. It is also the school attended by Fernwood's police officer, Dennis Foley, in the TV series *Mary Hartman, Mary Hartman*.
Princip, Gavrilo
    (1893–1918) Serbian student who by his assassination of Austrian Archduke Francis Ferdinand on June 28, 1914, set off World War I. He was portrayed in the 1977 movie *The Day That Shook the World* by Irfan Mensur.
Prinze, Freddie
    (1954–1977) Stand-up comedian who co-starred with Jack Albertson in the TV series *Chico and the Man*. He committed suicide on January 29, 1977. Prinze was portrayed in the 1979 TV movie *Can You Hear the Laughter?* by Ira Angustain.
Pvt. Braddock
    Infantry soldier played by Shecky Greene in the 1962–1967 TV series *Combat*.

*Also known as *The Warriors*.

Pvt. Gripweed
British soldier played by John Lennon in the 1967 movie *How I Won the War.*
Pvt. Hannibal Shirley Dobbs
Bugler at Fort Courage, played by James Hampton, in the TV series *F Troop.*
Pro Bowl (1956)
Jack Christiansen of the Western Conference returned the opening kickoff for a 103-yard touchdown run. Ollie Matson of the Eastern Conference returned the opening kickoff of the second half for a 91-yard touchdown run.
Professor (George Edward) Challenger
Character in stories by Arthur Conan Doyle; "The Lost World" (1912); "The Poison Belt" (1913); "The Land of the Mist" (1926); "When the World Screamed" (1929); and "The Disintegration Machine" (1929). He was played by Wallace Beery in the 1925 movie *The Lost World,* and by Claude Rains in the 1960 remake, also called *The Lost World.*
Professor Horatio Tucker
Medicine man disguise of the Lone Ranger in the TV series *The Lone Ranger.* He used the disguise to gather information.
Professor Ludwig von Fossil
Nutty scientist played by Milton Berle in the TV series *Texaco Star Theater.*
Professor Ludwig von Humperdoo
Strange-acting scientist played by Red Skelton in his TV series *The Red Skelton Show.*
Professor O. G. Watasnozzle
Brilliant, bearded mad scientist and inventor in Elzie Crisler Segar's comic strips *Sappo* and *Thimble Theater.*
Professor Theobold
Scientist who gave Mandrake the power to travel through time (comic strip *Mandrake the Magician*).
Professor X (Xavier)
Head of the X-men crimefighters comprised of Cyclops (Slim Summers), The Angel (Warren Worthington III), Iceman (Bobby Drake), the Beast (Hank McCoy), and Marvel Girl (Jean Grey) (comic book series *X-Men*). Debut: *X-Men Comics* No. 1 (September 1963).
Profiles in Courage
Pulitzer Prize-winning book written by John F. Kennedy while he was a senator. It was made into a 1964–1965 TV series. *Profiles in Courage* was one of two books written by a U.S. President that was made into a TV series. The other was *Crusade in Europe* by Dwight D. Eisenhower.
Pro Flight
Brand of golf ball used by Dr. David Huxley (Cary Grant) in a mixup on the fairway with Susan Vance (Katharine Hepburn), who was hitting a PGA ball, in the 1938 movie *Bringing Up Baby.*

Project Sign

United States Air Force's first study of UFOs beginning in 1947. In 1949 the name was changed to Project Grudge, and in 1951 it was again changed, this time to Project Blue Book. In 1969 the UFO investigations were terminated.

Proof

Magazine for which Steve Roper works (comic strip *Steve Roper*).

Proteus IV

Gigantic computer that ran amok in the 1976 movie *Demon Seed*. Robert Vaughn provided the voice of Proteus.

Prudence Prim

President Calvin Coolidge's pet, a white collie dog. (See: **Peter Pan, Rob Roy, Beans**)

Prysock, Arthur

Deep-voiced singer of the Lowenbrau Beer commercial song "Here's to Good Friends."

Psycho-Neurotic Institute for the Very *Very* Nervous

California mental institution headed by Nobel Prize winner Dr. Richard H. Thorndyke (Mel Brooks) in the 1978 movie *High Anxiety*.

Pterodactyl Airlines

Airline company in the TV cartoon series *The Flintstones*.

Ptolemy

(A.D. 90–168) Claudius Ptolemaeus, Greek astronomer and mathematician. He was portrayed in the 1958 movie *Alexander the Great* by Virgilio Texeira.

Puccini, Giacomo

(1858–1924) Italian composer of operas who was portrayed in the movie *Puccini* by Marta Toren.

Puce Goose

CB handle of Dave Starsky (Paul Michael Glaser) in the TV series *Starsky and Hutch*. (See: **Blond Blintz**)

Puerto Rican Bombshell

Nickname of actress Rita Moreno. She is the only actress to have won an Oscar, an Emmy, a Tony, and a Grammy.

Punxsutawney Phil

Weather-watching groundhog of the Punxsutawney Groundhog Club of Punxsutawney, Pennsylvania. According to tradition, if he comes out of his hole on Ground Hog Day and sees his shadow, there will be 6 more weeks of winter.

Purple Code

Japanese secret code during World War II that was broken by U.S. Army code breaker Col. William F. Friedman. (Herbert O. Yardley had broken the Japanese code in 1920, but it was changed before World War II.)

Purple, Green, and Gold
Official colors of the New Orleans Mardi Gras.

Purple Staff for Distinguished Music Making in the Line of Duty
Medal hung around the neck of Sgt. Pepper in the 1978 movie *Sgt. Pepper's Lonely Hearts Club Band*.

Pursuit of Happiness
1934 movie starring Francis Lederer and Joan Bennett that was playing at the Strand Theatre in Tupelo, Mississippi, the day Elvis Presley was born (January 8, 1935).

Purvis, Melvin
FBI agent who helped to capture a number of wanted criminals and was involved in the killing of John Dillinger. During a radio program on which Purvis was a guest in 1935, he accidentally belched while reading a commercial, thus becoming the first person to belch on network radio. He committed suicide in San Francisco with the gun he had used to shoot Dillinger. Movie portrayals: *Dillinger* (1973) Ben Johnson, *The Story of Pretty Boy Floyd* (1974) Geoffrey Binney *Melvin Purvis, G-Man* (1974 TV movie) Dale Robertson; *The Kansas City Massacre* (1975 TV movie) Dale Robertson; and *The Private Files of J. Edgar Hoover* (1978) Michael Sachs.

Pushface
Carole Lombard's pet Pekingese that appeared with his mistress in the 1936 movie *My Man Godfrey*.

Putman's Landing
Connecticut hometown of Harry Bannerman (Paul Newman) in the 1958 movie *Rally 'Round the Flag, Boys!* The U.S. Army wanted to build a missile site there.

Puttin' on the Ritz
Song to which Dr. Frankenstein (Gene Wilder) and his monster (Peter Boyle) tap-danced at the Bucharest Academy of Science in the 1974 movie *Young Frankenstein*.

Pyle, Ernie
(1900–1945) Pulitzer Prize–winning World War II war correspondent who was killed on a small island off Okinawa on April 18, 1945. He was portrayed by Burgess Meredith in the 1945 movie *The Story of G.I. Joe*.

Quant, Mary

British fashion designer who created the miniskirt in the 1960s.

Quantrill, William Clark

(1837–1865) American Confederate guerrilla commander who led a band of ruthless men that included the James and Younger brothers. On January 21, 1863, he destroyed Lawrence, Kansas, killing over 100 townspeople. Quantrill was killed near Taylorsville, Kentucky, in May 1865. Movie portrayals: *The Dark Command* (1940) Walter Pidgeon (as Cantrell); *Renegade Girl* (1947) Ray Corrigan; *Kansas Raiders* (1950) Brian Donlevy; *Red Mountain* (1951) John Ireland; *Woman They Almost Lynched* (1953) Brian Donlevy; *Quantrill's Raiders* (1958) Leo Gordon; *Young Jesse James* (1960) Emile Meyer; and *Arizona Raiders* (1965) Fred Graham.

Quarterdeck

London home of M, the boss of spy James Bond (novel series).

Queen Elizabeth I

(1533–1603) Queen of England (1558–1603) called the Virgin Queen. She was the only child of Henry VIII and Anne Boleyn. Elizabeth I was the first person to wear a wristwatch, which was invented in 1571 by her court's official clockmaker, Bartholomew Nelson. Movie portrayals: *Fire Over England* (1937) Flora Robson; *The Private Lives of Elizabeth and Essex* (1939) Bette Davis; *Tower of London* (1939) Barbara O'Neill; *The Sea Hawk* (1940) Flora Robson; *Young Bess* (1953) Jean Simmons; *Anne of the Thousand Days* (1969) Amanda Jane Smythe (as a baby); *Mary Queen of Scots* (1971) Glenda Jackson; and *Elizabeth R* (1972 PBS-TV miniseries presented by *Masterpiece Theater*) Glenda Jackson.

Queen Elizabeth Hotel
> Montreal hotel where John Lennon and Yoko Ono recorded "Give Peace a Chance" on June 1, 1969. Singing in the background were: Timothy Leary, Derek Taylor, Murry the K, and several others.

Queenie
> Dondi's pet dog (comic strip *Dondi*).

Queen Isabella I
> (1451–1504) Spanish queen who with her husband, King Ferdinand, financed the first voyage to the New World by Christopher Columbus. She was portrayed in the 1949 movie *Christopher Columbus* by Florence Eldridge.

Queen Kelly
> Unreleased 1928 movie written and directed by Erich Von Stroheim and financed by Joseph Kennedy for $1 million. It starred Gloria Swanson. One of the movie's scenes was shown in the 1950 movie *Sunset Boulevard* which also starred Gloria Swanson. *Queen Kelly* was the movie debut of actor Walter Byron.

Queen Mallard
> Beauty contest winner crowned at the annual World Championship Duck-Calling Contest held at Stuttgart, Arkansas.

Queen Mary
> Nickname of President James Carter's armor-plated limousine.

Queen of the B's
> Title conferred on actress Lynn Bari.

Queen of Disco
> Title conferred upon singer Donna Summer.

Queen of Technicolor
> Nickname conferred upon actress Maria Montez.

Queen of the Gospel Singers
> Title conferred upon Mahalia Jackson.

Queen of the Hollywood Dress Extras
> Name conferred on actress Bess Flowers.

Queen of the Kentucky Derby—1972
> Title held by United Airlines pilot Gail Gorski.

Queen of the Surf
> Nickname conferred upon actress/swimmer Esther Williams.

Queen of the Swashbucklers
> Nickname of actress Maureen O'Hara.

Queensboro Realty Company
> Jackson Heights, New York City, real estate firm that sponsored the first radio commercial. It was broadcast over New York's WEAF on August 28, 1922. The 10-minute commercial cost $100.

Queen Umpateedle

King Guzzle's nagging wife (comic strip *Alley Oop*).

Queen Victoria

(1819–1901) Alexandrina Victoria, queen of the United Kingdom of Great Britain and Ireland from 1837 to 1901. Portrayals: *Disraeli* (1929) Margaret Mann; *Victoria the Great* (1937) Dame Anna Neagle; *Sixty Glorious Years* (1938) Dame Anna Neagle; *The Story of Alexander Graham Bell* (1939) Beryl Mercer; *The Mudlark* (1950) Irene Dunne; *Victoria Regina* (1961 TV "Hallmark Hall of Fame") Julie Harris; *The Great McGonagall* (1974) Peter Sellers; and *Edward the King* (1978 TV) Annette Crosbie.

Quick, Henry, the Flit!

Advertising slogan for Flit insecticide that became a popular saying of the 1920s. The slogan was created by Theodor Gisel, who then worked for an advertising firm.

Quinlan, Karen Ann

New Jersey girl whose parents went to court to gain permission to have her life-support system cut off, as she was comatose with no hope of recovery. The system was shut off but Karen Ann Quinlan did not die, though she remains in a coma to this day. Mr. and Mrs. Quinlan were portrayed by Brian Keith and Piper Laurie in the 1979 TV movie *In the Matter of Karen Ann Quinlan*.

Quinn and Cohon

Advertising agency where Sandy Stockton (Sandy Duncan) was employed in the TV series *The Sandy Duncan Show*.

Quintiphonic Sound

Special audio effect used in projecting the 1975 rock opera movie *Tommy*.

Rabin, Yitzhak
Israeli prime minister who was portrayed in the 1977 TV movie *Raid on Entebbe* by Peter Finch.

Rache
Word clue written in blood on the wall of a house at 3 Lauriston Gardens, off Brixton Road, London, that brought Sherlock Holmes and Dr. Watson to investigate in the novel *A Study in Scarlet*. Holmes declared the word *Rache* was German for *revenge*.

Rachel
Walt and Skeezix's black maid (comic strip *Gasoline Alley*).

Racing With the Moon
Theme song of the TV series *The Vaughn Monroe Show*.

Rademacher, Pete
Olympic Gold Medal winner in boxing. In his first pro bout in 1957 he fought against Floyd Patterson for the heavyweight championship. It was the first time that an amateur fought for the heavyweight championship in his first pro match.

Radziwill, Princess Lee Bouvier
Sister of Jacqueline Onassis who played the leading role in the TV play *Laura,* adapted by Truman Capote (televised on January 24, 1968).

Raft, George
American actor (born George Ranft in 1895) who played mainly gangster type characters in the movies. As a small boy, George Raft was the mascot of the New York Highlanders (New York Yankees) baseball team. In 1955 he appeared on the TV series *I Am the Law*. He was portrayed in the 1961 movie

The George Raft Story by Ray Danton. In the 1961 movie *The Ladies' Man* George Raft portrayed himself.

Raider

Horse ridden by the Durango Kid (Charles Starret) in B westerns.

Raiderettes

Cheerleaders for the Oakland Raiders football team.

Rainmaker, The

1956 Katharine Hepburn—Burt Lancaster movie. When Elvis Presley did his first screen test, opposite Frank Faylen, it was a scene from *The Rainmaker.* Lancaster's role was sought by Bing Crosby.

Raisin in the Sun, A

First Broadway play (1958) written by a black playwright, Lorraine Hansberry. It starred Sidney Poitier and Ruby Dee, who repeated their roles in the 1961 movie version.

Rajah

Horse that killed Samuel "Nails" Nathan (Leslie Felton) and was, in turn, killed by Tom Powers (James Cagney) in the 1931 movie *Public Enemy.*

Raleigh, Mississippi

Site of the annual National Tobacco Spitting Contest.

Raleighs

Attorney Perry Mason's favorite brand of cigarettes (novels).

Raleigh, Sir Walter

(1552–1618) English historian and navigator who explored the coast of America from Florida to North Carolina. He also authored a number of poems. Movie portrayals: *The Private Lives of Elizabeth and Essex* (1939) Vincent Price; *The Virgin Queen* (1955) C. Richard Todd; *The Story of Mankind* (1957) Edward Everett Horton; and *Elizabeth R* (1971 TV miniseries) Nicholas Selby.

Rambler

Grizzly Adams's pet hound dog.

Ramblin' Man

Allman Brothers' song that can be heard via a jukebox in a pub in the 1973 movie *The Exorcist* and in the 1978 movie *Casey's Shadow.*

Ranch Breakfast

Brand of cereal ("A Champ's Way to Start the Morning") owned by the AMPCO conglomerate that Norman "Sonny" Steele (Robert Redford) advertised in the 1979 movie *The Electric Horseman.*

Randall, Lenny

New York Mets third baseman who was at bat against Chicago at Shea Stadium when the New York blackout occurred at 9:34 P.M on July 13, 1977. When the lights went out, he dropped his bat, went to first base, and said to the umpire, "Let's see you argue about this one."

Rand, Sally

Fan dancer and actress (born Helen Gould Beck). In the 1927 movie *King of Kings* Sally Rand played Mary Magdalene's slave. She herself was portrayed in the 1928 movie *Sally of the Scandals* by Bessie Love.

Ranger, HMS

British nuclear submarine captured by the supership *Liparus* in the 1977 movie *The Spy Who Loved Me*. (See: **Wayne, USS**)

Rangers vs. Red Wings

Hockey game to which Oscar Madison took his bride, Blanche, on their honeymoon in the *The Odd Couple*.

Rankin, Jeanette

First woman to be elected to the U.S. House of Representatives (from Montana in 1916). She was the only member of Congress to vote against declaring war in both World War I and World War II. Rankin was portrayed in the 1944 movie *Wilson* by Hilda Plowright.

Raoul

Mystery man whom James Earl Ray claimed was his contact in the weeks before the assassination of Martin Luther King, Jr., in 1968.

Raoulle

Barking dog in the 1978 movie *The Buddy Holly Story*. He is mentioned in the movie credits.

Raphael

(1493–1520) Italian painter and architect who was portrayed in the 1965 movie *The Agony and the Ecstasy* by Tomas Milian.

Rapid Fire

Cotton Candy's rival band in the 1978 TV movie *Cotton Candy*. Rapid Fire's favorite song was the Eric Clapton classic "I Shot the Sheriff."

Rapture at Two Forty

Episode of *Kraft Suspense Theater* broadcast in April 1965. It became the pilot for the 1965–1968 TV series *Run for Your Life*.

Rare Stamps

Three rare stamps worth a total of $250,000 are the subject of a massive search and three deaths in the 1963 movie *Charade*; an 1854 Swedish 4 schilling (de Gula Fyraskillingen) stamp valued at $85,000; an 1850 Hawaiian Blue stamp valued at $65,000; and an 1852 3 penny British Guiana (Gazette Guyanne) stamp valued at $100,000.

Raskind, Dr. Richard

Name of eye surgeon and tennis pro Renee Richards before a sex-change operation.

Rasputin

Dog that lived in Ivan Petrovsky's (Lou Jacobi) apartment (although he was never seen) in the TV series *Ivan the Terrible*.

Rastus
Smiling black chef on the front of Cream of Wheat packages.

Rattler
Sloop skippered by David Grief (Maxwell Reed) in the TV series *Captain David Grief*.

Raunchy
Instrumental that George Harrison played when he auditioned in 1958 for the Quarrymen, which was then the name of John Lennon's band. The song was a hit in 1957 for Ernie Freeman, Bill Justis,* and Billy Vaughn.

Raven, The
Professor Waldo Cunningham's (Burgess Meredith) futuristic submarine pursued by the sub *The Nautilus* in the TV series *The Return of Captain Nemo*.

Rayburn, Sam
(1882–1961) Speaker of the U.S. House of Representatives for 17 years. Four U.S. presidents attended his funeral in November 1961: Harry S. Truman (past), Dwight D. Eisenhower (past), John F. Kennedy (present), and Lyndon B. Johnson (future).

Raymond
Code name of chemist Harry Gold, to whom scientist-spy Klaus Fuchs passed the secrets of the atomic bomb between 1941 and 1949. Harry Gold passed the information on to "John" (Anatoli A. Yakovlev), who also was the Rosenbergs' contact. FBI chief J. Edgar Hoover referred to Fuchs's sellout as "the crime of the century." The first time Gold and Fuchs met in New York City (January 1944), Gold carried a pair of gloves in his left hand and a book with a green cover in his right to identify himself. Fuchs carried a tennis ball in his right hand. Gold's identifying words were: "My name is Raymond."

Ready to Take a Chance Again
Song by Barry Manilow sung as the theme of the 1978 movie *Foul Play*.

Real McCoy, The
Expression that originated with welterweight boxer Kid McCoy (1873–1940) to distinguish him from another fighter also named McCoy. The words also appeared on posters. Kid McCoy spent time in prison for murdering his girlfriend. After his release, he committed suicide.

Reavis, James Addison
Con artist who in 1868 forged documents that showed he owned 10,800,000 acres of land in Arizona. In 1895 he went to prison. Reavis was portrayed in the 1949 movie *The Baron of Arizona* by Vincent Price.

Rebel
German shepherd friend of the horse Champion, owned by Ricky North (Barry Curtis), in the TV series *The Adventures of Champion*.

---

*Composed by Bill Justis, the song was originally titled "Backwoods."

Red Cloud
(1822–1909) American Indian chief of the Oglalas and of the Sioux and Cheyenne bands who fought against American soldiers. He was portrayed in the 1955 movie *Chief Crazy Horse* by Morris Ankrum.

Red Herring, The
Newsletter of the Crime Writers Association.

Red Lightning
Racehorse that Nikki Arane (Timothy Carey) shot with a rifle (at 4:23 p.m.) during the 7th race in the 1956 movie *The Killing*.

Redskinettes
Cheerleaders for the Washington Redskins.

Red Suspenders Awards
Annual awards given by *Rolling Stone* magazine in numerous categories.

Regal Order of the Golden Door to Good Fellowship
Fraternal organization of which Andy Taylor (Andy Griffith) was a member in the TV series *The Andy Griffith Show*.

REgent 5598
New York City phone number of producer George S. Kaufman (Jason Robards, Jr.) in the 1963 movie *Act One*.

Regie
Detective Philo Vance's imported Turkish cigarettes (from Constantinople) with rose-petal tips (novels).

Reginald Van Gleason III
Rich, snobbish character played on TV by Jackie Gleason. Sedgwich Van Gleason, Reginald's father, was played by Art Carney.

Rego Park Lanes
Bowling alley in Queens, New York, that was the setting for TV's first bowling show, *Bowling Headlines,* telecast in 1949.

Rehton
Planet of midget-sized people in the 1962 movie *The Phantom Planet*.

Reilly, Peter
18-year-old youth who was arrested for the slaying of his mother on September 30, 1973. He signed a confession, which he later repudiated, stating that he had been harassed into signing it by the authorities. He was portrayed by Paul Clemens in the 1978 TV movie *A Death in Canaan*.

Reluctant Dragon, The
B29 on which actor Tim Holt served as bombardier in raids over Tokyo during World War II.

Rem
Humanlike android played by Donald Moffat in the TV series *Logan's Run*.

Rembrandt
(1606–1669) Great Dutch painter whose full name was Rembrandt Harmensz

van Rijn. He was portrayed in the 1936 movie *Rembrandt* by Charles Laughton.

Remington
Typewriter used by Mark Twain to type the manuscript of *The Adventures of Tom Sawyer* in 1875. It was the first book ever composed on a typewriter. Margaret Mitchell also used a Remington portable to type *Gone with the Wind*.

Remuda Golf Club
Private club of which attorney Perry Mason is a member (novels).

Renaldo and Clara
1978 4-hour movie written, directed, co-edited by and starring Bob Dylan.

Renfro, Marti
Woman who doubled for Janet Leigh in the deadly shower scene in Alfred Hitchcock's 1960 movie *Psycho*.

Reno Brothers, The
Title considered originally for Elvis Presley's first motion picture, *Love Me Tender* (1956).

Reno, Maj. Marcus
(1823–1862) American Army officer who graduated from West Point. He was attached to Custer's 7th Cavalry, but was not involved in the Battle of Little Big Horn. Reno's son, Jesse, invented moving stairs in 1892. Marcus Reno was portrayed in the 1965 movie *The Great Sioux Massacre* by Joseph Cotten, and in the Hallmark Hall of Fame TV presentation of *The Courtmartial of George Armstrong Custer* by William Daniels.

Rescue
Irene Bailey's (Arlene Dahl) pet Great Dane in the 1953 movie *Here Come the Girls*.

Resorts International Hotel Casino
First major gambling casino in Atlantic City, New Jersey (May 26, 1978). The building was formerly the Chalfonte-Haddon Hall Hotel.

Restful
Wild West town setting of the 1954 movie *Destry*, starring Audie Murphy.

Retlaw Yensid
Author of the story on which the 1966 Disney movie *Lt. Robin Crusoe, U.S.N.* is based. Retlaw Yensid is Walter Disney spelled backward.

Reuter, Julius
Organizer of the first news agency in England in 1858. Reuter was portrayed in the 1940 movie *A Dispatch from Reuters* by Edward G. Robinson (Dickie Moore as a child).

Revenge, The
Pirate ship of buccaneer Jaimie Waring (Tyrone Power) in the 1942 movie *The Black Swan*.

Revenue Marine

Previous name of the U.S. Coast Guard, founded August 4, 1790, 8 years before the U.S. Navy was established. The Coast Guard (name changed on January 18, 1915) is under the Department of the Treasury. Alexander Hamilton, the first secretary of the treasury, is considered the father of the U.S. Coast Guard. The Coast Guard's first ship was the cutter *Massachusetts*.

Reverend Galsworthy

Minister who performed the marriage ceremony in the 1950 movie *Father of the Bride*. He baptized the couple's baby in the 1951 sequel, *Father's Little Dividend*. Galsworthy was played by Paul Harvey.

Reverend Scot Sloan

Religious man who runs a coffee shop in G. B. Trudeau's comic strip *Doonesbury*.

Revlon Girl

Woman who modeled Revlon products on the TV quiz show *The $64,000 Question*. Two Revlon Girls were actresses Wendy Barrie and Barbara Britton. Evelyn Patrick, a third, was the wife of comedian Phil Silvers.

Reynolds, Quentin

American journalist and author who was the European representative for *Collier's* magazine during World War II. Reynolds was portrayed in the 1978 movie *The Private Files of J. Edgar Hoover* by George Plimpton.

Rhett K. Butler, Capt.

Lover and third husband of Katie Scarlett O'Hara in Margaret Mitchell's novel *Gone With the Wind*. Butler was played in the 1939 movie by Clark Gable. He had been expelled from West Point Academy.

Rhinestone

Gem that was set in cement to dot the "i" in Marilyn Monroe's name at Grauman's Chinese Theater when she and Jane Russell left their handprints there at the debut of their 1953 film *Gentlemen Prefer Blondes*. A sightseer later chiseled the gem out of the cement.

Rhodes Scholarships

Scholarship named for British colonist Cecil Rhodes for study at Oxford University. It was first awarded in 1904. Kris Kristofferson was a Rhodes scholar, as was U.S. Supreme Court Justice Byron "Whizzer" White, Senators Bill Bradley and J. W. Fulbright and news commentator Howard K. Smith. Alexander Scott (Bill Cosby) in the TV series *I Spy* was also a Rhodes scholar.

Rhythm Movies

Four rhythm movies in which Bing Crosby appeared: *Rhythm on the Range* (1936) (Roy Rogers can be seen playing guitar); *Dr. Rhythm* (1938); *Rhythm on the River* (1940); and *Star-Spangled Rhythm* (1942).

Ribbentrop, Joachim von
(1893–1946) German diplomat who served under Adolf Hitler during World War II. He negotiated the Italian-German-Japanese alliance in 1940. In 1946 he was hanged by the Allies as a war criminal. Ribbentrop was portrayed in the 1943 movie *Mission to Moscow* by Henry Daniell.

Rice, Grantland
(1880–1954) Sports editor of the *New York Tribune*. Rice announced the first broadcast of a World Series Game, in 1921, from the Polo Grounds. He portrayed himself in the 1951 movie *Follow the Sun,* and by Byron Morrow in the 1975 TV movie *Babe*.

Richelieu, Cardinal
(1585–1642) Armand Jean du Plessis, French statesman called the Red Eminence. He controlled King Louis XIII and during his reign made domestic and foreign policy for France. He became prime minister in 1629. Movie portrayals: *Richelieu* (1914) Lon Chaney; *The Three Musketeers* (1921) Nigel De Brulier; *The Iron Mask* (1929) Nigel De Brulier; *The Three Musketeers* (1934) Nigel De Brulier; *Cardinal Richelieu* (1935) George Arliss; *Under the Red Rose* (1937) Raymond Massey;*The Three Musketeers* (1939) Miles Mander; *The Three Musketeers* (1948) Vincent Price; *The Three Musketeers* (1974) Charlton Heston; and *The Four Musketeers* (1975) Charlton Heston.

Ricketts, Dr. Howard Taylor
(1871–1910) American pathologist who studied spotted fever, discovering that ticks transmit Rocky Mountain Spotted Fever and that lice transmit typhus. He died of typhus. Ricketts was portrayed in the 1937 movie *Green Light* by Errol Flynn.

Rickey, Branch
Member of Baseball's Hall of Fame who, as vice president of the Brooklyn Dodgers in 1947, integrated baseball when he signed Jackie Robinson, the major league's first black player. Rickey never played ball or managed on a Sunday because of his religious convictions. He was portrayed in the 1950 movie *The Jackie Robinson Story* by Minor Watson.

Rick Jones
The Hulk's lone friend. The Hulk (Dr. Bruce Banner) saved Rick from the explosion of the G Bomb (Gamma Bomb), which changed Banner into *The Hulk* (*The Hulk* No. 1, May 1962).

Ride 'em Cowboy
1941 movie in which Ella Fitzgerald sang "A Tisket, A Tasket."

Rideout, John
First man to go on trial in the United States for raping his wife on October 10, 1978. The trial began in December 1978. He was acquitted. After the trial he and his wife, Greta, went back together, but later they were divorced.

John and Greta Rideout were portrayed by Mickey Rourke and Linda Hamilton in the 1980 TV movie *Rape and Marriage: The Rideout Case.*

Ridgemont College

Learning institute where Jim Nash (Mark Miller) taught English in the TV series *Please Don't Eat the Daisies.*

Ridgeville University

College for which Junior Jackson, No. 66 (Jerry Lewis), played football in the 1951 movie *That's My Boy.* Ridgeville beat Wilton College in the final scene (score 9–7).

Ridout,.Jack

Survivor of the crash between two Boeing 747 aircraft at Tenerife Airport in the Canary Islands on March 27, 1977, in which 582 people were killed. It was the worst aviation accident in history. On September 25, 1978, Jack Ridout purchased tickets for PSA Flight 182, but canceled out. PSA Flight 182, a Boeing 727, crashed into another aircraft in San Diego, killing 147 people, the worst aviation accident in the air up to that time. Thus Jack Ridout escaped both the worst air and the worst ground accident in aviation history.

Rimsky-Korsakov

(1844–1908) Russian composer of classical music and operas. He was portrayed in the 1947 *Song of Scheherezade* by Jean-Pierre Aumont.

Ringer Bowl

Wildwood, New Jersey, location of the annual National Marbles Tournament.

Ringo

Real name of the horse ridden by Steve McQueen in the TV series *Wanted—Dead or Alive.*

Ringo's Theme

Subtitle of Beatles song "This Boy."

Rings

Room service at the Cheyenne Social Club in the 1970 movie *The Cheyenne Social Club:*

1 Ring—Sara Jean (Sharon De Bord)
2 Rings—Pauline (Elaine Devry)
3 Rings—Opal Ann (Sue Ane Langdon)
4 Rings—Carrie-Virginia (Jackie Russell)
5 Rings—Annie Jo (Jackie Joseph)
6 Rings—Jenny (Shirley Jones)

Riordon, Con

Heavyweight boxer who died in the 2nd round of a bout with Robert Fitzsimmons at Syracuse, New York, on November 19, 1894.

Rising Star

$6 million champion stallion owned by AMPCO and stolen by Norman "Sonny" Steele (Robert Redford) in the 1979 movie *The Electric Horseman*.

Ritty, James

Inventor of the cash register in 1884.

Ritz Plaza Hotel

Sophisticated hotel where Susan Vance (Katharine Hepburn) met Dr. David Huxley (Cary Grant) for the second time in the 1938 movie *Bringing Up Baby*.

River Bird

Vessel commanded by Capt. Bounce (Walter Brennan) in the 1954 movie *Dakota*.

River Gulch

Hometown of Cherie (Marilyn Monroe) in the 1956 movie *Bus Stop*.

River of No Return, The/I'm Gonna File My Claim

Only single-record release by Marilyn Monroe; from the 1954 movie *River of No Return*.

River Ouse

River in Sussex Downs in which author Virginia Woolf drowned herself on March 28, 1941. She had just finished her last work, *Between the Acts*.

River Queen

Capt. Sam Jackson's (Henry Travers) showboat on which Dexter Broadhurst (Bud Abbott) and Sebastian Dinwiddie (Lou Costello) worked as performers in the 1945 movie *The Naughty Nineties*.

Rivers End

Small town in which Dr. Mark Christian (MacDonald Carey) and his uncle, Dr. Paul Christian (Jean Hersholt), practiced medicine in the TV series *Doctor Christian*.

Rizzuto, Phil

New York Yankees shortstop who in 1950 was the first recipient of the Hickok Belt and the first Mystery Guest to appear on the TV quiz show *What's My Line*. His voice can be heard announcing a Yankee game on Meat Loaf's 1978 hit single "Paradise by the Dashboard Light."

Roberts, Peter

Inventor who successfully sued Sears Roebuck for $60 million in 1979, claiming that the company bought a wrench he had invented. Sears originally told him that it wouldn't sell well, but it did.

Robertson, Don

Singer/composer who whistled the theme song "The Happy Whistler" for the TV series *The Andy Griffith Show*. Robertson is a prolific songwriter who wrote 12 songs for Elvis Presley.

Robespierre
Little brother of Baby Snooks (Fanny Brice) on the radio series *The Baby Snooks Show.* Robespierre's voice was provided by Leone Ledoux and Jerry Hausner.*

Robin
Kermit the Frog's 5-year-old nephew (voice: Jerry Nelson).

Robin
4-year-old horse that pulled Mr. Neeley's (Chill Wills) ice wagon (Donovan's Ice) in the 1944 movie *Meet Me in St. Louis.*

Robin Hood
Movie starring Douglas Fairbanks. It was first shown at Grauman's Egyptian Theatre in Los Angeles in 1922 at the opening of the theater.

Robinson, Eugene "Tony"
Bag boy and disco dancer after whom John Travolta's character in the 1978 movie *Saturday Night Fever* was modeled. Robinson played a bit role in the movie.

Robinson, Mack
Jackie Robinson's older brother who finished second behind Jesse Owens in the 200-meter race in the 1936 Olympics in Berlin.

Rob Roy
President Calvin Coolidge's sheep dog. (See: **Peter Pan; Beans; Prudence Prim**)

Rob's Place
Favorite hangout of the characters in the TV series *What's Happening.*

Rock-a-Bye Baby
Theme song of the radio series *The Baby Snooks Show.*

Rock and Roll
Title of a song sung by the Boswell Sisters in the 1934 musical movie *Transatlantic Merry-Go-Round.*

Rockfeller, Nelson, and Patty Hearst
Two celebrities whose picture adorned the first issue of the revitalized *Look* magazine (February 19, 1979). Rockefeller was on the cover in the East, while Patty Hearst was on the cover in the West.

Rocking Chair Lady, The
Nickname of big band vocalist Mildred Bailey (wife of Red Norvo). Her name was taken from the title of her theme song, "Rockin' Chair."

Rockne, Knute
(1888–1931) Captain of the Notre Dame football team (1913), assistant coach (1914–1917) and head coach (1918–1931). In 13 years he won 105, lost 12,

---

* Jerry Hausner played Ricky Ricardo's agent, Jerry, in the *I Love Lucy* TV series.

and tied 5. Rockne was killed in an airplane crash on March 31, 1931. Movie portrayals: *Knute Rockne—All American* (1940) Pat O'Brien (Johnny Sheffield as a boy*); and *The Long Gray Line* (1955) James Sears.

Rock Ridge

Western town setting of the 1974 movie *Blazing Saddles*. Some of the town's residents were Dr. Samuel Johnson, Howard Johnson, George "Gabby" Johnson, Olsen Johnson, Van Johnson, Harriet Johnson, Reverend Johnson, and Lili Von Shtupp.

Rocky

Horse of Kermit "Tex" Maynard in B westerns.

Rodale, J. I.

Health food expert and editor of *Prevention* magazine who died shortly after suffering a heart attack while a guest on the TV show *The Dick Cavett Show*.

Rod Brown Rocket Ranger Pledge

1. I shall always chart my course according to the Constitution of the United States of America.
2. I shall never cross orbits with the Rights and Beliefs of others.
3. I shall blast at full space-speed to protect the Weak and Innocent.
4. I shall stay out of collision orbit with the laws of my State and Community.
5. I shall cruise in parallel orbit with my Parents and Teachers.
6. I shall not roar my rockets unwisely, and shall be Courteous at all times.
7. I shall keep my gyros steady and rectors burning by being Industrious and Thrifty.
8. I shall keep my scanner tuned to Learning and remain coupled to my Studies.
9. I shall keep my mind out of free-fall by being mentally alert.
10. I shall blast the meteors from the paths of other people by being Kind and Considerate.

Rodia, Simon

Builder of the Watts Towers in Los Angeles between 1921 and 1954.

Rodgers, Richard

(1902–1980) American composer who, with lyricist Oscar Hammerstein II, wrote many popular tunes and musicals, such as *Oklahoma!* (1943), *Carousel* (1945), *South Pacific* (1949), *The King and I* (1949), *Flower Drum Song* (1958) and *The Sound of Music* (1959). He also composed a special musical score for the 1952 TV documentary series *Victory at Sea*. Rodgers was portrayed by Tom Drake in the 1948 movie *Words and Music*.

Rodney Hotel

New York City building from which Robert Cosick (Richard Basehart)

---

*Others who portrayed him as a child in the film were Bill Sheffield (age 4), David Mado (age 7), and Billy Dawson (age 12).

threatened to jump from a 15th-floor ledge in the 1951 movie *Fourteen Hours*.

Roger Ramjet

Inept superhero in TV cartoon series (voice: Gary Owens). His Proton Pill gives him the power of 20 atom bombs for 20 seconds. Lotta Love is his girlfriend, Lance Crossfire is his rival. Ramjet's assistants are The American Eagle Squadron, and his enemies include "Noodles" Romanoff and the Solenoid Robots.

Rogers, Will

(1879–1935) Political humorist who talked to his audience as he performed rope tricks. Rogers was killed in a plane crash with Wiley Post. Movie portrayals: *The Great Ziegfeld* (1936) A. A. Trimble; *You're a Sweetheart* (1937) A. A. Trimble; *Look for the Silver Lining* (1949) Will Rogers, Jr.; *The Story of Will Rogers* (1952) Will Rogers, Jr. (Robert Scott Cornel as a boy); *The Eddie Cantor Story* (1953) Will Rogers, Jr.; and *Ziegfeld: The Man and His Women* (1978 TV) Gene McLaughlin. He was also portrayed by James Whitmore in the one-man show *Will Rogers U.S.A.* It was Will Rogers who, after opening the envelope that contained the name of the best director at the 1933 Academy Awards ceremony, announced, "Come up and get it, Frank." Frank Capra, who had been nominated for *Lady for a Day,* was almost to the stage when Rogers announced that Frank Lloyd was the winner for *Cavalcade*.

Rolex

Wristwatch worn by private-eye Mike Hammer (novels).

Rolling Stone

Largest magazine dedicated to rock 'n' roll music. It was founded by Jann Wenner and its first issue appeared on November 9, 1967, with a picture of John Lennon (from his movie *How I Won the War)* on the cover.

Romanoff, Mike

(1892–1971) Born Harry Gerstefson. Self-proclaimed Russian prince who was a Hollywood restaurant owner and good friend of many actors and actresses. He was a member of Humphrey Bogart and Lauren Bacall's Holmby Hills Rat Pack. Romanoff was portrayed in the 1980 TV movie *Bogie* by Alfred Ryder.

Romberg, Sigmund

(1887–1951) Hungarian composer who after immigrating to the United States wrote such classic light operas as *Student Prince* (1924) and *Desert Song* (1926). He was portrayed in the 1954 movie *Deep in My Heart* by Joseph Ferrer.

Romeo and Juliet

Shakespearean tragedy (1597) about two young lovers, Romeo Montague and Juliet Capulet, that was based on an earlier story in Arthur Brooke's poem

The Tragicall Historye of Romeus and Juliet. In 1867 Charles Gounod composed an opera about the same pair, *Roméo et Juliette.* Movies: *Romeo and Juliet* (1936) Leslie Howard* and Norma Shearer; *Romeo and Juliet* (1954) Laurence Harvey and Susan Shentall; *Romeo and Juliet* (1966) Leonard Whiting and Olivia Hussey†; and *Romeo and Juliet* (1966), ballet with Rudolf Nureyev and Margot Fonteyn.

Rommel, Ed
First major league baseball umpire to wear glasses while umpiring (at a game between the Yankees and Washington on April 18, 1956).

Rommel, Erwin
(1891–1944) German field general, nicknamed the Desert Fox. He committed suicide after being implicated by the SS in an attempt on Hitler's life. Movie portrayals: *Five Graves to Cairo* (1943) Erich von Stroheim; *The Desert Fox* (1951) James Mason; *The Desert Rats* (1953) James Mason; *The Longest Day* (1962) Werner Hinz; *Hitler* (1962) Gregory Gay; *The Night of the Generals* (1967) Christopher Plummer; *Patton* (1970) Karl Michael Vogler; and *Raid on Rommel* (1971) Wolfgang Preiss. In 1974 Manfred Rommel, his son, was elected mayor of Stuttgart.

Romulus
Stephen Tolliver's (Ray Milland) pet Scottish terrier in the 1942 movie *Reap the Wild Wind.*

Romulus and Remus
Mythological founders of Ancient Rome. The pair was played in the 1963 movie *Duel of the Titans* by musclemen Steve Reeves** and Gordon Scott.

Ronald
Charger ridden by the 7th Earl of Cardigan†† (James Thomas Cardigan) at Balaklava on October 25, 1854. The horse's head was later stuffed. In the 1936 movie *The Charge of the Light Brigade* Lord Cardigan was portrayed by Charles Crocker King.

Room 222
Title of a popular ABC TV series (1969–1974). Room 222 was also the room occupied in the Riggs House by Charles Guiteau the day he assassinated President Garfield. (Garfield's parlor on the train car that day was 222.)

Room 1123
Douglas A. MacArthur's room at West Point.

Room 1472
Room in the Hotel La Reine Elizabeth in Montreal, Canada, where, on June

---

*Clark Gable had turned down the part, saying ''I don't look Shakespeare, I don't talk Shakespeare, and I won't do Shakespeare.''
†Whiting, age 17, and Hussey, age 16, were the two youngest actors to play the roles professionally.
**Steve Reeves was the 1947 AAU Mr. America.
††The cardigan sweater is named after him.

2, 1969, John Lennon, Yoko Ono, Tommy Smothers, Derek Taylor, Timothy Leary, and the Plastic Ono Band recorded "Give Peace a Chance."

Roosevelt, (Anna) Eleanor

(1884–1962) Maiden name of Eleanor Roosevelt, who was a niece of President Theodore Roosevelt (the daughter of his younger brother, Elliott). Theodore Roosevelt gave Eleanor away at her wedding to Franklin D. Roosevelt. Portrayals: *Sunrise at Campobello* (1960) Greer Garson; *Eleanor and Franklin* (1976 TV) Jane Alexander (MacKenzie Phillips at age 14); *Eleanor and Franklin: The White House Years* (1977 TV) Jane Alexander; *Backstairs at the White House* (1979 TV) Eileen Heckart; and *F.D.R.: The Last Year* (1980 TV play) Eileen Heckart.

Roosevelt Hotel

Hollywood site of the first Academy Awards presentation, May 16, 1929.

Rooster

Tony Baretta's informant, played on the TV series *Baretta* by Michael D. Roberts.

Rosa Mine Gold Pearlman "Reba"

Wife of Abie (comic strip *Abie the Agent*).

Rose, Billy

(1899–1966) Producer and lyricist who wrote "Barney Google," "Without a Song," and "It's Only a Paper Moon." He produced many Broadway musicals, including *Jumbo* (1935) and *Carmen Jones* (1943). Beginning in the late 1930s, he produced the *Aquacades*. Rose was portrayed in the 1975 movie *Funny Lady* by James Caan (Robert Blake was originally considered for the part).

Roseburg High

School attended by Mary Richards (Mary Tyler Moore) in her hometown of Roseburg, Minnesota, in the TV series *The Mary Tyler Moore Show*.

Rosecliff

Mansion on Bellevue Avenue in Newport, Rhode Island, designed by Stanford White. It was this house that was used as the home of Jay Gatsby in the 1974 version of *The Great Gatsby*. The house was also used as the home of Sarah Bernhardt in the 1977 movie *The Incredible Sarah*. Diana Barrymore's mother, Michael Strange, was born in Rosecliff.

Rosenberg, Julius and Ethel

Husband and wife who were arrested, tried, and executed for spying in the United States in the 1940s. They were electrocuted at Sing Sing Prison on June 19, 1953. The Rosenbergs were portrayed in the TV movie *The Trial of Julius and Ethel Rosenberg* by Allan Arbus and Brenda Vaccaro.

Rose of Tralee

Theme song of the radio series *Backstage Wife*, performed by Chet Kingbury.

Ross, Barney

(1909–1967) Born Barnet Rasofsky, he was the lightweight and junior welterweight boxing champion in 1933, and the welterweight champion in 1934. Ross was awarded the Distinguished Service Cross, the Silver Star, and the Presidential Citation for killing 20 Japanese soldiers on Guadalcanal when he was a Marine. He was portrayed in the 1957 movie *Monkey on My Back* by Cameron Mitchell.

Ens. George Ross, one of John F. Kennedy's crew members on *PT109* when it was rammed on August 2, 1943, by the Japanese destroyer Amigiri, was nicknamed "Barney" after the boxer. At Princeton George Ross had been the intramural heavyweight boxing champion. George Ross was portrayed in the 1963 movie *PT109* by Robert Culp.

Ross, Diana
Lead singer of the Supremes and then a solo artist. She was the first entertainer to be invited to the Imperial Palace in Japan where, in 1973, she had an audience with the empress.

Ross, Leonard
12-year-old boy who won the top prize on the TV quiz show *The $64,000 Challenge*. His subject was the stock market.

Rossmore
Ohio hometown of the Jackson family in the TV series *That's My Boy.* Jack Johnson, Jr. (Gil Stratton, Jr.), attended Rossmore College.

Roth, Lillian
(1910–1980) American actress (born Lillian Rutstein) who married eight times, eventually became an alcoholic. She described her tragic life in her autobiography *Beyond My Worth*. Roth was portrayed in the 1956 movie *I'll Cry Tomorrow* by Susan Hayward (by Carole Ann Campbell as a child and by Gail Ganley at age 15).

Rotolo, Suze
Woman with whom Bob Dylan is walking arm and arm down West 4th Street in New York on the cover of his second album *The Free Wheelin' Bob Dylan* (1963).

Rothschild, Meyer
(1743–1812) Jewish financier who founded the famous House of Rothschild. His sons and descendants to the present have been bankers, members of Parliament, members of the House of Lords, and successful businessmen. Meyer was portrayed in the 1934 *The House of Rothschild* by George Arliss (the actor portrayed both father and son). In the Broadway musical titled *The Rothschilds*, Meyer Rothschild was played by Hal Linden.

Rothstein, Arnold
New York gambler blamed for the rigging of the 1919 World Series. He always carried no less than $100,000 in cash on him. He was shot to death while playing poker at the Park Central Hotel. Arnold Rothstein was the only real gangster mentioned by name in the 1972 movie *The Godfather*. He was

portrayed in the 1961 movie *King of the Roaring Twenties* by David Janssen (Jim Baird as a boy), and (loosely) in two other movies: *Street of Chance* (1930) by William Powell (as Natural Davis) and *Now I'll Tell* (1934) by Spencer Tracy (as Murray Golden). Portrayed in the TV series *Gangster Chronicles* by George DiCenzo.

Roux, Emile
(1853–1933) French physician and bacteriologist who worked with Louis Pasteur on a number of experiments. Movie portrayals: He was portrayed by Henry O'Neill in the 1936 movie *The Story of Louis Pasteur.*

Rover
Call sign of the PBY (VMB611) flown by Cmdr. Paul Eddington (Kirk Douglas) when he spotted the Japanese battleship in the 1965 movie *In Harm's Way.* The home base call sign was "John Paul."

Rover
Special-built lunar vehicle used by *Apollo* astronauts on the moon.

Rover's Bar
Pub located at 11 Coronation Street that was the setting of the British TV series *Coronation Street.*

Rowan, Andrew Summers
Volunteer sent by President McKinley in April 1898 to deliver a message to Cuban rebel leader Garcia during the Spanish-American War.

Rowe, Dick
London Decca Records executive who turned down the Beatles when they auditioned for him. A few weeks later he did sign Brian Poole and the Tremeloes. (He was not the only record company executive to turn down the Beatles—but he did hear the group in two auditions.)

Rowe, Gary Thomas Jr.
FBI informant on the Ku Klux Klan during the civil rights movement in the 1960s. He was portrayed in the 1979 TV movie *My Undercover Years With the Ku Klux Klan* by Don Meredith.

Roxy Theatre
New York City theater named after Samuel Rothafel that opened in 1927.

Royal Hawaiian
Hotel (Room 108) in Hawaii that was the setting of the 1978 movie *Goin' Coconuts* starring Donny and Marie Osmond.

Royal Order of Camels
Fraternal organization to which the men of Hooterville belonged in the TV series *Petticoat Junction.*

Royal Order of the Mystic Nile Lodge
Fraternity of which Amos McCoy (Walter Brennan) was a member in the TV series *The McCoys.*

Royal Rascal, The
   1927 silent film being premiered at Grauman's Chinese Theatre in the
   opening scene of the 1952 movie *Singin' in the Rain*.
Royce, Betty
   Singer who dubbed Debbie Reynolds's dubbing of Jean Hagen's singing
   voice in the 1952 movie *Singin' in the Rain*.
Roy Powers
   17-year-old Eagle Scout comic hero who appeared as the official symbol of
   the Boy Scouts of America in 1935. He was a member of the Beaver Patrol.
   Roy Powers was played in the 1939 movie serial *Scouts to the Rescue* by
   Jackie Cooper (as Eagle Scout Bruce Scott).
Rubáiyát
   Poem written by the Persian poet Omar Khayyám. In a 1958 movie *I Want
   to Live!* Barbara Graham (Susan Hayward) used a phrase from the *Rubáiyát*,
   "I came like water," to identify her contact, Ben (Peter Breck), who replied,
   "And like wind I go."
Ruby, Harry
   (1895–1974) Co-writer with Bert Kalmar of many songs, including "Who's
   Sorry Now," "I Wanna Be Loved by You," and "Three Little Words."
   Ruby was portrayed in the 1950 movie *Three Little Words* by Red Skelton.
   His wife, actress Eileen Percy, was portrayed by Arlene Dahl.
Ruditsky, Barney
   New York City police detective of the 1920s–1940s whose exploits were
   recounted in the TV series *The Lawless Years* in which Ruditsky was por-
   trayed by James Gregory.
Rudolph, Wilma
   Child polio victim who became the first woman to win three Gold Medals in
   the Olympics for track, in 1960. She was also the first female to be named
   UPI Athlete of the Year. Rudolph was portrayed in the 1978 TV movie *Wilma*
   by Shirley Jo Finney.
Rudy
   Ostrich in *Barney Google* comic strip (named for Rudolph Valentino).
Rufus
   Prime Minister Winston Churchill's pet dog.
Rugg, Micah
   Blacksmith who took out the first patent for nuts and bolts (August 31,
   1842).
Rugley, North Dakota
   Town that includes the site (indicated by the U.S. Geological Survey) of the
   geographical center of North America.
Runyon, (Alfred) Damon
   (1880–1946) American journalist and writer of several short stories and

plays. He was portrayed in the 1978 movie *The Private Files of J. Edgar Hoover* by Jack Cassidy, and in the 1978 TV movie *Ring of Passion* by Allen Garfield.

Ruppelt, Edward J.
First director of the Air Force's Project Blue Book. He coined the term *UFO*.

Russell, Lillian
(1861–1922) Soprano born Helen Louise Leonard and called the American Beauty Rose. Movie portrayals: *Diamond Jim* (1935) Alice Faye; *The Great Ziegfeld* (1936) Ruth Gillette; and *Lillian Russell* (1940) Jean Arthur.

Russia
Country described by Winston Churchill as "a riddle wrapped in a mystery inside an enigma" (in a broadcast on October 1, 1939); and by Czar Peter the Great as a country in which things that just don't happen, happen.

Rusty's
Manhattan restaurant (1271 Third Avenue) owned and run by baseball player Daniel "Rusty" Staub.

Rutland Township, Montgomery County, Kansas
Location of most of Laura Ingalls Wilder's *Little House on the Prairie* (novels).

Rutledge, Ann
(1816–1835) Fiancée of Abraham Lincoln who died suddenly of malarial fever. Movie portrayals: *Abraham Lincoln* (1924) Ruth Clifford; *Abraham Lincoln* (1930) Una Merkel; *Young Mr. Lincoln* (1939) Pauline Moore; and *Abe Lincoln in Illinois* (1940) Mary Howard.

Rutles, The
Takeoff on the Beatles in Eric Idle's 1978 TV movie *All You Need Is Cash*. The four are: Dirk McQuickly (Eric Idle), bass guitar; Stig O'Hara (Rikki Fataar), lead guitar; Barry Wom (John Halsey), drummer; and Ron Nasty (Neil Innes), rhythm guitar. The original fifth member was named Leopo. The original drummer was Barrington Womball. George Harrison played an interviewer in the film. The group's four movies were: *A Hard Day's Rut; Ouch!; Yellow Submarine Sandwich;* and *Let It Rot.* Their manager was Leggy Mountbatten.

Ruz, Juanita Castro
Cuban leader Fidel Castro's sister, who immigrated to the United States in 1954.

Ryan, Leo
U.S. representative from California who was killed at Jonestown, Guyana, on November 18, 1978. He was laid to rest in Golden Gate National Cemetery in a grave next to Adm. Chester W. Nimitz. Ryan was portrayed in the 1980 TV movie *Guyana Tragedy: The Story of Jim Jones* by Ned Beatty, and in the 1979 movie *Guyana: Cult of the Damned* by Gene Barry (as Leo O'Brien).

Rydell High

Los Angeles high school featuring the Class of 1959 in the 1978 movie *Grease*. The football team was the Rangers, and the school's principal was Principal McGee (Eve Arden). The Rangers were teamed against the Gladiators. The movie was actually filmed at two Los Angeles high schools, Venice and Huntington.

6

Number of people who can utilize the Enterprise's transporter at the same time in the TV series *Star Trek*.

6

Seconds left in the 15-round championship fight when Sugar Ray Leonard TKO'd defending WBC welterweight title defender Wilfred Benitez in Las Vegas, on November 31, 1979. The Filippino referee, Carlos Padilla, stopped the fight with just 6 seconds to go.

6

Identification of the prisoner (played by Patrick McGoohan) in the TV series *The Prisoner*. No. 6 gave his birthday as March 19, 1938, at 4:31 a.m.

6T423

Special automobile license plate given to George Temple, father of actress Shirley Temple, in 1936. The 6 stood for Shirley's age, the T for Temple, the 4 for her month of birth (April), and the 23 for her day of birth.

6:50 (p.m.)

Time that the clock always reads in front of the Lenin Mausoleum in Moscow. It is fixed at the time of Lenin's death.

7 Blocks of Granite

Nickname of the football line at Fordham University in the 1930s. John Druze (end), Leo Pacquin (end), Ed Franco (tackle), A. Barbatsky (tackle), Alex Wojciechowicz (center), Nat Pierce (guard), and Vince Lombardi (guard).

Seven Faces of Dr. Lao, The

1964 George Pal movie (based on the 1935 Charles Finney novel, *The Circus of Dr. Lao*) starring Tony Randall. The 7 faces are: Dr. Lao, Merlin, Medusa, Pan, Appolonius, Giant Serpent, and Abominable Snowman.

7th floor
Setting of the action in the TV serial *General Hospital*.

7 Mary 3
Motorcycle call letters of California highway patrol officer Jon Baker (Larry Wilcox) in the TV series *Chips*.

7 Mary 4
Motorcycle call letters of California highway patrol officer Frank "Ponch" Poncherello (Erik Estrada) in the TV series *Chips*.

7 Lt–26 Rt–14 Lt
Combination of the safe on board the train robbed in the 1965 movie *Cat Ballou*.

7:15 p.m.
Exact time each evening that detective Nero Wolfe begins his dinner. (In some novels it is given as 7:30.)

16
Apache Indians shot by the members of the Overland Stage before they ran out of ammunition in the 1939 movie *Stagecoach*.

16 Pounds
Weight of a shot put, and maximum legal weight of a bowling ball.

16 Months, 13 Days, 4 Hours, 23 Minutes
Time that Joe Bell (John Garfield) served for a crime he never committed in the 1939 movie *Dust Be My Destiny*.

17
Uniform number of quarterback Ron Catlan (Charlton Heston) of the New Orleans Saints football team in the 1968 movie *Number One*

17 Castle Heights Road
Los Angeles home address of Blanche Tyler (Barbara Harris) in the 1976 movie *Family Plot*.

17 Inches
Scarlett O'Hara's waist size, the smallest in three Georgia counties, in Margaret Mitchell's novel *Gone With the Wind*.

$62
Weekly income of both Ralph Kramden (bus driver) and Ed Norton (sewer worker) in the TV series *The Honeymooners*.

60A Half Moon Street
London home address of Capt. Hugh Drummond (detective series by H. C. McNeile).

70
Number of the red Porsche 935 Twin Turbo with 650 hp that Paul Newman drove to second place in the 24-hour Le Mans race in 1979. Newman, at 54, was the oldest driver in the race.

78

Number of episodes of *Star Trek* filmed from September 8, 1966, until the TV series was canceled, April 4, 1969. The episode "The Menagerie" was broadcast in two parts, making 79 telecasts of 78 episodes.

606

Nickname of Salvarsan, a cure for syphilis created by Dr. Paul Ehrlich, who discovered it on his 606th experiment. He received a Nobel Prize in 1908. Dr. Ehrlich was portrayed by Edward G. Robinson in the 1940 movie *Dr. Ehrlich's Magic Bullet*. Some famous victims of syphilis: Napoleon, Beethoven, Custer, Wild Bill Hickok, Christopher Columbus, and Al Capone (who died from it).

616

Rodney Harrington's (Barry Coe) 1941 Maine automobile license plate in the 1957 movie *Peyton Place*.

625 Morris Street

San Francisco address of the house in which Patty Hearst was finally found by the FBI in September 1975.

632 Elysian Fields

New Orleans address of Stanley and Blanche Kowalski's apartment in Tennessee Williams's play *A Streetcar Named Desire*.

635 QHH

California automobile license plate of the 1963 green low-rider Chevy that trailed private eye Moses Wine (Richard Dreyfuss) in the 1978 movie *The Big Fix*.

636 North Beach Street

Central City home address of Corey Anders (voice of Marc Hamil) in the animated TV series *Jeannie*.

653

Number of fans who watched the Oakland A's play the Seattle Mariners in a night game on Tuesday, April 17, 1979. It was the A's smallest crowd ever.

666

Diabolical Trinity: Devil, Anti-Christ, False Prophet (from the Book of Revelation 13:18). The numbers were found on the scalp of Damien (Harvey Stephens) in the 1976 movie *The Omen*.

685

Number of drinking fountains inside the Pentagon building.

699

Record number of at-bats for one season, held by Dave Cash (established in 1975).

721 Lombard Street

Home address in Zenith of Lulu Bains (Shirley Jones) in the 1960 movie *Elmer Gantry*.

6,270 Pounds
World record weight lifted (backlift off trestles) by 23-year-old Paul Anderson on June 12, 1957, in Toccoa, Georgia.

$64,000 Challenge
TV quiz show hosted by Sonny Fox and later by Ralph Story. Patty Duke once won $32,000 on the program.

655321
Alex's (Malcolm McDowell) prison number in the 1971 movie *A Clockwork Orange*.

628-3297
Chief's phone number in the TV series *Get Smart*.

652-1652
Home phone number in Los Angeles of John Norman Howard (Kris Kristofferson) in the 1977 movie *A Star Is Born*.

$776,330
Amount CBS-TV was forced to pay to Tom and Dick Smothers in 1973 for breach of contract in the cancellation of the *Smothers Brothers* TV show. The award was decided by a Los Angeles Federal District Court jury.

6977859
U.S. Army serial number of Pvt. Robert E. Lee Prewitt (Montgomery Clift) in the 1953 movie *From Here to Eternity*.

68° 45′ N 76° 10′ W
Crash site of B52 in the 1955 movie *Strategic Air Command*.

S
Letter that Professor Bertrom Potts (Gary Cooper) was researching for the encyclopedia he was editing in the 1941 movie *Ball of Fire*.

SAM 1
California automobile license plate number of Samantha Taylor's (Julie Andrews) Mercedes Benz in the 1979 movie *"10"*.

SAM 27000
Call sign that *Air Force One,* carrying Richard Nixon, changed to while en route from Andrews Air Force Base to San Clemente, California, on August 9, 1974. The call sign change occurred at 38° 35.5′ N, 92° 26.6′ W (13 miles southwest of Jefferson City, Missouri) at 12:03:25 p.m., when Gerald Ford became the 38th president of the United States. SAM = Special Air Mission, 27000—the tail number of the Boeing 707.

SOS
Southland Oil System—the gas company that W. W. (Burt Reynolds) robbed, using his 1955 two-tone (gold and black) anniversary Olds (only 50 were built), in the 1975 movie *W.W. and the Dixie Dance Kings*.

S. Peter Prior Junior College
School attended by both Dobie Gillis and his good buddy Maynard G. Krebs

after the two got out of the Army in the TV series *The Many Loves of Dobie Gillis.*

S.W.I.N.E.

*S*tudents *W*ildly *I*ndignant about *N*early *E*verything—radical group of protesters that appeared in Al Capp's *Li'l Abner* comic strip in the late 1960s.

Sabich, Vladimir "Spider"

One-time world champion skier who, on March 21, 1977, was shot to death by Claudine Longet (ex-wife of singer Andy Williams) at Aspen, Colorado. For the accidental shooting with a .22 pistol, Longet was sentenced to 30 days in the county jail.

Sabor

Tiger in Tarzan novel series (though tigers are not found in Africa).

Sabre Tooth Tigers

Barney Rubble's Boy Scout troop when he was a young lad in the TV series *The Flintstones.*

Sacajawea

(1787–1812) American Indian woman who accompanied Lewis and Clark on their 1805 expedition as interpreter. Sacajawea, a member of the Shoshone tribe, was called Bird Woman. She was portrayed in the 1955 movie *The Far Horizons* by Donna Reed.

Sachem

387-ton American ship in which the Siamese twins Chang and Eng first traveled to the United States in 1829. They arrived on August 16, after a 138-day voyage.

Sacramento Register

Newspaper for which Tom Bradford (Dick Van Patten) worked in the TV series *Eight Is Enough.*

Sacred Emily

Poem by Gertrude Stein that contains the oft-quoted line: "A rose is a rose is a rose is a rose."

Sade, Donatien Alphonse François de

(1740–1814) French soldier and author of such perverted novels as *Justine* (1791) and *Juliette* (1798). He spent most of his life in prison and died in an insane asylum. The Marquis de Sade was portrayed in the 1969 movie *De Sade* by Keir Dullea (Max Kiebach as a boy).

Sadie McKee

1934 movie starring Joan Crawford. This was the movie that Blanche Hudson (Joan Crawford) watched on TV in the 1962 film *What Ever Happened to Baby Jane.* (See: **Ex-Lady**)

Sadie Thompson

Wayward woman who is the central character of Somerset Maugham's novel *Rain,* in which she is stranded on the Pacific island of Pago Pago. Jeanne

Eagels played the part on the stage. Gloria Swanson (*Sadie Thompson*, 1928), Joan Crawford (*Rain*, 1932), and Rita Hayworth (*Miss Sadie Thompson* 1953) played Sadie Thompson in the movies.

Sadler, Sgt. Barry

Vietnam veteran who in 1966 had a million-selling record, "The Ballad of the Green Berets," which was composed by Sadler and author Robin Moore, who wrote the book *The Green Berets*. Sgt. Sadler posed for the picture on the cover of Moore's book.

Safari Club

Chicago nightclub where Molly (Kim Novak) worked in the 1955 movie *The Man with the Golden Arm*.

Safe Combination

8Rt-27Lt-18Lt-11Rt was the combination of the safe that held the arming keys of the missiles in the 1977 movie *Twilight's Last Gleaming*.

Sahara Tahoe Hotel

Nevada hotel where Ann-Margret fell 22 feet to the stage during a rehearsal in September 1972. She broke her jaw and had a brain concussion.

St. Botolphs, Massachusetts

Small village setting of two novels by John Cheevers: *The Wapshot Chronicles* (1957) and *The Wapshot Scandal* (1964).

St. Clair County

U.S. Navy LST (No. 1096) of which Lt. Victor Donald (Pat Boone) was the executive officer in the 1961 movie *All Hands on Deck*.

St. Francis

(1182–1226) Francis Bernardone, Italian friar, founder of the Franciscan order, who is popularly known for his love of animals. He is the patron saint of ecology. He was portrayed in the 1961 movie *Francis of Assisi* by Bradford Dillman, and in the 1973 movie *Brother Sun, Sister Moon* by Graham Faulker.

St. Francis Hotel

San Francisco Hotel where movie comedian Roscoe "Fatty" Arbuckle was alleged to have raped Virginia Rappe on September 5, 1921, in Suite 1221. She died on September 10. After three trials, Arbuckle was acquitted of the charge. Al Jolson died in this same hotel, of a heart attack, on October 24, 1950, while playing cards* (rummy). Drummer Gene Krupa was arrested there by the FBI on January 18, 1943, for possession of narcotics. The St. Francis was also the site of the attempted assassination of President Ford by Sara Jane Moore, on September 22, 1975. It was the first San Francisco hotel to serve ice cubes and the only hotel that hires a full-time coin washer ($2,000 worth of coins are washed each day).

---

*With accompanist Harry Akstad and arranger Martin Fried.

St. Joseph, Missouri
Departure point for the 1957–1965 TV series *Wagon Train* on the westward trek to California.

St. Jude
Patron saint of the impossible. It was his medal that Father Devers (John Marley) gave to Barbara Graham (Susan Hayward) hours before her execution in the gas chamber at San Quentin in the 1958 movie *I Want to Live!*

St. Louis
Passenger liner (Hamburg-American Line) that departed from Hamburg, Germany, on May 27, 1939, for Havana, Cuba, with 937 Jewish passengers. They were not permitted to land at that or any other port until finally, on June 17, the ship was allowed to dock at Antwerp. The ship's commander was Capt. Gustav Schroeder. The story is retold in the 1976 movie *Voyage of the Damned* (based on the 1974 book of the same name).

St. Louis Blues
Gangster Louie Brook's (George Raft) favorite song in the 1932 movie *Dancing in the Dark*.

St. Louise Cardinals
Baseball team featured in the movie *Death on the Diamond*. The Cards were the favorite team of Gus (William Bendix) in the 1943 movie *Lifeboat*.

St. Nicholas
14th-century bishop of Myra who became the inspiration for Santa Claus. St. Nick is the patron saint of children, pawnbrokers, thieves, and of Russia.

St. Peter
Simon Peter, disciple of John the Baptist and later of Jesus, died a martyr in A.D. 67. Movie portrayals: *King of Kings* (1927) Ernest Torrence; *The Robe* (1953) Michael Rennie; *Demetrius and the Gladiators* (1954) Michael Rennie; *King of Kings* (1961) Royal Dano; *Barabbas* (1962) Harry Andrews; *Jesus of Nazareth* (1978) James Farentino; and *The Day Christ Died* (1980 TV) Jay O. Sanders.

St. Swithin's Teaching Hospital
London setting of the TV series *Doctor in the House*.

Salcedo, Teresa
First baby to be born in Disneyland. When she was born on July 4, 1979, Donald Duck presented her with Disneyland Birth Certificate No. 1.

Sallie Gardner
Racehorse used to prove that Leland Stanford was correct in his bet that, at a central point while racing, all four legs of a horse are off the ground at the same time. The photographer was Eadweard Muybridge, who used 24 cameras (1872).

Salome
(A.D. 14–62) Granddaughter of Herod the Great who asked for and received

the head of John the Baptist as a gift for her dancing. She is the subject of the 1905 opera by Richard Strauss. Movie portrayals: *Salome—Where She Danced* (1945) Yvonne DeCarlo; and *Salome* (1953) Rita Hayworth.

Salter, Susanna
27-year-old woman who in 1887 became the first female mayor in the United States. She served a one-year term as mayor of Argonia, Kansas.

Salinas Valley
Original title of John Steinbeck's 1952 novel *East of Eden*.

Salt Peanuts
Song that President Carter joined in singing with John Birks "Dizzy" Gillespie during a White House Jazz Festival on June 18, 1978, in which more than 30 musicians took part.

Salty
Sinbad Jr.'s pet parrot (voice of Mel Blanc) in the TV cartoon series *The Alvin Show.*

Sam Benedict
1962–1963 TV series starring Edmond O'Brien. The character Sam Benedict was based on an actual San Francisco lawyer, Jacob Jake Ehrlich.

Sam Diamond
Detective played by Peter Falk in the 1976 movie *Murder by Death.*

Samson
Francis Gary Power's dog as a young boy. He gave this information in order to prove to the Americans that he was indeed Francis Powers when he was about to be exchanged for Col. Rudolf Abel on February 10, 1962, at 8:52 a.m. on the Glienicker Bridge in East Germany. He volunteered the dog's name after he couldn't remember the name of his high school football coach when asked.

Samson
Biblical hero of enormous strength who was captured and enslaved by his enemies because of the treachery of Delilah. His eyes were then put out. Samson was portrayed in the 1949 movie *Samson and Delilah* by Victor Mature.

Samson and Delilah
The 1949 movie starring Victor Mature and Hedy Lamarr that was being directed by Cecil B. DeMille in a scene in the 1950 movie *Sunset Boulevard*. A movie marquee advertised the film as the circus rode through town in DeMille's 1952 movie *The Greatest Show on Earth.*

Sand, George
Pseudonym of French novelist Amandine Aurore Lucie Dupin (1804–1876), who was romantically involved with composer Frederic Chopin. She was

portrayed in the 1945 movie *A Song to Remember* by Merle Oberon, and in the 1960 movie *Song Without End* by Patricia Morison.

Sandhurst

British equivalent of West Point. Ian Fleming and David Niven were graduates of Sandhurst.

Sands of Time

Theme song of 1949–1952 TV series *The Clock,* narrated by Larry Semon.

Sandy Harbor

Town setting of the radio series *Ethel and Albert.*

San Francisco Earthquake

It began at 5:13 a.m. on April 18, 1906, and lasted about 75 seconds. It registered 8.3 on the Richter scale. The San Francisco earthquake is featured in the following movies: *San Francisco* (1936) Clark Gable; *The Sisters* (1938) Errol Flynn; and *Flame of the Barbary Coast* (1945) John Wayne. Comedian Joe E. Brown, then age 14, was awakened by the quake. Film producer Sol Lesser was a 15-year-old boy when the quake hit his home. Comedian Leon Errol was performing in the city when the quake struck. Enrico Caruso was so shaken by the quake that he left San Francisco the next day, swearing to never return. (He never did.)

San Francisco Memorial Hospital

Medical facility where Dr. John McIntyre (Pernell Roberts) practices medicine in the TV series *Trapper John, M.D.*

San Francisco vs. Los Angeles

In the 1968 movie *Bullit* a radio at the Hotel Daniels gave the baseball score of a double header: the San Francisco Giants defeated the Los Angeles Dodgers 2–0 and 4–1. In the 1962 movie *Experiment in Terror* the San Francisco Giants were playing the Los Angeles Dodgers at Candlestick Park. In the 1954 movie *The Bridges at Toko-Ri* the football score of a San Francisco 49er and Los Angeles Rams game was given over the ship's radio (the 49ers were leading). In the 1978 movie *The Big Fix* the San Francisco 49ers defeated the Los Angeles Rams 49–24.

Sanger, Margaret

(1883–1966) Pioneer in the birth-control movement. She was portrayed by Bonnie Franklin in the 1980 TV movie *Portrait of a Rebel: Margaret Sanger.*

San Marco

Fictitious country in which the 1971 Woody Allen movie *Bananas* is set.

San Pascal

California town setting of the 1972 TV series *Me and the Chimp.*

San Paula

Passenger liner on which William Powell and Joan Blondell were married on September 19, 1936, in San Pedro Harbor.

Santa Claus
Jolly man who delivers gifts to the children of the world every Christmas. Also known as Kris Kringle and Jolly Old Nick. In 1890 James Edgar became the first department store Santa Claus (for the Boston store in Brockton, Massachusetts). Saint Nicholas, a 4th-century bishop, is often credited with inspiring the character of Santa Claus, since he delivered gifts at Christmastime. Some movie portrayals: *Babes in Toyland* (1934) Ferdinand Munier; *Miracle on 34th Street* (1947) Edmund Gwenn; *The Seven Little Foys* (1955) Oliver Blake; and *Miracle on 34th Street* (1973 TV) Sebastion Cabot. Errol Flynn wore a Santa Claus suit in the 1946 movie *Never Say Goodbye*. Bob Hope wore a Santa Claus suit in the 1951 movie *The Lemon Drop Kid*. Producer Phil Spector wore a Santa Claus suit on the cover and back of the reissue of *Phil Spector's Christmas Album*.

Santa Fe Chief
Passenger train that once ran from Hollywood to New York.

Santa Monica
California community in which Drs. Marcus Welby (Robert Young) and Steven Kiley (James Brolin) practiced medicine in the TV series *Marcus Welby, M.D.*

Sapphire
Wife of the Kingfish, George Stevens, played in the radio/TV series *Amos 'n' Andy* by Ernesta Wade, the mother of rock musician Billy Preston.

Sarteret, Raoul
Prisoner in the city jail of St. Pierre who became the sole survivor of the volcanic eruption of Mt. Peleé on May 8, 1902. He was blinded for life.

Saturday Night Massacre
October 20, 1973: The night that President Nixon ordered Attorney General Eliot Richardson to fire the special prosecutor for the Watergate investigation, Archibald Cox. Richardson refused and resigned in protest. Deputy Attorney General William Ruckelshaus also refused and was fired. U.S. Solicitor Robert Bork was then named acting attorney general, and he fired Cox.

Saunders, William "Smokey"
Youngest jockey to win the Triple Crown (1935). He was 17.

Savrola
Sir Winston Churchill's only novel, written in 1900.

Sawfish, USS
Nuclear submarine (No. 623) commanded by Cmdr. Dwight Lionel Towers (Gregory Peck) in the 1959 movie *On the Beach* (based on the 1957 novel by Nevil Shute).

Scamp
President Theodore Roosevelt's terrier.

Scar

Horse ridden by Britt Ponset (James Stewart) on the radio series *The Six Shooter.*

Scarecrow

Scarecrow in L. Frank Baum's *The Wizard of Oz.* The character was played in both the 1902 silent movie and the 1903 musical play by Fred Stone, and in the 1939 movie by Ray Bolger. He was played by Hinton Battle on Broadway in *The Wiz,* and by Michael Jackson in the 1978 movie *The Wiz.* The Scarecrow asks the Wizard for brains.

Scarlett O'Hara

Southern belle played in the 1939 movie *Gone With the Wind* by Vivien Leigh. Her father called her Katie. Her three married names were: Hamilton, Kennedy, and Butler. Before the release of the 1939 movie, Robert Montgomery and Constance Bennett played Rhett Butler and Scarlett O'Hara in a single scene heard on the radio series *Sears-Roebuck Hour.*

Scatter

Elvis Presley's pet monkey. He died from cirrhosis of the liver.

Schlitz Light

Only two words spoken by James Coburn in Schlitz beer TV commercials. Coburn received $500,000 for the ad.

Schenck, Joseph M

Russian-born Hollywood director who in 1933 founded 20th-Century Motion Pictures with Darryl Zanuck. Schenck was married to actress Norma Talmadge. He was portrayed in the 1980 TV miniseries *Moviola* by John Marley.

Schmeling, Max

German Heavyweight Champion of the World after he beat Jack Sharkey on a foul on June 12, 1930. On June 21, 1932, Schmeling lost his title to Sharkey. As a member of Germany's paratroops in World War II, Schmeling parachuted onto the island of Crete. Movie portrayals: *The Joe Louis Story* (1953) Buddy Thorpe; and *Ring of Passion* (1978 TV) Stephen Macht.

Schmid, Al

U.S. Marine who was blinded by a Japanese grenade at Guadalcanal during World War II. Before his injury, he had reportedly killed over 200 Japanese soldiers. Schmid was portrayed in the 1945 movie *Pride of the Marines* by John Garfield.

Schockley, William

Inventor of the first transistor on July 5, 1951.

School Days

Theme song of the radio series *The Quiz Kids.*

Schubert, Franz Peter

(1797–1828) Austrian composer who wrote over 600 songs in his short life. He was portrayed in the 1934 movie *Blossom Time* by Richard Tauber.

Schultz, Dutch

Nickname of Chicago Gangster Arthur Flegenheimer (1902–1935). His last dying words (never explained) were: "A boy has never wept, or dashed a thousand krim." Movie portrayals: *Mad Dog Coll* (1961) Vincent Gardenia; *Portrait of a Mobster* (1961) Vic Morrow; and *Lepke* (1975) John Durren.

Schumann, Clara Josephine Wieck

(1819–1896) Pianist and music teacher whose husband was the German composer Robert Schumann. She was portrayed in the 1947 movie *Song of Love* by Katharine Hepburn.

Schumann, Robert

(1810–1856) German composer and pianist who married Clara Josephine Wieck. He was portrayed in the 1947 movie *Song of Love** by Paul Henreid.

Schwarzenegger, Arnold

Six-time winner of the title "Mr. Olympia" (1970–1975) who is featured in the 1977 movie *Pumping Iron*. The bodies of Schwarzenegger and Franco Columbo (Mr. Universe) were used on the cover of the Grand Funk Railroad album *All the Girls in the World Beware*.

Scooter

Nickname of baseball player Phil Rizzuto.

Scooter

Nickname of muppet Simon Smith (voice: Richard Hunt) in the TV series *The Muppet Show*. His uncle, J. P. Grosse (voice: Jerry Nelson), owns the theater in which the muppets perform. Scooter's dog is Muppy (voice: Dave Goetz.)

Scott, Blanche

First woman to solo in an airplane, on October 23, 1910, in Fort Wayne, Indiana. Her instructor was Glen Curtiss.

Scott, Col. Robert L.

World War II American fighter pilot who began flying in combat at the age of 34 with the Flying Tigers in China. He was portrayed in the 1945 movie *God Is My Co-Pilot* by Dennis Morgan (Buddy Burroughs as a boy). After the war he authored a number of World War II–related books.

Scott, Wendell

First black stock car champion. He always drove No. 34. Scott was portrayed in the 1977 movie *Greased Lightning* by Richard Pryor.

Scott, Winfield

(1786-1866) American Army officer who was general-in-chief of the U.S. Army in 1841 and the American commander during the Mexican War. He was defeated for the presidency in 1852 by Franklin Pierce. Scott was

---

*14-year-old choirboy George Chakiris made his movie debut in *Song of Love*, singing as part of a chorus.

portrayed in the 1941 movie *They Died With Their Boots On* by Sydney Greenstreet.

Scrambled Egg

Original title of the Beatles' hit ballad "Yesterday" (composition by Paul McCartney, though credited to Lennon-McCartney).

Screen's Perfect Lover, The

Nickname of actor John Gilbert who failed to go from silents to talkies.

Scuber

Ship featured in the TV series *Follow the Sun*.

Seacliff

Barbour family's home near San Francisco in the radio series *One Man's Family*.

Sea-Cook, The

Original title of Robert Louis Stevenson's 1883 novel *Treasure Island*.

Sea Crab

Two-man self-propelled sub belonging to the atomic sub *Seaview* in the TV series *Voyage to the Bottom of the Sea*.

Sea Gals

Cheerleaders of the Seattle Seahawks football team.

Seale, Bobby

Member of the Black Panthers. He was one of a group of people who attempted to negotiate a solution to the Attica Prison riot (August 22–September 13, 1971). Seale was portrayed in the 1980 movie *Attica* by Noble Lee Lester.

Seaport

Town setting of the 1939 Mickey Rooney–Judy Garland movie *Babes in Arms*.

Sears and Roebuck

Largest chain of commercial retail stores in America. It was founded on September 16, 1893, by Richard Sears and Alvah C. Roebuck. They first sold watches. Vincent Price was once an art purchaser for the firm in Los Angeles, and John Davidson was once a Sears catalogue model. Gloria Swanson, Ginger Rogers, Lauren Bacall, and Susan Hayward all modeled for the Sears catalogue.

Sears Radio Theatre

Radio drama series begun in 1979, running 5 nights a week, hosted each evening by a different person:

Night	Presentation	Host
Monday	Western Night	Lorne Greene
Tuesday	Comedy Night	Andy Griffith
Wednesday	Mystery Night	Vincent Price

| Thursday | Love and Hate Night | Cicely Tyson |
| Friday | Adventure Night | Richard Widmark (later Howard Duff) |

Sears, Roebuck Catalog (1962)
In this edition not one woman modeling Sears maternity lingerie wore a wedding ring.

Seattle
Theme song of the TV series *Here Come the Brides*. It became a hit record for Perry Como in 1969.

Sea Witch
Tugboat run by Capt. John Sands (Charlton Heston) in the 1959 movie *The Wreck of the Mary Deare* (based on the Hammond Innes novel of the same name). The *Mary Deare* sank the tug.

Sebastian
Everett family rooster in the TV series *Nanny and the Professor*.

Sebastian
Pet cat of the rock 'n roll group Josie and the Pussycats (animated TV series).

Secoma
Puget Sound hometown of Tugboat Annie (Marjorie Rambeau) in the 1940 movie *Tugboat Annie Sails Again*.

Seconds Out
Title of heavyweight champion Jack Johnson's vaudeville act.

Secrets
Novel written by attorney F. Lee Bailey (1978).

See How They Run
First made-for-television movie. It was first shown on TV on October 7, 1964, and it starred John Forsythe. *The Killers* was to have been the first TV movie, but because it contained so much violence, it was released theatrically instead.

Seeley, Blossom
Broadway dancer and singer who was married to Hall of Fame pitcher Rube Marquard, and later to Lew Fields. She and Rube composed the song "Marquard Slide." Seeley was portrayed in the 1952 movie *Somebody Loves Me* by Betty Hutton (Lew Fields by Ralph Meeker).

Seeress of Washington
Nickname of psychic Jeane Dixon.

See See Rider and Can't Help Falling in Love
Opening and closing songs sung by Elvis at most of his live concerts in the 1970s.

See the Jaguar
Play in which James Dean made his Broadway debut. It opened on December 3, 1952, at the Cort Theatre and lasted for only five performances.

Segretti, Donald

Head of the dirty tricks department of the Republican Committee to Re-elect the President in 1972. He was portrayed by Robert Walden in the 1976 movie *All the President's Men*.

Selznick, David O.

(1902–1965) American movie producer, founder of Selznick International Pictures in 1936. At Selznick's funeral some of the pallbearers were: Samuel Goldwyn, William S. Paley, Alfred Hitchcock, Sam Spiegel, and William Wyler. Selznick was loosely portrayed by Kirk Douglas as Jonathan Shields in the 1952 movie *The Bad and the Beautiful*. He was portrayed by Tony Curtis in the 1980 TV miniseries *Moviola*. His agent brother, Myron, was portrayed by Bill Macy.

Senator

Silent western film hero Leo Maloney's horse. His dog was named Bullet.

Sennett, Max

(1884–1960) American producer of numerous silent comedy films, nicknamed the King of Comedy. He produced the Keystone Kops, Charlie Chaplin, and others. Sennett was portrayed loosely in the 1939 movie *Hollywood Cavalcade* by Don Ameche, and in the Broadway musical *Mack and Mabel* by Robert Preston.

Sensation House

New Orleans saloon where Diamond Lil (Mae West) sang in the 1933 movie *She Done Him Wrong*.

Sentimental Journey

One of several theme songs of Les Brown. It was also the theme song of the TV series *Garroway at Large*.

September Song

Classic song composed by Kurt Weil and first introduced on record in 1938 (from the musical *Knickerbocker Holiday*) by actor Walter Huston.

September 13, 1999

Date on which the Earth's moon is blown out of orbit in the TV series *Space 1999*.

Sgt. Bernie Vincent

Policeman played by Eddie Egan in the TV series *Joe Forrester*.

Sgt. Edward Ryker

Supervisor of the rookies at Station No. 7 of the S.C.P.D., played in the TV series *The Rookies* by Gerald S. O'Loughlin. His wife was named Mary Kate.

Sgt. Ernest G. Bilko

Motor pool master sergeant at Fort Baxter, Kansas, and at Camp Fremont, California, played by Phil Silvers in the TV series *You'll Never Get Rich* and *The Phil Silver's Show*. The ribbons Bilko wore were: the Combat Infantry

Badge, Purple Heart, Asiatic Pacific, American Theater, European Theater, Victory Medal, Occupation Medal. Note: No good conduct medal.

Sgt. Nick Anderson
Los Angeles police detective played by Ben Gazzara in the TV series *Arrest and Trial*.

Sgt. Phineas Patrick Paul Pepper
Leader of the Lonely Hearts Club Band, played by Billy Preston in the 1978 movie *Sgt. Pepper's Lonely Hearts Club Band*. Heartland, U.S.A., was his hometown. His daughter was Saralinda.

Sgt. Steve Nelson
Police officer played by Adam West in the TV series *The Detectives*.

Sgt. Warnicki
Role played by Freddie Steele, the ex-middleweight boxing champion, in the 1945 movie *The Story of G.I. Joe*.

Sgt. William "Bumper" Morgan
Los Angeles veteran police officer played by George Kennedy in the 1975 TV movie and TV series *The Blue Knight*. The character was played by William Holden in the pilot movie, also titled *The Blue Knight* (based in part on the 1972 Joseph Wambaugh novel of the same name).

Serpico, Frank
Real New York City plainsclothes policeman who was portrayed in the 1973 movie *Serpico* by Al Pacino, and in the 1976 TV movie *The Deadly Game* and the TV series *Serpico* by David Birney.

Serron and Akita
Only two words spoken by Loana (Raquel Welch) in the 1966 movie *One Million Years B.C. Serron* means "giant bird," while *Akita* means "help."

Sevareid, Eric
CBS-TV news anchorman who during World War II bailed out of a crippled aircraft over the Himalayas. He lived with a tribe of head hunters for a month.

Seven Japanese Gods of Luck
Benten, Bishamonten, Daikoku, Ebisu, Fukurokuju, Hotei, and Jurojin.

Seven Lakes Country Club
Palm Springs golf course on which former President Dwight Eisenhower hit his first and only hole-in-one. He used a nine iron on the 104-yard 13th hole in February 1968.

Seven Million Dollar Man
Bionically rebuilt racing driver Barney Miller (Monte Markham) who has nuclear-powered parts in a 1974 episode of the TV series *The Six Million Dollar Man*. He was the only living man stronger than Steve Austin.

Seven Pleiades
Maia, Celeno, Merope, Alcyone, Electra, Sterope, and Taygeta.

Seven Sages of Greece
Bias, Chilon, Cleobulus, Periander, Pittacus, Solon, and Thales.

Sex for Newlyweds
Book that Mooney Lynn (Tommy Lee Jones) gave to his young bride, Loretta (Sissy Spacek), in the 1980 movie *Coal Miner's Daughter.*

Sex Kitten, The
Nickname of French actress Brigitte Bardot.

Seymour
Man-eating plant in the cartoon TV series *George of the Jungle.*

Shacove, Gene
Hair stylist who was supposedly the inspiration for Warren Beatty's role in the 1975 movie *Shampoo.*

Shadrack
Airedale given to actress Olivia De Havilland by director John Huston.

Shain, Eva
First woman to judge a heavyweight boxing championship fight. She was one of the judges for the Muhammad Ali–Ernie Shavers fight held on September 29, 1977.

Shake Rattle and Roll, and Rock Around the Clock
Titles of hit songs by Bill Haley and His Comets (1954 and 1955), which then became titles for rock 'n' roll movies (both in 1956).

Shakespeare, William
(1564–1616) English dramatist and poet born in Stratford-upon-Avon, perhaps the most respected playwright of all time. He was portrayed in the 1957 movie *The Story of Mankind* by Reginald Gardiner.

Shamus O'Flynn
Capt. R. Fred Clancey's (Henry Beckman) sailing vessel in the TV series *Here Come the Brides.*

Shanghai, SS
Ocean liner on which Arthur Ferguson Jones (Edward G. Robinson) and his wife, Wilhelmina "Bill" Clark (Jean Arthur), sailed in the closing scene of the 1935 movie *The Whole Town's Talking.*

Shangri-La
Theme song of character Reginald Van Gleason (Jackie Gleason) in Gleason's TV series.

Shangri-La Lil
B25 that took part in the Doolittle raid on Tokyo, piloted by Col. Harry Broderick, OR 28202275 (Andy Griffith), in the TV series *Salvage-1.*

Shaughnessy, Ed
Drummer with Doc Severinsen's band. His name is on the drums. He played on the 1973 LP *Maria Muldaur.*

Shawani

Singer John Denver's pet California golden eagle.

Shaw, Artie

Popular band leader whose theme song is "Nightmare." His seven wives: Margaret Allen (1930–1940); Lana Turner (1940–1942); Betty Kern (Jerome Kern's daughter) (1942–1945); Ava Gardner (1945–1946); Kathleen Windsor (author of *Forever Amber*) (1946–1952); Doris Dowling (1952–1956); and Evelyn Keyes (1957–   ). Artie Shaw and Evelyn Keyes made a cameo appearance in the 1972 movie *Across 110th Street*.

Sheffield, Washington

Inventor of the toothpaste tube in 1892.

She-Hulk

Secret identity of Jennifer Walter; she is the cousin of Dr. David Banner (*The Hulk*; created by Stan Lee for Marvel Comics).

Shelley, Mary Wollstonecraft

(1797–1851) English novelist and wife of poet Percy Bysshe Shelley. She authored *Frankenstein* in 1818. Mary Shelley was portrayed in the 1935 movie *The Bride of Frankenstein* by Elsa Lanchester and in the 1973 TV movie *Frankenstein: the True Story* by Nicola Pagett.

Shelley, Norman

British actor who on June 4, 1940, delivered over radio the famous Churchill speech after the British defeat at Dunkirk: "We shall fight on the beaches, We shall fight in the streets...." Winston Churchill sound-a-like Shelley delivered the speech that evening because the prime minister was too busy to go on radio himself.

Shepherd One

Nickname of the TWA Boeing 747 used by Pope John Paul II on his visit to the United States in October 1979.

Sheppard, Sam

Cleveland osteopath who in 1954 was convicted of murdering his wife, Marilyn. F. Lee Bailey served as his lawyer at the retrial, at which Sheppard was acquitted. George Peppard portrayed Sheppard in the 1975 TV movie *Guilty or Innocent: The Sam Sheppard Murder Case* (Claudette Nevins portrayed Marilyn Sheppard). While in prison, Sheppard became the first human being to be inoculated with live cancer cells. After his release, he was involved in several malpractice suits; finally he became a professional wrestler.

Sheridan Military Academy

Santa Barbara School where Maj. Bernard Benson (Charlton Heston) headed the ROTC program in the 1955 movie *The Private War of Major Benson*.

Sheridan, Philip

(1831–1888) American Civil War general who in 1884 succeeded Gen.

Sherman as commander-in-chief of the Union Army. Actress Anne Sheridan is a direct descendent of Philip Sheridan. Movie portrayals: *Abraham Lincoln* (1930) Frank Campeau; *In Old Chicago* (1938) Sidney Blackmer; *Union Pacific* (1939) Ernie Adams; *Santa Fe Trail* (1940) David Bruce; *They Died With Their Boots On* (1941) John Litel; *Rio Grande* (1950) J. Carrol Naish; and *Custer of the West* (1968) Lawrence Tierney.

Sheriff Buford T. Justice
Texas sheriff who chased after the Bandit (Burt Reynolds) in the 1977 movie *Smokey and the Bandit* and in the 1980 sequel *Smokey and the Bandit II*. He was played by Jackie Gleason.

Sherlock
Actual name of the basset hound to which Elvis Presley sang "Hound Dog" on the TV series *The Steve Allen Show* July 1, 1956.

Sherman, William Tecumseh
(1820–1891) American Union Civil War general who led the famous March to the Sea in 1864. In 1869 he succeeded Grant as general and commander of the Army. Sherman was portrayed in the 1963 movie *How the West Was Won* by John Wayne.

Sherrill, Charles
Yale University track man who first utilized the crouching start, on May 12, 1888.

Shields and Yarnell
Comic couple who are popularly known for their mime act. Robert Shields and Lorene Yarnell are both left handed and both are Aries.

Shikahr
Mr. Spock's hometown on the planet Vulcan in the TV series *Star Trek*.

Shiloh
Real name of the Arabian horse that Lee Majors rode in the TV series *The Men from Shiloh*. The horse actually belonged to Majors.

Shithead
Navin R. Johnson's (Steve Martin) pet dog in the 1979 movie *The Jerk*. He originally wanted to name him Lifesaver.

Shore Leave
Only episode of the TV series *Star Trek* in which the USS *Enterprise* is shown orbiting from right to left.

Short, Bobby
Singer of the Charlie perfume TV commercials.

Should a Girl Tell?
Movie playing on TV starring Mae Busch; during the commercial breaks Stanley R. Sogg (Jackie Gleason) sold Mother Fletcher's homely products (in Gleason's TV series).

Sicily Beaches

Cent, Dime, and Joss: Code names for the beaches on which Allied troops landed in Sicily on July 10, 1943.

Sidewalks of New York

Campaign song of presidential candidate Al Smith (1928).

Sidney Wang

Oriental detective played by Peter Sellers in the 1976 movie *Murder by Death*.

Siegel, Benjamin "Bugsy"

(1906–1947) Syndicate gangster and hit man who in 1945 built in Las Vegas the Flamingo Hotel. He was once engaged to actress Wendy Barrie. He was executed by the Syndicate on June 20, 1947.

Movie portrayals: *The George Raft Story* (1961) Brad Dexter; and *The Virginia Hill Story* (1974 TV) Harvey Keitel. Portrayed by Joe Penny in the TV series *Gangster Chronicles*.

Sieg Heil, Sieg Heil

One of the marches used by Adolf Hitler to rally his audience. The tune was taken from the Harvard University "Fight, Fight, Fight" song.

Sievers, Roy

Onetime outfielder for the Washington Senators and 1949 American League Rookie of the Year. He was President Nixon's favorite baseball player.

Siger and Violet Holmes

Sherlock and Mycroft Holmes's parents (novels).

Silver

Horse ridden in B westerns by Sunset Carson.

Silver Bowl

Award given to animal actors that are inducted into the Animal Hall of Fame.

Silver Bullet

White horse ridden by Whip Wilson in B westerns.

Silvercreek

California hometown where Benji, the dog that starred in the 1974 movie *Benji*, lives.

Silverheels

Gray steed of Thomas James Smith, the first marshal of Abilene, Texas. He tamed the town before Wild Bill Hickok took up residence there as U.S. marshal.

Silver Keystone

Highest award given by the Boys' Clubs of America.

Silver Mask

Italian equivalent of the Oscar.

Silverplate

U.S. Army's code name for the program whereby 15 bomber crews were trained to drop the first atomic bomb (393rd Heavy Bombardment Squadron). The program was headed by Lt. Col. Tibbets and the crews trained at Wendover, Utah.

Silver Queen
Clipper plane that crash-landed in the 1939 movie *Five Came Back*.

Silver Sandal
Nightclub where "Lucky" John Garnett (Fred Astaire) and Penny Carrol (Ginger Rogers) worked as dancers in the 1936 movie *Swing Time*. The Mafia-run club in the movie was the Club Raymond.

Silver Spur Award
Annual award for the best actor in a western movie.

Silver Threads Among the Gold
Billy the Kid's favorite song.

Silver Triangle, The
Original title of the musical play *The Music Man*.

Sinbad
Sailor adventurer in the *Arabian Nights* who made seven voyages. Movie portrayals; *Arabian Nights* (1942) Shemp Howard; *Sinbad the Sailor* (1947) Douglas Fairbanks, Jr.; *Son of Sinbad* (1955) Dale Robertson; *The Seventh Voyage of Sinbad* (1958) Kerwin Matthews; *The Golden Voyage of Sinbad* (1974) John Phillip Law; and *Sinbad and the Eye of the Tiger* (1977) Patrick Wayne.

Singin' in the Rain
Song composed in 1929 by Nacio Herb Brown and Arthur Freed. It is this song that Alex (Malcolm MacDowell) sang as he robbed a family in their home in the 1971 movie *A Clockwork Orange*. During the closing credits of the film, Gene Kelly sang the original version. "Singin' in the Rain" can also be heard in the following movies: *Hollywood Revue of 1929* (1929); *Little Nellie Kelly* (1940); *Hi Beautiful* (1944); *The Babe Ruth Story* (1952); *Singin' in the Rain* (1952); *That's Entertainment!* (1974) and *Fame* (1980) Roger Thornhill (Cary Grant) whistled the song in the bathroom of Room 463 of Chicago's Ambassador Hotel in the 1959 movie *North by Northwest*.

Singing Capon, The
Nickname of singer Nelson Eddy.

Sipple, Oliver
Bystander who knocked the .38-caliber revolver out of the hand of the would-be assassin of President Ford, Sara Jane Moore, on September 22, 1975.

Sirica, John J.
Chief judge of the U.S. District Court for Washington, D.C., Sirica presided over the trial of the seven men who broke into the Watergate offices of the Democratic National Committee in June 1972. He later ordered President

Nixon to turn over to the court tape recordings of White House conversations pertaining to the incident. The judge was portrayed in the 1979 TV miniseries *Blind Ambition* by Al Checco.

Sir Lancelot du Lac

Mythical character who was a member of King Arthur's Round Table and the father of Sir Galahad.

Movie portrayals: *Knights of the Round Table* (1953) Robert Taylor; *Prince Valiant* (1954) Don Megowan; *Sword of Lancelot* (1963) Cornel Wilde; and *Camelot* (1967) Franco Nero. William Russell played the character in the TV series *The Adventures of Sir Lancelot*.

Sirocco

Errol Flynn's 75-foot yacht from 1938 to 1943. It was originally named *Arop*.

Sister Kenny

Australian nurse (Elizabeth Kenny) who dedicated her life to the treatment of infantile paralysis. She was portrayed in the 1946 movie *Sister Kenny* by Rosalind Russell.

Sitting Bull

(1834–1890) American medicine man and Indian chief who was present at the Battle of the Little Big Horn in 1876. In 1890 he was killed by Indian guards. Movie portrayals: *Hands Up!* (1926) Nobel Johnson; *Annie Oakley* (1935) Chief Thunderbird; *Custer's Last Stand* (1936) Howling Wolf; *Annie Get Your Gun* (1950) J. Carrol Naish; *Fort Vengeance* (1953) Michael Granger; *Sitting Bull* (1954) J. Carrol Naish; and *The Great Sioux Massacre* (1965) Michael Pate.

Six Shooter, The

1952 radio series starring Jimmy Stewart as cowboy Britt Ponset.

Skeeter

Bantam rooster mascot of Bing Crosby's racehorse, Broadway Joe, in the 1950 movie *Riding High*.

Skinner, Cornelia Otis

Broadway actress and humorist whose most famous work was *Our Hearts Were Young and Gay*. She was portrayed in the 1944 movie *Our Hearts Were Young and Gay* and the 1946 sequel *Our Hearts Were Growing Up* by Gail Russell. She was portrayed in the 1950 TV series *The Girls* (a/k/a *Young and Gay*) by Bethel Leslie and Gloria Stroock.*

Skinner, Deborah

Daughter of behavioral psychologist B. F. Skinner. During her childhood she lived in a climate-controlled box designed by her father for 2 years (1942–1943).

Ski Nose

Nickname of Bob Hope, conferred on him by Bing Crosby.

---

*Sister of actress Geraldine Brooks.

Skippy Dugan
Charlie McCarthy's friend at school.
Skoda Lasky
Czech song meaning "Lost Love." When Lew Brown created English lyrics for the tune in 1934, it became the song "Beer Barrel Polka."
SKyler 7-8941
Phone number of Midge Kelly (Kirk Douglas) in the 1949 movie *Champion*.
Skyliner
Retractable hard-top Ford convertible, produced 1958–1959.
Skypad Apartments
Home of the Jetson family in the TV cartoon series *The Jetsons*.
Slapsie Maxie
Nickname (coined by Damon Runyon) of punch thrown by the light-heavyweight (later actor) Maxie Rosenbloom.
Slaughter, John
Civil War officer who later became a Texas Ranger. He was played by Tom Tryon* in episodes titled "Texas John Slaughter" of the TV series *Walt Disney Presents*.
Sleep 'n' Eat
Demeaning name bestowed on actor Willie Best when he first appeared in films.
Slimey
Oscar the Grouch's pet worm in the TV series *Sesame Street*.
Sluggy
Humphrey Bogart's 36-foot cabin cruiser, nicknamed for his third wife, Mayo Methot.
Smile
1954 hit song co-written by Charles Chaplin. In 1953 Chaplin also composed the song "Limelight," for his movie of the same name.
Smile and Show Your Dimple
Original title of Irving Berlin's "Easter Parade," which he composed for the 1917 play *As Thousands Cheer*.
Smile, Darn Ya, Smile
Theme song of *The Fred Allen Show* (radio).
Smith, Al(fred) Emanuel
(1873–1944) American politician who served as governor of New York for four terms and was the Democratic nominee for president in 1928. He tossed out the first baseball for the first game ever played at Yankee Stadium (1923). Movie portrayals: *Beau James* (1957) Walter Catlett; and *Sunrise at Campobello* (1960) Alan Bunce.
Smith, Charley
(1842–1979) Black man, born in Liberia in 1842 and brought to America on

---

*Tom Tryon has authored four best-selling novels: *The Other, Harvest Home, Lady,* and *Crowned Heads*.

a slave ship, who witnessed the launching of *Apollo 17* at Cape Kennedy on December 7, 1972. Smith was believed to have been the oldest person living in the United States at that time. The life of the 135-year-old Florida man was told in a series of 1977 TV plays called *Charley Smith and the Fritter Tree*. He was portrayed by Richard Ward and Glynn Turman (as a boy). Charley Smith died on October 5, 1979, at the age of 137.

Smith, Edward

Man who committed the first bank robbery, on March 19, 1831, when he robbed the City Bank of New York of $245,000. He was sentenced to Sing Sing Penitentiary for 5 years of hard labor.

Smith, Gladys

Real name of two actresses: Mary Pickford and Alexis Smith. Gladys Smith was also the maiden name of Elvis Presley's mother.

Smith, Joseph

(1805–1844) Founder of the Mormon Church (Church of Jesus Christ of Latter-Day Saints) at Fayette, New York, on April 6, 1830. He was portrayed in the 1940 movie *Brigham Young—Frontiersman* by Vincent Price.

Smith, Margaret Chase

(1897–   ) U.S. politican who served as senator from Maine for 23 years (1949–1973). She was the first Republican to attack the demagogic Wisconsin Senator Joseph McCarthy on the floor of the Senate. Margaret Chase Smith was portrayed by Patricia Neal in the 1977 TV movie *Tail Gunner Joe*.

Smith, Gen. Walter Bedell

(1895–1961) Chief of staff to Gen. Dwight D. Eisenhower during World War II. He served as U.S. ambassador to the Soviet Union (1946–1949) and as director of the CIA (1950–1953). Gen Smith was portrayed in the 1979 TV miniseries *Ike* by J. D. Cannon.

Smitty

Sidekick of Cheyenne Bodie (Clint Walker) in the TV series *Cheyenne*. He was played by L. Q. Jones (for only the first season—1955).

Smokey Corners

Area in the Big Piney Hills of West Virginia that the McCoy family called home before they moved to California in the TV series *The Real McCoys*.

Snert

Hagar the Horrible's pet dog (comic strip).

Sniffles

Little cartoon mouse in Warner Bros. cartoons; created by Chuck Jones, voice of Sara Berner.

Snow

Monroe family dog in the TV series *The Monroes*.

Snowflake

Only known white gorilla in the world; kept at the Barcelona Zoo.

Snowflake
White mare ridden by Texas Guinan in B westerns.
Snowman
Cledus's (Jerry Reed) handle in the 1977 movie *Smokey and the Bandit.*
Snuffy Smith
Friend of Barney Google who was introduced in 1934 (comic strip *Barney Google*). Loweezy is Snuffy's wife. Snuffy was played by Bud Duncan in the movies *Snuffy Smith, Yard Bird* (1942) and *Hillbilly Blitzkrieg* (1942).
Soapie
Annual award given to the best daytime television drama.
Soapsuds
Political humorist Will Rogers' favorite horse.
Society of Union Hunters
Lake Superior State College group favoring the extinction of words and phrases that are misused and overused.
Sock it to me
Phrase said on the TV series *Laugh In* by Marcell Marceau, Bing Crosby, Dick Gregory, Pat Boone, Jack Benny, and President Richard Nixon, among others.
Soda
Col. Smolletts' (Monty Woolley) pet dog in the 1944 movie *Since You Went Away.*
Soda Fountain Rag
First song written by Duke Ellington. It was composed in 1913 when he was 14.
Sofie
Seal that Dr. Dolittle threw back into the sea, an act that precipitated his arrest as the accused murderer of a woman in the 1967 movie *Doctor Dolittle* (based on the Hugh Lofting novels of the same name).
Soma
Happiness drug taken by future people in Aldous Huxley's novel/1980 TV movie *Brave New World.*
Somebody Loves Me
Song composed in 1924 by George Gershwin, Bud DeSylva, and Ballard MacDonald. It can be heard in the following motion pictures: *Broadway Rhythm* (1944), sung by Lena Horne; *Rhapsody in Blue* (1945); *Lullaby of Broadway* (1951), sung by Doris Day and Gene Nelson; *Somebody Loves Me* (1952); and *Young at Heart* (1955).
Someone to Watch over Me
Song composed by George and Ira Gershwin in 1926. The song can be heard in the following movies: *Rhapsody in Blue* (1945); *John Loves Mary* (1949); *Backfire* (1950); *Young at Heart* (1955), sung by Frank Sinatra; and *Three for the Money* (1955).

Somers, USS

U.S. naval vessel on which Philip Spencer, the son of the Secretary of War, made a mutiny with 20 other men in December 1842. Spencer was hanged, along with two other mutineers. The ship's captain, Cmdr. A. S. MacKenzie, was later tried and found not guilty.

Something That Happened

Original title of John Steinbeck's 1937 novel *Of Mice and Men*.

Sometime Sweet Susan

Porno movie that Travis (Robert De Niro) took Betsy (Cybill Shepherd) to see in the 1976 movie *Taxi Driver*.

Sonny

White House janitor played by Flip Wilson in comedy routines.

Son-of-a-gun

Detective Bulldog Drummond's water pistol, which he used to squirt ammonia at his enemies (novels).

Son of a Gun

Words whispered by Carly Simon at the beginning of her 1972 hit record ''You're So Vain.''

Son of Sam

Confessed killer David Berkowitz, also called the .44-caliber killer. He murdered six persons and wounded seven more in 1977. He was sentenced to 547 years in jail (315 years to be served consecutively).

Son of the Sheik

Silent Rudolph Valentino movie that Louis Jordan took Linda Christian to see in the 1952 movie *The Happy Time*.

Sonora

Vessel that Dwan (Jessica Lange) was aboard when it exploded, blowing her overboard, in the 1976 movie *King Kong*. The crew were all below watching the movie *Deep Throat*.

Sonora Desert

Mexican desert where the five missing Avenger bombers were found in the 1977 movie *Close Encounters of the Third Kind*. (See: **Flight 19**)

Sons-in-Law

Past and Present (a sampling):
Noah Beery, Jr., of Buck Jones
Peter Lawford of Dan Rowan
Rick Nelson of Tom Harmon
Pat Boone of Red Foley
Frank Sinatra of Maureen O'Sullivan
Artie Shaw of Jerome Kern
Robert Walker of John Ford

Oskar Werner of Tyrone Power
Tommy Sands of Frank Sinatra
Mervyn LeRoy of Harry Warner
George Stanford Brown of James Daly
Burt Ward of Mort Lindsay
Johnny Cash of Maybelle Carter
Rand Brooks of Stan Laurel
Robert Walker of Ward Bond
Sidney Lumet of Lena Horne
Gabe Dell of Henry Daniell
Tom Ewell of George Abbott

Sons of Italy Hall
New York establishment where the Kramdens first met the Nortons in the TV
series *The Honeymooners*.

Sony 800B
Tape recorders installed to record all of President Nixon's conversations in
the Oval Office.

Sordelet, James
Electrician's mate first class who reenlisted in the U.S. Navy under the North
Pole when the atomic sub *Nautilus* cruised there on August 3, 1959.

Sorrow and the Pity, The
Movie that Alvy Singer (Woody Allen) and Annie Hall (Diane Keaton) saw
several times in the 1977 film *Annie Hall*.

So this is the little lady who made this big war
Words said by President Abraham Lincoln upon first meeting Harriet Beecher
Stowe, the author of *Uncle Tom's Cabin*.

Soubirous, Bernadette
French peasant girl who claimed to have seen the Blessed Virgin Mary on
February 11, 1858. In the 1943 movie *The Song of Bernadette* she was
portrayed by Jennifer Jones, who won an Oscar for the role. The Virgin Mary
was portrayed by an uncredited actress.*

South American Bombshell
Nickname of Latin dancer and comedienne Carmen Miranda (real name:
Maria de Carno da Cunha).

Southern Cross
Charles E. Kingsford Smith's Fokker FVII, in which he flew from Oakland to
Australia, a trip of 7,281 miles, departing on May 31, 1928, and finishing the
flight 83 hours and 11 minuts later. He had a crew of four. Smith's portrait is
on the Australian $20 bill.

---

*It was later revealed that she was portrayed by Linda Darnell.

South Figuero Street Motel

Los Angeles motel at which singer Sam Cooke was shot to death with a .22 pistol by 55-year-old motel manager Bertha Franklin, on December 10, 1964.

South Fork

Ewing family Texas ranch in the TV series *Dallas*.

Southwest Trail Lines

(No. 275) Bus that Ben Shockley (Clint Eastwood) drove into Phoenix while being shot at by the city's police force in the 1977 movie *The Gauntlet*.

Spaak, Gen. Carl

(1891–   )U.S. Army officer who was chief of the U.S. bombing force in Germany (1944) and Japan (1945). He was portrayed in the 1955 movie *The Court Martial of Billy Mitchell* by Steve Roberts.

Space Cadet

Novel by Robert A. Heinlein that was the basis for the 1950–1952 TV series *Tom Corbett, Space Cadet*. *SHIP – POLARIS   COMM. ARCWRIGHT*

Spanish Bit

Million-acre Texas ranch of the McCanles family in the 1946 movie *Duel in the Sun*. The nearby town was called Paradise Flats.

Sparkplug

Houndcats' special automobile in the TV cartoon series *The Houndcats*.

Spartacus

Roman slave gladiator who led a slave uprising against Rome. He was killed in 71 B.C. Movie portrayals: *Sins of Rome* (1954) Massimo Girotti; and *Spartacus* (1960) Kirk Douglas.

Specht, Paul

First dance band to broadcast over radio (Detroit's WWJ in the late 1920s).

Speedway

John Norman Howard's (Kris Kristofferson) rock band in the 1976 movie *A Star Is Born*. The band was previously named the Noble Five; later they became Freeway. In the film Booker T. Jones was a member of Speedway (in real life he is married to Priscilla Coolidge, sister of Rita Coolidge, who was Kris Kristofferson's wife).

Speedy

Secret identity of Roy Harper, Green Arrow's boy partner (comic books). Debut: *More Fun Comics* No. 76 (February 1943).

Spencer, Philip

Midshipman aboard the brig *Somers* who in 1842 was hanged by his captain for mutiny. At the time, Philip's father, John Canfield, was the U.S. secretary of war (1841–1843).

Spike

Frank Weatherwax's trained dog who played Yeller in the 1957 movie *Old Yeller* (PATSY award). He also starred in the 1960 movie *A Dog of Flanders*.

Spike Wilson

The capture of this escaped convict led to the promotion of Constable William Preston to sergeant in the Northwest Mounted Police in the radio series *Sergeant Preston of the Yukon*. Wilson had killed Preston's father.

Spinachovia

Kingdom ruled by King Blozo (comic strip).

Spingarn Medal

Annual award by the NAACP for the year's outstanding black person.

Spot

Black-and-white dog of Dick and Jane Harper (George Segal and Jane Fonda) in the 1976 movie *Fun With Dick and Jane*.

Spot

Henry's pet cat in the TV cartoon series *Hong Kong Phooey*.

Spot

The soldier's pet dog in the 1950 movie *Rocky Mountain*.

Spotsylvania, Virginia

Site of the plantation where Kunta Kinte was enslaved by his first master, John Reynolds, in the TV miniseries *Roots* (based on Alex Haley's book of the same name). It was also where Kunta was buried. His descendants finally settled in Henning, Tennessee.

Spray

37-foot boat in which Joshua Slocum of Nova Scotia made the first solo voyage around the world. He left Boston on April 24, 1895, and arrived in Newport, Rhode Island, on June 27, 1898.

Springdale

Setting of the radio series *Mayor of the Town*, starring Lionel Barrymore as his honor.

Springtime for Hitler

Play intended to be written off as a failure for tax purposes in the 1968 Mel Brooks movie *The Producers*. (Brooks made a cameo appearance in the show's chorus.) Later, in prison, Max Bialystock (Zero Mostel) and Leo Bloom (Gene Wilder) produced the play *Prisoners of Love*.

Spruance, Raymond Ames

(1886–   ) American admiral who commanded the task force at the Battle of Midway, June 1942. In 1945–1946 he became the commander-in-chief of the U.S. Pacific fleet. Spruance was portrayed in the 1976 movie *Midway* by Glenn Ford.

Spunky

The Fonz's white cocker spaniel (The Spunk) in the TV series *Happy Days*. His girlfriend is Peaches.

Spy Who Laughed at Danger, The

Movie for which Sonny Hooper (Burt Reynolds) is the head stunt man in the 1978 movie *Hooper.*

Squaw Man

Only movie to have been successfully filmed three times by the same producer/director, Cecil B. DeMille. In the first version (silent, 1913), which was DeMille's first movie, he appeared as an extra (a gambler). (The 1913 *Squaw Man* was the first Hollywood movie to list credits.) The second version, also silent, was made in 1918. The third version, filmed in 1931, was a talkie.

Squeaking Door, The

Original name of the radio series *Inner Sanctum* when it was first aired in 1941.

Stabalize

Theme song of the TV series *Flatbush.*

Stag Party

Name Hugh Hefner originally intended to call *Playboy* magazine when it was begun in December 1953.

Stained Glass

Best-selling novel written in 1978 by William F. Buckley, Jr.

Stanford, Leyland

(1824–1893) Governor of California (1861–1863) who helped to build the Central Pacific Railroad (1863–1869). He built Leland Stanford Junior University in memory of his son. Stanford was portrayed in the 1939 movie *Union Pacific* by Guy Usher.

Stanford-Michigan

College football game that singer Buddy Clark (real name Samuel Goldberg) had just finished watching when the airplane he was leaving Los Angeles in crashed on Rampart Boulevard on October 1, 1949. Buddy died a few hours later.

Stanford, Sally

Marcia Jane Busby, San Francisco madam of the 1930–1940s. Between 1976 and 1978 she was mayor of Sausalito, California. She adopted the name Stanford from a newspaper headline: "Stanford Wins." She claimed in her autobiography that the very first time she ever hit a golf ball, at the age of 8, she made a hole-in-one. Sally Stanford was portrayed in the 1978 TV movie *Lady of the House* by Dyan Cannon.

Stanley R. Sogg

One of the characters played by Jackie Gleason on TV. He was an announcer for the *Late, Late, Late, Late, Late, Late, Late, Late Show.* He also advertised Mother Fletcher's products.

Stanleyville Steamer
First zebra trained as a trotting horse. His trainer was Jim Papon.

Stanton, Edwin
(1814–1869) American politician and Secretary of War under President Lincoln. He had in his possession the diary of John Wilkes Booth, with 18 pages mysteriously missing. Movie portrayals: *Abraham Lincoln* (1930) Oscar Apfel; *The Lincoln Conspiracy* (1977) Robert Middleton; and *The Ordeal of Dr. Mudd* (1980 TV) Richard Dysart.

Starbuck, Jo Jo
Figure skating star, wife of Pittsburgh Steelers quarterback Terry Bradshaw.

Starkweather, Charles
(1940–1959) Murderer and thief who, with his girlfriend, Caril Ann Fugate, went on a crime spree of murder and robbery in Nebraska in 1958. He was portrayed loosely in the 1973 movie *Badlands* by Martin Sheen (as Kit Carruthers).

Starlight
Horse ridden by Bob Livingston in B westerns.

Star of Delhi
World's largest emerald, which was delivered to the Tower of London from Delhi on the British cruiser the *Invincible,* in the 1939 movie *The Adventures of Sherlock Holmes.*

Starr, Belle
(1848–1889) Notorius female outlaw of the West called the Outlaw Queen. Her real name was Myra Belle Shirley. Her daughter, Pearl, was fathered by outlaw Cole Younger. Movie portrayals: *Court Martial* (1928) Betty Compson; *Belle Starr* (1941) Gene Tierney; *Montana Belle* (1952) Jane Russell; *Badman's Territory* (1946) Isabel Jewell; *Belle Starr's Daughter* (1947) Isabel Jewell; *The Outlaws Is Coming* (1965) Sally Starr; *Zachariah* (1971) Pat Quinn; and *Belle Starr* (1980 TV) Elizabeth Montgomery (with Michelle Stacy as Pearl).

Starr, Ringo
Drummer for the Beatles who replaced Pete Best. Born Richard Starkey, July 7, 1940, he was the oldest member of the Fab Four. Ringo was portrayed in the 1979 TV movie *Birth of the Beatles* by Ray Ashcroft.

Stars Over Broadway
Opening theme song of the TV series *Your Show of Shows.*

Star Wars
Highly successful 1977 science fiction movie directed by George Lucas (it is the biggest-grossing movie of all time). The comic strip *Star Wars,* by Russ Manning, debuted on March 16, 1979.

Statue of Enlightening the World, The
Official name of the Statue of Liberty

Statue of Libido
Nickname of actress Mae West.

Stauffenberg, Count Claus Schenk von
German staff officer who was part of the Generals' Plot on Hitler's life. On July 20, 1944, he carried a brown briefcase containing a bomb into a conference room in Berlin where Hitler was presiding. At 12:42 p.m. the bomb exploded, killing four men but only injuring Hitler.

Stayin' Alive
Bee Gees hit heard sung in the 1977 movie *Saturday Night Fever*, on a phonograph in the 1978 movie *Foul Play*, and on a jukebox in the 1980 movie *Airplane*. The song was originally going to be titled "Saturday Night, Saturday Night."

Steamboat 'Round the Bend
1935 John Ford movie starring Will Rogers. The film was advertised on a marquee in the 1973 movie *Paper Moon*.

Steed
Name of Dudley Do-Right's horse (TV cartoon). The name Horse is also used.

Steel
Horse ridden by the following actors in the following movies: Joel McCrea, *Buffalo Bill* (1944); Joel McCrea, *The Virginian* (1946); Clark Gable, *The Tall Man* (1948); Ben Johnson, *She Wore a Yellow Ribbon* (1949); Gary Cooper, *It's a Big Country* (1951); Robert Taylor, *Westward the Women* (1952); and John Wayne, *The Conqueror* (1956).

Steinhagen, Ann Ruth
19-year-old woman who shot Phillies baseball player Eddie Waitkus in a Chicago hotel room on June 15, 1949.

Steller Todler
Dumb, unsexy woman who mumbles when she talks, played by Carol Burnett in her TV series *The Carol Burnett Show*.

Stetson, John B.
Man who created the Stetson hat.

Steve
Name that Marie Browning (Lauren Bacall) called Harry Morgan (Humphrey Bogart) in the 1944 movie *To Have and Have Not*. It is also the name that Judy Maxwell (Barbra Streisand) called Howard Bannister (Ryan O'Neal) in the 1972 movie *What's Up Doc?* Humphrey Bogart and Lauren Bacall named their only son Steve.

Stevenson, Adlai Ewing
(1900–1965) Two-time Democratic candidate for the presidency (1952 and 1956). He was also a delegate to U.N. (1949), governor of Illinois (1949–1953),

and U.S. Ambassador to the U.N. (1961–1965). Stevenson was portrayed by Ralph Bellamy in the 1974 TV play *The Missiles of October.*

Stevenson, Iowa
Setting of the 1942 movie *The Major and the Minor.*

Steverino
Name of Greyhound dog that appeared in advertisements for the Greyhound Bus Company on the TV series *The Steve Allen Show.*

Steve Roper
Cartoon strip hero created by Harold Anderson and Eugene Conley. He debuted as a photographer in the comic book strip *Big Chief Wahoo* in late 1936. In 1946 the series became *Chief Wahoo and Steve Roper*; and finally it was called *Steve Roper.*

Stewart, James, and Margaret Sullavan
Films in which the pair appeared: *Next Time We Love* (1936); *The Shopworn Angel* (1938); *The Shop Around the Corner* (1940); and *The Mortal Storm* (1940).

Stillman, Lou
Founder of the famous New York City gym for boxers, Stillman's Gym. It was originally the location of a charity mission. Lou Stillman was portrayed in the 1956 movie *Somebody Up There Likes Me* by Matt Crowley.

Stilwell, Joseph W.
Probably one of the ablest American generals of World War II. (1883–1946) He was Chang Kai-shek's chief of staff and later deputy supreme commander (under Mountbatten) of the Southeast Asia Command. Stilwell opposed Chiang's and Chennault's tactics in the war (he habitually referred to Chiang as "the Peanut"). Movie portrayals: *Objective Burma!* (1945) Erville Anderson: *Merrill's Marauders* (1962) John Hoyt; and *1941* (1979) Robert Stack.

Sting, The
1973 movie starring Paul Newman and Robert Redford. The film's six segments were titled: "The Set-Up," "The Hook," "The Tale," "The Wire," "The Shutout," and "The Sting."

Stingley, Darryl
New England wide receiver who, after being hit by Oakland Raider Jack Tatum in a 1978 preseason game, became paralyzed from the neck down.

Stix Nix Hix Pix
Famous *Variety* headline about the rejection of cornball comedies by rural audiences.

Stockbridge, Massachusetts
Onetime hometown of Norman Rockwell, who included the town in many of his paintings. Also the site of Alice's Restaurant, made famous by Arlo Guthrie in song and director Arthur Penn in film.

Stonewall Jackson
Old riverboat featured in the 1928 Buster Keaton comedy *Steamboat Billy, Jr.*

Stoneway
Brand of piano owned by Fred and Wilma Flintstone in the TV series *The Flintstones*.

Storm Warning
1950 movie that is the only film in which Doris Day dies (she is accidentally shot by Steve Cochran).

Stormy Weather
1952 song recorded by the Five Sharps on Jubilee Records. It is considered the rarest R & B record; a 78 rpm copy (Jubilee 5104) is valued at $4,000.

Story of the Family Weis, The
Subtitle of the TV miniseries *Holocaust*.

Strange, Michael
Poet (real name: Blanche Oelrichs Thomas Barrymore) who married John Barrymore and became the mother of actress Diana Barrymore. Her own children had to call her Miss Strange. She was portrayed in the 1959 movie *Too Much, Too Soon* by Neva Patterson.

Strangler, The
Nickname of 1920s wrestler Ed Lewis.

Stratton, Monty
Major league pitcher who played for the White Sox. After the 1938 season, he lost a leg in a hunting accident. He was portrayed in the 1949 movie *The Stratton Story* by James Stewart.

Strauss, Johann
(1825–1899) Austrian composer and orchestra leader, one of whose most famous works is "The Blue Danube." Portrayals: *The Great Waltz* (1938) Fernand Gravet; *Vienna Waltzes* (1951) Anton Walbrook; *Great Waltz* (1972) Horst Bucholz; and *The Strauss Family* (1973 TV miniseries) Eric Woolfe.

Strawberry
Secret Service code name for President Nixon's secretary Rose Mary Woods.

Strawberry Springs
Small town (population 1,472) where Bill Haley and the Comets were discovered playing at the town hall in the 1956 movie *Rock Around the Clock*.

Street Gang
Mission name of the patrol boat in the 1979 movie *Apocalypse Now*. The code name of mission control was Almighty.

Strickland Foundation
Estate headed by Goldie Appleby (Betty Hutton) in the TV series *The Betty Hutton Show*.

Strigas Affair, The
    Episode of the TV series *The Man from U.N.C.L.E.* in which William Shatner
    and Leonard Nimoy both appeared.
Strike Up the Band
    1940 Mickey Rooney–Judy Garland movie, advertised on a theater marquee
    in the 1941 Marx Brothers film *The Big Store*.
Struck, Hudson
    First American to scale Mt. McKinley in Alaska, on June 7, 1913.
Stuttgart, Arkansas
    Site of the Annual World Duck Calling Championship.
Stuyvesant Club
    Private New York club of which detective Philo Vance is a member (novels).
Stuyvesant Museum of Natural History
    Museum where Dr. David Huxley (Cary Grant), a zoologist, was putting
    together a brontosaurus in the 1938 movie *Bringing Up Baby*.
Suaviter in Modo, Fortiter in Re
    "Gently in Manner, Strongly in Deed"—placque that sat on President
    Eisenhower's desk in the Oval Office.
Subaru
    Foreign automobile company for whom Gerald Ford's daughter Susan appeared
    in a TV commercial in 1979.
Success
    Title of Loretta Lynn's first hit record (1962).
Suellen O'Hara
    Younger sister of Scarlett O'Hara (Vivian Leigh), played in the 1939 movie
    Gone With the Wind by Evelyn Keyes, whose 1977 autobiography is titled
    Scarlett O'Hara's Younger Sister.
Sugar Daddy
    Lollipop advertisement that Bobby Riggs wore on his yellow jacket at the
    "Battle of the Sexes" tennis match with Billie Jean King, on September 20,
    1973, at the Houston Astrodome. Riggs lost the match to King.
Sukiyaki
    Hit song by Kyu Sakamoto released in 1963. It is the only Japanese song ever
    to reach No. 1 in the United States (May 25, 1963).
Sullavan, Margaret
    (1911–1960) American actress and wife of producer Leland Hayward. She
    was portrayed in the 1980 TV movie *Haywire* by Lee Remick. The movie,
    based on the book of the same title by Sullavan and Hayward's daughter,
    Brooke Hayward, was produced by their son, Bill Hayward. In the 1980 TV
    miniseries *Moviola* Sullavan was portrayed by Jean Gilpin.
Sullivan, Ed
    Newspaper columnist turned TV variety show host. He was portrayed by Will

Jordan in the following: Broadway play *Elvis—The Legend Lives;* 1978 movie *The Buddy Holly Story;* 1979 TV movie *Elvis*; 1979 movie *I Want to Hold Your Hand.*

Sullivan, John Lawrence

(1858–1918) American heavyweight champion who was defeated in 1892 by James (Gentleman Jim) Corbett. Movie portrayals: *My Gal Sal* (1942) John Kelly; *Gentleman Jim* (1942) Ward Bond; and *The Great John L* (1945) Greg McLure.

Sultana

Pirate vessel commanded by Capt. Dan Tempest (Robert Shaw) in the TV series *The Buccaneers.*

Summerfield High School

Summerfield, California, high school that Robert T. Ironside (Raymond Burr) graduated from in 1940 in the TV series *Ironside.* He played center on the football team, wearing Jersey No. 34.

Summersby, Kay

Gen. Dwight D. Eisenhower's personal driver during World War II with whom he is supposed to have had a love affair. She drove his Packard and Cadillac. By executive order, she was the only British citizen given an officer's commission in the U.S. WAFs (lieutenant). Kay Summersby was portrayed in the TV miniseries *Ike* by Lee Remick.

Sumner, Charles

(1811–1874) U.S. senator who led the opposition against slavery. He was physically assaulted by Representative Preston Brooks of South Carolina on May 22, 1856, and suffered permanent injury as a consequence. Sumner was portrayed in the 1915 movie *The Birth of a Nation* by Sam De Grasse.

Sundancers

Name of the cheerleaders for the Los Angeles Rams when the team was formed. In 1979 they changed their name to the Embraceable Ewes.

Sun Day

Government day first declared on May 3, 1978 (a Wednesday), with the object of emphasizing the importance of solar power.

Sunja

First elephant to water-ski, trained by Dave Blasko.

Sunset

Horse ridden by Jimmy Wakely in B westerns.

Sunset Magazine

Magazine founded in 1898 by the Southern Pacific Railroad.

Sunshine Cab Company

Taxi firm in the TV series *Taxi.* Its phone number: 555-2387.

Sunshine Girls

Club to which Hazel Burke (Shirley Booth) belonged in the TV series *Hazel.*

Sunwest Airlines

Airline company for which the three stewardesses flew in the TV series *Flying High.*

Super Chicken

Secret identity of Henry Cabot Henhouse III (TV cartoons).

Super Electronic Age

Time setting of the TV cartoon series *The Jetsons.*

Super Fly

Nickname of the bad-dude drug dealer named Priest, played in the movies *Super Fly* (1972) and *Super Fly T.N.T.* (1973) by Ron O'Neal.

Super Goober

Pill swallowed by Goofy to change him into Super Goof (comic books).

Super Sauce

Liquid that turns Henry Cabot Henhouse III into Super Chicken (TV cartoon series).

Superior Hotel

Hotel in Iron Mountain, Montana, that became the first recipient of a Gideon Bible on July 1, 1899.

Supertrain

Possibly the most expensive TV series ever made, averaging $1 million per episode (NBC). (Some sources say *Battlestar Galactica* was the most costly TV series.)

Surf Ballroom

Clear Lake, Iowa,* location where, on February 2, 1959, Buddy Holly, Ritchie Valens, and the Big Bopper made their final public appearances. All three were killed in a plane crash the next day. At the performance Buddy played drums for Valens, the Big Bopper, and Dion and the Belmonts. The admission price that night was $1.25.

Susan Hilton

Fictitious name that Agent 99 (Barbara Felton) gave as her own on the episode "99 Loses Control" (February 17, 1968) of the TV series *Get Smart.* On the episode 99 later denied that name was her own.

Susanne Langen

Name that Nancy Drew, the hero of juvenile novels, is called in Germany. In France she is named Alice.

Susanne Onstad

Supertanker used to transport King Kong back to the United States in the 1976 movie *King Kong.*

Sutcliffe, Stu

"The Fifth Beatle." He was a member of the original Beatles band in

---

*Clear Lake, California, was the site of the drowning of singer Johnny Burnette on August 1, 1964.

Liverpool and Hamburg, where he died after suffering a head concussion. Sutcliffe was portrayed in the 1979 TV movie *Birth of the Beatles* by David Wilkinson.

Sutton Place Apartments
Affluent New York City apartment house whose servant entrance opened on the docks in the 1937 movie *Dead End*.

Suwannee River
Official song of the state of Florida, adopted in 1935.

Suzie-Q
Name given to heavyweight boxer Rocky Marciano's overhand right punch. It was coined by manager Charley Goldman.

Suzie Sorority
Collegiate character played in comedy skits by Lily Tomlin.

Suzy Chapstick
Character played in Chapstick TV commercials by world championship skier Susy Chaffee.

Swan, Joseph W.
Inventor of the light bulb in 1879.

Swan Lake
Excerpts from this classical ballet score composed by Tchaikovsky are played during the opening credits of the 1931 Bela Lugosi movie *Dracula*.

Swanee
Song composed by George Gershwin and first performed professionally at the opening of New York's Capitol Theatre in 1919. The song can be heard in the following movies: *Rhapsody in Blue* (1945), sung by Al Jolson; *The Jolson Story* (1946), sung by Al Jolson; *Jolson Sings Again* (1949), sung by Al Jolson; and *A Star Is Born* (1954), sung by Judy Garland.

Swann, Lynn
Football player who played in the 1973 and 1974 Rose Bowl games with USC and in the 1975 and 1976 Super Bowl games with Pittsburgh.

Swayback, USS
Cruiser commanded by Cmdr. Rockwell "Rock" Torrey (John Wayne) and used as his flagship when he was made an admiral in the 1965 movie *In Harm's Way* (filmed aboard the USS *St. Paul*).

Sweater Girl, The
Publicity nickname for actress Lana Turner.

Sweet Adeline
Song composed in 1903 by Richard H. Gerard and Harry Armstrong, sparring partner of heavyweight champion John L. Sullivan. It was the favorite song of Mayor John F. (Honey Fitz) Fitzgerald of Boston (grandfather of President John F. Kennedy). He often sang it at political rallies.

Sweet & Fragrant Soap
Advertisement on the side of Porgy's (Sidney Poitier) wooden cart, made from a packing crate, in the 1959 movie *Porgy and Bess*.

Sweetest Story Ever Told, The
Theme song of the radio series *John's Other Wife*.

Sweetman, Elizabeth
Baby girl who played Superman as a baby boy in the 1978 movie *Superman*.

Sweet Sue and Her Society Syncopaters
All-girl band that Sugar Kane Kumulchek (Marilyn Monroe) sang with, which was joined by Joe (Tony Curtis) and Jerry (Jack Lemmon) disguised as a female saxophonist (Josephine) and bass player (Daphne), in the 1959 movie *Some Like It Hot*.

Sweetwater
Seaport hometown of Popeye the Sailor.

Swift, Joseph
First cadet to graduate from West Point (1802). He later became the academy's superintendent.

Swinetrek
Spaceship commanded by Capt. Link Hogthrob (voice: Jim Henson) in episodes of "Pigs in Space." (TV series *The Muppet Show*). The other two crew members are Miss Piggy (voice: Frank Oz) and Dr. Julius Strangepork (voice: Jerry Nelson).

Swingin' Safari, A
Theme song of the TV game show *Match Game*. The song had been a 1962 hit for Billy Vaughn.

Sy
Jack Benny's Mexican gardener (Mel Blanc) in the *Jack Benny Show* on radio. Sy's sister was Sue who sews.

Sydney Bridge
Bridge in Sydney, Australia, from which singer Richard Penniman (known as Little Richard) threw all his diamond rings prior to quitting rock 'n' roll to become a minister in 1957.

Sykes, Gloria
Woman who was awarded $50,000 in 1971 as a result of a San Francisco cable car accident that she claimed caused her to sleep with over 100 men.

Sylvester
Pet chimpanzee of Capt. Safari (Randy Knight), played by Zippy, in the 1955 TV series *Captain Safari*.

Symbol
Allied code name of the January 14–23, 1942, conference at Casablanca between Winston Churchill and Franklin D. Roosevelt.

T

2:15 p.m.
Time that Charlie's wife goes down to Scollay Square station each day to hand Charlie a sandwich as his train passes through in the song "M.T.A." by the Kingston Trio.

3
Number of years that the singer of the song "Tie a Yellow Ribbon Around the Old Oak Tree" spent in prison (in song lyrics).

3 B's of Rock Music
Beatles (1960–1970); Beach Boys (1961–   ); and Bee Gees (1956–   ).

3 C's of Credit
Character, Capacity, and Credit (financial code).

3 D's of the Fighting Man
Discipline, Decision, and Devotion to Duty (West Point Military Academy).

12
Number of letters in the Hawaiian alphabet (a,e,h,i,k,l,m,n,o,p,u,w).

13
Number of steps to a gallows and the number of loops in a hanging noose.

13
Number of stars on the Federation Flag in the TV series *Star Trek*.

20 Feet Square
Size of a regulation boxing ring.

20 Inches
Size of Popeye's forearms and calves. His biceps and thighs are 7 inches, his neck is 8 inches, and his chest 30 inches (60 inches when expanded).

£20
Reward given by the British authorities for the capture of Frankie McPhillip

in the 1935 movie *The Informer*. It was collected by Gypo Nolan (Victor McLaglen).

21 Beacon Street
Boston address of the David Chase Detective Agency in the TV series *21 Beacon Street*.

22

Burt Reynolds' football jersey at West Palm Beach High School and at Florida State. He wore this jersey number in the films *The Longest Yard* (1974) and *Semi Tough* (1977). In the 1978 movie *Hooper* Reynolds wore a Florida State University sweatshirt.

22 Long Island Cove
House address at Paradise Cove in Long Island of the Quaker Alexander Austin (Alan Ladd) in the 1958 movie *The Deep Six*.

22 miles, 1,470 yards
Distance that Pheidippides ran from Marathon to Athens in September 490 B.C. to tell the people of the Greek victory over the Persians. Upon reaching Athens, Pheidippides fell over dead. In 1924, for the Olympic run, the distance was set at 26 miles, 385 yards.

23 hours
Length of the filibuster by Sen. Jefferson Smith (James Stewart) in the 1939 movie *Mr. Smith Goes to Washington*.

24th Precinct
Manhattan precinct for which Rocky King (Roscoe Karns) worked in the 1950 TV series *Rocky King, Detective*.

24 Sussex Drive
Ottawa, Canada, address of the Canadian prime minister.

25 Cents
First minimum wage (per hour) set by Congress in 1938.

27th Precinct
Manhattan setting of the 1967 TV series *N.Y.P.D.*

29 Cove Road
Malibu address of Jim Rockford's (James Garner) $7,000 trailer in the TV series *The Rockford Files*.

$29

Cost of Princess Margaret's divorce from her husband of 18 years, Lord Snowdon, in May 1978. The proceedings took 53 seconds.

30

Symbol that means the end of a newspaper story: "and that's 30." The number was used for a 1959 Jack Webb/William Conrad movie.

32

Number on the train engine that the Marx Brothers tore apart to use as fuel in the 1940 movie *Go West*.

32

Number worn on the uniform of MVP winners Sandy Koufax (NL) and Elston Howard (AL) in 1963. Also that year, the MVP winner in NFL football, Jim Brown, wore number 32.

32

Football jersey number worn by both Jim Brown and O.J. Simpson.

32

Football jersey worn by Nick Bonelli (Tony Curtis) in the 1953 movie *The All Americans*.

32 East River

Sutton Place, New York City, home of Godfrey Parke (William Powell) in the 1936 movie *My Man Godfrey*.

33 Kosciusko Street

New York City home address of Alice Kramden's mother, Mrs. Gibson, in the TV series *The Honeymooners*.

33 Riverside

New York City apartment (4A) address of Paul Kersey (Charles Bronson) in the 1974 movie *Death Wish*.

33 Rue Dunôt, Faubourg St. Germain

French home address of detective C. Auguste Dupin in Edgar Allan Poe's *The Murders in the Rue Morgue* (1841).

$33.31

Astronaut Edwin E. Aldrin's travel voucher payment on his trip from his home to the moon and back home again (July 7–July 27, 1969).

35

Minimum age set by the Constitution to be elected president of the United States. It is also the maximum age to begin training to become an astronaut (the height limit is 6 feet, the weight limit 190 pounds).

35 Wood Dale Lane

Santa Barbara, California, address of the Loud family in the TV series *An American Family*.

39

Marching band uniform retired in honor of member Dolly Parton at Sevier County High School on October 13, 1977. Dolly played snare drums.

39

Number worn by President Carter in the Cancoctin Mountain Park 6-mile race he ran on September 15, 1979. He dropped out after 4 miles.

209 East 106th Street

New York City house address where Burton Stephen Lancaster was born on November 2, 1913. Tony Curtis was also born on East 106th Street, at Flower and Fifth Avenue Hospital on June 3, 1925.

211 Pine Avenue

Mayfield home address of the Cleaver family in the TV series *Leave It to Beaver*. Their home phone number was Whitney 1-2738 (in some episodes, KLondike 5-4763).

214 Brookline Avenue

Address of the Fields Rooming House in the TV series *The Abbott and Costello Show*.

216 South Emory Street

Address of the Baltimore, Maryland, house where George Herman Ruth was born on the 3rd floor on February 6, 1895.

220 pounds

Weight of Fred Flintstone (TV cartoon series).

220 to 0

Final score in the football game between Georgia Tech and Cumberland College in October 1916. John Heisman was the coach for Georgia.

221

Wally Cleaver's (Tony Dow) locker number at Mayfield High School in the TV series *Leave It to Beaver*. The combination was: Lt 10—Rt 3—Lt 11.

234

Papillon's (Steve McQueen) solitary confinement cell on Devil's Island in the 1973 movie *Papillon*.

251 feet

Distance of the foul line running from home plate to left field in the Los Angeles Coliseum, where the Dodgers first played when they moved to Los Angeles in 1958.

258

First draft number drawn for recruitment of U.S. troops in 1917 (World War I). Alden C. Flagg, Sr., of Boston held this number. Twenty-three years later, in 1940 (World War II), his 27-year-old son held the first draft number (158).

272

Number of words in Abraham Lincoln's Gettysburg address.

282

Number of consecutive football games that 6-foot-4-inch Jim Marshall played in professional football. He retired at age 42 in 1979, after 19 seasons.

285 Norwood Street

Central City home address of the Gillis Grocery Store in the TV series *The Many Loves of Dobie Gillis*.

289

Number of cookbooks owned by detective Nero Wolfe.

318th

U.S. Marine Corps platoon to which Pvt. Gomer Pyle (Jim Nabors) was assigned in the TV series *Gomer Pyle, U.S.M.C.*

326

IQ of Popeye's hamburger-loving friend, J. Wellington Wimpy.

327 North Robin Hoot Roach

Home address in the Sherwood Forest Estates in San Fernando, California, of the Wilson family in the TV series *Love Thy Neighbor.*

341 Brockner Street

Fernwood, Ohio, home address of Martha, George, and Cathy Shumway in the TV series *Mary Hartman, Mary Hartman.* Their phone number was (614) 555-7335.

367 IRQ

California automobile license plate number of Lionel Whitney's (Jeff Goldblum) green Triumph TR7 in the TV series *Tenspeed and Brownshoe.*

1060 W. Addison

Chicago address of Wrigley Field. Elwood Blues (Dan Ackroyd) many times falsely gave this as his home address in the 1980 movie *The Blues Brothers.*

1069

Name that Michael Herbert Dengle of Minneapolis wished to change his name to in a court application. A judge turned down his request in February 1978.

2001: A Space Odyssey

1968 Stanley Kubrick movie being shown in a movie theater that Joe Buck (Jon Voight) and a "friend" (Bernard Hughes) attend in the 1969 movie *Midnight Cowboy.*

2001 Odyssey Ballroom

Bay Ridge, Brooklyn, dancehall setting of the 1977 movie *Saturday Night Fever.* The house DJ was Monty Rock III.

2015

Time setting of the 1965 movie *Spaceflight IC-I.*

2020

Time setting of the 1978 movie *Deathplot.*

2022

Time setting of the 1973 movie *Soylent Green.*

2024

Time setting of the 1960 movie *Beyond the Time Barrier* and of the 1976 movie *A Boy and His Dog.*

2036

Time setting of the 1936 movie *Things to Come.*

2053

Time setting of the 1971 Irwin Allen movie *City Beneath the Sea.*

2072

Time setting of the 1972 movie *Silent Running.*

2101 South 33rd Street
Omaha, Nebraska, home where Montgomery Clift was born on October 17, 1920.

2173
Time setting of the 1973 Woody Allen movie *Sleeper.*

2200
Time setting of the 1956 movie *Forbidden Planet.*

2212
Number of performances that the Broadway musical *Oklahoma!* played during its original run, which began on March 31, 1943.

·2220–2222 Fairview Avenue
Los Angeles duplex in which Stan Laurel and Oliver Hardy lived with their wives in the 1934 movie *Sons of the Desert.*

2222
Time setting of the TV series *Quark.*

2293
Time setting of the 1973 movie *Zardoz.* (Note: Wizard of *Oz.*)

2311
Hijacked police unit chased throughout the 1974 movie *Sugerland Express.*

2319
Time setting of the 1976 movie/TV series *Logan's Run.*

2356 Vinewood
Hollywood home address of Lionel "Brownshoe" Whitney (Jeff Goldblum) in the TV series *Tenspeed and Brownshoe.*

2369
Time setting of the TV series *The Lost Saucer.*

2434 fans
Smallest crowd ever to attend a heavyweight championship bout—the May 25, 1965, match between Sonny Liston and Muhammad Ali in Lewiston, Maine.

2476
Time setting of the TV series *Ark II.*

2508
Time setting of the 1956 movie *World Without End.*

2790
Time setting of the TV series *The Starlost.*

2814
Sector, including Earth, patrolled by Green Lantern Hal Jordon (comic books). There are numerous Green Lanterns in the Universe.

3085
Time setting of the TV series *Planet of the Apes.*

3100 Willow Road

Los Angeles home address of Jonathan (Robert Wagner) and Jennifer Hart (Stephanie Powers) in the TV series *Hart to Hart*.

3218½ Washington Boulevard

Los Angeles address of private eye Moses Wine's (Richard Dreyfuss) home and office in the 1978 movie *The Big Fix*.

3632½ La Hamber Street

Los Angeles home address of the Valdez family in the TV series *Viva Valdez*.

3701

Population of Sugarland, Texas, in the 1974 movie *The Sugarland Express*.

3732

Time setting of the Saturday morning series *Space Academy*. The spacecraft is called *Seeker,* while the small computer robot is named *Peepo*.

20013

Zip code of Resurrection City, the temporary camp set up in Washington, D.C., by civil rights leader Ralph Abernathy and his followers in June 1968.

30-30100

Telephone number used in order to get in touch with·Jefferson Keyes (James Farentino) through his contact Elena (Adele Mara) in the TV movie *Cool Million* (on the *NBC Wednesday Mystery Movie*).

315–406–296

Social security number of Jake Blues (John Belushi) in the 1980 movie *The Blues Brothers*.

3911810

Corp. Walter ''Radar'' O'Reilly's (Gary Burghoff) U.S. Army serial number in the TV series *M*A*S*H*.

266-8765

Phone number of CONTROL'S chief in the TV series *Get Smart*. The numbers correspond to the letters (CONTROL) on the telephone dial.

275-0817

Beverly Hills home phone number of George Webber (Dudley Moore) in the 1979 movie *''10''*.

3,200,000

Number of bricks that originally made up the racing track of the Indianapolis Speedway, which at one time was owned by Eddie Rickenbacker.

362-9296

Allen Felix's (Woody Allen) home telephone number in San Francisco in the 1972 movie *Play It Again Sam*.

31326933

U.S. Army serial number of Pvt. Braddock (Shecky Greene) in the TV series *Combat*.

39729966

Capt. B. J. Hunnicut's (Mike Farrell) U.S. Army serial number in the TV series *M*A*S*H*.

259-20-7368

Social Security number of President James Earl Carter.

$2,775,395.12

Value of the heist in the famous Brink's robbery in Boston on January 17, 1950, by seven masked bandits. ($1,218,211.29 of the loot was in cash.)

TAB

Trans-Atlantic Broadcasting Company, the New York–based TV network for which Ellen Cunningham (Pamela Bellwood) was an executive in the TV series *W.E.B.*

T-Birds (Thunderbirds)

Rydell High School black-leather-jacket gang led by Danny Zucko* (John Travolta) in the 1978 movie *Grease*. Their rival gang was The Scorpions. In the Broadway production of *Grease* Zucko's gang was called the Burger Palace Boys.

T.H.U.M.B.

Tiny Humans Underground Military Bureau in the cartoon TV series *Tom of T.H.U.M.B.*

THX 138

California license plate number of John Milner's (Paul Le Mat) Yellow '32 Ford Coupe in the 1973 movie *American Graffiti*. The movie was directed by George Lucas, who had previously directed a 1971 film titled *THX1138*.

T & T Combined Circus

Traveling circus of the 1800s owned by Col. Casey Thompson (Chill Wills) and Ben Travis (John Derek) in the TV series *Frontier Circus*.

TMA-1

Tycho Magnetic Anomaly-One—name given by scientists to the monolithic slab on the moon in the 1968 movie *2001: A Space Odyssey*.

TVU566

California license number of Jaime Sommers' blue Datsun 280Z in the TV series *The Bionic Woman*.

Tabasco Film Company

Havana, Cuba, firm from which Col. Henry Blake (McLean Stevenson) ordered stag movies in the TV series *M*A*S*H*.

Tadpole

Frog's (Smiley Burnette) young sidekick, who looked and dressed like Frog, in Gene Autry movies. His horse also had a ring around its left eye. Tadpole was played by Joe Strauch, Jr. He made his debut in *Home in Wyoming* (1942).

---

*Henry Winkler was originally considered for the movie role.

Taff

White pony featured in the 1976 Disney movie *Ride a Wild Pony.*

Tag

Tom Mix's dog, which appeared with him in the movies.

Tail Gunner Joe

Nickname of Senator Joseph R. McCarthy. He was portrayed in the 1977 TV movie *Tail Gunner Joe* by Peter Boyle.

Taj Mahal

World-famous structure built in 1650 by Emperor Shan Jehan as a memorial to his wife, Mumtaz Mahal.

Take Down

1978 movie that became the first Walt Disney movie to be rated PG.

Talleyrand-Périgord, Charles Maurice de

(1754–1838) French statesman who served the monarchy, the Revolution, and the Directorate, but opposed Napoleon. He became prime minister of France in 1815, after Napoleon's defeat at Waterloo. Movie portrayals: *The Fighting Eagle* (1927) Sam De Grasse; and *Conquest* (1937) Reginald Owen.

Tall Ships

Large sailing vessels that passed through New York harbor on July 4, 1976, in honor of the Bicentennial: *The Mircea* (Rumanian); USS *Eagle* (American); *Esmeralda* (Spanish); *Christian Radich* (Norwegian); *Kruzenshtern* (Russian); *Nippon Maru* (Japanese); and *Amerigo Vespucci* (Italian).

Taming of the Shrew

1929 movie in which Douglas Fairbanks and Mary Pickford made their only screen appearance together.

Tammy

Tammy Tarleton, a fictional character whose adventures are depicted in the following movies: *Tammy and the Bachelor* (1957) Debbie Reynolds; *Tammy Tell Me True* (1961) Sandra Dee; and *Tammy and the Doctor* (1963) Sandra Dee. Debbie Watson played her in the TV series *Tammy*. (Four of the TV episodes were made into the 1967 TV movie *Tammy and the Millionaire*.) Debbie Reynolds' recording of "Tammy" became the No. 1 song of 1957.

Tampico

Mexican town in the opening scenes of the 1948 movie *The Treasure of the Sierra Madre*. It was the birthplace of actress Linda Christian (1923). Ronald Reagan was born in Tampico, Illinois, on February 6, 1911.

TARDIS

Time and Relative Dimensions In Space. Dr. Who's flying police call box in the TV series *Dr. Who*.

Tarzana

Southern California community that grew around Edgar Rice Burroughs'

550-acre ranch of Tarzana.* It was the setting of the 2nd episode of the TV series *The New Dick Van Dyke Show.*

Tater
Loweezy and Snuffy Smith's only child (comic strip *Snuffy Smith*).

Tattoo
3-foot 10-inch midget servant (played by Herve Villechaize) of Roarke (Ricardo Montalban) in the TV series *Fantasy Island.* His first two words each episode are "La plane, la plane."

Taylor, Chip
Recording artist and composer of such popular songs as "Wild Thing" and "Angel of the Morning." He is the brother of actor Jon Voight.

Taylor, Glen
U.S. senator from Idaho (1944–1950) who was called the Singing Cowboy. He and his wife, Dora, sang with the Glendora Ranch Gang band before Taylor entered politics. After retiring from politics, Glen Taylor founded the Taylor Topper, a business specializing in custom hair pieces.

Taylor, Robert and Alfred
Brothers who in 1886 ran against each other for the governorship of Tennessee. Robert, a Democrat, defeated his Republican brother. In 1921 Alfred became governor.

Taylor, Ted
Lancashire butcher who recorded the Beatles at the Star Club in Hamburg, Germany, in 1962. It was a crude tape, but electronic engineering improved it so that it could be released in 1976 as an album.

Taylorville, Illinois
Hometown of UCLA student Sandy Stockton (Sandy Duncan) in the TV series *Funny Face.*

Tchaikovsky, Peter
(1840–1893) Russian composer of the ballet scores *Swan Lake* and *The Sleeping Beauty* and such piano pieces as the Piano Concerto No. 1. He was the guest conductor when Carnegie Hall opened on May 5, 1891. Tchaikovsky was portrayed in the 1970 movie *The Music Lovers* by Richard Chamberlain (Alex Brewer as a boy).

Teabiscuit
Winning racehorse in the 1943 Abbott and Costello movie *It Ain't Hay.*

Teeka
Sheena's pet chimpanzee (comic strip *Sheena Queen of the Jungle*).

Tee-Tot
Nickname of black musician Rufe Payne, who taught Hank Williams to play the guitar when Williams was a small boy. In the 1964 movie *Your Cheatin'*

---

*There is also a Tarzan, Texas.

Heart Tee-Tot was portrayed by Rex Ingram. Rufus Thomas portrayed him in the 1980 TV special *Hank Williams—The Man and His Music*.

Tegtight
Carter Primus's (Robert Brown) home base in the TV series *Primus*.

Telek
Scotty given to Gen. Eisenhower by his London staff on his 52nd birthday.

Tell the Story
Theme song of the radio series *Big Town*.

Telstar
1962 instrumental recording by the Tornados that became the first British instrumental to top the U.S. charts.

Tempo
Power boat driven by band leader Guy Lombardo to win the Gold Cup in 1946, 1947, 1948, and 1949. He also won the Silver Cup and the President's Cup. Lombardo raced several boats, all named *Tempo*.

Ten Commandments, The
Cecil B. DeMille's 1956 religious spectacular, a remake of his 1923 silent version. This was the movie that Roy Neary's (Richard Dreyfuss) children were watching on TV in the 1977 movie *Close Encounters of the Third Kind* (the scene was of the Red Sea being parted). The movie was also advertised in the animated opening of the 1978 movie *Grease*.

Tennis Cabinet
Nickname given to the political advisers of President Theodore Roosevelt.

Tennison
Servant to agents Jim West and Artemus Gordon in the TV series *The Wild Wild West*.

Tereshkova-Nikolayev, Valentina
First woman to orbit the earth, on June 16, 1963, in her Russian spacecraft *Vostok VI*. She married fellow cosmonaut Adrian Nikolavev, who had in 1962 orbited the earth 64 times in *Vostok III*.

Terminal
Allied code name for the July 17–August 2, 1945, conference at Potsdam between Churchill, Attlee, Truman, and Stalin.

Terminus
Planet setting of Isaac Asimov's *Foundation* trilogy.

Texas
Only state to have had six flags fly over it: Spanish, French, Mexican, Lone Star Republic, Confederate States of America, and the United States.

Texas Gold
Savings stamp stolen by Lou Jean (Goldie Hawn) in the 1974 movie *The Sugarland Express*.

Texas, Our Texas
   Official song of the state of Texas, adopted in 1930.
Texas Rangers Hall of Fame
   Located in Waco, Texas.
Texas School Book Depository
   Building at 411 Elm Street in Dallas, Texas, from which Lee Harvey Oswald
   shot both John F. Kennedy and John Connally. He fired from the 6th-floor
   window with an Italian 6.5-mm Mannlicher-Carcano rifle on November 22,
   1963.
Texas Wheelers, The
   Short-lived (1974–1975) TV series in which both Gary Busey and Mark
   Hamill appeared.
Thackeray, William Makepeace
   (1811–1863) English novelist who wrote *Vanity Fair* and *Henry Esmond*,
   among other works. He was portrayed in the 1946 movie *Devotion* by Sydney
   Greenstreet.
Thackery Realty Company
   Real estate agency for which Robert S. Beanblossom (Robert Cummings)
   worked as a salesman in the TV series *My Hero*.
Thalberg, Irving Grant
   (1899–1936) The "boy genuis" who became head of Universal pictures at
   the age of 20. He was married to actress Norma Shearer. Thalberg was F.
   Scott Fitzgerald's model for the character Monroe Stahr in the novel *The
   Last Tycoon*. He was portrayed in the 1957 movie *The Man of a Thousand
   Faces* by Robert Evans (who later became head of Paramount Pictures). In
   the 1976 movie *The Last Tycoon* Thalberg was characterized by Robert
   DeNiro as Monroe Stahr. John Rubinstein portrayed Thalberg in the 1980 TV
   miniseries *Moviola*.
Thanagar
   Home planet of Hawkman and Hawkgirl (Silver Age series of comic books).
Thatcher, Margaret
   Britain's first female prime minister, who took office in 1979. Portrayed by
   Janet Brown in the 1981 movie *For Your Eyes Only*.
That Night in Rio
   1941 movie starring Carmen Miranda. It was the movie being shown at the
   theater attended by F. Scott Fitzgerald (Gregory Peck) and Sheila Graham
   (Deborah Kerr) in the 1959 movie *Beloved Infidel*. Scenes from *That Night in
   Rio* appeared in the 1970 movie *Myra Breckinridge*.
That Old Black Magic
   Song Charles Manson sang at his murder trial on October 3, 1970. (On
   October 1 he had been removed from court after singing "Old Grey Mare" to
   the judge.) It was the song sung by Cherie (Marilyn Monroe) in an Arizona

café in the 1956 movie *Bus Stop*. "That Old Black Magic" was originally sung by Johnnie Johnston in the 1942 movie *Star Spangled Rhythm*.

That school up north
Words used by Ohio State football coach Wayne "Woody" Hayes to describe Ohio's closest rival, the University of Michigan. Hayes refused ever to mention Michigan by name.

That's What You Jolly Well Get
Song sung by Errol Flynn in the 1943 movie *Thank Your Lucky Stars*.

That Wonderful Year
Nostalgic sequence, featuring a different year each week, presented in the TV series *The Gary Moore Show*.

The bigger they come, the harder they fall
Remark made by Bob Fitzsimmons, who weighed 167 pounds, about his 206-pound opponent, heavyweight champion James J. Jeffries, before their July 25, 1902, fight. Jeffries won.

The Case of the Headless Bride
Novel by Wayne Morgan that was being read by Nicki (Deanna Durbin) while riding in a train in the 1945 movie *Lady on a Train*.

Thee I Love
Original title of the 1956 motion picture *Friendly Persuasion*. Perry Como was approached to sing the theme song (which did retain the title "Thee I Love"), but turned down the offer. Pat Boone sang it instead.

The Fool
Group of artists who painted the mural on the Beatles' Apple Boutique in London. They also ran the boutique.

There and Back Again: A Hobbits' Holiday
Title of Hobbit Bilbo Baggins' memoirs of his journey to the land of Murkwood in J. R. R. Tolkien's *The Hobbit*.

There's a New Girl in Town
Theme song of the TV series *Alice*.

There's Nothing That I Haven't Sung About
Song written for Bing Crosby to sing to Ralph Kramden and Ed Norton in *The Honeymooners* TV series. Crosby later recorded the song.

Theron
Master of Magic who taught Mandrake the Magician his secret tricks.

The World Is Yours—Cook Tours
Flashing electric sign across the street from Tony Camonte's (Paul Muni) apartment in the 1932 movie *Scarface*.

They're Either Too Young or Too Old
Song sung by Bette Davis in the 1943 movie *Thank Your Lucky Stars*.

Thief of Bad Gags
Nickname conferred on comedian Milton Berle by columnist Walter Winchell.

Thief, The
1952 movie starring Ray Milland in which no dialogue is spoken.

Third Degree, The
Newsletter of the Mystery Writers of America.

This Is Cinerama
First Cinerama movie, narrated by Lowell Thomas. It debuted at the Broadway Theater in New York City on September 30, 1952.

This Is the Army
1943 movie in which George Murphy (future U.S. senator) played the father of Ronald Reagan (future president).

This Is Today
Theme song of the TV series *The Today Show*.

This Machine Kills Fascists
Slogan on the guitar of folk singer Woody Guthrie.

Thomas Bolt (Old Thunderball)
Assumed name often used by pulp detective Nick Carter.

Thomas Flyer
Automobile (1907 Model 35) that finished first (by 26 days) in the 1908 New York City–to–Paris road race. The five other cars in the race were an Italian Brixia Zust, a French De Dion-Bouton, a French Motobloc, a German Protos, and a French Sizaire-Naudin. The race lasted from February 12, 1908, to September 17, 1908. The automobile is presently in Bill Harrah's automobile collection.

Thompson, Robert L.
U.S. soldier who was driving the military truck that was struck by the sedan in which Gen. George S. Patton was a passenger on the Frankfort-Mannheim road at 11:48 a.m. on December 9, 1945. Pfc. Horace Woodring was the driver of the sedan. Patton died on December 21, 1945, from injuries sustained in the crash.

Thor
Son of Odin, the Norse Thunder god, and secret identity of Dr. Donald Blake, whose cane turns into the URU Hammer. Debut in comics: *Journey into Mystery Comics* No. 83, August 1962.

Thornton Corporation
Company whose dividends provide Mrs. Mary Worth with her income, (comic strip *Mary Worth*). She was left the stock by her husband.

Thorton, Stan
17-year-old Australian who flew to San Francisco on July 13, 1979, to collect the *San Francisco Examiner's* reward of $10,000 for bringing to the paper the first chunk of *Skylab*.

Those Redheads from Seattle
1953 3D movie, the only film in which singer Teresa Brewer ever appeared.

Those Who Care
TV soap on which Dick Preston (Dick Van Dyke) played Dr. Brad Fairmont at Pleasant Valley Hospital in the TV series *The New Dick Van Dyke Show.*

Threat, The
Publicity nickname of actress Lizabeth Scott.

Three Days of the Condor
1975 Robert Redford movie based on James Grady's novel *Six Days of the Condor.*

Three Mile Island Reactor
Harrisburg, Pennsylvania, nuclear power plant that went critical on March 28, 1979. The accident occurred shortly after the release of the Michael Douglas–produced movie *The China Syndrome*. In the film mention is made of the fact that a nuclear power plant accident could wipe out the state of Pennsylvania.

Three Musketeers, The
Classic story by Alexandre Dumas. It was the first story published by *Classic Comics* (No. 1, October 1941). With issue No. 35, March 1947, the title of the comics changed to *Classics Illustrated*. No. 35 was *The Last Days of Pompeii*.

Three Rivers
Locale for the radio soap *The Brighter Day.*

Three Texas Steers
Movie poster on a wall of Florence Jean Castleberry's (Polly Holliday) nightclub, Flo's Yellow Rose, in the TV series *Flo.*

Thunderbolt
Favorite TV canine star of the 101 Dalmations in the 1961 cartoon movie *101 Dalmations.*

Thunderbolt
Code name of the Israeli assault on Entebbe Airport in Uganda on July 4, 1976, to free 103 hostages.

Thunderfish, USS
(No. 502)—submarine commanded by Lt. Comdr. Duke E. Gifford (John Wayne) in the 1951 movie *Operation Pacific.*

Thurman, John S.
Inventor of the vacuum cleaner in 1899.

Tiberius (Claudius Nero Caesar)
(42 B.C.–A.D. 37) 2nd emperor of Rome (A.D. 14–37) who was portrayed in the 1953 movie *Salome* by Sir Cedric Hardwicke, and in the 1980 movie *Caligula* by Peter O'Toole.

Tie
Twin Ion Engines—fighter planes flown by the rebel force in the 1977 movie *Star Wars.*

Tiger

Lane family's pet dog in the TV series *The Patty Duke Show*.

Tigerfish

U.S. nuclear submarine commanded by Cmdr. James Ferraday (Rock Hudson) in the 1968 movie *Ice Station Zebra* (loosely based on the Alistair Maclean novel of the same title).

Tigris

Papyrus craft in which Thor Heyerdahl sailed in 1970 from Safi, Morocco, to Barbados.

Tillie

Nickname of the mobile crane on the flightdeck of the aircraft carrier *Savo Island* in the 1954 movie *The Bridges at Toko-Ri*.

Tillis, Mel

Country singer (Entertainer of the Year, 1976) who stutters acutely when he talks; yet when he sings, the stuttering totally disappears.

Tilly

Strawberry Fields' (Sandy Farina) pet goose in the 1978 movie *Sgt. Pepper's Lonely Hearts Club*.

Time Magazine

Lyndon B. Johnson's picture is on the cover of the issue of *Time* magazine shown on the cover of the Bob Dylan album *Bringing It All Back Home*. Fictitious people on fictitious covers of *Time* magazine: Professor Clayton Forrester (Gene Barry) in the 1953 movie *War of the Worlds;* Rod Anderson (Robert Mitchum) in the 1964 movie *What a Way to Go!;* Romer Treece (Robert Shaw) in the 1977 movie *The Deep;* John Kovak (Sylvester Stallone) in the 1978 movie *F.I.S.T.;* and Sgt. Pepper's Lonely Hearts Club Band (Bee Gees) in the 1978 movie *Sgt. Pepper's Lonely Hearts Club Band*.

Timex

Wristwatch worn by Lois Lane (Margot Kidder) in the 1978 movie *Superman*. The time shown was 8:05 p.m.

Tim Tyler's Luck

Comic strip begun on August 13, 1928, by Lyman Young, the brother of Murat "Chic" Young, the creator of *Blondie*.

Tina

Female drone that Twiki (Felix Silia) fell in love with on the TV series *Buck Rogers in the 25th Century*. Tina was played by Patty Maloney.

Tina's Joy

Dinghy in which Doug (Keith Gordon*) was sailing when attacked by a giant shark in the 1978 movie *Jaws 2*.

---

*Son of actor Barry Gordon.

Tingler, The
  1959 movie starring Vincent Price. When the film was shown in many
  theaters, the seats were wired to give the audience a mild shock.

Tin Goose
  Nickname affectionately given to the 1947 Tucker automobile. It had three
  headlights.

Tinker Air Force Base
  Military base where Buddy Holly and the Crickets recorded "Maybe Baby"
  and three other songs in the Officers' Club in 1957.

Tin Pan Alley
  New York City locale (between 5th and 6th avenues on 28th Street) where
  numerous old-time music publishers were located. The term was coined by
  journalist Monroe H. Rosenfeld in an article written in 1903. Denmark Street
  in London's West End is the British equivalent of Tin Pan Alley.

Tiny Petite Pheasant Feather Tea Shoppe
  Three-tabled restaurant where Sade Gook went for lunch in the radio series
  Vic and Sade.

Tippit, J. D.
  Dallas policeman who was shot and killed by Lee Harvey Oswald the same
  day he assassinated President Kennedy—November 22, 1963.

Tirpitz, (Adm.) Alfred von
  (1849–1930) German naval commander who created the modern German
  Navy. He was portrayed by Lon Chaney in *Beast of Berlin* (1918).

Tisdale, Marie M.
  Albany, New York, reader of *Movie Weekly* magazine whose contest entry
  to change Lucille Le Sueur's name won her the $500 prize. Her suggestion was
  Joan Crawford. (The previous winning name was Joan Arden, but it was discovered that there already was an actress of that name on the MGM lot.)

Toby
  Prime Minister Winston Churchill's pet canary.

Toby
  Dog that helped Sherlock Holmes to solve a number of cases (novel).

Toe, The
  Nickname of NFL player Lou Groza.

To hell with Roosevelt, to hell with Babe Ruth, to hell with Roy Acuff!
  Insult yelled by Japanese soldiers to American GIs during World War II.

Tomahawk
  Trophy given to the winner of the annual University of Illinois–Northwestern
  football game.

Tomaszewski, Stanley
  16-year-old busboy who accidentally started the fire that destroyed Boston's
  Cocoanut Grove Nightclub on November 18, 1942.

Tom, Dick, and Harry
　　First names of the three Byrd Brothers: Thomas Byrd, Adm. Richard Byrd, and Harry Byrd.

Tom, Dick, and Harry
　　Original title of the 1930 song "Time on My Hands."

Tommy
　　Racehorse belonging to Tip Scanlon (Clark Gable) that won the Kentucky Derby in the 1931 movie *Sporting Blood*.

Tommy Chan
　　Charlie Chan's No. 3 son. He was played in the movies—with Sidney Toler as father Charlie—by Benson Fong, and—with Roland Winters as father Charlie—by Victor Sen Young, who had previously played the No. 2 son, Jimmy, in movies with Sidney Toler as the father.

Tom Thumb
　　5½-inch-high boy in stories by the Brothers Grimm. He was played by Russ Tamblyn in two George Pal movies—*Tom Thumb* (1958) and *The Wonderful World of the Brothers Grimm* (1962)—and by Sumner Getchell in the 1934 movie *Babes in Toyland*.

Tom Thumb Golf Course
　　First miniature golf course, built by Garnet Carter in 1929.

To My Friends: My work is done. Why wait?
　　Suicide note left by George Eastman, inventor of the Kodak camera (1888), who shot himself in 1932.

Tonight You Belong to Me
　　Song written by Billy Rose that Steve Martin and Bernadette Peters sang to each other along the beach in the 1979 movie *The Jerk*.

Tony Crombie and the Rockets
　　First professional British rock 'n' roll band. They began playing rock music in 1956.

Too Hot to Handle
　　Title of Ian Fleming's first James Bond novel in 1954 when it was distributed in the United States. The title was changed from the British edition because it was feared that Americans could not correctly pronounce *Casino Royale*. When Fleming's boss, William Stephenson (known as Intrepid) read the manuscript he told Fleming that it would never sell.

Too Marvelous for Words
　　George Gershwin composed this love song for Vincent Parry (Humphrey Bogart) and Irene Jason (Lauren Bacall) in the 1947 movie *Dark Passage*.

Toonder
　　Nickname of right-hand punch thrown by heavyweight champion Ingemar Johansson.

Toonerville Trolley That Meets All the Trains, The
Full title of Fontaine Fox's comic strip *Toonerville Trolley*. In silent movies Dan Mason played the skipper.

Toot, Whistle, Plunk, and Boom
First Cinemascope cartoon, and winner of the 1953 Oscar for Best Short Subject.

Top Hatters
Name of Jan Savitt's big band of the 1930s–1940s.

Topper
Cosmo B. Topper—character created by Thorne Smith in novels. Movie portrayals: *Topper* (1937) Roland Young; *Topper Takes a Trip* (1939) Roland Young; and *Topper Returns* (1941) Roland Young. Roland Young played the part in the radio series, and Leo G. Carroll played Topper in the TV series. Jack Warden played the part in the 1979 TV movie *Topper*. GHOSTS - KIRBY'S
MRS KIRBY (COOK)

Top 10 Movies
Results of a 1977 vote by 35,000 members of the American Film Institute:
1. *Gone With the Wind* (1939)
2. *Citizen Kane* (1941)
3. *Casablanca* (1942)
4. *The African Queen* (1951)
5. *The Grapes of Wrath* (1940)
6. *One Flew over the Cuckoo's Nest* (1975)
7. *Singin' in the Rain* (1952)
8. *Star Wars* (1977)
9. *2001: A Space Odyssey* (1968)
10. *The Wizard of Oz* (1939)

Torrent, The
Greta Garbo's first American movie (1926 MGM). In the film Joel McCrea doubled for Garbo in a horse-riding sequence.

Torsk, USS
Submarine that fired the last shot (torpedo) of World War II (21:17 GMT, August 14, 1945), sinking a Japanese vessel.

Tortuga
Thomas Hudson's (George C. Scott) fishing vessel in the 1977 movie *Islands in the Stream*.

Toselli's Serenade
Theme song of the radio series *The Goldbergs*.

Tossy
Circus pony that Jack Griffith (Jackie Gleason) bought for his daughter, Corrine, in the 1963 movie *Papa's Delicate Condition*. In order to get her the pony and cart, he bought an entire circus.

Touch

Nickname of actor Krekor Ohanian (Mike Connors) as a University of California basketball player. His agent, Henry Wilson, named him Touch Connors, and that is the name by which he was billed in films in the early 1950s.

Touchdown for LSU and Darling of LSU

Football fight songs of Louisiana State University written by Huey P. Long and Castro Capazo.

Touhy, Roger

Underworld figure of the 1930s who was convicted of kidnapping. He was portrayed in the 1944 movie *Roger Touhy, Gangster* by Preston Foster.

Toulouse-Lautrec

(1864–1901) Henri Marie Raymond de Toulouse-Lautrec Monfa. French painter and lithographer who had the physical disability of underdeveloped legs. His depictions of Paris and Parisian night life have become classics. Toulouse-Lautrec was portrayed in the 1952 movie *Moulin Rouge* by José Ferrer.

Tournament of Roses and Rose Bowl

Annual January 1 parade and football game that, in 1948, was the subject of the first color newsreel (shown January 5). On January 1, 1954 the parade was the first coast-to-coast color show ever telecast from the West Coast (NBC).

T'Pring

Vulcan to whom Spock was married in a parent-arranged ceremony in the TV series *Star Trek* ("Amok Time" episode). Spock was 7 years old at the time.

Traci

15-year-old daughter of Helen Reddy who can be heard at the end of the 1974 record "You and Me Against the World." Both mother and daughter have a gold record for the song.

Trader

Skipper's (Martin Huston) dog in the TV series *Jungle Jim*.

Tralfamador

Planet 423 billion miles from Earth in the 1972 movie *Slaughterhouse Five* (based on the Kurt Vonnegut, Jr., novel of the same name).

Trans-Globe News

Wire news service for which Dean Evans (George Brent) and Katherine Wells (Mercedes McCambridge) worked in the 1956–1957 TV series *Wire Service*.

Transoceanic Airways

Four-engine aircraft (Flight No. 4) shot down by the German destroyer *Bon Sheer* 300 miles off the coast of England in the 1940 movie *Foreign Correspondent*. Only six people survived the crash.

Trapp, Maria von
Austrian tutor and eventual wife of Baron von Trapp who was portrayed in the 1965 movie *The Sound of Music* by Julie Andrews. The family fled Nazi Germany during the 1930s.

Trapshooting Hall of Fame
Located in Vandalia, Ohio.

Travels With a Donkey
Book written by Robert Louis Stevenson in 1879 while he was on his honeymoon.

Travis, William "Buck"
(1809–1836) American soldier and lawyer who commanded the Texas forces at the Alamo when it was wiped out by Santa Anna's troops on March 6, 1836. Movie portrayals: *Man of Conquest* (1939) Victor Jory; *Davy Crockett* (1954 TV) Don Megowan; and *The Alamo* (1960) Lawrence Harvey.

Travolta, John
First male to be on the cover of *McCall's* magazine in over 100 years. He appeared on the July 1978 issue.

Treasure House, The
Captain Kangaroo's museum (TV series).

Tree and the Blossom, The
Original working title of Grace Metalious's 1956 novel *Peyton Place*.

Triangle Films
Movie company founded in 1915 by D. W. Griffith, Mack Sennett, and Thomas Ince. In 1919 the company folded.

Triangle Publications
Publisher (in Radnor, Pennsylvania) of the largest-selling weekly magazine, *TV Guide*.

Tribal Rites of the New Saturday Night
Article by Nik Cohn in *New York* magazine, that was made into the 1977 movie *Saturday Night Fever.*

Tricky Dick
Uncomplimentary nickname given to Richard M. Nixon. It was first used by the *Independent Review* on September 29, 1950. ABC announcer "Dandy" Don Meredith referred to Nixon in this manner on *Monday Night Football,* and had to apologize the following week.

Trinity
Code name for the first A-bomb explosion at Alamogordo, New Mexico, at 5:30 a.m. (New Mexico time) on July 16, 1945.

Triple A Airlines
Small company for which Spud Barrett (Tim Conway) was the chief pilot in the 1970 TV series *The Tim Conway Show.* The company's motto was: "The Anywhere Anytime Airlines."

Triple Crown of Fillies

Acorn (1 mile); Mother Goose (1½ mile); and Coaching Club (1½ mile).

Tripoli

Dog picked up by the crew of the B17 *Mary Ann* in the 1942 movie *Air Force*. Tripoli barked whenever Moto's name was mentioned.

Triton, USS

First submarine to circumnavigate the globe (30,708 miles), from February 16,1960 to May 10, 1960. It was commanded by Capt. Edward L. Beach, who authored the novel *Run Silent, Run Deep*. He also co-directed (with Robert Wise) the 1958 movie of the same name.

Triumph

Motorcycle ridden by Johnny (Marlon Brando) in the 1954 movie *The Wild One*. It is also the motorcycle shown on the cover of Bob Dylan's *Highway 61 Revisited* album.

Trix Cereal

Colors of cereal puffs: Raspberry Red, Lemon Yellow, Orange Orange.

Trixie Norton

New York sewer worker Ed Norton's ex-burlesque queen wife. Trixie was played by Elaine Stritch on "Cavalcade of Stars," and then by Joyce Randolph, Patricia Wilson, and Jane Kean in the TV series *The Honeymooners*.

Trolley Series

Name given to the 1944 World Series played in Sportsman's Park in St. Louis between the Cardinals and the Browns.

Trooper

Douglas C. Neidermeyer's (Mark Metcalf) white horse that died of a heart attack in Dean Warner's office in the 1978 movie *Animal House*. He was played by Junior.

Troop No. 25

Boy Scout troop in Plains, Georgia, for which Jimmy Carter served as a scout master.

Tropicana Hotel

Hotel in Tropical Springs, California, that was held up by Roy Earle (Humphrey Bogart) and his gang in the 1941 movie *High Sierra*.

Tropic of Cancer

Henry Miller novel read by Frank Michaelson (James Stewart) in the 1963 movie *Take Her, She's Mine*.

Trotsky, Leon

(1877–1940) Russian Communist leader (born Lev Davidovich Bronstein) who was driven out of Russia in 1929 by Stalin. He was finally assassinated in Mexico on August 20, 1940, by Ramon Mercader. Trotsky was portrayed in the 1971 movie *Nicholas and Alexandra* by Brian Cox, and in the 1972 movie *The Assassination of Trotsky* by Richard Burton.

Troubadour
Los Angeles nightclub where Elton John made his U.S. debut in August 1970. John Lennon was thrown out of the club in March 1974 for heckling the Smothers Brothers. Cheech and Chong were discovered there by Lou Adler. The last group to play the Troubadour before it closed down was Orleans, in June 1975.

True Love
Bing Crosby's yacht.

Truman, Harry
83-year-old man who refused to leave his lodge home at Spirit Lake when Mount St. Helens erupted on May 18, 1980. He was killed by the explosion and buried under 60 feet of mud. Portrayed in a 1981 TV movie by Art Carney.

Truman, Harry S
(1884–1972) 33rd president of the United States. The S is an initial merely; it does not signify a name (hence no period). Truman was the first president to broadcast from the White House (1947). Portrayals: *The Beginning of the End* (1946) Art Baker; *The Man from Independence* (1974 TV special) Robert Vaughn; *Collision Course* (1975 TV) E. G. Marshall; *Give 'Em Hell Harry* (1976) James Whitmore; *MacArthur* (1977) Ed Flanders; *Tail Gunner Joe* (1977) Robert Symonds; *Harry S Truman: Plain Speaking* (1977) Ed Flanders; *Backstairs at the White House* (1979 TV miniseries) Harry Morgan (Bess Truman was portrayed by Estelle Parsons); *Enola Gay* (1980 TV) Ed Nelson; and "Truman at Potsdam" (1976 *Hallmark Hall of Fame* play) Ed Flanders.

Trushcross Grange
Linton family estate in Emily Brontë's 1845 novel *Wuthering Heights*.

Truth or Consequences
TV game show hosted by Bob Barker from December 31, 1956, to January 12, 1973 (3,524 consecutive performances). The radio version of the show appeared in the 1942 Victor Mature movie *Seven Day's Leave*.

Trysting Place, The
Play at Whittier College in which Richard M. Nixon played the male lead.

Tubby the Tuba
1947 million-selling album on Cosmopolitan Records, narrated by Victor Jory. Paul Tripp, who hosted the TV series *Mr. I Magination*, authored the book *Tubby the Tuba*. It is the only gold record recorded by Victor Jory.

Tubman, Harriet Ross
(1820–1913) Fugitive slave who ran an underground railroad to transport slaves across the Mason-Dixon line to freedom. She was portrayed in the 1978 TV movie *A Woman Called Moses* by Cicely Tyson.

Tubular Bells
Theme music by Mike Oldfield used in the 1973 movie *The Exorcist*.

Tucker, Sophie
> (1884–1966) Heavyset singer nicknamed The Last of the Red Hot Mamas. She was portrayed in the 1978 TV movie *A Love Affair: The Eleanor and Lou Gehrig Story* by Lainie Kazan.

Tucker, William
> First black child born in English America. His parents were Anthony and Isabella and he was baptized in 1624 at Jamestown.

Tudor, Mary
> (1496–1533) Queen of Louis XII of France. She was portrayed in the 1953 movie *The Sword and the Rose* by Glynis Johns.

Tuffy
> Gail's pet dolphin in the cartoon series *Sealab 2020* (voice of Ann Jillian).

Tumbleweed
> Character played by Elvis Presley in a sketch on the TV series *The Steve Allen Show,* July 1, 1956.

Tun Tavern
> Philadelphia pub, not far from Independence Hall, where the U.S. Marine Corps was born on November 28, 1775. Samuel Nicholas, commissioned a captain, was the first Marine.

Turkey One
> Lone B58 bomber that bombed Moscow in the 1964 movie *Fail Safe*.

Turkish Tom Toms
> Original title of the classic song "Dardanella," composed by Felix Bernard, Johnny Black, and Fred Fisher.

Turn On
> ABC television series that debuted and was canceled on February 5, 1969. It was considered too risqué. Tim Conway was the guest host that evening.

Turpin, Dick
> (1706–1739) English legendary robber, smuggler, and cattle thief who rode a horse called Black Bess. He was portrayed in the 1925 movie *Dick Turpin* by Tom Mix and in the 1951 movie *The Lady and the Bandit* by Louis Hayward.

Tusky
> Aquaman's pet walrus in the animated TV series *Aquaman* (voice of Marvin Miller).

Tut
> President Herbert Hoover's German shepherd. (See: **Pat, Wegie**)

Tut
> Isis' pet crow in the TV series *Isis*.

Tutter
> Hometown of Jerry Todd (children's books)

Tweed, George R.
World War II Navy radio man who worked undercover against the Japanese. He was portrayed in the 1962 movie *No Man Is an Island* by Jeffrey Hunter.

Tweed, William "Boss'
(1823–1878) American politician who headed the infamous New York City Boss Tweed Ring. He was portrayed in the 1948 movie *Up in Central Park* by Vincent Price.

Twiki
Buck Rogers's (Gil Gerard) companion robot (TWKE 4) in the 1979 movie *Buck Rogers,* as well as in the TV series *Buck Rogers in the 25th Century.* Twiki was played by Felix Silla (voice of Mel Blanc). On the episode titled "A Blast for Buck" (January 17, 1980) Patty Maloney played Twiki (previously she had played the robot Tina in an episode titled "A Cruise Ship to the Stars," aired on December 27, 1979).

Twin Sisters
Bette Davis has twice played the dual role of twin sisters in movies: *A Stolen Life* (1946) and *Dead Ringer* (1964).

'Twixt Twelve and Twenty
Book written by singer Pat Boone in 1958.

Two minutes to curtain
Only line said by Richard Dreyfuss in the 1967 movie *Valley of the Dolls,* his film debut.

Two Orphans, The
Play presented at the Brooklyn Theater on the night of December 5, 1876, when a fire broke out, killing 295 of the 900 members of the audience.

Two People
Theme song of the 1973 TV series *Adam's Rib.*

Tyler, John
(1790–1862) 10th president of the United States and the first to be married while in office (1844). Tyler is the only former U.S. president who served as a member of the Congress of the Confederate States (1861–1862).

Tyrone F. Horneigh
Dirty old man (Arte Johnson) who bothered Gladys Ormphby (Ruth Buzzi) on the park bench, usually offering her a Walnetto, in the TV series *Laugh In.* In the TV cartoon *Baggy Pants and the Nitwits* Tyrone and Gladys are married.

U

U-31

CIA agent impersonated by Henry Wadsworth Phyfe (Red Buttons) in the 1966 TV series *The Double Life of Henry Phyfe*.

U2513

Captured World War II German submarine in which President Harry S Truman took a ride on November 21, 1946.

UBS

United Broadcasting System, fictitious TV network ("The network that puts U before the BS") that presents *America 2Night,* a talk show, in the 1976 movie *Network.* Actor Charleston Heston was the first guest on the talk show. Some of the network's other programs were: *Celeb Canasta, Grand Guignol, Howard Beale Show, Shirley Pedro Putz, Holy Mackerel, 2 Plus 2, Death Squad, Celeb Mah-Jong, The Wilsons, Young Shyster.*

U.G.S.P.

United Galaxy Sanitation Patrol—the organization for which Capt. Adam Quark (Richard Benjamin) piloted an interplanetary garbage scow in the TV series *Quark.*

URO 913 E

British license place number of the Beatles' Magical Mystery Tour bus.

USMC 037773

U.S. Marine Corps serial number of baseball player Ted Williams during World War II and the Korean War.

Ultra

British code name of the German cipher machine Enigma, which the British Secret Service obtained in 1938, thereby allowing them to decipher the

German code during World War II. The Americans' code name for their copy of the machine was Magic.

Ulysses
Ben Calhoun's (Dale Robertson) pet raccoon in the 1966 TV series *Iron Horse*.

Umbrella Man
Mysterious man who was seen at Dealey Plaza with a black umbrella, which he opened briefly, as President Kennedy was assassinated (November 22, 1963). Years later Louie Steven Witt came forward to identify himself as the umbrella man. He had brought the umbrella to use to heckle Kennedy.

Uncle Bim
Uncle Benjamin Gump, an Australian billionaire relative of the Gump family, in the comic strip *The Gumps*. His wife, since 1934, has been Millie.

Uncle Duke
Zonker's uncle in the *Doonesbury* comic strip. Duke's three occupations were: writer for *Rolling Stone* magazine, ambassador to China, and governor of American Samoa. His character is loosely based on real-life journalist Hunter S. Thompson.

Uncle Luigi's Good Time Bar and Pizza Parlor
San Francisco restaurant through which Tony (Chevy Chase) drove a car in the 1978 movie *Foul Play*. The same building can be seen in the 1923 Eric von Stroheim film *Greed*.

Uncle Max
Relative whom Gabe Kotter (Gabe Kaplan) often referred to in telling a joke in the TV series *Welcome Back Kotter*.

Uncle Ralph
Long-distance telephone caller whose 6-year-old nephew, Johnny (played by Matthew Licht), hangs up on him in the 1979 Clio-winning Pacific Telephone commercial.

Uncle Sam
Personification of the United States. Silent western actor William S. Hart posed for the original Uncle Sam recruiting poster of World War I. On February 6, 1868, *Harper's Weekly* published a caricature of Uncle Sam, showing him for the first time with whiskers.

Uncle Sherman
Raincoat-wearing doll that "flashes"; produced by Flasher Fashion Inc.

Un-Cola Man
Jamaican man who advertises 7-Up. He is played by Geoffrey Holder.

Undercover Woman
Television series starring Joyce Whitman (Betty White) within the TV series *The Betty White Show*.

Underwood

1920 era black typewriter used by writer Grantland Rice for his newspaper columns. The typewriter is now on display at the College Football Hall of Fame.

Union Marine Bank (UMB)

Manhattan bank at 36th and Broadway held up by Al (Art Carney), Joe (George Burns), and Willie (Lee Strasberg) for $35,555 in the 1980 movie *Going in Style*.

United States Ski Hall of Fame

Located at Ishpeming, Michigan.

University Medical Center

Setting of the TV series *Medical Center*.

University of Arkansas

College attended by Martha Mitchell, wife of Nixon's attorney general, John Mitchell. As a young student, she was once disciplined by the school's president, J. William Fulbright. In later years Martha Mitchell made one of her famous 2:00 a.m. phone calls to an Arkansas newspaper demanding that Fulbright (then a U.S. senator) be "crucified."

University of Ingolstadt

Learning institute in Transylvania attended by Victor Frankenstein (novel *Frankenstein*).

University School

Los Angeles school where Michael Rhodes (Gary Collins) taught parapsychology in the TV series *The Sixth Sense*.

Unknown Comic

Corny television comedian who tells jokes with a paper bag over his head. (His similarly masked pet dog is referred to as Doggie Bag.) He began on the TV series *The Gong Show*. His real name is Murray Langston.

Uphold the Right

Maintiens le Droit: Motto of the Canadian Royal Mounted Police.

Ursula

George of the Jungle's girlfriend (voice of June Foray) in the TV cartoons.

Uru Hammer

Comic book hero Thor's magic weapon (*Thor* Comic books). Written on his hammer is: "Whosoever holds this hammer, if he be worthy, shall possess the power of Thor."

Usual Gang of Idiots, The

Uncredited artists and writers for *MAD* magazine.

Uz

Shortest name in the Bible.

V

V-Blue
  License plate of the blue Cadillac that Charlie Finley presented to Vida Blue on Vida Blue Night at the Oakland Coliseum.

VET 210
  California license plate of Luke Martin's (Jon Voight) 1971 white Boss 351 Mustang in the 1978 movie *Coming Home*.

VGV and 11th Street
  Two rival Puerto Rican gangs in the 1979 movie *Boulevard Nights*.

Vale, Jerry
  Singer of the national anthem heard via recording at many sporting events.

Valens, Ritchie
  (1941–1959) Popular singer of the 1950s (born Ritchie Valenzuela) whose three biggest hits were "Come On, Let's Go," "Donna," and "LaBamba." He was killed on February 3, 1959, in the same plane crash that took the lives of Buddy Holly and J. P. Richardson. Valens was portrayed in the 1978 movie *The Buddy Holly Story* by Gilbert Melgar.

Valhalla
  Sally Stanford's restaurant in Sausalito, California.

Valli, Violet Popovich
  Woman who shot Cubs baseball player Billy Jurgens in a Chicago hotel room on July 6, 1932.

Valse Triste
  Classical piece by Sibelius that is the theme of the 1934 movie *Death Takes a Holiday*.

Vamp
  Nickname of silent screen star Theda Bara (born Theodoshia Goodwin).

Vamp was taken from the word *vampire*. Kipling's *The Vampire* was the basis for the 1915 movie *A Fool There Was* in which Theda Bara appeared.

Van Buren, Martin

(1782–1862) 8th president of the United States and the first president to be born a citizen of the United States. According to John Q. Adams' diary, Martin Van Buren was reputed to be the illegitimate son of Aaron Burr. Van Buren was portrayed in the 1936 movie *The Gorgeous Hussy* by Charles Trowbridge.

Vanderbilt, Cornelius

(1794–1877) American financier and founder of the famous Vanderbilt fortune, which had its beginnings in the freight and ferryboat business. He was portrayed in the 1937 movie *Toast of New York* by Clarence Kolb.

Vander Meer, John

Cincinnati Reds pitcher who pitched two consecutive no-hitters—the first on June 11, 1938 (against Boston) and the second on June 15 (against Brooklyn). The second game was the first night game ever played at Ebbet's Field.

Van Doren, Charles

Very popular contestant on the TV quiz show *Twenty-One*. At a press conference he admitted that he had been given the answers ahead of time, after denying this for a year. During 1958 he served as host of the TV series *The Today Show;* he was Dave Garroway's summer replacement.

Van Gogh, Vincent

(1853–1890) Dutch painter whose works are highly valued by art lovers. He committed suicide after going insane in 1890. Van Gogh was portrayed in the 1956 movie *Lust for Life* by Kirk Douglas, and in the 1980 TV movie *Gauguin the Savage* by Barrie Houghton.

Vardon Trophy

Annual award presented to the player with the lowest average in the PGA. Lee Trevino won it in 1970, 1971, and 1972. It was first awarded to Harry Cooper in 1937.

Ventana Nuclear Power Plant

Southern California setting of the 1979 movie *The China Syndrome*.

Ventura Air Force Base

California military facility where Jaime Sommers (Lindsay Wagner) taught school in the TV series *The Bionic Woman*.

Venture

NASA space ship on which three astronauts traveled ahead in time in the animated TV series *Return to the Planet of the Apes*.

Verdi, Giuseppe

(1813–1901) Italian opera composer who was portrayed in the 1953 movie *Life and Music of Giuseppe Verdi* by Pierre Cressoy.

Vesti la giubba

Aria (from the opera *I Pagliacci*) on a 1902 recording by Enrico Caruso that became the first million-selling record.

Vice President of United States Steel

Position held by John "Bluto" Blutarski, after graduating from Faber College in 1963, in the 1978 book *Animal House*. In the 1978 movie Blutarski (John Belushi) became a U.S. senator.

Vice Presidents of the United States, Fictitious

Lew Ayres portrayed the vice president in *Advise and Consent* (1962) and in the TV movie *The Man* (1972). In the 1931 play *Of Thee I Sing* Victor Moore played Vice President Alexander Throttlebottom.

Vicious, Sid

(1958–1979) Born John Simon Richie, he was a member of the British punk rock group the Sex Pistols. He murdered his girlfriend, Nancy Spungen, and was defended by attorney F. Lee Bailey. Vicious died from an overdose of heroin shortly after being released from jail (February 2, 1979).

Victoire, La

Ship upon which the Marquis de Lafayette sailed for America from Bordeaux, France, on March 26, 1777.

Victory Bell

Trophy for the winner of the annual UCLA and Southern California football game.

Viennese Teardrop, The

Nickname of two-time Oscar-winning actress Luise Rainer.

Vigilante

Motorcycle-riding western hero who made his debut in *Action Comics* No. 42 (November 1941). The character was played by Ralph Byrd in the 1947 movie serial *The Vigilante*.

Village, The

Setting of the TV series *The Prisoner*. In reality, the Village was a resort in North Wales called the Hotel Portmeirion.

Villa, "Pancho" Francisco

(1877–1923) Born Doroteo Arango, Pancho Villa was a Mexican bandit and revolutionary leader who, on March 9, 1916, raided the American town of Columbus, New Mexico, killing 16 persons. He was then pursued by American troops under Gen. Pershing. Pancho Villa was portrayed in the 1934 movie *Viva Villa!* by Wallace Beery (Phillip Cooper as a boy), in the 1952 movie *Viva Zapata!* by Alan Reed, and in the 1968 movie *Villa Rides* by Yul Brynner.

Vince Lombardi High

School that the rock-crazed students burn to the ground in the 1979 movie *Rock 'n' Roll High School*. The principal was Miss Togar. Filmed at Mount

Carmel High School in Los Angeles where the 1956 movie *Rock Around the Clock* was filmed.

Vinci, Leonardo da

(1452–1519) Florentine painter, architect, scientist, engineer, and sculptor. He was portrayed in the TV series *The Life of Leonardo da Vinci* by Philippe Leroy (as a boy, by Alberto Fiorini; as a young man, by Arduino Paolini).

Vine Street

Street mentioned in the lyrics of the following songs: "Kansas City" (Wilbert Harrison); "Love Potion No. 9" (Clovers); "Dead Man's Curve" (Jan and Dean).

Viper

Colonial fighter spacecraft launched from Galactica in the TV series *Battleship Galactica*.

Virgin

Because this word was used in Otto Preminger's 1953 movie *The Moon Is Blue*, the Catholic Legion of Decency condemned the movie. Preminger released it anyway, despite the disapproval of the Hollywood establishment.

Virginia of Sagadahoc

30-ton vessel launched in Maine in 1607 that was the first ship built in America.

Viscuso, Sal

Actor who provided the voice over the PA system at the 4077th in the TV series M*A*S*H. He also played Father Tim Flotsky in the TV series *Soap*.

Voice, The

Publicity nickname of actress Lauren Bacall. She was also referred to as The Look.

Volcano

Secret Service code name for President Johnson's ranch in Texas.

Voltafiore,

Small Italian town setting of the TV series *McHale's Navy*. Before they arrived in the European theater, Torpedo Boat Squadron 19 had been stationed on the island of Taratupa in the South Pacific.

Voltaire

(1694–1778) Pseudonym of French writer and philosopher François Marie Arouet. He was portrayed in the 1933 movie *Voltaire* by George Arliss.

Vote for Townsend Phelps

Neon sign atop a building from which Lou Costello knocks out letters until it reads, "Send Help," in a scene from the 1942 Abbott and Costello movie, *Who Done It?*

Voyager 6

Explorer satellite launched by NASA in the 20th century in the 1979 movie

Star Trek: The Motion Picture. It was this satellite that the crew of the USS *Enterprise* encountered while it was seeking its creator.

Vulcan

Mr. Spock's home planet in the TV series *Star Trek*. The names of all males on Vulcan began with an "S," consisted of 5 letters, and ended in a "K" or an "N." The names of the males of Spock's generation had a vowel in the position of the 3rd letter, while older-generation males' names had vowels in the 2nd and 4th letter positions. (The system alternated from generation to generation.) All the females' names began with "T" or "P" and consisted of from 3 to 7 letters (a letter was added in each successive generation, up to a maximum of 7). In names of 4 to 7 letters a vowel was always in the 4th position and a consonant in the 5th.

Vulture Island

Home of the Sea Hag (comic strip *Thimble Theater*).

W5645022460H

Serial number of Warrant Officer Ripley (Sigourney Weaver*), lone survivor of the space tug *Nostromo* in the 1979 movie *Alien*.

WAVES

Women Accepted for Volunteer Emergency Service (Navy).

WBL Women's Basketball League

Western Division	*Eastern Division*	*Midwest Division*
Houston	New York	Minnesota
San Francisco	New Jersey	Iowa
New Orleans	Washington	St. Louis
Dallas	Philadelphia	Chicago
California		Milwaukee

WBN

D. B. Norton's (Edward Arnold) radio station in the 1940 movie *Meet John Doe*.

WBP

New York City television station that Alice Martin (Jane Fonda) worked for in the 1979 movie *The Electric Horseman*.

W. C. Fields College for Orphaned White Boys and Girls, Where No Religion of Any Sort Is to Be Preached

School W. C. Fields wanted established with his $800,000 estate after his death. However, his will was contested and the school never materialized.

---

*Daughter of onetime NBC president Sylvester Pat Weaver, creator of the *Today* and *Tonight* TV Series.

WDIA

Memphis radio station where singers Rufus Thomas and B. B. King were both employed as disc jockeys before they became recording artists.

WHB

Kansas City radio station that in 1955 became the first station to play solely rock 'n' roll music 24 hours a day.

WHN

New York City radio station over which Otis Driftwood (Groucho Marx) spoke in the 1935 movie *A Night at the Opera*.

WHO

Des Moines, Iowa, radio station on which the Williams Brothers (Andy and his three brothers: Richard, Robert, and Donald) made their professional debut in 1942. Ronald Reagan was once a broadcaster at the station.

WMPD

Voice of Mt. Pilot—Mt. Pilot radio station on the TV series *The Andy Griffith Show*. WMPD broadcast the singing of Leonard Blush.

WOFF

Danville, Illinois, radio station where Rob Petrie worked before being hired by Alan Brady in the TV series *The Dick Van Dyke Show*.

WROL

New York radio station for which Alan Freed (Tim McIntire) was a DJ in the 1978 movie *American Hot Wax*. Freed actually worked for WINS radio in New York City.

WZAZ

Fernwood, Ohio's, only TV station (Channel 6) in the TV series *Mary Hartman, Mary Hartman*. The manager was Clete Meizenheimer.

Wabash Cannonball, The

Baseball announcer Dizzy Dean's favorite country song, which he would sing to his listeners in between giving a play-by-play report of the game.

Wagner, Richard

(1813–1883) German composer of operas. He was the son-in-law of composer Franz Liszt. Wagner was portrayed in the 1956 movie *Magic Fire* by Alan Badel, in the 1960 movie *Song Without End* by Lyndon Brook, and in the 1973 movie *Ludwig* by Trevor Howard.

Wagonmaster

Actual name of the palomino horse ridden by Stewart Granger in the TV series *The Men from Shiloh*.

Wags

(Admiral Wags) Rear Adm. Frederick Sherman's black cocker spaniel that, with his master, was aboard the carrier USS *Lexington* at the Battle of the Coral Sea, May 1942.

Wainwright, Jonathan Mayhew

(1883–1953) Commanding general of Corregidor when it fell to the Japanese in 1942. He became a prisoner of war and was not rescued until 1945. Wainwright was portrayed in the 1977 movie *MacArthur* by Sandy Kenyon.

Waist Deep in the Big Muddy

Antiwar song by Pete Seeger that CBS cut from his September 1967 appearance on the *Smothers Brothers Comedy Hour* as too controversial.

Waitt, Charles C.

Boston player who is credited with being the first player to wear a baseball glove (1875).

Wakefield, Ruth G.

Inventor of the chocolate chip cookie in 1930.

Wake Up and Sleep

Book written by Dr. Siegfried von Sedative, the world's expert on sleep, played by Sid Caesar in the TV series *Your Show of Shows*.

Walcott, Jersey Joe

(Arnold Raymond Cream). Oldest fighter to win the heavyweight title. He defeated Ezzard Charles on July 18, 1951, at the age of 37. He was, in turn, defeated by Rocky Marciano on September 23, 1952. After retiring, Walcott became a parole officer. He played George in the 1956 movie *The Harder They Fall*. He himself was portrayed by Melo Alexandria in the 1979 TV movie *Marciano*.

Waldorf and Statler

Two grouchy old men who heckle the muppet performers from a balcony in the TV series *The Muppet Show*. Waldorf (voice by Jim Henson) wears a mustache and a brown suit, while Statler (voice by Richard Hunt) wears a blue suit.

Waldorf Astoria

New York City hotel where, in Suite 1162, the country of Panama was born in 1903. The Waldorf Astoria was torn down and was replaced by the Empire State Building in 1957. Count Basie headed the first band to play at the new Waldorf Astoria.

Walker, Jerry

At age 20, he became the youngest pitcher to win an All Star Game (1959).

Wallace, Lew

(1827–1905) American Army officer, politician, and author. He was the son of David Wallace, governor of Indiana (1837–1840). Lew Wallace served as a major general in the Civil War. He was on the court-martial board for the trials of Lincoln's assassins and Henry Wirz, commandant of Andersonville. While serving as governor of the New Mexico Territory (1878–1881), he wrote the classic *Ben Hur: A Tale of the Christ* (1880). Wallace was

portrayed in the 1973 movie *Pat Garrett and Billy the Kid* by Jason
Robards, Jr.

Wallendas
Family circus high-wire act, billed as the Great Wallendas. In a tragic fall on
January 30, 1962, at the Detroit Coliseum, two members of the family died
and one became paralyzed. Karl Wallenda was portrayed in the 1978 TV
movie *The Great Wallendas* by Lloyd Bridges. On March 22, 1978, Karl (at
age 73) fell to his death at San Juan, Puerto Rico. That same day, his nephew,
Steve, walked a wire at the Oakland (California) Zoo.*

Wall Street Blues
Theme song of the TV series *The Associates*, sung by B. B. King.

Wally Ballou
Radio interviewer in Bob and Ray sketches. Wally's mike cuts in and out
at inappropriate times.

Wally's Service
Gas station in Mayberry, North Carolina, where Gomer Pyle (Jim Nabors)
worked before joining the Marines in the TV series *The Andy Griffith Show*.

Walther 7.65
Pistol used in fiction by both John Steed and James Bond. It was also the
pistol used by Adolf Hitler when he shot himself on April 30, 1945, at 3:30
p.m.

Wambaugh, Joseph
Ex-Los Angeles policeman who authored the following novels: *The New
Centurions* (1972 movie); *The Blue Knight* (1975 movie/TV series/1973
TV movie); *The Choirboys* (1977 movie); *The Onion Field* (1979 movie);
and *The Black Marble* (1980 movie). Wambaugh also created the TV series
Police Story, in which he made cameo appearances. *Police Woman* was a
spinoff of *Police Story.*

WAMPAS Baby Stars
Western Association of Motion Picture Advertisers who, beginning in 1922,
sponsored an annual selection of new starlets. A few of the WAMPAS babys:
Clara Bow, Fay Wray, Mary Astor, Janet Gaynor, and Joan Crawford.

Wand'rin' Star
Million-seller record by Lee Marvin in 1970. He sang the song in the 1969
movie *Paint Your Wagon* (loosely based on the Lerner-Lowe Broadway play
of the same name).

Wankel, Felix
Inventor of the rotary engine who has never owned a driver's license.

War Is Hell
1964 Korean War movie starring Tony Russell that was being shown
at the Texas Theatre in Dallas when Lee Harvey Oswald entered the

*He set a distance record of a quarter mile.

theater after assassinating President Kennedy on November 22, 1963.

War Is Over! If You Want It—Happy Christmas from John and Yoko
Billboard sign paid for by John Lennon at Times Square (Christmas of 1969).

Warm Springs
President Franklin D. Roosevelt's Georgia retreat located 60 miles north of Plains. It was here that Roosevelt died during his fourth term in office on April 12, 1945.

Warner, Emily
First female commercial airline pilot in the United States. She was hired by Frontier Airlines in 1973.

Warner, Glen "Pop"
(1871–1954) Football coach for Georgia, Cornell, Carlisle, Pittsburgh, Stanford, and Temple. After Amos Alonzo Stagg, he won the most football games (313). He portrayed himself in the 1940 movie *Knute Rockne—All American*, and was portrayed by Charles Bickford in the 1951 movie *Jim Thorpe —All American*.

Washington Americans
Major league baseball team for which Jim Barton (Jim Bouton) pitched in the TV series *Ball Four*.

Washington, Booker Taliaferro
(1856–1915) Black American educator, born into slavery. He helped to found the Tuskegee Institute in Alabama in 1881. During World War II Marion Anderson christened the Liberty ship *Booker T. Washington*, the first American ship with an all-black crew.

Washington, George
(1732–1799) 1st president of the United States. He commanded the Continental Army during the Revolutionary War. Washington was the first person to be elected to the American Hall of Fame. Movie portrayals: *Alexander Hamilton* (1931) Alan Mowbray; *The Remarkable Andrew* (1942) Montagu Love; *Where Do We Go from Here?* (1945) Alan Mowbray; *Unconquered* (1947) Richard Gaines (as Col. Washington); *Lafayette* (1963) Howard St. John; *Independence* (1976 short) Patrick O'Neal; *The Adams Chronicles* (1976 PBS TV) David Brooks.

Watch and Ward Society
Organization in Boston, that officially bans novels, movies, music, etc.

Watch on the Rhine
(*Wacht am Rheim*) German song sung by the Nazi officers that is drowned out by the French singing "La Marseillaise" in Rick's Café Américain in the 1942 movie *Casablanca*.

Watch Your Body, Buddy
Physical fitness book written by Professor von Muscle (Sid Caesar) on the TV series *Your Show of Shows*.

Waterfield, Bob
Quarterback for the Cleveland Rams who married his childhood sweetheart, actress Jane Russell.

Watership Down
The 11 original rabbits in the novel/1979 movie were: Hazel (chief rabbit), Fiver, Bigwig, Blackberry, Silver, Buckthorn, Acorn, Dandelion, Pipkin, Speedwell, and Hawkbit. The group was joined by other rabbits along the way.

Watson, Thomas Augustus
(1854–1934) Assistant to inventor Alexander Graham Bell. It was to Watson that Bell yelled, "Mr. Watson, come here, I need you"—the very first message over the telephone. Watson was portrayed in the 1939 movie *The Story of Alexander Graham Bell* by Henry Fonda.

Watson, Whipper
Wrestler who beat Gorgeous George in March 1959 in Toronto. Because of his loss, George had a barber shave off his golden locks in front of the crowd. George's wife, Cherie, lost her hair when Gorgeous George was defeated in a match on which he had bet her hair.

Wattenscheid
German town in which James Bond was born on November 11, 1920.

Waverly High School
School in Eastfield, Wisconsin, where Joe Casey (Joe Namath) was a history teacher and coach in the TV series *The Waverly Wonders*.

Wayfarer's Inn
Largest hotel in the town of Cimarron in the TV series *Cimarron Strip*.

Wayne, John
Movies in which John Wayne died: *Reap the Wild Wind* (1942), killed by an octopus; *The Fighting Seabees* (1944), from gunshot and explosion; *The Wake of the Red Witch* (1948), by drowning; *Sands of Iwo Jima* (1949), gunshot wounds; *The Alamo* (1960), killed by lance and explosion; *The Man Who Shot Liberty Valance* (1962), of natural causes; *The Cowboys* (1972), of multiple gunshots inflicted by Bruce Dern; and *The Shootist* (1976), he was shot in the back twice with a shotgun by a bartender named Murray.

Wayne, John, and Maureen O'Hara
Movies in which the pair appeared: *Rio Grande* (1950); *The Quiet Man* (1952); *The Wings of Eagles* (1957); *McLintock!* (1963); and *Big Jake* (1971).

Wayne, USS
American nuclear submarine (No. 593) captured by the supership *Liparus* in the 1977 movie *The Spy Who Loved Me*. (See: **HMS Ranger**)

Waxworks
Group of bridge players who play each week in the home of Norma Desmond (Gloria Swanson) in the 1950 movie *Sunset Boulevard*. The players, all

of whom had acted in silent film days, were: Gloria Swanson, Buster Keaton, H. B. Warner, and Anna Q. Nilsson.

Wead, Frank "Spig"
U.S. naval officer during World War II who was a proponent of jeep carriers and pursuit planes. After falling down a flight of stairs, Wead suffered a spinal injury and became paralyzed from the waist down. He was portrayed by John Wayne in the 1957 movie *The Wings of Eagles*. Frank Wead wrote the screenplay for the 1945 movie *They Were Expendable*, starring John Wayne and Robert Montgomery.*

Weatherly, Jim
University of Mississippi quarterback who penned the hit songs "Best Thing That Ever Happened to Me" and "Midnight Train to Georgia," both recorded by Gladys Knight and the Pips.

Webber, Mary
14-year-old American who became the first girl to caddy in a professional golf tournament (the Greater Milwaukee Open Tournament).

Webster, Daniel
(1782–1852) American lawyer and statesman, Secretary of State (1841–1843), and unsuccessful Whig candidate for U.S. presidency in 1852. He was portrayed in the 1934 movie *The Mighty Barnum* by George MacQuarrie, in the 1936 movie *The Gorgeous Hussy* by Sidney Toler, and in the 1941 movie *All That Money Can Buy* by Edward Arnold.

Wednesday Afternoon Fine Arts League
Woman's club to which Lucy Ricardo and Ethel Mertz belong in the TV series *I Love Lucy*.

Weed, Steven
Fiancé of heiress Patricia Hearst when she was kidnapped by the SLA on February 4, 1974. He was portrayed in the 1979 movie *The Ordeal of Patty Hearst* by David Haskell.

Weehawken Heights
Site where Aaron Burr shot and mortally wounded Alexander Hamilton on July 11, 1804. Previously, at the same spot, using the same pistols ("Church Pistols"), Hamilton's son, Philip, had been mortally wounded in a duel with George Eacker.

Weekly Advertiser, The
Local paper for which Kate Columbo (Kate Mulgrew) was a free-lance writer in the TV series *Mrs. Columbo*.

Wegie
President Herbert Hoover's Elkhound dog. (See: **Tut, Pat**).

Weiss, Carl Austin
Doctor who on September 8, 1935, assassinated Louisiana governor Huey P.

---

*Montgomery had actually commanded PT boats during World War II.

Long. Weiss shot Long once with a .32 automatic. Weiss was shot 61 times *after* he had been disarmed.

Welch, George
Pilot at Pearl Harbor on December 7, 1941, who, after taking off three times, shot down 4 Japanese planes. Only 12 Japanese planes were shot down that day. Hap Arnold recommended Welch for the Medal of Honor, but he never received it because his commanding officer said that he had taken off without orders. Welch was portrayed in the 1970 movie *Tora! Tora! Tora!* by Rick Cooper.

Welcome to Berlin
Original title of the musical play *Cabaret*.

Well blow me down
Popeye's adopted son Swee' Pea's first words, spoken on June 23, 1938.

Welles, Billy
Muscular man who strikes the gong in the introduction to J. Arthur Rank movies.

Welles, Orson
Talented American actor, writer, director, and producer who was born in 1915. His debut film, *Citizen Kane* (1941), is considered by many to be his best work. Welles was portrayed in the 1975 TV movie *The Night That Panicked America* by Paul Shenar.

Wellington, Duke of
(1769–1852) Arthur Wellesley, called the Iron Duke. He defeated Napoleon at Waterloo in 1815 and later served as prime minister of England (1828–1830). Movie portrayals: *The House of Rothschild* (1934) C. Aubrey Smith; *Sixty Glorious Years* (1938) C. Aubrey Smith; *Devotion* (1946) Brandon Hurst; *Waterloo* (1969) Christopher Plummer; and *Lady Caroline Lamb* (1972) Laurence Olivier.

Wells, H. G.
(1866–1946) Herbert George Wells. English novelist of science fiction stories such as: *The Time Machine* (1895); *The Island of Doctor Moreau* (1896); *The Invisible Man* (1897); *The War of the Worlds* (1898); and *Kipps: The Story of a Simple Soul* (1905). He was portrayed in the 1979 movie *Time After Time* by Malcolm McDowell.

Wells, Henry
(1805–1878) American businessman who founded the Wells Fargo Stagecoach lines and in 1852 organized Wells, Fargo & Co. He was portrayed in the 1937 movie *Wells Fargo* by Henry O'Neill.

Wendt, Hans
Professional photographer who, while at a service station, took the last photos of PSA Flight 182 before it crashed in San Diego on September 25, 1978. He used a Nikkormat El camera.

Werwolf

Adolf Hitler's headquarters in the Ukraine (1942).

West Catholic High School

The girls who appeared on *American Bandstand* in uniforms were students of this school near the WFIL-TV studio in Philadelphia.

Westland Bank

San Francisco Bank where Lucy Carmichael (Lucille Ball) worked in the TV series *The Lucy Show* (second format). Her boss was Vice President Theodore J. Mooney (Gale Gordon).

West Point

U.S. Army Academy. Robert E. Lee set a record there that no one has equaled: He was not given a single demerit and later served as a superintendent at the Academy. Dwight Eisenhower was a punt kicker for West Point in 1912. Edgar Allan Poe and James Whistler were both dismissed from West Point. Some fictional characters who attended West Point: Jason McCord (Chuck Connors) in the TV series *Branded*. Lt. Craig Garrison (Ron Harper) in the TV series *Garrison's Gorillas, and* Rhett Butler (Clark Gable) in the 1939 movie *Gone With the Wind*.

Westside Clinic

New York City medical facility where Dr. Joseph Bogert (Barnard Hughes) practiced medicine in the TV series *Doc*.

What a Country

Song written for the play *All American*. It is now the theme song of Amtrak.

What a World

Message that Trisha (Lily Tomlin) put into a bottle in the 1978 movie *Moment by Moment*.

What da ya hear? What da ya say?

Greetings of William "Rocky" Sullivan (James Cagney) in the 1938 movie *Angels with Dirty Faces*.

What Goes On

Only Beatle song (with lyrics) composed by John Lennon, Paul McCartney, *and* George Harrison. Ringo Starr sang the lead.

What's for breakfast?

First words of Winnie-the-Pooh after he wakes up each morning.

What's up, Doc?

Bugs Bunny's favorite expression. Bob Clampett, Bugs's creator, borrowed the saying from the line, "What's up, Duke?," said by Carole Lombard to William Powell in the 1936 movie *My Man Godfrey*.

Whenever I'm with You

Theme song of the TV series *The Paul Winchell Show*.

When I Fall in Love

Song introduced by Victor Young in the 1952 movie *One Minute to Zero*.

When Irish Eyes Are Smiling
Theme song of the radio series *Duffy's Tavern*.
When You Wish upon a Star
Academy Award–winning song, sung by Cliff Edwards in the 1940 movie *Pinocchio*. Edwards sang the song in what was to be the closing scene of the 1977 movie *Close Encounters of the Third Kind*, but the scene was cut from the final release. It was included in the later-released special edition in 1979.
Where Do You Think You Are?
Weekly puzzle in the *Saturday Evening Post* in which readers were to identify what states the map segments were taken from.
Where or When
Alice Hyatt's (Ellen Burstyn) favorite song in the 1975 movie *Alice Doesn't Live Here Anymore*.
Whiffenpoofs
Yale University's singing society; James Whitmore was once a member.
Whiskey
Jack Burns's (Kirk Douglas) palomino horse in the 1962 movie *Lonely Are the Brave*.
Whistling Death
Nickname of Gregory "Pappy" Boyington's Corsair fighter which he flew during World War II.
White, Andrew
President of Cornell University who on October 2, 1873, refused to let his school football team travel to Cleveland to play a game. "I will not permit 30 men to travel 400 miles to agitate a bag of wind."
White Antelope
Indian girl married to Josh Randall (Steve McQueen) in an episode of the TV series *Wanted Dead or Alive*. She was played by Lori Nelson.
White, Byron R.
Associate justice of the Supreme Court of the United States. Nicknamed "Whizzer White," he was an All-American halfback from the University of Colorado who led the National Football League in rushing in his rookie year with the Steelers. He was also a Rhodes Scholar winner. In the Pacific during World War II, as a member of naval intelligence, White wrote the report on the mishap of *PT 109* (commanded by John F. Kennedy).
White Cloud
Eddie Dean's horse in B Westerns. He also rode Flash.
White, Dan
Ex-supervisor who killed San Francisco Mayor George Moscone and Supervisor Harvey Milk on November 27, 1978.

White Fang
Biggest and meanest (puppet) dog in the United States in the TV series *Soupy Sales*. Clyde Adler is the puppeteer.

White Fury
Silent film western hero Jack Hoxie's (brother of Al Hoxie) horse. (See: **Pardner)**

Whitehead, J. Gordon
Boxer who hit magician Harry Houdini in the stomach during a show in Montreal in October 1926. Houdini died 5 days later as a result.

White Horse Tavern
Pub on Marlboro Street in Newport, Rhode Island, built in 1673. It is the oldest tavern in the United States.

White, Pearl
(1899–1938) American actress called the Queen of the Silent Serials. She was portrayed in the 1947 movie *The Perils of Pauline* by Betty Hutton.

White Rats
Social club of vaudeville comedians and others circa 1900. Some of its members were Fred Stone, DeWolf Hopper, Maurice Barrymore, James J. Corbett, and (Joe) Weber and (Lew) Fields. Buster Keaton was their mascot.

White, Stanford
(1853–1906) Millionaire architect murdered on June 25, 1906, by Harry K. Thaw because of his relations with Thaw's wife, Evelyn Nesbitt. White was portrayed in the 1955 movie *The Girl in the Red Velvet Swing* by Ray Milland.

Whitney, Eli
Inventor of the cotton gin in 1793.

WHitney 1-2738
Home phone number of the Cleaver family in the TV series *Leave It to Beaver*. (In some episodes the number was KLondike 5-4763.)

Whitman, Charles
(1941–1966) Man who, on August 1, 1966, shot 46 people, killing 16, from the University of Texas campus tower in Austin, Texas. He was shot and killed by Officer Ramiro Martinez, who worked his way up the tower. Whitman was portrayed in the 1977 TV movie *The Deadly Tower* by Kurt Russell, officer Martinez by Richard Yniguer.

Whitmore, James
American actor born in 1921. He made his movie debut in the 1949 movie *Undercover Man*. In the 1950s he headed an acting school in New York City. In addition to several one-man shows where he has portrayed such immortals as Will Rogers, Harry Truman, and Teddy Roosevelt, he has also starred in three TV series—*The Law and Mr. Jones, My Friend Tony,* and *Temperatures*

Rising. Whitmore was portrayed in the 1976 TV movie *James Dean* by Dane Clark.

Who could ask for anything more
Phrase used by Ira Gershwin in three songs: "I Got Rhythm" *(Girl Crazy);* "I'm About to Become a Mother" *(Of Thee I Sing);* and "Nice Work If You Can Get It" *(Damsel in Distress).*

Who Killed . . .
How each episode of the TV series *Burke's Law* began.

Who Killed Cock Robin?
1935 Disney cartoon being shown in a London movie theater in the 1936 Alfred Hitchcock film *Sabotage.*

Who Killed Miss U.S.A.?
Pilot movie for the *McCloud* TV series.

Whole World Is Watching, The
1969 pilot for *The Bold Ones* TV series (lawyers' segment).

Why Do Fools Fall in Love?
1956 hit song by Frankie Lymon and the Teenagers on Gee Records. It was this song that was playing on the radio when private eye Amos Wine (Richard Dreyfuss) went to visit two people in prison in the 1978 movie *The Big Fix.* To cover up what they were saying, Wine, his companion, and the two inmates sang along with the song.

Wicksville
Hometown of Mark Tidd (children's books).

Wicked Witch
Evil witch who tries to poison Snow White in the Disney movie *Snow White and the Seven Dwarfs* (1937). Her voice is that of Lucille LaVerne.

Wiggy
Rhinoceros friend of George in the TV cartoon series *George of the Jungle.*

Wilbur
Reginald Van Gleason III's brother (both played by Jackie Gleason in his TV series).

Wilbur
Jiminy Cricket's grasshopper nephew (cartoons).

Wild Blue Yonder
Tioga recreational vehicle (Nevada license HBC514) driven by Sonny Steele (Robert Redford) in the 1979 movie *The Electric Horseman.*

Wildcats
(VMF 247) U.S. Marine fighter squadron headed by Maj. Dan Kirby (John Wayne) in the 1951 movie *The Flying Leathernecks.* Their call sign was Jigsaw.

Wilde, Oscar
(1854–1900) Irish-born writer and celebrated wit. His best known work of

fiction is *The Picture of Dorian Gray* (1891). Movie portrayals: *Oscar Wilde* (1959) Robert Morley; and *The Trials of Oscar Wilde* (1960) Peter Finch.

Wildfire

Canine subject of the 1955 movie *It's a Dog's Life*.

Wild Goose I

Director John Ford's yacht.

Wild Goose II

Actor John Wayne's 136-foot converted U.S. Navy mine sweeper.

Wild One, The

1954 movie starring Marlon Brando as the leader of the Black Rebels Motorcycle Club. The movie was banned in Britain for 11 years. It was originally released in the United States as *Hot Blood*, but quickly withdrawn and rereleased as *The Wild One*.

Wilhelm, Hoyt

Major league pitcher. In 1952 while playing for the New York Giants, he hit a home run his first time at bat in the major leagues. He never hit another home run in the next 20 years of his career.* Hoyt holds numerous records for relief pitching. Some have called him the greatest relief pitcher in history.

Wilkerson, David

Country minister and author who went to New York City to help youths involved in crime. He was portrayed in the 1970 movie *The Cross and the Switchblade* by Pat Boone. The movie also was the debut of actor Erik Estrada, who played Nicky Cruz.

Willert, Lauren

Stunt driver who drove the AMC Hornet that made a 360-degree flip across an old bridge in the 1974 movie *The Man With the Golden Gun.*

William

Goat rescued by the paramedic team and operated on by the doctors at Rampart General in the TV series *Emergency*.

Williams, Bert

(1876–1922) Black songwriter and comedian who, in 1909, became the best known comedian in the Ziegfeld Follies. He was portrayed by David Downing in the 1978 TV movie *Ziegfeld: The Man and His Women*.

Williams, Edy

Woman who streaked the Muhammed Ali–Leon Spinks bout (February 15, 1978).

Williams, Hiram "Hank"

(1923–1953) Country singer and composer. He and Jimmie Rodgers were the two most influential artists in country music. Williams died in the back seat of his Cadillac on New Years Day 1953. He was only 29 years old, yet he

---

*Wilhelm hit a triple in his 2nd year; it was both his first and his last.

had recorded over 100 successful songs. He was portrayed in the 1964 movie *Your Cheatin' Heart* by Donald Losby as a boy and by George Hamilton as an adult.

Williams, Lionel
Man who was arrested for the stabbing murder of actor Sal Mineo in Los Angeles on the night of February 12, 1976.

Williams, Marsh "Carbine"
Inventor of the 30-M1 carbine rifle used in World War II. He developed the rifle while in prison. In the 1952 movie *Carbine Williams* he was portrayed by James Stewart. In the movie Carbine's prison serial number was 91768.

Williams, Randy
1972 U.S. Olympic Gold Medal winner for the long jump who keeps a teddy bear nearby whenever he is to perform.

Williams, Sandy
First winner of the Miss Black America contest (1968). Sandy represented Pennsylvania.

Williams, Walter
Last known survivor of the Civil War. He died on December 19, 1959, at the age of 117.

William Tell
Legendary Swiss hero who was forced to shoot an apple from his son's head. He helped to win Swiss independence in the 1300s. *William Tell* was an unfinished 1954 movie financed by, and starring, Errol Flynn. It would have been the first Cinemascope movie. William Tell was played by Conrad Phillips in the TV series *The Adventures of William Tell;* his son, Walter Tell, was played by Richard Rogers.

Willie
Whale in the 1946 Disney cartoon movie *Make Mine Music*. (Willie's voice by Nelson Eddy).

Willie
Gen. George Patton's white English bull terrier, played in the 1970 movie *Patton* by Abraxas Aaran.

Willie
Hansen family dog in the TV series *Mama*.

Willie Mays
Woody Allen's answer to Diane Keaton's question, "What are you thinking about while we are doing it?" in the 1972 movie *Play It Again Sam*.

Willoughby's
Weaverville drugstore where Dennis Day worked as a soda jerk for $8 a week in the radio series *A Day in the Life of Dennis Day*.

Willow Road Farm
Setting of the radio series *Aunt Mary*.

Willows High School
School attended by Barbie the doll (Mattel doll).

Willson, Henry
Hollywood agent who renamed the following actors: Roy Fitzgerald (Rock Hudson); Art Gelien (Tab Hunter); Merle Johnson (Troy Donahue); Francis Timothy Durgin (Rory Calhoun); and Jimmy Ercolani (James Darren).

Will the Circle Be Unbroken?
Last song performed in the last show of The Grand Ole Opry presented at the Ryman Auditorium in Nashville on March 15, 1974. The song was sung by Maybelle Carter, Johnny Cash, and June Carter.

Wilson
Ernie Stanley Douglas's (Barry Livingston) pet dog in the TV series *My Three Sons*. Ernie was adopted. His real last name was Thompson.

Wilson, Edith
(1860–1914) President Woodrow Wilson's second wife, who acted as chief executive during her husband's illness. She claimed to have been descended from John Rolfe and Pocahontas. Movie portrayals: *Birdman of Alcatraz* (1962) Adrienne Marden; and *Backstairs at the White House* (1979 TV miniseries) Claire Bloom.

Wilson, (Thomas) Woodrow
(1856–1924) 28th president of the United States. He had previously been president of Princeton University. Wilson is the only president buried in Washington, D.C., at the National Cathedral. His favorite comic strip was *Krazy Kat*. Movie portrayals: *General Pershing* (1919) R. A. Faulkner; *Wilson* (1944) Alexander Knox; *The Story of Will Rogers* (1952) Earl Lee; *Oh! What a Lovely War* (1969) Frank Forsyth; and *Backstairs at the White House* (1979 TV miniseries) Robert Vaughn. Wilson was played by G. Wood on "Ordeal of a President," an episode on the TV series *You Are There*.

Winchester
Horse ridden during the Civil War by Gen. Sheridan.

Winchester 73
1950 James Stewart movie that Gen. Douglas MacArthur (Gregory Peck) was watching when told that North Korea had invaded South Korea in the 1977 movie *MacArthur*.

Wingfield, Walter C.
British Army officer who invented tennis in 1873. He originally called the game Sphairistike.

Wings of the Morning
First British movie to be made in color (1937).

Wings of the Navy
Film watched by the prison convicts in the movie *Each Dawn I Die* (1939).

Winning isn't everything—it's the only thing
Line said by Steve Williams (John Wayne), coach of St. Anthony's football team, in the 1953 movie *Trouble Along the Way*. Although pro football coach Vince Lombardi has often been credited with first saying the line, it was originally said by Henry (Red) Sanders. What Lombardi did say was, "Winning isn't everything, it's how you react to losing."

Winston
Margo's (Lily Tomlin) lost pet cat in the 1977 movie *The Late Show*. She hired detective Ira Wells (Art Carney) to search for the cat, for $25 a day plus expenses.

Winston
Pet lion of actress Tallulah Bankhead.

Winston Motor Car Company
First automobile manufacturer to advertise. The ad, "Dispense with a Horse," appeared in the July 30, 1893, edition of the *Scientific American*.

Wirz, Henry
Confederate major who commanded the military prison Andersonville, where 13,000 Union prisoners died because of the horrible conditions. Wirz was the only Civil War soldier to be executed for war crimes. He was portrayed by Richard Basehart in the May 7, 1970, TV play *Andersonville*.

Wise, Dennis
24-year-old man who underwent plastic surgery to make himself look like Elvis Presley. In February 1978 he unveiled his new face.

Wise Owl
Indian played by Milton Berle in the TV series *F Troop*.

Wizard of Westwood
Nickname of UCLA basketball coach John Wooden.

Wo Fat
Detective Steve McGarrett's (Jack Lord) archenemy in the TV series *Hawaii Five-O*. Wo Fat was played by Khigh Dhiegh, and was finally arrested by McGarrett in the last episode of the series.

Woffington, Margaret "Peg"
(1714–1760) Irish actress, portrayed by Anna Neagle in the 1935 movie *Peg of Old Drury*.

Wojtyla Disco Dance
Disco record by Freddie van Stegeran, a Dutch disc jockey, about Pope John Paul II. It was released in July 1979.

Wolfgang von Sauerbraten
German disc jocket played by Ernie Kovacs on TV.

Wolfie
Eddie Wolfgang Munster's (Butch Patrick) wolfman doll in the TV series *The Munsters*.

Wolf's Lair
(*Wolfsschanze*) Adolf Hitler's headquarters in East Prussia.
Wolf von Frankenstein
Dr. Henry Frankenstein's son, played by Basil Rathbone in the 1939 movie
Son of Frankenstein.
Wolsey, Cardinal Thomas
(1475–1530) English statesman who attempted to secure Pope Clement VII's
consent for Henry VIII's divorce from Queen Catherine. He was later
arrested for treason and died in 1530. Movie portrayals: *The Sword and the
Rose* (1953) D. A. Clarke-Smith; *A Man for All Seasons* (1966) Orson Welles;
and *Anne of the Thousand Days* (1969) Anthony Quayle.
Woman of Paris, A
1923 silent movie that was the only film Charles Chaplin directed but did not
appear in.
Woman of the Year
Title of the 1942 movie for which Katharine Hepburn was nominated for an
Oscar as best actress. She played Tess Harding, a journalist who was named
Woman of the Year. Ironically, that same year Hepburn herself became
McCall magazine's first Woman of the Year.
Woman's Journal
Magazine for which Christine Massey (Loretta Young) was a writer in the TV
series *The New Loretta Young Show*.
Women's Sports
Magazine founded by tennis star Billie Jean King.
Wonderful World
Song sung by Sam Cooke as Bluto (John Belushi) made a pig out of himself
in the college cafeteria in the 1978 movie *Animal House*.
Wonderland Zoo
Home of the Hair Bears in Cave Block No. 9 in the TV cartoon series *Help!
It's the Hair Bear Bunch*.
Wonder Rocket
Col. Bleep's spaceship in the 1957 cartoon series *Colonel Bleep*.
Woodhull, Victoria Claflin
In 1872 she became the first woman to run for the office of president of the
United States.
Wood, Natalie
American actress (born Natasha Gurdin) who married actor Robert Wagner in
1957, divorced him in 1963, and remarried him in 1972. She was portrayed
in the 1979 TV movie *Elvis* by Abi Young.
Woodstock
Typewriter (No. 230,099) owned by Alger Hiss. At his trial for treason the
typewriter was entered as evidence—it was alleged that Hiss had used it to

type State Department papers, which he then gave to the Russians, between 1936 and 1937. The Hiss case made Richard M. Nixon famous—he was then a young Congressman who helped gather evidence against Hiss. Alger Hiss is the first lawyer ever to have been disbarred and readmitted to the bar (in August 1975) in Massachusetts.

Woodstock Music and Art Fair
New York State rock 'n' roll festival held on the weekend of August 15–17, 1969, on a Bethel, New York, dairy farm. It was financed by John Roberts. The festival was the subject of a documentary movie released in 1970. In the 1971 movie *The Omega Man* Robert Neville (Charleston Heston) attended this movie in Los Angeles. It was in Woodstock, New York, that Bob Dylan was seriously injured in a motorcycle accident on July 29, 1966.

Woodward, Bob, and Carl Bernstein
Washington Post reporters who broke the Watergate story. Their dogged pursuit of the story resulted in the revelation that many key Nixon advisers were involved in the affair. The 1976 movie *All the President's Men* was based on Woodward and Bernstein's book of the same name. Robert Redford portrayed Woodward and Dustin Hoffman portrayed Bernstein.

Woodward, Roger
7-year-old boy who survived a fall over Niagara Falls in 1960.

Woody Sez
Daily column written by folk singer Woodrow "Woody" Guthrie for the *People's Daily World*.

Woollcott, Alexander
(1887–1943) American journalist and writer of numerous stories and anthologies. Portrayals: *Act One* (1963) Earl Montgomery; *Star!* (1968) Jock Livingston; and *Backstairs at the White House* (1979 TV miniseries) Tom Clancy.

Woolworths
(F. W. Woolworth) A 5 and 10-cent store. The first store was opened in Utica, New York, on February 22, 1879. The Woolworth store in Greensboro, North Carolina, was the site of the first black sit-in at a lunch counter. It was done on February 1, 1960, by four men from the North Carolina Agricultural and Technical College: Joseph McNeil, David Richmond, Franklin McCain, and Jibreel Khazan.

World Illustrated
London magazine for which Shirley Logan (Shirley MacLaine) worked in the TV series *Shirley's World*.

Worlds
Theme song of the TV series *Bracken's World,* performed by the Lettermen.

World's All-Around Champion Cowboy (1912)
Title held by rodeo rider Hoot Gibson.

World's Greatest Actor, The
Nickname of actor John Barrymore.

Worlds in Collision
Paperback book by Immanuel Velikovsky that was read by Mr. Giovanni while he was taking a mudbath in the 1978 movie *Invasion of the Body Snatchers*.

World Wide Studios
Hollywood picture company run by Lew Lord (Orson Welles) in the 1979 movie *The Muppet Movie*.

Wretched, Colorado
Setting of the TV series *Pistols 'n' Petticoats* in the year 1871.

Wright, Stan
University of California track coach who in the 1972 Olympics failed to get Reynaud Robinson and Eddie Hart to the stadium in time to run in the 100-meter dash.

Wright, Wilbur and Orville
Inventor brothers who on December 17, 1903, made the first power-driven flight, with Orville at the controls of the 120-foot, 12-second flight. In *The Wings of Kitty Hawk* (1978 TV) Wilbur was portrayed by Michael Moriarty and Orville by David Huffman.

Wyckoff, Douglas
Sacramento, California, man who in September 1978 canceled his seat aboard PSA Flight 182 from Sacramento to San Diego. The airliner collided with a small plane, resulting in the worst aviation accident in U.S. history. On May 25, 1979, Douglas Wyckoff again canceled his flight aboard American Airlines Flight 191, which crashed after takeoff from Chicago when an engine fell off. This tragedy became the worst air accident in U.S. history, with 273 casualties.

X-23
Allied submarine that was the first vessel to arrive at Normandy at the beginning of the D-Day invasion on June 6, 1944. It dropped dye markers.

X-27
Secret agent played by Marlene Dietrich in the 1931 movie *Dishonored*.

X-70
Missile silo complex near Marysville, Texas, that killer bees attacked in the opening scene of the 1978 movie *The Swarm*.

X371
Pacific island on which the Seabees were building an airfield, and where Lt. Cmdr. Wedge Donovan (John Wayne) was killed, in the 1944 movie *The Fighting Seabees*. Events earlier in the film took place on Island X214.

XQ2591
License plate number of the blue Cadillac driven by Linda Lovelace in the X-rated movie *Deep Throat*.

X-R-Z
Cmdr. Buzz Corey's (Ed Kemmer) space ship in the TV series *Space Patrol*.

Yamamoto, Isoroku
    (1884–1943) Japanese admiral during World War II, commander-in-chief of
    the Japanese fleet, and former Harvard student. He was shot down and killed
    on April 18, 1943, by American P38s. Movie portrayals: *Admiral Yamamoto*
    (1968 Japanese) Toshiro Mifune; *Tora! Tora! Tora!* (1970) So Yamamura; and
    Midway (1976) Toshiro Mifune.
Yankee Doodle
    Official song of the state of Connecticut, adopted in 1978.
Yankee Doodle Society
    Organization of freedom fighters in the TV series *The Young Rebels*. Its
    members were Jeremy Larkin (Rick Ely), Isak Poole (Lou Gossett), Henry
    Abington (Alex Hentloff); and Elizabeth Contes (Hilarie Thompson).
Yankee Girl
    10-foot sloop in which Gerry Spiess sailed from White Bear Lake, Minneso-
    ta, to Falmouth, England, in 54 days (3,500-mile trip).
Yasgur, Max
    Dairy farmer who leased his 600-acre Bethel, New York, farm for the
    Woodstock Festival held August 15–17, 1969. (See: **Woodstock Music and
    Art Fair.**)
Yeager, Charles E.
    First man to officially exceed the speed of sound (on October 14, 1947). He
    flew the *Bell X-1*. Yeager was the person who taught Jacqueline Cochran to
    fly jet aircraft.
Yellowstone Sentinel
    Yellowstone, Dakota, town newspaper published by Adam MacLean (Rex
    Reason) in the 1957 TV series *Man Without a Gun*.

Yes I Can

1965 autobiography of singer Sammy Davis, Jr. This is the book that Rosemary Woodhouse (Mia Farrow) was attempting to read when visitors interrupted her in the 1968 movie *Rosemary's Baby.* (In the novel Rosemary was interrupted reading *Manchild in the Promised Land.)*

Yes, Sir, That's My Baby

Theme song of 1965–1966 TV series *Mona McCluskey.* This was the favorite song of Curly the caterpillar in the 1944 movie *Once Upon a Time.*

Yonda

Ship on which the crew passed through time in the TV series *The Fantastic Journey.*

York

Lone slave who accompanied the Lewis and Clark expedition (1804–1806). He belonged to William Clark.

York, Hugh

Stylist who created Farrah Fawcett's hairstyle.

You and I

Theme song of the radio series *Maxwell House Coffee Time.*

You and I Know

Theme song of the radio series *Front Page Farrel.*

You Can't Take It With You, and Going Places

Two American movies playing at Paris's Champs Elysées on June 27, 1940, the day France surrendered to Germany.

You Deserve a Break Today

One of several McDonald Hamburger jingles. It was originally sung by Barry Manilow.

You Dirty Rat

Line never used by (but often attributed to) James Cagney in any movie.

You, Dominique

Pirate Jean Lafitte's second-in-command. Movie portrayals: *The Buccaneer* (1938) Akim Tamiroff; and *The Buccaneer* (1958) Charles Boyer.

You Light Up My Life

Oscar-winning song from the 1977 movie *You Light Up My Life,* produced, written, and directed by Joseph Brooks. Kacey Cisyk dubbed the song for actress Didi Conn in the movie, though Cisyk never received credit. Debby Boone's version of the song won a Grammy in 1978; it set a record for a single by a female artist by staying in No. 1 place for 10 weeks. The original title of the movie was *Sessions.*

You'll Never Know

Classic song penned by Mack Gordon and Harry Warren. Alice Faye introduced it in the 1943 movie *Hello, Frisco, Hello* and sang it again in the 1944 movie *Four Jills in a Jeep.*

Young, Andrew

Outspoken U.S. ambassador to the United Nations who was asked to resign in 1979 by President Carter, because of his undiplomatic statements. Young was portrayed in the 1978 TV movie *King* by Howard Rollins.

Youngblood, Rufus

Secret Service agent who flung his body upon Vice President Johnson on November 22, 1963, the day on which President Kennedy was assassinated. His code name was Dagger.

Young, Brigham

(1801–1877) American Mormon leader who succeeded Joseph Smith as head of the Mormon Church. He was the first governor of the territory of Utah. Young was portrayed in the 1940 movie *Brigham Young, Frontiersman* by Dean Jagger.

Young Dr. Jekyll Meets Frankenstein

Horror movie watched by the sailors in the 1964 movie *Ensign Pulver.* The movie's actual title is *The Walking Dead* (1938).

Younger, Thomas "Cole"

(1844–1916) American bank robber who was a Confederate officer during the Civil War and later a member of the Jesse James gang. Portrayals: *Cole Younger, Gunfighter* (1958) Frank Lovejoy; *The Great Northfield, Minnesota Raid* (1972) Cliff Robertson (his brothers Jim and Bob Younger by Luke Askew and Matt Clark, respectively); *Belle Starr* (1980 TV) Cliff Potts; *The Long Riders* (1980) David Carradine (brothers Bob and Jim by Robert Carradine and Keith Carradine, respectively); and TV series *The Legend of Jesse James* John Milford (Bob Younger by Tim McIntire).

Young Ricardo

Name under which actor Victor Mature boxed in his youth. He once fought Jack Johnson in a nontitle bout.

Young Widder Jones

Title of the NBC radio soap *Young Widder Brown* when it was originally heard on Mutual radio.

Young, William

Philadelphia man who on October 16, 1800, created separate shoes for the right and left foot.

You Plug 'Em—I Plant 'Em

Motto of the undertaker Claude Clay in the comic strip *Tumbleweeds.*

You're a Grand Old Rag

Original title of George M. Cohan's classic song "You're a Grand Old Flag." He changed the title because of numerous protests.

You're My Greatest Love

Theme song of the TV series *The Honeymooners,* music by Jackie Gleason, lyrics by Bill Templeton.

You're the Flower of My Heart, Sweet Rosalie
Original title of the 1903 song "Sweet Adeline."

Your First Impressions
TV game show on which Richard Nixon appeared in 1962.

Your Kaiser Dealer Presents Kaiser-Frazer Adventures in Mystery Starring Betty Furness in Byline
Title of the 1951 TV series starring Betty Furness. It was more commonly referred to as *Byline*.

You Too Can Fly
Noted book written by the world's expert on aviation, Professor Rudolf von Rudder, played by Sid Caesar in the TV series *Your Show of Shows*.

You Wanted to See It
TV variety show on which Fonzie attempted to set a new world's record by jumping his motorcycle over 14 garbage cans in the TV series *Happy Days*.

You Were Meant for Me
Song written in 1929 by Arthur Freed and Nacio Herb Brown. It can be heard in the following motion pictures: *The Broadway Melody* (1929); *Hollywood Revue* (1929); *Show of Shows* (1929); *You Were Meant for Me* (1948); *Let's Make It Legal* (1952); *Singin' in the Rain* (1952).

Yow-suh, Yow-suh, Yow-suh
Catchline of 1930s band leader Ben Bernie. The line was used in the 1970s disco song "Dance, Dance, Dance" by Chie.

Yvonne
Alice Cooper's pet boa constrictor that performed on stage with her musical master.

Z

000 Cemetery Land
Address of the haunted home on North Cemetery Ridge of the Addams family in the TV series *The Addams Family*.

00077181
Federal prisoner number of Patricia Hearst while she was incarcerated at Pleasanton, California.

01489-163 (B)
H. R. Haldeman's prisoner number at the federal prison camp at Lompoc, California.

054-22-5457
Social Security number of the talking horse Mr. Ed in the TV series *Mr. Ed*.

051-246-4379
Phone number of Liverpudlian private detective Eddie Ginley (Albert Finney) in the 1971 movie *Gumshoe*.

Z
Stanley McLaurel's (Stan Laurel) middle initial in the 1935 movie *Bonnie Scotland*.

ZR-3
Home planet of Fi (Ruth Buzzi) and Fum (Jim Nabors) in the TV series *The Lost Saucer*.

ZX-99
Captain Z-RO's (Roy Steffins) spacecraft in the TV series *Captain Z-RO*.

Zaca
Errol Flynn's 118-foot schooner. It was used as the vessel in the 1948 movie *The Lady from Shanghai*, in which Errol Flynn played an unbilled extra as a crew member. Robert Taylor became owner of the vessel after Flynn. In 1952

Warner Brothers produced a 20-minute film titled *Cruise of the Zaca* about Flynn's 1946 voyage on the vessel.

Zapata, Emiliano

(1877–1919) Mexican revolutionary who was portrayed in the 1952 movie *Viva Zapata!* by Marlon Brando. His brother, Eufemio, was portrayed by Anthony Quinn.

Zapple Records

Only subsidiary record label of Apple Records. (See: **Apple Records**).

Zatopek, Emil and Dana

Husband and wife who both won Gold Medals in the Olympics in 1952, Emil for the marathon and Dana for the javelin throw.

Zebra 3

Call sign of David Michael Starsky's (Paul Michael Glaser) red and white Ford Torino in the TV series *Starsky and Hutch*.

Zenker, Arnold

Network executive who gave the evening news in place of Walter Cronkite during the 1967 AFTRA strike.

Zero

Chauffeur played by Sugar Ray Robinson in the 1968 movie *Candy*.

Zero

World War II Japanese fighter based on an aircraft designed by Howard Hughes but turned down by the U.S. government. The aircraft was called the Zero because it was designed in the 2600th year of the Nipponese dynasty (1940).

Zero

Name of the computer in the 1975 movie *Rollerball*.

Zero Records

Small Nashville record label on which Loretta Lynn (Sissy Spacek) recorded her first song, "Honky Tonk Girl," in the 1980 movie *Coal Miner's Daughter*.

Ziegfeld, Florenz

(1867–1932) American theatrical producer who as a boy was a survivor of the Chicago fire. He was married to Anna Held (1897–1913) and Billie Burke (1914). Movie portrayals: *The Great Ziegfeld* (1936) William Powell; *The Jolson Story* (1946) Eddie Kane; *Ziegfeld Follies* (1946) William Powell; *The Story of Will Rogers* (1952) William Forrest; *The Eddie Cantor Story* (1954) William Forrest; *Deep in My Heart* (1955) Paul Henreid; *The Helen Morgan Story* (1957) Walter Woolf King; *Funny Girl* (1968) Walter Pidgeon; *W.C. Fields and Me* (1976) Paul Stewart; and *Ziegfeld: The Man and His Women* (1978 TV movie) Paul Shenar (James Francis at age 4).

Ziegler, Ron

President Richard M. Nixon's press secretary. He was portrayed by James Sloyan in the 1979 TV miniseries *Blind Ambition*.

Zing, Went the Strings of My Heart

Song that Judy Garland sang at her MGM audition for Louis B. Mayer in 1934. Her father, Frank Gumm, accompanied her on piano. Garland later sang the song in the 1938 movie *Listen Darling*.

Zinn, Jeff

John Travolta's stand-in. It was Zinn's legs that were first shown walking down the street at the beginning of the 1977 movie *Saturday Night Fever*.

Zodiac Club

Greenwich Village nightclub that was the hangout of witches and warlocks in the 1958 movie *Bell, Book and Candle*.

Zola, Emile

(1840–1902) French writer who, while in exile in Britain, wrote about the wrongful conviction of Alfred Dreyfus. Movie portrayals: *The Life of Emile Zola* (1937) Paul Muni; and *I Accuse!* (1958) Emlyn Williams.

Zombie

First racehorse bought by Bing Crosby, acquired in 1935. Crosby was supposedly the first actor to own a racehorse.

Zonk

Booby prize "won" by contestants on the TV game show *Let's Make a Deal*.

Zot!

Sound of a thunderbolt in Johnny Hart's comic strip *B.C.*

ZOWIE

Zonal Organization World Intelligence Espionage: organization for which Derek Flint (James Coburn) worked in the 1966 movie *Our Man Flint* and in the 1967 series *In Like Flint*. It was headed by Cramden (Lee J. Cobb).

Zylberberg, Rachel

Woman who opened the first disco in Paris in 1961. She also appeared in the 1976 movie *The Seven Percent Solution*.